MODERN INDIA

FOR CIVIL SERVICES AND OTHER COMPETITIVE EXAMINATIONS

About the Author

Poonam Dalal Dahiya is one of the finest authors who have been helping and mentoring students develop their knowledge, skills and confidence for different public service examinations. An alumna of University of Delhi, she holds a postgraduate in Humanities and is also a certified teacher who possesses rich and varied administrative experience of different professions. To her credit, she has cleared different competitive examinations ranging from SBI P.O., SSC Graduate Level, State Civil Services and UPSC. After working in Indian Revenue Service (Income Tax) for about 4 years, she has now switched over to policing and is presently working as the Assistant Commissioner of Police in Gurugram.

MODERN INDIA

FOR CIVIL SERVICES AND OTHER COMPETITIVE EXAMINATIONS

Poonam Dalal Dahiya

McGraw Hill Education (India) Private Limited

Published by McGraw Hill Education (India) Private Limited
Registered Office: Anjana Complex No: 5/90 A, Butt Road, St. Thomas Mount, Chennai – 600016, Tamil Nadu, India

Modern India

Second reprint 2022

Print-Book Edition
ISBN-(13): 978-93-5460-002-9
ISBN-(10): 93-5460-002-6

E-Book Edition
ISBN-(13): 978-93-5460-010-4
ISBN-(10): 93-5460-010-7

03 04 05 06 07 RAJ 26 25 24 23 22

Typeset at TNQ Technologies Pvt. Ltd., 4/600, Phase II, Dr. Vikram Sarabhai Instronics Estate Kottivakkam, Chennai 600 041 and printed and bound in India at Rajkamal Electric Press, Kundli, Sonepat, Haryana.

Cover Image Source: Shutterstock

Cover Designer: Creative Designer

Cover Printer: Rajkamal Electric Press

Visit us at: www.mheducation.co.in

Write to us at: info.india@mheducation.com

CIN: U80302TN2010PTC111532
Toll Free Number: 1800 103 5875

To my dear son

Vikramaditya Dahiya

Preface

The syllabus of the General Studies for the UPSC and State Service examinations is pretty exhaustive in nature and modern Indian history has emerged as one of the important components of this syllabus. To many of the aspirants, modern Indian history is a boring factual subject which has to be crammed and is not fun to learn. It is indeed difficult for any new aspirant to cover it comprehensively and, that too, in a short span of time. In fact, the very purpose of writing this book was to break this myth about learning about history and making it a joyful process.

This book offers a completely new approach to study towards modern Indian history. It attempts **to make the learning not only simple and interesting** but also **quick**. The book is structured in sync with **each and every topic in the syllabus**, presenting the information in an interesting format which will make the aspirants comfortable.

Special Features of the Book

1. **Comprehensive coverage** of the entire syllabus pertaining to Modern Indian History of UPSC, State Services and other competitive exams.
2. Inclusion of two comprehensive detachable quick **revision charts** pertaining to the topics taught in the book to simplify the learning process.
3. In every chapter, the **keywords** have been highlighted so that it becomes easy for the reader to make a quick reference to important points.
4. Ample use of **tables**, **information boxes**, **maps**, **pictures** in the chapters to provide conceptual clarity about historic events.
5. **Previous years' questions** are provided for each chapter so that students can practise, assess and master the particular topic.
6. Use of a **simple and lucid language** to cater to the needs of all the students.

I sincerely hope all the readers of the book will appreciate and benefit from its contents and find it useful for their preparation.

Any suggestion for further improving the content of the book will be most welcome and eagerly awaited. Your valuable suggestions will go a long way in enhancing the quality of this book in future. Please feel free to reach me at *poonamrandhawasingh@gmail.com.*

All the very best!

Poonam Dalal Dahiya

Acknowledgements

I wish to thank a multitude of people whose lives have intersected with mine in one way or another and inspired me to write this book. To begin with, I would like to express my heartfelt gratitude to my dear husband Aseem Dahiya, who has been a source of constant inspiration and encouragement ever since I have known him. Aseem has seen from close quarters the crests and troughs of my struggle, all the while prodding me to never give up. Without his unflinching support, I would not have been able to complete this challenging task or anything else in life. I am especially indebted to my dear son Vikramaditya Dahiya, after all, I have stolen time from his precious childhood to write this book! He has been a constant source of both joy and inspiration for me. I sincerely hope that I could prove to be the mother whose efforts my son would be proud of and the daughter, my late father Shri Randhawa Singh, would be equally proud of and shower blessings upon.

My gratitude is also due to my dear younger brothers Amit and Ajay Dalal who have always believed in me and motivated me to develop my notes written over the years during the preparation of various exams which I have used while writing this work. I would also like to thank everyone else in my family especially my mother, in-laws, teachers, colleagues and friends who, in their own unique ways, have helped me form my views on various issues as delineated in this book and without their support it would not have been possible for me to create this book.

I am also indebted to every teacher of mine who has not only relentlessly mentored me in this endeavour but also helped me during the course of my own UPSC preparation, especially Pavan Sir (Pavan Kumar IAS Academy), Ravindran Sir (Vajiram and Ravi), Praveen Bansal Sir (Abhimanu IAS Study Group) and Anil Narula Sir (Anil Narula's IAS Study Center).

I would also like to express my true appreciation for McGraw Hill Education, India and their entire team for their support and cooperation during the preparation of the book. My special thanks go to Tanweer Ahmad, Ridhi Gupta, S. Srivatsan, Sachin Kumar, Jinia Dasgupta, Suhaib Ali and Atul Gupta for their continued support and patience.

I hope that this book will help the readers for a better conceptual understanding and help all those civil service aspirants who have passion in their hearts, fire in their eyes and who dare to dream!

Poonam Dalal Dahiya

Contents

CHAPTER 4 – The Revolt of 1857 4.1–4.26

CHAPTER 5 – Emergence of Indian Nationalism 5.1–5.23

Appendices

The British Conquest of India

1

The British rule firmly established in the latter half of the 18th century changed the course of history in India as it was for the first time that India became a colony of a foreign power since all those who had come earlier such as the Turks, the Afghans and the Mughals have made India their home. Unlike those, the British colonial rulers always remained foreigners to this land. Nonetheless, the two centuries of colonial rule brought profound social, economic and political changes and in the process left deep imprints on many aspects of the Indian society and the nation as a whole and quite interestingly helped to build a modern India as well. However, in order to appreciate the history of Modern India, it is equally important to trace and understand the nature of the British conquest of India as the same has been a matter of serious debates and discussions among historians and scholars.

While the Colonial historians like **James Mill**, **John Seeley and Vincent Smith** stress that the British conquest of India was accidental, unplanned and more situational based, the Nationalist historians like **Dadabhai Naoroji**, **M. G. Ranade**, **R. C. Dutt and G. K. Gokhale** have strongly opposed this interpretation and rather emphasised that the establishment of British rule was the result of careful planning and design by the colonial masters. However, closer examination of the history of the events reveals a **mix of both** in a way and can be easily related to *continuity and change* paradigm as during the early phase of their association with India, the British concentrated mostly on trading and commercial activities but gradually in order to have a stronghold, they started participating in political and military affairs which further intensified by more careful planning and design once the vision of British ruled India started fascinating the English. Thus, the British conquest of India was built upon successive phases:

- **Phase with focus on Trading and Commercial Activities** (roughly from 1600 to 1746): The first phase consisted of taking hold of the Indo-European trade, since the British came to India for making profits through trade. They bought Indian goods at very low prices and sold them in the Western markets at very high prices, thereby making enormous profits, and hence during this phase, their entire thrust was on increasing their **commercial profit** and to ensure this, they sought special privileges and concessions from Indian rulers, for instance the royal *farman* of **1717** received by the Company from Mughal Emperor **Farrukhsiyar** securing valuable trading privileges. In order to further their commercial motives, they purchased several zamindari rights and established fortified settlements. A detailed scrutiny easily establishes that during this phase there was **no clear attempt** on the part of the East India Company to establish any colonial Empire in India.
- **Phase of Participation in Political and Military activities** (roughly from 1746 to 1813): In the second phase, a number of wars and battles were fought by the East India Company to save their interests in India but these were rather more of a **reaction** towards prevailing circumstances than a thorough planned expansion on the part of the British. The prominent battles and wars belonging to this phase included the **Carnatic Wars** (1740–63), **Battle of Plassey** (1757), **Battle of Buxar** (1764), **First**

and Second Anglo–Mysore Wars (1767–69 and 1780–84) and **First and Second Anglo–Maratha Wars** (1775–82 and 1803–05). In most of the cases, these wars and battles fought by the British were largely situational and the Company got involved to save their political and military interests.

- The political fragmentation and instability after the decline of the Mughal power actually facilitated the territorial expansion of the Company. In the 18th-century political scenario, it was beyond the imagination of Indian regional states to combine as a nation against an alien power. Rather, they often entered into diplomatic alliances with the Company in order to turn the balance of power in their favour against other regional states. Thus, in the late 18th century, the English were mostly responding to the developments of 18th-century Indian politics and exploiting advantageously the opportunities that came their way.
- During this phase, the elements of **proper planning** or **vision** of establishing a British India Empire were largely absent as during this phase, the English were more interested in **safeguarding** their **gains** instead of expanding their territories in India. Interestingly, the East India Company's obsession with stable frontiers, as a necessary precondition for smooth operation of trade, served as another motivation behind the conquest as one annexation brought them to more unstable frontiers and, which thus necessitated more conquests.
- However, as a result of these battles, the British slowly gained political and economic control of the majority areas of the country and soon it emerged as the supreme power and they utilised the political control very effectively to eliminate both Indian as well as foreign rivals to their newly established authority.

- **Phase of Planned Expansion of British Empire** (roughly from 1813 to 1858): The third phase was an **intensified** phase of British imperialism and colonial exploitation. An element of planning and design to control India is clearly evident in the activities of the British Empire during this phase, as the offensive wars and battles were now not compelled by circumstances but were rather fought to expand the frontiers of British India and to complete the conquest of India. If we take a look at the **Third Anglo–Maratha War** (1816–17) through which Peshwaship was abolished, **annexation of Mysore** (1831) on account of misgovernance, the **First Anglo–Afghan War** (1839–42), **annexation of Sindh** (1843) and **conquest of Punjab** (1849) and **annexation of Satara** (1848), **Jaitpur and Sambhalpur** (1849), **Nagpur and Jhansi** (1854), **Tanjore and Arcot** (1855) and **Awadh** (1856) through Lord **Dalhousie's** notorious policy of Doctrine of Lapse, it clearly emerges that now the British were using every possible method to annex maximum number of native states and complete their quest for a British Empire in India.

  It is also interesting to note that till 1813, the British Governor General used to address himself as the loyal servant of the Mughal Emperor, but starting from the tenure of Lord **Hastings** (1813–23) there was a clear emphasis on the idea of **British paramountcy** and as matter of fact, Hastings even refused to meet Mughal Emperor **Akbar II** without the terms of equality, and consequentially Lord **Amherst** (1823–28) became the first Governor General to meet the Mughal Emperor on equal terms. Gradually, by 1835, the face of the Mughal Emperor was removed from the coins issued by the British. Slowly, but rapidly, the entire Indian sub-continent came under British rule and they were now recognised as a paramount as well as the sovereign power.
- **Phase of Direct Rule by British Government** (1858–1947): The last phase, which continued for almost a century, was the culminating and final step of British imperialist dream of having India as a jewel in its hegemonist crown. Through the provisions of the **Government of India Act, 1858**, the *facade* of the rule of East India Company was removed and the **British Crown** took over the reins of India. Now, India was officially a part of the British Empire and was clearly reduced to the status of a colony. The master of Indian people was now the foreign British Government who ruled India till it achieved its independence in 1947.

Thus, it can be safely concluded that for the Company, commerce provided the **will to conquer** and political disunity provided the opportunity. So, it was a mix of varied factors ranging from quest for trading privileges, search for further revenues along with imperatives of military exigencies, which all accelerated the process of territorial conquest and finally erected in India the most magnificent empire that the British ever had.

The important events, battles and wars belonging to each phase will be further explained and discussed in detail. However, in order to clearly understand the background of British conquest of India, its nature and the way it was achieved, we need to revisit certain pages of **medieval history**, which carry the imprints of the advent of Europeans and Indo-European trade, the transitions of the 18th century, which culminated in the decline of the Mughals and emergence of regional states.

The Advent of Europeans and Intricacies of Indo-European Trade

With the discovery of a new sea route via Cape of Good Hope by Vasco da Gama in 1498, many trading companies came to India and established their trading centres. At the outset, they entered India as traders but with the passage of time, in order to safeguard their commercial interests, they tried to dominate the politics of India. Thus, the commercial rivalry among the European powers led to political rivalry and this not only brought them in conflict with each other but with Indian rulers too.

The Portuguese

The Portuguese hold the distinction of being the first Europeans to reach India and ironically, were also the last to leave in 1961, when Indian Government took the reigns of Goa, Daman and Diu from them. **Prince Henry** of Portugal encouraged voyages for discovery of a sea route to India. The first Portuguese who succeeded in reaching the Cape of Good Hope was **Bartholomew Diaz** in 1487. Later, following his footsteps, **Vasco da Gama** reached the port of **Calicut** on 21 May 1498, making it a landmark day in the history of India's maritime trade. He was warmly received by **Zamorin**, the Hindu ruler of Calicut, and he returned to Portugal the next year making huge profits. The Portuguese established trading stations at **Calicut, Cannanore** and **Cochin** (first Portuguese fort) with the dream of monopolising eastern trade and excluding their competitors, especially the Arabs.

The first governor of the Portuguese in India was **Francisco de Almeida** who pursued the famous '**Blue Water Policy**' through which he advocated 'making Portuguese the master of the Indian Ocean by being powerful at sea instead of building fortresses on Indian land'. Later in 1510, the second governor, **Alfonso de Albuquerque**, the real founder of the Portuguese power, captured Goa from the ruler of Bijapur (during reign of Sikander Lodhi), and thereafter Goa became the capital of the Portuguese settlements in India and, interestingly, also the first territory to be under Europeans since the times of Alexander. Albuquerque not only captured Malacca and Ceylon but also gained strategic control of the Indian Ocean by establishing Portuguese bases overlooking all the entrances to the sea such as Malabar, Ormuz, East Africa and the Red Sea. He also encouraged his countrymen to marry Indian women probably to secure permanent Portuguese population in India. At the time of his death in 1515, he left the Portuguese as the strongest naval power in India.

In 1530, **Nino da Cunha** acquired Diu and Bassein from Bahadur Shah of Gujarat. Later, Portuguese settlements were also established in Daman, Salsette and Bombay on the west coast and at San Thome near Chennai and Hooghli in Bengal on the east coast. However, the Portuguese power declined in India by the end of the 16th century and they lost all their possessions in India **except** Goa, Diu and Daman. The Portuguese acts of piracy and prosecution of Muslims brought them in conflict with the Mughals. In 1631, the Portuguese lost Hooghly during the reign of **Shah Jahan**. In 1661, the Portuguese king gave **Bombay** as a gift to **Charles II** of **England** for marrying his sister. In 1663, the Dutch ousted the Portuguese from the Malabar Coast. The Marathas captured Salsette and Bassein in 1739 and Portuguese power declined substantially, never coming back to its glory days.

Reasons for Decline of the Portuguese

- **Emergence of More Powerful Trading Competitors Such As the English and the Dutch**: Gradually, other European traders like the Dutch and the English emerged on the scene, and due to fierce struggle for control of trade among them, the less resourceful and comparatively weak Portuguese had to give up its territories to its opponents. Also, the emergence of powerful dynasties circumventing the Indian Ocean, like Persia and Egypt, caused a setback to the monopoly of the Portuguese over the Indo-European trade. The rise of conflicts with strong local powers such as the Marathas further endangered their position.
- **Religious Intolerance**: The religious policies of the Portuguese further weakened their position in the Indian subcontinent, because with their proselytising activities and antagonistic attitude towards Muslims, they alienated both Hindus and Muslims. The Jesuit activities gave rise to political fears, and some instances of forceful conversion to Christianity added fuel to the fire.
- **Clandestine Practices in Trade and Piracy**: Due to their dishonest trade practices and sea piracy, the Portuguese were resented by all, ranging from the mighty Mughals to rulers of small states along with the other European competitors too. The regular naval assaults by the Portuguese brought them in conflict with all these powers and, thus, further weakened Portuguese territorial occupation.
- **Discovery of Brazil**: It diverted the focus of Portugal to the West as it was easy for them to colonise Brazil, devoid of any other troubling competition. Brazil soon emerged as an economic centre of the overseas empire of Portugal, gradually superseding Goa.

Portuguese Gifts to India

- Cultivation of tobacco and potato
- First printing press in India (1556)
- First scientific work on Indian medicinal plants
- Introduced various military innovation techniques like body armour, matchlock men and drilling groups of infantry

The Dutch

The first Dutch expedition which reached the East Indies was led by **Cornelis de Houtman** in 1596. In March 1602, the Dutch East India Company amalgamating many other trading companies was formed. Interestingly, it is often considered to be not only the first multinational corporation in the world but also the first company to issue stock. In 1605, the Dutch set up their first factory at **Masulipatnam** (Andhra Pradesh). Other Dutch factories were at Pulicat, Chinsurah, Kasim Bazar, Patna, Balasore, Surat, Karaikal, Nagapattinam and Cochin. In fact, **Pulicat** emerged as the headquarters of Dutch operations in India and from 1617, the Chief of Pulicat also functioned as the Dutch Governor in India, and the factory at Pulicat was known as **Fort Geldria**. However, Pulicat was later replaced by **Nagapattinam**, which they had captured from the Portuguese.

The credit of dislodging the Portuguese from India's maritime trade and establishing Indian textiles as the premier export of India goes to the Dutch. In 1619, the Dutch company conquered Java, and by 1623 effectively controlled the **English** competition in the Malaya Archipelago (though by the infamous massacre of Englishmen at Amboyna). Soon, the Dutch monopolised the trade in black pepper and spices though they also traded in cotton, indigo, rice, silk and opium. The Anglo–Dutch rivalry lasted for about 7 decades during which period the **Dutch** lost their settlements to the **British** one by one and the final collapse of the Dutch came with their defeat by English in the **Battle of Biderra** in 1759.

The English

The **English East India Company** was established on 31 December 1600 as 'The Company of Merchants of London Trading into the East Indies' by a royal Charter issued by Queen **Elizabeth I**. Initially, the company had rights of exclusive trading for fifteen years, but in 1609 CE, through a fresh charter, the monopoly of the company was extended indefinitely. In 1609 itself, Captain **William Hawkins** arrived at the court of Mughal Emperor **Jahangir** to seek permission to establish a *factory* (store house of goods) in Surat. But, it was refused by the Mughal Emperor due to **Portuguese** opposition. The English, thus, started trading at Masulipatnam (located on the southeastern coast) in 1611, which was developed into a factory in 1616. However, in 1612, impressed by the defeat of the Portuguese at the hands of Captain **Thomas Best** in the sea off Surat, Jahangir issued a *farman* (permission letter) to the English and they established a trading factory in Surat in 1613. Later in 1615, Sir **Thomas Roe** came to the Mughal court as the ambassador of James I, the King of England, and obtained permission from Jahangir to establish English trading factories at Agra, Ahmedabad and Broach.

- The company's position was further improved in 1632 when they earned the privilege of trading freely in the ports of Golconda through the ***golden farman*** issued to them by the Sultan of Golconda. The Company established its first factory in East India at **Balasore** (Orissa) in **1633**.
- In 1639, **Francis Day** obtained the site of Madras from Raja of Chandragiri (which was later renamed as **Fort St. George**). Madras soon replaced Masulipatnam as the headquarters of English in the Coromandel Coast.
- The English East India Company acquired Bombay from Charles II, the then King of England on lease at an annual rent of £10 in 1668 and Bombay became the headquarters of the company in the west coast.
- In 1690, **Job Charnock**, an agent of the East India Company, purchased three villages, namely Sutanuti, Gobindapur and Kalikata, which, in course of time, grew into the city of Calcutta (**Fort William**, renamed after the English King, William III) and which later became the capital of British India.
- The factories and trading centres that the English established all along the sea coast of India were, thus, grouped under three presidencies, namely Bombay, Madras (**Fort St. George**) and Calcutta (**Fort William**).
- In 1701, Emperor **Aurangzeb** ordered the general arrest of all the Europeans in India due to their aggressiveness on mughal ships and territory but the English could be controlled only for a short time. In 1715, an English surgeon, **William Hamilton**, cured Mughal Emperor **Farukhsiyar** of a disease and as result of this, in 1717, the English mission led by the Governor of Calcutta, **John Surman** secured three valuable *farmans*, which were also regarded as **Magna Carta** of the company (since they provided a large number of trade concessions to Company at Bengal, Gujarat and Hyderabad).

Important highlights of 1717 Magna Carta of the Company

- The Company's imports and exports were exempted from additional customs duties excepting the earlier settled annual payment of ₹3,000.
- The Company was permitted to issue dastaks (passes) for the movement of their goods.
- The Company was permitted to rent more lands around Calcutta.
- The Company was permitted to mint its own coins and it was decreed that the coins minted by the company at Bombay were a legal currency throughout the Mughal empire.
- In Hyderabad, the Company retained its existing privilege of no duties and had to pay only for the prevailing rent for Madras.
- In Surat, for an annual payment of ₹10,000 the Company could secure exemption from levy of all duties.

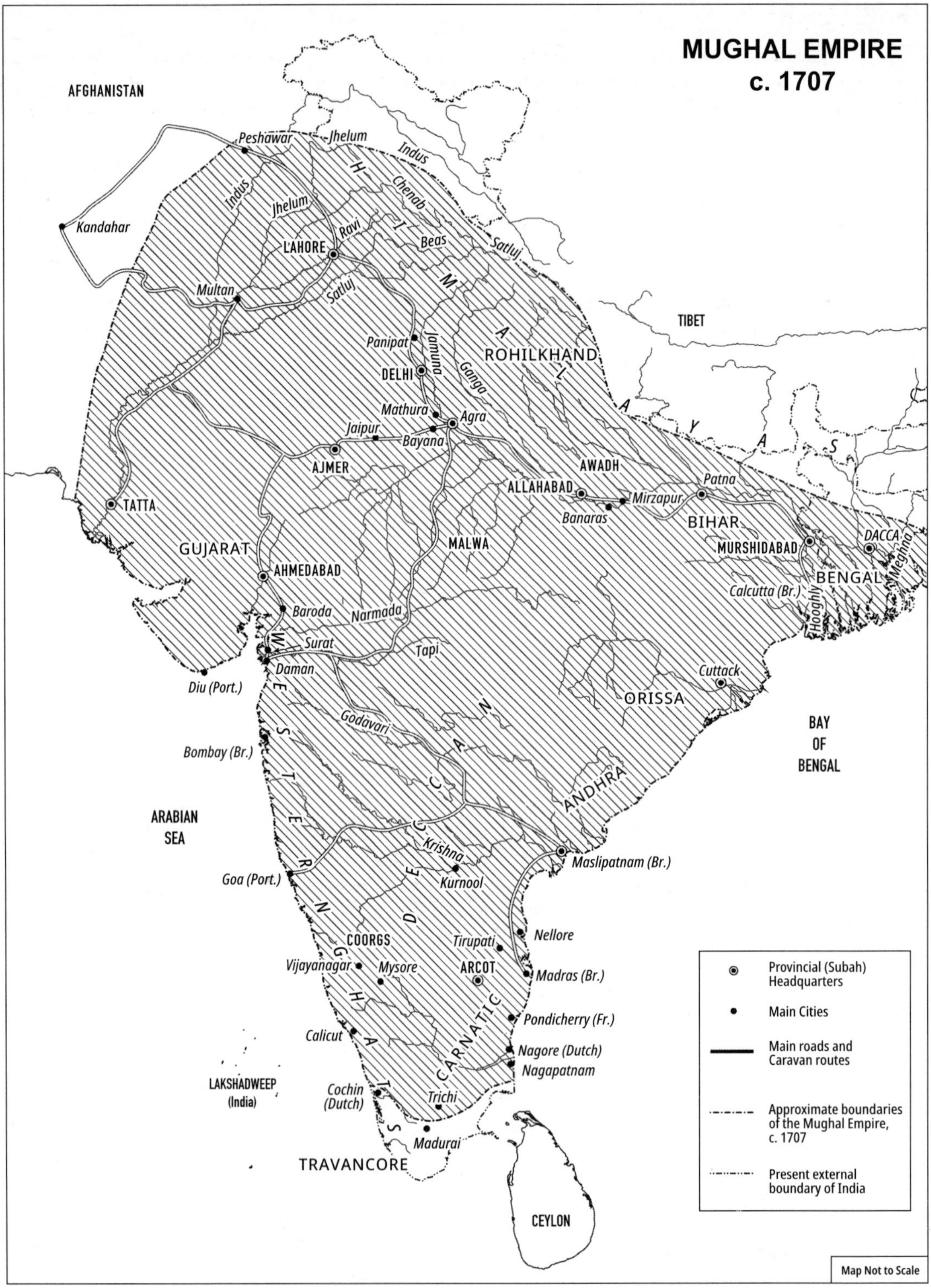

The Mughal Empire in 1707

The Danes (from Denmark)

The Danes formed an East India Company in 1616. They established a settlement at Tranquebar (Tamil Nadu) in 1620 and at Serampore (Bengal) in 1676. Serampore was their headquarters in India. However, they failed to strengthen themselves and were forced to sell all their settlements of India to the British in 1845. They are known more for their **missionary activities** than commerce.

The French

The French were the **last** Europeans to arrive in India for sharing the fruits of Indo-European trade. The French East India Company *La compagnie des Indes Orientales* was formed in 1664 by **Colbert**, a minister under Louis XIV. In 1667, **François Caron** established the first French factory in India at Surat and then, in 1669, **Marcara**, a Persian who accompanied Caron, succeeded in establishing another factory at Masulipatinam. Later, in 1673 **François Martin** founded **Pondicherry** (Fort Louis), the headquarters of the French possessions in India and became its first governor too. He gradually transformed Pondicherry from a small fishing village to a flourishing and important port town. In 1690, Chandernagore (in Bengal) was acquired from Shaista Khan, the Mughal governor. Other French factories in India were Mahe, Balasore, Qasim Bazar and Karaikal. The French had to face perpetual conflict from both the Dutch and the English. The arrival of **Dupleix** as the French Governor in India in 1742 saw the beginning of **Anglo–French** conflict that resulted in the famous ***Carnatic* Wars**.

Anglo–French Rivalry

In the beginning of the 18th century, the English and the French were competing with each other to establish their supremacy in India. The Anglo–French rivalry, taking the form of three ***Carnatic* Wars**, were decisive in terms of the British conquest in south India. *Carnatic* was the name given by the Europeans to the Coromandel Coast and its nearby hinterland. A part of the fallout of the events of the Carnatic Wars was that the weaknesses of the Indian regional powers, in particular their inability to make naval interventions and the ineffectiveness of their large unorganised, indisciplined armies against smaller European forces became manifest and this had grave implications in the political history of the rest of the 18th century.

1. ***First Carnatic* War** (1746–1748)

↓

English under **Commodore Barnett** captured French ships	**Dupleix** (French Governor of Pondicherry) (a) Appealed for help to French Governor of Mauritius La Bourdonnais (b) Madras was captured by French

Cause of the First *Carnatic* War

The First Carnatic War was the Indian theatre of war for the **Austrian succession**. In 1742, war broke out between **France** and **Britain** in Europe over the **Austrian** War of Succession and in 1746 the English Navy under **Commodore Barnett** started the war in India by seizing some French ships. France retaliated by seizing **Madras** (St. George) with the help of the fleet from Mauritius, under French Governor Admiral La Bourbonnais while the English sought help from the Nawab of *Carnatic* **Anwar-ud-din**.

The English under Commodore Barnett captured the French ships.

Important Battles and Treaty Pertaining to the First *Carnatic* War

1.a **Battle of Adyar** (1746, also known as Battle of St. Thome which exposed the indiscipline of Indian Army): It was fought between the **French** and **Mehfuz Khan** (representative of Nawab **Anwar-ud-din**) to capture/restore Madras in which a small disciplined French army defeated a much larger unorganised Indian army.

Later, in 1748, the Austrian war of succession ended in Europe, so battle also stopped in India, resulting in the Treaty of Aix-la-Chapelle.

1.b **Treaty of Aix-la-Chapelle** (1748) →
- Madras was restored to English.
- Louis-burg in North America was given to France.

2. ***Second Carnatic* War** (1749–1754)
↓

English supported **Nasir Jung** for Hyderabad and Nawab **Anwar-ud-din** for Carnatic	**Dupleix** supported **Muzzaffar Jung** for Hyderabad and **Chanda Sahib** for Carnatic

Cause of the Second *Carnatic* War

Both the French and English wanted to increase their political influence in southern India so they frequently indulged in interfering in local dynastic disputes. When the Nizam of Hyderabad died in 1748, it resulted in a war of succession among different contenders to the throne, similarly in the *Carnatic*, the appointment of Anwar-ud-din as the Nawab was resented by Chanda Sahib. This all culminated in the Second *Carnatic* War as both the English and French supported opposite camps.

Important Battles and Treaty Pertaining to the Second *Carnatic* War

2.a Battle of Ambur (1749)

The **French** side defeated Nawab Anwar-ud-din at Ambur and his son Mohammed Ali escaped to Tiruchirappalli for safety and surrendered to the English. Meanwhile, Chanda Sahib, the Nawab of *Carnatic*, rewarded Dupleix by giving Valudanoor, Villianoor and Bahur, near Pondicherry and marched towards Tiruchirappalli to capture Muhammed Ali. Since Nasir Jung (British ally) lost his life in an encounter in 1750, Muzaffar Jung became Nizam and he amply rewarded the French.

2.b Battle of Arcot (1751)

Robert Clive (an English officer) suggested a plan to attack **Arcot** (capital of *Carnatic*), which was approved by Governor Saunders, and he sent a small army with Robert Clive and Major Lawrence. Clive captured Arcot and earned the tag of Hero of Arcot. Meanwhile, French forces and Chanda Sahib were defeated at Arni and Kaveripakkam and Chanda Sahib was beheaded in 1752. Since, Dupleix failed to capture Tiruchirappalli, and also due to heavy financial losses, he was recalled to France in 1754.

Godeheu succeeded Dupleix as the French Governor and he adopted a policy of negotiations with the English.

2.c Treaty of Pondicherry

- The English and the French agreed not to interfere in the quarrels of the native states.
- The English emerged as the real winner in *Carnatic*, but still French possessions were given back to France, and each party was left in possession of the territories actually occupied by them at the time of the treaty.

  A key change in Indian authority during the course of the Second *Carnatic* War was that it became dependent on European support, and regional rulers like Muhammad Ali (*Carnatic*) and Salabat Jung (Hyderabad) functioned more as clients rather than patrons to these European powers.

3. ***Third Carnatic* War** (1756–1763)

- French **Count de Lally** captured English Fort St. David and recalled Bussy (French General in Hyderabad) to assist him at Madras. Due to this mistake, French lost political influence in Hyderabad. Later, Lally lost Madras too.
- English attacked Northern Circars when Bussy left and forced **Salabat Jung** (Nizam of Hyderabad) to change sides.

The Third *Carnatic* War decisively put an end to the French ambitions in India, and its political influence completely disappeared after the war. Henceforth, the French, like the Portuguese, the Dutch and the Danes, were confined to only commercial pursuits and that too in a small periphery. Hereafter, the **English** emerged as supreme power across the Indian subcontinent. It is pertinent to note that unlike the earlier two *Carnatic* wars, which were limited to Deccan only, the Third *Carnatic* War spread to Bengal too.

Cause of the Third *Carnatic* War

- As a result of the Seven Year's War (1756–63) in Europe, the French and English settlements in India also became involved in open hostilities.

Important Battles and Treaty Pertaining to the Third *Carnatic* War

3.a. Battle of Wandiwash (1760): The French under Counte de Lally were defeated by Sir Eyre Coote at Wandiwash (in Tamil Nadu) and this battle gave the British trading company a far superior position in India compared to the other Europeans. Later, in 1761, the French had to eventually surrender Pondicherry too. The Battle of Wandiwash is regarded as an equally decisive battle as the Battle of Plassey (1757) in terms of the British conquest of India because with their victory at Wandiwash, the British could eliminate their last, most important and strong European rival, that is, the French, from the Indian subcontinent (since they had already defeated the Dutch at the Battle of Biderra in 1759). With this win, they clearly emerged as a supreme European power across the Indian subcontinent.

3.b. Treaty of Paris

- Pondicherry, Karaikal and other French possessions were returned to the French on condition that they should not fortify them.

Causes for the English Success and French Failure in Anglo–French Rivalry

- Commercial and naval superiority of the English, combined with good leadership skills of able commanders such as Robert Clive, Sir Eyre Coote and Major Lawrence as compared to only a few such as Dupleix on the French side. Difference of opinion between the French generals at times also hampered their military strategies.
- Private nature of the English Company with less governmental control aided in quick decision-making as opposed to the French Company, which being state concern, had to face more controls and regulations which at times, resulted in delayed decision-making. Also, at certain instances, the French could not muster adequate support at the right time from the French government.
- The French had support only in the Deccan but the English had a strong base and larger resources at its command in Bengal.
- The English had three important ports – Calcutta, Bombay and Madras – but the French had only Pondicherry.
- England's victory in the European wars decided the destiny of the French in India.

The Transitions in the 18th Century

The 18th century was characterised by two critical transitions that not only altered the structure of power in India but also initiated important social and economic changes. The first was the transition in the first half of the century from the **Mughal Empire** to the **regional political orders**, and the second was the establishment of the **English** East India Company as the dominant **influential power** and perpetuation of its colonial order.

The gradual weakening of the central Mughal authority (especially after the death of Aurangzeb) set in motion a new type of power dynamics that ultimately resulted in the emergence of a number of independent regional states, some of which were built on the older local or regional tradition of state formation such as **Bengal**, **Awadh** and **Hyderabad**, whereas others were primarily based on ethnic identity and associated notions of community such as the **Marathas**, the **Jats** and the Sikhs. These states that arose during the phase of Mughal decline (roughly from 1700 to 1850) varied greatly in terms of resources, longevity and essential character, **but** the symbolic hegemony of Mughal authority was still recognised by all these states along with the continuity of varied traditions. They can be easily grouped under the following categories:

- **Successor States**: These states were founded by **Mughal provincial governors** who, though never formally severed their links from the Mughal imperial authority, governed these states with full autonomy and authority. These erstwhile Mughal provinces proved to be most stable polities and had the administrative system worth emulating, and in certain instances even better than the Mughal Empire. Bengal, Awadh and Hyderabad were the three successor states.
- **Independent Kingdoms**: These states were previously functioning as autonomous but dependent polities, and with the destabilisation of the Mughal control over these principalities, these kingdoms had asserted their independence and became completely independent. For instance, the Rajput kingdoms, Mysore and Travancore.
- **New States/Rebel States**: Few states were set up by the rebels against the Mughal state such as the Marathas, the Jats, the Sikhs and the **Afghan** kingdoms of Farrukhabad and Rohilkhand.

The rulers of these states established law and order and viable administrative states while the politics of these states was invariably secular and their rulers did not discriminate on religious grounds in public appointments, civil or military. It is, however, noteworthy to add that though some states were very prosperous, and some achieved considerable military success, yet **none** could achieve resources and power to maintain an all-India polity or to take the place of the Mughals. One of the major reason behind this was the mutual rivalry and conflicts among these states that prevented these states from consolidating their interests into an effective challenge to the growing British dominance. Each state, in proportion to its strength, looked for and seized opportunities to establish its dominance over the others. At the same time, while these states did prevent any breakdown of internal trade, unfortunately they **did nothing** to modernise the basic industrial and commercial structure of their states.

Prominent Regional States of the 18th Century

Bengal

In 1705, Aurangzeb appointed **Murshid Quli Khan** as the Governor of Bengal and later placed Orissa too under his authority. Murshid Quli Khan shifted the capital from Dacca to Murshidabad, and after the death of Aurangzeb, Murshid Quli Khan founded an independent state and became virtually independent but kept sending tribute to the Mughal emperor. After his death in 1727, his son-in-law **Shuja-ud-Din** started ruling Bengal. However, in 1739, **Alivardi Khan** deposed the family of Shuja-ud-Din and became the Nawab himself.

These Nawabs brought stability and peace to Bengal and at the same time **promoted** agriculture, trade and industry. During their reign, equal opportunities were given to both Hindus and Muslims in the administration. But the Nawabs could not foresee the long-term implications of the presence of the European trading companies. Their ignorance of contemporary world affairs cost them a lot as they were totally ignorant about the devastation caused by the western trading companies in Africa and Latin America. Also, they neglected to build a strong army and failed to check the growing corruption among their officials. The foreign trading companies, especially English East India Company, took full advantage of their weakness and thus, started interfering in their affairs. The successor of Ali Vardi Khan, **Siraj-ud-Daulah** had to fight the English East India Company over the trading rights and his defeat at the **Battle of Plassey** in 1757 paved the way for subjugation of Bengal as well as India, the details of which will be subsequently discussed.

Awadh

The weakened control of the Mughals also resulted in the emergence of the provincial kingdom of Awadh (1722) under governor **Saadat Khan**, popularly known as **Burhan-ul-Mulk** who was an energetic, bold and intelligent ruler. He not only disciplined the rebellious zamindars but also improved the lot of the peasants by levying equitable land revenue. His administration was efficient and troops were well paid, well-armed and well-trained. Before his death in 1739, Saadat Khan made his position hereditary. His successors **Safdar Jung** and **Asaf-ud-Daulah** not only played a very decisive role in the politics of northern India but also gave a long-term administrative stability to the Awadh province. Under the Nawabs, firstly Faizabad and then Lucknow emerged as the centres of cultural excellence comparable to Delhi in the spheres of arts, literature and crafts. Regional architecture too reflected itself in the form of *imambarahs* and certain other buildings. In fact, the evolution of the dance form **Kathak** was the outcome of this cultural synthesis.

Punjab

Even though the Mughal forces suppressed the Sikhs under **Banda Bahadur** and he was executed, the Sikh resistance against Mughal authority continued. After invasions of Nadir Shah and Ahmad Shah Abdali, the Sikhs once again asserted their authority and organised themselves into 12 *misls* or confederacies ruled by **chiefs** who exercised control over different parts of the kingdom. It was one such chief, **Ranjit Singh**, of the **Sukerchakia *misl***, who eventually welded these principalities into a larger entity lasting though for a brief time. He captured Lahore in 1799 and Amritsar in 1802. Later, he conquered Kashmir, Peshawar and Multan.

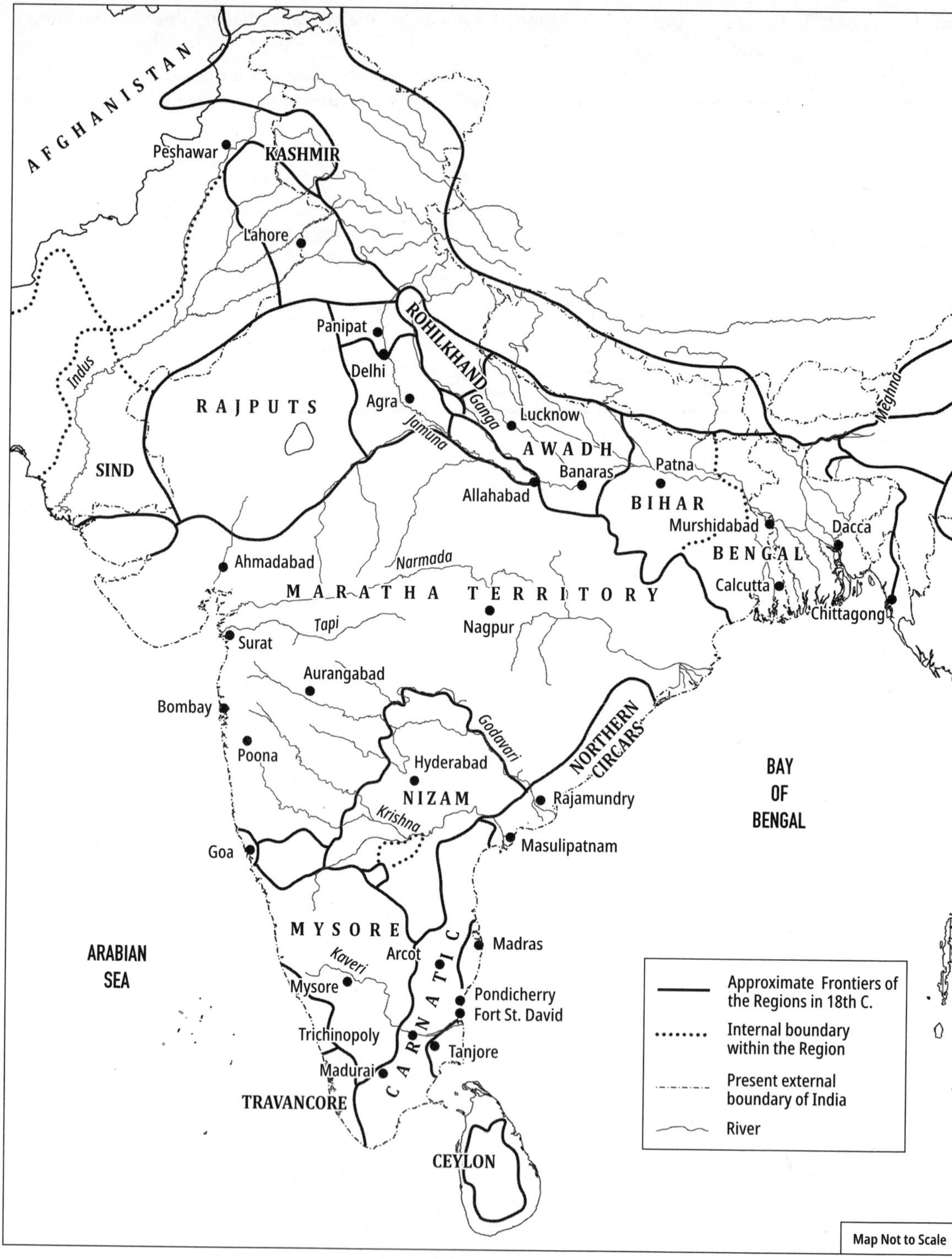

Regional Powers of the 18th Century

His rise to power was based on superior military force, partly serviced by European mercenaries, intelligent application of the principles of statecraft and by the strategic location of his territories. It is said that he possessed the second best army in Asia, next only to English East India company army. By 1809, he was the undisputed master of most of Punjab. His effective rule lasted four decades, from 1799 to 1839 however, within 10 years of his death, the British annexed Punjab, the details of which along with the annexation of Sindh will be further discussed later in the chapter.

Rajputs

The Rajputs had proved to be a great support to the Mughals, especially in control of the peripheral areas. However, during the reign of **Aurangzeb**, the Mughal relations with Rajputs suffered, particularly over the issue of the Aurangzeb's interference in the succession dispute of Marwar. His support to the rival candidate antagonised the Rajputs and his occupation of Jodhpur further put a dent on the Mughal–Rajput relation alienating the Rajputs totally from the Mughal rule. However, most of the larger Rajput states like the other regional states were constantly involved in petty quarrels and civil wars. In fact, Ajit Singh of Marwar was killed by his own son.

One of the principalities that came into prominence in the early 18th century was of **Jaipur** (earlier Amber) located in eastern Rajasthan. Its remarkable ruler **Sawai Jai Singh** (1699–1743, after whom Jaipur came to be named) was a distinguished statesman and reformer. He tried to enforce a law to reduce lavish expenditure which a Rajput had to incur on a daughter's marriage which often indirectly resulted in female infanticide. Interestingly, he was a great **astronomer** and a man of science in an age when Indians were oblivious to scientific progress. He erected observatories with accurate and advanced instruments, some of which were his own invention, at Jaipur, Delhi, Mathura, Ujjain and Varanasi. He drew up a set of tables, titled **Zij-i Muhammad Shahi**, to enable people to make astronomical observations, and as matter of fact his own astronomical observations were remarkably accurate. He translated Euclid's *Elements of Geometry* in Sanskrit along with Napier's work on construction and use of logarithms and other various works on trigonometry. But after his death, the second half of the 18th century was marked by an economic depression on the account of series of crop failures in the 1750s and 1760s, which further led to the decline of political power of Jaipur and it became a vulnerable target for the ambitions of the Marathas, and of **Mahadji Scindia** in particular.

Hyderabad

The state of Hyderabad was founded by *wazir* **Chin Qilich Khan** himself, who was one of the leading nobles of the post-Aurangzeb era and had earlier played a key role in the overthrow of the Saiyyad brothers. However, frustrated by his failure to reform the administration under Emperor Muhammad Shah, he relinquished his office of *waziriyat* and in 1724 marched south to establish the state of Hyderabad in the Deccan and took the title of **Nizam-ul-Mulk Asaf Jah**. Similar on the lines of Murshid Quli Khan of Bengal, he never openly declared his independence from Mughals but acted more like a sovereign ruler who waged wars, concluded peace, conferred titles and gave *jagirs* and offices without any reference to Delhi. He established an orderly administration in the Deccan and successfully not only kept the defaulting zamindars in line but also kept the powerful Marathas out of his dominions. However, after his death in 1748, the power of Hyderabad also declined and the state was not able to maintain its affairs independently. The control of the coastal districts was quickly lost, leaving the kingdom in economic loss.

Mysore

Originally a vice royalty under the Vijayanagara Empire in the 16th century, Mysore emerged as an important state under the rulers of the Wodeyar dynasty, such as **Kanthirava Narasaraja** and **Chikka Devaraja**. However, it reached its real period of glory under **Hyder Ali**, a cavalry commander of migrant origin, who assumed effective power in the kingdom in 1761 when he took over the political power in Mysore by ousting the corrupt *dalwai*, that is, the prime minister **Nanjaraja** (who had in the meanwhile usurped real power in the state by reducing the Wodeyar's to mere figureheads).

Hyder modernised his army with **French** experts and infused European discipline into the Mysore army which was organised on a European model through the system of *risalas*, with a clear chain of command going up to the top commander, that is, the Sultan himself. He, and later his son **Tipu Sultan** (around 1782), made attempts to consolidate Mysore and make it a kingdom with access to not one but both the coasts of peninsular India. In fact, they were relatively successful against the **Kodavas** (the inhabitants of the upland kingdom of Kodagu, that is, Coorg), Coastal Karnataka and northern Kerala, enabling Tipu to open diplomatic and commercial relations on his own with the Middle East. However, both Hyder and Tipu were always resisted by **Poligars**, the local chiefs and the Marathas, and on top of that, they had to also face a formidable military adversary in the form of the English East India Company. Their detailed rivalry culminating in Anglo–Mysore wars will be discussed later in the chapter.

Travancore

Marthanda Varma who ruled Travancore (southern Kerala state of Venad) from 1729 to 1758 initiated many measures to strengthen his authority such as to build a substantial standing army, reducing the power of the Nayar aristocracy on which rulers of the area had earlier depended militarily, and fortifying the northern limits of his kingdom at the so-called 'Travancore line'. In order to limit European involvement in trade, he extended patronage to the Syrian Christians, a large trading community within his domains and also organised a strong army on the western model with the help of European officers. He defeated the Dutch and ended their political power in Kerala. In order to further keep the trade under his watch, he declared many goods as royal monopoly items, requiring a licence for trade, such as pepper. He also built roads and canals and undertook many irrigation works. These policies were also continued by Marthanda's successor, **Rama Varma** (1758–98), who was himself a poet, scholar and a man of great knowledge. He conversed fluently in English, took keen interest in European affairs and regularly read newspapers and journals published in London. The 18th century saw a remarkable revival in Malayalam literature and Trivandrum, the capital of Travancore, became a famous centre of Sanskrit scholarship. However, around 1766, the kingdom of Travancore had to face invasions from Mysore that affected the state as Hyder Ali was able to annex northern Kerala up to Cochin.

Marathas

The most important challenge to the decaying Mughal power came from the **Marathas** who alone possessed the strength to fill the political vacuum created by the disintegration of the Mughal Empire, but due to the lack of unity and an outlook necessary for founding an all India empire, they failed to do so. In the crucial **Third Battle of Panipat** (1761), the Maratha forces under **Sadashiv Rao** were defeated by **Ahmad Shah Abdali**, and this defeat somehow marked the beginning of the decline of Maratha power. However, along with Mysore, they too offered formidable challenge to the English East India Company, but the British divided the mutually warring Maratha sardars through clever diplomacy and then overpowered them in separate battles during the subsequent **Anglo–Maratha wars**, which we will study in detail shortly. It is believed that one of the major reasons for the decline of Maratha state was inherent in its own structure as its nature was that of a confederacy wherein the power was shared among different chiefs like the Bhonsle of Nagpur, Gaikwad of Baroda, Holkar of Indore or Scindias of Gwalior and the factional rivalry among the Maratha chiefs ultimately sealed their doomed fate.

Jats

The Jats were an agriculturist and pastoral caste who inhabited the region around Delhi, Agra and Mathura. Caste affinity with their zamindars brought solidarity within the community and they began to revolt against the Mughal state from the time of Jahangir. In fact, the first revolt of the Jat peasants took place in 1669 and the Emperor himself had to proceed to suppress the rebellion. Later using the discontent of their peasants against the Mughal state, local zamindars, first **Gokula** and then **Raja Ram** and **Churaman Jat** founded the Jat kingdom in Bharatpur. However, the Jat power reached its highest glory under King **Suraj Mal** (1756–63) who consolidated the Jat power during his reign and compelled the Mughal authorities to recognise him. He was not only an extremely able administrator and a wise statesman but a great warrior too. He successfully withstood **Ahmad Shah Abdali's** army siege and supported the **Marathas** in the Third Battle of Panipat. He tried to centralise his powers and bring key reforms in the administration by reducing the state's dependence on the over mighty kinsmen, by raising an army with foreigners and introducing the Mughal system of revenue collection. But, with his untimely death, there was a virtual collapse of the Jat state.

Rohilkhand and Farrukhabad

A couple of small **Afghan kingdoms** were also established in north India following the weakening of the Mughal Empire. The Afghans were bands of roving warlords who had initially started migrating to India from the 15th century. In the 18th century, due to political instability and economic dislocations in Afghanistan, Afghani migration to India increased. Also, the breakdown of authority in north India that followed Nadir Shah's invasion gave the opportunity to another Afghan leader, **Ali Muhammad Khan**, to establish a small kingdom of **Rohilkhand** at the foothills of the Himalayas between the Ganga in the south and the Kumaon hills in the north with its capital at first at Aonla in Bareilly and later at Rampur. But, the new kingdom had hardly any influence, as it suffered heavily at the hands of stronger neighbouring powers like Awadh, the Jats and later the English.

Another independent Afghan kingdom to the east of Delhi in the area around Farrukhabad (between Aligarh and Kanpur) was established by **Ahmad Khan Bangash**, during the reigns of Farrukhsiyar and Muhammad Shah. Both the Rohillas and Bangash helped Ahmad Shah Abdali during the Third Battle of Panipat, but their power declined quickly as Abdali retired from the Indian stage leaving Najib-ud-Daula in charge of affairs at Delhi.

The Conquest of Bengal

The **struggle with the French** for supremacy in south India marked the first phase of the British conquest of India and proceeding further in the sequence of events, the **conquest of Bengal** proved to be the second and the most decisive step. Bengal was one of the most fertile and richest of India's provinces, and the English East India Company had highly profitable trading interests in the province as Bengal goods came to comprise nearly 60 per cent of English imports from Asia. As we have earlier discussed that, through the royal *farman* of **1717**, the Company secured valuable trading privileges but this *farman*, however, became a **perpetual source of conflict** between the Company and the Nawabs of Bengal.

The *farman* granted the Company the freedom to export and import their goods in Bengal without paying taxes and also the right to issue passes or *dastaks* for the movement of such goods. It is pertinent to note that, though the Company's servants were also permitted to trade but they were not covered by this *farman* and were required to pay taxes as Indian merchants. Since, the Nawabs on multiple occasions had refused to extend the duty-free provision to private trade of the Company officials, the latter, therefore took to rampant misuse of *dastaks*, which led to development of hostilities towards each other. Matters came to a head in **1756**, when young **Siraj-ud-Daulah** succeeded his grandfather, **Alivardi Khan**, and threatened the lucrative English private trade by stopping all misuse of *dastaks*. The breaking point came with the grant of asylum to Krishna Ballabh, who was charged with fraud by the Nawab and the new fortifications at Calcutta by the Company without taking Nawab's permission.

Background of Battle of Plassey (1757)

Paved the way for foundation of British Rule in India.

In Bengal, as we have already discussed:

Murshid Quli Khan
↓
Shuja-ud-din Khan (son-in-law of Murshid Quli Khan)
↓
Sarfaraz Khan (son)
↓
Alivardi Khan
↓
Death of Alivardi Khan
↓
Siraj-ud-Daulah (Alivardi's Grandson)

- As compared to Alivardi Khan, Siraj-ud-daulah was a young, inexperienced and quick-tempered ruler, who had to face continuous opposition from **Ghasiti Begum** (widow of Alivardi Khan), **Shaukat Jung** (his rival cousin, who was also Nawab of Purnea) and **Mir Jafar** (rebellious commander of the army whom Siraj-ud-daulah dismissed and replaced by Mir Madan).
- Came in conflict with British as was against misuse of **dastaks** (that is, seals of trading).
- Prevented British from fortifying **Fort William** (Calcutta).
- Attacked English factory at Kasimbazar on British refusal of fortifying and occupied the Fort William on 20 June 1756. Some references of Black Hole tragedy (wherein, many English prisoners were holed up in one room and as a consequence they died of suffocation).
- He then retired from Calcutta to celebrate his easy victory, letting the English escape with their ships to Fulta near the sea protected by their naval superiority, a mistake for which he paid dearly later.

This precipitated in a crisis, and in the meantime, the English organised a web of intrigue and treachery with the leading men of the Nawab's court such as **Mir Jafar** (Commander in chief of Siraj), **Khadim Khan** (commanded large number of the Nawab's troops), **Manik Chand** (Officer in charge of Calcutta), **Amichand** (Rich merchant), **Jagat Seth** (Biggest banker of Bengal) and **Robert Clive** along with **Admiral Watson** now arrived with a strong force from Madras. Clive reconquered Calcutta in the beginning of 1757 and apprehensive of an Afghan attack under Abdali, Siraj now preferred a negotiated settlement, but a confident Clive decided on a *coup d'etat* and conspired to replace Siraj with Mir Jafar resulting in the fateful **Battle of Plassey** which marked the beginning of political rule of the Company and laid the foundation of the British empire in India.

Battle of Plassey (23 June 1757)
↓

Siraj-ud-daulah (was captured and was put to death by Miran, Mir Jafar's son).	**Robert Clive** and **Mir Jafar** (Commander in chief of Siraj).

- Was a battle only in name as the English victory in the battle was predecided, much before the first shot was fired since a major part of the Nawab's army remained inactive and took no part in the fighting. It was not a great battle but was rather a great betrayal.
- Only a small group of Nawab soldiers led by Mir Madan and Mohan Lal fought bravely but could hardly bring a difference to the outcome of the battle, that is, victory of English and Mir Jafar.
- The Nawab was forced to flee and was captured and put to death by Miran, Mir Jafar's son.

Outcomes of Battle of Plassey

- The English proclaimed **Mir Jafar** as Nawab of Bengal and indulged in plunder of vast resources of Bengal, often referred to as the '**Plassey Plunder**'.

- The Company was granted undisputed monopoly over the right to free trade in **Bengal, Bihar** and **Orissa**. It also received the *zamindari* of the 24 *Parganas* near Calcutta and a whopping sum of ₹17,700,000 as compensation for the attack on Calcutta.
- In addition, Mir Jafar also paid large sums of bribes disguised as 'gifts' to the high officials of the Company. Clive himself got a personal jagir and over ₹2 million.
- Moreover, it led to the tacit understanding that British officials and merchants would no longer be asked to pay any taxes on their private trade.
- Robert Clive was appointed Governor of Bengal (1758–60) and he consolidated the British power both in Bengal and in the Deccan.

Significance of Battle of Plassey

- Immense **historical importance** as it paved the way for the British mastery of Bengal and eventually whole of India. Boosted British prestige and at a single stroke raised them to the status of a major contender for the Indian Empire.
- The **economic significance** of Battle of Plassey was far greater than the immediate political one. The rich revenues of Bengal enabled them to organise a strong army, and thus also, played a decisive role in Anglo-French struggle.
- Brought major change in the nature and structure of British trade as prior to 1757, the English trade in Bengal was largely financed through import of bullion from England, but after 1757, interestingly not only bullion import stopped but reversely bullion was exported from Bengal to China and other parts of India, which gave a competitive advantage to the English Company over its European rivals.

> *"Night of Eternal gloom for India"*
>
> Poet Nabin Chandra Sen

> *"Bengal in particular was not to know peace again in until it had been bleed white"*
>
> British historians Edward Thompson and G. T. Garrett

> *"The single aim of the Company officials was to grasp all they could; to use Mir Jafar as a golden sack into which they could dip their hands at pleasure"*
>
> Colonel Malleson

Mir Jafar

- Mir Jafar soon discovered that his treasury was getting emptied by not only the unnecessary regular presents and bribes to the Company officials but also due to the unreasonable demands of the Company officials as they wanted Bengal to pay for the expenses of the Bombay and Madras Presidencies and purchase out of Bengal's revenue all the Company's exports from India, which were almost impossible for him to meet.
- The Company officials too started criticizing Nawab for his incapacity in fulfilling their expectations and thus, in 1760, he was forced to resign in favour of his son-in-law Mir Qasim.

Mir Qasim

- Mir Qasim on securing the throne, rewarded Company by granting the **zamindari** of the districts of Burdwan, Midnapore, and Chittagong, and also gave handsome presents totalling around ₹29 lakhs to higher officials. But, he was not as docile as British had hoped.
- He was an able, efficient and a strong ruler who soon emerged as a threat to English position in Bengal. He tried to maintain public order, increase revenues by removing corruption from the administration, raise a modern and disciplined army on European lines and also tried to free himself from English control.
- In order to ward off company's influence, he shifted his capital from Murshidabad to Munger and also established a gun factory at Munger.
- He tried to check the misuse of the *farman* of 1717 by the Company officials through which they not only used to evade customs duty but also compelled the Indian artisans, peasants and merchants to sell their goods cheap but forced them to buy dear from them. This used to hurt the Indian merchants as they had to pay taxes from which the foreigners got complete exemption from. Thus, in order to address the recurrent problem of misuse of *dastaks* by the Company officials while giving his own subjects a concession that the English had seized by force, he took the drastic step of **abolishing all duties** on internal trade, thus, providing a equal level playing field to Indian merchants too. The English, however, did not like this display of independence and as a retaliatory measure, again replaced him with Mir Jafar.

Mir Jafar

- In 1763, Mir Jafar was again placed on the throne and again huge sums were extorted from him by Company Officials.
- After Mir Jafar's death, British placed his second son **Nizam-ud-daulah** on the throne.

Nizam-ud-Daulah

- He was made to sign a new treaty with British through which, most of the army of Nawab was disbanded and he was required to administer Bengal through a Deputy *Subahdar* (nominated by the Company and who could not be dismissed without its approval). The Company, thus gained supreme control over the *nizamat* that is, administration of Bengal specially over the law and order and criminal justice.
- In December 1763, **Mir Qasim** fled from Bengal and tried to form a grand alliance with the fugitive Mughal Emperor **Shah Alam II** and Nawab of Awadh **Shuja-ud-daulah** against the British. The three allies clashed with the Company's army at Battle of Buxar but were thoroughly defeated.

Battle of Buxar (1764): made the English virtually the masters of Bengal, Bihar and Orissa

Battle of Buxar (22 October 1764)

↓

Mir Qasim, Mughal Emperor **Shah Alam II** and **Shuja-ud-daulah** (Nawab of Awadh)	English led by Major **Hector Munro**

Outcome and Significance of the Battle of Buxar

- One of the most **decisive battles** of Indian history as it demonstrated the superiority of English arms over the combined army of two of the major Indian powers and firmly established the British as masters of Bengal, Bihar and Orissa and placed Awadh at their mercy.
- The victory of British in Battle of Buxar not only **confirmed** the verdict of Plassey, that is, establishing the British as one of the prominent political powers in India but also somehow sealed the fate of India by demonstrating superiority of Company over the other Indian contenders.

- **Treaty of Allahabad** (1765): Victory of British made it *defacto* power in Bengal; however, the Treaty of Allahabad converted the company into *dejure* power too as through this treaty, Mughal Emperor Shah Alam II legitimised the company's control over Bengal.
  - Shah Alam II was forced to grant the **diwani rights** (that is, revenue collecting rights) of **Bengal, Bihar** and **Orissa** to the English. The districts of Kara and Allahabad were given to Shah Alam II and English accorded pension of ₹26 lakhs per year to him.
  - Province of Awadh was returned to Nawab Shuja-ud-Daulah but he had to pay war indemnity of ₹50 lakhs to English. A British resident was posted at his court and he was forced to maintain English troops for the defence of his state. The Company also secured free trading rights in Awadh (a clause which in later years created tensions and prepared the grounds for annexation of Awadh itself).
  - The **British resident** posted at the court of Murshidabad, thereafter became the locus of real administrative power in the province, and thus from Bengal started the system of indirect rule or **Dual Government**.

Dual Government (1765–72)

- Robert Clive introduced a new administrative system in Bengal called the **Dual Government** or the rule of two in which:
  - Nominal Head – **Nawab of Bengal**
  - Real **Power – English**

This dual government was ended later by **Warren Hastings** in 1772.

- Dual Government can also be understood as dual system of administration, wherein the East India Company was enjoying all the politico-military-economic authority in Bengal while the Nawab of Bengal was only a nominal/titular head.
- The East India Company became real masters of Bengal at least from 1765 as they controlled the finances and army of the province directly and its administration indirectly. The Nawab and his officials had the responsibility of administration but not the power to discharge it. On the other hand, the British had all the power without any responsibility.
- In this kind of arrangement[1]:
  - British army was in sole control of Bengal defence.
  - Supreme political power was in British hands.
  - As the *Diwan*, Company directly collected revenues.
  - Through right to nominate the Deputy *Subahdar*, it controlled the *nizamat,* that is, judicial and police functions.

Impact of Dual Government

- It resulted in great exploitation of the people of Bengal as neither the Company nor the Nawab cared for their welfare. The Company officials used its politico-military-economic authority to exploit the peasants, craftsman and traders which further resulted in ruining of Indian agriculture and handicrafts industry.
- The Company starting draining Bengal of its wealth as the Company officials used Bengal wealth to not only finance Indian trade but also wars fought on Indian soil. They stopped sending money from England to purchase Indian goods, rather they started purchasing the Indian goods from the revenues of Bengal and sold them abroad. In three years (1766 to 1768) alone, nearly 5.7 million pounds were drained from Bengal.

[1]Interestingly, under this system, the same person acted in Bengal as the deputy *Diwan* on behalf of the Company and as deputy *Subahdar* on behalf of the Nawab.

- The abuses of Dual Government and drain of wealth further led to the impoverishment of the people of Bengal and when in 1770 Bengal suffered from famine, then its effects on the already exhausted population were a lot gruesome and it proved to be one of the most terrible famines known in Indian history resulting in annihilation of about one-third of Bengal's population.

The Conquest of Mysore

In the 16th century, after the famous **Battle of Talikota** (1565), the great kingdom of **Vijayanagara** disintegrated and many small kingdoms emerged from its remnants. Mysore was one such independent kingdom ruled by Hindu Wodeyar dynasty. We have already discussed how during the second half of the 18th century, under the able leadership of **Hyder Ali**, and later his son **Tipu Sultan**, Mysore emerged as a formidable power in south India, much to the annoyance of the British who considered it as a major threat to their expansion plans. Hyder Ali was an **able general** who strengthened his army by including French soldiers and also set up an arms factory at **Dindigul**. He also maintained tight control over the rich trade of the Malabar coast, which was another cause of concern for the British.

First Anglo–Mysore War (1767–69)

After the conquest of Bengal, the British were looking for ways to further their conquests and expand their influence. Hyder Ali was already having disputes with his neighbouring states such as the Nizam of Hyderabad, Nawab of Arcot and Marathas due to clash of territorial interests. Taking advantage of their hostilities, the British in 1766 entered into a treaty with the **Nizam of Hyderabad** to help him in attacking Hyder Ali in lieu of cession of the region of *Northern Circar*s. The Nizam, the English and the Marathas allied together against Hyder Ali resulting in the First Anglo–Mysore War.

1. **First Anglo-Mysore war** (1767–1769)

↓

Rapid rise of Haider Ali naturally excited the jealousy of the **Marathas**, **Nizam of Hyderabad** and the **English**. They joined together and formed a triple alliance and declared a war on Haider Ali.

Haider Ali

However, by considerable tact and diplomacy, Hyder Ali won over the Marathas and Nizam and the First Mysore War ended with the **defeat of the British** and they were forced to sign the Treaty of Madras.

1.a Treaty of Madras

Both sides restored each other's conquest and promised mutual help[2] in case of an attack by a third party.

Second Anglo–Mysore War (1780–84): During the Time of Lord Warren Hastings

Mysore was attacked by the Marathas in 1771 and as per the terms of the Treaty of Madras, the English were supposed to help Hyder Ali. However, the British under Verelst did not come to his help. So, this added to the already created rift between the two. Hyder Ali, thus, wanted an opportunity to strike at the English. During

[2]However, after only eleven years, the Second Anglo–Mysore War broke out.

the course of the American War of Independence, there was an outbreak of hostilities in India too between the English and the French (who were allies of Hyder).

Immediate Cause of the Second Anglo–Mysore War

When **Mahe**, a French possession in the dominion of Hyder Ali was attacked by the **English**, Hyder Ali considered it as a direct challenge to his authority. He formed a grand alliance with the **Nizam of Hyderabad** and the **Marathas** against the British in 1779 and declared war on the English in 1780, when without Hyder's permission, the British led their forces through his territory to capture Guntur in the northern *Circars*. Hyder Ali defeated English force in *Carnatic* under **Colonel Baillie** and captured **Arcot** in 1780. However, by a clever stroke of diplomacy in 1781, **Warren Hastings** divided the confederacy, consequently isolating Hyder without any alliance. He was, thus, defeated by Sir Eyre Coote at **Porto Novo** in 1781.

2. **Second Anglo-Mysore war** (1780–1784)

English
English under **Sir Eyre Coote** defeated Haider Ali at Porto Novo in 1781.

Haider Ali
Haider Ali defeated English force in Carnatic and made them surrender but was defeated at Porto Novo. Also in the meantime, Haider Ali died of cancer in 1782. His son, **Tipu Sultan** continued the war with English for more than 2 years.

2.a Treaty of Mangalore (1784)

Fed up with inconclusive war, both sides opted for peace under the Treaty of Mangalore wherein both sides agreed to exchange the captured territories and war prisoners.

Third Anglo–Mysore War (1790–92): During the Time of Lord Cornwallis

The peace of 1784 was not able to permanently end the traditional hostility between Tipu Sultan and the East India Company. After the Second Anglo–Mysore War, Tipu Sultan undertook several internal reforms to strengthen the state of Mysore. He also made attempts to seek external assistance against the British by sending envoys to **Turkey** (1784–85) and **France** (1787). All of these acts alarmed the British and especially worried its Governor General Cornwallis, who after his debacle in the American War of Independence, did not want to take any risk in India. Cornwallis was, thus, waiting for an opportunity to wipe out the challenge of Tipu forever. In 1789, the British also secured the necessary support[3] of the Nizam of Hyderabad and the Marathas since they were also anxious about Mysore's rise.

Immediate Cause of the Third Anglo–Mysore War

In April 1790, Tipu attacked his neighbouring state **Travancore**, which was an ally of the British. The British used this act as a pretext for declaring war on Mysore in May 1790. The Third Anglo–Mysore War was fought in three phases:

[3] However, interestingly after the conclusion of war the British gave only a small territory on the banks of river Krishna to the Nizam of Hyderabad and on similar lines offered a negligible area of land to Marathas on the banks of Tungabhadra which Marathas refused to accept. That is why even Cornwallis commented on the Third Anglo–Mysore War that *We have crippled our enemy effectively without making our friends too formidable.*

- The first phase commenced when the Governor of Madras, **Medows**, initially directed the campaign to invade Mysore but Tipu's rapid movements halted the progress of the English troops and inflicted heavy losses on them.
- The second phase of the war started when in the meantime, **Cornwallis** himself assumed command in December 1790 and Marching from Vellore, he captured Bangalore in March 1791, but Tipu's brilliant strategies prolonged the war and Cornwallis was forced to retreat to Mangalore due to lack of provisions.
- The third phase of the war began when timely aid from the **Marathas** with plenty of provisions helped Cornwallis to resume his campaign and he marched against Seringapatnam again. Unfortunately, now Tipu was at a disadvantage and the English forces quickly occupied the hill forts near Seringapatnam and seized it in February 1792.

3. **Third Anglo-Mysore war** (1790-1792)

↓

English along with **Nizam of Hyderabad** and **Marathas**
English under Cornwallis defeated Tipu Sultan and captured Bangalore.

Tipu Sultan

3.a Treaty of Seringapatnam (1792)

- Tipu Sultan lost almost ½ of his territory, that is, Malabar, Coorg, Dindigul, Baramahal (now Salem and Erode).
- He was compelled to pay huge war indemnity of ₹3 crore and had to surrender two of his sons as hostages to the English until he paid the indemnity.
- Both the sides agreed to release the prisoners of war.

Fourth Anglo–Mysore War (1799): During the Time of Lord Wellesley

The Third Anglo–Mysore War had dealt a severe blow to Mysore's dominant position in the south and Tipu Sultan too was never able to reconcile with the loss of half of his territory. He, therefore, worked incessantly to make Mysore a strong state. He also wanted to avenge his humiliating defeat and the harsh terms imposed on him by the British. He, thus, not only entered into negotiations for an alliance with revolutionary **France** (1798) but also sent missions to **Afghanistan**, **Arabia** and **Turkey** to forge an anti-British alliance. In fact, he started a **Jacobian Club** at Seringapatnam where even the flag of the French Republic was hoisted and the tree of Liberty was planted. Later, Tipu also received a friendly letter from **Napoleon** (who was in Egypt at that time). This increased the suspicions of Lord **Wellesley** who wanted to prevent any possibility of the French re-entering India and he was now more than determined to annihilate Tipu Sultan completely.

Immediate Cause of the Fourth Anglo–Mysore War

Tipu refused to accept the Subsidiary Alliance of Lord Wellesley. As a part of his strategy, Wellesley tried to revive the **Triple Alliance** of 1790 with the Marathas. Though his proposal was not accepted by the **Marathas**, they, however, promised to remain neutral. Meanwhile, a subsidiary alliance with the **Nizam of Hyderabad** was concluded by the British and consequently French force at Hyderabad was disbanded.

Knowing fully well that proud Tipu Sultan would never agree to a subsidiary alliance, Wellesley asked him to dismiss the French, to receive an English envoy, and to make terms with the Company and its allies. As expected, Tipu refused to accept the humiliating terms and proudly declared that it was *better to die like a soldier, than to live a miserable dependent on the infidels, in the list of their pensioned rajas and nawabs*, and thus the Fourth Anglo–Mysore War started. The war was brief but fierce and decisive. As planned, the Bombay army under **General Stuart** invaded Mysore from the west while the Madras army, which was led by the Governor-General's brother, **Arthur Wellesley**, forced Tipu to retreat to his capital Seringapatnam. Unable to receive French help on time, on 4 May 1799, Tipu met a hero's end while defending his capital.

4. **Fourth Anglo-Mysore War** (1799)

English
English under Wellesley, General Stuart and General Harris defeated Tipu Sultan and besieged Seringapatnam.

Tipu Sultan

Results of the War[4]

- **Tipu Sultan** fought bravely but died in the battle and English annexed large portions of **Mysore**. Central part of Mysore was given to **Krishna Raja** of **Wodeyar's dynasty**, a five-year-old boy who was descendant of the dethroned Hindu Raja and Purnaiya, the previous minister was made *diwan.* Tipu's family was removed from Seringapatnam and sent to Vellore prison.
- The remaining parts of the kingdom, nearly half of Tipu Sultan's dominions, were divided between the British and their ally, the Nizam. The whole of Canara, Wynad, Coimbatore, Dharmapuri and Seringapatnam were retained by the British, whereas the Nizam was given the areas around Gooty and a part of Chittoor and Chitaldurg districts.
- A **British resident** was stationed at Mysore and a special treaty of **Subsidiary Alliance** was imposed on the new Raja. Under the system, Mysore would not henceforth enter into any relationship with any other European powers, a contingent of Company army would be stationed in Mysore and the provision for its maintenance would come from its treasury. Also, the Governor General was authorised to take over the administration of the state in case of necessity, using which **William Bentinck** in 1831 took control of Mysore on grounds of misgovernance. Later, however, in 1881, Lord **Ripon** restored the kingdom to its ruler.

British Struggle With Marathas

After the conquest of Bengal and Mysore, the **Marathas** were the only major Indian power left outside the sphere of British control. Meanwhile, with the growth of the Company's cotton trade with China through Bombay, control of Deccan (which was under the control of the Marathas) was a crucial requirement for the Company. A succession dispute among Marathas provided the first opportunity to the British for intervention which resulted in the First Anglo–Maratha War, a series of battles between 1775 and 1782 in which the British were ultimately defeated.

[4] An important result of the Fourth Anglo–Mysore War was the complete elimination of the **French threat** to British supremacy in India.

First Anglo–Maratha War (1775–82): During the Reign of Warren Hastings

In 1772, **Madhava Rao** (Maratha Peshwa) died who had no issue. **Narayan Rao**, the younger brother of Madhava Rao, succeeded him to the throne but his uncle Raghunath Rao alias Raghoba murdered him and announced himself the next Peshwa, but Maratha leaders disregarded the authority of Raghoba and under able leadership of **Nana Phadnavis** appointed **Madhava Rao Narayana**, the infant son of Narayan Rao.

- Infuriated by this harsh treatment, Raghoba went to the British to seek their help for obtaining Peshwaship. To fructify their agreement, the **Treaty of Surat** (1775) was signed between Raghoba and the Bombay Governor, without the knowledge of Warren Hastings under which Raghoba agreed to hand over islands of Salsette and Bassein to the British along with parts of revenues from the districts of Surat and Bharuch. In return, the British promised him a support of 2,500 soldiers.
- When the news of this treaty reached Calcutta, Governor General Warren Hastings strongly condemned the decision of Bombay Governor to indulge in the fight against the Marathas (as by the *Regulating Act of 1773*, it was imperative for the Bombay and Madras Councils to get their actions ratified by the Calcutta Council which was headed by Governor General Warren Hastings). Since, Hastings wanted to consolidate the control over the newly acquired province of Bengal first, he sent his representative **Colonel Upton** to settle the issue in 1776. Colonel Upton cancelled the Treaty of Surat and concluded the **Treaty of Purandhar** (1776) with **Nana Phadnavis**, which was much to the advantage of the Marathas and eventually raised the position of Nana Phadnavis among the Marathas. According to this treaty:
    - Madhava Rao Narayana was accepted as the new Peshwa and the English withdrew their support from Raghunath Rao.
    - The British, however, retained Salsette along with Broach.
- However, the **Bombay Council** authorities rejected the **Treaty of Purandhar** and kept giving refuge to Raghunath Rao. They even appealed against the Treaty of Purandhar to the Court of Directors in London. The Court of Directors, thus, did not recognise the Treaty of Purandhar and nullified it. Subsequently, Warren Hastings too discarded the Treaty of Purandar as a *scrap of paper* and sanctioned operations against the Marathas.
- In the meantime, the British forces sent by the Bombay Government were defeated by the Marathas under the able leadership of Mahadji Scindia at the **Battle at Talegaon** (1776). Mahadji Scindia lured the British army into the ghats (valleys) near Talegaon and after trapping them from all sides, attacked their base camp. He also made use of *scorched earth policy* technique wherein all the farmlands were burned and wells were poisoned cutting their necessary food and water supplies.
- Subsequently, by January 1779, the English **retreated** and surrendered near the village of *Wadgaon* and the Company had to sign the humiliating **Treaty of Wadgaon** (1779) that forced the Bombay government to relinquish all territories acquired by the East India Company since 1775.

First Anglo-Maratha War (1775-1782)

English under **Warren Hastings**	**Mahadji Sindhia**, **Tukojirao Holkar** along with **Nana Phadnavis**

- However, Warren Hastings again refused to accept the Treaty of Wadgaon by taking the plea that Bombay Council had no legal powers to sign such treaty and acting swiftly in February 1779, he dispatched British troops under the command of **Colonel Goddard** who captured Ahmedabad, and Bassein in 1780 and **Captain Popham** who defeated the Maratha chief, Mahadji Scindia, in a number of small battles and captured Gwalior in 1781. But the English could not stage a final victory, and war with different ups and downs on both sides continued till 1782.

- By this time, the hostile camp against Warren Hastings in the Calcutta Council became active and lodged a complaint against him at the Court of Directors. The English Company was also involved in the **Second Anglo–Mysore War** against Hyder Ali (1780–84) at the same time and, thus, realised that it was almost impossible to continue wars in two different fronts against two formidable enemies. Realising the complexities of the situation, the British proposed for peace with Mahadji Scindia. Scindia accepted the proposal and, thus, in May 1782, the **Treaty of Salbai** was signed between **Warren Hastings** and Mahadji Scindia. According to provisions of this treaty:
  - English returned all the Maratha territories except Salsette.
  - Raghunath Rao was pensioned off and Madhav Rao Narayana was accepted as the Peshwa.

Critical Examination of Treaty of Salbai (1782)

In immediate terms, it may appear that the **Treaty of Salbai** (1782) was not advantageous to the East India Company as its provisions were quite similar to **Treaty of Purandar** (1776) which was discarded by the Company six years ago. On the face of it, it may appear that accepting a similar treaty after suffering huge financial and military loss was no way a good deal for the British but in terms of the long run, the Treaty of Salbai proved to be much more beneficial to the British than the Marathas as it provided the British **20 years of peace** with the Marathas which also enabled them to concentrate all its energies against **Mysore**. The Treaty of Salbai guaranteed the Company crucial support of the Marathas, without which it was impossible for the British to defeat Tipu Sultan in the **Third** and **Fourth Anglo–Mysore Wars**. Thus, the British were not only able to save themselves from the combined opposition of Indian powers but also succeeded in dividing the Indian powers that eventually led to the consolidation and establishment of the British Empire in India.

Second Anglo–Maratha War (1803–05): During the Reign of Lord Wellesley

The Marathas remained largely disunited since the Third Battle of Panipat (1761). The great Maratha statesman **Nana Phadnavis** kept the internal differences of Marathas in check, but with his death in 1800 it appears even wisdom and moderation too departed from Maratha land. In April 1801, **Peshwa Baji Rao II** who lacked political wisdom got **Vithoji**, the brother of **Jaswant Rao Holkar**, murdered. This triggered a war between the Holkar and the Peshwa, who was also supported by Daulat Rao Sindhia. **Holkar** defeated the combined forces of Scindia and the Peshwa and seized the city of Poona. With rich booty, Holkar returned to his capital but the scared and weak ruler **Peshwa Baji Rao II** fled to Bassein and approached the English for protection where he signed with them the **Treaty of Bassein** (1802) which was a **subsidiary alliance** treaty according to which:

- The Peshwa agreed to keep a permanent subsidiary force in his capital at Poona and for the upkeep of this force agreed to surrender to East India Company, the city of Surat and neighbouring territory yielding revenue of ₹26 lakh.
- A English resident was stationed at Poona.
- Peshwa surrendered his foreign policy to British control and agreed to not to enter in any offensive or defensive alliances without the permission of the Company.
- He also agreed not to keep in employment any other Europeans.

As an immediate response to the Treaty of Bassein, the British troops marched under the command of **Arthur Wellesley** towards Poona and restored the **Peshwa** to his position.

But the proud Maratha chiefs **Daulat Rao Sindhia** and **Raghoji Bhonsle** took the Treaty of Bassein as an insult to the national honour of the Marathas. Soon the forces of both the chieftains were united and they crossed the River Narmada. Lord **Wellesley** seized this opportunity and declared war in August 1803 and this way the Second Anglo–Maratha War was started.

2. **Second Anglo-Maratha War** (1803-1805)

- **English** under **Wellesley** defeated
- **Daulat Rao Sindhia**, **Raghoji Bhonsle** and later **Yashwant Rao Holkar**

- **Arthur Wellesley** captured Ahmednagar in August 1803 and defeated the combined forces of **Sindhia** and **Bhonsle** at Assaye near Aurangabad. Subsequently, Arthur Wellesley carried the war into Bhonsle's territory and completely defeated the Maratha forces on the plains of Argaon. As a result, the **Treaty of Deogaon** was signed between Bhonsle and Wellesley according to which Bhonsle signed the subsidiary treaty, which forced him to give up the province of Cuttack in Orissa.
- In the north, **Lord Lake** routed **Scindia's** army at Laswari in November 1803 and occupied Aligarh, Delhi and Agra. He took the Mughal Emperor **Shah Alam II** under British protection. **Scindia** too had to sign a type of subsidiary treaty known as the **Treaty of Surji–Arjungaon** with the British.
- Wellesley now turned his attention towards **Yashwant Rao Holkar**, but Holkar proved more than a match for the British. Using traditional Maratha tactics of guerrilla warfare and in alliance with the **Jats**, he remained unsubdued. His ally, the **Raja of Bharatpur**, inflicted heavy losses on Lake who unsuccessfully attempted to storm his fort. The **British**, thus, **failed** to comprehensively defeat **Holkar**, and since all these wars meant huge expenses for the Company and also the Court of Directors were dissatisfied with the forward policy of Lord Wellesley, he was recalled from India. The Company then made peace with Holkar by the **Treaty of Rajpurghat** (1806) giving back to him most of his territories.

Significance of the Treaty of Bassein for the British (1802)

Even though the treaty was signed by a Peshwa who lacked political authority, but the direct and indirect implications of the Treaty of Bassein were of immense benefit to the **East India Company**. The provision of keeping British troops permanently in Poona proved to be a decision of great strategical benefit to the English as now the Company's troops were more evenly spread across the Deccan and with this newly added advantage of swift movement of English troops in times of need to any place, the Company was in a better position to expand its sphere of influence in the neighbouring areas. Also, the provisions of Treaty of Bassein subjugated the entire **Maratha** kingdom as even though titular but still theoretically Peshwa was the head of the entire Maratha Empire. So, the Treaty of Bassein paved the way for making the East India Company into strongest political power in not only western India but also the whole of India as well since Marathas were the only major Indian power left outside the sphere of British control and now with their subjugation too, there was hardly any other native power left in India who could stand up against British.

Third Anglo–Maratha War (1817–18): During the Reign of Lord Hastings

Even though the Second Anglo–Maratha War had shattered the power of the Maratha chiefs somehow their spirit of fight was still alive within them. The **Maratha chiefs** did not want to surrender their great tradition of independence without a struggle, and hence they made a desperate last attempt to regain their independence and lost prestige in 1817. But before that an important event had a prominent role to play in the **Third Anglo–Maratha War**, and that was the **Pindari War** (1816–18).

Pindari War (1816–18)

The Maratha army used to have two components, regular forces and irregular forces. The regular forces were maintained by the state and were given arms, horses and salary, whereas the **Pindaris** formed part of irregular forces who used to bring their own horses and weapons, did not receive any salary from the state but in lieu of that used to get the opportunity to plunder the conquered territory after the war. After the Second Anglo–Maratha War, when the Marathas accepted the Subsidiary Alliance system, they had to **disband** these irregular forces. Having lost their traditional profession, Pindaris took to **highway robberies**. They were mostly active in the areas of Rajputana and the Central Provinces and subsisted on plunder. It is worth mentioning that even though being mercenaries, the Pindaris never helped the British and also noteworthy is the fact that they did not belong to any particular caste or creed and their leaders belonged to both the Hindu as well as the Muslim communities, who had thousands of followers. Chief leaders amongst the Pindaris were **Wasil Muhammad**, **Chitu** and **Karim Khan**. In 1812, the Pindaris plundered the districts of Mirzapur and Shahabad, and in 1815 they raided the Nizam's dominions. In 1816, they plundered the Northern Circars. All these plundering activities of seemingly lawless Pindaris caught the attention of Governor General **Lord Hastings** who viewed these activities of Pindaris as a direct challenge to British Paramountcy. Thus, in 1816, he determined to suppress the Pindaris and assembled a large force to round up and exterminate their chiefs.

Pindari War (1816-18)

- **English** under lord **Hastings** defeated Pindaris
- **Pindaris**
  Major leaders were **Karim Khan** (submitted but was offered estate).
  Wasil Muhammad (forced to lay down arms and died in captivity)
  Chitu (defeated but was probably killed by atiger in a forest)

- By 1818, the **Pindaris** were mostly suppressed and all their bands disintegrated. **Karim Khan** was given a small estate in the Gorakhpur district of the United Provinces. **Wasil Muhammad** took refuge in the Scindia camp, but the latter handed him over to the British and Wasil committed suicide in captivity while **Chitu** escaped to the forest, where probably a tiger killed him.
- Even though the Pindari War was won by British, yet it created a rift between the Company and the Marathas. When the military campaign was organised against the Pindaris, the Company had expected full Maratha support for the same but since the Pindaris were former Maratha soldiers only, the Maratha commanders were somewhere emotionally attached to them.
- Subsequently, Lord Hastings accused the Marathas of not supporting the Anti-Pindari Campaign wholeheartedly. He, thus, asked them to sign a new treaty providing greater control and when the Maratha chiefs hesitated, it became one of the reasons for Hastings to declare a war on them. Thus, the Anti-Pindari War merged into the Third Anglo–Maratha War.

Immediate Cause of the Third Anglo–Maratha War (1817–18)

Peshwa **Baji Rao II**, fed up with the rigid control of the British Resident, made a last attempt to regain his independence and took the lead in organising a united front of the Maratha chiefs against the British resulting in the Third Anglo–Maratha War.

3. **Third Anglo-Maratha War** (1817–1818)

- **English** under **Hastings** defeated the Marathas
- **Baji Rao II**, **Appa Sahib**, **Malhar Rao Holkar** and **Daulat Rao Sindia**

- The **Peshwa**, thus, attacked the **British Residency** at Poona in November 1817, but was defeated at a place called Kirkee. His territories were annexed and the Presidency of Bombay was enlarged subsequently.
- Similarly, the Bhonsle chief, **Appa Sahib** of Nagpur, refused to abide by the **Treaty of Nagpur** (1816) signed by him with the British and hereafter, attacked the **Residency** at Nagpur. The **Battle of Sitabuldi** was fought between him and the British in November 1817, but he too was defeated.
- **Malhar Rao Holkar** too was defeated by the British on 21 December 1817 at Baroda.
- **Lord Hastings** also compelled the **Scindia** to accept British suzerainty and he surrendered Ajmer to the British who gave it further to the Nawab of Bhopal, who had also accepted the British suzerainty.
- The **Gaekwar** of **Baroda** too accepted the Subsidiary Alliance and handed over certain areas of Ahmedabad to the British.

Therefore, by December 1817, the dream of a mighty Maratha Confederacy was finally shattered and British emerged as the paramount power[5] in India.

Results of the War

- To satisfy Maratha pride, a small state of Satara was created under **Pratap Singh**, a descendent of Shivaji, but he ruled it as a complete dependent of the British.
- The **Peshwa** was dethroned and pensioned off at Bithur near Kanpur. Peshwaship itself was abolished.
- An indirect result of the war was that with the downfall of the Marathas, the Rajputana states who had been dominated for several decades by the Scindia and Holkar, too readily accepted British supremacy.

Causes of the Defeat of the Marathas

- **Lack of Capable Leadership**: Towards the end of the 18th century, the Marathas unfortunately lost nearly all of their wise and experienced leaders such as **Peshwa Madhav Rao II**, **Nana Phadnavis**, **Mahadji Scindia**, **Tukoji Holkar** and **Ahilyabai Holkar**. These leaders had earlier kept the Maratha confederacy together and had provided efficient leadership. But, with their demise, the later Maratha leaders were not able to fill in their worthy shoes and, thus, it proved to be a huge cost for the Maratha state.
- **Lack of Unity and Coordination amongst Maratha Chiefs**: The Maratha Confederacy consisted of five major chiefs, being the Peshwa at Poona, the Gaekwad at Baroda, the Scindia at Gwalior, the Holkar at Indore and the Bhonsle at Nagpur, the Peshwa being the nominal head of the confederacy. But, more often the chiefs were engaged in bitter fratricidal strife, totally ignoring the real danger from the rapidly advancing British. For instance, when the Scindia and Bhonsle fought the British, the Holkar stood on the sidelines while the Gaekwad gave help to the British. Consequently, when the Holkar fought against the British, the Bhonsle and Scindia refused to help the Holkar. Had they fought as a united front against their common enemy the British in the early stages, the outcome of the wars would have been definitely different.
- **Military weakness of the Marathas**: Though Marathas were great warriors full of personal prowess and valour, they were still inferior to the English in terms of artillery, organisation of the forces and in disciplined action. The Maratha use of age-old warfare techniques was no match against British sophisticated modern warfare methodology. Along with it, the well-knit spy system and better diplomatic skills of the British to win over allies helped them to isolate their adversary.
- **Failure to estimate correctly the political and diplomatic strategy of the British**: Maratha chiefs somehow lived in the false belief that the Company being primarily a trading body was a transitory power, while Mysore, Nizam of Hyderabad and other native powers were their real enemies. This proved to be a costly mistake for both Marathas and the rest of the rulers too.

[5] The year **1818**, thus, proved to be a significant year for both India and the British as the entire Indian subcontinent excepting the Punjab and Sindh had been brought under British control, making them the **paramount power** in India.

The Conquest of Sindh

Since the 18th century, Sindh was ruled by some Baluchi chiefs collectively known as '**Amirs of Sindh**'. The East India Company had tried as early as 1758 to open a factory at the strategic port of Tatta, situated in the Indus Delta in Sindh. Trade relations thus established continued till 1775, when, owing to the discouraging attitude of the new ruler, **Sarfaraz Khan**, the factory was abandoned. However, owing to political turmoil in Sindh, all relations of the British with Sindh thus came to an end and were revived only after two decades owing to European political developments.

- In June 1807, **Napolean** concluded the alliance of Tilsit with **Alexander I** of Russia, one of the details of which was a combined invasion of India by the land route. To provide against this fresh danger, it was thought necessary to have a barrier between British India and Russia. Accordingly, **Lord Minto I** dispatched missions, namely that of Metcalfe to Lahore, Elphinstone to Kabul and Malcolm to Tehran and Mr Hankey Smith to Sindh. Consequently, in 1809 a '**Treaty of Eternal Friendship**' was concluded with Amirs of Sindh. By this treaty, both sides agreed to maintain territorial integrity and unity of each other and also to exclude **French** from Sindh.
- This treaty was renewed in 1820 with the addition of some new articles which excluded the **Americans** also and purported to resolve some border disputes on the side of Kutch.
- Again to counteract and check the influence of Russia through Persia, the British decided to collect political and geographical information of the region for possibilities of future military movements. Thus, in 1831, the British sent Lieutenant **Alexander Burnes** out to India to explore the possibilities of navigation of the river Indus for the purposes of commercial intercourse between Northern India and Britain.
- Further in 1832, Lord **William Bentinck** sent Henry Pottinger to Sindh, who negotiated a **treaty with Amirs** through which the Company gained a number of commercial privileges as the lower part of the Indus and the whole of the Sutlej were thrown open to English trade.
- In order to further consolidate their position in Sindh, the English were looking for an opportunity which they got, when Maharaja Ranjit Singh of Punjab captured a frontier town of Sindh. Lord **Auckland** offered protection to the Amirs but forced them to sign a new treaty in 1838 under which the Company troops were kept in Sindh at the Amir's expense. The treaty also permitted the English to intervene in the disputes between the Amirs and the Sikhs, along with stationing of a British resident. Thus, very cleverly Sindh was turned into a British protectorate.
- Gradually in 1839, Sindh was made to accept Subsidiary Alliance and later acting quite cheap British even forced the Amirs to pay for their Afghan adventure too.
- However, to counter-balance their defeat in the **First Anglo–Afghan War** (1839–42), and to uplift his already precarious position due to the Afghan reverses, **Lord Ellenborough** chanced upon the easy target of Sindh since it was going through a period of internal turmoil and chaos due to certain succession dispute after the death of an Amir. Ellenborough imposed a totally outrageous treaty on Sindh and made the Amirs to cede more provinces.
- In 1842, Sir **Charles Napier** was appointed as British resident in place of Major James Outram. Napier, thereafter, unnecessarily provoked the Amirs, and in 1843 destructed their famous desert fortress Imamgarh. In retaliation to this, the **Baluchis** attacked the British resident and declared war on the British. The **Battle of Miani** ensued in which the Baluchi army was defeated by Napier and some Amirs had to surrender. Later, the **Battle of Dubbo** happened in which Napier defeated the Amir of Mirpur Sher Muhammad resulting in the formal **annexation of Sindh** (1843).
- Napier was appointed as the first Governor of Sindh and interestingly he sent a telegram to the British headquarters exclaiming, "I have Sin(ne)d". Thus, in spite of previous assurances that territorial integrity would be always respected, Sindh was annexed. Napier had himself written in his diary, "*We have no right to seize Sindh, yet we shall do so, and a very advantageous, useful humane piece of rascality it will be.*"

Critical Examination of Annexation of Sindh (1843)

Most historians believe that the pretexts and causes for the annexation of Sindh were deliberately manufactured by the British. They thus univocally condemned the Annexation of Sindh and considered it as a political sequential to the First Anglo–Afghan War, which if we analyse closely seems to be a quite justified theory. In 1838, to counter the Russian influence, Shah Shuja was placed on the Afghan throne, but since he was a mere puppet of the East India Company, a popular uprising against him broke out and the First Anglo–Afghan War (1839–42) started in which the Company was badly defeated. This notably broke the myth of English invincibility and also emboldened many rebellions in India as witnessed in the ranks of Madras army and in the Scindia territory. The British thought that these dissensions could only be countered by restoring the myth of English invincibility. Thus, they chanced upon the easy target of Sindh. Even the British official Elphinstone statement read, "*Coming from Afghanistan, when a bully was knocked in the street, he went home to beat his wife in revenge*," confirms this inference.

Causes for Annexation of Sindh (1843)

- Commercial possibilities of the River Indus.
- British fear of expansion of Russian Empire towards the east.
- British desire to increase influence in Persia and Afghanistan through control over Sindh.

The Conquest of Punjab

In the late 18th century, the consolidation of Sikh power had taken place under Maharaja **Ranjit Singh**, who was a capable ruler and administrator. During his lifetime, there was no major tension between Punjab and the British. In fact, in order to counter the Russian threat and to maintain Sikh state as a buffer between Company's north Indian possessions on the one end and the Muslim powers in Persia and Afghanistan on the other, **Lord William Bentinck** negotiated friendly relations with both Ranjit Singh and also with the Amirs of Sind and as an initial measure, an exchange of gifts took place between Lahore, the capital of Punjab, and Calcutta, the seat of the Governor-General. It was then followed by the meeting of **Bentinck** and **Ranjit Singh** (1831) at Ropar on the banks of the River Sutlej amidst great show and splendour. Both sides mutually promised perpetual friendship and respect for each other's territorial integrity and unity. They also concluded a commercial treaty known as **Indus Navigation Treaty** through which River Sutlej was also opened for navigation. We have already discussed above that a similar kind of treaty was also concluded with the Amirs of Sind. In 1838, a **Tripartite treaty** was signed by East India Company, Ranjit Singh and Shah Shuja of Afghanistan, and all parties professed friendship and agreed to respect each other's territorial integrity and unity.

Background of Anglo Sikh Wars

But things took a sudden turn in 1839 when **Ranjit Singh** died. His death was followed by **political instability**. A number of people ascended the throne in quick succession and the whole region was plunged into prolonged and bloody succession battles resulting in the breakdown of the delicate balance of power that Ranjit Singh had carefully maintained between the hereditary Sikh chieftains and between the Punjabi and Dogra faction of nobles. After the death of Ranjit Singh, the next three rulers Kharak Singh, Nau Nihal Singh and Sher Singh were **murdered** within next 6 years (1839–45).

- In such an unstable environment, without much effective control over the army, **Dalip Singh**, the 5-year-old son of Ranjit Singh, ascended the throne in 1843, under the regency of **Rani Jindan** and guardianship of wazir **Hira Singh Dogra**. But, by now the Khalsa Army became a power onto itself and began to control Punjabi politics. Hira Singh soon fell a victim to this power struggle and was assassinated in 1844. He was succeeded by new wazir **Jawahar Singh**, the brother of **Rani Jindan**, but he remained for all practical purposes, a puppet in the hands of the army.

- The British were now concerned about these new developments of continuous political instability in Punjab and increasing political influence of the Khalsa Army since all these issues were threatening their scheme of a strong buffer state. Meanwhile, British encirclement of Punjab had started from 1833, when they had appointed British residents at Ludhiana and Sindh.
- Hereafter, when the situation in Punjab did not stabilise and even **Jawahar Singh** was executed by the army in 1845, the English started preparations for war. Barracks for additional troops were built in a forward area and additional regiments began to be despatched to the Punjab frontier. The Punjab army, now convinced that the British were determined to occupy Punjab, took counter-measures and when they learnt that British Commander in chief, Lord **Hugh Gough** and Governor General Lord **Harding** were marching towards Ferozepur, they decided to strike and war between the two was thus declared on 13 December, 1845.

First Anglo Sikh War (1845–1846)

- English under Hardinge defeated Sikhs
- Sikh Chiefs fought under the name of Dalip Singh and Rani Jindan.

A series of battles that happened during the course between the British and Sikhs form part of the First **Anglo–Sikh War** (1845–46):

- **Battle of Mudki** (1845): It was fought between **Lal Singh** (Prime Minister of Sikhs) and Lord **Hugh Gough** in which the Sikh Army was defeated.
- **Battle of Ferozeshah** (1845): It was fought between the Sikh Army under **Tej Singh** (got defeated) and the **British**
- **Battle of Baddowal** (1846): It was fought between **Ranjodh Singh Majithia** (got defeated) and **Harry Smith**.
- **Battle of Guns/Battle of Sobraon** (1846). One of the decisive battles fought between the British (**Harry Smith**) and **Sikhs**. The British emerged victorious and they not only crossed Sutlej but occupied Lahore too.

This resulted in signing of **Treaty of Lahore** (1846) according to which:

- **Jalandhar Daob** was given to the British along with a demand for payment of ₹1.5 crores to the British. Sikhs paid only half of this amount and for settling the rest they sold **Kashmir** to the **British** who sold it further to the Raja of Jammu, Gulab Singh Dogra, for a cash payment of ₹5 million.
- Appointment of British Resident at Lahore (**Sir Henry Lawrence**), with a strong British force stationed there.
- Punjab army was reduced to 20,000 infantry and 12,000 cavalry.
- Dalip Singh was allowed to retain his throne, but was to be advised and guided by an English resident.

Rani Jindan, who was acting as regent of her son, Dalip Singh, had believed that, as stipulated in the treaty of Lahore, the British force would eventually leave Lahore. But the British, instead of quitting, started strengthening their authority over Lahore administration. This led to the signing of the **Treaty of Bhairowal** (1846) also known as the Second Treaty of Lahore through which **Rani Jindan** was removed and a regency council for Punjab was set up (consisting of eight Sikh Sardars and presided over by Sir Henry Lawrence) and moreover, the British were permitted to station their troops in any part of the state and the Sikh authorities had to even pay for their maintenance. Thus, the Treaty of Bhairowal transformed the Sikh kingdom into a virtual British protectorate and hence the grounds for another confrontation were set.

Second Anglo–Sikh War (1848–49)

In order to avenge humiliation of the first war and also bad treatment accorded to Rani Jindan, Punjabis rose up in numerous local revolts. Two of the prominent revolts were led by Sikh governors **Mul Raj** of Multan and **Chattar Singh** Attariwala of Haripur near Lahore. Lord **Dalhousie** seized this opportunity to annex Punjab and thus, this way the **Second Anglo–Sikh War** started.

Second Anglo Sikh War (1848–1849)

↓

- **English** under **Dalhousie** defeated Sikhs
- Two Prominent Sikh governors:
  a) **Mul raj** of Multan
  b) **Chattar Singh Attariwala** of Haripur near Lahore

In the first two rounds of the battle at Ramnagar in November 1848 and at Chillianwala in January 1849, the British suffered heavy losses but this was soon reversed in February-March, when the rebel Sardars had to surrender one after another.

The Second Anglo–Punjab War thus resulted in **annexation of Punjab** by Lord Dalhousie in 1849 and Dalip Singh and Rani Jindan were transported to England. A board of **three Commissioners** was established consisting of:

- Henry Lawrence
- John Lawrence
- Charles G Mansel

In 1853, this board was abolished and Sir **John Lawrence** was appointed as Chief Commissioner for Punjab who was subsequently made Lieutenant Governor of Punjab in 1859.

The conquest of Punjab was followed by the annexation of several other princely states such as Satara (1848), Jaitpur, Sambalpur (Orissa), Jhansi, Nagpur (1854) and Awadh (1856) on the basis of Lord **Dalhousie's** infamous **Doctrine of Lapse**. Thus by 1857, the British had annexed 63 per cent of the territories of the Indian subcontinent and brought under its authority 78 per cent of the population while the rest remained under the Indian princes who were autonomous only in name.

Ideology of Expansion: Annexation Through Diplomatic Alliances and Administrative Policies

The Conquest of India by the British was carried out using a two-pronged approach. The first approach being annexation by means of defeating Indian states in different **wars and battles** to emerge as paramount power in the Indian subcontinent, while the second approach focused on making effective use of **diplomatic alliances and administrative policies** to fulfil its dream of imperial expansion and consolidation of British paramountcy. Some of the effective diplomatic and administrative policies utilised by British were as follows:

- **The policy of Ring Fence**: This policy was initiated by **Lord Warren Hastings** (1773–85) and was aimed at creating buffer zones to defend the Company's frontiers. The friendly native states were used as a buffer to keep the unfriendly states away. It can also be understood as a policy of defence of British's neighbours' frontiers for safeguarding their own territories. The policy is clearly evident in Warren Hastings' action of creating Awadh as a buffer and securing Awadh frontiers in order to ward off the influence of Marathas and Mysore. Interestingly, though the buffer states were promised military assistance against external aggression, yet they were required to pay for the maintenance and expenses of the defending army.

- **Subsidiary Alliance**: The Subsidiary Alliance system was introduced by **Lord Wellesley** (1798–1805) and was in fact an extension of the policy of ring fence. It is rather interesting to note that the basic principles of Subsidiary Alliance were first formulated by French Governor **Dupleix** in southern India when he initiated the practice of lending European troops to his native allies in return for fixed amount of money. The **English** thereafter adopted and expanded the system. The system was initially based on the idea of supporting a friendly native ruler in his wars and battles which over the course of time gradually modified in reducing the subsidiary states to a position of dependence on the Company's support. Under this system, **subsidiary agreements** (*sanads*) were entered between the British and the local Indian rulers according to which the British agreed to protect the Indian rulers against **external threats** and **internal disorders** but, in return:
  - The Indian rulers who accepted the Subsidiary Alliance system were to agree to the stationing of **permanent subsidiary British force** in his capital for whose maintenance they would pay a subsidy to the British. The Indian state was called '**the protected state**' and the British hereinafter were referred to as '**the paramount power**'.
  - The protected state should give money or was asked to surrender a part of its territory yielding revenue equal to the cost of maintaining subsidiary force to the British.
  - The ruler under the system of alliance had to completely **surrender his foreign relations** to the East India Company. He could neither enter into offensive or defensive alliance with any other power nor can fight a war or sign peace without **prior permission** from the British Company.
  - The Indian ruler could **not employ** any European in his service without the prior approval of the British.
  - A **British resident** was stationed at these subsidiary states. While the British promised to adopt a policy of non-interference in the internal matters of the protected state, in reality they seldom followed it.

  The **Nizam of Hyderabad** (1798) was first to enter into a subsidiary alliance with the English (1798), followed by Tanjore (1799), Awadh (1801), the Scindhias (1804), the Rajput states of Jodhpur, Jaipur, Bundi, the ruler of Bharatpur (1818) and the Holkars (1818). It is noteworthy to add that **Tipu Sultan** rejected it summarily but eventually with his defeat in the Fourth Anglo–Mysore War, Mysore was brought under the Subsidiary Alliance system (1799), while **Baji Rao II**, the Maratha leader, entered into it (Treaty of Bassein, 1802) in a futile attempt to regain control over his warring chiefs.

  Wellesley's Subsidiary system is regarded as one of the master strokes of British imperialism. This system was suited best to the advantage of the British as:
  - It gradually and discreetly disarmed the Native states resulting in considerable loss of their autonomy, which further aided in enhancing the clout of British paramountcy.
  - It increased the military strength of the Company in India at the expense of the protected states. The system enabled the Company to maintain large force without incurring any additional cost. Moreover, this force could be used at shortest possible notice against its Indian and non-Indian enemies.
  - This system enabled the Company to weed out the foreign influence from the Indian courts.

  It thus helped in the expansion of the British Empire in India by bringing new territories under its influence without even fighting any battle or spending any penny enabling the British to become the paramount power in India.

- The **Doctrine of Lapse**: It was an annexation policy devised by Lord **Dalhousie** (1848–56). There was a widespread custom of adoption to secure an heir in the absence of a natural successor, that is, son among the Indian rulers. However, with his principle of Doctrine of Lapse, Dalhousie refused to recognise the authority of succession of an adopted heir. He cunningly maintained that there was a difference in principle between the right to inherit private property and the right to govern. As per his policy of Doctrine of Lapse:
  - Any Indian state under the direct influence of the British East India Company, or as a vassal state under the British Subsidiary System, would be **automatically annexed** if the ruler died without a natural male heir or was either incompetent and did not have natural heirs to the throne.

- In other words, the sovereignty of a native state lapsed to the paramount power in absence of natural heirs in a ruling family.
- Thus, by the Doctrine of Lapse not only the long-established right of the Indian sovereigns without an heir to choose a successor was taken over, but the British also took over the authority of deciding the competence of the Indian rulers.

With the help of the policy of Doctrine of Lapse, the Company annexed the states of Satara (1848), Jaitpur, Sambalpur (Orissa), Jhansi, Nagpur (1854) and Awadh (1856).

Reasons for the Success of the British

In less than a century, the British not only established but also consolidated their power over India. For this, they made use of each possible tactic available at their disposal ranging from diplomatic alliances, to exertion of military power to utilisation of administrative policies to at times also, using unjustified reasons to finally emerge as supreme rulers of India. However, there were certain factors responsible for the success of the British in the conquest of India:

- **Lack of political unity and statesmanship among Indian states**: After the political power vacuum created by the Mughal decline, no single regional Indian state could rise up to the occasion. Some regional Indian states like Mysore, Marathas and Punjab possessed the capability to counter British influence but they were so busy fighting with each other that they failed to foresee the dangers arising from the growing political clout of the British. At the critical time, they could **not unite** against the common foreign enemy and, thus, eventually had to surrender before the British one after another. Also, in the 18th century, they **lacked** the **statesmanship** of having a vision and consciousness of one nation, which eventually hurt them all.
- **Use of superior warfare techniques, modernised arms and ammunition along with brilliant leadership**: Having witnessed the Industrial Revolution in 16th century, the British had the advantage of the latest and most sophisticated weapons. As a matter of fact, their firearms were much better in terms of firing and in range as compared to Indian firearms. The English also had the advantage of brilliant leaders both in the political and military field. **Robert Clive, Warren Hastings, Cornwallis, Dalhousie, Wellesley,** Sir **Eyre Coote**, Lord **Lake** all had the foresight and sharpness of mind to lead from the front. Even though the Indian side too had some gems of leaders like Hyder Ali, Tipu Sultan, Nana Phadnavis, Mahadji Scindia and Yashwant Rao Holkar but they often had to face the crunch of talented second line commanders. The Company's military power that held the key to its political dominance was predicated not only on the superior fighting skills but also on effective recruitment strategies. Also, their civil administration was integrated with the military administration and this generated important fiscal and logistical benefits.
- **Better military discipline, training and regular salary to the troops**: It is indeed interesting to note that the British troops consisted of many Indian natives only. The high quality of military training imparted by British officers transformed these natives into well-disciplined troops who won for British so many wars and battles. A regular system of payment of salaries ensured their loyalty towards the English. The Indian armies, on the other hand, were inadequately trained and poorly paid, who often were no match for the disciplined and well-trained British troops.
- **Effective use of diplomatic policies like subsidiary alliance and doctrine of lapse**: These policies proved to be more effective instruments than bloody battles and wars for expanding the colonial footprint of the British. These diplomatic treaties not only allowed the British to establish their **spheres of influence** but also at the same time saved them precious millions required for maintaining their troops. Later, the British used one or the other excuse to insubordinate that state completely. The insubordination of states of Hyderabad, Awadh and Mysore is a clear testimony to this fact.
- **Benefit from Britain's global profile**: The British East India Company could always rely on huge assets that Britain possessed and could be used to bail the Company out if the occasion so demanded.

Chronological Order of Major Events

First Carnatic War (1746–48)

- Dupleix and Barnett
- Battle of Adyar
- Treaty of Aix-La-Chapelle (1748)

Second Carnatic War (1748–54)

- Dupleix + Chanda Sahib + Muzzafar Jang vs English + Nasir Jung + Nawab Anwar-ud-din
- Battle of Ambur (1749)
- Battle of Arcot (1751)
- Treaty of Pondicherry

Third Carnatic War (1756–63)

- Count de Lally (French) vs General Eyre Coote(English)
- Battle of Wandiwash (1760)
- Treaty of Paris

Battle of Plassey (1757)

- Siraj-ud-Daulah vs Robert Clive + Mir Jafar

Battle of Buxar (1764)

- Mir Qasim + Shuja-ud-daulah + Shah-Alam II vs English + Mir Jafar
- Treaty of Allahabad (1765)

First Anglo–Mysore War (1767–69)

- Hyder Ali vs English
- Treaty of Madras (1769)

First Anglo–Maratha War (1775–82)

- Maratha Nana Padhnavis vs English + Raghoba (Under Lord Warren Hastings).
- Treaty of Surat (1775)
- Battle of Talcgaon (1776)
- Treaty of Purandhar (1776)
- Treaty of Salbai (1782)

Second Anglo–Mysore War (1780–84)

- Hyder Ali vs English
- Treaty of Mangalore (1784)

Third Anglo–Mysore War (1790–92)

- Tipu Sultan vs English + Nizam + Marathas (under Cornwallis)
- Treaty of Seringapatnam (1792)

↓

Fourth Anglo–Mysore War (1799)

- Tipu Sultan + French vs English (under Lord Wellesley)

↓

Second Maratha War (1803–05)

- Baji Rao II + British vs Holkar + Sindhia (under Lord Wellesley).
- Treaty of Bassein (1802)
- Treaty of Rajpuraghat (1806)

↓

Pindari War (1816–18)

- British vs Pindari

↓

Third Maratha War (1817–18)

- Baji Rao II + Daulat Rao + Appa Sahib + Malhar Rao vs British (under Lord Hastings)

↓

Annexation of Sindh (1843)

↓

First Anglo–Sikh War (1845–46)

↓

Second Anglo–Sikh War (1848–49)

Previous Year's Questions (Prelims)

1. With reference to Pondicherry (now Puducherry), consider the following statements: (2010)
   1. The first European power to occupy Pondicherry were the Portuguese.
   2. The second European power to occupy Pondicherry were the French.
   3. The English never occupied Pondicherry.

   Which of the statements given above is/are correct?

   (a) 1 only
   (b) 2 and 3 only
   (c) 3 only
   (d) 1, 2 and 3

2. The ruler of which one of the following states was removed from power by the British on the pretext of misgovernance? (2008)

   (a) Awadh
   (b) Jhansi
   (c) French
   (d) Satara

3. Who among the following Europeans were the last to come to pre-Independence of India as traders? (2008)
   (a) Dutch
   (b) English
   (c) French
   (d) Portuguese

4. Consider the following statements: (2008)
   1. Robert Clive was the first Governor-General of Bengal.
   2. William Bentinck was the first Governor-General of India.

   Which of the statements given above is/are correct?
   (a) 1 only
   (b) 2 only
   (c) Both 1 and 2
   (d) Neither 1 nor 2

5. Which of the following was the first fort constructed by the British in India? (2008)
   (a) Fort William
   (b) Fort St. George
   (c) Fort St. David
   (d) Fort St. Angelo

6. Which of the following is the correct chronological order of the battles fought in India in the 18th Century? (2005)
   (a) Battle of Wandiwash, Battle of Buxar, Battle of Ambur, Battle of Plassey
   (b) Battle of Ambur, Battle of Plassey, Battle of Wandiwash, Battle of Buxar
   (c) Battle of Wandiwash, Battle of Plassey, Battle of Ambur, Battle of Buxar
   (d) Battle of Ambur, Battle of Buxar Battle of Wandiwash, Battle of Plassey

7. Consider the following statements: (2004)
   1. In the Third Battle of Panipat, Ahmad Shah Abdali defeated Ibrahim Lodi.
   2. Tipu Sultan was killed in the Third Anglo–Mysore War.
   3. Mir Jafar entered in a conspiracy with the English for the defeat of Nawab Siraj ud-Daulah in the Battle of Plassey.

   Which of the statements given above is/are correct?
   (a) 1, 2 and 3
   (b) 3 only
   (c) 2 and 3
   (d) None

8. Which of the following pairs are correctly matched? (2004)

List I	List II
1. AD 1767–69	First Anglo–Maratha War
2. AD 1790–92	Third Mysore War
3. AD 1824–26	First Anglo–Burmese War
4. AD 1845–46	Second Sikh War

   Select the correct answer using the codes given below:
   Codes:
   (a) 2 and 4
   (b) 3 and 4
   (c) 1 and 2
   (d) 2 and 3

9. With reference to the entry of European powers into India which of the following is not correct? (2003)
   (a) The Portuguese captured Goa in 1499.
   (b) The English opened their first factory in south Indian at Masulipatnam.
   (c) In Eastern India, the English company opened its first factory in Orissa in 1633.
   (d) Under the leadership of Dupleix, the French occupied Madras in 1746.

10. In India, among the following locations, the Dutch established their earliest factory at (2003)
   (a) Surat
   (b) Pulicat
   (c) Cochin
   (d) Cossimbazar

11. Consider the following Princely states of the British rule in India (2003)
   1. Jhansi

2. Sambalpur
3. Satara

The correct chronological order in which they were annexed by the British is:

(a) 1-2-3
(b) 1-3-2
(c) 3-2-1
(d) 3-1-2

12. Who among the following Indian rules established embassies in foreign countries on modern lines? (2001)

(a) Hyder Ali
(b) Mir Qasim
(c) Shah Alam II
(d) Tipu Sultan

Previous Year's Answers (Prelims)

1. (a)	2. (a)	3. (c)	4. (b)	5. (b)	6. (b)	7. (b)	8. (d)
9. (a)	10. (b)	11. (c)	12. (d)				

Consolidation and Governance: Key Changes and Their Impact (1757–1857)

2

In the previous chapter, we discussed that the British gradually emerged as the paramount power in the Indian subcontinent. It was now essential for the British to consolidate their rule and devise suitable methods of governance for controlling and administering the vast Indian Empire. The **two-fold** policy adopted by the British to consolidate their rule in India comprised both the establishment of a proper administrative system along with pursuing robust foreign and frontier policy aimed at securing the boundaries of the newly conquered territories. The British initially though ruled through indigenous institutions, over the period from 1757 to 1857 gradually brought tremendous changes in the administrative structure and organisation. However, at the same time, the main orientation of British administration remained the same which was designed and developed to further the core objective of increasing the Company's profits and to maintain and strengthen the British hold over India.

Changes in the Structure of the Government

The need for **greater Parliamentary control** over the East India Company's affairs arose during the decades after Plassey, when the Company emerged as an important territorial power across the Indian subcontinent. The company's character changed quite significantly over the years from a predominantly **commercial** to a predominantly **political** power. As the Company's empire and wealth in India expanded, the British Parliament was also eager to have a share of the Company's prosperity. As a matter of fact, there had been government interventions in the Company's affairs as early as 1767, when the rights of the state were exerted on the revenues of the territories conquered with the help of the royal army, which thus, resulted in the payment of 400,000 pounds annually to the government. However, with each passing year, there was an increased demand for greater control of British Parliament over the company's affairs. Various factors that further put pressure on the parliament to intervene were as follows:

- There was a growing concern about **misgovernance of the Indian affairs** by the corrupt servants of the Company. The public opinion was critical of the corruption in the Government in Bengal. The debate grew bitter, as the English gentry became jealous of the East Indian *nawabs* indulging in conspicuous consumption to force their way into English elite society. For instance, Robert Clive returned to England at the age of 34 with wealth and property yielding 40,000 pounds a year. On the other side, the Company officials like **Robert Clive** or **Hastings** in order to buttress their power and legitimise their authority were also in favour of some kind of formal constitutional relationship with the Crown.
- Many political thinkers and statesmen of Britain wanted to **regulate the activities** of the Company and its officials since they were afraid that the Company and its powerful rich officials would eventually lower the moral standards of the English nation, further leading to corruption in British politics. There were apprehensions that the Company, with the help of money brought from India, might achieve preponderant influence in the British Government and may indulge in the malpractice of buying the seats in the House of Commons for its agents.

- A new school of economists led by **Adam Smith**, author of *Wealth of Nations*, were advocating **free trade** and condemned companies enjoying exclusive monopolies. Emboldened by this ideology, certain other free enterprises were striving to have a share of the profitable Indian trade and exerted great pressure on the government to put an end to the monopoly rights of the Company.
- Continuous wars and mismanagement by the company officials landed it in deep **financial crisis**. The Company applied to parliament for financial loan of 10,00,000 pounds, which further raised the suspicion about the mismanagement of resources in India as it was ironical that even though the Company was facing a financial crisis, its officials were returning to London amassing huge personal wealth.

The British Government was, thus, no longer willing to allow the Company's affairs to continue unsupervised. The Parliament agreed for financial help but on the condition that it will regulate the basic policies of the Company's Indian administration. A select committee of **Parliament** was appointed in April **1772** to enquire into the state of affairs in India and to resolve some important constitutional problems like how to define the relationship between the British Government and the Company with its possessions in India, how would the Company's authorities in Britain exert control over the large number of officials and soldiers working for it in faraway India and how a single centre of power could be devised for widespread British possessions in Bengal, Madras and Bombay. Though the monopoly of the Company over Eastern trade was allowed to continue, the British Parliament for the first time formally **recognising** its right to control Indian affairs passed the Regulating Act of 1773.

The Regulating Act of 1773

- The Act made changes in the constitution of the **Court of Directors** of the Company and subjected their actions to the supervision of the **British Government**. The Directors were, henceforth, obliged to submit all correspondence received from India pertaining to civil, military and revenues matters before the Ministry.
- In India, some degree of **centralised control** was attempted as the status of Governor of Bengal was raised to that of **Governor-General**, to be assisted by an executive council of four members. All the decisions were to be taken by the Governor-General and his council through a majority vote, though in case of an equal division the Governor General had a casting vote. They were given the power to superintend and control the **Bombay** and **Madras Presidencies** in matters of war and peace, except in emergency situations. (Lord **Warren Hastings**, 1773–85 became the first **Governor-General**).
- The Governors of Madras and Bombay were required to send regularly to the Governor-General information connected with government, revenues or interests of the Company. The Governor-General in turn was under the direct control of the Court of Directors and was supposed to keep them fully informed of the affairs concerning the interests of the Company.
- Legislative powers were granted to the **Governor-General** and Council to make rules, ordinances and regulations for the civil government of Fort William and subordinate factories.
- It also provided for the establishment of a **Supreme Court of Justice** in Calcutta to administer justice to Europeans, their employees and the citizens of Calcutta.

The Regulating Act, however, when implemented, was exposed to certain defects and weaknesses. It **failed** to streamline Indian administration, and the supervision of the British Government too remained ineffective due to problems of communication. The administration in India was hampered by the disunity in the council and harmony between the council and the Governor-General. The Act placed the Governor-General at the mercy of his council and the disunity in the Council often resulted in deadlocks, which impeded the smooth working of the administration. The Act was also vague about the jurisdiction control over subordinate presidencies. The Governor-General had no power to override the provincial governors, who often took advantage of the wide manoeuvring space they had been offered by the vague wordings of the Act. As a consequence of the defects of the Act, Warren Hastings often found himself unable to carry out his administrative responsibilities smoothly. Also, there were ambiguities in the **jurisdiction of the Supreme Court** and the Council, resulting in serious conflicts between the two authorities.

The Amending Act of 1781

- The Amending Act tried to partially address the anomalies of the Regulating Act of 1773 as it attempted to define the jurisdiction of the Supreme Court more precisely. The Supreme Court jurisdiction was defined within territorial limits of Calcutta, and it was to administer the personal law of the defendant honouring the social and religious usages of the subjects. However, the government officials were provided immunity against charges while discharging their official duty.

The Pitt's India Act of 1784 (named After William Pitt, the then Prime Minister of Britain)

- The defects of the Regulating Act and the exigencies of British politics necessitated the passing of Pitt's India Act in 1784. The Act is sometimes described as the *half-loaf system* since, it was sort of a compromise between the **Parliament** and the **Company directors** as on one side, it enhanced Parliament's control over the Company's affairs and its administration in India by establishing the **Board of Control**, and on another side the Company's territorial possessions were left untouched.
- The Act established a Board of Control consisting of six commissioners, including two **Cabinet ministers** and transferred the greater part of the power of decision from the Court of Directors to the Board of Control.
- The Board of Control was to guide and control the work of the Court of Directors and all matters of civil and military nature of the Government of India. A secret committee consisting of three Directors was also created to take the place of the Court of Directors in political and military matters.
- The **Court of Directors** retained its control over commerce and patronage **but** needed the approval of the Crown in appointing its principal servants in India, such as the Governor-General, Governors and the Commander-in-Chief.
- The Government of India was placed under the Governor-General and a council of three with a casting vote to the Governor-General. It was done purposefully to strengthen the position of the Governor-General so that if the Governor-General could get the support of even one member, he could have his way.
- The Presidencies of Madras and Bombay were **clearly subordinated** to the authority of Governor-General in all matters of war, diplomatic relations and revenues.
- However, the Governor-General in council were made subordinate to the Court of Directors and the Board of Control. They were forbidden to declare war and enter into any treaty without the sanction of the directors or the secret committee. Thus, the Act laid down a clear hierarchy of command and a more direct parliamentary control over the Indian administration.

Pitt's India Act is **important** in many respects. The Government of India was to be carried on till 1857 according to the framework given in it. It helped in uniting India by giving supreme power to the Governor-General over the Governors of Presidencies. The Governor-General and Governors were given the authority to override their councils. But the Act had many **defects** too. The first and foremost was the provision of two masters for the Governor-General, that is, the Court of Directors and the Board of Control. Due to this **conflict of authority**, at times the Governor-General could easily play his two masters one against another, thus enjoying virtual autonomy to act on his own discretion even on matters of great importance. For instance, using this advantage, **Cornwallis** stretched his authority to the widest possible limit on many occasions, and it was often rumoured that the actual state of affairs was not known to anybody except him. Also, on the other hand a fractious council could make any effective governance impossible.

The Amending Act of 1786

- The Amending Act intended to correct the anomalies of Pitt's India Act. It gave the Governor-General power to override his council in extraordinary circumstances.
- It also authorised the Court of Directors to **combine** the two offices of **Governor-General** and **Commander-in-Chief** to the same person. Governor-General **Warren Hastings** thus became the first Governor-General to enjoy the position of Commander-in-Chief too.

The Charter Act of 1793

- The Charter Act renewed the charter of the Company for 20 years and allowed the Company to continue with possession of all territories in India along with retaining its political privileges and responsibilities during that period.
- The Governor-General's power to overrule the council was **extended**, and the Governors of Bombay and Madras were brought more decisively under his control. He was allowed to issue orders and directions to any Presidency during his absence from Bengal without previous consultation with his council and could exercise all executive powers vested in the Central Government.
- The Act of 1793 introduced in India the concept of a **civil law**, enacted by a secular human agency and applied universally since a regular code of all regulations that could be enacted for the internal government of the British territories was framed. The Regulation applied to all rights, persons and property of the Indian people, and it bound the Courts to regulate their decision by the rules and regulations contained therein. All the laws were to be printed with translations in Indian languages and prefixed with statements of grounds on which they were enacted, so that the people could become familiar with their rights, privileges and immunities. The interpretation of regulations and written laws was to be done by the **Courts**. Thus, a system of government by written laws and regulations in British India was initiated, which was in sharp contrast with the earlier followed system of personal rules dictated by past rulers.
- The salaries for the staff and paid members of the **Board of Control** were now charged to the Company.

Reason behind the title 'Charter'

The English East India Company was founded on the basis of a *Charter*. A Charter is the *grant of authority or rights*, stating that the granter formally recognises the prerogative of the recipient to exercise the rights specified. Since in the subsequent Charter Acts, the British Crown renewed the **Company's Charter of territorial authority** over the Indian dominions, hence the use of the title *Charter*. We have already discussed how the Company's acquisition of substantial territories in India forced the British Crown to redefine its status and privileges, giving way to two major acts, the Regulating Act of 1773 and the Pitt's India Act of 1784. However, in the following years, four Charter Acts were passed by the Crown, renewing the Company's Charter and thus the use of the title of 'Charter' in all these subsequent Acts. It is **noteworthy** to point out that even though all the Charter Acts renewed the Company's mandate to possess territories in India, all the Acts over the years gradually circumscribed the privileges enjoyed by the Company.

Background behind The Charter Act of 1813: In 1808, just before the due renewal of the Charter in 1813, the House of Commons appointed a Committee of investigations to enquire about the Company's affairs. Meanwhile, the teachings of Adam Smith and his philosophy of free traders had become more than dominant in British Politics and they were demanding free access to India, thus putting an **end** to the continuance of commercial monopoly of the East India Company over Indian trade. The Benthamite reformists, the Evangelicals and the Traditionalists tried to influence British politics and policies towards

British India. All of these aspirations for change in Britain's India policy gained a decisive voice over a period of time, and thus the Charter Act of 1813 tried to incorporate all of these sentiments in a significant way. The election of leading Evangelist **Charles Grant** to the Court of Directors further helped the cause. It was in these prevailing circumstances that the Charter Act of 1813 was passed.

The Charter Act of 1813

- The Charter Act of 1813 renewed the Company's Charter for 20 years, but at the same time, it **asserted** the undoubted sovereignty of the British Crown over the Indian territories held by the Company. Hence, the Company was allowed to have territorial possessions for another 20 years.
- The Company was, however, **deprived** of its monopoly of trade with India although its monopoly of tea trade and trade with China was **left untouched** for another 20 years. The Indian trade was thus thrown open to all British merchants.
- The Company's control over revenue, administration and appointments of its officials remained untouched.
- The Act was also an important benchmark in the push towards westernisation of India as the **Christian missionaries** were henceforth allowed to enter India, subject only to obtaining a licence either from the Court of Directors or the Board of Control.

The Charter Act of 1833

- When the Charter was again due for renewal in 1833, there was a fresh and more widespread agitation in Britain for the abolition of the Company and for direct takeover of the Indian administration by the Crown. The political atmosphere in Britain at that time was also fully charged with enthusiasm for reform as the well-known Reform Act of 1832 had just been passed. Britain was also enjoying the prosperity achieved with the Industrial Revolution and was finally in a position to afford to free trade from restrictions and monopolies.
- The Charter Act of 1833, thus, proved to be a great landmark in the constitutional history of India. Though, the lease of 20 years to the Company was further extended, but here too it was **emphasised** that the Indian possessions of the Company were to be **held in trust** for the British Crown. The Company henceforth disappeared as a **commercial agency** in India, and functioned only as a **political agent** for the Crown. Thus, the union of the trader and the sovereign was finally dissolved.
- The Company's monopoly of tea trade with China was also **abolished**. At the same time, the debts of the Company were taken over by the Government of India, which was also to pay its shareholders a dividend of 10.5 per cent per annum on their capital.
- The **President** of the Board of Control was now designated as the **Minister for Indian affairs**, while the Directors were to act as expert advisors to the Minister. The Board of Control was invested with authority to superintend, direct and control the affairs of the Company relating to the Government or revenues of the Indian territory.
- The Governor-General of Bengal became the **Governor-General of India**, who would in consultation with his council, control all civil, military, revenue and expenditure matters of the Company.
- The Act also **deprived** the presidencies of the **power to make laws**, concentrating legislative power with the Governor-General and his council. Bombay, Madras and other regions were subjected to complete control of the Governor General in Council. The Central government was to have complete control over raising of revenues, expenses of Provincial governments, creation of new offices and obedience of all members.
- The number of members of the Presidency Councils was reduced to two, and the Bombay and Madras Presidencies were supposed to keep their separate armies under the Commanders-in-Chief.
- The Governor-General in Council was also empowered to legislate for the whole of the British territories in India and the laws framed were enforceable by all courts with their applicability over all persons, British or Indian.

- The Act added one more member to the Executive council of the Governor-General, the **Law Member**, whose work was fully legislative. Even though the law member had no vote in the Council, he was able to influence many policies of the government. For instance, the first Law Member **Lord Macaulay** had a huge influence on the educational policy of the government.
- The Act provided for the **codification of laws** in India and the Governor-General was empowered to appoint the Law Commission to study, collect and codify various rules and regulations prevalent in India. The Indian Penal Code and Codes of Civil and Criminal Law were enacted by the efforts of Indian Law Commission.
- The **Company's services** in India were thrown **open** to the natives, but it was not of much practical importance, since nothing was done and Indians remained excluded from higher posts in civil and military services. Also, the Charter Act of 1833 made no provision to secure the nomination of Indians to the covenanted services of the company. Nonetheless, the clause proclaiming **non-discrimination in recruitment** was of great importance as it became the sheet anchor of political agitation in India in the years to come.

The Charter Act of 1853

- The Charter of 1833 was renewed in 1853, but this time **not** for another 20 years. The Company was allowed to retain the Indian possessions *in trust of Her Majesty, her heirs and successors until the Parliament shall otherwise provide*, thus keeping the option open for **future takeover**.
- The number of directors of the Company were **reduced** from 24 to 18 and out of them 6 were to be nominated by the Crown.
- The Act also provided for the **separation** of the executive and the legislative functions of the Governor-General's council by adding new members for the purpose of legislation. The *Legislative Councillors* were now clearly distinguished from the *Executive Councillors* and by doing so, **legislation** was for the first time treated as a **special function** of the government requiring special machinery and special procedure. In fact, the Law Member was made a **full member** of the Executive Council of the Governor-General.
- The business of the Council was conducted in public, and the procedure adopted by it for the transaction of business was much on the same pattern as followed in the British Parliament. It initiated a system wherein questions were put, papers were demanded and information was asked for along with criticism of the Government for its lapses and excesses.
- The consent of the Governor-General was made necessary for all legislative proposals. The Council in its legislative capacity was to consist of 12 members. These included the Governor-General, Commander-in-Chief, four members of his council and six legislative members.
- The Central Legislative Council was mandated to include one representative each from the Provinces and the measures concerning a province were to be considered in the presence of representatives from that province only.
- The Chief Justice of Supreme Court of Calcutta was made the ex officio member of the Council. There was also a provision for nominating two more civilians by the Governor-General; however, this authority was never exercised.
- The Company's control over the appointments was curtailed by the **introduction of competition** for the recruitment of the Indian Civil Service. In fact, all the vacancies in India were to be filled in by competitive examinations, and **Lord Macaulay** was appointed the President of the Committee overseeing the process.

The Government of India Act of 1858

We will study about the Government of India Act of 1858 brought in after the Revolt of 1857 in detail in our next chapter, The Revolt of 1857.

Administrative Structure and Organisation

We have already discussed in the previous chapter **how** through a series of conquests the East India Company came to gradually control the entire country and was thus transformed from being just a commercial body into a political force. **But**, mere conquests could not possibly hold the empire together for a long time, and it had to be sustained by developing a comprehensive system of administration. **Initially**, the British made no attempt to introduce any key changes in the Indian tradition, or working of the administration, since till 1813, British interests lay mainly in establishing vigilant control over extracting the agricultural surplus through taxation and eliminating other European competitors, and as both these objectives were fulfilled without disturbing the existing institutions and administrative apparatus, the Company thus acted more like a traditional ruler in the initial years and hence undertook no major innovation or intervention in the administrative structure, **but** as the British Empire grew in size and in terms of resources, the need was felt to assert **sovereignty** and exert control to ensure a steady flow of revenue.

Also, gradually the idea of cultural particularism began to lose ground in the face of evangelical attacks and utilitarian zeal for reform. Along with these developments, the **Industrial Revolution** in Britain necessitated an integration of the markets throughout India with regular supply of raw materials, which in turn required an unequivocal assertion of sovereignty and much greater penetration into the Indian economy, society and administration. Thus, the British now felt a strong urge for bringing reforms in the traditional administrative institutions so that a market economy promoting free commercial relations could be created and an administrative apparatus facilitating smooth regulation of the various economic transactions with the help of modern laws could be established. The Company directors felt that, with the introduction of efficient administration and individual rights and ownership focused Western laws, there will be further expansion in both labour and capital and more avenues for income would be opened, and thus, taking into account all these outcomes, the British started the process of the **transformation** of Indian administration and judiciary.

However, before we proceed further, we need to take into account two key **issues**, the first that, the imperial interests in India varied during the different stages of the British rule and these changes were reflected in the transformation and the working of administration, and the second issue being that, the administrative institutions which evolved in order to govern and control India did not take a shape tun overnight but were implanted through a series of measures and acts, based on the **trilogy** of ideology, pragmatism and individual orientation of the different British administrators.

Changes in the Administrative Organisation: Judicial System

The early *Charters* of the Company gave it the authority to make reasonable laws, 'constitutional orders' and 'ordinances' along with limited powers to punish offences committed by its servants, but they gave no territorial powers of jurisdiction. In 1661, **Charles** I authorised the Governor and Council of each factory to exercise criminal and civil jurisdiction, not only over the Company's servants but also over all persons employed under the respective Governor or Company. The **Mayor's Court** were established in 1727 for civil litigation in Bombay, Calcutta and Madras.

- With the grant of *diwani* in 1765, the East India Company secured the right to collect revenue in Bengal, Bihar and Orissa and established a **dual system of administration** in these provinces due to which the Company, to some extent, became responsible for civil justice. For instance, following the principle of dual administration, Robert Clive appointed Muhammad Reza Khan to represent the Company's civil jurisdiction, and like *Naib Nazim*, he too administered the criminal jurisdiction of the Nawab. However, during the period from 1765 to 72, the **judicial administration** of the *subah* largely remained in the hands of the Indian officers and the Mughal system was followed in both civil and criminal justice. The focus of this system was more on **mutual resolution of conflict** rather than punitive justice (except in cases of rebellion), and punishment meted out often depended on the **status** of the accused.

- However, the **first** concrete step in organising judicial administration was taken up by **Warren Hastings** when he took charge as governor and established an elaborate judicial system, in 1772, known as *adalat*, with civil and criminal jurisdictions. He, for the first time, made the **district** as a unit of judicial administration and tried to **centralise** judicial authority. It is pertinent to note that in criminal matters, the **Muslim law** was exclusively followed though in a modified and less harsh form, while in civil cases, the **personal law** of the parties was applied. As per Warren Hasting's 1772 judicial reforms, each district was to have two courts:
    - ***Mofussil Diwani Adalat*** or **Civil court**: It was the court of original jurisdiction in **civil or *diwani* matters** at district level such as property, inheritance, succession, marriage, castes, contracts and others. It was presided over by the **European District Collector** who was responsible not only for collection of revenue but also for looking after the general administration of the district including judicial system and thus also functioned as judge. He was assisted by *maulvis* and *pundits* who helped him in interpretation of indigenous laws of both Muslims and Hindus. The decisions of the court up to the monetary value of ₹500 were final. It is pertinent to note that this court did not handle the cases of succession of Zamindari and Talukdar properties as it was dealt by the **Governor-General** and his council (the principle of duality between the courts of the Crown and the Zamindari courts ended in 1861 when the Indian **High Court** Act established **High Courts** in Calcutta, Madras and Bombay).
    - ***Mofussil Faujdari Adalat*** *or* **Criminal court**: This court handled **all criminal cases** of district level and was presided over by a **learned *Qazi*** and a ***Mufti***, who were assisted by two *maulvis* well versed in Muslim law but the supervisory control of this court was vested solely with the **European District Collector**, who had the responsibility to ensure that the sessions of the court were held regularly, equitable justice is administered and the judgements are impartial and fair. The court had the power to decide all criminal cases and punish the criminals **except** in the cases of capital punishment, the proceedings of which needed to be submitted to the *Sadar Nizamat Adalat* for confirmation. There was **further provision** for appeal to the *nawab* or the *subedar* who could finally confirm, commute or reduce the punishment.
    - *Adalats of Small Causes*: They were established at **village level** and were presided over by the **head farmer** (generally the eldest farmer of the district) who could decide petty cases up to the value of ₹10.

  Along with these courts, the **Courts of Appeal** were also organised:
    - ***Sadar Diwani Adalat*** or **Civil court**: It was located in Calcutta and was presided over by the Governor-General who was assisted by two members of his council. This court heard all **appeals** from the *Mofussil Adalats* beyond the value of ₹500 and above.
    - ***Sadar Faujdari (Nizamat) Adalat*** *or* **Criminal court**: This was an appellate court having the right to hear appeals in criminal matters and was under the overall authority of the *Nawab*. It was presided over by an **Indian judge** known as *Daroga Adalat* who was further assisted by chief *Qazi*, chief *Mufti* and three *Maulvis*, but as with *Mofussil faujdari*, here too, the overall supervisory control was exercised by the **Governor-General** and his council members.
- Under the **Regulating Act of 1773**, the Supreme Court was set up in the Presidency town of Calcutta, which derived its power from the Crown and had the authority to exercise all types of jurisdiction in the region of Bengal, Bihar and Orissa, with the only caveat that in situations where the disputed amount was in excess of ₹4,000 their judgement could be appealed to the **Privy Council** in London. However, the establishment of the Supreme Court led to the emergence of **two rival sets** of judicial authorities: the Supreme Court and the *Sadar Diwani Adalat* and hence a **temporary solution** was chalked out by the appointment of the Chief Justice of the Supreme Court as President of the *Sadar Diwani Adalat.* With time its authority was confined to the city of Calcutta and to matters related to factories dependent on Fort William and gradually in its place *Sadar Diwani Adalat* was now **reconstituted** to serve as an Appeal Court, with Sir **Elijah Impey** taking over its superintendence in 1780. The Supreme Courts in Madras and Bombay were finally established in 1801 and 1823, respectively.

- In Civil justice system, further changes took place between 1773 and 1781, partly in deference to the Whig Principle of separating executive functions from the administration of justice and partly to focus exclusively on revenue collection and hence the district collectors were divested of their judicial duties. Instead of district courts, initially 6 provincial courts, later replaced by 18 *mofussil* courts, were created which were to be presided over by only the European covenanted officers of the Company, who were designated as 'Judges'. Also, an effort was made to institutionalise the civil justice system, for example through the **Code of 1781**, certain rules and regulations to be followed in all the civil courts down to the lowest level were prescribed and all judicial orders were henceforth instructed to be in writing. Also, efforts were made to standardise the laws in order to reduce the conflicting and varying interpretations of the indigenous and customary laws by compiling Code for both Hindu laws and Muslim laws. However, there was a certain reversal of this system in 1787, when once again the District Collector was given the duty of administering civil justice.
- It was **Lord Cornwallis** and his code of 1793 which stabilised the system of judicial reforms by separating **the executive** (revenue collection function) from the **judicial responsibility**. He separated the posts of the Civil Judge and the Collector. The new system provided for a hierarchy of courts starting from district level to four provincial courts and at the highest appellate level was located the *Sadar Diwani* or *Nizamat Adalat.* Also, all the courts were headed **only** by the **European judges**, and there was total exclusion of Indians from the whole system at the higher level.
- Thus, in each district was established a ***Diwani Adalat***, or **Civil Court**, presided over by the District Judge who belonged to the Civil Services. Below the district courts were **Registrar's Courts**, headed by the Europeans, and a number of **Subordinate Courts** headed by the Indian judges known as *Munsifs* and *Amins.* For all the civil cases, appeals from the district court lay first to four **Provincial Courts** of Civil Appeal in Calcutta, Dacca, Murshidabad and Patna and, then, finally, to the ***Sadar Diwani Adalat***. To deal with criminal cases, Cornwallis divided the Presidency of Bengal into four divisions, in each of which a **Court of Circuit** in Calcutta, Dacca, Murshidabad and Patna presided over by the **civil servants** was established. A large number of magistrates were appointed to deal with petty criminal cases. The appeals from the Court of Circuit went to *Sadar Nizamat Adalat* in Calcutta. Broadly the structure of the new judiciary was something like this:

New Judiciary Structure[1]

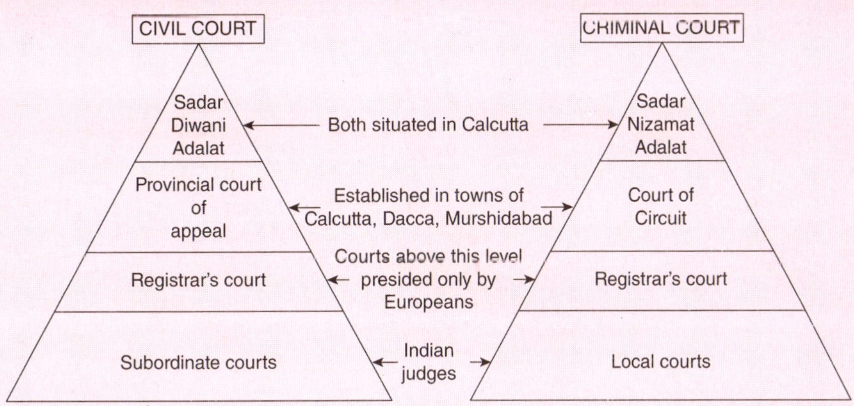

[1] The *Sadar Diwani Adalat* and *Sadar Nizamat Adalat* formed the top of the pyramid and were situated in Calcutta. Below these were the provincial courts of appeal (in the case of civil courts) and the courts of circuit (in the case of criminal courts) which were established in the towns of Calcutta, Dacca, Murshidabad and Patna. Below these were the registrar's courts and all those were presided over only by the Europeans. The participation of Indians was confined to subordinate positions such as *Munsifs*, *Amins*, the *Qazis* and the *Pandits* who merely advised the judges on the existing Mohammedan and Hindu laws.

- **However**, in 1831, **William Bentinck** abolished the four **Provincial Courts of Appeal** and **Circuit** and redistributed their work to Commissioners and District Collectors. Also, by the **Charter Act of 1833**, all law-making power was conferred on the Governor-General and his council and a welcome change was introduced in the judicial administration by opening of all the judicial positions for **Indians**. The status of Indians in the judicial services was thus elevated and they were now being appointed as Deputy Magistrates, Subordinate Judges and Principal *Sadar Amins*. A **law commission** was also constituted in 1833 for **codification of laws** (which was appointed under Lord Macauley and its labours eventually resulted in the India Penal Code of 1861, the Codes of Civil and Criminal procedures).

Critical Analysis of the New Judicial System

The traditional judicial system hitherto to British rule was based on either customary laws founded on traditions and social practices or religious laws based on *shastras* and *shariat* or royal laws flowing from the will and authority of the rulers. But, with the emergence of the new judicial system, the regulations and existing laws were not only codified but also made open to judicial interpretations and subsequent amendments. The important key features of the new judicial system were thus as follows:

- **The establishment of a whole network of uniform laws through the process of enactment and codification of laws**: For instance, the Indian Penal Code was uniformly applicable throughout the country and thus there came into being, for the first time, a set of laws which included into its fold every Indian, irrespective of caste, class or sex.
- **The recognition of the right to be judged by one's personal law**: One important feature of the system of law that was erected was that enough tolerance was displayed towards the existing traditional and religious laws. The criminal courts did not altogether abolish the Muslim criminal law but applied it in a somewhat modified form, so as to make it less harsh. Similarly, the civil courts also did not do away with the customary laws which had been followed by the local people.
- **Growth of the professional and trained judicial hierarchy**.
- **Inclusion of the theoretical legal principles of the rule of law and equality before law**: The two main theoretical principles underlying the entire British judicial system in India were the notions of the Rule of Law and Equality before law. As per theory, Rule of Law basically signified that no one was above the law and the law clearly defined the rights, privileges and obligations of the people, whereas **equality before** law signified that all the citizens irrespective of their caste, class and other status were now equal before the law. The natural upshot of the Rule of Law was the Equality before the Law, which subsequently followed the Rule of Law.

The Rule of Law and the Equality before Law

The Rule of Law: The Rule of Law meant that the administration was now to be carried out strictly according to certain laws which defined the rights, privileges and obligations of the people, and not according to the personal desires of the rulers. It also meant that in theory at least, nobody was above the law. Even the official and those who supervised law were, in theory, accountable to the same set of laws and could be brought before a court of law for violating any law. The law, once formulated, could place restrictions on the actions of the rulers. For instance, the principle of *Habeas Corpus* provided that no person could be arrested or kept in prison without a written order from the local executive or the judicial authority.

The Equality before Law: The Equality before law meant that in the eyes of the law, all men were equal. In theory, it signified that all the citizens, irrespective of their caste, class or status, and others, were now placed at an equal footing in the eyes of the law. The Equality before law appeared as a novel feature in the caste- and class-ridden Indian society, as, previously, the judicial system had to pay heed to caste and class distinctions which was now no longer done. There was, however, **one exception** that the Europeans and their descendants had separate courts and even different laws. In criminal cases, they could be tried only by European judges and, consequently, often miscarriage of justice happened as they were given indirect and undue protection.

However, in practice, the Indian people had to pay a heavy price for the new streamlined judicial system, which further resulted in emergence of another type of legal inequality as follows:

- **Justice now became distant**, not just **physically**, because of the geographical distance of one's village from the district courts, but also **psychologically**, as the native people found it often difficult to understand the complex judicial procedures, dominated by a new class of lawyers. As a result, **justice also became very expensive** and therefore out of reach for most people. For instance, it was now mandatory to pay the costly stamp fee which was as high as ₹1,000 to file suit in a court on a property worth ₹50,000. Moreover, the new laws were quite complicated and most people could not understand or interpret them. Lawyers, therefore, had to be employed and that added to the expenses. To seek justice, people now had to come to the district towns or the provincial centres and, as a result, one of the major setbacks was to the Village committees and panchayats who lost their importance even in the village matters.
- **The legal process too became very lengthy** and as the huge number of court cases started piling up, for most people justice became inordinately delayed too, sometimes even by 50 years.
- It was only the public side of the personal laws that upheld the laudable principles of the Rule of Law and Equality before Law but, unfortunately in most cases of interpretation of personal laws by *pundits* and *maulvis*, mostly **an element of continued benefit to conservative and feudal elements was witnessed**. Also, a disturbing fact was that the concept of equality before law often did not apply to the Europeans, and even though efforts were made for greater equality in the civil justice system, the racial privilege for the rulers remained in place in various forms in the criminal courts, as in criminal cases they could be tried only by the European judges.
- Gradually, **legality itself became an instrument of power and oppression**, as often within the defined parameters of the law, the law could be easily manipulated and violated to the advantage of the corrupt officials. For instance, certain significant domains of public activity like the police and the army almost remained practically outside the realm of the definition of the 'Rule of Law and Equality before Law' and was largely unaffected by the restrictions following from these principles. A great deal of extra-legal oppression continued to be exercised by the police and civil servants.
- Also, **the laws framed were often defective and contained the element of harassment** since they were not framed by people through a democratic process but autocratically by the foreign rulers.

However, the newly introduced judicial system marked a great step forward as it was based on not only the laudable principles of the rule of law and equality before law but also on rational and humane man-made **laws**, which also did have the merit of saving in motion the process of the unification of India. Now, it was possible to conceive India, in judicial terms at least, as one unit. Despite the British having formulated and used the idea of legality as an instrument of controlling India, as we will see later, in the 20th century, the same instrument of legality was effectively utilised by the leaders of the National Movement to defend civil liberty and to challenge the oppressive government authority within the limits of law.

Pillars of British Administration

Since the British being foreigners could not hope to win the affections of the Indian people, they, therefore, relied on superior force rather than public support for the maintenance of their control over India. The chief aim of British–Indian administration being the **maintenance of law and order** and the **perpetuation of the British rule**, the British administration in India was based on three pillars: the **Civil Service**, the **Army** and the **Police**, and they brought gradual changes suiting their needs in each of them. Affirming the same, the Duke of Wellington, who had served in India under his brother, Lord Wellesley, had once remarked *The system of Government in India, the foundation of authority, and the modes of supporting it and of carrying on the operations of government are entirely different from the systems and modes adopted in Europe for the same purpose ... the foundation and the instrument of all power there is the sword.*

Changes in Administrative Organisation: Indian Civil Service

The term **Civil Services** was used for the first time by the East India Company mainly to demarcate its civilian employees from their military and ecclesiastical counterparts. The service which was initially only commercial in nature did gradually transform into a public service; however, the main job of the civil services was mostly limited to a collection of maximum possible **revenue** along with **implementing policies** framed in faraway Britain. But, with the distance between London and India, the difficulties of communication and with their command over information from the field, the **civilian bureaucracy** enjoyed the advantage of considerable amount of discretion and initiative and thus, eventually emerged as very powerful. As Clive Dewey has rightly observed, *in their heyday they were the most powerful officials in the empire, if not the world.*

As we have discussed earlier in the chapter, the East India Company had from the beginning carried on its trade in the East through servants who were paid low wages but were permitted to trade privately. Later, when the Company became a territorial power, the same servants assumed administrative functions.

- It was a '**patronage bureaucracy**' at the outset, as the method of recruitment, as outlined by the India Act of 1784 and the Charter Act of 1793, was only through **nomination** by the members of the Company's Court of Directors. These nominated civil servants indulged in corruption, bribery and illegal private trade. By extorting bribes and gifts from *nawabs* and *rajas*, by indulging in illegal private trade and by oppressing local weavers and artisans, merchants and zamindars, they amassed huge unaccountable wealth with which they retired to England.
- **Lord Cornwallis**, who came to India as the Governor-General in 1786, tried to check this corruption and imposed certain restrictions with strictness on the civil servants like **forbidding private trade** and **acceptance of presents** and bribes by officials, **enforcing promotions through seniority** to ward off outside influence. At the same time, realising the fact that the Company's servants would not give honest and efficient service so long as they were not given adequate salaries, **he increased their salaries** as a compensation. For instance, the collector of a district was to be paid ₹1500 a month, besides the one percent commission on the revenue collected from his district. In fact, the Company's Civil Service was perhaps the highest paid service in the world that time. Thus, the basic structure of Civil Services was laid down by Lord Cornwallis, earning him the tag of *Father of Civil Services in India*.
- But, unfortunately, Indians were carefully excluded from Civil Services, as laid down officially in 1793 that 'no position worth an annual salary of 500 pounds or more could be held by them'. The Indians were accommodated in administrative structure at subordinate positions only, known as the **Uncovenanted Civil Service**. After 1813, under Warren Hastings, a gradual process of *indianisation* of the subordinate services had begun, mainly in the judiciary. Later, Lord Bentinck too advocated for inclusion of Indians in the administration.
- The gradual expansion of the empire increased the responsibilities of governance and required an efficient bureaucracy, trained in Indian languages and laws. **Lord Wellesley**, who arrived in 1798, took significant steps in this direction. He established the **Fort William College** in Calcutta on 24 November 1800 for the training of young recruits to the Civil Service. The Directors of the Company, however, disapproved of his action and in 1802, Fort William College was closed and instructions were issued to utilise it as a language school only, and in its place, in 1805 the **East India College** was established in Hertford near London, which was later moved to Haileybury in 1809. All the candidates nominated by the Court of Directors had to undergo two years of training at this college and were mandated to pass the final examination to secure an appointment to Civil Services in India. However, it should be **noted** that the method of recruitment was still the patronage system and all high-level posts were reserved for the British while the native Indians were excluded.

Reasons behind Exclusion of Indians from the Civil Services

- The British were mostly convinced that an administration based on British ideas, institutions and practices could be firmly established only by the English personnel.
- The British did not trust the ability and integrity of the Indians. As evident in Lord Cornwallis statement that *every native of Hindustan is corrupt.*
- It was part of a deliberate policy of the British as these services were required at the time to establish and consolidate British rule and obviously, the task could not be left to Indians who did not possess the same instinctive sympathy for, and understanding of, British interests as Englishmen.
- Also, the influential classes of British society were keen to preserve the monopoly of lucrative appointments in the Indian Civil services for their near and dear ones.

- The idea of '**competition**' for recruitment (as against nomination practised earlier) was introduced for the first time by the **Charter Act of 1833**. But it was limited competition among the candidates nominated by the directors and could be termed as *nomination-cum-competition* for recruitment. The Court of Directors were to first nominate four times the number of civil servants required. These nominated candidates had to go through a competitive examination through which one-fourth could ultimately be selected to join the coveted Civil Services.
- But gradually the demand for open competition started gaining ground and, finally, the **Charter Act of 1853** made provision for open competition. Subsequently, the college at Haileybury was abolished in 1858 and the **Civil Service Commission** assumed the sole responsibility of recruiting civil servants through a competitive examination held annually in England. The introduction of competitive examination though technically opened the gates to the Indians, they were still effectively barred, as the recruitment examination was held only in England in the English language, was based on classical learning of Greek and Latin and the maximum permissible age for appearing in examination was gradually lowered from 23 (1859) to 19 (1878). In 1863, **Satyendra Nath Tagore** became the first Indian to qualify for the Indian Civil Services.
- In the late 19th century, the nationalists demanded that the competition examination should be held in India but owing to the opposition by the European bureaucracy, the government could not do much about it. But as a compromise, it introduced the '**Statutory Civil Service**' in 1870, which provided for nomination of Indians of ability and merit to a few positions hitherto reserved for the European covenanted civil servants. But, usually Indians chosen for such positions were either those with a respectable family background or belonging to the indigenous princely families.
- The structure of the Civil Service was ultimately reformed in 1892 on the basis of the recommendations of **the Aitchison Committee on Public Services** (**1886**). The Committee recommended to do the following:
  - Drop the terms 'covenanted' and 'uncovenanted' and classify the Civil Services into:
    - **Indian Civil Services** (ICS) retaining the exclusive status of the covenanted civil service with its examination to be conducted in England.
    - **Provincial Civil Services** (PCS) retaining the nature of uncovenanted civil service and having examination in India.
    - **Subordinate Civil Services** having the examination in India.
  - The Statutory Civil service was abolished, and in its place certain higher positions which were previously reserved for the ICS were now filled in through promotion from the PCS.
  - The age limit for recruitment was raised to 23 years.
- The **Government of India** Act, 1919, finally provided for a separate, not simultaneous, recruitment examination to the Indian Civil Services, that is, ICS to be held in India; and thus under its provision, the first examination was held in Allahabad in February 1922. Later, on the basis of recommendations of **the Lee Commission**

(1924), direct recruitment to ICS on the basis of 50:50 parity between the Europeans and the Indians in the next 15 years was to be achieved and a Public Service Commission was to be established. The **Government of India Act, 1935,** recommended establishment of a Federal Public Service Commission and Provincial Public service Commission. As a result, by 1941, the Indian representation in Indian Civil Services increased from just about 15 per cent in 1922 to the situation where the Indian officers outnumbered the European officers.

The Indian Civil Services in years to come developed into one of the most efficient and powerful civil services in the world. Its members played a very crucial role in the framing of the British policies in India and also in maintaining and running the mighty British Empire in India and thus is often called as the *steel frame* which reared and sustained British rule in India. On the other hand, the Indianisation of the Civil Services made it possible to continue to serve even after Independence when the service only changed its nomenclature to the Indian Administrative Service.

Changes in Administrative Organisation: Army

The second most important pillar of the British regime in India was the **Army**, which also claimed the largest share of the Company's expenditure in India, devouring about 40 per cent of the central revenue. It was considered to be the most important apparatus of rule for the Company's administration in India as it not only conquered territories but also protected the empire against real or imagined internal threats by acting as the most effective instrument of coercion against all sorts of civil disturbances such as peasant rebellions, worker strikes or nationalist agitations and at times also collected information about Indian society and economy, which helped the British to form policies. Hence, the evolution of the Company's army was integrally connected to the development of its Indian empire.

The bulk of the Company's army consisted of Indian soldiers, recruited chiefly from the area at present in Uttar Pradesh and Bihar. For instance, in 1857, the Indians constituted about 86 per cent of the total strength of the Company's army. The main reason for this **large share of Indians** lay in the expenses involved in maintaining an exclusively British army as given the Company's expansionary policy, it needed to maintain a large army. Also, the population of Britain was perhaps too small to provide the large soldiery required for the conquest of India. However, as a counterweight, the army was officered entirely by British officials and a certain number of British troops were maintained to keep the Indian soldiers under control. In 1856, only three Indians in the army received a salary of ₹300 per month and the highest an Indian could reach was the post of a Subedar. Training and appointment of Indian officers started hesitatingly and selectively in 1931 after the First Round Table Conference; however, it was only in the 1940s under the pressure of the military needs of World War II and as a delayed concession to the nationalists, that the issue was given full consideration, but it was probably too late by then. Visible signs emerged in the cracking of the loyalty of Indian army (issues which we are going to discuss in later chapters), which further attributed to the end of the British Raj in 1947.

How Could a Handful of Foreigners Conquer and Control India with a Predominantly Indian Army?

It was possible due to two factors:

- There was an absence of modern nationalism in the country at that time since a soldier from Bihar or Avadh did not consider it to be anti-Indian activity if he was helping the Company defeat the Marathas or the Punjab troops.
- The people also joined the Company's army because the pay, allowances, pension and resettlement provisions offered by the Company were much better than those offered by the regional states, and the most important fact was that salaries were paid well and regularly, something which the other Indian regional rulers and chieftains were no longer doing. In other words, the Company was a good paymaster and the Indian soldier on his part was a good mercenary.

Changes in Administrative Organisation: Police

The third pillar of the British administration was the **police**, whose creator was again **Lord Cornwallis**. He tried to adapt the indigenous system of policing to the needs of the colonial state. Prior to him, the function of the Police was performed by the zamindars through their armed retainers. He divested the zamindars of their police functions, disbanded their armed retainers and established a regular police force to maintain law and order. He divided the districts into *thanas* or units of police jurisdiction of 20–30 square miles, each placed under an Indian officer called a *daroga*, who was appointed and supervised by the magistrates. Later, the post of *District Superintendent of Police* (SP) was created to head the police organisation in the district. In the villages, the duties of the police continued to be performed by the *village watchmen* who were maintained by the villagers. One of the major achievements of the Police was the suppression of the thugs who robbed and killed travellers on the highways, particularly in Central India and reducing major crimes like dacoity.

- The *daroga* system was formally abolished in 1812, and the supervision of the police was vested to the Collector, who was now responsible for revenue, police and magisterial functions at the same time. This arrangement of extreme concentration of power not only resulted in badly organised police force but also led to other problems. The subordinates in the revenue department, who were now in charge of revenue collection as well as supervision of rural policing, became the new agents of oppression and coercion. The same was revealed in the report of the Madras Torture Commission (1854). In the words of Marshman, 'These officials enjoyed almost unlimited power of extortion and became the scourge of the country'.
- Thus, the need for an appropriate and uniform police system grew with time as the effective implementation of various judicial reforms too required the reorganisation of police administration. The new model was first experimented in Sindh (1843) when it was conquered by **Sir Charles Napier**. He created a separate police department with its own officers, following the model of the **Royal Irish Constabulary**. Under this model, the whole territory was to be under the supervision of an **Inspector General**, while the districts would have their own Superintendents of Police, answerable to both the Inspector General and the District Collector, representing the civilian authority. While the rank and file were to be Indians, the officers were to be invariably Europeans. The Sindh model was later introduced in Punjab (1849), and later with various modifications to Bombay (1853) and Madras (1859).
- The Police Commission appointed in 1860 provided for a basic structure of a police establishment for the Indian Empire that was enacted in the **Indian Police Act**, 1961, and that structure with only minor adjustments continued unchanged till Independence. Under the new system:
    - The civilian police was organised on a provincial basis, with the inspectors general answerable to the provincial governments, and the district superintendents to the Collector.
    - A well-defined hierarchy of command was established with the **Inspector General** being the head of police in a province, the **Deputy Inspector General** functioned as the head in a range and the **District Superintendents** were to be in charge of rural Police in a district while the *daroga* became the **sub-inspector** heading a *thana*. But, Indians were systematically excluded from these positions of authority.
- Gradually, in 1902, the Police Commission provided for the appointment of educated Indians to the position of officers in the police force; but here too they 'stopped in rank where the European officer began'. The Commission also recommended for the establishment of **CID** (**Criminal investigation Department**) in the provinces and a **Central Intelligence Bureau** at the centre.

However, the Police became the foremost tool of coercion and repression to tackle the growing unrest, recurrent peasant rebellions and mounting political resistance. A Committee of the parliament reported in 1813 that the police committed 'depredations on the peaceable inhabitants of the same nature as those practised by the dacoits whom they were employed to suppress'.

British Economic Policies in India (1757–1857) and Their Effects

The economic policies of the British government led to rapid transformation of India's economy into a colonial economy, whose nature and structure were determined by British needs with its core revolved around economic exploitation in every sense.

Changes in the Revenue Administration

Since time immemorial, the Indian state had taken a part of the agricultural produce as land revenue, either directly through its officials or indirectly through intermediaries, such as zamindars, revenue farmers, and others, who collected the land revenue from the cultivator and kept a part of it as their commission. After securing the *diwani* rights of Bengal, Bihar and Orissa in 1765, the East India Company too depended on agricultural taxation for providing money for trade and profits of the Company, along with paying for dividends to the Company's investors in Britain, and at the same time sustaining the cost of administration and the wars of British expansion in India and abroad. Therefore, with the sole intention of maximising its revenue, the East India Company initiated certain far-reaching changes in the country's agrarian structure by introducing new systems of land tenures and policies of revenue administration.

Initially, the Company made an attempt to continue with the old system of revenue collection; however, in its drive to secure revenue, it accorded supervisory authority to European officers over the native officials who were in charge of revenue collection and also increased the revenue amount to be collected to an exponentially high level. For instance, between 1766 and 1769, the revenue collection increased by 53.8 per cent. This put severe pressure on zamindars, who became increasingly indebted to local creditors as well as European officers. This, combined with the disastrous famine of 1770 in which one-third of the population was wiped out, forced the Company to seriously review the situation in terms of both its responsibility and the land revenue settlements that could be introduced.

Thus, in 1772, the dual nature of administration came to an end, when the Company decided to take actual control of revenue collection and the Governor of Bengal, **Lord Warren Hastings**, introduced the annual lease system of revenue farming, known as the *farming system*, wherein the right to collect revenue was 'farmed' out or auctioned to the highest bidder. Under this system, the government gave out the collection of land revenue on a contract basis. The contractor who offered to pay the largest amount from a certain district or subdivision was given full powers for a certain number of years. But, the experiment proved to be a total failure as even though the amount of land revenue was pushed high by zamindars and other speculators bidding against each other, the actual collection varied from year to year and seldom came up to official expectations, which resulted in further instability in the Company's revenues at a time when the Company was fighting different wars and was thus hard-pressed for money. The *farming system* also led to corruption as happens with many government contracts even today, since profitable contracts on very easy terms were given to the friends and favourites and *benamidars* of men in power, leading to loss to the government. It adversely affected the cultivators too, since due to arbitrarily high revenue demands, not much was left with them. Moreover, neither the peasant nor the zamindar could do anything to improve the cultivation as the taxation had the character of an 'uncertain, arbitrary imposition', and thus everybody was clueless about next year's assessment, its rates or who is going to get the contract.

In order to address this chaos of revenue administration, it was at this stage that the idea first emerged of fixing the land revenue at a permanent amount, and in 1786, when **Lord Cornwallis** was sent to India, he was given one of the specific mandates of streamlining the revenue administration. Rather as a matter of fact, it was since 1770, that is, even before Cornwallis arrived, that a number of Company officials and European observers, like Alexander Dow, Henri Patella, Philip Francis and Thomas Law, were advocating for the land tax being permanently fixed.

Lord Cornwallis's Permanent Settlement (1793)

Lord Cornwallis made thorough enquiry into the usages, tenures and rents prevalent in Bengal for over three years and realised that the existing system was impoverishing the country, ruining agriculture and was not producing the large and regular surplus that the Company had hoped for. Also, since the production of two of the Company's major export items, Silk and Cotton, were mainly agro based, decline in agriculture was also resulting in decline of handicrafts production, which ultimately meant loss for the Company's trade as due to shortage of supply there was difficulty in procuring Indian goods for export to Europe. Thus, in 1793, after prolonged discussion and debates with his colleagues like Sir John Shore and James Grant, Lord Cornwallis finally decided to abolish the annual lease system and introduced the **Permanent Settlement** System in Bengal, Bihar and Orissa, which was initially a decennial (10 years) settlement, but subsequently this arrangement was declared to be continuous or 'assessment for ever' and hence got the title 'permanent settlement'. The sums to be paid as land revenue was thus fixed in perpetuity, and every bit of agricultural land in these provinces became part of some zamindari or estate. The main features of the Permanent Settlement, also known as the *Zamindari system*, were as follows:

- The state's demand for land revenue was permanently fixed and the *zamindars*, who earlier only had the right to collect revenue, were established as the proprietors or owners of land. Their right of ownership was made hereditary and transferable. Thus, the zamindars could sell, mortgage or transfer their rights.
- On the other hand, the cultivators were reduced to the low status of mere tenants and were deprived of long-standing rights to the soil and other customary rights such as rights over use of pasture and forest lands, irrigation canals, fisheries, homestead plots.
- There was also a provision of *patta* or written agreement between the **cultivator** and the *zamindar*, providing a record of the amount of rent to be paid; however, it was rarely followed by the *zamindars*, and the peasants were wholly at the mercy of the *zamindars*.
- The amount of revenue that the *zamindars* had to pay to the Company was firmly fixed and was not liable for any further revision on any account. The *zamindars* were to give to the state **10/11th of the pre-fixed rental** that was derived from the peasantry and could retain only 1/11th for themselves. However, if the rental of a *zamindar's* estate increased due to extension of cultivation and improvement in agriculture, or his capacity to extract more from his tenants, or any other reason, he would keep the entire amount of the increase and the state would not make any further demand upon him. At the same time, it also implied that the state was excluded from agricultural expansion and development, which hereafter came wholly under the purview of the *zamindars*.
- The *zamindar* had to pay a fixed amount of revenue rigidly on the due date (the so-called '**sunset**' law which provided that a zamindar has to deposit the agreed amount of land revenue by the sunset of the due date) and there was no margin for shortfalls due to flood, drought or other calamity. If the *zamindars* were unable to pay the full tax on time, their lands would be taken away and auctioned by the state and all the rights would vested in the new owner. Thus, the land now became a negotiable private property.

Critical Analysis of the Permanent Settlement

The decision to recognise the *zamindars* as the proprietors of land was basically determined by political, financial and administrative expediency. Several effects were expected from the measure of the Permanent Settlement, such as follows:

- **Creation of political allies**: It was a clever statecraft move to bring into existence a wealthy, powerful and privileged class of *zamindars* who owed their existence to British rule and therefore be compelled by their own basic interests to support it. In fact, the expectation was justified later when the *zamindars* as a class proved loyal to the British administration and supported the foreign government in opposition to the rising movement for freedom.

- **Financial Security**: The Permanent Settlement guaranteed the stability of income against the earlier arrangements of land revenue before 1793, where the revenue income from land was rather fluctuating. Moreover, the Permanent Settlement enabled the Company to maximise its income as land revenue was now fixed at a high level – the absolute maximum than it had ever been in the past, and the scope for corruption was greatly reduced as compared to the earlier system that existed prior to this wherein the Company officials could alter the assessment at will. Additionally, the collection of revenue through a small number of *zamindars* seemed to be much simpler and cheaper than the process of dealing with lakhs of cultivators and finally, Cornwallis also believed that even if the tax was fixed, the government could always levy taxes on trade and commerce in order to raise more money if it was needed.
- **Increase in Agricultural Productivity**: Furthermore, through this system, the state tried to create an enterprising class of landowners who would try to improve crop production in their fields to earn profits. Since, now that the state would not demand anything extra even if the production increased, it was hoped that the landholders or the *zamindars* would invest money in improving the land as the whole of the benefit from increased production would accrue to them, resulting further in improved agricultural activity and greater extension of cultivated lands. Lord Cornwallis expected that it would result in a system of benevolent landlordism.

However, the Permanent Settlement was bitterly criticised on various points:

- **Adopted with 'undue haste' with arbitrary fixation of land revenue**: The flagrant defect of this arrangement was that no attempt was made ever either to survey the lands or to assess their value. The initial fixation of revenue was made arbitrarily and without any consultation with the *zamindars*.
- **Abnormally High Rates of Land Revenue**: Since the land revenue was fixed in perpetuity, it was fixed at a very high level, rather absolute maximum. Even John Shore, the man who planned the Permanent Settlement and later succeeded Cornwallis as Governor-General, estimated that *if a piece of land produced crops worth ₹100, then the government claimed ₹45, zamindars and other intermediaries below them received ₹15 and only ₹40 remained with the actual cultivator*.
- **Impoverishment of the tenant cultivator**: The burden of high revenue assessment was thus shifted to the cultivators and peasants, who were often asked by oppressive *zamindars* to even pay for illegal cesses such as ***abwabs*** on top of the regular land revenue rates, which ultimately resulted in great misery for them.
    - The Permanent Settlement system also encouraged '**subinfeudation**', that is, many layers of intermediaries between the *zamindar* and cultivator, that further complicated the tenurial structure to an absurd level and adding to the woes of the already overburdened peasantry.
    - With the subsequent regulations of 1799 and 1812, the coercive power of the zamindars were increased, legally further worsening the condition of the actual cultivator as it gave the zamindars the '**right to seize property**' of the tenants in case of non-payment of rent without any permission of a court of law. In addition to this, the *zamindars* often resorted to illegal methods, such as locking up or beating tenants who did not pay whatever was demanded. Thus, Cornwallis' expectations of benevolent landlordism were totally belied, and ascertaining the same Baden Powell had remarked that, *the zamindars as a class did nothing for the tenants*.
    - Since the poor peasants were perennially harassed and excluded from any control over land and power, thus as a result, a number of peasant uprisings took place in these provinces, prominent among them being in Panchet (1795), Raipur (1798), Balasore (1799) and Midnapore (1799–1800). It was, however, only in 1859 and 1885 did the State take some steps to protect the rights of tenants and passed tenancy legislations which bestowed limited protection on old tenants, by recognising their occupancy rights.

But these reforms also strengthened the position of a group of powerful rich peasants who were actually controlling the landholding at the village level – the *jotedars*, while the power of the *zamindars* remained largely unrestrained and unhindered.

- **Difficulty for Zamindars**: It may seem that the settlement was greatly in favour of the *zamindars* but they too had to face a number of difficulties as follows:
  - The *zamindars* were now obliged to pay a fixed amount of revenue by a particular date, and any failure on their part meant the sale of the zamindari. Often, they found it difficult to collect the rent, as either the demands were too high or there were the uncertainties of nature but the Company accepted no reasons or margins for any shortfalls.
  - As a result, there was frequent sale of the *zamindari* estates. In Bengal alone, it is estimated that 68 per cent of the *zamindari* land was sold between 1794 and 1819, while in Orissa, between 1804 and 1818, 51.1 per cent of the original *zamindars* were wiped off because of auction sales. This resulted in collapse of most of the old traditional *zamindari* houses, while some of the old houses managed to survive by resorting to techniques of subinfeudation, which further complicated the tenurial structure to an absurd level. For instance, one such zamindar, the Raja of Burdwan, divided most of his estate into 'lots' or fractions called *patni* taluqs and each such unit was permanently rented to a holder called a *patnidar*, who promised to pay a fixed rent. If he did not pay, his *patni* could be taken away and sold.
  - These subinfeudatory *patni* tenures sometimes proliferated up to twelve grades between the *zamindars* and the peasants, thus increasing the demand to an abnormally high level for the latter. In the process, old zamindars were gradually parcelled out to new group of *zamindars* who were mostly urban-based merchants, speculators, money lenders, and others, having no permanent interests in the development of land or the welfare of peasantry.
- **Financial Loss for Company**: Though initially the Company gained financially, in the long run the Company too suffered financial loss as the revenue income from land was fixed; thus even though the productivity may increase in the future, it was of no benefit to the Company, and also due to the presence of intermediaries like *zamindars*, the portion of the land revenue was being shared between the Company and the intermediaries, resulting in subsequent loss to the Company.

Nevertheless, this system proved to be a great boon to the *zamindars* and to the government of Bengal. It formed a regular income and stabilised the government of the Company. On the other hand, since the tax payable to the government was fixed, the position of the zamindars improved and they were able to lead lives of indolence and luxury at the expense of their poor tenants. The Permanent Settlement was later extended to Orissa, the Northern districts of Madras and the districts of Varanasi. In parts of Central India and Avadh, the British introduced temporary settlement under which the zamindars were made owners of the land but the revenue paid by them was revised periodically.

Emergence of Alternate Systems of Land Tenure and Revenue Collection

Meanwhile, the establishment of British rule in South and South-western India brought new problems of land settlement. Here the problem was to find a sizeable zamindar class with whom the settlement of land revenue could be made as in Bengal. Also, there was growing disillusionment with the Permanent Settlement since there were no means to raise the income of the government, while the increased income from the land was being garnered by the zamindars. Moreover, the cultivator was left at the mercy of the zamindar who could oppress him at will, and thus need was felt for devising other ways of assessment and collection of the land revenue. However, a more powerful reason for a new settlement was the perennial financial crisis of the Madras Presidency, which was further worsened by the rising expenses of the war. The Company was, thus, on the lookout for a method which could result in a larger revenue income than the Permanent Settlement by eliminating the role of intermediaries like zamindars completely and squeezing from the cultivator directly. The **Ryotwari System** was thus intended to address all these issues.

Thomas Munro's Ryotwari Settlement (1801)

The Ryotwari experiment was started by **Alexander Reed** in Baramahal in 1792 and was continued by **Sir Thomas Munro** from 1801 in the provinces of Madras. The system was extended to Bombay Presidency under the supervision of Munro's disciple **Mountstuart Elphinstone**. Instead of collecting land revenue from the zamindars, they began to collect revenue directly from each cultivator or *ryot* and thus evolved the **Ryotwari System**. Under this settlement:

- The peasant or *ryot* was recognised as the proprietor of the land and the settlement was thus made directly with the actual cultivator rather than any intermediary like a zamindar. Every peasant was held personally responsible for direct payment of land revenue to the government. So long as the *ryot* paid the revenue in time, he was not evicted from the land.
- The settlement under the Ryotwari System was not made permanent, and it was revised periodically after 20 to 30 years.
- The **assessment** of each field depended on the nature of soil, its location, payments made in the immediate past and expected price rise.
- It evolved eventually as a field assessment system, as rent payable on each field was to be permanently assessed through a general survey of all lands and then annual agreements were made between the government and the cultivator, who had the choice of accepting or rejecting the agreement. If he agreed, he would get a *patta*, which would become a title to private property and if no cultivator was found, the land might lie fallow. Thus, the cultivator had the 'right of contraction or relinquishment', that is, freedom to take as much or as little land as one wants to. However, even this right was effectively dropped by 1833.
- The British also recognised the privileged rents of the *Brahmanas* and special rights of the *Mirasidars* (that is, large landholders of southern village communities who had the power to command retainers who tilled his land and received their subsistence from him).

Critical Analysis of the Ryotwari System

The supporters of the Ryotwari Settlement insisted that the system would reduce the revenue burden for farmers, while it would yield larger amount of land revenue for the state, as no intermediaries would be having a share of the surplus. They claimed that the Ryotwari System was the ancient Indian land tenure system and therefore best suited to Indian conditions. It was a continuation of the state of affairs that had existed in the past as Munro exclaimed 'It is the system which has always prevailed in India'. This reference to the past was done intentionally as it was felt that it was in the interest of the British empire to relate the Ryotwari System with the concept of British sovereignty. Since historically land in India was owned by the state, which collected revenue from individual peasants through a hierarchy of officials, thus, to create the same figment of impression would help in creating a foundation for the British empire.

However, quite contrary to Munro's instance that the Ryotwari settlement would benefit both Company and ryots equally, the system proved to be a **failure** as:

- The settlement was very good in theory but when implemented practically it opened a pandora box of issues as, in order to be an attractive and equitable system, it required a detailed land survey wherein everything ranging from the quality of the soil, the area of the field and the average produce of every piece of land had to be assessed and on the basis of that the amount of revenue was to be fixed. **But**, this was hardly followed in practice wherein the estimates were often guesswork and the revenue demands were often so high they could not be collected at all or collected with great difficulty. In many areas, no surveys were carried out and the tax of a *ryot* was assessed on an arbitrary basis, based on the village accounts. Known as the '**putout**' settlement, the revenue to be paid by a *ryot* was fixed on his entire farm, not on each field, which might have been carrying varying irrigation facilities and therefore different levels of productivity. And where the survey was actually undertaken, it was often ill conceived and hastily executed resulting in over-assessment. Thus, the cultivators were gradually impoverished and increasingly indebted and could not invest for the extension of cultivation. It resulted in scrapping of land market in Madras as buying land would mean paying extortionate land revenue.

- The Ryotwari System did not eliminate village elites as intermediaries between the government and the peasantry. As privileged rents and special rights of the *Mirasidars* were recognised and caste privileges of the Brahmanas respected, the existing village power structure was hardly altered, and indeed even more strengthened by the new system. David Ludden's study of the Tirunelveli district, for example, shows *how the locally powerful Mirasidars manipulated the system to get privileged rents and convert their collective rights into individual property rights.*
- The Ryotwari System promoted differentiation within the peasantry too as an affluent group of big landlords called as *peasant bourgeoisie* emerged who controlled large farms and leased out surplus lands to landless tenants and sharecroppers.
- It is also pertinent to note here that the *Ryotwari* Settlement did not bring into existence a system of **peasant ownership** as specified by David Ludden that *The state itself is the supreme landlord and individual peasants landowners obtained titles by paying annual cash rents, or revenue assessments, to the government.* The government openly claimed that land revenue was rent and not a tax. The *ryots*' **rights of ownership** of his land were also negated by three other factors:
    - **Exorbitant land revenue**: In most areas, the land revenue fixed was exorbitant and the *ryot* was hardly left with bare maintenance even in the best of seasons. For instance, in Madras the Government claim was fixed as high as 45–55 per cent of gross production in the earlier settlement and the situation was equally bad in Bombay too.
    - The Government's right to **enhance land revenue at will**.
    - The *ryot* had to pay revenue even when his produce was partially or wholly destroyed by drought and floods. The peasant soon discovered that the large number of zamindars had been replaced by **one giant zamindar**, that is, the state. The pasture and wasteland which belonged to the village communities were now appropriated by the state.

Holt Mckenzie's Mahalwari Settlement of 1822

Holt Mckenzie believed that the original property rights of land belonged to the village community and, thus, the responsibility of revenue collection should be given to them only. His recommendations became part of the **Regulation VII of 1822** that provided for a detailed field to field survey for revenue assessment. The Mahalwari Settlement was thus introduced in Punjab, the Central Provinces and parts of North Western Provinces. The settlement, however, did not work, and coinciding with a period of agricultural depression of 1828, the land remained largely uncultivated and buyers non-existent. This set the stage for revision, which was initiated by **R.M. Bird** and **James Thomson**, who modified and redesigned the **Mahalwari System** in 1833 on the following parameters:

- The basic unit of revenue settlement was the **village** or the *Mahal* or, in some cases, the traditional *taluqdar*. As the village lands belonged jointly to the village community, the responsibility of paying the revenue rested with the entire *Mahal* or the village community.
- A detailed survey to assess the revenue of an entire *Mahal* or fiscal unit, based on the net value of potential produce of the field was recommended.

- The total revenue thus fixed was to be shared by the members of a co-sharing body, and the settlement was to be made village by village with landlords or heads of families, who collectively claimed to be the landlords of the village or estate.
- Two-thirds of the net revenue for the land was to be designated as the **state share** while the duration of the settlement was 30 years.
- Under this system, recognition was given to **collective proprietary rights**.

Critical Analysis of the *Mahalwari* System

Though the *Mahalwari* system eliminated intermediaries between the government and the village community and brought about improvement in irrigation facility, yet it proved beneficial more to the Company only as this time around too, the settlements were based on faulty surveys, imperfect calculations resulting in over assessment and hardships for the members of co-sharing body.

Area under Each System

According to a rough estimate, in 1928–29, roughly 19 per cent of the total area under the British rule, that is, Bengal, Bihar, Varanasi, division of the Northern Western Provinces and northern Karnataka, were brought under the **Zamindari System** or the **Permanent Settlement**, while the **Mahalwari Settlement** was introduced in about 30 per cent of the total area under British rule, that is, in major parts of the North Western Provinces, Central Provinces and the Punjab with some variations, whereas the **Ryotwari System** covered about 51 per cent of the area under British rule comprising part of the Bombay and Madras Presidencies, Assam, Sindh and Coorg along with certain other parts of British India.

Thus, by the middle of the 19th century, the Company's administration had devised three systems of land revenue administration, creating private property in land and conferring the proprietary rights on three different groups:

- In the case of **Permanent Settlements** with the zamindars
- In the case of **Ryotwari Settlements** with the ryots or peasant proprietors
- In the case of **Mahalwari Settlements** with the village community

Since the primary motive of the Company's government was to maximise revenue income, a common feature among all these settlements was thus **over-assessment**, resulting in **arrears of payments**, **mounting debts** and increased **land dispossession**. The figure of the moneylender became strongly entrenched in the countryside and they along with zamindars became an important class and collaborators of British colonial rule. The British made land a commodity which could be freely bought and sold and thus introduced a fundamental change in the existing land systems of the country. In fact, the stability, autonomy and continuity of Indian villages were deeply shaken by the introduction of these new settlements.

British Commercial Policy

As witnessed with agriculture and land revenue policies, the commercial policies too reflected classical colonial economic relationship between Britain and India wherein the Indian Empire was supposed to pay for itself and at the same time, the country's resources were meant to be available for the imperial cause too. Over a period of time, India was cleverly reduced to a mere status of a **market** for Britain's manufactured goods and a **source of agricultural raw materials** for its industries. Not only this, India was also drained of her wealth on various accounts such as **interest on foreign debt** incurred by the East India Company,

military expenditure, **guaranteed interest on foreign investments** in railways, irrigation, road transport and various other infrastructural facilities, the **government purchase policy** of importing all its stationery from England and finally, the '**home charges**' or paying for the secretary of state and his establishment at the India Office in London, as well as pay, pension and training costs for the civilian and military personnel. Lawrence Sullivan, Deputy Chairman of the Court of Directors, had once remarked, 'Our system acts very much like a sponge, drawing up all the good things from the banks of the Ganges and squeezing them down on the banks of the Thames'.

Phases of British Economic Colonialism

The colonial economic exploitation of India can be categorised in certain phases[2] owing to its varied nature and character exhibited during each phase. Due to changes within Britain, the phases varied over the course of British reign, and these in turn had specific economic, social and political consequences for India too.

- The '**first phase**' (**1600–1757**), wherein the role of East India Company's in India was that of a **trading corporation** which brought goods or precious metals into India and exchanged them for Indian goods like textiles, spices which it used to sell abroad. Since, its profits came primarily from the sale of Indian goods abroad, it did try to open new markets for Indian goods in Britain and other countries along with emphasising on increase in export of Indian manufactures. However, quite soon the British manufacturers put pressure on their government to restrict and prohibit the sale of Indian goods and hence as a result, by 1750, laws had been passed either prohibiting or imposing heavy duties on the import of Indian cloth. For instance, in 1760, an English lady had to pay a fine of 200 pounds for possessing an imported handkerchief. In spite of these laws, Indian silk and cotton textiles still held their own in foreign markets, until the middle of the 18th century when the English textile industry began to develop on the basis of new and advanced technology.
- The '**second phase**' (**1757–1813**) was initiated just after the Battle of Plassey when the Company's commercial relations underwent a qualitative change and the British East India Company acquired the rights to collect revenue from its territories in the eastern and southern parts of the subcontinent and it lasted till 1813, when the Company's monopoly over trade with India came to an end. After 1757, the company started using its political control to push its Indian trade and utilised the revenues of Bengal to finance its export of Indian goods, which was nothing less than a kind of direct plunder. The Company also financed the additional burden of expeditions and war to consolidate its own position in the territories it possessed and to extend its influence from Indian revenues.
- The **'third phase'** (**1813–58**) is generally regarded to have begun with the Charter Act of 1813, when the Company lost its monopoly trading rights in India, and ended in 1858, when the British Crown took over the direct control and administration of all British territory in India. This phase is marked essentially by the **Free Trade** era wherein India was converted into a source of raw material and a market for British manufactured goods.
  - With the initiation of the 19th century, a new school of economic thought based on the ideology of **Adam Smith** favouring free trade or *laissez faire* gained ground. In his famous book, *An Inquiry into the Nature and Causes of the Wealth of Nations*, Adam Smith had critiqued the idea of companies enjoying exclusive monopolies and lobbied for a government policy of *laissez faire*. Within no time, the 'Free Traders' gained dominance in the parliament and demanded free access to India, which led to the passing of the **Charter Act of 1813**, thus ending the monopoly enjoyed by the Company in India and subordinating its territorial possessions to the overall sovereignty of the British crown.

[2] *However, one should keep in mind that even though the process of economic colonisation has been divided into phases, this periodisation is in some ways arbitrary and most of the characteristics are heavily overlapping, where new and more subtle forms of exploitation existed alongside older, cruder forms.*

- The free trade changed the nature of the economics of the Indian colony completely. **First**, it threw open Indian markets for the entry of cheap, mass-produced, machine-made British goods, which enjoyed little or almost no tariff restrictions, and **second**, the Indian territory was developed as a source of raw material for Britain, which fuelled rapid growth in its manufacturing sector, crucial to the emergence of a powerful capitalist economy. **Ironically** at the same time, to Britain were subjected the popular Indian textiles and handicrafts that exported prohibitive tariff rates and high import duties. For instance, in 1824, a duty of 67.5 per cent was levied on Indian calicos, a duty of 37.5 per cent on Indian muslins, while on Indian sugar was levied duty three times its cost price, and in some cases duties in England on Indian goods went up as high as 400 per cent.
- These changes gradually reversed the favourable **balance of trade** that India had enjoyed earlier and laid the foundations of a classic colonial economy. The unfairness of British commercial policy has been summed up by the British historian, **H. H. Wilson**, in the following words *British goods were forced upon India without paying any duty; and the foreign manufacturer employed the arm of political injustice to keep down and ultimately strangle a competitor with whom he could not have contended on equal terms.*

- The '**fourth phase**' **(1858 onwards)** began when British India was placed directly under the control and sovereignty of the British crown. This period was one of '**finance-imperialism**', when British capital was invested in India through a closed network of British banks, foreign trading firms and managing agencies, in **railways, jute industry, tea plantations and mining**. In fact, the fourth phase was merely a consolidation of the trends that were already witnessed clearly in the second and third phase. Most economic initiatives undertaken by the colonial state in this phase, even though couched in the language of development and 'modernisation', had a differential impact on India's economy, **often leading to backwardness rather than growth**.
  - The Indian money market during this phase was dominated by **British banking houses** while the British trading interests were well organised through **Chambers of Commerce** and **Managing Agencies**. While British entrepreneurs had easy access to capital made available by this banking network, Indian traders had to depend on family or caste organisations for their capital needs. Thus, although the colonial government spoke about 'free trade', the indigenous enterprise faced many obstructions perpetuated by the state's discriminatory policies. For instance, before World War I, British managing agencies controlled 75 per cent of industrial capital, and most of the profits from this limited industrialisation were also sent back to Britain.
  - **But**, in spite of such heavy odds, **Indian entrepreneurs** like G.D. Birla and father–son duo Swarupchand Hukumchand (the cotton prince of India), J. D. Tata found opportunities to expand and grow, more particularly whenever Britain underwent periods of economic hardship such as during World War I. Gradually, their control started expanding into other areas like coal mines, sugar mills and paper industry, and they could even buy up some European companies. The Tata Iron and Steel Company too made its mark in the iron and steel sector.
  - The greatest success of Indian capital was seen in the **cotton industry** in western India, which took advantage of high demands during the war years (1914–18) to consolidate its successes, and eventually was in competition with Lancashire itself. Also, gradually certain traditional trading communities like Gujarati *Banias*, *Parsis, Bohras* and *Bhatias* became important stakeholders in many industries.
  - After World War I, links with the foreign market was re-established, but again in the depression years (1929–33), the domestic market became relatively free to be exploited by indigenous industry, as foreign trade declined. Indians also ventured into the field of insurance and banking. Again, during World War II (1939–45), as foreign economic influence declined, Indian entrepreneurs managed to make huge profits.

But, to place these markers of success in perspective, on an overall level, these developments remained confined to the domestic market and indigenous capital still had a long battle ahead, against the structural weaknesses of a colonial economy. The potential for growth remained depressed given the massive poverty of the Indian people who were still primarily dependent on agriculture and here too, the British policies of **commercialisation of agriculture** and **de-industrialisation** further worsened their position.

Commercialisation of Agriculture and De-industrialisation

In the latter half of the 19th century, a significant development in the form of commercialisation of agriculture occurred, which had far-reaching effects on the Indian economy. Prior to this development, agriculture had been a way of life, but after the 1860s, it became more of a business enterprise as the nature of agricultural production was determined by the demands of the overseas markets for Indian primary products. The items exported in the first half of the 19th century included **cash crops** like indigo, opium, cotton and silk. Gradually raw jute, food grains, oil seeds and tea replaced indigo and opium; however, raw cotton remained in much demand then too. Also, due to high demands of payment of revenue, rents and debts in cash, many farmers started growing cash crops.

It is often believed that due to the commercialisation of agriculture, the position of peasants was improved. But, that was surely not the case, as commercialisation in colonial India was mainly a forced artificial process that led to very limited growth in the agricultural sector. On the contrary, it resulted in differentiation within the agricultural sector, and even failed to create the figure of the *capitalist landowner* as was prevalent in Britain. Also, due to the lack of any simultaneous large-scale industrial development, the accumulated agrarian capital neither had any viable channels of investment nor could it be converted into industrial capital. Commercialisation, thus, **increased the level of sub-infeudation** in the countryside, and the surplus money was channelised into trade and usury. In fact, the only people who benefited by this process were big farmers, some Indian traders, moneylenders, commission agents and bankers.

Another ill effect of the process of commercialisation was that it was often carried out through very exploitative forms of labour. For instance, tea was grown in plantations in Assam, owned by whites who made use of indentured labour, which was almost like slavery. Similarly, British planters used to force farmers to grow indigo despite their aversion to it. Also, the shift away from food crops like jowar, bajra and pulses to cash crops often created disaster in famine years. Although causes of these famines have been widely debated by historians, it is undeniable that the aggregate production of food crops remained far behind population growth, and millions of people died of starvation and epidemics.

Colonial rule also led to **de-industrialisation** or destruction of indigenous handicraft industries, further impoverishing the people who were dependent on these secondary industries. The primary cause behind deindustrialisation being the disappearance of export demand as well as invasion of the home market by cheap manufactured goods from England. Also, with the rise of British paramountcy in India, the power and status of Indian rulers declined, resulting in the reduction of demand for the luxury goods like royal attires, armory and objects of art, which till now was a major market for Indian handicrafts.

Consolidation of the Raj: Frontier and Foreign Policy

As we have discussed at the start of this chapter that after completing the empire building process, the British followed a twofold policy for the consolidation of the Raj, namely the introduction of a suitable administrative system and making arrangements for securing the boundaries of the newly conquered territories. The latter aspect constitutes the **frontier and foreign policy;** however, it should be carefully noted that although the British relations with Indian states were also regulated by the Foreign Department, they were clearly not a part of this policy as they were under the '**indirect rule**' of the Company and later the Crown.

The frontier and foreign policy adopted by the British was an imperialistic one as it was formulated to serve the British imperial interests and often led India into conflicts with its neighbouring countries and that too at the cost of Indian resources, as the blood shed in the battlefield was of the Indian soldiers and the money spent was from Indian coffers. There were primarily two reasons behind these conflicts:

- Need for internal cohesion and defence: With the introduction of modern means of communication and political and administrative consolidation of the country, it was natural for the British to consolidate their position at a geographical frontier too. India was surrounded by small states which in themselves were not a threat to India's security but being militarily weak they could not provide effective resistance against foreign powers like Russia which constantly posed a danger to British interests in India and thus it was imperative for the British to take charge of their frontier states.
- The British Indian foreign policy had also been largely shaped by the power struggle British had with other European imperialist powers, whose colonial interests came in conflict with those of the British, namely Russia and China, and their relations at a given time determined the political, diplomatic and military developments in India.

Thus, the desire to defend their Indian Empire, to promote British economic interests and to keep the other European powers at arm's length from India, often led the British Indian Government to commit aggression on India's neighbours.

The Anglo–Afghan Relations

In the early 19th century, the Anglo–Afghan relations were inextricably mixed up with **Anglo–Russian rivalry** as the British were skeptical about increasing Russian influence in Afghanistan and were anxious to protect the emporium of their trade, and the only entrance to Central Asia from their side. Throughout the 19th century, the British feared that Russia would launch an attack on India through Afghanistan and the North West frontier of India, and thus, in order to thwart the Russian presence and to make Afghanistan a buffer state against the growing Russian expansion in the 1830s, the British adopted the '**Forward Policy**'. Under the aegis of this policy, the British took initiatives to protect the boundary of British India from a probable Russian attack by securing commanding influence in Afghanistan by either entering into treaty with neighbouring states or by annexing them to bring under their direct control.

The British policy towards Afghanistan entered into active phase in 1835 when the *Whigs* came to power in Britain and **Lord Palmerston** became the Foreign Secretary. The idea of *Russian Peril* was widely propagated by Lord Palmerston and the term was for the first time mentioned by **William Bentinck**, the then Indian Governor-General who believed it to be a real danger to British authority. British aim at this point of time was not only to merely guard India against Russia but also to penetrate Afghanistan and Central Asia to promote British commercial interests. Afghanistan was being ruled by **Dost Muhammad** at this time, who had brought about partial stability to the country which was otherwise torn between internal rebellions and external challenges. Initially, he discouraged the Russian envoy and instead adopted a friendly attitude towards the British envoy Captain Burns. Dost Muhammad was interested in genuine support of the British and wanted to be an ally of the British Indian Government on the basis of complete equality, but **Lord Auckland**, the then Governor-General, offered him an alliance based on the subsidiary system, nowhere being near the status of equal partners. Thus, having tried his best to acquire British friendship and failed, he reluctantly, turned towards Russia, which alarmed the British.

Also, in 1838, the British entered into a **tripartite treaty** with Sikh Chieftain Maharaja Ranjit Singh and Shah Shuja (the deposed Afghan ruler who had been living as a British pensioner in Ludhiana since 1809) by which the first two promised to help Shah Shuja capture power in Afghanistan and in return, Shah Shuja promised not to enter into negotiations with any foreign state without the consent of the British or Punjab governments. Thus, without any genuine reason or excuse, as a part of its forward policy, the British government decided to interfere in the internal affairs of Afghanistan, which ultimately resulted in the First Afghan War.

The First Anglo-Afghan War (1839–42)

- As a result of the Tripartite treaty, the three allies launched an attack on Afghanistan in February 1839, but Maharaja Ranjit Singh cleverly hung back and the British forces had to not only take the lead but to do all the fighting.

- Even though in the initial phases of the war, the British gained advantage as the English army after a successful attack entered triumphantly into Kabul resulting in the surrender of **Dost Mohammad** (1840) and anointment of **Shah Shuja** as Amir, **but** ultimately the war ended as a disaster for the British as the British were soon compelled by the patriotic freedom-loving Afghan chiefs to sign a humiliating treaty by which they had to agree to not only evacuate but also restore Dost Mohammad on the throne of Afghanistan.
- The British suffered huge losses in the war both in terms of economic and human resources without much to gain in return. As per an official estimate, *the First Anglo-Afghan War resulted in net loss of one and a half crores rupees and nearly 20,000 men*. Thus, the entire Afghan adventure ended in total failure and proved to be one of the greatest disasters suffered by the British armies in India.

Later, in 1855, a new period of **Anglo–Afghan friendship** was initiated when a treaty of friendship was signed between **Dost Muhammad** and the British Indian Government, according to which the two sides promised to maintain friendly and peaceful relations, to respect each other's territories and to abstain from interfering in each other's internal affairs. In fact, to the distinct advantage of British, Dost Muhammad loyally followed the treaty and maintained absolute neutrality when England was fighting against Russia in the Crimean War (1854–56) or was facing in India the Revolt of 1857.

Policy of Non-Interference or Masterly inactivity (1863–75)

During 1863–75, the British Government of India, under this second policy of **non-interference** or **masterly inactivity** preferred to meet the danger of Russian domination on the Indian frontier itself since it was dangerous to strive for political domination over Afghanistan. This policy was vigorously pursued by Governor-General **John Lawrence** and his two successors too, more so on the account of learning from the disastrous outcome of the First Anglo-Afghan War and practical commonsense arising due to underlying knowledge of Afghan's passion for independence. As a matter of fact, when Dost Muhammad died in 1863, there was no interference in the war of succession. The policy of non-interference was primarily laid on two fundamental preconditions:

- the peace at the frontier was not to be disturbed and
- no candidate in civil war will seek any foreign help.

And as a result when **Sher Ali** emerged successful as Amir out of all contenders, John Lawrence tried to maintain friendly relations with him and ensured him complete British support. Thus, by a policy of non-interference and occasional help, the Amir was prevented from aligning himself with Russia.

The Second Anglo-Afghan War (1870–80)

- The policy of non-interference, however, did not last long. From **1870** onwards, along with the resurgence of imperialist ambitions, the Anglo–Russian rivalry also intensified again. The British statesman once again thought of bringing Afghanistan under direct political control for letting it serve as a base for British expansion in Central Asia. The ghostly fears of a Russian invasion added fuel to the fire and thus the pretext for the Second Anglo-Afghan War was set.
- Soon after the Crimean War, the Russians advanced swiftly in Central Asia. Making the Russian intention clear, Prince Gortchadoff wrote in his 1864 memorandum that *in approaching Afghanistan, Russia was influenced by the same imperious law that had led the British armies across the plains of Hindustan and Punjab*. **Sher Ali**, the Afghan ruler, was fully conscious of the Russian danger to his independence and was, therefore, quite willing to cooperate with the British in eliminating any threat

from the North. He approached British India for extensive military aid against internal and foreign enemies and in return offered a defensive cum offensive alliance against Russia, but the British Indian Government refused to enter into any such unconditional commitment and instead demanded unilateral right to keep a British mission at Kabul along with control over Afghanistan's foreign relations.

- When Sher Ali refused to comply, he was declared anti-British and pro-Russian in his outlook, and thus in 1876, **Lord Lytton** proposed to effect the gradual disintegration and weakening of the Afghan power, and thus an attack on Afghanistan was launched in 1878, signalling the start of the Second Anglo-Afghan War, although the results of this war too were almost similar to that of the First Anglo-Afghan War.
- Initially, the British were able to secure all they had desired by the **Treaty of Gandamak**, 1879 (signed between Sher Ali's son Yakub Khan and the British Indian Government). Through the treaty, the British secured certain border districts, the right to keep a Resident at Kabul and control over Afghanistan's foreign policy, but the British success was short-lived as very soon the freedom-loving Afghans rose into rebellion and on 3 September 1879 killed the British Resident, Major Cavagnari, and his military escort.
- Though Afghanistan was again invaded and occupied, the Afghans had made their point and when Lord Lytton was replaced by a new Viceroy, **Lord Ripon**, he reversed Lytton's aggressive policy and went back to the policy of non-interference in the internal affairs of Afghanistan. He recognised **Abdur Rahman**, the grandson of Dost Muhammad, as the new ruler, *Amir* of Afghanistan, and also withdrew the demand of a British Resident. The British Indian Government also agreed to pay the Amir an annual subsidy and to come to his aid in case of foreign aggression. In return, Afghanistan agreed not to maintain political relations with any other power except the British. Thus, the Amir even though losing control of his foreign policy at the same time retained complete control over his country's internal affairs.

The Third Anglo-Afghan War (1919–21)

- The First World War and the Russian Revolution of 1917 again changed the dynamics of Anglo–Afghan relations. With the disappearance of imperial Russia, the perpetual fear of aggression from the Russian side was removed and the Afghans now have no need to look to the British for support. Moreover, the war gave rise to strong anti-British feeling in Muslim countries, and the Russian Revolution also inspired anti-imperialist sentiments in Afghanistan. The Afghans now demanded full independence from British control. **Habibullah**, who had succeeded Abdur Rahman in 1901 as *Amir*, was assassinated in 1919, and his son, **Amanullah**, the new *Amir*, declared open war on British India. Peace came in 1921 when by a treaty, Afghanistan recovered its independence in foreign affairs.

North West Frontier

The annexation of Sindh and Punjab brought the British into direct contact with the North West frontier, which was an undefined border and beyond which lay the tangle of great hills, cut by deep winding valleys, inhabited by different hill tribes. The northern part of the North West frontier was inhabited by the *Pathans* and was administered by the **Punjab province**, while the southern part known as the Sindh frontier was occupied by the *Baluchis* and was then under the administration of **Bombay**. The hill tribes, however, were practically free, owing only nominal allegiance to the Amir of Kabul. Inhabiting dry and difficult terrain, living on meagre resources but endowed with courage, endurance and military skill, these tribal people frequently indulged in mass raids and plundering of the British Indian border areas. However, to encourage tribesmen to forsake plunder, the government allowed them to trade in the British Indian territory.

Since the North West frontier was under two different provincial governments, namely Punjab and Bombay, there developed two distinct methods of administering the frontier and conducting relations with the tribes. On the Sindh frontier, where the valleys were broader and less tortuous than in the Punjab and where the cultivated land was not very close to the tribal areas, the closed frontier system was adopted. Under this system, the frontier was patrolled, and no tribesman from beyond the border was allowed to enter

British territory without a pass. The Punjab frontier, on the other hand, was kept an 'open frontier' and for its protection, forts and garrisons were built to guard the narrow passes.

During the early phase, it was **Lord Dalhousie's** policy which served as a grand strategy to keep the frontier under control. His policy can be explained in three words, namely fines, blockades and expeditions. Fines were imposed as a punishment for plunder and murder, blockades for keeping crisis within certain limits; and expeditions were led against the tribes which resorted to mass plunder and rampage. The policy of sending punitive expeditions and blockades was described as 'butcher and bolt policy' and was criticised as a barbarous style of reprisal. However, to strengthen their control and conciliate the local tribal people, the government indulged in certain confidence building activities such as:

- By holding fairs to promote internal trade
- By making provision for free medical treatment by opening dispensaries and hospitals
- By creating employment opportunities and encouraging the tribals to enlist themselves in military and paramilitary forces
- By constructing roads and railway lines, which also helped in strengthening the hold of the British on the region

However, establishment of peace on the North West frontier was a complex issue as usually the *Amir* of Kabul was intrigued with the frontier tribes. On Lord Lansdowne's insistence, Sir **Mortimer Durand** was appointed to negotiate a boundary agreement with the *Amir* of Kabul, settling forever the responsibility of the Kabul Government concerning the tribes on the Indus border. The agreement concluded in 1893, dividing the tribal area between the Afghans and the British.[3] The line of demarcation known as the **Durand Line** was drawn between Afghan and British territories. But, the Durand Agreement failed to keep the peace, and there were soon rebellions against the British. To check these, a permanent British garrison was established in Chitral.

Later, the viceroy **Lord Curzon** (1899–1905) proposed for the replacement of British Indian regular troops by the bodies oftribal levies. This measure was well appreciated, as besides creating local responsibility for maintaining law and order, the proposed change had the additional advantage of being less costly. Further, for administrative efficiency and effective control, he carved out a new province known as **North-Western Frontier Province** (NWFP) and was thus successful in establishing protracted peace. In January 1932, NWFP was constituted as a governor's province and since 1947, the province belongs to Pakistan.

The Anglo–Nepal Relations

The British desiring to extend their India Empire to its natural geographical frontier brought them into conflict with the northern Kingdom of Nepal too. The valley of Nepal had been conquered in 1768 by the Gorkhas, a western Himalayan tribe, known for their vigour and bravery. Under the **Gorkhas**, Nepal began to expand its dominion beyond the Nepal *tarai* region and tried to push towards the south since the northern side was well defended by the Chinese.

The First Anglo-Nepal War (1814–16)

- In 1801, the English conquered *Gorakhpur* which brought the two expanding powers face to face across the common boundary and it was just a matter of time that a conflict happened.
- In October 1814, a border clash between the two countries led to open war. Initially, British armies were defeated by the Gorkhas under the able leadership of Commander Amar Singh Thapa but gradually the Gorkhas lost to the British since they were far superior in terms of men, money and resources. Thus, in the end, the Nepal Government had to make peace on British terms and had to sign the Treaty of Sagauli.
- As per the treaty:

[3] • The Amir of Kabul was to retain Wakhan, Asmar, Kafiristan, Mohmand and a portion of Wazirstan;
• The British were allowed to retain Swat, Bajaur, Darwaz Kurrum Valley, Chalgeh and New Chaman. The tribal areas of Gomal Pass were also given to the British.

- Nepal accepted a British resident at Kathmandu.
- Nepal ceded the districts of Garhwal and Kumaon and abandoned its claims to the *tarai* region.
- Nepal also withdrew from Sikkim.

This treaty had many advantages for the British as not only their Indian Empire now reached to the Himalayas but they also gained greater facilities for trade with Central Asia. Along with it, they also obtained important hill station sites like Shimla, Mussoorie and Nainital. The *Gorkhas* further added to the strength of the British Indian army and proved themselves to be valuable military assets for the British.

The Anglo–Sikkim Relations

Owing to its geographical position, the state of Sikkim holds strategic importance for the security of India's northern frontier. In 1835, the territory of Darjeeling was ceded to the British by the Raja of Sikkim in return for an annual money grant. Later, in 1849, due to a minor quarrel along the border, **Lord Dalhousie** sent troops to Sikkim and forced the Raja to cede nearly 1700 square miles of his territory to British India. The relations between the two again soured in 1860 when another clash occurred between the troops of Diwan of Sikkim and the British. Eventually, a peace treaty was signed between the two in 1861, by virtue of which the following occurred:

- Sikkim was reduced to the status of a **virtual protectorate**,
- The Raja of Sikkim not only expelled the Diwan and his relations from Sikkim but also agreed to pay ₹7,000 as fine as well as full compensation for British losses in the war,
- The Raja was also forced to open his country fully to British trade and was made to agree to limit the transit duty on goods exchanged between India and Tibet via Sikkim.

The peace bought through this treaty, however, lasted only till 1886 when fresh trouble arose between British India and Sikkim. It was alleged by the British that Tibetans were trying to increase their influence and control in Sikkim, and instead of resisting them, the Pro-Tibet rulers of Sikkim were extending support to them. Consequently, in 1888, the British carried out military operations against the Tibetans in Sikkim and later in 1890, a final settlement came with the signing of an Anglo–Chinese agreement through which Sikkim was recognised as a British protectorate over which the British had exclusive rights of control in terms of internal administration and foreign relations.

The Anglo–Bhutan Relations

Around 1774, Bengal Governor-General Warren Hastings succeeded in establishing friendly relations with Bhutan as the ruler of Bhutan permitted Bengal to trade with Tibet through its territory. However, after 1815, when the British occupied Assam and came in more close contact with the mountain state of Bhutan, due to mutually exclusive interests, the relations started straining between the two countries. The probable reasons behind the tension being the following:

- The dispute over the *duars* or passes in the Bhutan hills: At the base of the Bhutan hills lay a narrow strip of territory of about 1,000 square miles containing a number of *duars* or passes. This area was strategic not only from the viewpoint of a well-defined and defendable border but also held significance of being useful as fertile tea lands to the British planters. Considering all this, Lord Auckland in 1841 annexed the Assam *duars*, further increasing the tensions between the two countries.
- Frequent raids by the Bhutiyas on the Bengal side of the border: The relations between India and Bhutan were further strained by the frequent raids by the Bhutiyas on the Bengal side of the border. This tension kept on growing, and finally in 1865, a brief war broke out between the two. The fighting was mostly one-sided and was followed by a treaty signed in November 1865 through which Bhutan ceded all the Bengal and Assam *duars* in return for an annual subsidy of ₹50,000. British India gained control over Bhutan's defence and foreign relations though it promised not to interfere in Bhutan's internal affairs.

The Anglo–Burma (Myanmar) Relations

The independent kingdom of Burma was systemically annexed by the British through three successive Anglo–Burmese wars during the 19th century. Even though the conflict between Burma and British India was initiated by border clashes, the real and deeper reasons lay elsewhere and those being: the expansionist urges of the British further strengthened by the lure of forest resources of Burma, market potential for British manufacture in Burma coupled with the desire to check the spread of French commercial and political influence in Burma and the rest of South-East Asia.

The First Anglo-Burmese War (1824–26)

- The First Anglo-Burmese War was in part the result of border clashes and some part being the interest clashes between the Burma and the British. The pretext to the war was being set from the time when the Burmese King **Bodawpaya** conquered the border states of Arakan in 1785 and Manipur in 1813 bringing Burma's border up to that of British India and finally, in 1822 he annexed Assam. The Burmese occupation of Manipur and Assam was considered by the British authorities as a serious threat to their position in India and thus in order to counter this threat, the British started strengthening their position over the strategic border states of *Cachar* and *Jaintia*. This action of the British angered the Burmese and they marched their troops into *Cachar*, resulting in a clash between the two forces, which finally led to withdrawal of Burmese into Manipur.
- Also, for several decades, the British had been trying to persuade the Burmese authorities to sign a commercial treaty with them and exclude French traders from Burma, but Burma was not complying to British wishes. Thus, the British Indian authorities now seized this opportunity to declare war on Burma on 24 February 1824.
- After an initial setback, the British forces drove the Burmese out of Assam, *Cachar*, Manipur and Arakan. The British forces occupied Rangoon in May 1824 and reached within 45 miles of their capital at Ava. But, Burmese posed strong resistance, specially in terms of effective guerrilla warfare in the jungles. Interestingly, the rainy climate and virulent diseases like fever and dysentry killed more people than war. For instance, in Rangoon, 3160 died in hospitals and 166 on the battlefield.
- The war was also proving to be financially costly and thus in February 1826, both sides were more than glad to make peace by signing the **Treaty of Yandabo** through which the Government of Burma agreed:
  - to pay one crore rupees as war compensation
  - to cede its coastal provinces of **Arakan** and **Tenasserim**
  - to abandon all claims to **Assam**, ***Cachar*** and ***Jaintia***
  - to recognise **Manipur** as an independent state
  - to negotiate a commercial treaty with Britain
  - and to accept a British Resident at Ava while posting a Burmese envoy in Calcutta

The treaty proved to be advantageous to the British as through this treaty, the British not only deprived Burma of its coastline but also acquired a firm base in Burma for future expansion.

The Second Anglo-Burmese War (1852)

- The Second Anglo-Burmese War was mostly the result of British commercial greed and Lord **Dalhousie's** imperial aggressive policy. The British, already in control of Burma's two coastal provinces, now wanted to establish commercial relations with the rest of the country and take in possession left over on the coastal province of Pegu to further its imperial agenda. Two critical reasons behind the war were:

- The growing interest of British timber firms in exploiting the vast timber resources of Upper Burma.
- Commercial penetration of Burma for the sale of British goods and manufacture.

- On the basis of a frivolous and petty complaint, the British under Lord Dalhousie took the excuse for armed intervention in Burma in 1852 through which **Rangoon** was immediately captured and British authority over Pegu, the only remaining coastal province, was established. The Burmese King, **Mindon**, was hardly in a position to fight the British as he was himself indulged in the power struggle with his half brother King Pagan Min for Burma's throne, and thus there were no official negotiations for peace and war ended without a treaty.
- There was, however, an intense guerrilla resistance for three years before Lower Burma could be brought under effective control and finally, the British established their control over the whole of Burma's coastline as well as its entire sea trade. As evident in the outcome, the Second Anglo-Burmese War was ironically though much shorter but at the same time more decisive than the First Anglo-Burmese War (1824–26).

The Third Anglo-Burmese War (1885)

- The relations between Burma and Britain remained peaceful for several years after the annexation of Pegu, but the tables were again turned when King Mindon was succeeded by his son King **Thibaw**, who adopted an uncompromising attitude towards British selfish demands. The hostile attitude of the King coupled with the unresolved desire of British timber merchants to gain full control of Upper Burma along with the demand for exclusion of all foreign rivals from Burma, further intensified the issues of contention between the two states and war seemed again inevitable.
- The background to the Third Anglo-Burmese War had started almost a decade back, in 1871, when the British Government humiliated the Burmese King and reduced him to a mere status of ruler of one of the Indian states when it announced that the relations with him would be conducted through the Viceroy of India only. They were also apprehensive about the growing French influence in Burma. So, when in 1885, King Thibaw signed a commercial treaty with France which would also enable Burma to import modern arms, the British officials were alarmed and were on the lookout for a pretext for war.
- This was provided by the *Bombay Burma Trading Corporation*, a British concern which held a lease of the teak forests in Burma. The Burmese Government had demanded compensation from the concern on the grounds of extracting more than double the quantity of teak contracted. The British Government decided to seize this opportunity and in turn put forward untenable demands to the Burmese Government, the rejection of which led to British invasion of Burma on 13 November 1885.
- The Burmese Government was unable to put up effective resistance to the British forces and thus the British conquered Burma with great ease. However, as with previous Anglo-Burmese wars, the freedom-loving Burmese people refused to surrender and carried on widespread guerrilla warfare and rose up in rebellion. It took nearly 5 years and a 40,000 strong army to suppress the revolt.

After World War I, a vigorous modern nationalist movement similar on the lines of Indian National Movement arose in Burma. A wide campaign of boycotting British goods and administration was organised, and the Burmese nationalists joined hands with the leaders of the Indian National Congress demanding Home Rule. Alarmed at this unity and to weaken the camaraderie, the British separated Burma from India in 1935, however, the Burmese nationalist movement reached new heights under the leadership of U. Aung Sen and won its independence on 4 January 1948.

The Anglo–Tibet Relations

Tibet, also known as the *Hermit Kingdom*, is a landlocked country encircled by a chain of mountains with average height of 10,000 feet above the sea level and forms a strategic part of the northern frontier of India.

With meagre economic resources, its people loved isolation and was ruled by a theocracy of Buddhist monks (the ***lamas***) under the nominal suzerainty of China. (The Chinese had granted protection to Tibet in 1728 to ward off foreign dangers.) Out of commercial interests only, Warren Hastings sent two missions, one in 1774 and another in 1783, but the suspicious Tibet ruler, the *Dalai Lama*, declined the offer of establishing trade relations with the British East India Company and thus, not much was achieved by the British. Meanwhile, towards the end of the 19th century, the Chinese suzerainty on Tibet was being ineffective, and in view of the declining power of China, and scramble among the foreign powers to divide it into spheres of influence, Tibet assumed great strategic importance particularly for the British and the Russians. Also, during the 19th century, British interest in tea and shawl wool increased considerably, and there was a tremendous pressure of the traders on the government to develop regular traffic with Tibet through Bhutan.

The British policy towards Tibet was thus governed by both economic and political aspects as economically, the British wanted to develop Indo-Tibetan trade and to exploit mineral resources and politically, it wanted to exercise political control over Tibet to safeguard the northern frontier of British India. But, the British were not able to achieve much on both aspects. Also, further adding to British woes, it was being speculated that the Russian influence in Tibet was on the increase as suggested by the confidential reports received by the British Government that Russian arms and ammunition were entering Tibet. The British Indian Government, under **Lord Curzon**, decided to take immediate action to counter Russian influence and thus, in March 1904, dispatched a military expedition to **Lhasa**, the Capital of Tibet, under **Colonel Francis Younghusband** to bring Tibet under its system of protected border states. The virtually unarmed Tibetans offered non-violent resistance but without any success. Younghusband pushed his way into Lhasa (interestingly, without coming across any Russians on the way) and after prolonged negotiations the **Treaty of Lhasa** was signed through which:

- Tibet was to pay ₹25 lakhs as indemnity.
- The Chumbi Valley (lying between Bhutan and Sikkim) was to be occupied by the British for 3 years.
- British trade mission was to be stationed at Gyantse.
- The Tibetans agreed not to admit the representatives of any foreign power into Tibet and in return the British agreed not to interfere in Tibet's internal affairs.

On examining the British Tibetan scheme of things, it can be safely deduced that the British achieved very little by their Tibetan expedition as even though it was successful in securing the withdrawal of Russia from Tibet, but since it was achieved at the cost of confirming Chinese suzerainty, it held very little significance. Later, in the Anglo-Russian convention of 1907 too, China's suzerainty over Tibet was reaffirmed as one of the clauses of this Convention laid down the condition that both Russia and Britain would not negotiate with Tibet directly, but only through the mediation of China. Thereafter, with the Chinese revolution of 1911 and founding of new Chinese Government, China asserted its control over Tibet with more vigour and declared Tibet as an integral part of China, which prompted the *Dalai Lama* to announce his independence but ironically, the British instead of recognising Tibet as an independent state, invited representatives of China and Tibet to a **tripartite conference** in **Shimla** in May 1913 and concluded two agreements. By one of them, the British accepted China's suzerainty over the eastern zone or the inner zone while the outer zone or the western zone was declared autonomous. By another treaty, it was decided to draw a boundary line between Tibet and British India, which is named after the British delegate Henry McMohan.

British Relations with the Indian Princely States

About 2/5th of the territory of the Indian subcontinent were under 'indirect rule' of the Company and later the Crown where even though the indigenous princes ruled, the actual governance was done by the **British Political Agents** and **Residents**. Initially, when the role of the East India Company was primarily commercial, the Residents took the role of Commercial Agents, looking after the Company's trading interests **but** as the role of the Company over the years changed from commercial to political, the Residents' role too functionally enhanced from commercial nature to handling political relations between the Company Raj and Indian princes. As rightly stated by Sekhar Bandyopadhyay, *The Residency system involved a redefinition of sovereignty, which was encoded in the new terminology of "Paramountcy", under which the Indian states were left with "domestic sovereignty", while sovereignty beyond their borders lay with the Company as the superior imperial power.*

The responsibilities and privileges of the princes were in all cases defined in **treaties** between them and the Company, the provisions of which varied according to the **circumstances** in which they were signed, the **status** of the princes and the **size** of their states but certain features of indirect rule were common across all states. For instance, all the princes **recognised** the Company and later the Crown as the suzerain power, relinquished their right to enter into diplomatic relations with or declare war against any other state or to employ any other European, to direct all their communications with the outer world through the British Agents, to pay for a contingent of Imperial Service Troops and **contribute militarily** when there was a need for military assistance for the defence of the empire. In return, they were to be protected against external aggression and internal revolt, and enjoy internal autonomy. However, the internal autonomy of the princes was in practice seriously constrained by the overbearing presence of the Residents in the case of larger states and the Political Agents in cases of the smaller states. However, a question do arises why the British who were in a position of direct rule over these princely states preferred to keep many of these states under indirect rule. Well, there are pragmatic reasons for the same:

- The control and administration of these states required extensive resources – both financial and human – and thus it was **practically prudent** on the part of the English to keep these states under indirect rule, often reducing these so-called 'sovereigns' to the de facto status of puppets or virtually confining them within their own palaces. Rather, it was more beneficial to the British to keep them this way where they enjoyed the authority without any accountability or administrative responsibility.
- The choice of letting certain states function under indirect rule also rested on certain **other factors** such as follows:
  - The states which were not in a position to challenge the military power of the British were left to themselves;
  - The states situated in remote corners or on hostile terrains were also left alone;
  - The states having little arable land, and thus having limited prospects of revenue generation, also held little attraction for direct administration.
- The association with the princes also gave the British Raj some amount of **legitimacy** and due to this reason only, the traditional practices of holding a *durbar* were duly incorporated into the imperial rituals as evident in the holding of Imperial Durbar of 1877.

Phases in the Evolution of Indirect Rule in India

Michael Fisher has identified four distinct phases in the evolution of indirect rule in India until the Revolt of 1857.

- **The first phase** (1764–97) starts with the initial placement of the Company's Residents at the courts of Awadh, Murshidabad and Hyderabad after the Battle of Buxar (1764). The role of Residents during this period was more restricted, cautious and primarily focused on maintaining diplomatic relations since the Company had just started its imperial expansion and its authorities were not yet confident and clear-sighted about its forward policy in India.
- **The Second phase** (1798–1840) was marked by aggressive expansionism in contrast to initial hesitation of the first phase. Under Lord Wellesley and his policy of Subsidiary Alliance, the role of Residents changed from maintaining diplomatic relations to that of supervising indirect control, and in many cases, the Residents themselves facilitated further territorial expansion. However, this trend

was temporarily halted by the recall of Wellesley and the arrival of Lord Cornwallis with a mandate to follow a policy of non-interference. But, after his departure, the British again indulged in territorial expansion and the role of Residents became prominent again as many of the newly conquered territories were left to be indirectly controlled by them. This growth continued till 1841, when due to the disastrous Afghan campaign (1838–42), the British for the first time failed to establish indirect rule in Afghanistan.

- **The Third Phase** (1841–57) was marked more by 'Consolidation' rather than expansion since there is clear policy shift towards direct annexation as spearheaded by **Lord Dalhousie's** forward policies such as the Doctrine of Lapse through which a number of states like Awadh, Jhansi, Nagpur, Satara were annexed and brought under direct rule of the Company. This phase continued till the Revolt of 1857, after which the British policy towards Indian States changed. The **Revolt of 1857**, therefore, constitutes an important watershed in the evolution of British policies towards the Indian states since it was found that the territories under indirect rule were not only less affected by the Revolt than those under the direct rule but some states like Gwalior and Hyderabad had even rendered valuable service in containing the Revolt.
- **The Fourth Phase** (1857 onwards) was when the rule passed over from Company to the Crown, the Queen recognising the *princes as natural allies* made a commitment under her **proclamation of November 1858** to respect the rights, dignity and honour of the native princes. **Lord Canning**, thus, reassured the princely states by recognising their adopted heirs and issued 150 adoption *sanads*.
  - But, at the same time, the British made good governance a pre-requisite for continued political support to these states on the pretext of assuming greater responsibility for the welfare of the princely subjects and with the coming of **Lord Mayo** (1869–72) as viceroy, this reformist mission became a dominant official policy. Most indigenous rulers tried to adapt and initiated certain key social and revenue reforms in their states, and those who chose to resist were rudely reminded of the 'omnipotence of the Paramount Power'. For instance, Malhar Rao Gaikwad of Baroda was deposed in 1875 on charges of gross misrule.
  - However, towards the end of the 1870s when nationalism gradually began to surface in Indian politics, reform and modernisation were put on the back burner and specially from 1878 to 86, the states had to withstand systematic intervention and contraction of their domestic sovereignty. They had to relinquish control over the railway tracks and other communication systems like post and telegraph within their territories, although they had to pay for their construction, refrain from exporting salt to other parts of British India and accept British Indian currency as legal tender.
  - Along with it, they were also regularly reminded of the grandeur of British power and were placed according to their importance within the imperial order, which was further institutionalised into an elaborate hierarchy. For instance, by the 20th century, the King emperor was entitled to 101 gun salutes, the Viceroy 31 and the important Indian princes somewhere between 21 and 9 gun salutes. The Imperial Durbar of 1877 and Grand Coronation Durbar of 1903 were a testimony to the maintenance of this pecking order.
  - This interventionism reached its height during the administration of **Lord Curzon** (1898–1905), who brought the Princes under stricter control and deposed rulers of around 63 states and brought them under temporary British administration. For instance, in 1900, he prohibited their foreign travel; and in 1902, he pressurised the Nizam of Hyderabad to sign a more favourable treaty regarding the administration of Berar and forced the Princes to pay more for the Imperial Services Troops. However, this policy of interventionism was soon replaced by the policy of *laissez faire* when **Lord Minto** took over as the viceroy. However, it should be noted that the policy was more oriented towards isolating the states from the prevailing political currents and the Princes were considered to be reliable allies in the fight against political extremism.

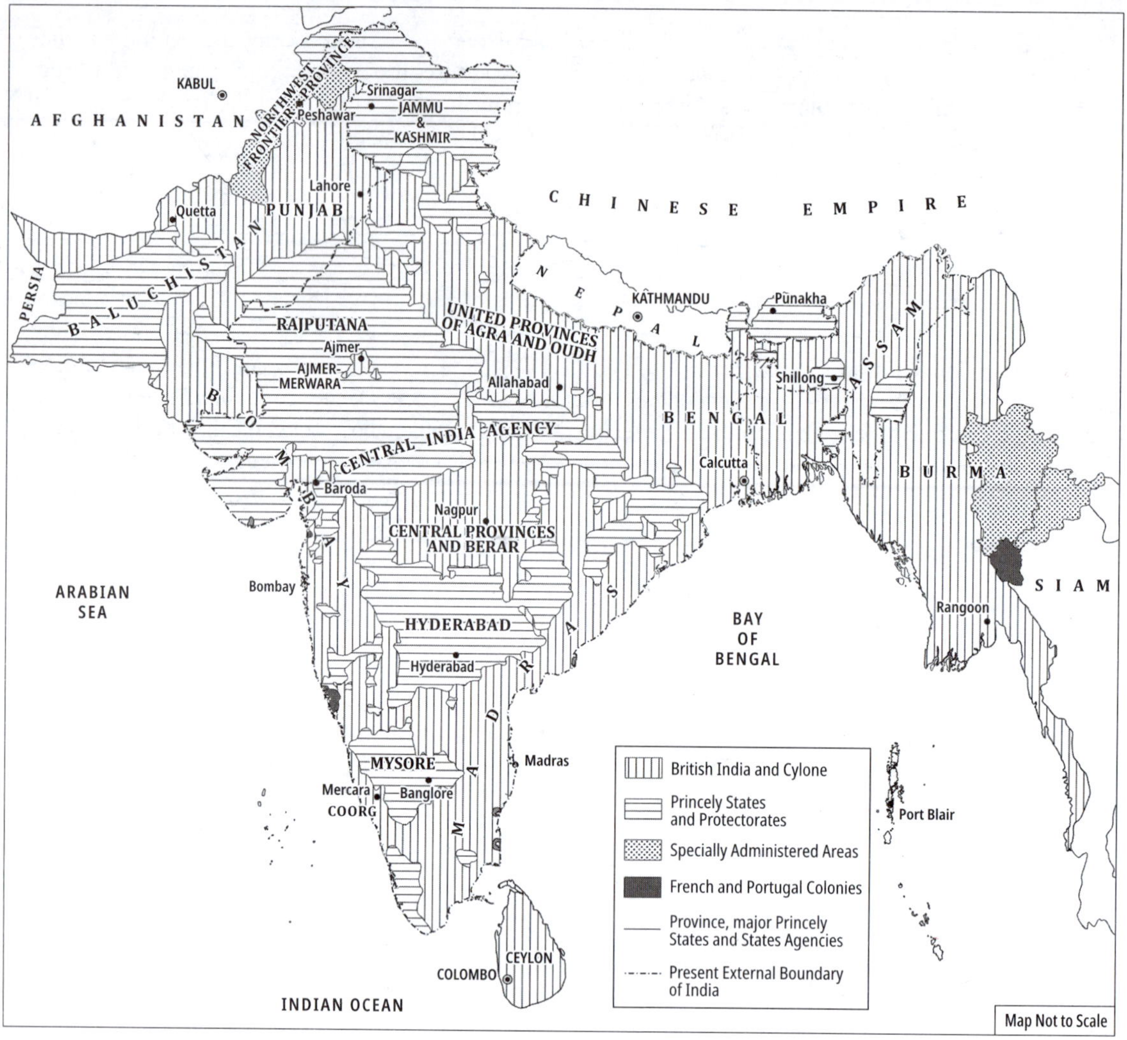

British India and the Princely States, 1904

Governors-General From 1773 to 1857 and Significant Events During Their Rule

Warren Hastings (1773–85)

- He was a gifted personality endowed with strong will, great energy and resourcefulness. He laid the foundation of the mighty British empire in India, over which others erected a 'stately edifice'.
- **Abolition of the Dual System of Governance** (earlier introduced by Robert Clive): The East India Company decided to act as Diwan and to undertake the collection of revenue by its own agents. For that purpose, a Board of Revenue was established in Calcutta to supervise the collection of revenue, and English Collectors were appointed in each district.

- **Reorganisation of the Judicial System**: Each district was provided with a civil court under the Collector and a criminal court under an Indian Judge. The highest civil court of appeal was called *Sadar Diwani Adalat*, which was to be presided over by the Governor and two judges recruited from among the members of his council. Similarly, the highest appellate criminal court was known as *Sadar Nizamat Adalat* which was to function under an Indian judge appointed by the Governor-in-Council. Experts in Hindu and Muslim laws were provided to assist the judges. A digest of Hindu law was prepared in Sanskrit by learned Pandits and it was translated into Persian. An English translation of it – Code of Hindu Laws – was prepared by Halhed.
- Trade Regulations and other Reforms: Warren Hastings abolished the system of *dastaks*, or free passes and regulated the internal trade. He reduced the number of custom houses and enforced a uniform tariff of 2.5 percent for Indian and non-Indian goods. Private trade by the Company's servants continued but within enforceable limits.
- **The Regulating Act of 1773**: Brought the affairs of the Company under the control of the Parliament and the Governor of Bengal was styled as the Governor-General of India.
- **The Amending Act of 1781**: Defined the jurisdiction of the Supreme Court more precisely, and divided the powers of jurisdiction between the Governor-General in council and the Supreme Court.
- **The Pitt's India Act, 1784**: A Board of Control consisting of six members was created who were appointed by the Crown. The Court of Directors controlled its commercial functions, whereas the Board of Control maintained its political affairs. Thus, the Board represented the King, while the directors symbolised the Company.
- **Expansionist policy of Warren Hastings**:
    - The Rohilla War (1774)
    - The First Anglo-Maratha War (1775–82)
    - The Second Anglo-Mysore War (1780–84)
- Since he considered Indian culture as a basis for sound Indian administration, he patronised the learning of Indian languages and arts. He was also instrumental in the foundation of the **Asiatic Society of Bengal** (1784) by Sir William Jones.
- The **Impeachment of Warren Hastings**: In 1787, Warren Hastings was impeached in the Parliament for his administrative excesses and 22 charges were brought forward against him. The most important of them were related to the:
    - The Rohilla War of 1774
    - The case of Nanda Kumar: It was contended that Warren Hastings and Sir Elija Impey, the judge of the Supreme Court, conspired against Nanda Kumar, who was an influential official of Bengal and was hanged to death by the verdict of the Supreme Court for a petty offence of forgery.
    - The treatment of Raja Chait Singh of Benaras: It was alleged that Warren Hastings imposed heavy penalty on the Raja for his delay in payment of tribute and deposed him in an unjust manner.
    - The pressures on the Begums of Awadh: Warren Hastings was accused of highhandedness when he helped the Nawab of Awadh by sending his troops to extort money from the Begums (the mother and grandmother of the Nawab of Awadh).
- However, after a long trial which lasted till 1795, Warren Hastings was completely acquitted from all charges and also received pension from the Company till his death in 1818.

Lord Cornwallis (1786–93)

- A blue-blooded aristocrat, an able warrior-statesman who not only consolidated the Company's position in India but as an administrator laid the foundation of an efficient and clean administration. He is often regarded as the **Father of the Indian Civil Services** and is credited with many administrative, revenue and judicial reforms.

- **Administrative Reforms**: Cornwallis, aiming at cleansing the administration and in order to address the issue of corruption, persuaded the Directors of the Company to pay handsome salaries to the Company servants and adopted a stern policy against any sort of default. He initiated the policy of making appointments mainly on the basis of merit thereby laying the foundation of the Indian Civil Services. Though, he was also responsible for Europeanisation of administrative machinery.
- **Revenue Reforms**: Cornwallis is credited with introduction of the system of Permanent Settlement (1793). He also tried to reform the Board of Trade, which managed the commercial investments of the Company and eradicated numerous abuses and corrupt practices.
- **Judicial Reforms**: With the support of Sir William Jones, who was a judge and a great scholar, Cornwallis completely reorganised the Civil and Criminal courts and appointed district judges. In criminal cases, Muslim law was improved and followed while in civil cases, Hindu and Muslim laws were followed according to the religion of the litigants. He also tried to abolish barbarous punishments like mutilation and trial by ordeal.
- **Police Reforms**: He established a regular police force to maintain law and order and divested the zamindars of their police functions by disbanding their armed retainers. He divided the districts into *thanas*, each placed under an Indian officer called *daroga*, who was appointed and supervised by the magistrates.
- **Cornwallis Code of 1793**: With the help of his colleague, George Barlow, Cornwallis prepared a comprehensive code based upon the principle of Montesquieu, *the Separation of Powers*, and covered all areas of administration, that is, judicial, police, commercial and fiscal. As a result, the collectors, the kingpins of the administrative system were deprived of their judicial powers, and collection of revenue became their primary task. Also, in order to curb undue exercise of authority Cornwallis made all officials answerable to the courts.
- During his reign, **the Third Anglo-Mysore War** (1790–92) was fought and the famous Treaty of Seringapatnam was signed.

Sir John Shore (1793–98)

- The period of Shore's rule as Governor-General was comparatively uneventful. He adopted the policy of neutrality, which greatly affected the prestige of the English and contributed much to the growth of anti-British feelings. The two major events during his reign were:
  - The Charter Act of 1793
  - The Battle of Kharda between the Nizam and the Marathas

Lord Wellesley (1798–1805)

- The appointment of Lord Wellesley as Governor-General marks an epoch in the history of British India. He called himself 'a Bengal tiger' and was a great imperialist who reversed the policy of non-intervention of his predecessor and played one of the finest master strokes of British imperialism, namely the 'Subsidiary Alliance' to accomplish his dream of converting 'the British Empire in India' into 'the British Empire of India'.
- Wellesley's diplomatic initiative of Subsidiary Alliance (1798) not only increased the military strength of the Company at the expense of the protected states but also established the British as the paramount

power in India. Hyderabad was the first state to be brought under this system, followed by Tanjore (1799), Surat (1800), Awadh (1801) and the Carnatic (1801).

- He is often called as the maker of the erstwhile Madras Presidency as with the annexation of Carnatic and Tanjore, the way for formation of Madras Presidency was paved.
- Fought and won crucial wars such as:
  - The Fourth Anglo-Mysore War (1799)
  - The Second Maratha War (1803–05)

Sir George Barlow (1805–07)

- During his administration, the Vellore Mutiny of 1806 took place.

Lord Minto I (1807–13)

- He concluded the Treaty of Amritsar with Maharaja Ranjit Singh of Punjab in 1809. Also, the Charter Act of 1813 was passed during this period.

Lord Hastings (1813–23)

- He not only completed and consolidated the work of Wellesley but also adopted a vigorous forward policy himself and waged wars extensively, which further expanded the frontiers of the British Empire.
- **War against the Gorkhas/Anglo-Nepal War (1814–16)** and Treaty of Sagauli (1816): Nepal had emerged as a powerful Gorkha state in 1768, and when in 1801, the British acquired the districts of *Gorakhpur* and *Basti* from the Nawab of Awadh, the boundary of Nepal was brought directly in touch with the British frontier, which resulted in regular confrontations and culminated in war in 1814. Hastings forced Amar Singh Thapa, the able General of the Nepal Army, to surrender and thus in March 1816, the Treaty of Sagauli was concluded. According to provisions of this treaty, the Gorkhas gave up their claim over the *Tarai* region and ceded the areas of Kumaon and Garhwal to the British, along with agreeing to keep a British Resident at Kathmandu and prohibiting employment to any other foreigner except the English. After this victory, Hastings was honoured with English peerage and he became *Marquis of Hastings*.
- Suppression of the Pindaris (1817–18)
- Third Maratha War (1817–19) and dissolution of Maratha confederacy; along with creation of Bombay Presidency (1818). As a matter of fact, Hastings is often considered as the maker of the Bombay Presidency.
- Reforms undertaken during Hastings reign: Apart from territorial expansion, there was a marked progress in the working of administration under Governor-Generalship of Lord Hastings such as follows:
  - He approved the Ryotwari System of land revenue introduced in the Madras Presidency by Sir Thomas Munroe.
  - In the sphere of judiciary, the Cornwallis Code was improved and the police system of Bengal was extended to other regions, though the principle of separation of judicial and revenue functions was not rigidly followed as the District Collector started again acting as Magistrate too.
  - Hastings had liberal views on education as he wholeheartedly encouraged the foundation of vernacular schools by missionaries and others. In 1817, the Hindu College was established in Calcutta for the teaching of English and Western science, and Hastings was the patron of this college.
  - He also encouraged the freedom of the Press and abolished the censorship introduced in 1799. It was during Hastings rule that the Bengali Weekly, *Samachar Darpan*, was started in 1818 by a Serampore missionary, Marshman.

Lord Amherst (1823–28)

- The principal events during his tenure include the annexation of Assam leading to the First Anglo-Burmese War (1824–26), resulting in the cession of Arakan and Tenasserim to the British Empire.

Lord William Bentinck (1828–35)

- As Governor-General, Bentinck initiated an era of progress and reforms. Not only was he the **first Governor-General of India** but also was undoubtedly the first Governor-General of British India who acted on the dictum that *the welfare of the subject peoples was a main, perhaps the primary, duty of the British in India.* Although his tenure of office covered only a short span of seven years, it saw a period of enduring reforms such as:
  - **Social Reforms**: He was the key initiator of a number of social reforms such as:
    - Abolition of Sati and other cruel rites like female infanticide and child sacrifice (1829): Bentinck was a crusader against the inhuman practice of *Sati*, the age-old custom of burning of widows alive on the funeral pyre of their husbands, and aghast at the report of 800 cases of *Sati* in a single year from Bengal, he promulgated his Regulation XVII on 4 December 1829 prohibiting the practice of *Sati*. Those who practiced *Sati* or were accomplice in the process were made liable for punishment by the courts, and by 1830, the Regulation was extended to the Madras and Bombay Presidencies. Similarly, he put a ban on female infanticide and child sacrifice and declared it illegal.
    - Suppression of *Thugs* (1830): One of the other commendable measures taken by Bentinck which further contributed to the material welfare of the people was the suppression of the *thugs. They were highway hereditary robbers who over the period of time had increased in number and went about in small groups of fifty to hundred posing as commercial gangs or pilgrims 'strangling and robbing peaceful travellers*'. From 1830, under the able guidance of Bentinck, a campaign against the thugs was systematically organised by Colonel Sleeman and during the course of five years nearly 2000 of them were captured who were either exterminated or transported to the Andaman and Nicobar Islands. Interestingly, for his role in the suppression of thugs, Sir William Sleeman was known as the *Thugee Sleeman.*
    - Introduction of English Education: His educational reforms heralded a new age in India, and the introduction of English Education was a significant event of Bentinck's administration. He appointed a committee headed by **Lord Macaulay** to make recommendations for the promotion of education and in his report, Macaulay emphasised the promotion of European literature and science through English medium among the Indian people. This recommendation was wholeheartedly accepted by William Bentinck and through the Government Resolution of 1835, the English language was made the official and literary language of India. In 1835, William Bentinck also laid the foundation of the Calcutta Medical College.
  - **Administrative Reforms**: He introduced local languages in the lower courts and English in the higher courts in the place of Persian, and abolished the provincial courts of appeal established by Cornwallis, that were largely responsible for the huge arrears of cases. In the matters of revenue too, he launched a peasant friendly settlement in the North West Province with the help of **R. M. Bird**. This settlement was for a period of 30 years, and it was made either with the tillers of the soil or with the landowners.
  - **Financial Reforms**: When Bentinck had assumed the Governor-Generalship in 1828, the financial position of the Company was very unstable, the exchequer was very weak and the state budget showed a deficit of one million rupees. In order to improve the financial condition, he adopted financial reforms such as reducing the salaries and allowances of all officers, removal of additional staff

and abolition of double *batta* (allowance to troops on active service). By all these measures, he left the treasury with a surplus of ₹1.5 millions at the time of his departure.

- **The Charter Act of 1833**, a significant constitutional instrument defining the scope and authority of the East India Company, was passed during his reign. One of the major reforms adopted by the Act was the Indianisation of public services as it categorically stated *that no native of India, nor any natural born subject of His Majesty, should be disabled from holding any place, office, or employment, by reason of his religion, place of birth, descent or colour.*
- **Policy Towards Indian States**: Though he mostly adopted a policy of non-intervention and non-aggression towards Indian states, at times, in order to safeguard British interests, he even annexed the states of Mysore (1831), Coorg (1834) and Central Cacher and Jaintia (1834).
- Treaty of 'perpetual friendship' with Ranjit Singh: The Governor-General was successful in winning the friendship of Ranjit Singh and concluded the Indus Navigation Treaty through which the river Sutlej was opened up for navigation. A similar treaty was also concluded with the *Amirs* of Sind.

Lord Metcalfe (1835–36)

- His brief tenure of just 1 year is memorable for giving entire liberty to the press. It was during his reign that the new press law removing restrictions on the press in India was executed (though it was initiated by his predecessor, Lord William Bentinck). Due to his liberal policy towards the press, Lord Metcalfe is known as the Liberator of Indian Press.

Lord Auckland (1836–42)

- During his reign, the two major events were:
  - Death of Maharaja Ranjit Singh (1839)
  - The First Anglo-Afghan War (1836–42), in which the British were defeated, and due to his failure in Afghanistan he was recalled in 1842.

Lord Ellenborough (1842–44)

- He succeeded Auckland and ended the Afghan War. Two other major events during his reign were:
  - Annexation of Sindh (1843)
  - War with Gwalior (1843)

Lord Hardinge I (1844–48)

- He fought the First Anglo-Sikh War (1845–46) and concluded the Treaty of Lahore (1846).
- He introduced the policy of giving preference to English-educated Indians in public employment.
- He is credited for suppressing the barbarous practice of making human sacrifices that prevailed among the primitive tribe of Gonds.

Lord Dalhousie (1848–56)

- He was the youngest Governor-General of India when he assumed charge at the age of 36 in 1848, but defying his age, he proved to be one of the most brilliant Governor-General for the British Empire.
- **Policy of Annexation**: Dalhousie was able to consolidate British rule in India by following his policy of annexation and with the support of his famous diplomatic masterstroke 'the Doctrine of Lapse'. His crucial wars and annexations include the following:

- Second Anglo-Sikh War (1848–49) and annexation of Punjab (1849).
- Second Anglo-Burmese War and the annexation of Lower Burma (1852)
- Introduction of the Doctrine of Lapse and annexation of Satara (1848), Jaitpur and Sambhalpur (1849), Udaipur(1852), Jhansi (1853), Nagpur (1854) and Awadh (1856)

- **Domestic Reforms of Dalhousie**: Dalhousie was an able administrator and visionary who inaugurated an era of progress and process of modernisation of India on many fronts and is rightly hailed as "the maker of modern India". Some of the key reforms initiated by him are as follows:
    - **Railways**: The introduction of railways in India inaugurated a new economic era, and Lord Dalhousie's contribution in the development of railways is worth commending. In 1853, he penned *Railway Minute* formulating the future policy of railways in India and for attracting investment for railways, introduced the "guarantee system" by which the railway companies were guaranteed a minimum interest of five percent on their investment. In fact, the first railway line running from **Bombay to Thane** was opened to traffic in 1853. Later, railway lines connecting from Calcutta to the Raniganj coal fields was opened in 1854 and from Madras to Arakkonam in 1856.
    - **Telegraph**: The use of Telegraph not only brought marvellous changes in the communication system but it also proved to be of great strategic military value during the 1857 Revolt. During Dalhousie's tenure, about 4000 miles long telegraph lines were laid and the main cities of the country like Calcutta, Peshawar, Bombay and Madras were telegraphically connected.
    - **Postal Reform**: The foundation of modern postal system was laid down by Lord Dalhousie. A new Post Office Act was passed in 1854, and consequently, irrespective of the distance over which the letter was sent, a uniform rate of half an anna per postcard was charged throughout India. Also, postage stamps were introduced in India for the first time during Dalhousie's reign.
    - **Education**: It was during Dalhousie's tenure that the *Intellectual Charter of India*, that is, the famous Educational Despatch of Sir Charles Wood (1854), was introduced. It provided an outline for the comprehensive scheme of education at primary, secondary and collegiate levels. Dalhousie fully accepted the views of Charles Wood and took steps to carry out the new scheme, some of the key projects being Organisation of the Departments of Public Instructions.
    - **Public Works Department**: Before the tenure of Dalhousie, the job of the Public Works Department was done by the Military Board. Dalhousie, however, realised the importance of public works and laid the foundations of the engineering service by creating a separate Public Works Department and allotting more funds to it for building canals and roads. The Upper Ganges Canal was completed in 1854 and many bridges were constructed.
    - **Social Reforms**: He was instrumental in passing of the Widow Remarriage Act (1856).
    - His other achievement was the molding of the new provinces into a modern centralised state. For the newly acquired territories, he introduced the centralised control called Non-Regulation System. Under this system, a commissioner was appointed to a newly acquired territory.

Lord Canning (1856–57)

- Establishment of the Universities of Calcutta, Bombay and Madras in 1857.
- Revolt of 1857.

After the Revolt of 1857, fundamental changes were brought in the character of Indian administration as the power was transferred from the East India Company to the Crown by the Queen's Proclamation of 1858. At the same time, the Governor-General received the new title of Viceroy. Thus, Lord Canning had the unique opportunity to become the **Governor General as well as the first Viceroy**.

Reasons behind Development of Railways

The primary consideration behind development of Railways in India had its roots in serving the economic, political and military interests of British imperialism as evident in the study of the real reasons behind the development of Railways:

- Commercial Reason: The railway network made it easier to penetrate the interior markets and also linked the sources of raw materials to port cities and thus, the railway network served the British interest of foreign trade very aptly. Moreover, the railway rates were fixed in a manner so as to favour imports and exports and to discriminate against internal movement of goods. Also, the British bankers and investors looked upon railway development as a channel for safe investment of their surplus capital since they were guaranteed a minimum of 5 per cent return on their capital by the Government of India, while the British manufacturers regarded it as an outlet for their products since most of the railway equipment like plant and machinery, rail wagons, railway lines, high level expertise and even coal to an extent were imported from Britain.
- Defence Reason: At the time of revolt and disturbances, mobilisation and movement of the troops was much easier through railways and this way, the British regime was better prepared to handle internal rebellion or external aggression.
- Administrative Reason: Railways aided in more effective and efficient administration.

Previous Year's Questions (Prelims)

1. Who among the following was/were associated with the introduction of Ryotwari settlement in India during the British rule? (2017)
   1. Lord Cornwallis
   2. Alexander Read
   3. Thomas Munro

   Select the correct answer from the following options.
   (a) Only 1
   (b) 1 and 3
   (c) 2 and 3
   (d) 1, 2 and 3

2. What was/were the object/objects of Queen Victoria's Proclamation (1858)? (2014)
   1. To disclaim any intention to annex Indian states
   2. To place the Indian Administration under the British Crown
   3. To regulate East India Company's trade with India

   Select the correct answer from the following options.
   (a) 1 and 2 only
   (b) 2 only
   (c) 1 and 3 only
   (d) 1 2 and 3

3. With reference to Ryotwari settlement, consider the following statements. (2012)
   1. The rent was paid directly by the peasants to the government
   2. The government gave pattas to the Ryots
   3. The land was surveyed and assessed before being taxed.

   Which of the statements given above is/are correct? Select the correct answer from the following options.
   (a) 1 only
   (b) 1 and 2 only
   (c) 1, 2 and 3
   (d) none

4. Consider the following statements. (2012)
   1. Assessment of land revenue on the basis of nature of the soil and the quality of crops
   2. Use of mobile cannons in warfare

3. Cultivation of tobacco and red chillies which of the above was/were introduced into India by the English?

Select the correct answer from the following options.

(a) 1 only
(b) 1 and 2
(c) 2 and 3
(d) none

5. With reference to the period of colonial rule in India, 'Home Charge' formed an important part of drain of wealth from India. Which of the following funds constituted 'Home Charges'? (2011)

1. Funds used to support the India office in London.
2. Funds used to pay salaries and pensions of British personnel engaged in India.
3. Funds used for waging wars outside India by the British.

Select the correct answer from the following options.

(a) 1 only
(b) 1 and 2 only
(c) 2 and 3 only
(d) 1, 2 and 3

6. The tendency for increased litigation was visible after the introduction of the land settlement system of Lord Cornwallis in 1793. The reason for this is normally traced to which of the following provisions? (2011)

(a) Making Zamindars position stronger vis-a-vis the Ryot
(b) Making East India Company an overlord of Zamindars
(c) Making judicial system more efficient
(d) None of the above

7. Under the permanent settlement of 1793, the Zamindars were required to issue pattas to the farmers which were not issued by many of the Zamindars. Which among them was the reason for this? (2011)

(a) The Zamindars were trusted by the farmers
(b) There was no official check upon
(c) It was the responsibility of the British government
(d) The farmers were not interested in getting pattas

8. By a regulation in 1793, the District Collector was deprived of his judicial powers and made the collecting agent only. What was the reason for such regulation? (2010)

(a) Lord Cornwallis felt that the District Collector's efficiency of revenue collection would enormously increase without the burden of other work.
(b) Lord Cornwallis felt that judicial power should compulsorily be in the hands of Europeans while Indians can be given the job of revenue collection in the district.
(c) Lord Cornwallis was alarmed at the extent of power concentrated in the District Collector and felt that such absolute power was undesirable in one person.
(d) The judicial work demanded a deep knowledge of India and a good training in law and Lord Cornwallis felt that District Collector should be only a revenue collector.

9. The ruler of which one of the following states was removed from power by the British on the pretext of misgovernance (2007)

(a) Awadh
(b) Jhansi
(c) Nagpur
(d) Satara

10. Consider the following statements: (2005)

1. Warren Hastings was the first Governor-General who established the regular police force in India on the British Pattern.
2. Supreme Court was established at Calcutta by the Regulating Act 1773.
3. The Indian Penal Code came into effect in the year 1860.

Which of the statements given above are correct?

(a) 1 and 2
(b) 2 and 3
(c) 1 and 3
(d) 1, 2 and 3

11. Which one of the following provisions was NOT made in the Charter act of 1833 (2003)

(a) The trading activities of the East India Company were to be abolished

(b) The designation of the supreme authority was to be changed as the Governor-General of India-in-Council

(c) All law-making powers to be conferred on Governor-General-Council

(d) An Indian was to be appointed as a law member in the Governor-General's Council

12. Match List-I (Acts of Colonial Government of India) with List-II (Provisions) and select the correct answer from the options that follow the list. (2002)

	List-I (Acts of Colonial Government of India)		List-II (Provisions)
A.	Charter Act, 1813	1.	Set up a Board of Control in British to fully regulate the East India Company
B.	Regulating Act, 1773	2.	Company's trade Monopoly in India was ended
C.	Act of 1858	3.	The power to govern was transferred from the East India Company to the British Crown
D.	Pitt's India Act	4.	The Company's Directors were asked to present to the British Government all correspondence and documents pertaining to the administration of the company

Codes:

	A	B	C	D
(a)	2	4	3	1
(b)	1	3	4	2
(c)	2	3	4	1
(d)	1	4	3	2

13. Which one of the following Acts of British India strengthened the Viceroy's authority over his executive Council by substituting 'portfolio' or departmental system for corporate functioning? (2002)

(a) Indian Councils Act, 1861

(b) Government of India Act, 1858

(c) Indian Councils Act,1892

(d) Indian councils Act, 1909

14. Match List-I with List-II (2000)

	List-I		List-II
A.	Land allotted to big feudal landlords	1.	Jagirdari System
B.	Land allotted to revenue farmers or rent collectors	2.	Ryotwari System
C.	Land allotted to each peasant with the Right to subject, mortgage, transfer gift or sell	3.	Mahalwari System
D.	Revenue settlements made at village level	4.	Zamindari System

Select the correct answer from the following options.

	A	B	C	D
(a)	1	3	2	4
(b)	1	4	2	3
(c)	3	4	1	2
(d)	2	1	3	4

Previous Year's Answers (Prelims)

1. (c)	2. (a)	3. (c)	4. (d)	5. (a)	6. (d)	7. (b)	8. (c)
9. (b)	10. (b)	11. (d)	12. (a)	13. (a)	14. (b)		

Early Indian Responses: Reform and Rebellion

3

In the earlier chapters, we discussed about the process of British conquest of India and the consequent transformation British rule brought in the diverse fields of polity, law, economy and administration. Indian society was also not left untouched by the impact of these changes, and a process which further triggered significant societal responses was thus initiated. However, quite interestingly, the early Indian responses to these changes varied from one end of the spectrum to the another. While the **urban intelligentsia** elites, who were also the chief beneficiaries of colonial rule, responded to the moralistic critiques of the indigenous culture and institutions by initiating **introspection** about the strengths and weaknesses of Indian culture and bringing social and religious reforms to change their society from within, the response of the **rural** traditional elite and the peasantry, who were losing out as a result of colonial impositions, was that of **resistance** and **defiance**, resulting in a series of unsuccessful tribal and peasant rebellions. In this chapter, we are going to study both these responses in detail, that is, the reform movements and the rebellions.

State of Indian Society in the 19th Century

Unfortunately, **Indian society** in the 19th century was caught in a vicious web of religious superstitions and social obscurantism and was divided into multi-layered identities on the basis of religion, region, tribe, language, class and caste, with caste being a major divisive force. Inter-caste marriages and inter-caste dining was forbidden, and even people who converted to other religions could not escape the clutches of the caste system, which sought to maintain a system of segregation, hierarchically ordained on the basis of ritual status. The rules and regulations of caste hampered social mobility, fostered social divisions and limited individual initiative. The presence of the practice of untouchability further shamed human dignity. Almost all the religions suffered from innumerable inhuman and insensible practices marked by constraint, credulity, status, bigotry and blind fatalism. The social life of both Hindus and Muslims was strongly influenced by religious tenets. The *purohits* and the *qazis* exercised an overwhelming and unhealthy influence on the minds of the people. Their monopoly of scriptural knowledge and of ritual interpretation imparted a deceptive character to all religious systems.

Equally depressing and distressing was the **social condition of women**, as from womb to tomb they were subjected to all forms of torture and brutality. Their birth was considered unwelcome, and there were unfortunate attempts to kill girl infants. Their marriage was considered a burden, and most of them were married at a very tender age. Often, the marriage was a device to escape social ignominy, hence, marital life for most of them was also a harrowing experience. Polygamy and dowry were widely prevalent, further reducing the women to the status of an object, and several women hardly had a married life worth the name. For instance, *an 80-year-old Brahmin had as many as 200 wives, the youngest being just 8 years old.* Yet, when their uncaring worthless husbands died, they were expected to commit *sati*, and if they somehow succeeded in overcoming this social coercion, they were condemned as inauspicious widows and were resigned to lifelong misery, neglect and humiliation. Irrespective of any religion or caste, the women across all stratas were expected to suffer silently and live as the role models of ideal daughters, wives and mothers, without having any individual existence of their own.

The **education system** was also lagging behind and could not change according to the requirements of the time. The traditional curriculum was confined to literature, languages, law, religion, philosophy and logic, but excluded the crucial studies of physical and natural sciences, technology and geography. There was dominance of theoretical framework and a general lack of progressive ideas in the syllabus. Even though elementary education was widespread, the education system excluded females and low caste people. Mediums of instruction at higher education level was limited to Sanskrit and Persian only, which kept even the educated masses unaware of the latest developments in science and technology.

Thus, **India**, in contrast to an enlightened Europe, presented the picture of a stagnant civilisation and a static and decadent society. However, the British conquest and the consequent dissemination of western culture and ideology led the intellectual Indians to question the status quo and to undertake an honest introspection about the strengths and weaknesses of the indigenous culture and social institutions. As a consequence, several individuals and movements sought to bring about changes in the social and religious practices with a view of reforming and revitalising Indian society. These efforts, collectively known as the **Renaissance**, were complex social phenomena which aimed at creating a social climate for modernisation of Indian society. The **social base** of this quest was the newly emerging middle class and the traditional as well as Western-educated intellectuals, and the **ideological base** of this quest was the foundation of rationalism, religious universalism and humanism.

Was This Entire Process of Reform a Manifestation of Western Ideology?

Even though the importance of Western impact on the socio-cultural regeneration in the 19th century was undeniable as most of the stimulating forces were almost exclusively Western, namely English education and literature, Christianity, Oriental research, European science and philosophy, yet regarding this entire process of reform as a manifestation of Western ideology would limit ourselves to view only one dimension of this multi-dimensional issue, and we shall fail to do justice to the complex character of this social phenomenon. To grasp its true essence, due consideration should be given to the fact that there was never just a blind imitation of Western cultural norms and the reform movements never totally rejected tradition. Because the aim of the reformers was modernisation rather than Westernisation, the cultural ideological struggle was **both** against backward elements of traditional culture, on one hand, and the hegemonising colonial culture and ideology, on the other. Thus, it should be duly noted that the process of socio-cultural regeneration was not **created by the colonial presence, but was occasioned by it**.

British Social Policy and Major Governmental Interventions

Initially, the British interest was limited to trade and commercial activities, and also because of the fear that they might lose trade advantage, they adopted the **policy of extreme precaution** and **indifference** towards social issues in India. Broadly till 1813[1], they followed a **policy of non-interference** in the religious, social and cultural life of the country and did not evince any interest in taking the issue of social or religious reforms. However, the policy of non-interference was never followed in the strictest sense, as even before 1813, certain British administrators did try to progressively and cautiously intervene in Indian social institutions, but the underlying objective was always being maximisation of the Company's interests.

Therefore, initially along with pragmatism that demanded continuation of existing systems, there was also an attempt to learn about Indian culture through a study of scriptures in Sanskrit and Persian languages to use that knowledge in matters of governance. The same was expressed in **Warren Hastings's** policy of Orientalism through which he advocated *to govern the conquered in their own ways and resist anglicisation,*

[1] Through the Charter Act of 1813, the concept of Western education in India was introduced, which was the first and important area of intervention by the British.

which was a clear reflection of combination of Orientalist ideological preferences along with political pragmatism. He felt that the knowledge about the subject population and their social customs, manners and codes was a necessary perquisite for developing permanent institutions of rule, and thus, was in favour of creating an English bureaucracy, well versed in Indian languages and traditions.

> *"Every accumulation of knowledge and especially such as is obtained by social communication with people over whom we exercise dominion founded on the right of conquest, is useful to the stage: it is the gain of humanity."*
>
> Warren Hastings, 1784

Hastings insisted that the young officials of the East India Company should learn the vernacular languages and know something of the history and culture of the people his countrymen were to dominate. This insistence led to the emergence of **Indology** and the birth of a historical consciousness about India's cultural past. The result of this endeavour was the establishment of the Asiatic Society of Bengal[2], the Calcutta Madrassa and the Sanskrit College in Banaras. **Nathaniel Halched**, a close aide of Hastings, compiled and translated a set of Hindu customary and religious laws into English and, in 1788, he published a **book called *Grammar of the Bengali Language.***

However, since the end of Hasting's tenure as Governor General, there was a gradual move towards **cautious intervention** in Indian social institutions. *Orientalism*, which was the characteristic feature of Hastings' period, now came to be criticised by a variety of ideological streams such as **utilitarianism, evangelicalism** and **free trade thinking**, which shared the conviction that Indian society needed urgent modernisation and westernisation. While the **utilitarians** such as Jeremy Bentham, James Mill and John Stuart Mill stressed on appropriate social engineering and authoritarian reformism, the **evangelists** led by William Wilberforce and Charles Grant argued about the necessity of government intervention to liberate Indians from their religion that was full of superstitions, idolatry and tyranny of priests, while the **free trade thinkers** advocated government intervention to free Indian economy from the shackles of tradition to ensure a free flow of trade. Gradually, these contending ideologies contributed in the shift from cautious intervention in Indian social life. However, still pragmatic considerations of not provoking wide-scale resentment acted as a severe constraint for socio-religious reforms. The British, thus, followed a delicately balanced policy of partial modernisation, that is, introducing modernisation in some respects and blocking and preventing it in other respects.

The conscious attempts at state intervention in India's social practices and customs were done only after prolonged procrastination and immense pressure, which often resulted in very limited impact. Some specific instances of governmental intervention in social practices are as follows:

Infanticide

The first traditional social custom which was suppressed by the Company's government was the practice of infanticide, mainly female infanticide, which was rampant in many parts of the country, particularly in Rajputana, Punjab and the North Western Provinces. Factors such as family pride, the fear of not finding a suitable match for the girl child and the hesitation to bend before the prospective in-laws were some of the major reasons responsible for this practice. Therefore, immediately after birth, the female infants were being killed either by feeding them with opium or by strangulating or by purposely neglecting them.

Governmental Intervention in Case of Suppression of Infanticide

- In the case of suppression of infanticide, initially the initiative for change came from local-level officials and missionaries such as Colonel Todd, Johnson Duncan and John Malcolm. **Jonathan Duncan**, the Resident of *Banaras*, was the first British official who tried to curb this social evil by persuading the local *Rajkumars* to abandon this barbarous practice. Instead of getting passed a legislation

[2] It was founded by Sir William Jones in 1784 for furthering the cause of oriental research.

for abolition of infanticide, Duncan tried to convince them by pointing across the fact that the killing of female infants was against the tenets of Hindu scriptures. In addition, to address the main cause of considering female children as economic liability, he promised monetary compensation from the Government if the community abandons the practice.

- Later, **William Carey**, a missionary in the College of Fort William, vehemently argued for the abolition of infanticide. He, after prior consultation with Hindu *pundits*, submitted a petition to the government for immediate suppression of the practice. Meanwhile, the Calcutta magistrates sent a letter to the Vice-President-in-Council stating that infanticide had never enjoyed sanction under the Mughal or the British governments, and there was no likelihood of any public opposition for the same. Ultimately, a law banning infanticide was enacted as **Regulation VI of 1802**. Thus, the Governor General gave his assent to legislation prohibiting infanticide only after ascertaining the views of the Hindu *pundits* and ruling out the possibility of such a measure causing public hostility.

Although, due to the laws enacted against this practice in 1795, 1802, 1804 and 1870, the British were able to stamp out the practice of infanticide from Bengal easily, the practice could not be completely eradicated from other parts of the country. However, with support of legal measures, education and public opinion, gradually, this evil practice was done away with.

Sati

The next significant state intervention in Indian social life was the suppression of practice of ***Sati*** or self-immolation of widows on the funeral pyres of their deceased husbands. Although *Sati* had been in vogue since ancient times, it was more of an exception rather than rule in Hindu life. As a matter of fact, a number of Indian rulers such as **Akbar**, **Jahangir**, **Guru Amardas**, **Ahilyabai**, the **Peshwas**, the **King of Tanjore** and the **Portuguese** in Goa tried to discourage this practice. Even then, this practice was widespread in all the three Presidencies, and no sustained and systematic efforts were made to suppress this inhuman practice till the 19th century.

Governmental Intervention in Case of Suppression of Sati

- The government's early attitude towards this practice was that of caution and restraint as evident in the Governor General **Cornwallis**' advice of *avoiding coercion and using persuasion* to the Collector of Shahabad, H. T. Colebrooke, in 1789, and to Midnapore District Magistrate, in 1797, when they had disallowed the act of *Sati* in their respective districts. Later, **William Carey,** the founder of Serampore Missionaries, conducted a survey on the *Sati* system in the vicinity of Calcutta and studied Hindu *shastras* containing information on *Sati*, concluding that, whereas Hinduism did not forbid it, it did not make it obligatory either. He then sent a memorial to **Lord Wellesley** for curbing *Sati*. In 1805, Wellesley asked the judges of the *Nizamat Adalat* to find out to what extent the practice of *Sati* was based on Hindu religion. The *pundits* of the court not only declared that forcible burning of widows was not permitted but also confided to the Governor General that as *Sati* was being widely practised and popular among Hindus, any measure to abolish it would result in considerable dissatisfaction amongst them and cause public hostility.
- However after some vacillation, in 1813, the government fixed the minimum age for a widow to become *Sati* as 16 years and declared that a mother of a child less than 3 years could not become *Sati* unless another person undertook to look after the child. Later, in 1819 and 1821, two Judges of the Supreme Court pleaded for an immediate suppression of *Sati*, arguing that such a measure would not result in any serious public resentment, but this plea was rejected by the government as **Lord Hastings** in 1821 refused to authorise the total abolition of *Sati*, fearing it would incite religious fanaticism. A similar approach was adopted by his successor Lord Amherst.
- Meanwhile, as the government was dithering over this issue, the Westernized Bengali intelligentsia led by **Raja Rammohan Roy** actively agitated for the abolition of *Sati*. In 1818, he sent a petition

to the government urging them to abolish this practice and also to counter orthodox Hindu demands against its prohibition. A vigilance committee was organised to strictly implement the age restrictions on the practice of *Sati*, and along with all these measures, to create mass awareness about the issue, Roy also engaged in polemical debate with the supporters of *Sati* such as **Kashinath Tarkavagish** (1819), wrote pamphlets and newspaper articles to mobilise public opinion against this custom. On this issue, he also received support from the Christian missionaries who were also demanding prohibition of *Sati*.

Finally, it was Governor General **William Bentinck** who took the plunge and brought in the legislation against the *Sati* system in December 1829[3].

Important Milestone in Education and Development of Women	Legislative Measures for Women Emancipation in Free India
Calcutta Female Juvenile Society, 1819 ↓ - by Christian missionaries. **Bethune School, 1849** ↓ - founded in Calcutta by JED Bethune, who was President of the Council of Education in Calcutta. **Charles Wood Despatch on Education, 1854** ↓ - stressed on female education. **Dufferin Hospitals, 1880s** ↓ - providing health facilities to women. **Training of Nurses and Midwives, 1914** ↓ - done by the Women Medical Service. **Indian Women University, 1916** ↓ - by the efforts of D. K. Karve. **Lady Hardinge Medical College, 1916** ↓ - for training of lady doctors. **All India Women Conference, 1927**	**Article 14 and 15 of the Indian Constitution** ↓ - provides equality to women and prohibits any discrimination by the State. **Special Marriage Act, 1954** ↓ - permits inter-caste and inter-religious marriage. **Hindu Marriage Act, 1955** ↓ - abolished bigamy and permitted dissolution of marriage on specific grounds. **Hindu Succession Act, 1956** ↓ - daughter is equal co-heir as son. **Equal Remuneration Act, 1976** ↓ - women entitled to get equal pay for equal work. **Factories (Amendment) Act, 1976** ↓ - establishment of creches where 30 women were employed. **Dowry Prohibition Act, 1961 amended in 1986** ↓ - lady training of lady doctors. **Act against glorification of Sati, 1987**

Slavery

Slavery was another institution which came under attack in the 19th century. Slavery as a system of labour exploitation was prevalent in India till its abolition in 1843. Although the awareness about this issue was from as early as 1774, yet procrastination was once again the most evident feature in the Company Government's attitude towards the abolition of slavery. In addition, surprisingly even though Britain abolished slave trade in her dominions in 1820, the Company in India acknowledged the legality of slavery on the grounds that it was a traditional practice with religious sanction.

[3] Although the incidence of Sati declined gradually after the legislation, the idea and myth of Sati persisted in popular culture through epics, ballads and folktales, to reappear again in public life as late as in 1987 in the much publicised Sati of Roop Kanwar at Deorala in Rajasthan.

Governmental Intervention in the Case of Suppression of Slavery

- Evangelical propaganda against slavery led by **William Wilberforce** helped in attracting public attention in Britain on the evils of slavery in India. Consequently, **Regulation X of 1811** (prohibition of import of slaves by land) and **Regulation IV of 1832** (prohibition of inter-provincial movement of slaves) were passed.
- In addition, the Charter Act of 1832 directed the Company's Government *to ameliorate the condition of slaves as soon as extinction shall be practicable and safe and to prepare drafts of laws and regulations for the purposes aforesaid.* This led to the appointment of the Indian Law Commission (1835), which along with its primary task of framing penal code, also drew up an anti-slavery Report in 1841. A draft act was also submitted by the Law Commission in 1839 whereby inflicting corporal punishment on slaves was made a penal offence, but before taking any action on the Draft Act, the Commissioners discussed the possibility of such a measure exciting public disaffection. However, under pressure of parliamentary opinions and anti-Slavery atmosphere, the Law Commission was again asked to frame a new Act, which was eventually passed as **Act V of 1845**, abolishing slavery in India.
- The impact of the Act was, however, very limited since even the most crucial provision in the Act merely stated that *no claim to the labour of a slave was to be recognised in a British court of law and that a government official could no longer force a slave to return to his master*. But, gradually slavery declined mostly owing to the generation of sources of alternate employment in the later 19th century in plantation and public works.

However, governmental interventions were just not enough for removal of superstitions and abhorrent customs. The real change was brought only in the **19th century** when a series of reform movements were undertaken in various parts of the country that stood for the democratisation of society, spread of enlightenment, development of a rational and modern outlook and were oriented towards re-structuring of Indian society along modern lines.

Significance of the 19th Century

The 19th century was a very significant phase in the history of modern India as it was during this period that the country witnessed the emergence of many intellectual currents for national regeneration in all its aspects: religious, social, cultural, economic and political. Although the intellectual endeavours aimed at achieving holistic improvement, the social and cultural problems acquired predominance over economic and political ones. The major plank of the 19th-century-intellectual movement was based on **socio-cultural reform** which started from identification of the socio-cultural evils such as the Sati, degraded position of women, child marriage, enforced widowhood, caste system, untouchability, idolatry, polytheism, ritualism, and others. These defective social practices were then brought under intellectual scrutiny followed by attempts to renovate the social order.

Socio-Religious Reform Movements of the 19th Century[4]

In the evolution of modern India, the socio-religious reform movements of the 19th century have made a very significant contribution. During the initial decades of the century, the movement started as a small affair of a limited number of individuals who initiated fight against social obscurantism and posed a challenge to the advocates of orthodoxy. Gradually, the movement picked up momentum and reached its peak during the

[4] These reform movements could broadly be classified in two categories: Reformist movements like the Brahmo Samaj, the Prarthana Samaj, the Aligarh movement, and the Revivalist movements like Arya Samaj and the Deoband movement.

second-half of the 19th century resulting in mass awareness about different social evils. To understand the comprehensive nature of the intellectual, social and religious movements of the 19th century, it is better to first discuss the ideas and activities of individual intellectuals who initiated and led these movements and later we can have a detailed analysis of the movement. In addition, it would be advisable to look beyond the strict chronological limits and consider developments in the later decades of the 19th century and early years of 20th century to arrive at the holistic picture of the Socio-Religious Reform Movements.

Individual Intellectuals and Their Key Movements

The dawn of the 19th century witnessed the birth of a new vision – a modern vision among some enlightened individuals of the Indian society who were to shape the course of events in modern India history. Here, we would discuss the ideas of these reformers on various socio-religious issues and their contribution to the socio-reform movements. Along with their ideas, brief background of the intellectual is also discussed to make the learners appreciate the great lives of these noble souls and how they made a difference. To initiate and undertake these reforms which today may appear to be modest was not an easy proposition back then since breaking the bonds of tradition created emotional and sentimental crises for all involved in the process. For instance, the first widow remarriage in Bengal attracted thousands of curious spectators, and in Maharashtra the police had to give lathis to the first such couple to protect themselves.

Eastern India

In Eastern India, the first significant step to eradicate the social evils was taken by **Raja Rammohan Roy**, whose spirit of reform rather embraced almost whole of India. The process of reform that started with Rammohan Roy was carried forward by men like **Henry Vivian Derozio**, **Debendranath Tagore**, **Ishwar Chandra Vidyasagar**, **Keshab Chandra Sen**, **Swami Vivekanand** and others in the 19th century.

Rammohan Roy (1772–1833)

Raja Rammohan Roy

- Rammohan Roy is aptly regarded as the Father of Indian Renaissance who touched on nearly every aspect of Indian social life and struggled for its regeneration. He was an erudite scholar who knew over a dozen languages including Sanskrit, Persian, Arabic, Latin, English, French, Greek and Hebrew.
- He was born in 1774 into a wealthy zamindar *kulin* Brahmin family in a village called Radhanagar of district Burdwan, Bengal, and had been married off thrice as polygamy was a common practice amongst *kulin* Brahmins, which was then called *kulinism*. The tradition was enforced on the child Rammohan too who years later expressed his abhorrence for the same and wrote forcefully against the practice of *kulinism* as *this horrible polygamy amongst Brahmins is directly contrary to the law given by the ancient authors.*
- Rammohan's reform activities were accelerated after he settled down in Calcutta in 1815 where he started the ***Atmiya Sabha*** (Society of Friends) and carried on a consistent struggle against the religious and social malpractices prevalent among the Hindus in Bengal. In particular, he opposed the practices of idolatry, caste rigidities and prevalence of meaningless rituals. He blamed the priestly class for encouraging and inculcating these practices by keeping people ignorant about the true teachings of the indigenous scriptures.

- He held that all the principal ancient texts of the Hindus preached ***monotheism*** or worship of one God. To prove his point, he published the Bengali translation of the Vedas and some Upanishads and also wrote series of tracts and pamphlets advocating monotheism. In addition, his translations into and writings in the vernacular promoted the growth of the Bengali language.

> *"The superstitious practices which deform the Hindu religion have nothing to do with the pure spirit of its dictates."*
>
> Raja Rammohan Roy

- Rammohan also composed devotional songs about his monotheistic beliefs, these songs are today called *Brahmo Sangeet*. For instance, one of his famous compositions, '*Mon Eki Branti Tomar*' asks *How can you blunder my heart, by welcoming or wishing goodbye to God who is everywhere and ever present?* Another song, *Ki Swadeshi, Ki bideshi*, says *Either at home or abroad I live here and there, and I see you everywhere in the middle of your own creation, As each moment declares your glory through endless space and time, I see you everywhere.*
- Rammohan Roy was an ultimate rationalist who relied completely on the power of human reason and considered it as the touchstone of the truth of any doctrine, be it Eastern or Western. He believed that one could depart from holy books, scriptures and inherited traditions if human reason so dictates and if such traditions are proving harmful to the society. His writings focus on reason and consider it as the touchstone of reality.
- He understood the causes underlying the development of Western intellectual progress and wanted India guided by reason to acquire and treasure all that was best in the West along with accumulating the best from the East too. Thus, he neither did rely on India's own past nor support blind imposition of Western culture.
- He did want India to learn from the West, but the learning was to be an intellectual and creative process enriching Indian culture. He, therefore, stood for the reform of Hinduism but at the same time opposed any effort of its suppression by Christianity. Along with it, he believed in universal brotherhood and adopted a friendly attitude towards other religions.
- In 1828, he along with Dwarkanath Tagore[5] established a new society, ***the Brahma Sabha*** which later came to be known as **Brahmo Samaj**, a community dedicated to anti-idolatry, abolition of meaningless rituals and customs, monotheism, that is, the worship of one God, and the worship of *Brahman*, the Supreme Being. It was based on the foundation of reason and incorporated the best teachings of both the *Vedas* and *Upanishads* along with other religious texts. The society acted as a powerful plauorm for the advocacy of humanism, monotheism and social regeneration.

> *"Brahmo Samaj is committed to the worship and adoration of the Eternal, Unsearchable, Immutable Being who is the Author and Preserver of the Universe."*
>
> Goals and purposes of the Brahmo Samaj according to its Trust Deed

[5] He was the paternal grandfather of Rabindranath Tagore.

- He was extremely concerned with the pitiable plight of women in society and in particular about the inhuman practice of *Sati*, the burning of a widow on her husband's funeral pyre. In 1812, the incident of burning of his elder brother's wife on her husband's funeral despite the best efforts of Rammohan disturbed him greatly and left a profound impact on Rammohan's mind who started working tirelessly for its abolition.
- To rouse public opinion on the issue, on one hand, he cited the **ancient Hindu texts** to prove their lack of sanction for the same, while simultaneously, he appealed to the **reason**, **humanity** and **compassion** of the people over the same. Along with these measures, he indulged in **polemic debates** with the orthodox over the issue, organised **vigilante groups** of like-minded people to keep a strict check and to prevent any attempt to force the widows to become *Sati*. He also kept sending regular petition to the Company's Government seeking a ban on the practice. Eventually, his tireless efforts bore fruit and finally in 1829, Lord **William Bentinck**, the then Governor General of India, enacted a law against the practice of *Sati*. However, quite surprisingly, the solution which he put forward for the living widows was not widow remarriage but ascetic widowhood.

> *"Sati is murder according to every shastra."*
>
> Raja Rammohan Roy

> *"What I lament is, that seeing the women thus dependent and exposed to every misery, you feel for them no compassion, that might exempt them from being tied down and burnt to death."*
>
> Raja Rammohan Roy

- Being a stout champion of women's rights, he **condemned** polygamy, early marriage and opposed the subjugation of women and their inferior status in society. He related their problems to the root cause of absence of property rights and thus **demanded** the right to inheritance and property for women. To him, female education was another effective method to free Indian society from social stagnation.
- At times, Rammohan even had to endure personal loss and hardship for his fight against social injustice and inequality. He often faced social boycott by his friends and family including his mother too and was branded a heretic and an outcaste over his liberal views and democratic opinion. For instance, in 1817, a law suit was filed in the Supreme Court to disinherit Rammohan from the ancestral property by his deceased elder's son who was instigated by Rammohan's mother Tarini Devi, as a furious reaction to her son's campaign against idol worship. However, all this could never stop him for supporting a just cause or fighting a social evil.
- He also rooted vociferously for the introduction and spread of modern education which he considered as a major vehicle for the dissemination of modern ideas in the country. For the same purpose, he provided enthusiastic support to **David Hare** who, along with many Indian notables of Calcutta, founded the famous Hindu College in 1817. In addition, he also maintained at his own cost an English School in Calcutta in which, among other subjects, Mechanics and philosophy of Voltaire were taught. Since he laid stress on India's need for western scientific knowledge, Mathematics, Natural philosophy, Chemistry, Anatomy and other useful sciences, in 1825, he founded the Vedanta College in which courses both in Indian learning and in Western social and physical sciences were offered.
- Rammohan took up not only social and religious problems but also political and economic issues of the times, in fact he was first among the intellectuals who initiated **discourse on political questions**

in the country. He not only condemned the oppressive practices of the Bengal zamindars but also demanded that the maximum rents paid by the actual cultivators of land should be permanently fixed so that they too would enjoy the benefits of the Permanent Settlement of 1793.

- He protested against the attempts to impose taxes on tax-free lands and demanded the abolition of the Company's trading rights and the removal of heavy export duties on Indian goods. Along with these, he strongly petitioned for the Indianisation of the superior services, trial by jury, separation of powers between the executive and the judiciary and judicial equality between Indians and Europeans.
- He was a staunch supporter of freedom of the press and fought for the rights of vernacular press seeking removal of all restrictions imposed on them. He brought out a newspaper in Persian called ***Mirat-ul-Akbar***, that is, the Mirror of News and a Bengali Weekly called ***Sambad Kaumudi***, that is, the Moon of Intelligence.
- Rammohan was also progenitor of **nationalist consciousness** and ideology in India. It would not be wrong to assume that his every effort of social and religious reform was aimed at nation-building because through his reforms, he wished to lay the foundations for the unity of Indian society, divided into divergent groups. More particularly, he attacked the rigidities of the caste system which, according to him, had been the source of disunity among Indians. He held that the caste system not only created inequality and division among the people on the one hand but also deprived them of patriotic feeling on the other.

"I regret to say that the present system of religion adhered to by the Hindus is not well calculated to promote their political interest. The distinctions of castes introducing innumerable divisions and sub-divisions among them has entirely deprived them of patriotic feeling, and the multitude of religious rites and ceremonies and the laws of purification have totally disqualified them from undertaking any difficult enterprise. It is, I think, necessary that some change should take place in their religion atlas for the sake of their political advantage and social comfort."

Raja Rammohan Roy, 1828

- Rammohan took keen interest in international affairs and was a firm supporter of liberty, justice, democracy, internationalism and in free cooperation between nations. He opposed oppression and tyranny in every form and related himself to the just causes of movements happening across the globe. For instance, he cancelled all his social engagements when he came to know of the failure of the Revolution in Naples in 1821, whereas he celebrated the success of the Revolution in Spanish America in 1823 by giving a public dinner.
- The poet Rabindranath Tagore has rightly remarked about him, '*Rammohan was the only person in his time, in the whole world of man, to realise completely the significance of the Modern Age. He knew that the ideal of human civilisation does not lie in the isolation of independence, but in the brotherhood of inter-dependence of individuals as well as nations in all spheres of thought and activity*'.
- In 1830, he travelled to England as the Mughal Emperor **Akbar II'd** envoy for both taking up the petition for increase in his pension and also for ensuring that Lord William Bentick's law banning the practice of Sati was not overturned due to the counter-petitions by the orthodox Hindu organisations such as Dharma Sabha which used to issue a periodical *Samachar Chandrika* to counter *Sambad Kaumudi*. Because of his services to the nation, the Mughal Emperor awarded him princely title of *Raja*. In 1833, this maker of Modern India passed away in England leaving behind his ideas and the message of modernisation for others to pursue.

Although Brahmo Samaj remained a society of the intellectual elites rather than masses, yet because of its espousal of liberal ideas that spanned science, literature, nationalist consciousness, education, social reform and women's rights, its influence in Bengal through the 19th and 20th centuries, and its place in the awakening of the Indian mind was far excess of its size. Many of the key players of the Socio-Awakening movement were members of Brahmo Samaj and the rational, puritan Brahmo ethos permeated many bright minds. Whatever be the limitations, Rammohan Roy was certainly one of the most luminous star on the Indian intellectual firmament of the 19th century.

Major Works of Raja Rammohan Roy

- In 1805, he published his first philosophical work ***Tuhfat-ul Murahhiddin*** in which he analysed the major religions of the world in the light of 'reason' and 'social comfort'. He vehemently denied that religion was merely a matter of faith outside reason and attempted to expose the myth of miracles associated with it.
- In 1809, he wrote in Persian ***Gift to Monotheists*** in which he put forward weighty arguments against belief in many gods and for the worship of single God.
- In 1820, he published ***Precepts of Jesus*** in which he applied rationality to Christianity too, particularly to the elements of blind faith in it. He stressed on the moral and philosophic message of the New Testament as opposed to the miracle stories and thus earned for himself the hostility of the Christian missionaries.

Young Bengal Movement and Henry Louis Vivian Derozio (1809–31)

- During the late 1820s and the 1830s, new and radical ideas began to be propagated by a band of young Bengali intellectuals known as the '**Young Bengal**'. This movement was largely initiated by an Anglo-Indian teacher of the Hindu College, **Henry Louis Vivian Derozio** (1809–31), who was inspired by the ideals of the French Revolution.
- A free thinker and a rationalist, he helped promote a radical and critical outlook among his students whom he inspired to think rationally and freely, to question all authority, to love liberty, equality and freedom and to worship truth. His followers known as the **Derozians** attacked old and decadent customs, rites and traditions, and being staunch rationalists measured everything with the yardstick of reason thereby questioning the existing social and religious structure of Hindu society.
- The prominent members of this group, Dakshinaranjan Mukherjee, Ram Gopal Ghose and Krishna Mohan Banerjee, stood for rejection of tradition and revolt against accepted social norms. They were highly influenced by *the regenerating new thought from the West* and displayed an uncompromisingly rational attitude towards social problems. Ram Gopal Ghose expressed the rationalist stance of this group when he declared: *He who will not reason is a bigot, he who cannot is a fool and he who does not is a slave.*
- They were passionate advocates of women's rights and rooted tremendously for female education. Interestingly, they were also fiery patriots and perhaps, Derozio was the first nationalist poet of modern India. For instance, Derozio in his famous poem *To India – My Native Land* talks of the past glory of India and how the country that was once called the Golden Eagle has been chained and enslaved.

"To India – My Native Land
My country! In thy days of glory past.
A beauteous halo circled round thy brow
and worshipped as a deity thou wast—
Where is thy glory, where the reverence now?
Thy eagle pinion is chained down at last,
And grovelling in the lowly dust art thou,
Thy minstrel hath no wreath to weave for thee
Save the sad story of thy misery!
Well—let me dive into the depths of time
And bring from out the ages, that have rolled.
A few small fragments of these wrecks sublime
Which human eye may never more behold.
And let the guerdon of my labour be,
My fallen country! One kind wish for thee!."

Henry Vivian Derozio

- Derozio was dismissed from the Hindu college in 1831 because of his radical views, and shortly afterwards he died of cholera at the young age of 22. The Derozians were able to make their presence and good work felt as they carried forward the Rammohan Roy's legacy of fighting for different social, political and economic issues.
- In 1838, the Derozians formed the *Society for the Acquisition of General Knowledge*, where they discussed various aspects of Western Science, and stood for a number of social reforms, such as the prohibition of caste taboos, child marriage, *kulin* polygamy or the ban on widow remarriage. They staged agitation on various **public questions** such as the freedom of the Press, better treatment for Indian labour in British colonies abroad, employment of Indians in the higher grades of service, trial by jury, protection of the peasants from oppressive zamindars and revision of the company's Charter.
- Another remarkable contribution of the Derozians was the establishment of the **Calcutta Public Library**, which later developed into National Library, the biggest library in the country. No wonder regarding Derozians, Surendranath Banerjee has remarked, *they were pioneers of the modern civilisation of Bengal, the conscript fathers of our race whose virtues will excite veneration and whose failings will be treated with gentlest consideration.*
- However, one of the major shortcomings of the Young Bengal Movement was that they forgot to maintain their links with the people and their radicalism was often labelled as more bookish than practical. Because their ideas were much advanced of their times and the social conditions were not yet ripe for their ideas to flourish, the Derozians were unable to create a mass movement.

Debendranath Tagore (1817–1905)

- Debendranath Tagore, the father of Rabindranath Tagore, was a product of the best in the traditional Indian learning and the new thought of the West. In 1839, he founded the ***Ta[vabodhini Sabha*** (Truth Seekers Society) to carry on Rammohan's ideals independent of the Brahmo Samaj.

- The Sabha advocated the development of more rational and humanist form of Hinduism based on the *Vedanta* and the *Upanishads* and distanced themselves from the earlier outdated version based on meaningless rites and rituals.
- The Sabha had emerged in the background of increased missionary presence in Calcutta who used to criticise the classical branch of *Vedanta* as amoral and renunciatory. Thus, to counteract **missionary influences** and reaffirm faith in the doctrines of reason and humanism of their reformed faith, the Sabha was formed.

> *"It was to counteract influences like these (missionary) and inculcate on the Hindu religious inquirer's mind doctrines at once consonant to reason and human nature, for which he has to explore his own sacred resources, the Vedanta, that the society was originally established."*
>
> Debendranath Tagore, 1843

- Interestingly, they also display a marked stress on the role of 'householder' as a religious path over that of the renouncer or hermit as according to them *if the householder person being surrounded by all material wealth has the ability to detach himself from the same is equally worthy*. Similarly, they viewed that if material wealth was made and possessed with the correct intention, that of helping society and others, it was in fact not only ethically sound but an utter necessity for harmonious society.
- It laid emphasis on indigenous language and culture and through its journal, ***Tattvabodhini Patrika***, promoted a systematic study of India's past in the Bengali language. The Sabha also helped to spread a rational outlook among the intellectuals of Bengal and gradually it came to include most of the prominent followers of Rammohan and Derozio and other independent thinkers like Ishwar Chandra Vidyasagar and Akshay Kumar Dutt.
- In the meanwhile, Debendranath Tagore became a *Brahmo* in 1843 and reorganised the Brahmo Samaj in the same year providing impetus to the reform movement initiated by Rammohan which had otherwise lost much of its momentum by then. He again put new life into the organisation by providing it with a better organisational structure and ideological consistency actively supporting the cause of abolition of polygamy, promotion of female education, widow remarriage and improvement in the peasants' condition.

Keshab Chandra Sen (1838–84)

- Keshab Chandra Sen was another influential social reformer of Bengal in the 19th century, who infused new energy and vigour in the Brahmo Samaj. Being an impressive speaker, he possessed special ability of simplifying the *Brahmo* philosophy to the common people which soon made him immensely popular among the members of Brahmo Samaj and he also became a close associate of Debendranath Tagore, who was leading the Brahmo Samaj after the death of Rammohan Roy.
- Keshab was made the *acharya* of the Samaj in 1858 and was quite instrumental in popularising the movement outside Bengal, and consequently branches of the Samaj were opened in the United Provinces, Punjab, Bombay, Madras and other states. He brought in some amount of radicalism in the movement, by attacking caste system, by focussing on women's rights, by promoting widow remarriage and inter-caste marriages and by raising the issue of caste status of the Brahmo preachers, who were invariably Brahmins.

> *"No country on earth has ever made significant progress in civilisation whose females were sunk in ignorance."*
>
> Keshab Chandra Sen

- However, differences soon emerged between Sen and Tagore, as **Keshab's** emphasis on universalism and social radicalism was considered by Tagore as overreach of his authority. Keshab's strong views against the caste system and his open support to inter-caste marriages clashed with the moderate views of **Tagore** whose act of allowing *Brahmos* conducting services to wear their sacred threads further broadened the conflict between the two, and with this, the first schism happened in Brahmo Samaj as the loyal people to Tagore who were more conservative in their approach grouped themselves into the **Adi** (original) **Brahmo Samaj** and Keshab Chandra Sen and his followers soon established the **Brahmo Samaj of India** on 15 November 1866.

> *"It was a schism between Keshab followers, for whom social progress and reform were more important than anything else, and the followers of Debendranath, who preferred to maintain their identification with Hindu society."*
>
> Meredith Borthwick, researcher on Bengal of the 19th century.

- With his ability to impress people and encourage them, Keshab Chandra Sen soon expanded the network of **Brahmo Samaj of India** across the country, and by 1872, branches were established in Bihar, United Provinces, Punjab, Assam, Orissa, Madhya Pradesh and other southern and western cities of India. He was also instrumental behind the foundation of the **Indian Reform Association**, which worked for improving the life of peasants.
- However, after 1875, Keshab strongly demonstrated a new interest in strictly religious issues and organised a seminar to study different religions and their prophets. During 1875–76, he also began to propagate a new type of **Brahmoism** which included elements of ecstatic religious experience and *shaktism* (the worship of female power). During the same time, he also met the famous Hindu religious leader, **Ramakrishna Paramhansa**, and it is often speculated that it was Ramakrishna who had motivated Sen for devotional worship.
- Sen's inclination for devotional worship disoriented his followers and along with certain other controversial events such as Keshab's inexplicable act of getting his 13-year-old daughter married to the minor Hindu Maharaja of Cooch-Behar with all the orthodox Hindu rituals in 1878, consideration of Keshab as an incarnation by some of his followers, while the authoritative nature of Keshab created further discontent among the progressive followers and Brahmo Samaj was again headed for a split. The disgruntled followers of Keshab set up a new organisation, the ***Satharan Brahmo Samaj*** on 15 May, 1878.
- In 1881, Keshab formed his ***Naba Bidhan***, that is, New Dispensation and started moving towards a new universalist religion. He also published a journal *New Dispensation* to disseminate his ideas and philosophy and his own vision of religion.

> *"Religion is essentially universal. If God is our common father, His truth is our common property. But the religious world may be likened to a vast market, where every religious sect sells only a portion of truth. Religion is many sided; but each individual, each nation, often at times adopts and represents only one side of religion. In different times and in different countries, therefore, we see not the entire religious life of humanity, but only partial religious life.*
>
> *Whoever worships the True God daily must learn to recognise all his countrymen as brethen."*
>
> Keshab Chandra Sen

- He died in 1884 and after his death, the Brahmo movement also broke down quickly, confining to a small elite group due to successive ideological rifts and organisational divisions.

Although he was responsible for many splits in the Brahmo Samaj including the first schism, he was undoubtedly one of the key transitional figures in the history of socio-religious movements of the 19th century. Despite doctrinal differences among themselves, the Brahmo Samajists collectively contributed to the propagation of modern ideas and helped in creating support in the society about female emancipation, widow remarriage, monogamy, women's education and monotheism.

Pandit Ishwar Chandra Vidyasagar (1820–91)

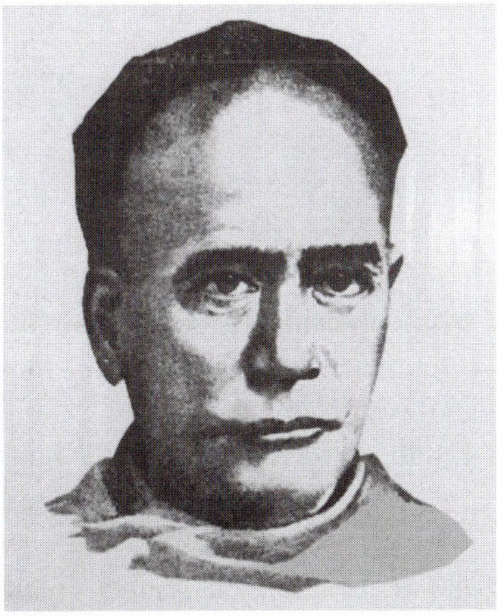

Pandit Ishwar Chandra Vidyasagar

- The second-half of the 19th century witnessed the emergence of Pandit Ishwar Chandra Vidyasagar, the great scholar and reformer who dedicated his entire life to social reform.
- He was born in 1820 in a very poor family and had to struggle through hardship to educate himself. However, being a brilliant student, he defied all odds and received the title of ***Vidyasagar*** (Ocean of Knowledge) from Sanskrit College, Calcutta, when he was merely 22 years old. Later, he became the principal of the same Sanskrit College in 1851, where he introduced the study of Western thought, evolved a new technique of teaching Sanskrit and opened its gates to non-Brahmin students. He wrote a Bengali Primer '*Barnaparichay*' which is used till this day and helped evolve a distinct modern, prose style in Bengali.
- His great contribution, however, lay in the field of **female emancipation**. He devoted his entire life to the specific social issue of **widow remarriage** and waged a long struggle to fetch support of the enlightened sections from various parts of the country over the same. Finally, his agitation for legalising the remarriage of widows bore fruit and **Hindu Widows Remarriage Act** was enacted in 1856, and in the same year, the first legal Hindu widow marriage among the upper castes in India was celebrated under the supervision of Vidyasagar. To set an example, he even married his own son Narayan Chandra to a widow. Between 1855 and 1860, through his efforts, which included the grant of monetary help to needy couples, nearly 25 widow remarriages were solemnised which was certainly a major breakthrough in the history of radical social reform, and was a great advance from Rammohan's idea of ascetic widowhood.
- He was also deeply interested in the cause of **female education** and was one of the pioneers of higher education for women for their general uplift. As Secretary to the Bethune School, founded in Calcutta in 1849 exclusively for girls' education, he was instrumental in leading the movement for women's education. In addition, as Government Inspector of Schools, he organised 35 girls schools, many of which he ran at his own expense.

> *"Education does not only mean learning, reading, writing, and arithmetic, it should provide comprehensive knowledge. Education in geography, geometry, literature, natural philosophy, moral philosophy, political economy, and others is very much necessary. We want teachers who know both Bengali and the English language, and at the same time are free from religious prejudices.*
>
> *I have no time to think about God, since there is so much to be done on earth."*
>
> Pandit Ishwar Chandra Vidyasagar

- He also campaigned against child marriage and polygamy and was a great humanist who possessed immense sympathy for the poor, the unfortunate and the oppressed. In Bengal, innumerable stories regarding his simple behaviour, high character, moral qualities and deep humanism are related till this day. It is often quoted that *he seldom possessed a warm coat for himself as he invariably gave it to the first beggar he met on the street*. In fact for his generosity, Poet Michael Madusudan Dutt gave him the epithet of ***daya sagar*** (ocean of generosity).
- The great scholar and reformer, however, passed away in 1891 at the age of 70.

> *"One wonders how God, in the process of producing forty million Bengalis, produced a man!"*
>
> Rabindranath Tagore's statement shortly after Vidyasagar's death

Ramakrishna Paramhansa (1834–86)

While the didactic nationalism of the Brahmo Samaj appealed more to the intellectual elite in Bengal, the average Bengali found more emotional satisfaction in the cult of *bhakti* and *yoga* which were popularised in the 19th century by a priest of the Kali temple in Dakshineswar, Calcutta: **Ramakrishna Paramhansa** (1836–86) originally named Gajadhar Chattopadhyaya, whose teachings formed the basis of Ramakrishna Movement. Although his education did not proceed beyond the elementary stage and he had no formal education in philosophy and *shastras*, yet his knowledge about spirituality was not only unparallelled but also universalistic in orientation. Ramakrishna stressed on religious universalism and recognised the fundamental oneness of all religions emphasising on the fact that all lead to the same God. He taught that *jatra jiv tantra Shiv,* that is, 'wherever there is a living being, there is Shiva' and *jive daya noy, Shiv gyane jib seba meaning* 'not kindness to living beings but serving the living beings as Shiva himself matters more', that is, **service to man is the service to God**, for man is the embodiment of God himself'. Later, the teachings of Ramakrishna were spread across the world by his devoted discipline, Swami Vivekanand, who tried to reconcile them with the needs of contemporary Indian society.

Swami Vivekananda (1863–1902)

- The last of the great thinkers of 19th century Bengal who created a stir in Hindu society was Swami Vivekananda, who was known in his pre-monastic life as Narendra Nath Datta. His spiritual preceptor or guru was **Ramakrishna Paramhansa** who sought salvation through traditional religious ways of renunciation, mediation and *bhakti* amidst increasing westernisation and modernisation. Vivekananda too, like his Guru, proclaimed the essential oneness of all the religions and condemned narrowness or parochial attitude.
- As a child, young Narendra had boundless energy and was fascinated with many aspects of life, especially wandering ascetics. He received a western education at the Ishwar Chandra Vidyasagar's Metropolitan Institution and became well versed in Western and Eastern philosophy. His teachers remarked him to have a prodigious memory and tremendous intellectual capacity.

Swami Vivekananda

- Although initially he had joined the Brahmo Samaj, after a few years he left the organisation when he accepted Sri Ramakrishna Paramhansa as his Guru whom he had met in course of his search for spiritual quest. Interestingly, at first, his mind could not accept the ways and teachings of Ramakrishna as he followed the devotional path and was particularly devoted to idol worship of Mother Kali but over time, Narendra's spiritual experiences in the presence of Ramakrishna caused him to whole-heartedly accept Ramakrishna as his Guru. As per the wishes of Ramakrishna, after his death in 1886, Narendra was chosen as the leader of the monastic disciples and he founded a *math* that is, monastery at **Belur** near Calcutta. Vivekananda then threw himself into intense spiritual practices and would spend many hours in meditation and *japa*. In 1888, he left the monastery to become a wandering *sannyasin*, visiting various holy places around India. He began accepting disciples and, in 1893, accepted an invitation to speak at the World Parliament of Religions in **Chicago**.

- Vivekananda made a strong impression at the inaugural World Parliament of Religions in Chicago, 1893, as a representative of the Hindu religion, giving a powerful speech underlying universality and harmony of the world religions. He thus introduced the world to the *Vedanta* philosophy whom he considered to be a fully rational system and to the superior approach of the Indian philosophical tradition.

After getting up on the stage, Vivekananda bowed to Saraswati, the goddess of learning and then begin with the greeting *Sisters and Brothers of America!* - Something in Vivekananda's address and personality caused the crowd of 7,000 to stand in ovation for 2 minutes before he continued his speech.

Some excerpts from the historic speech.

It fills my heart with joy unspeakable to rise in response to the warm and cordial welcome which you have given us. I thank you in the name of the most ancient order of monks in the world; I thank you in the name of mother of religions; and I thank you in the name of millions and millions of Hindu people of all classes and sects….

I am proud to belong to a religion which has taught the world both tolerance and universal acceptance. We believe not only in universal toleration, but we accept all religions as true. I am proud to belong to a nation which has sheltered the persecuted and the refugees of all religions and nations of the earth….

Sectarianism, bigotry, and its horrible descendant, fanaticism, have long possessed this beautiful earth. They have filled the earth with violence, drenched it often and often with human blood, destroyed civilisation and sent whole nations to despair. Had it not been for these horrible demons, human society would be far more advanced than it is now….

But their time has come; and I fervently hope that the bell that tolled this morning in honour of this convention may be the death-knell of all fanaticism, of all persecutions with the sword or with the pen, and of all uncharitable feelings between persons wending their way to the same goal….

Vivekananda attracted widespread attention among the press covering the event, which called him the '*handsome oriental monk*'. The New York Herald noted Vivekananda is undoubtedly the greatest figure in the Parliament of Religions. After hearing him we feel how foolish it is to send missionaries to this learned nation.

Vivekananda's other famous quotes:

"I do not come to convert you to a new belief. I want you to keep your own belief; I want to make the Methodist a better Methodist, the Christian a better Christian; the Unitarian a better Unitarian. I want to teach you to live the truth, to reveal the light within your own soul."

"Religion is realisation; not talk, not doctrine, nor theories, however beautiful they may be. It is being and becoming, not hearing or acknowledging; it is the whole soul becoming changed into what it believes."

"No other religion preaches the dignity of humanity in such a lofty strain as Hinduism and no other religion on earth treads upon the poor and the low in such a fashion as Hinduism."

- He spent another 2 years giving speeches in America and accepting disciples to follow *Vedanta* philosophy. In 1895, he travelled to England, where he met Professor Max Muller and also Margaret Noble (later Sister Nivedita, one of closest disciples of Vivekananda who devoted her entire life to the education of Indian women and India's independence). From abroad too, he was in touch with his disciples through correspondence and exhorted them to indulge whole-heartedly into social service, helping the poorest to gain an education.
- He returned to India in 1897 to a hero's welcome and founded the Ramakrishna Mission to carry on humanitarian and social work. The main motto of the Mission was to provide social service to the people, and it carried on its mission by opening schools, hospitals, orphanages, libraries, and others in different parts of the country.
- While, on one hand, he was passionate about India's immense spiritual and philosophical heritage, on the other hand, he had the wisdom to accept its shortcomings. He criticised the degeneration of India's status due to the caste system, lack of education, poverty, colonial rule, subjugation of women and superstitious traditions.
- He strongly disapproved of the caste system and people's obsession with rituals, ceremonies and superstitions. He lamented the isolatonist tendencies and the *touch me not* attitude of Hindus in religious matters and urged the people to imbibe the spirit of liberty, equality and free thinking.
- Vivekananda was a great humanist who frowned at religion's tacit approval of the oppression of the poor by the rich. He believed that it was an insult to God and humanity to teach religion to starving men. He stressed on social action and believed that knowledge without action is useless.
- He also installed a sense of national pride and national fervour among the Indians and influenced many Indian nationalists and leaders such as Mahatma Gandhi, Aurobindo Ghosh, Bal Gangadhar Tilak, Netaji Subhash Chandra Bose, and others. He also drew attention to the extent of poverty in the country and maintained that addressing such poverty was a pre-requisite for national awakening.

"If superstitions enters, the brain is gone."

"There is a danger of our religion getting into the kitchen. We are neither Vedantists, most of us now, nor Pauranics, nor Tantrics. We are just 'don't touchiest'. Our religion is in the kitchen. Our God is in the cooking-pot, and our religion is 'Don't touch me, I am holy.' If this goes on for another century, everyone of us will be in a lunatic asylum."

"A country where millions have nothing to eat and where few thousand holy men and brahmins suck the blood of the poor and do nothing at all for them, is not a country but a living hell. Is this religion or dance of death?"

"This is the gist of all worship - to be pure and to do good to others. He who sees Shiva in the poor, in the weak, and in the diseased, really worships Shiva; and if he sees Shiva only in the image, his worship is but preliminary."

"The fact of our isolation from all other nations of the world is the cause of our degeneration and its only remedy is getting back into the current of the rest of the world. Motion is the sign of life."

"Liberty in thought and action is the only condition of life, growth and well being: Where it does not exist, the man, the race, and the nation must go down."

"So long as the millions live in hunger and ignorance, I hold every man a traitor who, having been educated at their expense, pays not the last heed to them."

> *"We want education by which character is formed, strength of mind is increased, the intellect is expanded, and by which one can stand on one's own feet."*
>
> *"Education is the manifestation of perfection present already in man. Religion is the manifestation of the divinity already in man."*
>
> *"This life is short, the vanities of the world are transient, but they alone live who live for others, the rest are more dead than alive."*
>
> Swami Vivekanand

- Vivekananda is regarded as the patriot saint of modern India and an inspirer of her dormant national consciousness. Subhash Chandra Bose considered him to be the maker of modern India, while Mahatma Gandhi counted him among the few Hindu reformers who could maintain Hindu religion in a state of splendour by cutting the dead wood of tradition. About him, French Nobel laureate Romain Rolland wrote *His words are great music, phrases in the style of Beethoven, stirring rhythms like the march of Handel choruses. I cannot touch these saying so this, scattered as they are through the pages of books, at 30 years' distance, without receiving a thrill through my body like an electric shock. And what shocks, what transports, must have been produced when in burning words they issued from the lips of the hero!.*

Why Bengal was the Centre of all the Activities?

Being the headquarters of the Company's government in India and its early subjugation to British rule, Bengal provided a laboratory where the government developed many of its early state policies. Because of the economic activities of the British in Calcutta and the spread of Western education, it was also the region where there existed a substantial number of educated middle-class people who not only actively discussed and responded to British policies but also played a key role in socio-cultural reforms.

Western India

In contrast to **Bengal** where the socio-religious movement had a religious and philosophical overtone, the main focus of reform movements of **Western India** was strictly on social issues. The early intellectuals of Western India were not essentially religious thinkers, concerned with the philosophical subtleties, but were practical social reformers who tried to develop a general awareness among the various lower castes against the prevalent forms of social discrimination. Prominent Reformers like Dadoba Pandurang, Jyotiba Phule, M. G. Ranade and others played very significant role in the development of this social awareness as a means to end all sorts of social disabilities.

Early Phases of the 19th Century

The first soundings of intellectual revolt in Maharashtra were heard in the early decades of the 19th century. Among the early intellectuals who initiated and led the movement, the most prominent were Bal Shastri Jambhekar, Dadoba Pandurang, Atmaram Pandurang, Bhasker Pandurang Tarkhadkar, Gopal Hari Deshmukh better known as ***Lokahitwadi*** and Vishnu Bhikaji Gokhale, popularly known as Vishnubawa **Brahmachari**, for he remained a life long bachelor.

Bal Shastri Jambhekar (1812–46)

- Jambhekar was the pioneer of the intellectual movement in Maharashtra who laid its foundations through his numerous writings, in the early 1830s.
- He is also known as the father of Marathi journalism who started the weekly ***Darpan*** in 1832. Through *Darpan*, he tried to create positive awareness about the social issues such as widow remarriage and rational outlook towards social problems.

Dadoba Pandurang (1814–82)

- Dadoba founded the first socio-religious reform organisation of Maharashtra ***Paramhansa Mandali*** in 1849, which was a secret gathering of like-minded people following seven principles outlined by Dadoba in his book *Dharma Vivechan*:
  - God alone should be worshipped.
  - Real religion is based on love and moral conduct.
  - Spiritual religion is one.
  - Every individual should have freedom of thought.
  - Our actions and speech should be consistent with reason.
  - Mankind is one caste.
  - Right kind of knowledge should be given to all.

> *"When we went for long walks in the evening, we talked about the evils of caste distinctions, how much damage was done by this division between high and low, and how true progress for this country could never be achieved without removing these distinctions."*
>
> R. G. Bhandarkar recalling his *mandali* days

- These principles denied polytheism of popular Hinduism, the caste system and the Brahmanical monopoly of knowledge. All members of the *mandalis* were required to take a pledge that they would abandon caste restrictions and at their meetings, communal meal prepared by lower caste people was taken by all. Branches of these *mandalis* existed in Poona, Satara and other prominent towns of Maharashtra. However, for fear of facing the wrath of the orthodox, the *mandali* being a secret society could not bring much of a difference as participation was limited to its few members only.
- Dadoba is also known as *Panini* (a well-known Sanskrit grammarian) of Marathi language because he laid the foundation of Marathi syntax and also wrote a volume on Marathi grammar.

Atmaram Pandurang (1823–98)

- Dadoba's younger brother who was an Indian physician and social reformer opposed many Hindu traditions including child marriage. He believed that the minimum age for marriage of girls should be 20.
- He was under the strong influence of Keshab Chandra Sen, and when Sen visited Maharashtra in 1867, Atmaram founded the ***Prarthana Samaj*** along with **R. G. Bhandarkar**, with the aim to make people believe in one God. The Samaj became popular after **Justice Ranade** joined.

Bhaskar Pandurang (1816–47)

- Bhaskar Pandurang was the first person in Maharashtra to preach nationalist ideas in the 19th century, earning the distinction of '**militant nationalist critic**' of the colonial rule in India.

- It was he who first articulated the exploitative character of the British rule in India and wrote, in 1841, a series of eight long letters exposing nearly every aspect of colonial domination in the *Bombay Gazette*, one of the oldest newspapers in the Presidency.

Gopal Hari Deshmukh (1823–92)

- His concern for the masses earned him the title of *Lokahitwadi*. He broadened the scope of the socio-religious reform movement in Maharashtra by his hundred letters, the famous ***Shatapatren*** published in the *Prabhakar*, a Marathi Weekly between 1848 and 1850. These all-encompassing letters constituted the magnum opus of the early intellectual endeavours in Maharashtra and when taken together, leave hardly any aspect of the society which is untouched.
- Through his letters, he promoted emancipation and education of women, advocated a reorganisation of Indian society on modern, rational, humanistic and secular principles and values and wrote against the evils of child marriage, caste system, superstitious traditions, and others.

> *"If Religion does not sanction social reform, then change religion."*
>
> Gopal Hari Deshmukh 'Lokahitwadi'

Vishnu Bhikaji Gokhale (1825–71)

- Vishnubawa Brahmachari was a contemporary of Swami Dayanand and like him believed in the supremacy of Vedic religion. At the age of 23, he gave up his government service, abandoned society and became a *Sanyasi* for the realisation of higher self and knowledge.
- Disappointed at the false propaganda of the Christian missionaries demeaning the Hindu faith, he vowed to fight against the rumours and gossips spread by them but at the same time, talked about necessary amendments to be brought in the Hindu faith for retention of its core philosophy.
- Having strong belief in the oneness of humanity, he was against caste distinctions and worked all along his life for an equitable social order. Although himself a *Brahmin*, he employed a Muslim cook and ate food served by anyone, thus openly challenging caste system rigidity.

Later Phase of the 19th Century

The reform movement further gained strength during the second half of the century, and a host of towering personalities emerged on the intellectual scene. The most notable among them were Vishnu Shastri Pandit, Jyotiba Phule, Ramkrishna Gopal Bhandarkar, Narayan Mahadev Parmanand, Mahadev Govind Ranade, Vishnushastri Chiplunkar, K. T. Telang, Ganesh Vasudev Joshi and Gopal Ganesh Agarkar.

Vishnu Shastri Pandit (1827–76)

- Pandit was a leading figure in the sphere of the agitation for female emancipation, specially widow remarriage. He himself set an example by marrying a widow.
- He started the ***Punar Vivahtojak Mandal*** (Society for Encouragement of Widow Marriage) in 1865 and worked as its secretary.

Jyotiba Phule (1827–90)

- Phule, born in the *Mali* (gardener) caste, emerged as a champion of the depressed sections of the society and organised a powerful movement against upper caste domination. He was the first Indian to start a school for the untouchables in 1854.
- In 1873, he founded the ***Satyashodhak Samaj*** (Truth Seeker's Society) to liberate the less privileged *shudras* and *ati shudras* from oppression and exploitation. The Society worked for the spread of education among women and lower caste people.
- The leadership of the *Samaj* came from the backward classes such as *malis, telis, kunbis* and *dhangars*. The Samaj propounded the spread of rational thinking and rejected the need for a Brahman priestly class as educational and religious leaders. Phule used the symbol of *Rajah Bali* as opposed to the Brahmins symbol of Rama and refused to regard the Vedas as sacrosanct.

Jyotiba Phule

- Through the mouth piece of Satyashodhak Samaj ***Deenbandhu*** and other prominent works like ***Sarvajanik Satya Dharma*** and ***Gulamgin*** Phule tried to give a sense of identity to the depressed communities and spread awareness among them. In fact, he was given the title of *Mahatma* for his work for the cause of oppressed.
- He and his wife Savitribai Phule were the pioneers of women's education in India. The couple were among the first native Indians to open a school for girls in Poona in 1848. They also staunchly supported the widow remarriage movement in Maharashtra.

Ramkrishna Gopal Bhandarkar (1837–1925)

- R G Bhandarkar was not only a key social reformer but also a distinguished orientalist and Sanskrit scholar who earned the title of ***Maharishi*** for himself. He worked as Vice Chancellor of Bombay University and also Vice Chancellor of **first Women's University** in India, founded by **Maharishi Karve** in Pune.
- He founded ***Prarthana Samaj*** with Justice Ranade and Atmaram Pandurang in 1867, whose aim was abolition of caste system, widow remarriage and education of women. Working hard, he sought sanction in ancient Sanskrit and Pali texts in support of women education, widow remarriage and against child marriage.
- Believing more in practice than preaching, he set an example by encouraging his daughters and granddaughters to receive university education amidst social boycott enforced by then prevailing orthodox ambience and also arranged marriage of his widow daughter in 1891 in the teeth of conservative opposition. The opposition to his this action was so strong that even a social reformer like K. T. Telang did not dare to take meals at his place.
- He was one of the very few to strongly advocate Hindu–Muslim unity.

Narayan Mahadev Parmanand (1838–93)

- Paramanand, writing under the pen name of the 'Political recluse', was one of the constructive critics of the British administration, besides being a great social reformer.

Mahadev Govind Ranade (1842–1901)

- Ranade was a distinguished scholar and a founding member of the Indian National Congress (INC). An alumnus of the Elphinstone College, Bombay, he was a judge of the Bombay High Court during 1891–1901.
- He was a founder of the **Social Conference** movement which aimed against child marriage, heavy cost of marriages and other social functions, caste restrictions and advocated for female education and widow remarriage. He used to summarise the mission of the Indian social reform movement as to *Humanize, Equalize and Spiritualize*.
- He held that the social reform movement could not move the people unless it assimilated religious reform. He also held that if religious ideas were rigid, then there would be no success in social, economic and political spheres.

> *"This is the land of Religion, Be it be for good or for evil, we cannot do without religion. Religious thoughts are in our blood. If we try to flee from it, it will pursue us.*
>
> *Strength of numbers we cannot command, but we can command earnestness of conviction, singleness of devotion, readiness for self sacrifice, in all honest workers in the cause."*
>
> M. G. Ranade

- Under his able guidance, the *Paramhansa Sabha* was reorganised in 1867 under the name *Prarthana Samaj* which preached monotheism and denounced priestly domination and caste distinctions. Its activities also spread to south India through the efforts of the Telugu reformer, **Veeresalingam**.
- Apart from Prarthana Samaj, he was closely associated with **Poona Sarvajanik Sabha**, Ahmednagar Education Society, **Indian Social Conference** (which functioned as the social reform cell of INC and initiated Pledge Movement to inspire people against Child Marriage), Industrial Conference and **Widow Remarriage Association**.
- He was considered to be a great historian who played a decisive role in the modernisation of the Indian economy and also wrote books on Maratha history such as *Rise of Maratha Power*.
- Although Ranade criticised superstitions and blind faith, quite ironically, he was somewhat conservative in his own life. Upon the death of his first wife, his reform-minded friends expected him to marry a widow because he was an ardent supporter of widow remarriage but to their dismay, he adhered to his family wishes and married a child bride Ramabhai Ranade, whom he subsequently provided with an education and who continued his social and educational reform work after his death.

Vishnu Shastri Chiplunkar (1850–82)

- Chiplunkar was a Marathi writer whose writings have had a decisive influence on modern Marathi prose style, and most of his writings were devoted to the cause of social reform. In 1874, he started his famous ***Nibandhmala*** (A Garland of Essays), a monthly Marathi magazine covering diverse topics ranging from Marathi prose style to social reform articles.
- In 1880, he founded together with Gopal Ganesh Agarkar and Bal Gangadhar Tilak newspapers ***Kesari*** (in Marathi) and ***Mahratta*** (in English). He was also a co-founder of **The New English School** in Pune which aimed at providing a more patriotically inclined education as opposed to the schools run by the government in British India.

- In 1884, he along with Gopal Ganesh Agarkar created the **Deccan Education Society** and also established Fergusson College with Tilak and Agarkar as early lecturers.

K. T. Telang (1850–93)

- Telang started his career as a lawyer and later became a judge in the Bombay High Court. His equal command over English and Sanskrit made him an authority on Hindu laws as he used to quote Hindu law books with ease. He also translated the *Bhagavadgita* into the English language and was instrumental in introducing **compulsory primary education** in Bombay.
- He was the founding member of the INC and the first Secretary of the INC and belonged to the moderate groups of the INC. He was an important member of the ***Bombay Triumvirate*** comprising himself, Pherozeshah Mehta, and Badruddin Tyabji (who also founded the Bombay Presidency Association in 1885).

Ganesh Vasudev Joshi (1828–80)

- G. V. Joshi was a lawyer, social reformer and political activist who provided a brilliant critique of the economic policy of the British government. He was a founding member of ***Poona Sarvajanik Sabha*** and was called *Sarvajanik Kaka* with affectionate humour.
- He represented Vasudev Balwant Phadke in his trial and was courageous enough to ask the Viceroy Lytton at the Delhi Durbar of 1877 that the Queen might grant to India the same political and social status as is enjoyed by her British subjects.

Gopal Ganesh Agarkar (1856–95)

- Agarkar was the first editor of *Kesari*, a prominent Marathi language weekly newspaper that had been founded by Lokmanya Tilak in 1880–81. Later, due to ideological differences of primacy of social reform over political reform, he parted ways with Tilak and started his own periodical ***Sudharak***, in which he campaigned against the injustices of untouchability and the caste system.
- He was an iconoclast and uncompromising rationalist who was very pungent in his denunciation of any blind dependence on tradition or false deification of India's past.

Dr Bhimrao Ramji Ambedkar (1891–1956)

Dr Bhimrao Ramji Ambedkar

- Dr Bhimrao Ramji Ambedkar, affectionately and reverently known by his followers as *Babasaheb*, was an eminent jurist, social reformer and politician, whose efforts to eradicate social evils like untouchablity and caste restrictions were remarkable.
- He was born in the *Mahar* community, which at that time was one of the 'untouchable' castes. Throughout his childhood and youth, Dr Ambedkar had to suffer the humiliating treatment meted out to 'untouchables' by the 'upper castes' of society. Despite all difficulties, he completed his education in India, and having received a scholarship from the then **Maharaja of Baroda**, he proceeded abroad for his further studies. Having distinguished himself in his studies, Dr. Ambedkar then returned to India to practice law at the Bombay High Court. Unfortunately, in spite of his outstanding knowledge, qualifications and acumen, he had to face caste-based discrimination, ostracism and stigma once again, but all this strengthened Dr. Ambedkar's resolve to emancipate his fellow 'untouchables' from social slavery.
- He strove to bring about unity amongst the untouchables by founding and establishing political parties and organisations for their unity and upliftment, and publishing newspapers to disseminate

information and spread awareness amongst them, and espouse their cause. He founded the Marathi fortnightly, ***Mooknayaka*** (leader of the voiceless), in 1920, and the organisation, ***Bahishkrit Hitkarni Sabha*** in 1924.

- By 1927, Ambedkar launched full-fledged movements for Dalit rights. He demanded public drinking water sources open to all and right for all castes to enter temples. He openly condemned Hindu scriptures advocating discrimination and arranged symbolic demonstrations to enter the Kalaram Temple in Nashik. He also objected to the decision of the Congress and Mahatma Gandhi to call the untouchable community as *Harijan*, as according to him even the members of untouchable community are same as the other members of the society.
- In 1932, the **Poona Pact** was signed between Dr. Ambedkar and Pandit Madan Mohan Malviya, representative of the Hindu Brahmins relinquishing reservation of seats for the untouchable classes in the Provisional legislatures, within the general electorate. These classes were later designated as Scheduled Classes and Scheduled Tribes. In 1936, he founded the Independent Labor Party which won 15 seats in the 1937 Central Legislative Assembly elections. Later, the same party transformed into the **All India Scheduled Castes Federation**. In the house, he was instrumental in introducing several bills for the welfare of peasants, workers and the depressed classes.
- His famous literary works are:
    - *The Annihilation of Castes*
    - *Who were the Shudras*
- His reputation as a scholar led to his appointment as free India's first Law Minister and **chairman** of the committee responsible to draft a constitution for independent India. Later in his final years, he founded the *Bharatiya Buddha Mahasabha* and embraced Buddhism along with exhorting his followers to leave the fold of Hinduism so that they might get rid of the injustices and humiliation meted out to them in the name of caste.

North India

The social and religious reform in North India among Hindus was spearheaded by **Swami Dayanand Saraswati** who founded the *Arya Samaj* (the society of virtuous human beings, that is, *Arya*) in 1875 at Bombay which later established its headquarters in Lahore. North India also witnessed certain Muslim Reform and Revivalist movements such as the **Aligarh Movement** under the able guidance of Sir Syed Ahmed Khan, **Deoband School Movement**, a revivalist movement under the leadership of Mohd. Qasim Nanotovi and Rashid Ahmed Gangohi, **Wahabi Movement** under Shah Walliullah, **Ahmadiyya Movement** under Mirza Ghulam Ahmed, **Faraizi Movement** under Haji Shariatullah, **Sikh reform movements** and reform movements among Parsis, the details of which we are going to subsequently discuss in the following paragraphs.

Swami Dayanand Saraswati (1824–83)

Swami Dayanand Saraswati

- Swami Dayanand Saraswati was originally known as Mulshankar in his childhood and was born in the small town of Tankara belonging to Kathiawar of Gujarat in a conservative Brahmin family. He wandered as an ascetic in search of truth for 15 years and finally received education on *Vedanta* from a blind teacher named **Swami Virajananda** in Mathura.
- Dayanand's views were published in his famous work ***Satyarth Prakash*** (The True Exposition) where he talks about his vision of a classless and casteless society, united India, India free from foreign rule, with *Aryan* religion being the common religion of all. He considered Vedas as 'India's Rock of Ages' and gave the clarion call of '**Go Back to the Vedas**'.

- With an indigenous orientation, he wanted to bring a new social, religious, economic and political order in India. It should be noted that his call for Back to the Vedas was a call for a revival of Vedic learning and Vedic purity of religion and not just revival of Vedic times. Taking inspiration from the Vedas, he attacked superstitious practices like caste rigidities, belief in magic, charms and animal sacrifices, taboo on sea voyages, polytheism, Idolatry, untouchability, Brahmin-sponsored religious rites like feeding the dead through *shraddhas*, and others.

"The Vedas are the infallible and the true original seed of Hinduism. If men followed the teachings of Vedas, there would be India's Golden Age and so let's all of us go back to the Vedas.

I accept as Dharma whatever is in full conformity with impartial justice, truthfulness and the like; that which is not opposed to the teachings of God as embodied in the Vedas. Whatever is not free from partiality and is unjust, partaking of untruth and the like, and opposed to the teachings of God as embodied in the Vedas-that I hold as adharma.

All alchemists, magicians, sorcerers, wizards, spiritists, and others, are cheats and all their practices should be looked upon as nothing but downright fraud. Young people should be well counselled against all these frauds, in their very childhood, so that they may not suffer through being duped by any unprincipled person."

Swami Dayanand Saraswati

- He was a vehement opponent of child marriage and considered it to be one of the causes of the degeneration of the Hindus. He used to sometimes lament Hindu race as *the children of children*. He was a strong supporter of adult and inter-caste marriages and advocated fixing of marriageable age at 25 for boys and 16 for girls.
- Basing himself on the *Vedas* and *Shastras*, he showed that *women, being the emblem of creative power and representative of motherhood, must be treated with respect in married life*. He advocated equal rights for man and woman in all respects: in marriage, in matter of property and in the study of *Vedas* and *Shastras*. Discarding *purdah* completely, he believed in the complete emancipation of woman and considered man and woman equal in every respect.

"The family goes to rack and ruin where women are unhappy and miserable and that family enjoys perpetual prosperity where women are filled with joy and delight."

Swami Dayanand Saraswati quotes Manu on treating women with dignity.

- He repudiated caste system and denounced untouchability but at the same time upheld the fourfold varna division, thus retaining the core of Indian social organisation. **However**, he subscribed to the Vedic notion of *Chaturvarna* system where all the individuals were placed in different classes according to their qualifications, accomplishments and character. According to him, an evildoer, even if born of Brahmin parents, must be considered as Shudra, while a man, born of Shudra parents, must be classed a Brahmin, if his actions were pure.

"He deserves to be a Brahman who has acquired the best knowledge and character and an ignorant person is fit to be classed as Shudra."

Swami Dayanand Saraswati

- He strongly criticised the prevalent popular belief that every individual receives from the society according to the principles of *niyati* (destiny) and *karma* (deeds). Rather, he advocated that every individual had to work for his own salvation by right deeds and in the light of eternal principles governing human conduct.
- He advocated the cause of compulsory education and considered it the duty of the State to provide for education to all the boys and girls. While he wanted the traditional subjects to be taught, he was equally enthusiastic for modern subjects to be studied. It should be duly noted that although the Vedas were venerated as infallible, the reforms advocated by Swami Dayanand were the product of modern rational thinking.
- He was the first to advocate ***swadeshi*** clothes, Indian system of medical treatment and indigenous industries. He was also the first to use the term *Swaraj* as **India for Indians** in 1876, a call later taken up by Lokmanya Tilak. To promote an all-Indian national spirit, he recognised Hindi as the national language.
- He established different branches of Arya Samaj which played a progressive role in furthering the cause of social reform in India, especially Punjab and North Western Provinces. The organisation advocated social equality, denounced caste-rigidities and untouchability while simultaneously working for the upliftment of women. The Arya Samaj established a number of educational institutions like *Gurukuls, Kanya Gurukuls,* DAV (**Dayanand Anglo Vedic**) Schools and Colleges for the education of both males and females.

The ten guiding principles of the Arya Samaj are:

- God is the efficient cause of all true knowledge and all that is known through knowledge.
- God is existent, intelligent and blissful. He is formless, omniscient, just, merciful, unborn, endless, unchangeable, beginning-less, unequalled, the support of all, the master of all, omnipresent, immanent, un-ageing, immortal, fearless, eternal and holy, and the maker of all. He alone is worthy of being worshiped.
- The Vedas are the scriptures of all true knowledge. It is the paramount duty of all Aryas to read them, teach them, recite them and to hear them being read.
- One should always be ready to accept truth and to renounce untruth.
- All acts should be performed in accordance with Dharma that is, after deliberating what is right and wrong.
- The prime object of the Arya Samaj is to do good to the world, that is, to promote physical, spiritual and social good of everyone.
- Our conduct towards all should be guided by love, righteousness and justice.
- We should dispel *Avidya* (ignorance) and promote *Vidya* (knowledge).
- No one should be content with promoting his/her good only; on the contrary, one should look for his/her good in promoting the good of all.
- One should regard oneself under restriction to follow the rules of society calculated to promote the well being of all, while in following the rules of individual welfare all should be free.

The motto of the Arya Samaj taken from the Vedas is *'Krinvanto Vishwamaryam'*.

–Make all men Arya (noble and cultured)

- Arya Samaj tried to inculcate the spirit of self-respect and self-reliance among the masses of India and was successful in instilling feeling of nationalism. However, Swami ji's bent towards the Vedas which he regarded as infallible gave his teachings an orthodox hue. Emphasising on the superiority of Hinduism and in its zeal to protect the Hindu society from the onslaught of Christianity and Islam, the Arya Samajists started the ***Shuddhi* Movement** as a process of converting the people of other religions to Hinduism and also to reconvert those who have changed from Hinduism to other religions. This development marginalised the identity of the 'reformist' movement to 'revivalist' one which in turn led to certain unintended consequences.

Reform and Revivalism

The urge for reforms brought the much needed rejuvenation in the society and its institutions; however, this aspect of the reform movement also introduced an element of **revivalism,** a tendency to harp back on the Indian past, an attempt to reinvigorate traditional institutions and to defend Indian culture and civilisation. This concern embraced the entire cultural existence, the way of life and all signifying aspects of social life such as language, religion, art and philosophy. Two distinguished features characterising this concern were:

- **The creation of an alternate cultural ideological system**: This aspect involved features such as the development of vernacular languages, the creation of an alternate system of education, attempts to revitalise the Indian system of medicine, and the defence of religion.
- **The regeneration of traditional institutions**: Some of the expressions of this aspect included the efforts to regenerate Indian art and literature, the emphasis on Indian dress and food, the attempt to probe the potentialities of pre-colonial technology and to reconstruct traditional knowledge.

Although, at times, this tended to impart a conservative and retrogressive character to these movements, nevertheless, the Revivalist movements played an important role in creating cultural consciousness and confidence among the people. It is pertinent to note that the only difference between the reform and revivalist movement depended on the varying degree it relied its premise on reason and universalism as opposed to tradition and old ways.

Sir Syed Ahmed Khan (1817–98)

- The movement for reform arose relatively later among the Indian Muslims only after the 1860s. Sir Syed Ahmed Khan was deeply concerned at the depressing situation of the Muslims and raising them from their backwardness became his lifelong passion and aim. He urged the Muslims to reject the decadent medieval thought, and to imbibe modern scientific knowledge and outlook.
- Born in 1817 in a respectable Muslim family, he was a loyalist member of the judicial service of the Government. In 1878, he became a member of the Imperial Legislative Council and was awarded knighthood in 1888.
- He was greatly concerned with the promotion of modern education for which he worked throughout his life. In 1859, he founded a modern *madrassa* in Muradabad which was one of the first religious academies to incorporate scientific knowledge along the religious one, followed by an English High School in Ghazipur in 1863. In 1875, he founded the **Mohammedan Anglo-Oriental** (M. A. O) College at Aligarh for the spread of Western education, which later developed into the **Aligarh Muslim University**. He founded the **Scientific Society of Aligarh** modelling it on the Royal Society of England.

Aligarh Movement

The movement of Muslim awakening associated with Syed Ahmed Khan and M.A.O College came to be known as **Aligarh Movement**. It emerged as a liberal, modern wave of thinking among the Muslim intelligentsia based in M.A.O College, Aligarh, and soon **Aligarh** became an icon for religious and cultural reformation among Muslim community. Its followers primarily based their ideology on a liberal and rational interpretation of the Quran and sought to harmonise Islam with a distinct modern outlook. Thus, the movement focussed on two key areas:

- Spreading modern education among Indian Muslims without weakening their allegiance to Islam;
- Initiating Social reforms among Muslims relating to polygamy, purdah, slavery, easy divorce, women's education and widow remarriage.

- Even though he viewed the *Quran* as the most authoritative religious text for the Muslims, he wanted to reconcile the teachings of the Quran with the western scientific education in the light of contemporary rationalism and science. He wrote an interpretation on the *Quran* along the logical and scientific lines and started a magazine ***Tahzib-ul-Akhlaq*** which projected adoptable European manners.

"Religion should be adaptable with time or else it would become fossilised."

Sir Syed Ahmed Khan

"Religious tenets were not immutable."

Sir Syed Ahmed Khan

"The real greatness of the man consists in the fact that he was the first Indian muslim who felt the need of a fresh orientation of Islam and worked for it. Sir Saiyad was an ardent reformer and he wanted to reconcile modern scientific thought with religion by rationalistic interpretations and not by attacking basic belief."

Jawaharlal Nehru on Sir Syed Ahmed Khan

- He advocated for improvement in the position of women through the spread of education and condemned the patriarchal practices of *purdah*, polygamy and easy divorce system.
- He supported the British during the 1857 revolution and in 1859 published the booklet ***Asbab-e-Baghawat-e-Hind*** (The Causes of the Indian Revolt) to clear the Muslims of the charge of mutiny. He cited British ignorance and aggressive expansion policies as the chief causes of the revolt. In his another pamphlet 'The Loyal Muhammandans of India', he drew the attention of the British to the services of the Muslims families who had saved the lives of many Englishmen, women and children at the risk of their own lives.
- He **opposed** political activity by the Muslims because he felt that active participation in politics at that point of time would invite hostility of the Government towards the Muslim masses. Instead, he urged Muslims to utilise this time by concentrating on education and jobs to catch up with their Hindu counterparts. He believed, like many other leaders at that time, that Indians were not yet ready to govern themselves and that their interests would be best served by remaining loyal to the British rule. He founded the United Patriotic Association with the support of some Hindu and Muslim leaders to oppose the Congress.

- He also urged upon Muslims to remain at a distance from Congress because, in his opinion, it was a party that was solely devoted to the cause of Hindus and detrimental to Muslims and their ideologies. Unfortunately, in his enthusiasm to promote the educational and employment interests of the Muslims, he allowed himself to be used by the colonial government in its obnoxious policy of divide and rule. Sir Syed Ahmed Khan was one of the pioneers of the **Two Nation Theory** and his political visualisation guided the creation of the **All India Muslim League** in 1906.

Other Key Muslim Reform and Revival Movements

The Muslim community, like their Hindu counterparts, was equally caught by religious diktats and innumerable fatwas issued by Muslim cleric class. During the 19th century, a number of reform and revivalist movements emerged among the Muslims some of which are explained as follows:

Deoband Movement

- The Deoband Movement was established in Deoband in Saharanpur district (United Provinces) in 1866 by **Mohammad Qasim Nanotavi** and **Rashid Ahmed Gandhi** as a revivalist movement with the twin objectives of propagating **pure teachings of the *Quran*** and *Hadis* among Muslims and keeping alive the **spirit of *jihad* against the foreign rulers**.
- In contrast to the Aligarh Movement, which aimed at the welfare of Muslims through western education and British Government support, the aim of the Deoband Movement was moral and religious regeneration of the Muslim community. On the political front too, dissimilar to Aligarh Movement opposition to the Congress, the Deoband Movement **welcomed** the formation of the Indian National Congress. However, some critics attribute Deoband's support to the nationalists more to its determined opposition to Syed Ahmed Khan than to any positive philosophy.
- Later, under leadership of **Mahmud-ul-Hasan**, the movement received a new orientation as he tried to work out a synthesis between Islamic principles and nationalist aspirations. The Deoband School declared in unambiguous terms that the concept of nationality was based on the unity of all religious groups and did not contravene any Islamic principle.
- Another supporter of this new thinking in Deoband School was **Shibli Numani**, a profound scholar of Persian and Arabic who was in favour of reforming the traditional Islamic system of education by cutting down its formal studies and including the English language and European sciences. He founded the ***Nadwat-al-Ulama*** and ***Dar-ul-Uloom*** in Lucknow in 1894–96, where he tried to give effect to his educational ideas. He also held Congress in high esteem and was convinced that *the Muslims could, jointly with the Hindus, create a State in which both could live honourably and happily.*

Wahabi Movement

- This movement, centred around Patna, was an Islamic revivalist movement led by **Syed Ahmed Barelvi** (1786–1831), who was influenced by the teachings of Abdul Wahab of Arabia (1703–87) and Shah Walliullah of Delhi (1702–62). The actual name of the Wahabi movement was ***Tarikh-i-Mumammadia*** or the Path shown by Prophet Muhammad. Therefore, the movement originated as a religious movement, with the aim of purifying Islam and to condemn any change into the original Islam and return to its true spirit.
- Shah Walliullah was the first Indian Muslim leader of the 18th century to organise the Muslims around the twofold ideals of this movement:
  - Desirability of harmony among the four schools of muslim jurisprudence which had divided the Indian Muslims
  - Recognition of the role of individual conscience in religion where conflicting interpretations were derived from the *Quran* and the *Hathis*.

- Although Shah Walliullah started the movement, the actual founder of the movement in India was **Syed Ahmed Barelvi**, under whose guidance the religious movement soon assumed political proportions. Syed Ahmed called upon its followers to launch a crusade against India which was considered to be *dar-ul-Harb* (land of *kafirs*) and needed to be converted into *dar-ul-Islam* (land of Islam). Syed Ahmed had a countrywide organisation with an elaborate secret code for its working and the movement was strong at Sithana in the North-Western tribal belt and at Patna though it had its missions in Hyderabad, Madras, Bengal, Uttar Pradesh and Bombay too.
- Initially, the movement was directed against the Sikhs but after the death of Syed Ahmed Khan in the **Battle of Balakot** (1831) against the Sikhs and the British annexation of Punjab (1849), the movement was directed against the British and Patna became its new centre of activity.
- During the revolt of 1857, the Wahabi played a notable role in spreading anti-British sentiments and in 1860–70s, the Government launched a multi-pronged attack by organising a series of military operations in the Wahabi base of operations in Sithana and a number of court cases for sedition were registered against the Wahhabis and almost all the principal leaders of the movement were arrested. The **Ambala trial of 1864** and **Patna trial of 1865** were some notable trials of Wahabi Movement. Eventually, in the face of British military might, the movement soon fizzled out.
- Interestingly, the movement was responsible for introducing the term Sedition in Indian Penal Code as in 1870, British suspicious about Wahhabism and increasing Wahabi activities in the subcontinent introduced the term 'sedition' to outlaw speech that attempted to excite disaffection towards the government established by law in India.

Titu Mir's Revolt and Barasat Uprising

In Bengal, the Wahabi movement found its leader in Mir Nishar Ali or **Titu Mir** (1782–1831), a disciple of Syed Ahmed who organised the Muslim peasants of Bengal against the local Hindu zamindars and British indigo planters. He started an intense movement in the 24 Parganas, Nadia, Jessore, Rajshahi, Dhaka and Malda and declared end of British rule in extensive parts of Barasat and Basirhat and proclaimed himself as the *Badshah*. He started raising taxes from the zamindars of Taki and Gobardanga, and this is known in history as the **Barasat uprising**. The Company resented such attitude and eventually Lord William Bentick sent troops against him and Titu Mir with some of his followers died in the battle.

Ahmadiyya Movement

- The Ahmadiyya movement was launched by **Mirza Ghulam Ahmad** of Qadiyan, a small village in **Punjab** in 1889 to spread Western liberal education among Indian Muslims.
- It based itself, like the Brahmo Samaj, on the principles of universal brotherhood and tolerance of other faiths. Claiming to practice Islam in its pristine form, the movement was opposed to Islamic orthodoxy and *jihad*, that is, sacred war against non-Muslims.
- However, the Ahmadiyya movement suffered from certain controversies and mysticism because its founder proclaimed himself to be the *messiah* and prophet, as opposed to Quran view that Mohammad was the final prophet sent to guide mankind. Orthodox Muslims thus regard Ahmadiyya followers as heretical and the Ahmadiyya community faces restrictions in many countries even today.

Faraizi Movement

- This 19th-century movement was launched by **Haji Shariatullah** (1781–1837) in **East Bengal** (modern Bangladesh). The term Fairazi is derived from *farz* meaning obligatory duties enjoined by Allah. The Faraizas, therefore, aimed at enforcing the obligatory religious duties.

- Shariatullah insisted on the complete acceptance and strict observation of pure monotheism and condemned all deviations from the original doctrines as *xirk* (polytheism) and *bid'at* (sinful innovation). He stressed on justice, social equality and universal brotherhood of Muslims.
- The Faraizi movement spread with extraordinary rapidity in the districts of Dhaka, Faridpur, Bakerganj, Mymensingh, Tippera (Comilla), Chittagong and Noakhali as well as the province of Assam. The movement, however, gained the greatest momentum in those places where the Muslim peasantries were depressed under the oppressive domination of Hindu zamindars and European indigo planters.
- On the death of Haji Shariatullah in 1837, his only son **Dudu Miyan** was acclaimed head of the Faraizi movement, and it was under his leadership that the Faraizi movement assumed an agrarian character. He organised the oppressed peasantry against the oppressive landlords and transformed the Faraizi movement from being socio-religious to **socio-economic and political**.
- Dudu Miyan asked his disciples to abstain from paying taxes to the zamindar as according to him, *Allah was the owner of the land hence zamindar had no right to collect taxes*. The uniqueness of Dudu Miyan was that he had established his own law and law courts. A Munshi was appointed who exercised control over every two or three villages, adjudicated and settled civil as well as criminal cases.
- Gradually, the Faraizi movement spread all over East Bengal and for more than a quarter of century, Dudu Miyan remained a controversial figure in Eastern Bengal. The zamindars and indigo planters joined hands with the government to stop Dudu Miyan and between 1838 and 1847, he was imprisoned at least four times but had to be released owing to lack of witnesses against him. During the Revolt of 1857, he was imprisoned at Alipore Jail as a precautionary measure.
- Dudu Miyan died in Dhaka in 1862 and his son **Noah Mian** took up his task but his focus shifted from anti-British activities to religious activities. In the absence of a strong centre, the movement became sporadic and there were isolated actions against the landlords, particularly in places where the Faraizis had their traditional centres.

Some Orthodox Hindu Organisations of the 19th Century

Dharma Sabha (1830)

- An orthodox society based in Calcutta was founded by **Radhakant Deb**, the leader of Calcutta conservative Hindu society. The Dharma Sabha stood for preservation of the status quo in the socio-religious matters defending the traditional Hindu religious and social system from the sweeping wave of socio-religious reform currents.
- It sent a petition to the Privy Council in England urging repeal of the **anti-Sati regulation** and received support from many wealthy Hindu zamindars who held orthodox views and strongly opposed any interference by an alien government in the social and religious life of their community. However, it is pertinent to note that quite ironically, the society favoured promotion of Western education, even for girls.
- The chief public organ of the Dharma Sabha (Divine Society) was the Bengali newspaper ***Samachar Chandrika*** whose editor Bhawani Charan Banerjee was himself the Secretary of the Dharma Sabha.

Bharat Dharma Mahamandala (1887)

- It was a prominent all-India Hindu organisation having its headquarters in Varanasi and **Pandit Madan Mohan Malviya** was very closely associated with the Mahamandala.
- The objective behind the organisation was to bring together all leaders of the orthodox Hindu community and to work together for the preservation of *Sanatan Dharma* amidst the environment of radical teachings of the Arya Samajists, the Thesophosits and the Rama Krishna Mission. The *Sanatan Dharma Sabhas* were the offshoots of the Mahamandala, which aimed at the defence of Hinduism from critics both within the community and outside it. The organisation also sought to introduce proper management of Hindu religious institutions, open Hindu educational institutions, and others.

Sikh Reform Movements

During the 19th century, the tide of rationalist and progressive ideas swayed the Sikh community too and certain reform movements were initiated among them.

Nirankari Movement

- The first reform movement which was an initial offshoot of Sikhism in the 1840s was the Nirankari Movement, founded by **Baba Dayal Das** (1783–1855) and his disciples Darbara Singh and *Rattaji*. A man of humble origin, Baba Dayal Das preached against the rites and rituals that were creeping into Sikhism that posed a threat of assimilation of Sikhism within Hinduism.
- Emphasising on the worship of a formless God, ***Nirankar***, the movement advocated a ban on idolatry, meaningless Brahmin rituals, liquor, lying and cheating. Focussing on community morals and selfless service, Nirankaris established itself as a permanent sect among Sikhs.

Namdhari or Kuka Movement

- Like the Nirankari, this second reform movement known as the Namdhari or Kuka movement also had its origin in the north west corner of the Sikh kingdom. It is important to note that the Kuka movement was a small but important phase of the overall Namdhari movement. Initially started as a religious movement with a view of reforming Sikh religion by purging it of the degenerate features, the Kuka movement gradually turned into a political struggle against the British. Popularly known as Sian Sahib, **Bhagat Jawahar Mal** and his disciples **Bhai Balak Singh** and later **Baba Ram Singh** are believed to be leaders of this movement.
- The name *Namdharis* is derived from the fact that founder of Namdhari community, Bhai Balak Singh (1797–1862), did not believe in any religious ritual other than the repetition of God's name or *nam*, and thus for this reason members of the sect are called Namdharis. Namdharis were also called ***Kukas*** because of their peculiar style to recite the *Gurbani* (Sayings of the Gurus) in high-pitched voice called *Kook* in Punjabi.
- In the midst of national pride born of military glory and political power, the movement extolled the religious obligation for a pious and simple living and preached the spiritual way of life, shorn of tawdry customs and mannerisms. They stressed on caste abolition, inter-caste marriages, widow remarriages, abstinence from liquor, meat and drugs. Even to this day, Namdhari keep the distinct style of turban, wear only white attire, maintain their own Gurudwara, practice vegetarianism and marry at a fire altar.
- In the later years, one of the famous leaders of the movement, **Baba Ram Singh** (1816–85), gave a call to his followers for boycott of the British goods, government schools and government posts. Namdharis sought a resurgence of Sikh rule in Punjab and claimed that *it was not possible to be a Kuka and subject to British imperialism.*

Singh Sabha Movement

- One of the most effective reform cum revivalist movements which influenced the entire Sikh community and re-oriented its outlook and spirit focussing on the motivation for search for **Sikh identity** and **self-assertion**. The Singh Sabha was founded in Amritsar in 1873 with a twofold objective:
    - To make available modern Western education to the Sikhs
    - To counter the proselyting activities of Christian missionaries as well as Hindu revivalists
- Raising their voice against Hindu philosophers who had declared Sikhs as 'another sect of Hinduism', Singh Sabha established a network of **Khalsa schools** throughout Punjab and tried to re-establish rites and customs consistent with Sikh doctrine, along with rejecting everything that was against the Guru's teachings.
- The setting up of **Khalsa College** in Amritsar in 1892 helped promote *Gurmukhi*, Sikh learning and Punjabi literature.

Akali Movement or Gurdwara Reform Movement

- The Akali movement was an offshoot of the **Singh Sabha Movement**, which came into full swing in the early 1920s and aimed at bringing reform in the working and management of ***Sikh Gurdwaras***. The movement's focus was to free the Sikhs Gurdwaras from the control of corrupt *Udasi Mahants* who treated the gurdwara offerings and income as their personal income and were a loyalist and reactionary lot, supported by the government patronage.
- The British government supported these *mahants* as a counterpoise to the rising tide of nationalism among the Sikhs. The situation was so tragic that these *mahants* of the Golden Temple had issued a *hukamnama* (injunction) against the *Ghadarites*, declaring them renegades, and then honoured General Dyer, the butcher of Jallianwala Massacre with a *saropa*.
- In 1921, the Akalis launched a non-violent, non-cooperation **agitation** for freeing the gurudwara from these corrupt mahants and for handing over the gurudwara to a representative body of Sikhs. The British tried to use its repressive policies against them, but eventually it had to bow before popular demands and the **Sikh Gurdwaras Act** was passed in 1922 (amended to **Gurdwara Reform Act** in July 1925), which placed all Gurdwaras in Punjab under elected *Panthic* bodies like Shiromani Gurdwara Prabandak Committee and local Gurdwara Committees.

Reform Movement Among Parsis

The Parsis were the refugee Zoroastrians from Iran who had settled in India around 936 CE and gradually made India their home. Religious reform began among the Parsis in Mumbai in the middle of the 19th century.

Behramji Malabari (1853–1912)

- B. M. Malabari, a Parsi reformer, better known for his deep concern for the rights of women and for his staunch struggle against **child marriage**, which was largely responsible for the **Age of Consent Act** in 1891 forbidding marriage of girls below the age of 12 years. He also launched a journal called- *Mahapap Bal Vivah* (Child marriage: The Cardinal Sin) to fight against child marriage.
- In 1885, he established ***Seva Sadan***, for taking care of those women who were exploited and discarded by society.

Rehnumai Maz' Dayasan Sabha (1851)

- In 1851, the *Rehnumai Maz'dayasan Sabha* or Religious Reform Association was founded by Nairobi Furdonji, Dadabhai Naoroji, S. S. Bengalee, K. R. Cama and others. Achieving the 'regeneration of the social condition of the Parsis and the restoration of the Zoroastrian religion in its pristine purity' were the broad objectives of the Rahnumai Maz'dayasnan Sabha.
- They started a journal, ***Rast Goftar*** (Truth Teller), for the purpose of creating awareness about socio-religious reforms among the Parsis. The Sabha actively campaigned against the entrenched orthodoxy in the religious field and initiated the modernisation of Parsi social customs through breakdown of numerous religious prejudices that slowed down progress of community.
- The Sabha strongly criticised the elaborate ceremonies at marriages and funerals and opposed both infant marriage and use of astrology. It extensively worked towards spread of education, especially among girls, for uniform laws of inheritance and marriage, upliftment for social position of women in general.

Because of all these efforts, in due course of time, the Parsis became the socially most westernised section of Indian society.

Theosophical Society (1875)

Henry Steel Olcott

- The Society was first founded by a group of Westerners who were inspired by Indian philosophy and culture under the guidance of **Madame H. P. Blavatsky** (1831–91) and **Colonel H. S. Olcott** (1832–1907) in the United States in 1875. Later, in 1882, they shifted their headquarters to India in Adyar, near Madras.
- The word *theosophy* comes from two Greek words, *theos* and *sophia* which means 'God' and 'wisdom'. Thus, the main aim of the society was to attain wisdom to realise God. The Theosophists believed that the **Hindu *Upanishads*** were the storehouse of wisdom for the realisation of absolute truth and divinity. The society conducted systematic study of Hindu religious thoughts, mystic potencies of life and matter and translated and published Hindu scriptures stressing on the greatness of the ancient Hindu metaphysical doctrines. The society accepted the Hindu beliefs of *karma* and reincarnation and drew inspiration from the philosophy of the Upanishads and Vedanta.
- The key objectives of the Society were:
  - To form a nucleus of the universal brotherhood of humanity without distinction of race, creed, caste, sex or colour.
  - To encourage the study of comparative religion, philosophy and science.
  - To investigate the unexplained laws of nature and the powers latent in man.
- In 1889, **Annie Besant**, an Irish women, joined the Theosophical Society and became one of its prominent members, raising the society to new heights of glory. In 1893, Besant represented the Theosophical Society at the World Parliament of Religions in Chicago and in the same year she came to India and gradually turned a Hindu, not only in her views but also in her dress as well as social manners. Along with revival of Hindu traditions, she also focussed her energies on female education. In her book ***Wake Up India: A plea for Social Reform***, she pleaded the cause of widows remarriage and emancipation of the depressed classes.
- The greatest contribution of this society was the establishment of several educational institutions for spreading education among the masses as well as for promoting higher education. Besant opened a number of schools in Adyar and Benaras. In 1898, she laid the foundation of the Central Hindu College in Benaras where both Hindu religion and western scientific subjects were taught and which was later developed into Benaras Hindu University by **Madan Mohan Malviya** in1916.
- Although as religious revivalists, the Theosophists did not attain much success, but as a movement of Westerners glorifying Indian religious and philosophical traditions, they gave much needed self-respect to the Indians resisting foreign rule.

Southern India

One of the distinctive features of reforms initiated in south India was the presence of different caste associations and caste mobility movements of various kinds. By the turn of the century, a number of caste associations began to play a significant role in the reform movements. A notable feature of these caste associations, originally concerned with internal reforms, was that they slowly graduated into the form of **strong political forces** and were also often responsible for the social elevation of the caste concerned as observed in the case of, for example, the *Kongu Vellala Sangam* of the Gounder Caste in Tamil Nadu, the *Vokkaliga* and *Lingayat* Associations in Mysore, the *S. N. D. P. Yogam* of the *Iravas* of Kerala, and others. The caste leaders of the caste movements formed an elite, often in non-traditional careers, who stressed a common heritage of caste members and pushed forward changes in social and ritual practices.

Kandukari Veeresalingam (1848–1919)

- In the South of India, a leading light of the social reform movement in the early stages was Kandukari Veeresalingam. Unlike many of his contemporaries in the social reform movement in Calcutta or Bombay, Veeresalingam was born in a poor family; and for the major part of his life he was a school teacher by profession. Prolific in writing, he produced a large number of tracts and pamphlets on social reform in the Telugu language and is claimed to be the **father of modern Telugu prose literature**.
- His missionary zeal on issues like remarriage of widows, female education and generally on the upliftment of women and removal of social vices made him the father figure of the later generation of Andhra social reformers. It was under his supervision that the **first widow remarriage** in the whole of south India was performed at Rajahmundry, in 1881. During his lifetime, he arranged 40 widow remarriages and was even commended by Ishwar Chandra Vidyasagar for his efforts on widow remarriage. Recognising his immense service for the betterment of women, M. G. Ranade called him *Ishwar Chandra Vidyasagar of the Deccan*.
- In his seminars, he used verses from ancient scriptures to convince people that remarriage of widows was not forbidden by Hindu dharma and along with it, he equally stressed on the importance accorded to women education in ancient and medieval times, citing examples of Raja Krishna Deva Raya, whose courts had many prominent poets and scholars
- He started a monthly magazine in Telugu called *Vivekavardhini* and through his other publications like *Satihitabobhini*, he raised voice against superstition, child marriage, evils of caste system, devdasi system, bribery, and others.

Periyar E. V. Ramaswamy (1879–1973)

- Periyar E. V. Ramaswamy was a great social reformer, an iconoclast, thorough rationalist who is best known for his **Self-Respect Movement**, **Vaikom Satyagraha**, **Justice Movement** and **Dravidian Movement**.
- As a social reformer, he focussed on social, cultural and gender inequalities, and his reform agenda questioned matters of faith, gender and tradition. He urged people to be rational in their life choices and argued that women needed to be independent and not mere child bearers. In those times when birth control was a taboo, he advocated it not only for the health of women and population control but also for the liberation of women. He criticised the hypocrisy of chastity of women and argued that it should apply to both men and women alike.
- He was strongly against the system of *Devadasi* and viewed it as an example of degradation of women, attaching them to temples for the entertainment of others. He insisted that women be allowed an equal share in employment and pushed for their right to join the armed services and police force.

"We are fit to think of 'self respect' only when the notion of 'superior' and 'inferior' caste is banished from our land.

All are blessed with the tool of reasoning, but very few use it.

No other living being harms or degrades its own class, But Man, said to be a rational living being, does these evils. The differences, hatred, enmity, degradation, poverty and wickedness, now prevalent in the society ate due to lack of wisdom and rationality and not due to God or cruelty of time."

Periyar

- During the 1920s and 1930s, Periyar **combined** social and political reform and challenged the conservatism of the Congress and mainstream national movement in the Tamil region. He reconstructed the Tamil identity as an egalitarian ideal that was originally unpolluted by the caste system, and counterposed it against the Indian identity championed by the Congress. He argued that caste was imported to the Tamil region by *Aryan* Brahmins, who spoke Sanskrit and came from Northern India. Under him, the **Dravidian Movement** became a struggle against caste and an assertion of Tamil national identity. He founded the Tamil journals ***Kudiarasu***, ***Puratchi*** and ***Viduthalai*** to propagate his ideals.
- He was not happy with the Brahminical dominance in society as well as in Congress party. Subsequently in 1925, he started the '**Self-Respect Movement**' to assert the rights of non-Brahmins and to redeem the identity and self-respect of backward classes.

Self-Respect Movement

Two important aspects of Self-Respect Movement were Anti-brahmanism and Self-Respect Marriages. The movement encouraged inter-caste and inter-religious marriages, along with encouraging marriage ceremonies without a Brahmin priest or any rituals. Such marriages were known as 'Self-Respect Marriages'. Post independence, Tamil Nadu became the first state to legalise Hindu marriage without a Brahmin priest.

- Periyar's fame spread beyond the Tamil region during the **Vaikom Satyagraha** of 1924, a mass movement to secure for untouchables the right to use a road near a temple at Vaikom in Kerala. He was later referred to as ***Vaikom Veerar*** (Hero of Vaikom).
- He appealed to people to give up the caste suffix in their names, and not to mention caste. He used to give **secular names** to new born babies. He instituted inter-dining with food cooked by *dalits* in public conferences in the 1930s.
- He also focussed on the upliftment of the rural communities and advocated for the modernisation of villages by providing public facilities such as schools, libraries, roads, radio stations, bus transport and police stations. In 1938, at Tamil Nadu Women's Conference appreciating the noble services rendered by E. V. R, he was given the title ***Periyar***.
- In the 1940s, Periyar launched ***Dravidar Kazhagam***, which espoused an independent Dravida Nadu comprising Tamil, Malayalam, Telugu and Kannada speakers. The **Dravidian Linguistic Family** was

the foundation on which he based his idea of a Dravida national identity. Today, both major regional political parties of Tamil Nadu, DMK and AIADMK, proudly claim to be inheritors of Periyar's social and political vision, although they might have diluted his ideals.

Dravidian Movement

The root of the Dravidian Movement lies in the **Brahmin–non-Brahmin conflict**. The non-Brahmans started demanding their right and questioned the dominance of Brahmins in each and every sphere. Dravidian Movement was a culmination of many other major movements such as Justice Movement, Self-Respect Movement, Dravidar Kazhagam, Anti-Hindi Movement and others.

Justice Movement

- In 1916, *Zamindars* and *Maharajas* **to counter** growing clout of Brahmins in society and politics established South India Welfare Association in **Madras** Presidency. The organisation had eminent non-Brahman leaders such as **Dr T. M. Nair**, **Dr C. N. Mudaliar**, **P. Tyagaraja**, **Sir A. Ramaswamy Mudaliar** who started the English newspaper ***Justice*** for propagating its ideology and demanded separate representation for the lower castes in the legislature. With the passing of time, it gained popularity and the society came to be known as **Justice Party**. The Justice Party contested the election and for the first time in 1921, its members formed part of the cabinet in Madras Presidency.

Dravidar Kazhagam

- The Justice Party could not continue with its popularity, and in 1936, no party candidate was elected to the state legislature. After the defeat, Justice Party approached Periyar and it came under Periyar who decided to withdraw from politics and transform the Justice Party into a social organisation called ***Dravidar Kazhagam*** (Dravidian Organisation).

Anti-North Orientation and *Dravida Naidu*

- After independence, another dimension of *Anti-North Orientation* was attached to the Dravidian movement. Periyar fearing dominance of North India and Brahmin led Congress over the south, started demanding independent south nation or ***Dravida Nadu***. The movement for Dravida Nadu reached its height during the period of anti-Hindi protests. Use of Hindi as the official language was vehemently opposed by people and politicians of non–Hindi-speaking states in general and Tamil Nadu in particular. However, after the 16th Amendment (popularly known as the Anti-Secessionist Amendment), successionist tendency was declared illegal and the demand for politically independent nation faded away but still the issue of language was still not completely resolved.

Split in *Dravidar Kazhagam* and formation of DMK

- Periyar's view of demand for independent Dravida Nadu was not supported by other party leaders such as **C. N. Annadurai**. Because of certain other ideological differences, there was a split in Dravidar Kazhagam and C N Annadurai formed a new party **Dravida Munnetra Kazhagam** (Progressive Dravidian Organisation).

Formation of AIDMK

- Tamil movie star **M. G. Ramachandran** (MGR) was a key member of DMK and helped in propagation of the Dravidian ideology through his movies. However, after the death of C. N. Annadurai, the differences between MGR and party president **M Karunanidhi** reached new heights and MGR was suspended from the party. In retaliation, MGR formed a new party, **All India Anna Dravida Munnetra Kazhagam**.

Sri Narayana Guru (1856–1928)

- Sri Narayan Guru was forerunner of social renaissance in Kerala. He was an *Izhava*, a caste of toddy tappers which was considered to be an untouchable caste, though they were the single largest caste group in Kerala constituting 26 per cent of the total population. Having experienced the oppressive caste system, he devoted his life to the upliftment of the untouchables.
- **Aravipuram Movement**: To break the exclusive monopoly of Brahmins over installing images of God inside the temple, Sri Narayan Guru, in 1888, on the occasion of *Sivarathri*, installed a stone as idol of Shiva at **Aravippuram** in Kerala. It was a bold proclamation that everyone irrespective of his caste or religion has the right to realise God. The walls of the same temple carried the message – *Here is the place where all people live in fraternity without any caste distinctions and religious rivalry*. This event was of far-reaching importance in south India and inspired by its success, a number of socio-religious reform movements were launched in the South such as the **Temple Entry Movement.**

Temple Entry Movement

The Temple Entry Movement can be seen as the conclusive act of the civic rights movement for the depressed classes as access to *Savarna* temples was more a matter of civil rights than a question of freedom of worship for them. The movement which had begun with the plea of the lower caste women to wear garments, proceeded on with fresh demands such as the right to education, space in public service and freedom to use public roads, reached the high watermark with the loud clamour for temple entry.

In 1924, a beginning was made for opening the doors of the temples for the *avarnas* or the depressed classes. The Congress organised the vigorous 20-month-long Satyagraha at the Vaikom temple with the simple aim of securing the right to use the approach roads of the temple for untouchables, like the *Izhavas* and *Palayas*, who were otherwise forbidden to even pass through them. For the lower caste sections, it was a 'fight to finish' protracted struggle for their civil rights and to create a 'community of equals' around temples. Significant work was done by reformers and intellectuals like **Sri Narayan Guru**, **K. P. Kesava**, **N. Kumara Asan**, **T. K. Madhavan**, **M. K. Gandhi**, and others. in this direction. In fact, after 1924, the anti-untouchability programme became a part of the **Gandhi and constructive programme**, attracting a new popularity, and the temple entry movement used the techniques developed in the course of the nationalist struggle. As a result, in 1928, approach roads to all temples in **Travancore** were thrown open to all people.

The second Satyagraha struggle against caste-based population, to get temple open to all Hindus, was organised in 1931–32 at the **Guruvayur temple** in Malabar. The Satyagraha attracted countrywide attention and people from all over India reached Guruvayur to support the struggle. The *Zamorin* who was the trustee of the temple, refused to compromise over the issue, which led K. Kelappan, popularly known as '**Kerala Gandhi**', to start a fast unto death, which however, was withdrawn under the advice of Gandhiji. Although the agitation was unsuccessful, it created a climate in favour of temple entry. Nevertheless, very soon, in November 1936, the movement for temple entry registered its crowning victory when the Travancore government made the **temple entry proclamation** by which all temples in Travancore were thrown open to all Hindus irrespective of caste. Later, in 1938, **Madras** also followed suit when the C. Rajagopachari administration allowed the same.

> *"People call me 'The Mahatma' and I don't think I deserve it. But in my view, you have in reality become a 'The Mahatma'(great soul) by your proclamation at this young age, breaking the age old custom and throwing open the doors of the Temples to our brothers and sisters whom the hateful tradition considered as untouchables. I verily believe that when all else is forgotten, this one act of the Maharajah-the Proclamation-will be remembered by future generation with gratitude and hope that all other Hindu Princes will follow the noble example set by this far off ancient Hindu State."*
>
> *Mahatma Gandhi's open letter to the Maharaja Chithira Thirunal of* **Travancore** *on his Temple Entry Proclamation*

- In subsequent years, Sri Narayan Guru consecrated several temples in different parts of Kerala and even opened temples without any image of God. In one temple, instead of a deity, he installed a mirror for worship, revealing the truth that *God is within oneself and one should find salvation by the development of inner self.* In 1925, Guru supported the famous **Vaikom Satyagraha** movement, which demanded entry rights for lower caste people in the Vaikom and all temples in Kerala.
- He founded ***Sri Narayana Dharma Paripalana Yogam*** in 1903, an organisation which took up several issues such as
  - Right to admission to public schools
  - Recruitment to government services
  - Access to roads and entry to temples
  - Political representation.
- Over the years, the SNDP Yogam was able to bring transformative structural changes in Kerala society, leading to upward social mobility, shift in traditional distribution of power and turning the federation of 'backward castes' into a large conglomeration.
- Sri Narayan Guru popularised the belief ***One Caste***, ***One Religion and One God***, which was a clarion call to the mankind to unite, instead of breaking down in the name of caste and religion. Later, one of his disciple Saharan Ayyappan changed it into ***No Religion***, ***No Caste and No God for mankind***.

> *"Whichever the religion, it suffices if it makes a better man.*
>
> *Not Ask, Not Say and Not Think about Caste.*
>
> *Progress through Education and Strengthen through Organisation."*
>
> Sri Narayan Guru

Chembeti Sridharalu Naidu

- Naidu was one of the torch bearers of the reform movement in south India, who founded **Veda Samaj** in Madras in 1864, which was patterned along the same lines as Brahmo Samaj of Bengal. The Samaj worked for the abolition of caste distinctions and condemned the superstitions and rituals of orthodox Hinduism. It also made efforts to promote women's education and widow remarriage.
- Sridharalu Naidu translated the books of the Veda Samaj into Tamil and Telugu and renamed it as Brahmo Samaj of South India.

Ayyankali (1863–1941)

- Ayyankali belonged to *Pulaya* agricultural labour community of Kerala and was a leading labour leader and social reformer. He formed the *Sadhu Jana Paripalana Sangham* for voicing the concerns of the depressed community and creating awareness about the issues concerning them.
- Although he fought for Dalit rights in the Tranvacore kingdom, he never allowed bitterness to creep in the social fabric. **Gandhiji** was so impressed with his work that he came specially to Kerala to meet him.

Pandit K. P. Karuppan (1885–1938)

- Pandit Karuppan is fondly called the Lincoln of Kerala, and apart from being a distinguished playwright, poet and Sanskrit scholar, he was also one of the pioneers of the fight for dalit rights in Kochi kingdom. In Kochi, the *Pulayas* being considered untouchables by the upper caste Hindus were not allowed to assemble in any common place for meetings. To keep such meetings away from the eyes of the landlords, Karuppan organised ***Kayal Sammelan***, that is, meetings on boats.
- He asked the *Pulayas* to come in rowboats to the expanse of the Ernakulam backwaters and tie their boats together. There, he addressed them and charted out strategies for their emancipation by forming a sabha called the *Kochi Pulaya Maha Sabha*. This event proved to be a watershed event in **Dalit Rights Movement** in Kerala, similar to Gandhi's Dandi March.

C. Iyodhee Thass Pandithar (1845–1914)

- He was a Dalit social reformer of Tamil Nadu who ran a weekly ***Tamilan*** and reinterpreted Indian history by claiming that Dalits were originally Buddhists, but Brahmins stigmatised them as 'untouchables' because being Buddhists, they denounced caste system. He called them *Adi Dravidars* – original Dravidians and began *Dravid Buddha Sangam*. He criticised Indian National Congress as 'Brahmin Congress'. Later, Dr Ambedkar and E.V. Ramaswamy Periyar too had a similar stand.

Prominent Women Reformers

Pandita Ramabhai (1858–1922)

- Pandita Ramabhai was a truly remarkable women who pioneered women's education and rebelliously championed for women's rights and empowerment. She was born in an intellectual Brahmin family, and due to her father's progressive thinking and strong belief in female education, she received education in Sanskrit much against the established norms of that time. Her exceptional knowledge of Sanskrit texts astonished the scholars and she was awarded with the highest titles of ***Pandita*** (a wise person) and ***Sarasvati*** (Goddess of learning/wisdom) by the University of Calcutta.
- Her childhood was full of hardships; her father, mother and sister died of starvation during the famine of 1874–76. Still, she and her brother travelled around to spread awareness about female education and social reform and eventually ended up in Calcutta. After her brother's death in 1880, she married Bipen Behan Das Medhavi, a Shudra by caste, a lawyer and teacher by profession, but unfortunately her husband died the following year, after which she returned to Pune.
- At Pune, she founded the **Arya Mahila Samaj** in 1881, which is the very first Indian feminist organisation. She studied as well as taught about the issues which surround Indian women especially those involved in the Hindu traditions and spoke vehemently against the practice of child marriage and the resulting constraints on the lives of girl child who were either married young married or widowed early.
- In 1882, providing inputs to the **Hunter Commission**, she suggested that *teachers should be trained for their jobs and more women should be appointed by schools*. She also demanded that *there should be more*

women in the medical field for some treatments for women required the presence of other women. Such was the impact of her statements that these demands reached the office of Queen Victoria, and they were met in later years when **Women's Medical Movement** bore fruit under Lord Dufferin.

It is not strange, my countrymen, that my voice is small, for you have never given a women the chance to make her voice strong.

In ninety-nine cases out of a hundred, the educated men of this country are opposed to female education and the proper position of women. If they observe the slightest fault, they magnify the grain of mustard seed into a mountain, and try to ruin the character of a women.

Pandita Ramabhai's statements before The Hunter Education Commission (1882)

- Ramabai went to Britain in 1883 to start medical training and from there she travelled to the United States in 1886 to attend her cousin Anandibai Joshi's graduation ceremony, India's first woman doctor. A year later in December 1887, the American Ramabhai Association was formed in Boston by her admirers and she was able to garner financial support for residential schools for Hindu widows. She also wrote the book *The High Caste Hindu Women* highlighting Brahmanical patriarchy narrating the darkest aspects of the Hindu women, including child brides and child widows.
- In 1889, she started ***Sharda Sadan*** (Abode of wisdom), an institute for the education of young Hindu widows, where they were encouraged to be not only independent by learning variety of skills ranging from running carpentry to running a printing press but also taught science subjects like physiology and botany.
- Later, she also established the ***Mukti Mission*** in Pune as a refuge for people devastated in famine of 1889 specially for women and children who were left stranded due to the calamity and this mission is active even till this day providing education, housing, vocational trying and medical services to widows, orphans and the visually challenged. In 1919, she was awarded ***Kaiser-e-Hind*** Gold Medal for her contribution to community services.

Savitribai Phule (1831–97)

- Savitribhai Phule was a prominent social reformer, educationist and poet who played an instrumental role in women education and empowerment during the 19th century. Counted among few lite rate women of those times, Savitribai is credited for founding the first girl's school in **Pune** (Bhinde Wada) with her husband **Jyotirao Phule** and she became the first women teacher in the country too. In her lifetime, she built 18 such schools for girls in the region.

Savitribai Phule

- They later started schools for children from downtrodden castes who were regarded as untouchables. In spite of all the ostracism and humiliation hurled on her, she encouraged and inspired her students to excel in their studies. One of the essays written by a student of hers, Mukta Salve, became the face of Dalit feminism and literature during that period.
- A night school was also opened by the Pule couple in 1855 for agriculturist and labourers so that they can work in daytime and attend school at night. To check the school drop-out rate, Savitribai started

the practice of giving stipends to children for attending school. She conducted parent–teacher meetings at regular intervals to apprise the parents on the significance of education so that they send their children to school regularly.

- In 1863, the couple started a care centre called ***Balhatya Pratibandhak Griha*** to help pregnant rape victims and widows to deliver their children in a safe and secure place, thus preventing the killing of widows as well as reducing the rate of infanticide. She also started ***Mahila Seva Mandal*** with the objective of creating awareness among women regarding their rights, dignity and other social issues. To reduce the miseries of the widows, she organised and led a strike in Mumbai and Pune against the barbers to dissuade them from shaving the heads of the widows which was a norm back in those days.
- She worked in tandem with her husband in the latter's efforts in eradicating the custom of untouchability and the caste system, advocating equal rights for people of lower castes, and reform of the Hindu family life. The couple opened a well in their house for the untouchables during an era when the shadow of an untouchable was regarded as impure and people were reluctant to offer even water to the thirsty untouchables.
- She was also associated with ***Satyashodak Samaj*** founded by Jyotirao and as a part of the Samaj, the Phule couple organised marriages without a priest, without dowry and at a minimum cost. Even after the death of Jyotirao Phule in 1890, she carried forward the work of her husband.
- She was not just a social reformer but also a philosopher and a poet. Her poetry mostly revolved around nature, education and the abolition of caste system. Savitribai died of an infection while taking care of patients infected with the plague in 1897.

Other Key Reformers and Their Contributions

Reformer	Contribution/Famous Quote
• Akshay Kumar Dutt	• 'Rationalism is our only preceptor'. • cited Medical opinion against Child Marriage. • held very advanced ideas about marriage and family: courtship before marriage, partnership and equality as the basis of married life and divorce by both law and custom.
• Shiv Narain Agnihotri	• founded Deva Samaj in 1887, a society emphasising on the eternity of soul, the supremacy of the guru and ideal social behaviour such as non-accepting bribes, avoiding intoxicants and non-vegetarian food.
• Tulsi Ram alias Shiv Dayal Saheb	• started the Radhaswami movement in 1861, focussing on the belief in one supreme being, supremacy of the guru, a company of pious people (*satsang*) and a simple social life.
• Narayan Malhar Joshi	• founded Social Service League in 1911 in Bombay to secure for the masses better and reasonable conditions of life and work. • in 1921, started the All India Trade union Congress (AITUC) along with Lala Lajpat Rai and served as its general secretary. However, in 1931, he left AITUC and started All India Trade Union Federation (AITUF).
• Vitthal Ramji Shinde	• he established the Depressed Classes Mission in 1906.
• Prof D. K. Karve	• he established a widow's home in Poona in 1899. • in 1916, he opened India's first Women University in Bombay.

Reformer	Contribution/Famous Quote
• Karsondas Mulji	• to promote the cause of widow remarriage, he started *Satya Prakash* in Gujarati (1852).
• Jagannath Shankar Seth and Bhau Daji	• promoters of Girls' School in Maharashtra.

Social Reform Movements: An Analysis

The Social Reform Movements were a testimony to the intellectual and cultural turmoil of social life of the 19th century. They not only contributed towards liberation of the individual from the uncritical submission to exploitation by the priests but also helped to create a social climate for modernisation.

Factors Behind These Social Movements

- **Impact of Western thought and English Education**: The importance of Western impact on the regenerative process in the society in the 19th century is undeniable. Apart from the introduction of the idea of equality based on a conception of the individual as a repository of rights and values, this contact with the West gave to India, for the first time, a doctrine of social progress – *the belief that man can himself, through collective action, change the structure of society*. The introduction of English education helped a lot in bringing a great transformation in Indian society as the people who came in contact with the new system of education became familiar with the liberal and rational thinking of Europe and a spirit of rational enquiry was instilled into their minds.
- **Response to the challenge posed by colonial intrusion**: The presence of a colonial government on Indian soil played a complex, yet decisive, role in this crucial phase of modern Indian history. The consciousness of defeat by a foreign power gave birth to a new awareness that a vast country like India had been colonised by a handful of foreigners because of internal weaknesses within the Indian social structure and culture. Thus, what brought about the urge for reform was the need to rejuvenate the society and its institutions in the wake of the colonial conquest.
- **Criticism by Christian Missionaries and Western observers**: The Christian missionaries and Western observers often denounced Indian civilisation on account of its reliance on decadent old customs and rituals. This made the Indian intellectuals realise the need to purge the Indian society of existing social evils and practices. For instance, Indian society was under attack by both Western observers and missionaries on account of low status accorded to women. This gender question was a key issue for James Mill condemning Indian civilisation in his *The History of British India*. Therefore, the Indian intelligentsia responded to this civilisational critique by advocating and supporting reforms to improve the status of women in Indian society.
- **Indological Research**: The Indological research by scholars like William Jones, Max Muller, James Princep, Charles Wilkins, Max Muller and R. G. Bhandarkar supplied Indians with sufficient information regarding formidable cultural achievements in the past, which further resulted in the urge for achieving the old and lost glory.
- **Development of Press**: The rapid growth of newspapers in both English and Indian languages acted as an instrument for building opinion and disseminating nationalist and reformist ideas among the people.

Apart from all these factors, changes in physical infrastructure and semi-political unification of the country, rise of a middle class, personal interest of some British administrators like **Lord William Bentinck** in social welfare were certain others factors partly responsible for these Social Reform movements.

Characteristics of the Social Reform Movement

- **Emphasis on Modernisation and not Westernisation**: The Socio-Reform movements of the 19th century laid emphasis on modernisation and not westernisation. The reform movements never totally rejected tradition and never blindly imitated the Western cultural norms. Although Indian modernisers looked towards the colonial state for support and direction and their vision was being shaped by the Post-Enlightenment rationality, they could neither leave their tradition nor forget their Indian identity. Thus, the Indian modernity that was constructed was always located in the Indian cultural space.
- **Common Theme**: The issues taken by up the intellectuals involved in Socio-Religious Reforms had some common themes regarding upliftment of the position of women, abolition of infant marriage, elimination of caste distinctions, the end of social bigotry and superstitions, promotion of monogamy, widow remarriage, monotheism and spiritual worship. It should be noted that even though their target area and work differed from each other, the underlying concern of each individual intellectual was the all-round progress of Indian society based on the foundations of a reformed socio-cultural system.
- **Reformation and not Revolution**: Social Reform Movements in India did not ordinarily mean, as it did in the West, a reorganisation of the entire structure of society with a view to the alleviation of the conditions of the underprivileged; rather, it meant the infusion into the existing social structure of newer ways of life and modes of behaviour. The reform movement aimed at gradual changes and not rapid or fundamental changes since the course delineated by the reformers for transformation was evolutionary and not revolutionary.
- **Intellectual Premise**: Two important intellectual premises of the Socio-Reform movements were rationalism and religious universalism. The movements emphasised the human intellect's capacity to think and reason. The reformers not only adopted a rational approach to tradition but also tried to evaluate the socio-religious practices from the touchstone of social utility and rationality. The reformers across regions and religions strongly believed in universalism which also influenced the political and social outlook of that time. Be it Raja Rammohan Roy who considered 'different religions as national embodiments of universal theism' or Syed Ahmed Khan who echoed the idea that *all prophets had the same din (faith)*, almost all reformers stressed on development of secular ethos.
- **Urban phenomenon and Filtration theory**: Another unique aspect of the Socio-Reform movement was that social change in India was, for a very long time, initiated mostly by the upper classes and was based on the 'filtration theory' – the filtration of attitudes and modes of behaviour from the upper layers of society to the lower ones. The intellectual movement was mostly an urban phenomenon as it originated and operated mostly in urban areas.

Methods of Reform

Primarily four methods were adopted to reform the socio-religious practices:

- **Reform from Within**: The technique of reform focusses on the theory that any reform to be effective had to emerge from within the society itself. As a result, the main thrust of their efforts was to create a sense of awareness among the people. They tried to do this by publishing tracts and organising debates and discussions on various social problems. Rammohan's campaign against *Sati* and Vidyasagar's pamphlets on widow marriage are apt examples of this method.
- **Reform through Legislation:** The second method represented faith in the efficacy of legislative intervention and the advocates of this method believed that reform efforts cannot really be effective unless supported by the state. Therefore, they appealed to the government to give legislative sanction for reforms like widow remarriage, prevention of female infanticide and abolition of child marriage. Major proponents of this method were Keshab Chandra Sen in Bengal, Mahadev Govind Ranade in Maharashtra and *Veera salingam* in Andhra. However, the limitations of this method included the fact that the interest of the British

Government in social reform was linked with its own narrow politico-economic considerations and the legislative intervention was only done if it did not adversely effect its own interests and second, the role of the legislation as an instrument of change was limited because the lack of sanction of the people.

Child Marriage

Native Marriage Act/Civil Marriage Act, 1872
↓ - First legislation prohibiting child marriage but not effective as not applicable to Hindus/Muslims
Age of Consent Act, 1891
↓ - Because of the efforts of B M Malabari, a Parsi reformer, the Act forbade the marriage of girls below the age of 12 years
Sarda Act, 1930
↓ - Fixed the marriageable age of boys –18 years and girls – 14 years
Child Marriage Restraint Act, 1978
↓ - Increased the marriageable age of girls from 15 to 18 years and for boys from 18 to 21 years

- **Reform through Social Work:** The third method tried to develop the idea of supportive social work as a creed and advocated its use as a tool to disseminate ideas of reform and regeneration. *Arya Samaj* and *Ramakrishna Mission* are the best examples of this type of reform.
- **Reform through the Symbol of Change:** The fourth method was an attempt to create symbols of change through non-conformist individual activity. This was, however, limited to the *Derozians* or Young Bengal who represented a radical stream within the reform movement and manifested individual social rebellion through symbols of change like wining and dining in forbidden meat. They did pose an intellectual challenge to the religious and social orthodoxy of Hinduism, yet they never succeeded in organising any social movement in support of their proposed reforms as they failed to draw upon the cultural traditions of Indian society and their radical nature was taken in positive stride by many.

Dynamics of Socio-Reform Movements and Religion

The social life of both Hindus and Muslims was strongly influenced by the religious tenents. *The Hindu meets his religion at every turn, in eating, drinking, moving, sitting, standing, he is to adhere to sacred rules, to depart from which is sin and impiety*. Similar was the state of affairs of Muslims who were also equally tied to the chain of religion. Religion was the dominant ideology of the times, and it was not possible to undertake any social action without coming to grips with it. Thus, given the interconnection between religious beliefs and social practice, religious reformation was a necessary pre-requisite for social reform since the practices based on faith cannot be challenged without bringing faith itself into question. They attempted to make use of religious ideas to bring about changes in social institutions and practices. For instance, **Raja Rammohan Roy** demonstrated that *sati* had no religious sanction, **Ishwar Chandra Vidyasagar** took up his pen in defence of widow remarriage only after being convinced about its scriptural support and Swami **Dayanand** based his anti-casteism on Vedic authority.

However, it should be carefully noted that the perspectives on reform were not always influenced by religious considerations. A rational and secular outlook was very much evident in posing an alternative to prevalent social practices. For instance, in advocating widow marriage and opposing polygamy and child marriage, **Akshay Kumar Dutt** did not base his arguments on religious sanction or whether they existed in the past or not, instead he based his rationale on their effects on society and cited medical opinion against child marriage. Furthermore, in their attempt to *rationalise* the aspects related to religion, these reformers sought to distinguish the essential aspects of religion from the non-essential ones, to separate the pristine religion from the subsequent accretions.

In the religious sphere, the Socio-Reform movement sought to remove idolatry, polytheism and priestly monopoly of religious knowledge and to simplify religious rituals. All of these aspects had social implications too as it contributed to the liberation of the individual from the conformity born out of fear and the simplification of rituals made worship a more intense personal experience free from mediation of any intermediary. Although religious reformation was a major concern of these movements, none of them were exclusively religious in character. Strongly humanist in inspiration, the idea of other worldliness and salvation were not a part of their agenda, but instead their focus was on worldly existence. For instance, **Vivekananda** emphasised on the secular use of religion and used spirituality to take cognisance of the material conditions of human existence.

Socio-Reform Movements Versus Bhakti Movement

One of the unique features of the Social Reform Movement of the 19th century as compared to the Bhakti movements of the early years was that the Socio-Reform Movement was primarily based on positive social action as opposed to more of an isolated *sannyasin* renunciative type of Bhakti culture. The Socio-Reform movement appeal was more rational and focussed on social salvation as compared to the Bhakti movement's emotional appeal which centred more on individual salvation. For all its spiritual egalitarianism, the Bhakti movement failed to cure the diseased condition of the Indian social system, which was later addressed by the Social Reform Movement of the 19th century.

Contribution of the Socio-Reform Movements

In the evolution of modern India, the reform movements of the 19th century have made very significant contributions. They stood for the democratisation of society, removal of superstition and abhorrent customs, spread of enlightenment and the development of a rational and modern outlook.

- **Creating Awareness about Social and Religious Evils**: The reform movements attacked a number of social and religious evils such as polytheism, idolatry, animism, female infanticide, child marriage, Sati system, and others, which negated the development of individuality. These movements also subjected to strong criticism, the authority of religious leaders who induced the habit of conformity against irrational customs and traditions and claimed exclusive monopoly over the interpretation of the religious texts. As a redressal against this practice, the reform movements helped in the translation of religious texts into vernacular languages and laid emphasis on an individual's right to interpret the scriptures, making the rituals simplified and worship more of a personal experience.
- **Revival of Indigenous Cultural Personality**: By weeding out corrupt elements, religious beliefs and practices, the reformers enabled their followers to meet the official taunt that *their religions and society were decadent and inferior*. It gave the rising middle classes the much needed cultural roots to cling to, and served the purpose of reducing the sense of humiliation and inferiority which the conquest by a foreign power had produced. The cultural ideological struggle, represented by the socio-reform movements, proved to be an important instrument in the evolution of national consciousness.

Providing Social Climate for Modernisation: Promoting a modern, worldly, secular and rational outlook was another contribution. The reform movements sought to create a favourable social climate for modernisation and to some extent, these movements ended India's cultural and intellectual isolation from the rest of the world. Indian society was nourished by imbibing the best of the outer and inner world.

Key Achievements in certain social areas: The Social Reform Movements did achieve progress in terms of emancipation of women and extension of equal rights to them apart from removal of caste rigidities. These movements not only appealed to the moral and ethical values while opposing caste system but also highlighted the divisive character of the caste system. Ranade, Jyotiba Phule, Narayana Guru and Vivekanand denounced the existing system of caste in no uncertain terms.

Weaknesses and Limitations of the Socio-Reform Movements

Although the 19th-century reform movements aimed at ameliorating the social, educational and moral conditions, they too suffered from several weaknesses and limitations:

- **Confined to a narrow social space**: These movements were confined to a narrow social space, limited only to a small elite group. None of them could reach the vast masses of the peasantry and the urban poor who generally remained unaffected. For instance, in Bengal, the reform movement involved only a small number of Western educated elite who were known by the general term *bhadralok* (gentlefolk), similarly in western India, the members of Prarthana Samaj were the English educated *Chitpavan* and *Saraswat Brahmans*, some Gujarati merchants only and the Aligarh movement with those of the Muslim upper classes. With the exception of Arya Samaj, which had a broader influence, on the whole, the reform movements were thus limited to upper castes and classes.
- **More reliance on legislations for imposing reform**: Lacking in a broad social base, the reformers of the early 19th century exhibited more faith in the benevolent nature of colonial rule and relied more on legislation for imposing reform from above. In addition, being mainly reform from above, these reforms remained mostly on paper and a reformist social consciousness at the grassroots level was never as trained. For instance, even after the passage of the **Hindu Widows Remarriage Act of 1856**, not many widows were remarried, as for that social consent and acceptability was more required, which could not be generated by the power of the colonial state.
- **Overemphasis on 'glorified past'**: The third limitation primarily present in Revivalist Movements, which later became a major negative factor, was the overemphasis on the 'glorified past'. The appeal to past greatness, the tendency to look backward and to rely on scriptural authority which at times apart from encouraging mysticism and fostering pseudo scientific thinking also created false pride. But, most of all, these tendencies tended to divide Hindus, Muslims, Sikhs and Parsis as also high caste Hindus from low caste Hindus. In addition, the portrayal of medieval period of Indian history as an era of decadence was not only historically incorrect but also proved to be socially and politically harmful for the nation as unknowingly it created the notion of separate interests and resulted in growth of communal consciousness.
- **Colonial mirroring of the reforms**: Indian reformers' position in a significant way mirrored the colonial mind. The dominant colonial position of the time was that religion was the basis of Indian society and this religion was encoded in the scriptures. As the colonial rulers gave supreme importance to scriptures, most Indian reformers too, as well as their detractors, referred to ancient religious texts to argue their respective cases. The brutality or the irrationality of the custom, or the plight of women, whom the reform was intended for, were of lesser concerns in a debate, which was more focussed on the position that whether the custom was supported by scriptures or not. For instance, the whole debate over *Sati* was grounded in scriptures, and the colonial government decided to prohibit it only when it was convinced that the custom does not enjoy the sanction in the ancient texts. However, due regard should be given to the fact that scriptures were an easy methodology to sell the reform to both cautious colonial government and to a reticent Hindu society reluctant to accept change.
- **Inability to perceive the exploitative nature of the British rule**: Another limitation lay in the reformers' perception of the nature of the British rule and its role towards India. They believed quite erroneously that British rule was Godsent and would lead India to the path of modernity. Because

their model of the desirable Indian society was like that of 19th-century Britain, they felt that the British rule was necessary to make India Britain-like. Although they perceived the socio-religious aspects of Indian society very accurate, its political aspect, that of a basically exploitative British rule, was missed by the reformers.

Nevertheless, the Socio-Reform Movement was instrumental in bringing about the initial intellectual and cultural break which made a new vision of a modern India possible, and subsequently this vision got incorporated in the Indian National Movement.

Social Reform and Nationalism

The Socio-Reform Movement directly or indirectly resulted in nation-building and in a way acted as a prelude to the nationalism. It was not an isolated phenomenon but a phenomenon having wider political, economic and national ramifications. Social Reform and Nationalism are **irrevocably linked** because the cultural ideological struggle represented by the Socio-Religious Movements was an integral part of the evolving national consciousness, which apart from initiating the intellectual and cultural break also served as a crucial part of the resistance against colonial cultural and ideological hegemony.

Initially, the socio-religious reform movement and the political movement, although interacting, constituted separate and clearly distinguishable traditions **but** gradually, they came together to lay the intellectual foundations for the emergence of nationalism. At the onset, the Social Reform Movement was marked by the efforts on the part of individual intellectuals such as Raja Rammohan Roy, to incorporate awareness about social evils but slowly there also emerged the growth of a new desire for unity between the scattered and culturally diverse social groups. With the building up of the infrastructure of social mobility, a rapidly growing system of communication, the expansion of educational facilities and the increase in the number and circulation of newspapers, no longer was social protest confined to individual revolts against established patterns of conduct, but a new set of group loyalties began to sweep over the various sections of the educated populace.

In addition, with the turn of the century, social reform, specifically the revivalist movements, resulted in regeneration of the traditional spirit of the nation – a regeneration founded on religious revival and cultural xenophobia. It was, thus, the first glimmer of national consciousness on the horizon of the Indian intellectual canvas, but not all these progressive nationalist tendencies were able to outgrow the sectarian and obscurantist outlook which in the long run had its own costs.

Consequent Rebellions

While the **urban elites** of the Indian society silenced the moralistic critiques of the West by initiating religious and social rcform to change their socicty from within, thc **rural society**, especially the traditional elites and the peasantry, responded to British rule in an entirely different way. Losing out as a result of colonial impositions, they resorted to resistance and defiance, leading to a series of unsuccessful peasant and tribal uprisings.

Peasant and Tribal Uprisings

The processes that aided the consolidation of the Raj, its methods of governance and social and intellectual constructs which developed during this period laid the ground for colonial dominance as well as resistance to it. The changing economic relations in the colonial period attributed to various peasant grievances and often their anguish found expression in different rebellions. It is **important to note** that even in pre-colonial India, peasant revolts against the Mughal rulers and their officials was not uncommon but the tendency became even more pervasive as the colonial regime established itself and introduced a series of revenue experiments with the sole purpose of maximising revenue income. With the breakdown in the pre-colonial Mughal subsistence compromise, the peasants were left with no other option but to take to protest and revolt as they were not even left with enough provision for their own subsistence.

The **tribals** had their own special reasons to be aggrieved since the imposition of British rule resulted in loss of their autonomous domains of power, freedom and culture. The extension of the British land revenue system fully destroyed the autonomy of the tribal world and they were drawn into the larger economic nexus of non-tribal oppressive agents – **the zamindars** and **the moneylenders**. The new forest regulations encroached on their natural rights and the regular intrusion by outsiders – the ***suds*** and ***dikus*** threatened their control over local resources which further drove them to violent outbursts. Oppression and extortion by policemen and other petty officials further aggravated the tribals who often felt so oppressed that they had no alternative but to fight.

Some of the **major reasons** behind various peasant and tribal rebellions are as follows:

- **Colonial policies and Revenue Reforms**: In the late 18th and early 19th centuries, the colonial policies and revenue reforms of the Company's government had fundamentally altered and affected Indian rural society. The **high revenue demands** of the Company's government coupled with the **harsh attitude** of the tax-collecting officials provoked the peasants to rise in revolt.
    - The colonial rule resulted in *revitalisation of landlordism* as rightly pointed by **Ranajit Guha**. Because of changes in property relations, the peasants lost their occupancy rights and were reduced to a very low status of tenants-at-will, share croppers and landless labourers, while their lands, crops and cattle passed into the hands of landlords, traders, moneylenders and rich peasants. **Creation of property right in land** and consequently of a **land market** resulted in the replacement of **customary production relationship** with **contract** resulting in eviction of the tenants in the case of non-payment of increased revenue demand.
    - The development of **land market** resulted in a growing rate of land alienation as the landlords were more interested in extraction rather than in capitalist enterprise, as they too were under constant pressure of the sunset laws and the burden of high revenue demand of the state. The high land revenue demand particularly in the context of cash payments of land revenue increased the peasants, need for credit and gradually the **moneylenders** got complete control of the rural economy and society.
    - In case of the **tribals community**, the colonial administration ended their relative isolation and brought them fully within the ambit of colonialism as well as Christian missionaries. The colonial government transformed their centuries-old relationship of dependence with the forest by usurping their forest lands and placing restrictions on access to forest products, forest lands and village common lands. The tribals were no longer allowed to practise shifting cultivation and instead a new system of land revenue and taxation of tribal products was introduced. This complete disruption of the old agrarian order of the tribal communities provided a common factor for all tribal uprisings.
    - Colonial policies further accentuated the differences and created a sharper polarisation between those who owned lands; had access to the courts to defend themselves and their property and those whose customary rights got undermined. Even though social differentiation was not a new feature, this accentuation and polarisation of differentiation laid ground for future rebellions.
- **Transformation of the Indian economy to enhance Company's profits**: Colonial endeavour to draw Indian economy into the world capitalist system and attempts to develop capitalist agriculture also had a devastating impact on agrarian relations and was another reason behind peasant's grievances. Certain changes were brought in Indian economy to suit the Company's needs and to enhance the Company's profits:

- Commercial crops were encouraged in place of food crops with the obvious idea of providing raw material for British industries. This proved hazardous for the peasants who were forced to grow commercial crops (like indigo and cotton) instead of food grains, even in years of scarcity. The economic decline of the peasantry is clearly reflected in 12 major and numerous minor famines from 1770 to 1857.
- Local industries were suppressed to make way for the British manufactured goods, and as a result of the imposition of arbitrary free trade in India along with a levy of discriminatory tariffs against Indian goods in Britain, the local handicraft industry was completely ruined, resulting in pauperisation of millions of artisans. With the disappearance of their traditional patrons and buyers – the princes, chieftains and zamindars – and the destruction of indigenous industry, a large section of the artisans were thrown out of employment, who, to sustain themselves, turned to agriculture. The pressure on land increased but the land revenue and agrarian policy of the government allowed little scope for the improvement of Indian agriculture, eventually resulting in more distress for the peasants.

- **Exploitative character of the British administration**: While the British economic policy led to pauperisation and impoverishment of the Indian peasantry, the British administration turned a deaf ear to the peasants' grievances. The landlords, coercive authority to oppress the peasants was greatly expanded by British law, which was indirectly supported by newly established **courts** and lengthy judicial processes that mostly safeguarded the interest of the government and its collaborators – the landlords, the merchants and the moneylenders. There were regular instances of flogging, torture and jailing of the cultivators for arrears of land revenue. Thus, being the prey of colonial exploitation and being deprived of justice from the colonial administration, the peasants took up arms to protect themselves.
- **No check on the unholy nexus of the official, the landlord and the moneylender**: The high revenue demand and growing burden of taxation increased the peasants, need for credit and made them an easy prey to the moneylenders, revenue collectors and merchants. Gradually, moneylending got associated with a complete control of the rural economy and greatly enhanced the power of the moneylenders and the merchants over rural society. Growing indebtedness led to the eviction from land, which subsequently passed on to the hands of the non-cultivating classes. Thus, as summed by **Ranjit Guha**, *the landlords, money lenders and the state came to constitute a composite apparatus of dominance over the peasant*.
  - The situation in tribal society was no different as with the triumvirate of moneylenders, merchants and revenue farmers, the tribals were reduced to the position of agricultural labourers and share croppers and brought within the vortex of the colonial economy and exploitation. All this created discontent and resentment among both peasants and tribals which at various junctures took the form of rebellion.
- **Role of scholarly and priestly class and foreign character of the British rule**: The scholarly and priestly classes were also active in inciting rebellion against the colonial rule. One of the crucial reasons behind the attitude of these classes was the fact that with the coming of the British and the ruin of the traditional landed and bureaucratic elites, the financial patronage extended to these scholars, religious preachers, priests and men of arts and literature came to an end, seriously disrupting their way of life and eventually turned most of them against the foreign rule. In addition, the very foreign character of British rule inspired efforts to expel the foreigner from their lands.

Now, we would discuss in brief some of the important peasant and tribal uprisings. It should be duly noted that whatever may be the immediate cause of each uprising, by and large, all of these protest movements were largely due to a **shared experience of oppression**, specifically colonial oppression. These rebellions were not always directly anti-colonial movements, but were all related to the policies and conditions of colonial rule.

The Sanyasi Rebellion (1763–1800)

- Displaced peasants and demobilised soldiers of Bengal led by wandering bands of **armed monks** (*Sanyasis* and *Fakirs*[6]) and dispossessed small zamindars were the first to rise up against Company's rule in the famous Sanyasi rebellion that rocked northern Bengal and adjacent areas of Bihar between 1763 and 1800.
- Although the Sanyasis and Fakirs were religious mendicants, originally they were peasants who were affected by the Company's high revenue demands and commercial monopoly, provoking them to take up arms against the Company's rule. The **Bengal famine of 1770** brought a large number of sufferer peasants and rural poor into the ranks of these rebellious bands of Sanyasis and Fakirs, and the number of participants rose up to 50,000 at the height of insurgency.
- These *Sanyasi-Fakirs* travelled from place to place and adopting '**the guerilla technique**' made sudden attacks on the store houses of food crops and property of the local landlords and government officials. At times, they looted the local government treasuries and even established an independent government for some time at Bogra and Mymensingh. Encounter between the *Sanyasis-Fakirs* and the British forces became a regular feature all over Bengal and Bihar till 1800 and the British had to use its full force to suppress the rebels.
- One noticeable feature of these insurrections was the **equal participation of Hindus and Muslims** and the remarkable philosophical affinity between the two religious orders. Some of the important leaders of these movements were Manju Shah, Musa Shah, Bhawani Pathak and Debi Chaudhurani.
- The rebellion was the theme of famous novel ***Anand Math*** written by Bankim Chandra Chatterjee.

The Rangpur Rebellion (1783)

- In certain instances, peasants themselves on their own initiative offered resistance to the British rule. The Rangpur rebellion, in the northern districts of Bengal, is an apt example of such opposition.
- The establishment of the British rule over Bengal after 1757 along with various land revenue experiments in Bengal to extract as much as possible from peasants brought unbearable hardship to the poor peasants. Harsh attitude of the revenue contractors further added to their woes. Rangpur and Dinajpur were two such districts of Bengal where the revenue contractors like **Debi Singh** and **Gangagobind Singh** unleashed a reign of terror among the poor peasants who apart from paying high revenue demand also had to pay for illegal cesses. Debi Singh and his men used to beat and flog the peasants, burn their houses and destroy their crops not sparing even innocent women and children.
- The peasants initially appealed to the Company officials to redress their grievances but when their appeal for justice went unheeded, they took the law in their own hands. In this rebellion too, both Hindus and Muslim peasants fought side by side. They organised themselves, elected their own leader (**Dirjinarain**), raised a huge army, equipped themselves with primitive bows, arrows, swords and attacked the local *cutchery* (a court of law), looted grain stores of local agents of the contractors and government officials and forcibly released prisoners.
- The rebels sought to legitimise their movement by forming their own government and invoking what **Sugata Bose** has called *the symbols of the pre-colonial state system* that is, calling their leader *Nawab* and levying 'insurrection charges' to meet the expenses of the rebellion.
- On Debi Singh's appeal, the Company's government under Warren Hastings sent troops and brutally suppressed the revolt. However, owing to the peasants' pressure, some reforms in the revenue farming system were introduced.

[6] The Dasnami Sanyasis, known for their martial tradition, were involved in landholding, moneylending and trade in raw silk, broadcloth, copper and spices, while the Madari Fakirs traced their origin from the Sufi order initiated by Sha-i-Madar and enjoyed rent-free tenures.

The Uprising of the Bhils (1813)

- The Bhils were mostly concentrated in the hill ranges of Khandesh in the previous Maratha territory. British occupation of this region in 1818 brought in the outsiders and accompanying dislocations in their community life. Moreover, it was believed that **Trimbakji**, rebel minister of Baji Rao II, instigated the Bhils against the British occupation of Khandesh.
- There was a general insurrection in 1819 and the Bhils in several small groups ravaged the plains but it was crushed by the British military forces, and although some conciliatory measures were taken to pacify them, the situation remain unsettled until 1831 when the Ramosi leader **Umami Raje** of Purandar was finally captured and executed.

The Rebellion at Mysore (1830–31)

- The final overthrow of Tipu Sultan and reinstatement of the old ruling dynasty 'Wodeyar' brought in enhanced revenue demands, the burden of which ultimately fell on the poor cultivators. Rampant corruption and extortion by local officials further aggravated their desperate situation, provoking them to rise in an open revolt in the province of Nagar, one of the four divisions of Mysore.
- Peasants from other provinces too joined the rebellious peasants of Nagar and defied the authority of the Mysore rulers. The rebels elected their own leader **Sardar Malla**, the son of a common *ryot* of *Kremsi*. However, subsequently, they had to bow down to the British troops and ultimately the administration of the country passed into the hands of the British.

The Kol Uprising (1831–32)

- One of the major tribal revolts, the Kol Uprising, took place in the Chota Nagpur and Singbhum region of Bihar and Orissa. In these areas, the Kols had for centuries enjoyed independent power under their chiefs. They successfully resisted all attempts made by the Raja of Chota Nagpur and Mayurbhanjto to subdue them. However, with the British penetration into this area and the attempt to establish British law and order over the jurisdiction of the Kol Chiefs, the power of the hereditary tribal chiefs was threatened.
- In addition, the Raja of Chota Nagpur started evicting tribal peasants by farming out land to outsiders for higher rents. This settlement of non-tribals and constant transfer of land to traders and moneylenders – generally referred to as ***suds*** or **outsiders** – created great resentment among the tribal people and led to popular uprisings against the outsiders in the tribal area.
- The rebellion quickly spread over to Ranchi, Hazaribagh, Palamau and Manbhum. The forms of rebellion consisted of attacks on the properties of the outsiders, but not on their lives. Thus, although plunder and arson were the chief modes of peasant protest, the rate of killings was negligible. Unfortunately, the insurrection was ruthlessly suppressed by the British army.

The Faraizi Disturbances (1838–51)

- The Faraizi sect, founded by **Haji Shariatullah of Faridpur**, originated as a movement fuelled by the grievances of rack-rented and evicted peasants against landlords and British rulers. Gradually, under **Dudu Miyan**, the son of the founder of the sect, it progressed as a religious sect with an egalitarian ideology. His simple way of teaching and belief that *all men are equal and land belongs to god and no one has right to levy tax on it* appealed to the common peasants.

- The Faraizis set up parallel administration in some parts of Eastern Bengal and established local courts as alternatives to British judicial institutions. They protected cultivators from zamindars' excesses and motivated peasants not to pay taxes to the zamindars. Violent clashes with the zamindars and planters occurred throughout the 1840s and 1850s. There was a temporary lull in the movement after Dudu Miyan's death in 1862, but then it was renewed again at a different scale by his successor **Naya Mian** in the 1870s (the details had already been discussed above in the Socio-Reform Movement column).

The Mappila Uprisings (1836–54)

- Among the various peasant uprisings that posed serious challenge to the colonial rule, the **Mappila** uprisings of Malabar occupy a prominent place. The Moplahs or Mappilas were the descendants of the Arab traders who had settled in this region and had married local Nair and Tiyar women. Majority of them were cultivating tenants, landless labourers, petty traders and fishermen.
- When the British occupied Malabar in 1792, the land relations were revamped due to the consequent changes brought by the British in the land revenue administration. Earlier the traditional system stipulated an equal sharing of the net produce of the land by the ***janmi*** (holder of the *janmam* tenure), the ***Kanamdar*** or *Kanakkaran* (holder of *kanam* tenure) and the cultivator. However, with the introduction of new British system, the traditional arrangement was upset as now the *janmi* was recognised as absolute owners of land, with right to evict tenants, which did not exist earlier, and the other two categories were reduced to the status of tenants and lease holders. However, there was an important **religious touch** to *Moplah* uprising because the majority of the *janmi* were **high caste Hindus**, while the peasants were the **Muslim *Moplahs*.**
- Apart from that, over-assessment, illegal taxes and a pro-landlord attitude of the judiciary, police and the government officials further made the Moplahs rebel against the British and the Hindu landlords. Interestingly, in case of the Moplah rebellion, religion and economic grievances **intermingled** to produce open resistance as the Mosques became the centres of mobilisation, while the traditional Muslim intellectuals helped in strengthening the solidarity of Moplahs and the targets were the Hindu *janmi*, their temples and the British officials who came to their rescue.
- Between 1836 and 1854, there were about 22 uprisings in Malabar and the repressive measures adopted by British could restore peace for only 20 years, but then the Moplahs rose again in 1870 and the events followed a similar trajectory.

The Khonds Uprising (1837–56)

- In the early 1850s, there were some tribal movements in **Orissa** covering the Ghumsar and Baud areas. The Khonds retaliated under **Chakra Bisoi** against the British efforts to put an end to the Khonds' practice of human sacrifice known as ***meriah*** first through persuasion and later through force. However, the Khonds could also not match the superior arms of the British and the rebellion ended in failure though Chakra Bisoi could never be arrested and nothing was heard of him after October 1856.

The Santhal Rebellion (1855–56)

- The most effective tribal movement of this period was the Santhal *hool* (rebellion). The Santhals lived primarily in the area between Bhagalpur and Rajmahal, known as ***Daman-i-koh*** comprising the districts of Cuttack, Birbhum, Bankura, Murshidabad, Dumka, Bhagalpur and Purnea.
- They were gradually driven to a desperate situation as tribal lands were leased out to non-Santhal zamindars and moneylenders and along with this, they had to face the continuous oppression of the local police and European officers engaged in railroad construction. This gradual penetration by

outsiders – called ***dikus*** – brought misery and oppression for the simple living Santhals and forced them into action to take possession of their lost territory.

> *"Zamindars, the police, there venue and court all have exercised a combined system of extortions, oppressive exactions, forcible dispossession of property, abuse and personal violence and a variety of petty tyrannies upon the timid, and yielding Santhals. Usurious interest on loans of money ranging from 50 to 500 percent; false measures at the haut (weekly market) and the market; willful and uncharitable trespass by the rich by means of their untethered cattle, tattoos (small ponies), ponies and men elephants, on the growing crops of the poorer race; and such like illegalities have been prevalent."*
>
> The social conditions which drove them to insurrection was described by a contemporary writer in the Calcutta Review of 1856

- Initial protests of the Santhals were in the form of robbery and looting of Zamindars and moneylenders' houses. However, violent suppression of these activities and harassment of Santhals at the hands of police and local officials made them more violent.
- In July 1855, when their ultimatum to the zamindars and the government went unheeded, several thousand Santhals, armed with their traditional weapons of bows, arrows, axes, assembled under the leadership of two brothers, **Sido** and **Kanhu**, who were believed to have received blessings from the *Thakur* (God) to put an end to the ongoing oppression of the Santhals and to restore 'the good old days', started an open insurrection against the unholy trinity of their oppressors – the *zamindars*, the *mahajans* and the government.
- The insurrection spread rapidly in the whole Santhal Pargana, and Santhal rebels were joined by large numbers of low caste non-Santhals peasants too resulting in virtual collapse of the Company's rule and spread of panic in the government circles. This invited brutal counter-insurgency measures, the army was mobilised and Santhal villages were burnt one after another with vengeance. According to one estimate, out of 30,000 to 50,000 rebels, 15,000 to 20,000 were killed before the insurrection was finally suppressed.
- The heroic struggle of the Santhals ultimately failed but henceforth, the British government became more cautious about them and the Santhal inhabited areas were constituted into a separate administrative unit called the *Santhal Parganas*, recognising the distinctiveness of their tribal culture and identity.

Other Key Peasant and Tribal Uprisings

Peasant/Tribal Uprising	Causes	Significant Leader/Significant Consequence
	Bengal and Eastern India	
• Chuar Uprising (1760s–1820s) Midnapore District, Bengal	Famine, enhanced land revenue, oppressive demands and economic distress provoked Chuarab original tribesmen to take up arms.	Leader: Durjan Singh, a displaced zamindar.
• Ho and Munda Uprising(1820s–40s) Chota Nagpur Plateau and Singhbhum Region	Oppressive demands and economic distress provoked the tribesmen to challenge company's forces several times.	Leader: Raja Parhat

Peasant/Tribal Uprising	Causes	Significant Leader/Significant Consequence
• Ahoms Revolt (1828) Assam	Continued occupation of Assam by the British despite their pledge of withdrawal after the First Anglo-Burmese War (1824–26).	Leader: Gomdhar Konwar. Conciliatory policy adopted by the British and part of the kingdom was restored to the Assamese King.
• Khasi Uprising (1829–33)	Occupation of Khasi Hills by the British and consequently presence of large number of outsiders in these regions.	Leader: Tirath Singh, Nunklow Ruler.
• Singphos Rebellion (1830s and 1840s) Assam	Rose in rebellion against British oppressive policies many times during the 1830s and 1840s.	• Early 1830: which was suppressed after 3 months. • 1839: killed the British political agent. • 1843: Rebels attacked British garrison under their leader Nirang Phidu and killed several soldiers.
• Savara Rebellion (1856–57), Parliakamedi, Orissa	Against British interference in their cultural practices.	Leader: Radhakrishna Dandasena.
	Western India	
• Ramosi Risings (1822–39) Western Ghats	The hill tribes of Western Ghats, popularly known as Ramosis, had not reconciled to British rule and administration. Disturbances occurred again in 1839 over deposition and Banishment of Raja Pratap Singh of Satara.	Leader: Chittur Singh.
• The Cutch Rebellion (1819–31) Kutch and Kathiawar	Interference by British in the internal feuds of the Cutch when they defeated and deposed the Cutch ruler Rao Bharamal in favour of his infant and stationing of British Resident who acted as the de facto ruler.	Leader: Different Cutch Chiefs.
• Waghera Risings (1818–19) Oka Mandal	Resentment against the foreign rule coupled with the exactions of the Gaekwad of Baroda supported by the British Government.	
• Kolis Risings (1820s–1840s) Gujarat	Resentment against the Company's rule and administration which resulted in widespread unemployment and destruction of their forts.	
• Surat Salt Agitation (1844–48) Gujarat	Salt duty was raised from 50p to Re, resulting in widespread outrage.	Government was compelled to withdraw the additional salt levy.

Peasant/Tribal Uprising	Causes	Significant Leader/Significant Consequence
• Kolhapur and Savantvadi Revolts (1844)	Administrative reorganisation in Kolhapur resulted in disbanding of the Gadkaris, a hereditary military class which garrisoned Maratha forts, leading to a simmering discontent between them.	
	Southern India	
• Revolt of the Raja of Vizianagaram (1794)	Annexation of Raja's estate by the British along with certain outrageous demands such as tribute of 3 lakh and disbanding of Raja's troops,	Raja died in the battle but owing to popular pressure, the company restored the estate to the dead Raja's son and even reduced the demand for tribute and presents.
• Insurrection of Dewan Velu Thampi (1805), Travancore	Imposition of harsh conditions and high-handedness on the State of Travancore, after it agreed to a Subsidiary Alliance system.	Leader: Dewan Velu Thampi, the prime minister of Travancore State.
• Poligars Revolt (1801–06) Dindigal and Malabar Region	Against the oppressive land revenue system.	

Restorative Rebellions

During the first century of British rule, there were, first of all, a series of uprisings which Kathleen Gough has called '**Restorative rebellions**' as they aimed at restoring the old order and were started by deposed *rajas* and *nawabs* or their descendants, disaffected local rulers, Mughal officials, dispossessed *zamindars*, landlords and ***poligars*** (landed military magnates in south India), ex-retainers and officials of the conquered Indian states. In most cases, they were **supported by** the local peasants, ruined artisans and demobilised soldiers who were marginalised by the changes introduced by the British in the economy, administration and land revenue system and, hence, wanted to reinstate the old agrarian relations. Some instances of restorative rebellions were:

- The Revolt of Raja Chait Singh and other zamindars of Awadh in 1778–81
- Revolt of the Nawab of Awadh, **Vizier Ali** (1799)
- Rebellion of the Bundel Rajput chieftains (1842)
- Revolt of Pazhassi Raja in the Malabar region (1796–1805)
- Insurrection of Dewan Velu Thampi, the prime minister of Travancore State (1805).

Peasants and Tribal Uprisings: An analysis

These peasant and tribal uprisings of the early colonial period have been looked at in different ways. While on one hand, the **British administration** considered them as problems of law and order and the rebels as primitive savages resisting civilisation, on the other hand, the **nationalists** tried to project them as the 'pre-history of modern nationalism' ignoring certain other facets of the oppressed people's struggle. There was also considerable debate about the character of these movements. Some historians like **D. N. Dhanagare** regarded peasant rebellions as pre-political because of their lack of organisation, programme and ideology, while others like **Ranjit Guha** argued that *there was nothing in the militant movements of the rural masses that was not political*.

It is therefore necessary to understand the nature, characteristics and domain of peasant and tribalaction in its own terms. Equally important is to note that, although these rebellions took myriad forms, they often bore the same character as they represented common oppressed conditions though separated in time and space.

Nature and Characteristics of These Movements

- **Certain level of political and social consciousness**: Some features of the peasant and tribal protest movements demonstrate a certain level of political and social consciousness among them. As explained by **Ranjit Guha**, they exhibited, first of all, a clear awareness of the relations of power in rural society and a determination to overturn that structure of authority. The rebels were quite conscious of the political sources of oppression, and this was demonstrated in their targets of attack – the zamindars' houses, their grain stocks, the moneylenders, the merchants and ultimately the state machinery of the British, which came forward to protect these local agents of oppression. A clear identification of the enemies was matched by an equally clear marking of the friends. For instance, in the **Kol insurrection of 1832**, Kols of different regions rose in revolt simultaneously and the fellow tribals were not attacked in a clear recognition of who their allies were.

However, it should be carefully noted that the peasant rebellions before 1857 differed a lot from modern nationalism as the spread of the rebellion was limited to rebels, own perception of space, ethnic boundary and time. For instance, the ***Santhals***, battle was limited for their 'fatherland' and there was an urge for restoration of that imagined golden past.

- **Leadership, mobilisation and solidarity among different oppressed classes**: The leadership of these movements mostly came from the ranks of the rebels themselves who belonged to the same cultural world of the peasants and tribals whom they led and thus were in a better position to articulate their protest.

Interestingly, this is quite in contrast to the times of the national movement where leaders from various sections of upper strata consciously, on certain ideological premises, made an intervention into the peasant and tribal movements. In some movements, the leaders were the holy men who referred to the loss of a moral world and thus expressed the anxieties of the peasants in religious idioms and promised a new millennium to be achieved through supernatural means. For instance, the **Faraizi rebellion** was led by the holy men who sought to purify Islam by purging all un-Islamic beliefs and practices and mobilised the oppressed peasants around an egalitarian ideology by stressing on the fact that all land was god's land and levying taxes on it was therefore against divine law.

The mobilisation took place mostly along the community lines and in many cases, religion, ethnic ties and traditions played a positive role in mobilising the peasants and strengthening their solidarity. For example, when the **Dhangar Kols of Sonepur** were the first to rise in that region, they were promptly given support by the **Larka Kols of Singhbhum** where no disturbances had yet taken place. In addition, it is worth noting that initially the rebellion was triggered by certain local issues, but in the course of the development of the movement, its ambit was broadened to include issues beyond the immediate grievances. For example, the **Moplah rebellion** in the Malabar region started as a struggle against the Hindu landlords but ended up as a protest against British rule itself.

- **Restorative character of some movements**: One of the characters inherent in most of the uprisings was the 'restorative' character of some of these movements and attempts to look back into the past when life was much better. This did not necessarily mean that the protest movements were backward looking, rather this reflected a peasant utopia having hopes of 'imagined golden past', an ideal construct of fair and just society having no exploitation or oppression.

- **Role of religion in peasants and tribal uprisings**: Religion played an important role in many peasant and tribal movements as apart from providing an ideology for rebellion, legitimacy to their movements, it also provided a discursive field within which the oppressed understood colonial rule and conceptualised resistance. Religion at times defined their ideology of protest, and in many cases, it also provided the bond of unity among the poorer classes. The holy leaders referred to the loss of a moral world and thus expressed the anxieties of the peasants in religious idioms promising them a new millennium to be achieved through supernatural means. The rebellion was therefore divinely ordained and legitimised through reference to a higher authority. This provided both an ideology as well as motivation for peasant action. For instance, in the **Santhal rebellion**, the charismatic leaders Sido and Kanhu were thought to be endowed with magical power and their empowering was considered as an act of God.

Was It Communal?

There have been efforts to paint certain rebellions as communal because the rebels belonged to a particular religion and the dominant classes belonged to another religion, but making such a generalised assumption is definitely not in scholarly interest. Due respect should be given to the fact that protest of the oppressed also often involves redefinition of the relationship of the oppressed to the language, culture and religion of the dominant classes. This may take the form of denial of the convention of respect and submission in speech or the destruction of places of worship or of symbols of domination or oppression. Thus, protests took myriad forms in many spheres, from everyday life to organised insurgency. For instance, in the **Moplah rebellion**, religion forged a bond between the poorer sections of the peasantry to create grounds for a fight against landlord oppression.

Different from crime and social banditry: At times, these rebellions were labelled as acts of crime and social banditry, but it would be an injustice to adopt such an approach. There is no doubt that in the first century of British rule in India, violent armed rebellions, social banditry or general lawlessness were quite endemic but what needs to be stressed is that the reasons were quite different. The idea of hitting at their exploiters was conditioned by the rationality of setting things right and represented a kind of their own form of elemental protest against the oppressed system which otherwise paid no heed to their justified demands. In fact, many dispossessed peasants, especially individuals and small groups who found that collective action was not possible, preferred robbery and dacoity than to succumb to starvation and social degradation. Often an insurgency was preceded by the rise in the rate of rural crimes. For instance, in 1854, a year before the Santhal rebellion, a number of dacoities were committed against the local moneylenders. The Santhal leaders later justified them on moral grounds to the British court saying that their complaints against the moneylenders were never heeded by the officials.

In addition, in spite of the attempt of the officials to portray the rebellions as crime, the open and public character of rebellions and rebels' mode of action tell an entirely different story. For instance, **Santhals** gave ample warning in advance to the villages they attacked, while in most rebellions not all outsiders were attacked as enemies. Often there was no violence against the non-tribal poor, who worked in tribal villages in supportive economic roles like *telis, gwalas, lohars*, carpenters, potters, and others, and even where attacks were made, they were mostly on the properties of the outsiders but not their lives. Consequently these acts had a popular sanction and on occasions were collective acts.

Reasons for Failure of Rebellions

- These continuous peasant and tribal rebellions were, though massive in their totality, wholly **local in their spread** and **isolated** from each other. They were the result of local causes and grievances, and were also localised in their effects.
- Socially, economically and politically, the semi-feudal leaders of these rebellions were **backward looking** and **traditional in outlook**. The resistance offered was centuries old in form and ideological content aimed at restoring the earlier forms of rule and social relations, devoid of any modern vision. The rebels in fact did not have a future plan beyond the restoration of the old order and thus their resistance represented no societal alternative and was scattered, sporadic and disunited which itself was in capable of fending or overthrowing foreign rule.
- While many of these movements drew strength from ethnic or religious ties, that fact itself became a constraint. Their isolation, due to **failure to develop a higher order of integrating consciousness**, limited the impact of these movements at the national level.
- The warfare between the rebels and the British armed forces was totally unequal. On one side were drilled regiments armed with latest weapons and on the other were men and women fighting in roving bands armed with primitive weapons such as stones, axes, spears and bows and arrows, believing in the magical powers of their commanders who often claimed that they possessed powers to make the enemies' bullets ineffective.

Thus, the isolated nature of these episodes of rebellion, besides the technical superiority of the **British** armed forces and the law and order machinery supporting the established social order, ensured British success.

Significance of These Rebellions

Nevertheless, as the first expression of the protest of the oppressed in the colonial period, these movements are highly significant and, in spite of their limited objective and narrow world view, the rebels definitely **exposed the unpopular character** of colonial rule. In addition, the historical significance of these rebellions lies in that they established strong and valuable local traditions of resistance to British rule. The Indian people were to draw inspiration from these traditions in the later struggles for freedom. One such great struggle of freedom, **The Revolt of 1857**, we will be studying in our next chapter.

Previous Year's Questions (Prelims)

1. Satya Shodhak Samaj organised which of the following? (2016)
   (a) A movement for upliftment of tribals in Bihar.
   (b) A temple entry movement in Gujarat.
   (c) An anti-caste movement in Maharashtra.
   (d) A peasant movement in Punjab.
2. Consider the following: (2016)
   Keshab Chandra Sen is associated with the establishment of which of the above?
   1. Calcutta Unitarian Committee
   2. Tabernacle of New Dispensation
   3. Indian Reform Association

   Select the correct answer using the code given below.
   (a) 1 and 3 only
   (b) 2 and 3 only
   (c) 3 only
   (d) 1, 2 and 3
3. Annie Besant was (2013)
   1. responsible for starting the Home Rule Movement.
   2. the founder of the Theosophical Society.

3. once the President of the Indian National Congress.

Select the correct answer using the codes given below:

(a) 1 only
(b) 2 and 3 only
(c) 1 and 3 only
(d) 1, 2 and 3

4. Which of the following statement(s) is/are correct regarding Bramho Samaj? (2012)

1. It opposed idolatry.
2. It denied the need for a priestly class for interpreting the religious texts.
3. It popularised the doctrine that the Vedas are infallible.

Select the correct answer using the codes given below:

(a) 1 only
(b) 1 and 2 only
(c) 3 only
(d) 1, 2 and 3

5. Which of the following provided a common factor for tribal insurrection in India in the 19th century? (2011)

(a) Introduction of a new system of land revenue and taxation of tribal products.
(b) Influence of foreign religious missionaries in tribal areas.
(c) Rise of a large number of moneylenders, traders and revenue farmers as middlemen in tribal areas.
(d) The complete disruption of the old agrarian order of the tribal communities.

6. In collaboration with David Hare and Alexander Duff, who out of the following established Hindu College at Calcutta? (2009)

(a) Henry Louis Vivian Derozio
(b) Ishwar Chandra Vidyasagar
(c) Keshab Chandra Sen
(d) Raja Rammohan Roy

7. Who among the following wrote the book *Babuvivah*? (2007)

(a) Raja Rammohan Roy
(b) Ishwar Chandra Vidyasagar
(c) Pandita Ramabai
(d) RabindranathTagore

8. Who among the following started the newspaper *Shome Prakash*? (2007)

(a) Dayanand Saraswati
(b) Ishwar Chandra Vidyasagar
(c) Raja Ram Mohan Roy
(d) Surendranath Banerjee

9. Lectures from Colombo to Almora is based on the experiences of which of the following? (2006)

(a) Veer Savarkar
(b) Annie Besant
(c) Ramakrishna Paramhans
(d) Swami Vivekananda

10. Which one of the following revolts was made famous by Bankim Chandra Chatterjee in his novel *Anand Math*? (2006)

(a) Bhil Uprising
(b) Rangpur and Dinapur Uprising
(c) Bishnupur and Birbhum rebellion
(d) Sannyasin rebellion

11. Who among the following was a proponent of Fabianism as a movement? (2005)

(a) Annie Besant
(b) Michael Madhusudan Dutt
(c) A. O. Hume
(d) R. Palme Dutt

12. Consider the following statements: (2005)

1. Ishwar Chandra Vidyasagar founded the Bethune school at Calcutta with the main aim of encouraging education for women.
2. Bankim Chandra Chattopadhyay was the first graduate of the Calcutta University.
3. Keshav Chandra Sen's campaign against Sati led to the enactment of a law to ban Sati by the then Governor General.

Which of the following statements given above is/are correct?

(a) 1 only
(b) 1 and 2
(c) 2 and 3
(d) 1, 2 and 3

13. Which of the following mountain tribes did the British first come into contact with after the grant of Diwani in the year 1765? (2002)
    (a) Garos
    (b) Khasis
    (c) Kukis
    (d) Tipperahs

14. Consider the following statements: (2001)
    1. Arya Samaj was founded in 1835.
    2. Lala Lajpat Rai opposed the appeal of Arya Samaj to the authority of Vedas in support of its social reform programmes.
    3. Under Keshab Chandra Sen, the Brahmo Samaj campaigned for women's education.
    4. Vinobha Bhave founded the Sarvodaya Samaj to work among refugees.

    Which of the following statements given above is/are correct?
    (a) 1 and 2
    (b) 2 and 3
    (c) 2 and 4
    (d) 3 and 4

15. His principal forte was social and religious reform. He relied upon legislation to do away with social ills and worked unceasingly for the eradication of child marriage, the purdah system.... To encourage consideration of social problems on a National Social Conference, which for many years met for its annual sessions alongside the Indian National Congress? (1996)
    The reference in this passage is to:
    (a) Ishwar Chandra Vidyasagar
    (b) Behramji Merwanji Malabari
    (c) Mahadev Govind Ranade
    (d) B R Ambedkar

16. Who among the following was the leader of some anti-British revolts in Sambalpur? (1994)
    (a) Utirat Singh
    (b) Surender Sai
    (c) Kattabomman
    (d) Syed Ahmed Barelvi

Previous Year's Answers (Prelims)

1. (c)	2. (b)	3. (c)	4. (b)	5. (c)	6. (d)	7. (b)	8. (b)
9. (d)	10. (d)	11. (a)	12. (b)	13. (b)	14. (d)	15. (c)	16. (b)

The Revolt of 1857

4

In the previous chapter, we discussed about the various peasant and tribal rebellions that initiated traditions of resistance to British rule. However, it was the great Revolt of 1857 that posed for the first time, a serious challenge to the English supremacy and emerged as one of the most powerful act of resistance to the British rule. The Revolt of 1857, though was unsuccessful in eliminating foreign rule, yet it is considered as an important **watershed event** in the history of the Indian freedom struggle. It is primarily because of two reasons: firstly, it was historic in the sense that it ended the rule of the East India Company and transferred the power to govern to the British Crown and secondly, it paved the way for the emergence of the modern national movement as it sowed the seeds of Indian nationalism in the subconscious minds of the Indian people and served as a perennial source of inspiration to them.

In this chapter, we will be discussing in detail about the various causes pertaining to the Revolt of 1857, chronology of the Revolt, various reasons behind its failure, the nature of the Revolt and its significance and also about the different changes brought in the administration of the country after the Revolt of 1857.

Causes of the Revolt

C. A. Bayly has once rightly remarked that '*The Indian Rebellion of 1857 was not one movement … it was many*'. Thus, no single causal explanation can be provided for the Revolt of 1857 as multiple factors were at play. The revolt which started as sepoy mutiny was gradually joined by an aggrieved rural society of north India and therefore its causes need to be searched not only in the reasons responsible for disaffection of the army but also in the long-drawn process of fundamental social and economic changes that upset the peasant community during the first century of the Company's rule.

Disaffection of the Army

In the earlier years of mid-18th century, the Company's government used to respect the traditions and customs of the indigenous communities and deliberately encouraged the high caste identity of the army. Under instructions from Warren Hastings, the army administration used to scrupulously respect the sepoy's caste rules, dietary and travel restrictions. However, **from 1820s,** a more universalised military culture in the name of **army reforms** was introduced and some of the caste privileges and pecuniary benefits were curtailed. These reforms thus created discontent among the sepoys, and the disaffection of the Indian troops found articulate expressions from time to time in form of different mutinies.

Important Mutinies of Pre-1857 Era

- The mutiny of the sepoys in Bengal in 1764.
- The Vellore mutiny of 1806 when due to the replacement of the turban by a leather cockade caused the sepoys to raise a banner of revolt unfurling the flag of the ruler of Mysore.
- The mutiny of the sepoys of the 47th Native Infantry in 1824, when the sepoys were ordered to go to Burma. Since, to the religious Hindu, crossing the sea meant loss of caste, they refused to comply. The regiment was thus disbanded and those who led the opposition were hanged.
- The revolt of the Grenadier Company in Assam in 1825.
- The mutiny of regiment at Sholapur in 1838.
- The mutinies of the 34th Native Infantry in 1844.
- The mutinies of the 22nd Native Infantry in 1849.
- The mutinies of the 66th Native Infantry in 1850.
- The mutinies of the 37th Native Infantry in 1852.

The Indian sepoys were also not very happy with their **service conditions** and **emoluments**. As compared to their British counterpart, they were having very low salary, were made to feel a subordinate at every step and were discriminated against racially and in matters of promotion and privileges. To make the matters further worse, in 1856, a set of new service rules under General Service Enlistment Act were introduced, which abolished their extra allowance for service outside their own regions, thus creating further alienation among them.

"Though he might give the signs of a military genius of Hyder, he knew that he could never attain the pay of an English subaltern and that the rank to which he might attain, after 30 years of faithful service, would not protect him from the insolent dictation of an ensign fresh from England."

British Historian T.R. Holmes

"The officers and men have not been friends but strangers to one another. The sepoy is esteemed an inferior creature. He is sworn at. He is treated roughly. He is spoken as a 'nigger'. He is addressed as a 'suar' or 'pig' ... The younger men ... treat him as an inferior animal."

Contemporary English Observer

The discontent of the sepoys was not limited to military matters alone; they felt the general disenchantment with and opposition to British rule. As Bipin Chandra has rightly remarked '*The sepoy, in fact, was a peasant in uniform, whose consciousness was not divorced from that of the rural population and since every agricultural family in Oudh, perhaps without exception, . . . sends one of its members into the British army*', thus, whatever happened there was of immediate concern to the sepoy. The sepoy was thus anxious about the declining conditions of the peasantry due to the summary settlements in Awadh and due to the confiscation of lands attached to charitable institutions. It is thus no surprise that the revolt was preceded by about 14,000 petitions from the sepoys about the hardships relating to the revenue system. In fact, a proclamation issued by the Delhi rebels clearly reflected the sepoy's awareness of the misery brought about by British rule. The annexation of Awadh in 1856 further shook the loyalty of the sepoys and had a very adverse effect on the morale of the Bengal army, as about 75,000 of them were recruited from this region.

> *"Your army is derived from the peasantry of the country who have rights and if those rights are infringed upon, you will no longer have to depend on the fidelity of the army . . . If you infringe the institutions of the people of India, that army will sympathise with them; for they are part of the population, and in every infringement you may make upon the rights of the individuals, you infringe upon the rights of men who are either themselves in the army or upon their sons, their fathers or their relations."*
>
> Sir James Outram, a military officer cautioning Lord Dalhousie about the precarious situation

Also, to the discontent with service conditions and general disenchantment with British rule, was added another constant fear that the British were determined to **convert them into Christianity**. The official–missionary nexus[1], the rumours about mixing cow and pig bone dust with flour – all enhanced the sepoys growing disaffection with the Government and prepared the backdrop for the mutiny of 1857. Finally, the controversy about the **cartridge for Enfield rifles** provided the occasion for the simmering discontent to come out in the open and acted as a spark to set the fire. The cartridges of the new Enfield rifle had to be bitten off before loading and the grease was reportedly made of cow and pig fat, which confirmed the sepoy's old suspicion that British will destroy their religion and caste and convert them into Christianity.

Political Causes

The Company's policies of aggrandisement such as '**Effective Control**' and '**Subsidiary Alliance**' accompanied by broken pledges and promises created a group of disgruntled feudal lords who had every reason to join the ranks of the rebels. Lord Dalhousie's '**Doctrine of Lapse**'[2] further intensified their grievances as a lot of kingdoms were annexed on its pretext. For instance, Satara (1848), Nagpur, Sambalpur and Baghpat (1850), Udaipur (1852) and Jhansi (1853) were taken over in quick succession. Finally, in February 1856, Awadh was annexed on grounds of mis-governance and the king was deported to Calcutta. All these annexations did not merely affect the rulers and their family, but the entire aristocracy attached to them. In many cases, these deposed princes offered leadership to the rebels in their respective regions, thereby in the process also providing legitimacy to the revolt. For instance, Nana Sahib, the adopted son of Peshwa Baji Rao II, who was refused pension by the Company assumed leadership in Kanpur, Begum Hazrat Mahal in Lucknow, Khan Bahadur Khan in Rohilkhand and Rani Lakshmibai in Jhansi.

Economic Causes

One of the another key causes of the popular discontent was the economic exploitation of the country by the British who had completely destructed the traditional economic fabric and thereby, the **civil rebellion** which accompanied the revolt of the sepoys had a broad social base, embracing all sections of society, be it the territorial magnates such as *zamindars* and *taluqdars* or impoverished classes such as peasants, artisans, handicraftsmen, shopkeepers and religious mendicants and priests.

- **Exploitation of the Peasantry**

  The discontent and disaffection manifested in the form of revolts against the British Government were not confined to the ruling chiefs and royal families alone. Really hard hit by the **inordinately high revenue**

[1] The proselytising activities of chaplains often maintained on the Company's expenses were interpreted by Indian sepoys as interference in their religious affairs.

[2] The policy of Doctrine of Lapse interfered in the traditional system of inheritance and de-recognised the adopted sons of the deceased princes, thereby annexing the territory to British.

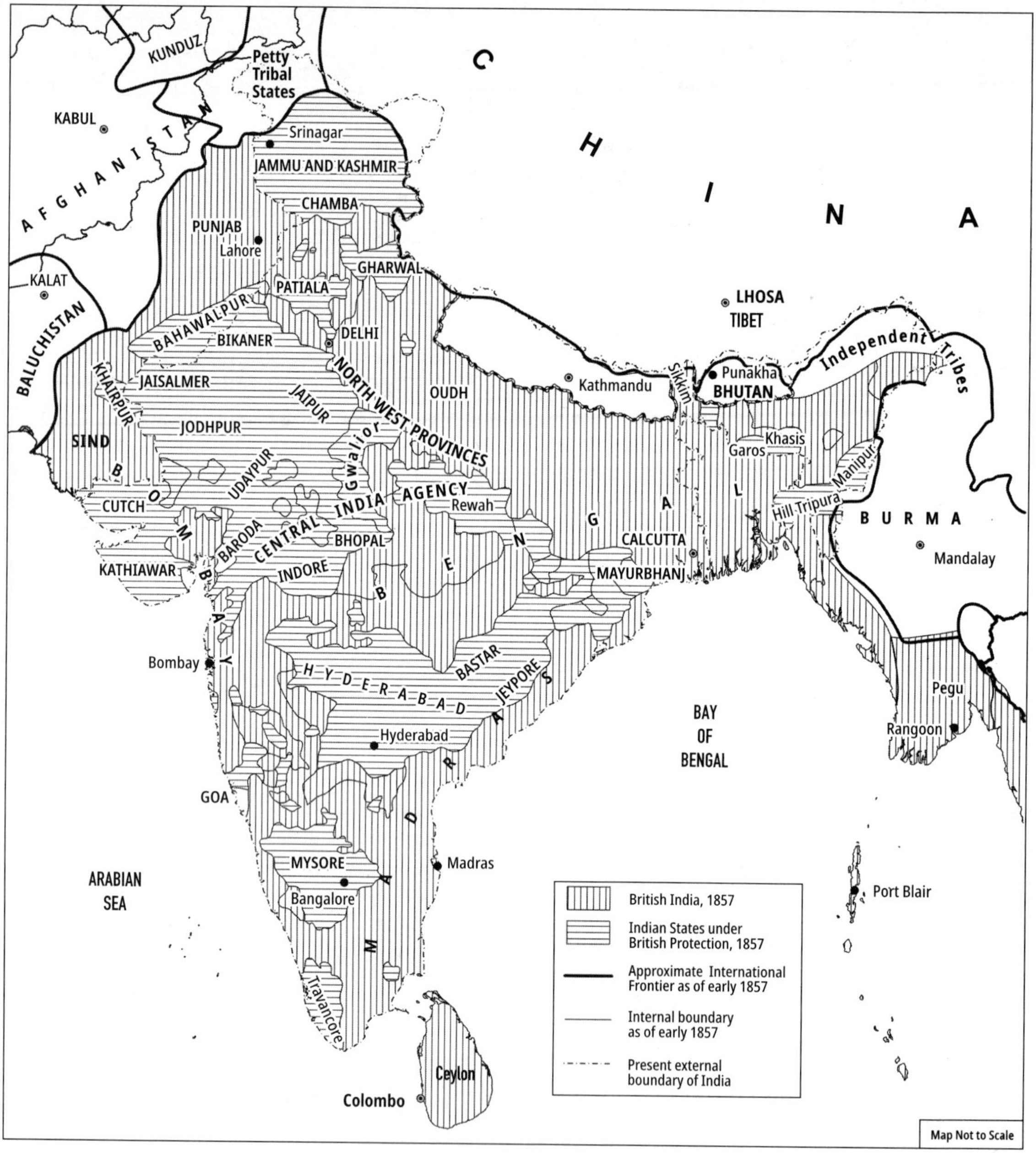

British Territories in India in 1857

demands of the state, the peasants had no other option but to join the rebellion since it was the owner-cultivators, rather than the rent-receiving landlords, who felt the burden of over-assessment more severely than others. For instance, in Awadh, though the revenue assessment overall was reduced, yet there were pockets of over-assessment, and here the *taluqdars* losses resulted in a '*talukdar–peasant complementarity*' of interests. The same situation existed in the north-western provinces too, where even though the village proprietors were supposed to be the beneficiaries of the new land revenue system[3], they were not satisfied due to high land revenue demand.

Also, where the agriculture was insecure, the high revenue demands inevitably drove the peasants into debt and eventually dispossession, the process of which was further aided by the new civil courts and the legal system. The increased public sales of landed rights can clearly serve as the index of this extraordinary pressure. In 1853, for example, in the north-western provinces alone, 110,000 acres of land were sold in auction and, therefore, when the revolt started, the *baniya* and the *mahajan* and their properties became the natural targets of attack by the rioting peasants.

> *"Thus the sale of land not merely uprooted the ordinary people from their small holdings but also destroyed the gentry of the country, and both the orders being the victims of the operations of British civil law were united in the revolutionary epoch of 1857–58 in a common effort to recover what they had lost."*
>
> S. B. Chaudhuri

- **Grievances of the traditional landed aristocracy, that is, *taluqdars* and *zamindars***

The other elements of rural society that joined the ranks of the rebels were the territorial magnates, that is, the *zamindars* and *taluqdars*. The annexation of Awadh was followed by a summary settlement in 1856, which like *Mahalwari* Settlement of north-western provinces, was made with the actual occupiers of the land or village co-parcenaries hereby disregarding all other proprietary rights which eventually resulted in the dispossession of a number of powerful *taluqdars*, who lost about half of their estates were disarmed and their forts demolished. For instance, in Awadh alone, about 21,000 *taluqdars* estates were confiscated and suddenly they found themselves *without a source of income, unable to work, ashamed to beg, condemned to penury*.

All this was a big blow to their prestige as they lost earlier enjoyed considerable status and power in local society, and were reduced to the ranks of humblest of the tenants. Therefore Awadh, as well as the North Western Provinces where too many *taluqdars* had lately been dispossessed, became the hotbed of discontent of the landed aristocrats. These dispossessed *taluqdars*, thus smarting under the humiliation heaped on them, seized the opportunity presented by the Revolt of 1857 to oppose the British and regain what they had lost. Interestingly, as the Revolt of 1857 progressed, these *taluqdars* did not face any resistance from their erstwhile tenants, and thus they quickly moved into the villages they had recently lost and laid claims to their earlier proprietary rights.

> *"Bound by ties of kinship and feudal loyalty, the villagers were happy to acknowledge the claims of their lords and joined hands against their common enemy, the British."*
>
> Thomas Metcalf

[3] The Mahalwari Settlement.

- **Deprivation of the Artisans, Handicraftsmen and other cultural personnel**

  It was not merely the peasantry and landed aristocracy that got alienated from the British rule, the artisans and handicraftsmen also felt oppressed as the annexation of Indian states by the Company cut off their **major source of patronage** and deprived them of their source of income. Along with this, the British policy of promotion of English goods and discouraging of Indian handicrafts further meant misery for them. Since, the destruction of Indian handicrafts was not accompanied by the development of modem industries, the highly skilled Indian craftsmen were left with no option but to look for alternate sources of employment that hardly existed.

> *"It was the British intruder who broke up the Indian handloom and destroyed the spinning-wheel. England began with depriving the Indian cottons from the European market; it then introduced twist into Hindustan and in the end inundated the very mother country of cotton with cottons."*
>
> Karl Marx, 1853

Furthermore, due to the annexation of the native states, those sections of the Indian society which derived their sustenance from cultural and religious pursuits like poets, dramatists, writers, musicians, religious preachers, *pandits* and *maulavis*, and others were also adversely affected and hence played an important role in spreading the hatred against the foreign rule.

- **Alienation of Middle and Upper Classes**

  The middle and upper classes of Indian society, particularly in the north, were hard hit by their exclusion from the well paid higher posts in the administration which were now taken mainly by the British. Even the most brilliant of Indians were made to serve at only subordinate positions which led them to join the revolt.

Social and Religious Causes

One of the most common trait that pervaded all the layers of Indian society especially rural at the time of Revolt was the factor of suspicion of British rule. British rule was mostly disliked by many and was perceived as a major threat to their religion. The social reforms of the earlier period such as abolition of *Sati*, support to widow remarriage and women's education indirectly created this suspicious environment and the proselytising efforts of Christian missionaries directly added fuel to the fire.

The attempts at socio-religious reform aroused considerable suspicion, resentment and opposition in the minds of both orthodox Hindus and Muslims who feared that the British through social legislation were trying to destroy their religion and culture. Moreover, they also believed that social legislation was undertaken to aid the missionaries in their quest for evangelisation. These fears were further compounded by certain government acts and legislations such as Government's decision to tax mosque and temple lands and making laws such as the Religious Disabilities Act, 1856, which modified Hindu customs[4], thereby arraying both orthodox religious Hindus and Muslims against the British who felt that their caste and religion was under serious threat. It is equally pertinent to note that since both Hindus and the Muslims felt they were equally affected by the British rule, therefore, **Hindu–Muslim unity** was all along maintained during the revolt.

[4] It declared that a change of religion will not debar a son from inheriting the property of his 'heathen' father thus enabling a convert to Christianity to inherit ancestral property.

"Like the sepoys of Jhansi, rebels everywhere fought for their 'deen [faith] and dharam [religion]'—to restore a moral order, which had been polluted by an intruding foreign rule."

Tapti Roy

"It is well known that in these days all the English have entertained these evil designs—first, to destroy the religion of the whole Hindustani Army, and then to make the people by compulsion Christians. Therefore, we, solely on account of our religion, have combined with the people, and have not spared alive one infidel, and have re-established the Delhi dynasty on these terms."

A proclamation issued at Delhi expressing the cultural concern of the rebels.

The Alien Nature of British Rule and Its Foreign Character

Another crucial reason behind the unpopularity of the British was the alien nature of their rule. The British remained perpetual foreigners in the country and unlike foreign conquerors before them, they never mixed with the Indian people and treated even the upper class Indians with contempt. They had a feeling of racial superiority and arrogance which at most occasions found expression in their demeaning behaviour towards Indians.

"Even natives of the highest rank never came into the presence of officials but with an inward fear and trembling."

Sir Syed Ahmad Khan

Moreover, it was pretty clear to Indians that the British had not come to settle in India or to make it their home and thus, their main aim was to enrich themselves at the cost of Indians and therefore, almost all Indians even those who proved loyalist to the British at some point of time had a vague sort of anti British feeling.

"Those who had grown rich under British rule showed hidden delight at British reverses."

Munshi Mohan Lal of Delhi, who remained loyal to British during the Revolt.

"In no instance is a friendly glance directed to the white man's carriage.. ..Oh! that language of the eye! Who can doubt! Who can misinterpret it? It is by it alone that I have learnt our race is not even feared at times by many and that by all it is disliked."

English Observer W. H. Russell

"People looked upon the British as foreign trespassers."

Another loyalist, Muinuddin Hasan Khan

> *"At length, the Hindustanees fell into the habit of thinking that all the laws were passed with a view to degrade and ruin them, and to deprive them and their fellows of their religion. Such acts as were repugnant to native customs and character, whether in themselves good or bad, increased this suspicion. At last came the time when all men looked upon the English Government as slow poison, a rope of sand, a treacherous flame of fire. They learned to think that if today they escaped from the hands of Government, tomorrow they would fall into them; or that even if they escaped on tomorrow, the third day would see their ruin … The people wished for a change in the Government, and rejoiced heartily at the idea of British rule being superseded by another."*
>
> Sir Syed Ahmed Khan summing up the widespread and intense dislike of Indian people against British in his Causes of the Indian Mutiny

Coincidence of Certain Events

The period of the growth of discontent among the people coincided with certain other events which shattered the general belief in the invincibility of the British. The British army suffered major reverses in the First Afghan War (1838–42), Punjab Wars (1845–49), and the Crimean Wars (1854–56) which provided the much needed confidence to the rebels that, with determined fighting, they too can defeat the British army.

Chronology of Events[5]

Crucial Date	Remark
February 1857	• **19th Native Infantry** at Berhampur refused to use the newly introduced Enfield Rifle.
29 March 1857	• At Barrackpur, a young sepoy of the 34th Native Infantry, **Mangal Pandey**, refused to use the greased cartridges and fired at a European officer. His comrades refused to arrest him when ordered by their European superiors, who were then apprehended, court martialed and hanged in early April while his regiment was disbanded. • But, the disaffection of the sepoys could not be contained and in the following days, a chain reaction was set in motion with incidents of disobedience, incendiarism and arson being reported from the army cantonments in Ambala, Lucknow and Meerut, until finally, the Meerut sepoys started the revolt on 10 May.
3 May 1857	• 7th Awadh Regiment defied officers and was disbanded.
10 May 1857	• The sepoys of the 3rd Cavalry regiment broke out in open rebellion, shot their officers, rescued their arrested fellow sepoys who had previously refused to accept the new cartridge and headed towards Delhi.

[5]It is pertinent to note that, wherever revolt broke out, the pattern of attack was the same everywhere. The government treasury was plundered, the magazine was sacked, barracks and court houses were burnt and prison gates were flung open. In the countryside, the peasants and dispossessed zamindars attacked the money lenders and new zamindars who had displaced them from the land. They destroyed the government records and money lender's account books. They tried to destroy all the symbols of colonial power and thus attacked the British established law courts, revenue offices, revenue records and *thanas* (police stations). It should also be noted that even where people did not rise up in revolt, they showed strong sympathy for the rebels and rejoiced in the successes of the rebels, whereas organised social boycott of these sepoys who remained loyal to the British.

Crucial Date	Remark
11 May 1857	• The rebels proclaimed the ageing nominal Mughal emperor Bahadur Shah Zafar as the '*Shahenshah-e-Hindustan*'. • From Delhi, the uprising soon spread to other army centres in the north-western provinces and Awadh and soon took the shape of a civil rebellion, as disgruntled rural population lent a helping hand.
First week of June 1857	• Mutinies broke out in Aligarh, Mainpuri, Bulandshahr, Etawah, Mathura, Lucknow, Bareilly, Kanpur, Jhansi, Nimach, Moradabad, Saharanpur, and others.
By mid-June and September 1857	• There were mutinies in Gwalior, Mhow and Sialkot and in Bihar, in Danapur, Hazaribagh, Ranchi and Bhagalpur, and Nagode and Jabalpur in central India.

"In Rohilkhand and the Doab from Delhi to Cawnpore and Allahabad the country is not only in rebellion against us, but is utterly lawless."

The despondent Governor General, Lord Canning's statement on 19 June 1857.

Prominent Storm Centres of the Revolt

Centre	Leaders of Rebels	Reason for Joining the Rebellion	Important Development during the Course of Rebellion	Final Result
Delhi	Symbolic leader – Mughal Emperor Bahadur Shah Zafar Real Leader – Court of Soldiers headed by General Bakht Khan, a descendant of the former ruler of Rohilkhand who led the forces at Bareilly and brought them to Delhi	Deprivation by British	Simon Fraser, the Political Agent and several other Englishmen at Delhi were killed.	• The combined effort of Nicholson, Wilson, Baird Smith and Neville Chamberlain enabled the recapture of Delhi by September 1857 (**first prominent centre to fall**). • Bahadur Zafar was exiled to Rangoon where he died in 1862 while after the British occupation of Delhi, Bakht Khan went to Lucknow and continued to fight British till he died in a battle on 13 May 1859.

Centre	Leaders of Rebels	Reason for Joining the Rebellion	Important Development during the Course of Rebellion	Final Result

Kanpur	• Nana Saheb (adopted son of last Peshwa Baji Rao II)
	• Nana Saheb in his efforts against the British was ably supported by two of his lieutenants:
	  • Tantia Tope
	  • Azimullah
		Refusal of family Pension	• Sir Hugh Wheeler, the commander of the British garrison at Kanpur. surrendered on the 27 June 1857 and Nana Saheb proclaimed himself the Peshwa and simultaneously acknowledged the suzerainty of Bahadur Shah Zafar.
			• But, soon Kanpur was recaptured by the British commander Sir Colin Campbell.
				• **Nana Saheb** was defeated and he escaped to Nepal in early 1859.
				• **Tantia Tope** joined Rani Laxmibai after fall of Kanpur and but after losing at Gwalior, he escaped into jungles of Central India from where he carried on successful guerrilla warfare against the British until April 1859 when he was captured because of betrayal by a zamindar friend and was subsequently put to death.

Lucknow	• Begum of Awadh Begum Hazrat Mahal and her son Birjis Qadar • The more popular leader was Maulvi Ahmadullah of Faizabad, who organised rebellions and fought against the British	Nawab Birjis Qadar was deposed	Henry Lawrence, the chief commissioner was killed in a bomb blast during the fight and it was Sir Colin Campbell who suppressed the revolt at Lucknow.	Begum was compelled to hide in Nepal while Maulvi Ahmadullah was treacherously killed by the Raja of Puwain who was rewarded ₹50,000 by the British.
Jhansi	Rani Laxmibai and Tantia Tope	Annexation of her state by Lord Dalhousie on the grounds to 'Doctrine of Lapse'	The combined efforts of Rani and Tantia Tope saw the capture of Gwalior.	• Meanwhile, Sir Hugh Rose defeated Tantia Tope and stormed Jhansi on 3 April 1858. He then captured Gwalior. • The Rani of Jhansi died a soldier's death on 17 June 1858 and Jhansi was recaptured by Sir High Rose.

Centre	Leaders of Rebels	Reason for Joining the Rebellion	Important Development during the Course of Rebellion	Final Result
Bihar (Jagdishpur)	Kunwar Singh (70-year-old *Zamindar* of Arrah)	Deprivation of his estates	One of the most outstanding military leader and strategist of the Rebellion, who, despite his old age, was too quick for the British troops and fought the British in Bihar, and also campaigned against them in Awadh and central India.	He sustained a fatal wound in the battle and thus, consequently, he died on 9 May 1858 at his ancestral house in Jagdishpur.

"Here lay the woman who was the only man among the rebels."

A tribute to the Rani of Jhansi from the man who defeated her, General Hugh Rose.

"If a patriot is a man who plots and fights for the independence, wrongfully destroyed, of his native country, then most certainly the Malawi was a true partot ... He had fought manfully, honourably, and stubbornly in the field against the strangers who had seized his country, and his memory is entitled to the respect of the brave and the true hearted of all nations."

British Historian Colonel G. B. Malleson on Maluvi Ahmadullah of Faizabad

Apart from these acknowledged leaders, who are remembered for their patriotism and courage, there were many unknown and unacknowledged martyrs who were no less valiant such as the countless Peasants and *Sepoys* who laid down their lives and fought the British with exemplary courage to expel them from India forgetting their religious prejudices and caste differences and rising above their narrow personal interests. However, by the end of 1859, the sepoys and the rural rebels were completely defeated and British authority over India was fully re-established.

Reasons for Failure of the Revolt

While the contemporary colonial explanations for the failure of the Revolt highlighted certain aspects such as 'British bravery, their superior national character, better leadership qualities and effective military strategies, as against the lack of unity, discipline and order among the rebels', however, the story was not perhaps that straightforward. There are certain crucial aspects that unfold the complexity of the situation such as:

Lack of Support for the Rebels

Even though the Revolt of 1857 was widely popular among the people and the rebels received the sympathy of the people, yet it **could not embrace the entire country** or all groups and classes of Indian society. Unfortunately, certain Indian rulers, big merchants and intelligentsia not only kept aloof but also actively supported the British. Indeed, the sepoys might have made a better fight had they received their support.

- **Lack of Support from the Indian rulers and other chieftains**: Most Indian rulers of the Indian states and the big *zamindars* who expected their future to be safer with the British did not support the Rebels. For instance, the *Sindhia* of Gwalior, the Holkar of Indore, the Nizam of Hyderabad, the Raja of Jodhpur and other Rajput rulers, the Nawab of Bhopal, the rulers of Patiala, Nabha, Jind and Kashmir, the Ranas of Nepal, and many other ruling chiefs, and a large number of big zamindars such as the zamindars of Bengal Presidency not only refused to join in but also gave active help to the British in suppressing the Revolt. In fact, no more than 1 per cent of the chiefs of India joined the Revolt. Even the *taluqdars of* Awadh who had joined the Revolt abandoned it once the Government gave them assurance that their estates would be returned to them.

> *"These rulers and chiefs acted as the breakwaters to the storm which would have otherwise swept us in one great wave."*
>
> Governor General Lord Canning

- **Lack of Support from the Big Merchants and Educated Indians**[6]: The modern educated Indians also did not support the revolt because, in their view, the revolt was backward-looking due to rebel's opposition for progressive social measures. Meetings were organised in Calcutta and Bombay by them to pray for the success of the British. Similarly, the big merchants of Calcutta, Bombay and Madras supported the British because as their main profits came from foreign trade and economic connections with the British merchants, so they felt that their future and interests were more secure with British.
- **Lack of Support from the Soldiers**: It was another irony that **almost half the Indian soldiers** not only did not revolt but fought against their own countrymen on the side of the British to crush these rebellions. The recapture of Delhi, for example, was effected by five columns consisting of 1,700 British troops and 3,200 Indians.

Lack of Definite Vision and Ideology

Apart from a commonly shared hatred for British rule, the rebels had no political perspective or a definite vision of the future. They were all prisoners of their own past, each fighting a different battle, having different grievances, having different perception about future and hence, their primary focus was more on regaining their lost privileges, rather than a united plan of action, which was the need of the hour. Unsurprisingly, in the absence of a unified and forward-looking plan, they proved incapable of ushering in a new political order.

Lack of Effective Coordination, Organisation and Leadership

The rebellions in different parts of the country were completely uncoordinated and poorly organised. The rebel units lacked a common plan of action, strategy and central leadership. They were also poorly served by their leaders apart from some honourable exceptions like Maulvi Ahmadullah, the Rani of Jhansi and Kunwar Singh, most of them failed to realise the significance of the Revolt and simply did not do enough. For instance, Bahadur Shah and Zeenat Mahal had no faith in the abilities of sepoys and negotiated with the British to secure their safety, similarly the Begum of Awadh frequently had difference of opinion with Maulavi Ahmadullah, while Azimullah, the political advisor of Nana Saheb, asked him not to visit Delhi lest he be overshadowed by the Emperor. Most of the *taluqdars* too tried only to protect their own interests and some of them, like Man

[6] It is pertinent to note that the educated middle class believed mistakenly that the British would lead the country towards modernisation, whereas the rebels on the other hand did not realise that the country had fallen prey to the foreigners because it had stuck to rotten and outmoded customs, traditions and institutions and failed to see that national salvation lay not in going back to feudal monarchy but in going forward to a modern society, a modern economy and modern political institutions.

Singh, changed sides several times depending on which side had the upper hand. All this ultimately led to the weakening of the Revolt and prevented its consolidation. Even at the places where they were able to overthrow the British, the rebels had no clear idea as to create what sort of power in its place.

> *"... Had a single leader of ability arisen among them (the rebels), we must have been lost beyond redemption."*
>
> John Lawrence

Superior Resources of the British

The resources of the British Empire be it constant supply of disciplined soldiers, superior arms, war materials and money or the sophisticated weapons and better equipments were all far superior to those of the rebels. In addition, the British were the masters of practically the whole of India, and had the support of most of the Indian princes and chiefs along with backing of a centralised administration and access to an efficient communication system, such as the telegraph system which further enabled them to keep in touch with all parts of the country and to manoeuvre their troops according to their needs. On the other hand, the rebels suffered from a desperate scarcity of cash, were having no constant source of arms and ammunition and being members of a peasant army were only equipped with primitive weapons, and lacked any formal military training in strategy, discipline and a central command, which made them lose even more men and material.

> *"They were often forced to fight with swords and pikes against an enemy supplied with the most modern weapons. They had no quick system of communication at their command and, hence, no coordination was possible. Consequently, they were unaware of the strength and weaknesses of their compatriots and as a result could not come to each other's rescue in times of distress. Every one was left to play a lonely hand."*
>
> Bipan Chandra

Localised Nature of the Revolt

The extremely localised nature of the uprisings proved to be a big advantage for the British as it helped them to tackle each one at a time. Furthermore, as Eric Stokes has also rightly pointed out that due to the rebel sepoy's centripetal tendency to congregate at Delhi, it prevented the rebellion from spreading as much as it could. So, when by March 1858 Delhi and Lucknow fell to the British, the rebellion entered its dying phase and the British succeeded in crushing the leaders of the Revolt one by one.

Nature and Character of the Revolt

The debate over the nature and character of the Revolt perhaps started instantaneously as it happened. While some contemporaries like **Major Outram** believed that '*it was a Muslim conspiracy exploiting Hindu grievances to restore the Mughal empire*', the more dominant official version stated that '*it was primarily a mutiny of the sepoys followed by civilian unrest which happened as the unruly elements took advantage of the breakdown of law and order*'. Some of the later Indian historians too, like **S.N. Sen** and **R.C. Majumdar**, supported the official version. For instance, R.C. Majumdar stated, '*What began as a mutiny, ended in some areas in an outbreak of civil population which was sometimes organised by self seeking local leaders and* *sometimes was only mob violence caused by the breakdown of the administrative machinery*'. Most of the British historians have, however, **underplayed the character** of the Revolt of 1857 and interpreted the revolt as a mutiny of the sepoys, some aggrieved landholders and princes having vested interests.

> *"The movement began as a military mutiny and then when the administration collapsed, the lawless elements ... took the upper hand."*
>
> S. N. Sen
>
> *"It was neither the first, nor national, nor a war of independence as large parts of the country remain unaffected and many sections of the people took no part in the upsurge. To regard the outbreak of 1857 as either national in character or a war of independence of India betrays a lack of true knowledge of the history of Indian people in the nineteenth century."*
>
> R. C. Majumdar
>
> *"The Revolt was purely a military outbreak, and not a conspiracy to overthrow British rule."*
>
> Sir John Lawrence
>
> *"It was a wholly unpatriotic and selfish sepoy Mutiny with no native leadership and no popular support."*
>
> John Seeley
>
> *"The passions of the mutineers were centred on their grievances, not on larger ideals."*
>
> British historian Percival Spear

However, differing views are also being voiced since the time of the revolt itself. For instance, **Benjamin Disraeli**, the conservative leader had raised doubts on it being labelled as mere sepoy mutiny as back as 27 July 1857 itself when he asked in the House of Commons, '*Is it a military mutiny, or is it a national revolt*?'. Similarly, **Karl Marx** had expressed the same doubts in the summer of 1857 when he wrote in *New York Daily Tribune* that '*what he [John Bull] considers a military mutiny is in truth a national revolt*'. Later, in a 1909 publication, **V.D. Savarkar** vociferously hailed the Revolt of 1857 as 'the First War of Indian Independence,' a war fought for '*swadharma*' and '*swaraj*'. His claim received serious academic support from **S.B. Chaudhari** in 1959, who held that '*The Revolt was the first combined attempt of many classes of people to challenge a foreign power. This is a real, if remote, approach to the freedom movement of India of a later age*'.

> *"The decline and fall of empires are not affairs of greased cartridges. Such results are occasioned by adequate causes, and by the accumulation of adequate causes."*
>
> Benjamin Disraeli statement in July 1857
>
> *"The crisis came: At first apparently a mere military mutiny, it speedily changed its character, and became a national insurrection."*
>
> Colonel G. B. Malleson who later completed J. W. Kaye's *History of the Sepoy War* that challenged the official theory of simple mutiny.

> *"First War of Independence it certainly was, as in the whole canvas of the recorded history of India it would be difficult to find a parallel to this gigantic anti-foreign combine of all classes of people and of many provinces of India. There was never a war in India lasting continuously for more than a year and simultaneously in all the regions which had for its objective the abasement and ejectment of the alien ruling power."*
>
> S. B. Chaudhuri
>
> *"The revolt of 1857 was a struggle of the soldier-peasant democratic combine against foreign imperialism as well as indigenous landlordism."*
>
> Marxist interpretation

Before arriving at the final analysis regarding the nature and character of the revolt, let us first discuss in detail certain crucial questions pertaining to the Revolt of 1857.

Whether National or Not?

Many historians argue that it was **not 'national'** because the popular character of the revolt was limited to Upper India alone, while the regions and groups that experienced the benefits of the British rule remained loyal such as the Bengali middle classes, the Punjabi Princes and certain other areas of central India, like Indore, Gwalior, Saugar or parts of Rajasthan, where the sepoys rebelled, but the princes remained loyal to the British. The proponents of this theory also point out to the fact that the mutiny mainly affected the Bengal Army; the Madras and the Bombay regiments remained quiet, while the Punjabi and Gurkha soldiers actually helped to suppress the rebellion. They also point out to another crucial issue that there was no premeditated plan or future strategy to bring in any alternative system to replace the British Raj.

> *"In their vision of the future, the rebel leaders were hopelessly at odds; some of them owed allegiance to the Mughal emperor Bahadur Shah, others to various regional princes. United in defeat, the rebel leaders would have fallen at each others's throats in victory."*
>
> Thomas Metcalf

They tried to restore the old Mughal rule by inviting Bahadur Shah II. It is said, '*Although Indian initiatives and priorities were so central in the experience of change there was no national revolt in 1857. The discontented were fractured in loyalty and intention, often looking back to a society and a policy which were no longer viable*'. Thus, it was not revolution but just a restoration. Also, those who rebelled had various motives, which were not always connected to any specific grievance against the British.

However, in the recent past, the **pendulum of historical interpretation** of the nature of 1857 has moved considerably to the opposite direction. The above-mentioned theory is now seriously being questioned by many historians. Though it is mostly accepted by all across the spectrum that in terms of modern sense of the term 'nationhood', the rebels of 1857 clearly lacked that, yet, unlike the earlier peasant revolts, there was certainly a greater interconnection between the territories and there was more better coordination and communication between the rebels from different parts of north and central India. All of them shared a common feature of distaste for the British state and, thus, anything that stood for the authority of the Company became their target of attack. They all felt that their caste and religion was under threat and thus each one was aiming to restore the moral order which had been polluted by an intruding foreign rule. The historians also point out crucial fact that if we look at total numbers, almost half of the Indian sepoys of the East India Company had rebelled since the maximum number of Indian sepoys were in the Bengal regiment at that time and almost all were nurturing common grievances against the British.

> *"It was the perception and day to day experience of the authority of the alien state in his immediate surroundings that determined the rebel's action."*
>
> Gautam Bhadra

Whether It Was Elitist Movement?

Some historians like **Eric Stokes** and **Judith Brown** believe that Revolt of 1857 was essentially elitist in character as during the revolt, mostly the feudal elements were the-decision makers and much of the revolt was determined and shaped by their presence. **However**, this position trivialises the role of masses. On the contrary, the initiative for the revolt and even its effectiveness did **not** really **depend** on the feudal leadership. In many cases, the feudal lords were reluctant to assume leadership and were indeed pushed by the rebels. For instance, it has been established across all historical accounts that Bahadur Shah was intact taken by surprise when approached by the rebel sepoys to become their leader and it was only with great hesitation did he agree to be their leader. On the same lines, it was revealed in the confession of Tantia Tope that Nana Sahib was seized by the rebel sepoys to join hands with them and was threatened with dire consequences in case he does not comply and the Rani of Jhansi was actually threatened with death if she did not assist the sepoys or collaborated with the British. All these examples clearly establish that the initiative for the revolt and even its effectiveness did not really depend on the feudal leadership.

Similarly, in the case of *taluqdars*, though it is true that in many areas, peasants followed them because of the existence of pre-capitalist symbiotic relationship between the two classes, yet in many areas, the peasants and the artisans forced the *taluqdars* to join the revolt, while at some places, the masses insisted on carrying the revolt even after the *taluqdars* had made peace with the British. The more recent studies on the Revolt of 1857, too clearly point out towards the large participation of rural peasantry in the revolt. It is therefore difficult to ignore the evidence of autonomous mobilisation of the peasantry in the Revolt of 1857.

Whether It Was Organised or Spontaneous?

It is very difficult to ascertain whether the 1857 revolt was a methodically planned event or not since the study of the history of the Revolt of 1857 is based entirely on British records as the rebels have left behind no records and their version of events probably died with them. However, prima facie from the attitude and activities of the leaders, it appears that there was hardly any planning or conspiracy on their part. For instance, when the sepoys arrived from Meerut, Bahadur Shah seems to be taken by surprise and instead of joining the rebels straightway, he conveyed the news to the Lt. Governor at Agra. Similarly, the theory of well-planned conspiracy on the part of rebels do not hold true as nor there is any no solid evidence that there was circulation of *chappatis* and red lotus flowers and neither there is any proof that as pointed out by some historians Nana Saheb and Maulvi Ahmad Shah had established links with various cantonments had instigated the revolt.

However, it is also **significant** to note that the first impulse of the rebels was always to proceed to Delhi whether they were at Meerut, Kanpur or Jhansi and Bahadur Shah was recognised as the

Emperor by all rebel leaders. It also seems probable that some kind of organised plan was in existence but it had not matured sufficiently when the revolt broke out. Some historians also argue that even if there was no planning and organisation before the revolt, the need to create an organisation and a political institution to preserve the gains was certainly felt. For instance, immediately after the capture of Delhi, a letter was addressed to the rulers of all the neighbouring states soliciting their support and participation. However, there was no chance to build on these nebulous ideas in the face of the British counter offensive.

Final Conclusion

The debate has been going on since then, with a gradual emerging consensus that even though the Revolt of 1857 was **not a nationalist movement** in the modern sense of the term yet it was definitely **much more than a sepoy mutiny**. As rightly put by Thomas Metcalfe in 1965, '*There is a widespread agreement that it was something more than a sepoy mutiny, but something less than a national revolt*'.

> *"It has to be admitted that the war against the British was not inspired by any sentiment of nationalism, for in 1857 India was not yet politically a nation. It is a fact that the Hindus and Muslims cooperated, but the leaders and the followers of the two communities were moved by personal loyalties rather than loyalty to a common motherland."*
>
> Tara Chand
>
> *"It was far more than a mutiny, ... yet much less than a first war of independence."*
>
> Stanley Wolpert

Significance and Impact of the Revolt

Even though the rebels failed and the Revolt of 1857 was completely suppressed, yet it proved to be a glorious landmark in history of Indian freedom struggle. Despite the various limitations and no immediate achievements, the Revolt of 1857 was the first great heroic effort on the part of Indian people to emancipate themselves from foreign rule and thus was indeed a progressive step. The Revolt of 1857 ended an era and sowed the seeds of a new one. The spirit of Indian nationalism which was at a formative stage in the second-half of the 19th century was greatly influenced by this Revolt.

> *"Even in failure, it served a grand purpose: a source of inspiration for the national liberation movement which later achieved what the Revolt could not."*
>
> Bipan Chandra

Another significant and remarkable aspect about the Revolt of 1857 was the **Hindu–Muslim unity**. Among the soldiers as well as the leaders and the common people, there was complete Hindu–Muslim cooperation. All the sepoys, whether Hindu or Muslim accepted the suzeranity of the Mughal Emperor and gave the call '*Chalo Delhi*' (onward to Delhi).They respected each other religious sentiments as for instance, wherever the Revolt was successful, orders were immediately issued banning cow-slaughter as a mark of respect to the sentiments of the Hindus. The same fact was indirectly acknowledged later by Aitchisin, a senior British official in his memoir where he bitterly complained, '*In this instance, we could not play off the Mohammedans against the Hindus*'.

The events of 1857 also compelled the British to re-examine their policy towards India and bring fundamental changes in the character of Indian administration. The rule of the East India Company was ended and through the **Royal Proclamation of 1 November 1858**, the administration of India was taken over directly by the British Crown which again had far-reaching repercussions.

Changes Introduced After the Revolt

As we have discussed above that the Revolt of 1857 gave a severe jolt to the British administration in India and made its reorganisation inevitable. As a matter of fact, varied aspects of the British rule, be it the structure and organisation of the administration, or the Army or the British policy of managing Indian affairs all underwent significant changes.

Administrative Changes

The first major change was that the power to govern India passed from the **East India Company to the British Crown** through an act of Parliament widely known as the '*Act for the Better Government of India*' which was passed by the British Parliament[7] on 2 August 1858 and which came into effect on 1st November when the Queen issued a Proclamation famously known as the '*Royal Proclamation of 1858*'. The salient features of this Act were:

- India was to be governed directly by and in the **name of the Crown** through a Secretary of State[8] for India, who was a member of the British Cabinet and as such was responsible to the British Parliament. He was further aided by a Council known as the India Council consisting of 15 members, most of whom were retired British-Indian officials[9].

> *"In conceptual terms, the British, who had started their rule as 'outsiders', became 'insiders' by vesting in their monarch the sovereignty of India."*
>
> P. Bernard Cohn summarising what this constitutional change meant for the status of British rule in India.

- The Central administration in India continued to remain in the hands of the Governor General who was given the new title of Viceroy[10] or Crown's personal representative. An Executive council[11] was formed to help the Viceroy, whose members were to act as the heads of departments and advisors to the Viceroy. The position of the members of the Council was similar to that of the Cabinet ministers. The Council discussed all important matters and decided them by a majority vote; but the Viceroy had the power to override any important decision of the Council.

[7] Much before the peace was fully restored in India.

[8] Earlier, this authority was wielded by the Directors of the Company and the Board of Control. Thus, the dual control of the President of the Board of Control; the Directors of the Company was abolished and all the authority was centred in the Secretary of State.

[9] It was laid down that out of the 15 members, at least 9 would have served in India for not less than 10 years, and would have left India not more than 10 years before their appointment to the Council.

[10] In accordance with the Queen's Proclamation, Lord Canning had the unique opportunity to become the Governor General as well as the first Viceroy.

[11] Originally, there were 5 members but by 1918 there were 6 members, apart from the Commander-in-Chief heading the Army. The Indian Councils Act of 1861 further enlarged the Governor General's council (from 6 to 12 members) for the purpose of making laws in which capacity it was known as the Imperial Legislative Council. The Governor General was authorised to add to his Executive Council between 6 to 12 members of whom attest half had to be non-officials who could be Indian or English. The Indian National Congress after its formation in 1885 demanded a number of changes in the administration. As a result, the Act of 1892 was passed by which the number of members in the Council was increased to 16.

- The Act of 1858 further strengthened the role of the supervision and control of the **Secretary of State** and a result proportional diminution in the powers of the Viceroy vis-a-vis the Home Government was brought about. The Royal Titles Act of 1877 clearly brought out the subordination of the Viceroy and his council to the authority of the Secretary of State[12]. For instance, when the Viceroy of India, Lord Mayo, tried to assert his Council's authority he was clearly told that: '*The principle is that the final control and direction of the affairs of India rest with the Home Government and not with the authorities appointed and established by the crown under Parliamentary enactment, in India itself*'.
- The Secretary of State was to present to the **House of Commons** periodically report on the moral and material progress of India. All matters concerning legislation, land revenue, public works, railways, jobs, new expenditure and policies were rigidly scrutinised and controlled by the Secretary of State.
- While the powers of the Secretary of State were increased, the checks upon his authority were weakened. Barring financial matters, where its approval was necessary, the India Council was reduced to mere advisory functions and the Secretary of State could easily overrule its decisions. He was given the power of sending and receiving secret messages and dispatched them from the Viceroy without the necessity of communicating them to the India Council. In fact, due to all these aspects, the Secretary of State began to be regarded as the 'grand Mughal'.

Changes Introduced in the Army

In order to prevent the recurrence of another revolt by the Indian soldiers, some major changes were initiated in the organisation of the army. With the takeover of the administration by the Crown, the Company's army was merged with the Crown troops. Several steps were taken to minimise, if not completely eliminate, the capacity of Indian soldiers to revolt.

- Firstly, the domination of the army by its European branch was carefully guaranteed. The number of European soldiers was increased and their ratio vis-a-vis Indian soldiers was fixed at **1:2** in **Bengal Army** and **2:5** in **Bombay and Madras Armies**. The crucial branches of the army like artillery and, later in the 20th century, tanks and armoured corps were put exclusively in European hands. Moreover, the European troops were kept in key geographical and military positions. The older policy of excluding Indians from the officer corps was strictly maintained. As a matter of fact, till 1914 no Indian could rise higher than the rank of a *Subedar*.
- Secondly, the organisation of the Indian section of the army was now based on the policy of '**balance and counterpoise**' or 'divide and rule' to prevent any chances of uniting again in an anti-British uprising. In the recruitment of army, community, caste, tribal and regional loyalties were encouraged in order to check the solidarity among soldiers. Regiments were thus created on the basis of caste, community and region to prevent the development of any nationalistic feeling among them.

> *"I never wish to see again a great Army, very much the same in its feelings and prejudices and connections, confident in its strength, and so disposed to rise in rebellion together. If one regiment mutinies, I should like to have the next regiment so alien that it would be ready to fire into it."*
>
> An excerpt of a letter written by Charles Wood, Secretary of State to Viceroy Canning in 1861, which sums up the British thrust on 'Divide and Rule' in Army.

[12]All of this became possible as a result of the laying of a direct cable line between England and India in 1870, the opening of the Suez Canal and the shortening of voyage time between the two countries by introduction of steam vessels. These crucial developments speeded the pace of communication and the Secretary of State could now control the minutest details of administration, sitting even at a distance of thousands of miles from India.

- A distinction of martial and non-martial races was made and the former were recruited in large numbers. The soldiers of Bihar, Awadh, Bengal and Central India who had participated in the Revolt of 1857 were declared **non-martial**, while the soldiers who supported the British like Sikhs, Gurkhas and Pathans were declared **martial**.

Changes Introduced in the Relations With Princely States

Another important change was in the British policies towards the Princely states. After the Revolt of 1857, the British realised that the Princely States could serve as useful allies in case of any revolt and can play an important role in checking the discontent of Indian masses. Therefore, the British deliberately put a **hold on the policy of annexation** of Indian states but as the price of their continued existence, the princes were made to acknowledge Queen as the paramount power.

> *"It was long ago said by Sir John Malcolm that if we made all India into zillah's (districts), it was not in the nature of things that our Empire should last 50 years. But that if we could keep up a number of Native States without political power, but as royal instruments, we should exist in India as long as our naval supremacy was maintained. Of the substantial truth of this opinion I have no doubt; and the recent events have made it more deserving of our attention than ever."*
>
> Viceroy Lord Canning, in 1860

The following were some key developments in this regard:

- The Queen's proclamation of 1858 declared that '*the British had no desire to extend their existing territorial possessions*' and Lord Canning dispensed with the policy of Doctrine of Lapse and allowed all rulers the right of adoption.
- Territorial and monetary awards were bestowed on princes who had remained loyal. For instance on Princes of Gwalior, Rampur, Patiala and Jind.
- In 1861, a special order of knighthood, the Star of India, was instituted, of which the recipients were the rulers of Baroda, Bhopal, Gwalior, Patiala and Rampur.
- In 1876, Queen Victoria assumed the title of the Empress of India to emphasise British sovereignty over the entire Indian subcontinent and later, Lord Curzon made it clear to the princes that they are ruling their states as merely agents of the British Crown.
- Through the **policy of Paramountcy**, the authority of the Princes was completely subordinated to the authority of the British and in reality, they were converted into a Board of privileged dependents. Also, from now onwards, no Indian ruler was allowed to maintain relations with other countries except through the British.
- As the paramount power, the British claimed the right to supervise the internal affairs of the princely states and thus, interfered in their day to day functioning through their agents called Residents. It was also made clear that in the event of 'misgovernment' or 'anarchy' the British would step in to take temporary charge of a native state. For instance, in 1873, the rulers of Baroda and in 1891, the dynasty of Manipur were removed.

Changes Introduced in the Civil Services

We have already studied in the previous chapters about the fact that **Lord Cornwallis** was the first to bring into existence the institution of Civil Services in India. But he had relegated the Indians to a subordinate position and this position did not alter in spite of the Charter Act of 1833 which theoretically threw open the Services to the Indians. The Queen's proclamation of 1858 also declared that the British intend to include the Indians freely and impartially in offices under the Civil Service. Though the doors were open for Indians but every year not more than one or two could join the coveted ranks of the Civil Service[13], and thus, their number was negligible compared with that of the English entrants. It was because of numerous challenges faced by the Indians:

- The competitive examination was held far away in London.
- The examination was heavily based on the knowledge of Latin, Greek and English (the Indians had little background of these languages).
- In addition, the maximum age for entry into the Civil Service was gradually reduced from 23 (in 1859) to 19 (in 1878).

All efforts of Indians to remove these hurdles bore little results. Apart from Civil Services, in other departments of administration like Police, Public Works Department, Forest, Post and Telegraph, Health services, Engineering, and later Railways too, all superior positions were likewise reserved for Europeans. It is pertinent to note that this preponderance of Europeans in all strategic posts was not accidental as the British generally believed it to be an essential condition for the maintenance of British supremacy in India.

"It is indispensable that an adequate number of the members of the Civil Service shall always be Europeans."

Statement of Lord Kimberley, Secretary of State, in 1893

"The absolute necessity of keeping the government of this widespread empire in European hands, if that empire is to be maintained."

Statement of Viceroy, Lord Lansdowne, in 1893

However, after 1918, under Indian pressure, the different administrative services were gradually Indianised; but then too not much was achieved as the key positions of control and authority still stayed mostly in British hands.

Changes Introduced in the Provincial Administration

In order to appreciate the changes incorporated in Provincial Administration, we need to have a basic understanding of the model of administration in Provinces prior to 1857. The British had divided India for administrative convenience into three provinces, three of which Bengal, Madras and Bombay were known as **Presidencies**. The Presidencies were administered by a **Governor** and his Executive Council of three members, who were appointed by the Crown. The Presidency Governments possessed more rights and powers than other provinces which were administered by Lieutenant Governors and Chief Commissioners appointed by the Governor General. The provincial governments enjoyed a great deal of autonomy before 1833 when their power to pass laws was taken away and their expenditure subjected to strict control.

However, a beginning in the direction of **decentralisation** was made by the Act of 1861, which provided **legislative powers** to the Presidencies of Bombay and Madras, but they had to obtain permission from the Governor General for passing an Act. Also, in the field of finance, strict control over the smallest details of provincial expenditure was exercised by Central Government. The first step in the direction of separating central and provincial finances was taken in 1870 by Lord Mayo. He for the first time granted fixed sums out of Central Revenues to provinces to spend on certain services like Police, Jails, Education, Medical Services, Roads, and others.

[13] Satyendranath Tagore, brother of Rabindranath Tagore, was the first Indian to do so successfully in 1863.

Lord Mayo's scheme was enlarged in 1877 by Lord Lytton who transferred to the provinces certain other heads of expenditure like Land Revenue, Excise, General Administration and Law and Justice. By 1882, the system of giving fixed grants to the provinces was put to an end and instead, the provinces were asked to generate a fixed income from the provincial taxes. According to these arrangements, some sources of revenue were fully handed over to the provinces, some partially and some reserved from Centre. The expenditure on war and famines was the responsibility of the centre. This arrangement continued till 1902. However, it is pertinent to note that in theory as well as in practice, the Central government remained supreme and continued to exercise effective and detailed control over the provincial governments.

Changes Introduced in the Local Bodies

Due to financial problems, the Government further decentralised the administration and promoted local bodies such as municipalities and district boards which were to generate revenue to be spent in their jurisdictions. The process started in 1864, when some of the local services like education, health, sanitation and water supply were transferred to the local bodies, who would finance them through local taxes. However, in the initial years, most of the members were nominated and the bodies were presided over by the District Magistrates.

The situation improved in 1882 during **Lord Ripon**'s tenure, when by a government resolution, the policy of administering local affairs through independent rural and urban local bodies was laid out. Now, the local boards were to be developed throughout the country which were assigned definite duties and funds. The official members were limited to one-third and majority of members were replaced by elected members wherein it was also provided that the Chairman of a local body can also be a non-official. But still it suffered from various lacunae such as the right to vote was restricted, the official control was firm and non-officials enjoyed very few powers.

"Except in the Presidency cities of Calcutta, Madras and Bombay, the local bodies functioned just like departments of the Government and were in no way good examples of local self-government."

Bipan Chandra

Changes Introduced in Respect of Other British Policies

Certain British administrative policies especially in the social arena changed for the worse after the Revolt of 1857. While before 1857, British had tried, however half-heartedly and hesitatingly, to modernise India, they now consciously began to follow reactionary policies.

- **Reversal in the Policy of Social Reform**: Since British believed that their measures of social reform, such as the abolition of the custom of Sati and allowing widows to remarry, had been a major cause of the Revolt of 1857, they gradually began to ally with the conservative classes and abandoned their previous policy of supporting the social reformers.

"The Indian Government's honeymoon with progress was over."

British Historian Percival Spear

"The earlier reformist zeal of a self-confident Victorian liberalism now evidently took a back seat, as many believed now that Indians were beyond reform."

Sekhar Bandyopadhyay

"This conservative brand of liberalism, rested upon the solid support of the conservative and aristocratic classes and upon the principle of complete non-interference in the traditional structure of Indian society."

Thomas Metcalf

"Because of this natural alliance of the British power with the reactionaries in India, it became the guardian and upholder of many an evil custom and practice, which it otherwise condemned."

Jawaharlal Nehru, in the Discovery of India

- **Lack of focus on Public Services**: While British spent most of its revenues on maintenance of Army and Civil Administration, it practically starved the fund flows for Public Services like education, public health, sanitation, water supply, irrigation and rural roads. For example, in 1886, of its total net revenue of nearly ₹47 crore the Government of India spent nearly ₹19.41 crore on the army and ₹17 crore on civil administration, but less than ₹2 crore on education, medicine and public health and only ₹65 lakh on irrigation.
- **Hostility towards Educated Indians**: Immediately after the Revolt of 1857, many British officials commended the refusal of educated Indians to participate in the Revolt of 1857. The Universities of Calcutta, Bombay and Madras were started in 1857 and, thereafter, higher education spread rapidly in the subcontinent. However, this favourable official attitude towards educated Indians soon **changed** when they began to organise a nationalist movement among the people and founded the Indian National Congress in 1885. British Administration now became hostile to higher education and to educated Indians when the latter begun to use their recently acquired modern knowledge to analyse the imperialistic character of British rule and to put forward demands for Indian participation in administration.

"This conservative reaction evidently made the empire more autocratic and denied the aspirations of the educated Indians for sharing power. This, therefore, also made the empire more vulnerable, as from this frustration of the educated middle classes arose modem nationalism towards the end of the nineteenth century.

Sekhar Bandyopadhyay

- **Favourable Attitude towards the Zamindars, Taluqdars and Landlords**: While being hostile to the forward-looking educated Indians, the British now tried to placate the *zamindars* and the landlords for utilising them as counterweights against the nationalist-minded intelligentsia. The British now hailed the zamindars and landlords as the traditional and 'natural' leaders of the Indian people and tried to protect their interests and privileges at the cost of the poor peasants. The zamindars and landlords in return became the firm supporters of British rule.

"The Crown of England should henceforth be identified with the hopes, the aspirations, the sympathies and interests of a powerful native aristocracy."

Viceroy Lord Lytton, in 1876

- **Restrictions imposed on the Press**: The credit for the growth and development of the modern printing press in India goes to the British[14]. But, as soon as the press started playing an important role in building public opinion and in criticising the reactionary government policies, a number of legislations were passed by the British to check its freedom. The Vernacular Press Act of 1878, which put serious restrictions on the freedom of the Indian language newspapers, was a serious attempt by the British government to curb the independence of the press. Though, after a series of protests and agitations, the Act was repealed in 1882. Later, again with the rise of the extremist ideological movements of Swadeshi and Boycott, repressive press laws were passed in 1908 and 1910.
- **Racial Antagonism towards Indians**: The British in India always considered themselves to be racially superior and, thus, they had always held aloof from the Indians believing that social distance from Indians had to be maintained to preserve their authority over them. The Revolt of 1857 and the atrocities committed by both sides further widened the gulf between the Indians and the British as from now on racial segregation became firmly entrenched and Indians were regarded not only different but also racially inferior. We have already discussed above how the Indian army and the Civil Services were re-organised to exclude Indians from an effective share in administration. Almost at all public places, there were visible manifestations of this racialism as most of the facilities such as waiting rooms at railway stations, Railway compartments, parks, hotels, swimming pools, clubs, and others, were reserved for 'Europeans only' and entry was denied to Indians.

> *"We in India have known racialism in all its forms ever since the commencement of British rule. More powerful than words was the practice that accompanied them, and generation after generation and year after year, India as a nation and Indians as individuals, were subjected to insult, humiliation and contemptuous treatment. The English were an imperial Race, we were told, with God-given right to govern us and keep us in subjection; if we protested we were reminded of the tiger qualities of an imperial race."*
>
> Jawaharlal Nehru

- **Adoption of the policy of 'Divide and Rule'**: After 1857, the British completely abandoned the idea of self-government for the Indians basing it on the rationale that India was not a nation and because of their inherent social and cultural disunity, representative bodies were impractical in India. Therefore, they carefully stirred divisions, primarily along religious lines but also along caste and regional identities for this purpose. Also, the British were greatly disturbed by the strong unity displayed by Hindus and Muslims during the Revolt of 1857. They were, thus, determined to break this unity and, hence, they introduced the policy of 'Divide and Rule' among the civilian population.

> *"We have maintained our power by playing off (up) one part against the other and we must continue to do so."*
>
> Sir Charles Wood, Secretary of State for India in a letter to Lord Elgin, the Viceroy.

---

[14] Prior to 1857, the Indian press was freed of restrictions in 1835 by Charles Metcalfe, popularly known as the Liberator of Press.

Initially, the British thought that the revolt was a conspiracy hatched by the Muslims, so immediately after the Revolt, they severely punished Muslims, confiscated their lands and property on a large scale, discriminated against them in public appointments and declared Hindus to be their favourites. In fact, so marked was the anti-Muslim attitude after the Revolt of 1857 that Syed Ahmad Khan felt the need to write a pamphlet titled '*Who Were the Loyal Musalmans*?' wherein he quoted numerous instances of Muslim collaboration with the British.

However, soon after 1870, this policy was reversed and a belated appeasement of Muslims began wherein an attempt was made to turn upper-class and middle-class Muslims against the growing nationalist movement. In order to encourage communal rivalry and hatred, the British government cleverly promised official favours like preferential treatment in terms of government service on a communal basis in return for loyalty and thus effectively played educated Muslims against educated Hindus.

Previous Year's Questions (Prelims)

1. What was/were the object/objects of Queen Victoria's Proclamation of 1858? (2014)
   1. To disclaim any intention to annex the Indian states.
   2. To place the Indian administration under the British Crown.
   3. To regulate East India Company's trade with India.

   Select the correct answer using the codes given below:

   Codes:
   (a) 1 and 2 only
   (b) 2 only
   (c) 1 and 3 only
   (d) 1, 2 and 3

2. Which of the following provided a common factor for tribal insurrection in India in the 19th century? (2011)
   (a) Introduction of a new system of land revenue and taxation of tribal products.
   (b) Influence of foreign religious missionaries in tribal areas.
   (c) Rise of a large number of money lenders, traders and revenue farmers as middlemen in tribal areas.
   (d) The complete disruption of the old agrarian order of the tribal communities

3. The ruler of which one of the following states was removed from power by the British on the pretext of mis-governance? (2008)
   (a) Awadh
   (b) Jhansi
   (c) French
   (d) Satara

4. With reference to the Revolt of the year 1857, who among the following was betrayed by a friend, captured and put to death by the British? (2006)
   (a) Nana Sahib
   (b) Kunwar Singh
   (c) Khan Bahadur Khan
   (d) Tantia Tope

5. Who was the Governor General of India during the sepoy mutiny? (2006)
   (a) Lord Canning
   (b) Lord Dalhousie
   (c) Lord Hardinge
   (d) Lord Lytton

6. Which one of the following revolts was made famous by Bankim Chandra Chatterjee in his novel *Anand Math*? (2006)
   (a) Bhil Uprising
   (b) Rangpur and Dinapur Uprising
   (c) Bishnupur and Birbhum rebellion
   (d) Sannyasin rebellion

7. Which one of the following territories was not affected by the Revolt of 1857? (2005)
   (a) Jhansi
   (b) Chittor
   (c) Jagdishpur
   (d) Lucknow

8. Which one of the following places did Kunwar Singh, a prominent leader of the Revolt of 1857, belong to? (2005)
   (a) Bihar
   (b) Madhya Pradesh
   (c) Rajasthan
   (d) Uttar Pradesh

9. Which one of the following mountain tribes did the British first came into contact with after the grant of Diwani in the year 1765? (2002)
   (a) Garos
   (b) Khasis
   (c) Kukis
   (d) Tipperahs

10. 'In this instance, we could not play of the Mohammedans against the Hindus'. To which of the following events did this remark of Aitchison relate? (2000)
   (a) Revolt of 1857
   (b) Champaran Satyagraha (1917)
   (c) Khilafat and Non-Cooperation Movement of (1919–22)
   (d) August Movement of 1942

11. The educated middle class in India: (1998)
   (a) Opposed the Revolt of 1857
   (b) Supported the Revolt of 1857
   (c) Remained neutral to the Revolt of 1857
   (d) Fought against native rulers

Previous Year's Answers (Prelims)

1. (a) 2. (c) 3. (a) 4. (d) 5. (a) 6. (d) 7. (b) 8. (a)
9. (b) 10. (a) 11. (a)

Emergence of Indian Nationalism

5

As we have studied in the previous chapter of Revolt of 1857, there is, as of now, **little disagreement** among nationalist leaders and historians that in a modern sense of the term, the Indian political nation, did not exist prior to the establishment of British rule. Most historians **agree** that the Indian Nationalism that confronted colonial rule and celebrated its victory in the formation of the Indian nation-state in 1947 **emerged** in India in the late 19th century. **However**, whether it was a product of colonial modernity or such a nation lay unselfconsciously embedded in Indian civilisation and then gradually evolved through history is a subject matter of **intense debate**. In this chapter, we will be discussing in detail about all these issues and will try to address the question of evolution of Indian Nationalism, factors facilitating the growth of national consciousness along with two other crucial historical events: foundation of the Indian National Congress and the peasants movements after 1857.

Evolution of Indian Nationalism

There are diverse ideological vantage points and historiographical perspectives to look at evolution of Indian nationalism. Some historians like **Benedict Anderson**[1] argue that nationalism in India as well as the developing world of Asia and Africa supposedly followed one or the other models developed in the West. Though there is no denial in the fact that rise of nationalism was certainly favoured by **industrialisation**, **urbanisation** and **capitalism**, yet mostly historians agree that understanding the evolution of Indian nationalism in terms of just **western modular influences** as Benedict Anderson had thought practically denies intellectual agency to the people of India in shaping their own history and certainly does not provide the complete picture.

Agreeing with the same, **Partha Chatterjee** asserted that the nation-state in India was no mere emulation of the Western model and the nationalism in India was essentially a '*different*' but '*derivative discourse*' from the West that developed through three distinct stages:

- The *Moment of Departure*: When the nationalist consciousness was constructed through the hegemonising influence of the 'post-Enlightenment rationalist thought',
- The *Moment of Manoeuvre*: When the masses were mobilised in its support, and
- The *Moment of Arrival*: When it became 'a discourse of order' and 'rational organisation of power'.

This theory has been further developed in his later book *The Nation and Its Fragments* (1993), wherein he has talked about two domains of action of Indian intelligentsia: **the material** and the **spiritual**. Chatterjee tries to persuade us that long before the political struggle for power began, the Indian society was imagining its nation in a private cultural sphere or the inner spiritual domain, where they refused to allow colonial intervention and imagined their own domain of sovereignty thereby **constructing an**

[1] He was an Irish historian and political scientist, best known for his 1983 book '*Imagined Communities*', wherein he explored the origins of Nationalism.

Indian modernity that was modern but not Western, whereas in the outer material world, defined by the institutions of the colonial state, there was, however, little scope for them to avoid the influence of Western models. Thus, it was from this cultural construction of a space for autonomy in the early 19th century that Indian nationalism initiated its journey.

C. A. Bayly (1998), on the other hand, has traced the roots of Indian nationalism to its pre-colonial days and has searched for the '***pre-history of nationalism***'. Indian nationalism, he thinks, emanated from 'traditional patriotism', which he describes as '*a socially active sentiment of attachment to land, language and cult*' that developed in the subcontinent long before the process of Westernisation had begun. According to Bayly, in India of the 18th and early 19th centuries, the traditional patriotism was built on pre-existing sense of territoriality as **homeland** was being defined by various terms like *desh*, *uatan* or *nadu*, and identities were gradually taking shape with the development of regional languages and religious affiliations rationalised by indigenous ideas of public morality and ethical government. Gradually, as the East India Company established its hegemony, this traditional patriotism manifested itself through various **indigenous critiques of foreign rule** and the regional solidarities too consolidated into a **broader cultural notion** of India. Finally, it burst forth through numerous acts of resistance, culminating in the great Revolt of 1857 and although the 'old patriotism' did not completely die out during this period, it was significantly reworked and reshaped to create a **new colonial modernity** that was different from that of the West.

Another striking theory about this process of nation-building is put forward by the **early nationalist School**[2], which points out to a national consciousness to which all other forms of consciousness were assumed to have been subordinated and which was based on a commonly shared antipathy towards colonial rule, a feeling of patriotism and a nationalist ideology rooted in a sense of pride in India's ancient traditions. This school, in other words, ignored the inner conflicts within Indian society which, among other things, led to its division into two nation-states – and assumed the existence of nation as a homogeneous entity with a single set of interests.

In opposition to this, a new interpretation emerged as the '**neo traditionalist**' school, which echoed the old imperialist assertion of authors like **Valentine Chirol**, that politicisation of Indian society developed along the lines of traditional social formations, such as linguistic regions, castes or religious communities, rather than the modem categories of class or nation. The institutional innovations of the colonial state, notably the introduction of **Western education** and **political representation** intersected with the traditional Indian social divisions and created new opportunities and new status groups such as the Western-educated elite, which drew its members from the existing privileged indigenous collective, such as the *Bhadralok* in Bengal, the *Chitpavan Brahmans* in Bombay or the *Tamil Brahmans* of Madras, whereas the backward regions or the under privileged groups remained outside of this limited political nation. This went on until the end of World War I, when for the first time **Mahatma Gandhi** flung open the gates of constitutional politics to initiate the new era of mass nationalism.

These divisions were tracked further down to the level of localities by the **Cambridge School** supported by the conservative colonial administrators and the imperial school of historians who **completely derecognised** the role of a nationalist ideology and sought to explain nationalist politics in terms of a **competition-collaboration syndrome**. According to them, *India was not a nation, but an aggregate of disparate interest groups who were united as they had to operate within a centralised national administrative framework created by the British and who regularly bargained with the British for power and patronage.* They, thus, viewed nationalism primarily as a mere ideology used by certain elite groups to legitimise their narrow ambitions and to mobilise public support.

By contrast to this, the **orthodox Marxist school** sought to analyse the class character of the nationalist movement and tried to explain it in terms of the economic developments of the colonial period, primarily

---

[2] Supported by Lajpat Rai, A. C. Mazumdar, R. G. Pradhan, Pattabhi Sitaramayya, Surendranath Banerjee, C. F. Andrews, Girija Mukerji, B. R. Nanda and Bisheshwar Prasad.

the rise of industrial capitalism and the development of a market society in India. It identified the bourgeois leadership, which directed this movement to suit their own class interests and neglected the interests of the masses and even to some extent betrayed them. This narrow class approach and economic determinism of the early Marxists like R. P. Dutt and Soviet historian V. I. Pavlov were qualified in later Marxist writings of S. N. Mukherjee and Sumit Sarkar.

Later, **Bipan Chandra**[3] and a few of his colleagues gave Marxist interpretation a distinctly nationalist orientation by arguing that even though Indian nationalist movement was a popular movement of various classes, it was not exclusively controlled by the bourgeoisie. According to them, in colonial India, there existed two types of contradictions: **the primary contradiction** that was between the interests of the Indian people and those of British rule and several **secondary contradictions** within the Indian society, between classes, castes and religious communities. With the gradual progress in the anti-colonial struggle, the secondary contradictions were compromised in the interest of the primary contradiction and in this way the **hegemony of a nationalist ideology** was established, though all the secondary conflicts were never satisfactorily resolved.

To conclude, rather than assuming any unilinearity of progress, due weightage needs to be given to the multiplicity of responses thereby accepting whole heartedly that India being a plural society, **Indian nationalism** was, therefore, bound to have many voices, as different classes, groups, communities and regions interpreted their 'nation' in various, sometimes even contradictory ways. Similarly, Indians had many identities, like class identity, caste identity, religious identity and, thus, at different historical conjunctures, different articulated identities intersected with each other. It is from this historiographical position of recognising that **India was not a structured nation but a nation in the making** and nation-building in India was a **process of continuous adjustment** and **accommodation** that one should look at the evolution of nationalism in India.

> *"It was common for colonial administrators and ideologues to assert that Indians could not be united or freed because they were not a nation or a people but a geographical expression, a mere congeries of hundreds of diverse races and creeds. The Indians did not deny this but asserted that they were now becoming a nation. India was as Tilak, Surendranath Banerjea and many others were fond of saying - a nation-in-the-making."*
>
> Bipan Chandra

Factors Facilitating Emergence of Indian Nationalism

The emergence of Indian nationalism might not have been the result of Western modular influences in the same way as Benedict Anderson had thought, but the role of British rule was **important** nevertheless. Certain measures adopted by the British for running an effective administration also became instrumental in providing favourable conditions for the rise and growth of Indian nationalism as through rapid spread of education, development of communication systems, such as the railways and telegraph, the uniform system of administration, printing press and the emergence of a new public space created by the colonial institutions, the groundwork was laid for a **critical public discourse** conducive for the growth of nationalism. Thus, it would not be wrong to assume that Indian nationalism grew partly **as a result of colonial policies** and partly as a **reaction to colonial policies**. Some of the factors that facilitated in the emergence of Indian Nationalism were:

[3] In his famous work '*India Struggle for Independence*' (1989).

- **Administrative and Economic Unification of the Country**: In order to meet the necessities of administrative convenience, considerations of military defence and to satisfy the urge for economic penetration and commercial exploitation, the British gradually introduced a uniform system of administration throughout the country. However, this unified system of governance that was basically intentioned for only British interests ironically also aided in the **development of national consciousness** among the people of India separated by vast distances. With a common land revenue administration, unified judiciary and police system, codified civil and criminal laws throughout the length and breadth of the country, a new dimension of **political unity** was achieved which further inter-linked the economic fate of the people of different regions. For instance, failure of crops in one region or famine occurred in one part of India affected the prices and supply in another region. Furthermore, with the introduction of the modern means of transport and communication, mutual contact among the people especially the leaders, from different regions, was increased which proved important for the exchange of political ideas and for mobilisation and organisation of public opinion on political and economic issues.
- **Western Thought and Education**: It is a well-accepted fact that the British introduced western education[4] in India due to their self-inherent need for efficient administration. The core purpose of such a move was to create a loyal section of Indians who would effectively carry out clerical and lower administrative tasks for the British.

> *"The idea was to form a class of persons, Indians in blood and colour, but English in taste, in opinions, in morals, and in intellect."*
>
> Lord Macaulay

However, due to the western education, the educated classes were exposed to a variety of ideological influences that further imbibed in them the spirit of **equality**, **liberty** and **nationalism**, which in turn created a critical discourse that held the colonial state under stringent scrutiny. The familiarisation with the works of liberal thinkers like John Milton, Shelly, Bentham, John Stuart Mill, Herbert Spencer, Rousseau, Voltaire, Mazzini and Garibaldi helped them adopt an outlook which was **modern**, **democratic**, **rational**, **secular** and **nationalist** in approach.

> *"If English education was introduced initially to inculcate a spirit of loyalty, it also exposed Indians, to the rationalist and democratic thoughts of the modem west."*
>
> A. R. Desai
>
> *"These ideas came to constitute an ideological package, called 'political modernity' consisting of such concepts as 'citizenship, the state, civil society, public sphere, human rights, equality before the law, the individual, distinctions between public and private, the idea of the subject, democracy, popular sovereignty, social justice, scientific rationality and so on."*
>
> Dipesh Chakrabarty

The educated Indians deployed these same ideas to construct their own critique of an autocratic and arrogant colonial state and later, the same critical **political consciousness** and **awareness** was spread throughout the whole country. The English language helped nationalist leaders from different linguistic regions to communicate with each other and form a common outlook towards the exploitation faced by India on multiple fronts due to the **inherent contradictions** existing in colonial policies. They came to realise that colonial rule was the major cause of India's economic backwardness, which further was compromising India's

[4] Higher education began to grow rapidly in India after universities were established in the three presidencies in 1857 and education became a free enterprise in 1882.

development at all other fronts. They could also compare the differential approach adopted by the British in their own country vis-a-vis India where even basic rights were denied to the citizens. Thus, the **middle-class intelligentsia**, which primarily benefitted from the western education, not only constituted the nucleus for the newly arising political unrest but in years to come also provided leadership to the Indian political associations. All this together provided a **new direction to the Indian political thinking** and later, mixed with an emotional patriotic belief in the superiority of Indian culture and civilisation, it acted as a precipitating factor on the emergence of nationalism. It is, however, pertinent to note here that in the initial years, the educated Indians were not questioning the imperial connection, but gradually these loyal subjects were turning into **conscious citizens**, demanding their rights from an authoritarian colonial state. Thus, it would not be wrong to conclude that, *if the education was designed to colonise the mind of the Indian intelligentsia and breed in them a sense of loyalty, the latter also selectively appropriated and manipulated that knowledge of domination to craft their own critique of colonialism.*

- **Role of Press and Literature**: In the second-half of the 19th century, there was an unprecedented growth of Indian-owned **English** and **vernacular newspapers** and eventually, press emerged as the chief instrument of creating national consciousness and awareness about different economic, social and political issues. For instance, by 1875 there were about 400 Indian owned newspapers, published in both English and the regional languages, with an estimated readership of 150,000.The prominent among these were the *Hindu Patriot*, the *Amrita Bazar Patrika*, the *Indian Mirror*, the *Bengalee*, the *Som Prakash* and the *Sanjivani* in Bengal; the *Native Opinion*, the *Rast Goftar*, the *Indu Prakash*, the *Mahratta* and the *Kesari* in Bombay; the *Hindu*, the *Andhra Prakasika, the Swadeshmitran* and the *Kerala Patrika* in Madras; the *Hindustani*, the *Advocate* and the *Azad* in U.P. and the *Tribune,* the *Akhbar-i-am* and the *Koh-i-noor* in Punjab. Through these newspapers columns, the official policies were constantly critically analysed the Indian point of view was put forward, the people were urged to unite and work for national welfare the ideas of self-government, democracy, civil rights industrialisation, and others were popularised among the people.

"The Indian is as strong enough ... in mind and knowledge to assert his right of citizenship."

Hindoo Patriot, June 1857

"We fight for our rights in India"

The Indian Mirror, July 1878

The newspapers, journals and pamphlets also enabled in the free exchange of political ideas among nationalist leaders from different regions thereby promoting inter regional solidarity. Meanwhile, **nationalist literature** in the form of novels, essays and patriotic poetry also played an important role in arousing national consciousness. For instance, **Dinabandhu Mitra's** play Nil Darpan sensitised the masses about the plight of Indigo cultivators, while **Bankim Chandra Chatterjee** work Anand Math was full of nationalist aspirations. Some other prominent nationalist writers of this period were Rabindranath Tagore in Bengali, Lakshminath Bezbarua in Assamese, Vishnu Shastri Chiplunkar in Marathi, Subramanya Bharati in Tamil, Bharatendu Harishchandra in Hindi and Altaf Husain Hali in Urdu who all produced significant works in regional languages written both in prose and poetry about the degrading conditions of the masses and need for Self Government.

- **Intellectual Awakening**: The growing racial tension, threat of conversion and the reforming zeal of the benthamite administrators in the 19th century made the educated Indians stand back and have a hard look at their own culture, ultimately leading to the initiation of the process of social reform and intellectual awakening. An attempt was made by intellectuals such as **Raja Ram Mohan Roy**, **Keshub Chandra Sen**, **Ishwar Chandra Vidyasagar**, **M. G. Ranade** and **Sir Syed Ahmed Khan** for critical and creative examination of the contemporary Indian society with the purpose of transforming it along modern lines. It further resulted in 'purification' and 'rediscovery' of an Indian civilisation that would be conformant with the European ideals of rationalism, empiricism, monotheism and individualism.

Efforts such as development of patriotic regional literature in Bangla, Marathi, Tamil, Telugu and Hindi, along with evolution of new art forms were undertaken to prove that Indian civilisation was by no means inferior to that of the West but in certain sense, such as in its spiritual accomplishments, was even superior to it[5]. As rightly asserted by Sekhar Bandyopadhyay '*this sense of pride in the spiritual essence of Indian civilisation as opposed to the material culture of the West not just helped Indians reorganise and sanctify their private spheres of life, its ideological inspiration also motivated them to confront the colonial state in a newly emerging public space. This, in other words, provided the ideological foundation of modem Indian nationalism that developed in the late 19th century*'.

- **Racial Arrogance of the Rulers and their Certain Reactionary Policies**: In the second-half of the 19th century, the racial arrogance adopted by the English in their dealings with Indians and certain reactionary policies of British made the Indians not only conscious of their constant humiliation at the hands of British but also concerned the educated Indians about their rights being continuously trampled by the colonial state. The English treated all Indians irrespective of their caste, religion, province or class with the badge of inferiority and all their actions towards Indian subjects were branded with racial arrogance. The Indians were not only kept out of exclusively European clubs but were often not permitted to travel in the same compartment in a train with the European passengers.

Meanwhile, certain groups of educated Indians started becoming politically active and established new associations, which began to fight for civil liberties along with organising countrywide agitations on various issues where their rights were being regularly marginalised. For instance, as early as 1850s, **protests against missionary interventions** and against the **Lex Loci Act**[6] were voiced from different parts of India simultaneously. Later, in 1867 a nationwide agitation against the proposed **income tax** was organised and demands were raised for a **balanced budget** and **right of control** by Indians over the expenditure of the revenue income. Similarly, certain other policies of the government incensed the educated Indians such as the Indian Councils Act of 1861, which even though had provided for the inclusion of a very limited number of non-official Indian members in the Governor General's council yet the members could not introduce any bill without the prior sanction of the Governor General, who also had, over and above this, the all-important power of veto the Bengal government's resolution of 1870 that proposed to cut back funding for English education in Bengal, allegedly to rechannel funding to promote mass education through vernaculars. The educated Indians were dismayed to find that increased taxation and fund cuts for higher education came at a time when the government continued to spend excessively on the army, the '*home charges*' and other public works serving the imperial needs. In 1876, the educated Indians were further alienated from the British when totally ignoring their older demand for a simultaneous examination in London and India, the maximum age for sitting in the Indian Civil Service examination was lowered from 21 to 19 much to their disadvantage and further reducing their chances of entering the Civil Services. Thus, by the 1870s, Indian nationalism had gathered enough strength and momentum to appear as a major force on the Indian political scene. However, it was under the reactionary regime of Lord Lytton that it take up an organised form.

During the Lord Lytton's viceroyalty from 1876 to 1880, certain acts were passed which helped intensify discontent against the foreign rule. For instance, in 1878 against the advice of his own law member, Lord Lytton passed the **Vernacular Press Act**[7], which was designed basically to gag the Indian press, which had become critical of the colonial policies. The Act, at once, became the target of a vehement

[5] It is, however, pertinent to note that this ideology was, of course, not without contradictions, as the sense of pride in the spiritual heritage was often reduced to an uncritical and obscurantist defence of all customs and practices of the past.

[6] Lex Loci Act of 1850 protected the right of a convert to inherit ancestral property.

[7] The Act provided for a deposit from all printers and publishers of regional language newspapers, which was to be forfeited and their machinery confiscated if they published anything objectionable.

countrywide agitation of the educated Indians and their various associations and even found support among some British parliamentarians like Gladstone, who raised a furore in the British parliament condemning it in the strongest words. The same year, that is, in 1878, Lytton also passed a new **Arms Act**, which introduced a licencing system throughout India for possessing firearms, but exempted the Europeans and Eurasians from its coverage, resulting in popular protests against the same all across the country. Certain other instances during Lytton reign like holding of the Imperial Durbar[8] at Delhi in 1877 in great splendour and pomp at a time when the country was suffering from a terrible famine, removal of import duties on British textile imports, Plantation Labour and Inland Emigration Act of 1881–82, which condemned the plantation labourers to serfdom, Second Anglo-Afghan War fought at the cost of Indian treasury further aroused vehement agitation against his reactionary rule.

"The reactionary administration of Lord Lytton had aroused the public from its attitude of indifference and had given a stimulus to public life. In the evolution of political progress, bad rulers are often a blessing in disguise. They help to stir a community into life, a result that years of agitation would perhaps have failed to achieve."

Surendranath Banerjee

"To Lord Lytton must belong the credit of having done much by his repressive measures towards stimulating the public life of this country and for this service certainly his Lordship will be entitled to the gratitude of our country."

Excerpt from article published in Bengalee newspaper (June 12, 1880)

Even later too, during the reign of Lord Ripon who was otherwise considered liberal, the controversy surrounding the Ilbert Bill[9] made it clear to the educated Indians that they could not expect racial equality from the colonial regime. The bill was bitterly opposed not just by the non-official Anglo-Indians but also by a large section of the British officials, including Rivers Thompson, the Lieutenant Governor of Bengal, who reportedly condemned the bill for '*ignoring race distinctions in order to establish equality by a stroke of pen*'. Ilbert Bill controversy, thus, emerged as an important benchmark in the history of the evolution of modern political activities as it made the educated Indians not only politically conscious but also painfully aware of their subordinate position in the imperial power structure, thereby, provoking them into counter demonstrations and press propaganda.

"The testimony of a single one of our countrymen has more weight with the court than that of any number of Hindus, a circumstance which puts a terrible instrument of power into the hands of an unscrupulous and grasping English man."

G. O. Travelyan, a historian and an influential civil servant pointed out in 1864

- **Impact of Contemporary Movements in the World**: The nationalist ranks were greatly influenced by the concepts of nationalism and right of self-determination initiated by the French Revolution and were further

[8] Where Queen Victoria assumed the title of the Empress of India.

[9] The Ilbert Bill introduced on 2 February 1883 by C.P. Ilbert, the law member in Lord Ripon's council, proposed to give Indian district magistrates and session judges the power to try European offenders in then *mofussil* (small towns), as they already did in the presidency towns.

inspired by the contemporary national liberation movements of different countries such as of Greece, Italy and Ireland. They were also emboldened by the fact that a lot of nations emerged on the ruins of the Spanish and Portuguese empires in South America, and felt that the time has come for India also to claim its share of self-determination.

- **Emergence of New Associations Dominated by Middle-Class Professionals**: Meanwhile, another major change in the organised political life of India started happening as the older associations controlled by a landed plutocracy were being gradually replaced by new associations dominated by middle-class professionals.

"The new middle class was a well-integrated all-India class with varied background but a common foreground of knowledge, ideas and values . . . It was a minority of Indian society, but a dynamic minority. . . . It had a sense of unity of purpose and of hope."

Percival Spear, an acclaimed British historian

The New Associations mostly Demanded, Among Other Things

- Indian representation in the legislative council.
- Separation of the Executive and Judicial functions of the government.
- Indianisation of the civil service and for that purpose simultaneous Indian Civil Service examination in India and England.
- Imposition of Import duties on cotton goods.
- Reduction of expenditure on 'home charges' and costly foreign wars, like the Afghan wars of 1878–79.
- Rationalisation of the financial relations between India and England and the extension of the permanent settlement to other pans of British India.

The **newness** of this politics of the second-half of the 19th century, lay in the new demands that were being raised by these associations. The demands now raised were most often of national significance though at times were also of a local or regional character.

Features of Political Associations during the first-half of 19th century	Features of Political Associations during the second-half of 19th century
• Dominated by wealthy, aristocratic landlords. • Were mostly local or regional in character. • Mainly demanded: · Admin reforms. · Association of indians with administration · Spread of education.	• Dominated by educated middle class such as lawyers, journalists, doctors. • Demands raised were most often of national significance. • Had wider agenda.

These associations also vehemently protested against the imposition of income tax, the draconian Vernacular Press Act and the racist Arms Act. Apart from raising such public issues, which concerned all Indians across the regions, these associations also took interest in the affairs of the peasantry[10] and were greatly

[10] Through such mediation, the Indian peasants, so far locked away in their localised existence, were being gradually connected to a wider national contest with colonial rule.

involved in the Indigo riots in Bengal, in the Deccan riots in Poona and in the protests against water tax in the Chenab Canal Colony in Punjab. It is, however, **pertinent to note** here that these new associations were not overtly anti-British and were not against British rule as such, as many of them sent messages of loyalty to Queen Victoria on the occasion of the Delhi Durbar. Equally important is another fact that even though these associations were fighting for limited reforms, nevertheless, they exhibited a **new public awareness** and, above all, demanded equality, representative government and a share in the administration of their own country and this is where the new politics differed from the earlier phase of landlord-dominated politics.

Political Associations Before the Indian National Congress

In the political history of Indian freedom struggle, the Indian National Congress, founded in December 1885, was the first organised expression of the Indian National Movement on an all-India scale however, it has many predecessors.

Year	Organisation (Region)	Proponent and Objective
1836	Bangabhasha Prakasika Sabha (Bengal)	• By Associates of Raja Ram Mohan Roy. • To discuss government policies and seek redressal through petitions and memorandums.
1837	Zamindari Association/Landholders Society (Bengal)	• An Association of the landlords of Bengal, Bihar and Orissa. • Founded by Dwarkanath Tagore, Radhakanta Deb and others. • To safeguard class interests of the landlords.
1843	Bengal British India Society (Bengal)	• To collect and disseminate information related to the actual condition of the people in British India.
1851	British India Association (Bengal)	• Was formed by the merger of Landholders Society and Bengal British India Society. • In 1852, its branches were also established in Bombay and Madras and were known as Bombay Association and the Madras Native association. • In general, they demanded reform of administration with focus on bigger share for Indians in administration, spread of education, and others. • Some of the demands raised by them were partially met in the Charter Act of 1853, wherein 6 members were added to the Governor General's Council for legislative purpose.
1866	East India Association (London)	• Organised by the Grand Old Man of India Dadabhai Naoroji, to discuss Indian question and to influence British publican to promote Indian welfare. • Later, branches of the association were opened in prominent Indian cities.

Year	Organisation (Region)	Proponent and Objective
1870	Poona Sarvajanik Sabha (Maharashtra)	• Formed by M. G. Ranade, Ganesh Vasudeo Joshi and S. H. Chiplunkar to represent the wishes of the people and within one year its members collected signed *muktiyamamahs* or power of attorneys from seventeen thousand people giving it a true representative character. • Mainly devoted to arousing political consciousness among the people along with criticism of important administrative and legislative measures. • Also involved in a variety of social work among the peasantry, like mobilising famine relief or organising arbitration courts.
1875	Indian League (Bengal)	• Founded by Sisir Kumar Ghosh, with the objective of stimulating nationalism and promoting political education among Indian people. He had earlier in 1868 also founded a noted Bengali newspaper, known as *Amrita Bazar Patrika.*
1876	Indian Association (Calcutta, Bengal)	• One of the most important pre-Congress nationalist organisation. • Founded by Surendranath Banerjee and Anand Mohan Bose, who both deriving inspiration from Mazzini, based it on the concept of United India. • It aimed at creating a strong public opinion in the country on political questions and unification of the Indian people on a common political programme. • In order to fulfil its avowed ambition of 'representing the people' and to establish contact with the masses, it kept its annual subscription low at ₹5. • One of the first major issues it took up for agitation was the reform of the Civil Service Regulations and raising of the age limit for its examination during Lord Lytton's tenure popularly known as the Indian Civil Service Agitation. Later, the organisation also staged protests against the Arms Act, the Vernacular Press Act, Rent Bill and the pathetic conditions of workers in the English-owned plantations. • In 1883, it sponsored an all India National Conference at Calcutta in December 1883, which was attended by many eminent leaders.

Year	Organisation (Region)	Proponent and Objective
1884	Madras Mahajan Sabha (Chennai)	• Political activities in Madras were revived after an interval of more than two decades with the foundation of the Madras Mahajan Sabha by M. Viraragharcheri, G. Subramaniya Iyer and P. Anandacharlu. • The Sabha aimed at collective action against the British policies harming their interests.
1885	Bombay Presidency Association (Bombay)	• Formed by Badruddin Tyabji, Pherozeshah Mehta and K. T. Telang.

Outside the presidencies too, organised political life revolved round the new associations like the Lahore Indian Association in Punjab or the Allahabad Peoples Association in the United Provinces. Later, in 1885, the first organised expression of Indian nationalism on an all-India scale, the Indian National Congress was formed, which was destined to play a dominant role in India's struggle for independence.

Foundation of the Congress

The Indian National Congress was formed at a national convention of 72 political workers[11] held in Bombay in December 1885 under the presidency of W. C. Bannerji. A retired British civil servant A. O. Hume played an important role in its formation, as it was he who toured across the subcontinent talked to prominent political leaders in Bombay, Madras and Calcutta and persuaded them to meet at a national conference that was initially supposed to meet at Poona[12]. But Hume's involvement also gave rise to a lot of controversy regarding the origins of Congress. For a long time, historians and even nationalist leaders across spectrum have linked the origins of the INC to the '**safety-valve theory**' or '**the conspiracy theory**'. But, of late, the same has been thoroughly discredited.

The Myth about Safety Valve Theory

The safety-valve theory originated from William Wedderburn's[13] biography of Hume published in 1913, wherein he pointed out that '*in the summer of 1878 at Shimla, Hume had come across seven volumes of secret reports which convinced him of the existence of 'seething discontent' among the lower classes and a conspiracy by them to overthrow British rule by violent force. Getting disturbed over the same, he met Lord Dufferin and together they decided to establish an organisation with educated Indians, which would serve as a safety valve and would thus prevent a mass revolution. The Congress was in this way the creation of British rule*'.

The **core of the myth**, that a violent revolution was on the cards at the time and was avoided only by the foundations of the Congress is accepted by most writers, the **imperialist historians** use it to discredit Congress, the **Marxist historians** use it to develop a conspiracy theory from it, the **radicals** use it to prove that the Congress has always been compromising and the **extreme right** use it to show that the Congress has been anti-national from the beginning.

[11] The regional distribution of the 72 delegates was as follows: 38 came from Bombay Presidency, 21 from Madras and only 4 from Bengal, since the Indian Association had convened its own national conference in Calcutta almost at the same time and most Bengal leaders such as Surendranath Banerjee were participating in the same.

[12] The outbreak of cholera deprived the Marathi town of this privilege, which was now passed on to the more cosmopolitan colonial city of Bombay.

[13] Another ex-civil servant and A. O. Hume's biographer.

> *"The Congress was a product of Lord Dufferin's brain and was started more with the object of saving the British Empire from danger than with that of winning political liberty for India. The interests of the British Empire were primary and those of India only secondary."*
>
> Lala Lajpat Rai, the extremist leader using the safety-valve theory to attack the moderates in the Congress in his Young India published in 1916
>
> *"Congress was brought into existence through direct Governmental initiative and guidance and through 'a plan secretly pre-arranged with the Viceroy' so that it (the Government) could use it 'as an intended weapon for safeguarding British rule against the rising forces of popular unrest and anti-British feeling. It was an attempt to defeat, or rather forestall, an impending revolution and the Indian bourgeois leaders were a party to it."*
>
> R. P. Dutt, a famous marxist historian in his widely acclaimed work in India Today
>
> *"What had led Hindus to enter the path of 'denationalization', were the aims and policy laid down by Hume, Cotton, and Wedderburn in 1885; the Congress they founded as a "safety valve" to "seething nationalism," as a toy which would lull the awakening giant into slumber, an instrument to destroy National consciousness, has been, as far as they are concerned, a success."*
>
> M. S. Golwalkar, the RSS chief in 1939

The Reality about Safety Valve Theory

However, in the 1950s, these safety valve or conspiracy theories were proved to be wrong as:

- First of all, those seven volumes of secret reports have not been traced in any of the archives either in India or London. Many historians also pointed out to the fact that except in Wedderburn's biography of Hume, nowhere else any reference to the existence of such reports could be found and he too mentioned that they were supplied to Hume by religious gurus, and were not procured from any official sources.
- Then, the opening up of Lord Dufferin's private papers in the late 1950s cleared up the confusion about Lord Dufferin's role in the sponsorship of the Congress or Hume. It was clearly established by his papers that even though he had met Hume in Shimla in May 1885, he did not take him seriously and indeed also gave definite orders to Lord Reay, the Governor of Bombay to be cautious about the delegates who were going to meet in his city. This clearly proves that Dufferin was suspicious and not much in favour of the proposed meeting of the 72 delegates, as he thought that they may start in India something like an Irish Home Rule League movement and soon after the formation of the Congress, Dufferin was openly castigating Congress for its dubious motives. In 1888, he criticised it for representing a '**microscopic minority**' and this statement clearly explodes the safety valve or conspiracy theory.

> *"He would consider in what way the happy despatch may be best applied to the Congress, for we cannot allow the Congress to continue to exist."*
>
> Lord Dufferin

Historians now more or less agree that the story of seven volumes of secret report was a **fiction** created by a friendly biographer Wedderbum to portray Hume as a British patriot who wanted to save the British empire from an impending crisis. So, as rightly remarked by Bipan Chandra '*It is high time that the safety-valve* *theory ... was confined to the care of the mahatmas from whom perhaps it originated*?'. It is now, thus, mostly accepted that even though Hume played a crucial role in the foundation of the Congress, his role has been grossly exaggerated in the safety valve or conspiracy theories. Also, now historians do point out to another crucial circumstantial aspect that even if Hume had not taken any initiative in 1870s and 1880s, the formation of a national organisation in India was clearly in the air.

The foundation of the Indian National Congress in 1885 was hence, neither a historical accident nor a sudden event. It was actually the **culmination** of a long **process of political awakening** that had its modest beginnings in the 1860s and 1870s, which further took a major leap forward in the late 1870s and early 1880s. We have already discussed about the different factors facilitating in the emergence of Indian Nationalism and about the new political associations initiated by the educated Indians which held countrywide agitations on various national issues. When majority of these demands raised by the associations remained unfulfilled, the regional leaders became all the more convinced about the need for an all-India organisation. So, the emergence of a national body was clearly on the cards, but there was still the need for a mediator who could bring all these regional leaders together under one organisational umbrella. **Hume** was ideally suited for this role as he was widely known for his liberal political opinions and moreover, his supra-regional identity made him acceptable to all the regional leaders.

Later, some historians while further clarifying about the role of Hume came up with another theory popularly known as the '**lightning theory**'. This new theory countering the safety valve controversy stressed on the possibility that the founders of the Indian National Congress cooperated with Hume due to their own self-inherent interest of survival as they felt that Hume's association would assuage official suspicion, which was a very crucial aspect of survival for the organisation in its early nascent stages of operations and any amount of official hostility at such an early stage would have otherwise proved fatal for the organisation. Thus, utilising Bipan Chandra's analogy, '*if Hume and other English liberals hoped to use Congress as a safety-valve, the Congress leaders hoped to use Hume as a lightning conductor*' and in this way, treading a safe path and representing a new and modern trend in Indian political tradition, the Indian National Congress was formed.

"They assumed that the British would be less suspicious and less likely to attack a potentially subversive organisation if its chief organiser was a retired British civil servant."

Bipan Chandra

"No Indian could have started the Indian National Congress . . . if an Indian had . . . come forward to start such a movement embracing all India, the officials in India would not have allowed the movement to come into existence. If the founder of the congress had not been a great Englishman and a distinguished ex-official, such was the distrust of political agitation in those days that the authorities would have at once found some way or the other to suppress the movement."

G. K. Gokhale wrote in 1913

Objectives of the Indian National Congress

- The first major objective of the Indian National Congress was the **promotion of national unity.** The Congress from the very beginning aimed at eliminating regional differences and for ensuring the same, it was decided to hold the Congress session every year in different parts of the country. Also, to ensure parity among the regions and to further break regional barriers, it was decided to choose the president from a region other than the one where the session was being held. The same fact was well substantiated by the conversation held between Russian traveller I. P. Minayeff and Mr Banerjee, the first President of INC as when Minayeff asked Banerjee, '*what practical results did the Congress leaders expect from the*

Congress', the first President had replied '*growth of national feeling and unity of Indians*'. Further, in order to carefully nurture the diversity of India and to reach out to the followers of all religions, specifically alleviating the fears of the minorities in 1888, it was decided that no resolution would be passed if it was objected to by an overwhelming majority of Hindu or Muslim delegates. Later, in 1889, a minority clause was added to a resolution adopted for demanding reform of the legislative councils. According to this clause, it was decided that wherever Hindus, Muslims, Parsis or Christians were a minority, their number elected to the Councils would not be less than their proportion in the Population.

"Congress is a mighty nationalizer and this was its most 'glorious' role."

P. Ananda Charlu in his presidential address to the Congress in 1891

"It was the beginning of a new life . . . it will greatly help in creating a national feeling and binding together distant people by common sympathy and common ends."

Indu Prakash of Bombay commenting on the first Congress session

"Out of three basic aims and objectives of the Congress, one of them was full development and consolidation of those sentiments of national unity."

W. C. Bannerji, first President of INC

- The second major objective of the early Congress was to create a **common political platform** and **a common programme** for political workers working in different parts of the country. Congress supported the early nationalists by providing them with an opportunity to gather together and take up their common grievances against the British and carry on their political aspirations along with educating and mobilising people on an all-India basis on political lines. It was because of the same reason that the Congress opted not to take up questions of social reform. As a matter of fact, at its second session, Dadabhai Naoroji[14] laid down this as a rule, '*A National Congress must confine itself to questions in which the entire nation has a direct participation and, therefore, not the right place to discuss social reforms*'.
- The '**internalisation of parliamentary democracy**' and '**indigenisation of political democracy**' were another two key objectives of the Congress. The politics preached by the Congress was based on the doctrine of the sovereignty of the people. The Congress functioned as a mini parliament wherein all the proceedings during the Congress sessions were conducted democratically and the issues were decided mostly through debate and discussion though occasionally through voting too.

"The new lesson is that Kings are made for the people, not peoples for their Kings."

Dadabhai Naoroji

"The basic objectives of the early nationalist leaders were to lay the foundations of a secular and democratic national movement, to politicize and politically educate the people, to form the headquarters of the movement, that is, to form an all-India leadership group, and to develop and propagate an anti-colonial nationalist ideology."

Bipan Chandra

[14] Then President of the Congress.

However, at the same time, the two most formidable challenges faced by the Congress from the very beginning were: **uneven representation** and total **exclusion of the non-elite groups** of Indian society. For instance, if we look at social composition data of the members of the early Congress, it is clearly established that the members belonged predominantly to the high caste Hindu communities, and this pattern continued unchanged for more than two decades of Congress's existence.

Major Peasants Movements and Tribal Uprisings after 1857

"Peasant movements of the earlier period should not be looked at as the pre-history of the Freedom Movement; they have a history of their own."

Ranajit Guha

Peasants Movements and Tribal Uprisings did not end with the suppression of the Revolt of 1857. We find a number of such movements taking place after 1857 and some prominent of them are discussed below.

The Indigo Rebellion of 1859–60

One of the most militant and widespread of the peasant movements was the Indigo Rebellion of 1859–60 in Bengal. We have already discussed in the earlier chapters about the oppressive aspects of the indigo plantation system and how it had been the targets of peasant protest in the central and eastern Bengal, be it Barasat protests of 1832 under **Titu Mir** or the Faraizi movement of **Dudu Mian**. Despite these protests, the oppressive system of Indigo plantation continued for long in Bengal as the planters who were mostly Europeans used to force the hapless peasants to grow **indigo** instead of any other crop and used to make them coercively enter into fraudulent contracts causing great loss to them. However, in the second-half of the 19th century, due to the **twin** factors of the failure of the Union Bank[15] in 1847, and the loss in Indigo's economic importance as an export item, the oppression of the coercive Indigo planters reached to unbearable levels. Meanwhile, in May 1859, emboldened by the support of the sympathetic Lieutenant Governor of Bengal, **John Peter Grant**[16] and some of his district officers who took a pro-peasant position, the oppressed peasantry refused to accept advances from the planters specifically in the districts of Nadia, Murshidabad and Pabna. Later, in the spring sowing season of 1860, they were joined by the Jessore district peasants too, thus, bringing the entire delta region of Bengal in protest against the oppressive plantation system.

"The root of the whole question is the struggle to make the ryots grow indigo plant, without paying them the price of it."

J. P. Grant, Lieutenant Governor of Bengal

"In case of disputes relating to Indigo Ryots, they (ryots) shall retain possession of their own lands, and shall sow on them what crops they please, and the Police will be careful that no Indigo Planter nor anyone else be able to interface in the matter."

Proclamation issued by Hem Chandra Kar,
Deputy Magistrate of Kalaroa to policemen on 17 August 1859

[15] It was the chief financier for the Europeans planters.

[16] He believed in the ethos of free enterprise and, thus, was against any coercive methods employed by the planters.

The peasants started the rebellion by refusing advances or entering into any contracts with the planters besides organising social boycott of their Indian agents. Leadership for the movement was provided by the more well-off *ryots* and in some cases by petty *zamindars,* moneylenders and ex-employees of the planters and at every stage, the peasants offered stiff resistance to the planters. For instance, when a planter of Nadia district sent a band of 100 *lathyals*[17] to attack the *ryots* of Govindpur village, then the villagers under the leadership of Digambar Biswas and Bishnu Biswas[18] organised a counter force armed with lathis and spears and bravely fought them back. Similarly, when the planters threatened the rebellious *ryots* with eviction or enhancement of rent, the *ryots* replied to the threats by going on a rent strike and physically resisting the attempts of eviction. They refused to pay the enhanced rents and the movement at this stage turned into a **no-rent campaign**. The peasants also fought their cases in **courts** against forceful eviction clearly establishing their right as occupancy *ryots* under the Rent Act X of 1859 along with initiating law suites on their own against the erring planters thereby learning to use the legal machinery for enforcement of their justful rights. Ultimately, the planters had to bow down before the united resistance of the *ryots* and the cultivation of indigo was virtually wiped out from Bengal[19] by the end of 1863.

Two major **reasons** responsible for the success of the Indigo Rebellion were: (a) tremendous cooperation, organisation and discipline of the *ryots* and (b) the complete unity among the Hindu and Muslim peasants during the movement. Another **significant feature** of the Indigo Rebellion was the intervention of the educated middle classes and some of the European missionaries who by organising a powerful campaign in support of the rebellious peasantry also succeeded in bringing the peasants issue to the wider arena of institutional politics. They not only prepared memoranda on peasants' grievances and supported them in their legal battles but also carried newspaper campaigns and wrote plays depicting the pitiful state of Indigo farmers, thereby, creating awareness among the general masses against the oppressive system of Indigo plantation. For example, **Dinabandhu Mitra** published in September 1860 a play in Bengali called Neel Darpan[20], which depicted the atrocities of the indigo planters in the boldest possible colour and later, the play was translated into English by the famous Bengali poet **Michael Madhusudan Dutta**. Similarly, **Harish Chandra Mukherji**, the editor of the Hindoo Patriot, published regular reports in his newspaper on instances of planters' oppression and acts of peasant resistance.

> *"Bengal might well be proud of its peasantry . . . wanting power, wealth, political knowledge and even leadership, the peasantry of Bengal have brought about a revolution inferior in magnitude and importance to none that has happened in the social history of any other country . . . With the Government against them, the law against them, the tribunals against them, the Press against them, they have achieved a success of which the benefits will reach all orders and the most distant generations of our countrymen."*
>
> Harish Chandra Mukherji, in May 1860 on the historical and political significance of the Indigo Rebellion

Pabna Disturbances of 1870s and 1880s

Large parts of East Bengal, more particularly Yusufshahi pargana of Pabna district were again engulfed by agrarian unrest during the 1870s and early 1880s. The unrest was caused by the oppression of a few new landlords, that is, *zamindars* who were in the practice of continually enhancing the rent, along with levying illegal cesses or *abwabs* thereby pushing the poor peasants to the threshold of tolerance. However,

[17] Armed retainers.

[18] Both were ex-employees of the planters.

[19] Later, it shifted to the relatively remote and backward region of Bihar, where it had to wait for Gandhi's intervention in 1917 for its complete demise.

[20] Literally meaning 'blue mirror'.

the main grievance of the peasantry was against the concerted attempts by the zamindars to prevent them from acquiring **occupancy rights**[21] under Rent Act X of 1859. The *zamindars* in order to achieve their ulterior motives were adopting all sorts of illegal coercive methods be it forced eviction or forcible written agreements or seizure of cattle and crops or dragging the poor peasants in costly litigation in the courts.

"The zamindars had recently resorted to 'high landlordism', that is, defying all laws in the management of their estates, enhancing rent at their will, imposing illegal abwabs and persistently trying to destroy the occupancy rights of the substantial peasants."

Benoy Chaudhuri

The peasants, discontent found expression in May **1873** when an Agrarian League was formed in *Yusufshahi pargana* of Pabna district with a mandate to organise **rent-strike** and to raise money to take the landlords to courts, which in no time were inundated with rent suites. The Pabna movement remained largely non-violent and within the bounds of law and was mainly spearheaded by the substantial peasants, but was also aided by the lower peasantry as well. What is worth noting is that the peasants were opposed to the harassment and not to the payment of dues and during the entire movement they not only exhibited a strong awareness of the law but also professed a profound faith in the British justice system. Thus, the main form of struggle adopted for securing the redressal of their grievances was that of **legal resistance** against the zamindars only and at no stage, the movement acquired an anti-colonial edge or raise any anti-British demands. Indeed, the Pabna peasants leaders often argued that they were against *zamindars* and not the British and declared that their ambition was to become the *ryots* of the '*Queen of England*'.

"The peasants want to be the ryots of Her Majesty the Queen and of Her only."

Slogan raised by the Pabna peasant leaders

The Pabna experiment was gradually replicated across eastern and central Bengal and Agrarian leagues came up in Dacca, Mymensingh, Tripura, Bakarganj, Faridpur, Bogra and Rajshahi districts. In fact, Naya Mian, the son of Dudu Mian[22], was himself active in organising the agrarian league in Mehendigunge in 1880. At all the places of Agrarian leagues, mass meetings of the peasants were organised, rents were withheld and the *ryots* challenging the *zamindars* in the courts fought for their legal rights. Subsequently, many peasants were able to resist enhanced rents and acquire occupancy rights. Later, in 1885 the **Bengal Tenancy Act** was passed, which provided for relatively greater protection of occupancy rights of the substantial peasants[23], however, it also failed to define the rights of the lesser peasantry, which again had further repercussions, the details of which we are going to study later in this book.

Another remarkable aspect about the Pabna Disturbances was the fact about the complete **Hindu–Muslim solidarity** during the entire movement despite the majority of the *ryots* being Muslim and the majority of *zamindars* being Hindu. The other interesting feature of the Pabna uprising was the ambivalence exhibited by the educated middle classes for the movement. While during the Indigo Rebellion, almost all the middle class intelligentsia took an unequivocal position against the European planters, in case of Pabna surprisingly they

[21] By denying them leases in the same plot of land continually for 12 years, which would otherwise entitle them to the protection of the law (Rent Act X of 1859).

[22] Associated with the Faraizi movement.

[23] Who leased land in the same village (not just the same piece of land) continuously for twelve years.

were divided in their opinion. For instance, the *Calcutta Native Press,* which had been vociferous supporter of the peasants during the entire campaign of Indigo movement, now was divided when the oppression of the indigenous landlords was under attack. The same was the case with *Hindoo Patriot* along with the *Amrit Bazar Patrika* both of which took an overtly pro-landlord position. However, not all were so ambivalent as a number of young Indian intellectuals supported the peasants' cause too. Intellectuals like Bankim Chandra Chatterjee, R. C. Dutt, Surendranath Banerjee, Anand Mohan Bose and Dwarkanath Ganguli all extensively campaigned for the rights of tenants and helped form *ryot* **unions** in different districts during the Pabna Movement. Similarly, there were also many newspapers like '*Bengalee*', the Anglo-Indian press and political associations like the *Indian Association* which were clearly taking up the cause of the peasants and were also exposing the double standards and grandiose reports on peasant violence of the landlord centric newspapers.

The Deccan Riots of 1875

The basis of the Deccan Riots, which erupted in 1875 in Maharashtra lay in the evolution of the Ryotwari system itself, as with its introduction, the relationship between the Maratha ***Kunbi*** peasants and the *sahukars* moneylenders (Vanis) who were mostly Marwari or Gujarati underwent a drastic change. Since the earlier times, the *sahukars* used to exercise intimate control over the village economy and were in the practice of lending money to the *Kunbi* peasants but now[24] with the creation of property rights in land, the moneylenders started the practice of lending money by mortgaging the land of peasants at high interest rates and in case of failure of repayment they used to easily take possession of mortgaged lands through a decree of the court. However, the caste prejudices present in the rural structure prevented the *sahukars* from touching the plough; so the same land was now leased out by them to their former owner-cultivators who unknowingly in this whole process became tenants in their own land.

> *"It took place, because of a redistribution of social power in the villages of Maharashtra."*
>
> Ravinder Kumar

A situation for open conflict was soon created in 1867 due to other three key developments:

- Succession of bad harvests
- Crash in the prices of cotton and acute depression in cotton exports due to the end of the American Civil War[25] in 1864
- Simultaneous increase in the land revenue rates by the government in 1867 on the grounds of extension of cultivation and rise in agricultural prices. In the taluka of *Indapur*, for example, the revenue rates were increased on the average of 50 percent, while in some villages it went as high as 200 percent.

All this inevitably led to further **impoverishment** and **indebtedness** of peasants who began to turn against the perceived cause of their misery, the moneylender. In order to compel the *sahukars* to accept their demands in a peaceful manner, they started their protest by organising a complete **social boycott** of the 'outsider' moneylenders and by also imposing **social sanctions** against those peasants and *ballutedars*[26] who would not join the boycott against moneylenders. This social boycott soon spread rapidly to the villages of Poona, Ahmednagar, Sholapur and Satara districts.

---

[24] Under the provisions of *Ryotwari System*, recognising peasant as the owner of his land, there was a direct settlement of land revenue with the peasant and due to this creation of property rights in land, subsequently a land market emerged thereby pushing for more demand for land.

[25] During the early 1860s, the American Civil War generated artificial demand of cotton further pushing the prices of cotton were pushed up resulting in great rise in cotton exports, thus, eventually leading to a cotton boom in Deccan.

[26] The Balutedari system was important part of socio-economic and cultural life in medieval Maharashtra. Balutedars were the village servants who received their wages as grain-share for the services to the members of the village community.

> *"They refused to buy from their shops. No peasant would cultivate their fields. The ballutedars (village servants) — barbers, washermen, carpenters, ironsmiths, shoemakers and others would not serve them. No domestic servant would work in their houses and when the socially isolated moneylenders decided to run away to the taluq headquarters, nobody would agree to drive their carts."*
>
> Bipan Chandra

However, when even the social boycott did not prove very effective, then the peasants were left with no other option but to take to agrarian riots. The riots first broke out on 12 May **1875** at a village known as Supe in Bhimthadi taluka with a systematic attack on the *sahukars* specifically *on* the houses and shops of Gujarati and Marwari[27] moneylenders. The peasants seized and publicly burnt **debt bonds**, **deeds**, **decrees** and other documents dealing with their debts that were signed either under pressure or in ignorance, or through fraud. Within days, the riots spread to other villages in Poona and Ahmednagar districts. However, due to the swift action on part of British to suppress the revolt, the rioting spirit could not spread to the whole of Maharashtra.

It is quite significant to note that in case of Deccan agrarian riots, there was very little violence against the *sahukars* or their persons but the instruments of oppression, that is, the **debt bonds** were seized and destroyed. Violence was resorted to in those cases only when there was resistance in handing over these legal documents and all through the movement there was an absence of anti-colonial consciousness. However, in order to protect the interest of peasants against such future land grabbing, the Bombay government soon came up with the **Deccan Agriculturists Relief Act of 1879**. It is also important to point out that peasant protests against moneylenders similar on the lines of Deccan Riots were quite common throughout India in the second-half of the 19th century and in the first-half of the 20th century. For instance, similar patterns of peasant behaviour, that is, little violence against moneylenders but destruction of their legal debt bonds, were adopted in 1857 in Saharanpur of western UP, in 1868 in Nasik, in 1874 in the ghat regions of Bombay and Poona, in 1891 in Ajmer of Rajasthan, in 1914 in Punjab and in 1930 in east Bengal.

Also as with Indigo and Pabna, in case of Deccan movement too, the middle-class intellectuals supported the peasants cause. The **Poona Sarvajanik Sabha** led by Justice Ranade organised a successful campaign among the *Kunbi* peasants and also presented before the government in 1873, a case for a revision of the revenue rates. Though the Bombay government did not concede to the rate revision demand but pressurised by their agitation, it granted a major concession to the peasants that in case of a failure to pay revenue, first only the movable properties of a peasant would be attached and his land would be put up for auction only if his movable properties proved to be insufficient.

> *"The riots of 1875 were not the result of one single factor, they stemmed from a combination of factors, such as the dislocation of the economy by the American Civil War, an ill-conceived revision of land tax, agitation initiated by the Poona Sarvajanik Sabha and finally the longstanding hostilities between the Kunbi peasants and the money lenders."*
>
> Ravinder Kumar

[27] Everywhere, the Gujarati and Marwari moneylenders were attacked not simply because they were 'outsiders' but because they were thought to be more avaricious. Also, unlike the Brahman moneylenders who usually resided in better-protected cities, the Gujarati and Marwari moneylenders lived in the villages and therefore were more exposed to such attacks.

Chenab Canal Colony Protests of 1907

A more effective and direct confrontation between the peasants and the British took place in Punjab in 1907, famously known as the Chenab Canal Colony Protests. In early 1907, the local Punjab government proposed to introduce a draconian new law for controlling the inheritance of land in the canal settlements along with enhancing the water taxes, thereby, severely hurting the prospects of Punjab peasants. What infuriated the peasants further was the inherent provision in the draft law about the imposition of heavy fine on all those who would break the canal colony regulations.

The peasants supported by the **Lahore Indian Association**[28], **Singh Sabha** and **Arya Samaj** held large demonstrations, sent petitions to the government and later withheld the payment of all sort of taxes. Soon, the protests turned violent and riots broke out in large cities like Lahore, Amritsar and Rawalpindi. Taking counter measures, the local government banned all public meetings and deported outside leaders such as Lajpat Rai and Ajit Singh but instead of any abatement of unrest, when the same started reflecting on the morale of the army[29], Viceroy Minto had to veto the new Act on 26 May 1907. The measure had an immediate miraculous effect on the peasantry who hailed it as '*a vindication of British justice*' as in the peasant consciousness, the distant ruler was still the saviour, while the enemy was the corrupt official closer at home. Later, no tax campaigns were reported from different parts of India, for example, from Awadh in 1879, from Cambay state in Gujarat in 1890, from Tanjore in 1892–93 and from Assam in 1893–94.

Moplah Uprisings

In the period from 1850 to 1900, we also witness a series of Moplah Uprisings in the region of **Malabar**. The reasons behind the uprisings were mostly similar to the causes discussed in Moplah Uprisings of 1836–54 (earlier ch 3). The Hindu *Janmis* landlords backed by the police, law courts and revenue officials were continuously harassing the poor Moplah Muslim peasants over illegal taxes, over assessment and, thus, there was a renewal of hostilities between the two groups. The Moplah peasants started targeting and looting the property of the Hindu *Janmis,* defiling their temples as well as attacking the British officials who came to their rescue. Unfortunately, all these acts gave an aggressively communal orientation to what was essentially a class conflict between the landlords and the peasants. The large factor played by Religion in the peasant rebellions was again witnessed in Punjab, when the attempts to purify Sikhism led to the Kuka revolt of 1872.

The Munda Ulgulan of 1899–1900

Along with the agrarian unrest movements, the earlier tradition of tribal uprisings also continued well into the post-1857 period. One such prominent tribal uprising was the Munda *Ulgulan* of 1899–1900. The Mundas were the inhabitants of the Chota Nagpur region of South Bihar and as with other tribal uprisings, the causes behind the Munda *Ulgulan* were more or less similar the **erosion of customary rights** of tribals and further **harassment** faced by them due to the **exploitative behaviour** of the dikus[30], landlords, the moneylenders and their patrons: both the British officials and the Christian missionaries. The movement was led by a charismatic religious leader, **Birsa Munda** who for two years mobilised the Munda tribal peasants against the colonial state. His initial popularity was based on rumours about his occult powers, ability to heal diseases and perform miracles and therefore gradually in tribal imagination, he was recognised as a *messiah* who could turn British bullets into water.

[28] Two of its prominent leaders were Lajpat Rai and Ajit Singh.

[29] Since Punjab was the most important catchment area for army recruitment.

[30] Means outsiders.

> *"He used to take the tribals on a pilgrimage to Munda holy places and on the way held large public meetings, talking about a golden past or satjug that was gone and the dark kaljug that had befallen, when the Munda land or disum was ruled by Queen Mandodari, the wife of the demon King Ravana-probably a metaphor for the Raj under Queen Victoria."*
>
> Sekhar Bandopadhyay on methodology adopted by Birsa Munda

Thus, under his leadership a massive anti-colonial uprising started during the Christmas of 1899, which targeted the established symbols of both the colonial regime as well as those pertaining to the *dikus* such as police stations, government offices, churches, temples, and others, since, according to the Mundas envisaged order of an ideal and just society, it was free from both the internal as well as European exploiters. The movement however could not survive for long and was ruthlessly suppressed by the government forces while the leader Birsa Munda was executed.

A striking aspect about the Munda *ulgulan* was its political awareness about the wider realities pertaining to the colonial state. Corroborating the same, Sekhar Bandopandhyay points out that '*the aim of the movement was not merely to drive out the dikus, but to destroy their enemies and put an end to the British Raj and establishing in its place a Birsa Raj and a Birsaite religion*'.

Shift in the Nature of Peasant and Tribal Movements after 1857

Even though there are some similarities in terms of different aspects of peasant ideology and political consciousness of the peasants and agrarian movements pre-1857 and post-1857, there was a certain shift in the nature of peasant movements after 1857 as these later movements acquired some new features too.

- Firstly, post-1857, there have been a **greater awareness of colonial policies**, **laws** and **institutions** among the peasants and tribals and more importantly, some of them even embraced those institutions, the law courts, for example, as an extended and legitimate space for seeking redress to existing injustices or for venting their anger.
- Secondly, in these agrarian movements the **peasant emerged as the main force** who had his own strong notions of legitimacy, specifically '*of what was justifiable and what was not*'. That is the major reason why in all these movements he never fought for land ownership or against landlordism but against eviction or undue enhancement of rent. Similarly, he never questioned the state's right to collect a tax on land but objected to it only when the level of taxation overstepped all traditional bounds.

> *"He did not object to paying interest on the sums he had borrowed; he hit back against fraud and chicanery by the moneylender and when the latter went against tradition in depriving him of his land. He did not object to the foreign planter becoming his zamindar but resisted the planter when he took away his freedom to decide what crops to grow and refused to pay him a proper price for his crop."*
>
> Bipan Chandra

- The other important feature was that these **struggles were directed towards redressal of some particular grievances** and once the specific objectives were achieved, the movement's organisation, along with peasant solidarity built around it, gradually dissolved and disappeared. For instance, the Indigo Rebellion, the Pabna agrarian leagues and the social-boycott movement of the Deccan *ryots* left behind no successors. Similarly, these movements remained largely disjointed, isolated and confined to particular localities lacking thereby wider linkages and continuity of struggle and, thus, at no stage did these movements ever undermine or threaten British supremacy.

> *"Peasant protest after 1857 often represented an instinctive and spontaneous response of the peasantry to its social condition. It was the result of excessive and unbearable oppression, undue and unusual deprivation and exploitation, and a threat to the peasant's existing, established position. The peasant often rebelled only when he felt that it was not possible to carry on in the existing manner."*
>
> Bipan Chandra

- Fourthly, in these movements, **colonialism was never the direct target** nor peasants ever directly challenged the British rule. In most cases, the peasants' focus of attention were their immediate oppressors, be it foreign planters or indigenous *zamindaris* and moneylenders. Due to this aspect, the colonial regime's treatment of the post-1857 peasant rebels was also qualitatively different and not that harsh as compared to its treatment of the participants of the pre-1857 rebellions who had otherwise posed a direct challenge to British authority. However, it is also pertinent to note that even though these movements never aimed directly at colonial rule yet at most instances they seriously contested the hegemony of the colonial state.
- Another striking new feature about these movements was the fact about **greater involvement of the educated middle class** in these peasant movements. These intelligentsia leaders most times acted as spokespersons for the aggrieved peasantry and as rightly pointed out by Ravinder Kumar '*performed an important and effective function as a channel of communication, between rural society and the administration at a time when the traditional channels and methods had become ineffective*' and in the process added new dimensions to agrarian protests thereby linking these movements to a wider struggle against the undesirable aspects of colonial rule.

However, certain **weaknesses** were common to peasants movements of both pre- and post-1857 era. The peasant movements in both timelines suffered from the **same lack of adequate understanding** of complex phenomenon of **colonialism**, its **real nature**, underlying **economic structure** and effects on **social framework**. The struggles inherent in these movements occurred within the framework of the **same old societal order** and as pointed out by some historians, the peasants identified themselves more with their **cultural groups** rather than with the economic category of 'class'. They not only **lacked a new ideology** but also an **all-India leadership** having vision of an alternative society – which would unite the people in a common struggle on a wide regional and all-India plane and help develop a strategy of struggle that would unify and mobilise peasants and other sections of society for nationwide *political* activity long-term political movements.

However, most of these weaknesses were overcome in the 20th century when peasant discontent was **merged** with the general anti-imperialist discontent and their political activity became a part of the wider anti-imperialist movement. And, of course, the peasants' participation in the larger national movement not only strengthened the fight against the foreigner but it also, simultaneously, enabled them to organise powerful struggles around their class demands and to create modem peasant organisation. In the absence of ideology, programme, leadership and strategy of struggle, it was not too difficult for the colonial state, on the one hand, to reach a conciliation and calm down the rebellious peasants by the grant of some concessions arid and on the other hand, to suppress them with the full use of its force. This weakness was, of course, not a blemish on the character of the peasantry, which was perhaps incapable of grasping on its own the new and complex phenomenon of colonialism. That needed the efforts of a modem intelligentsia which was itself just coming into existence. Nevertheless, the series of peasant uprisings that took place throughout the 19th and the early 20th centuries seriously **contested the hegemony** of the colonial state and as we would be witnessing in our later chapters, these sentiments were later channelised by the Indian National Congress under the able guidance of Gandhi ji in the coming years in its struggle against British rule.

Previous Year's Questions (Prelims)

1. Consider the following events: (1999)

1. Indigo Revolt
2. Santhal Rebellion
3. Deccan Riot
4. Mutiny of sepoys

The correct chronological sequence of these events is:

(a) 4, 2, 1, 3 (b) 4, 2, 3, 1

(c) 2, 4, 3, 1 (d) 2, 4, 1, 3

2. Match List-I with List-II and select the correct answer using the code given below the lists. (1997)

List-I	List-II
a. Moplah revolt	1. Kerala
b. Pabna revolt	2. Bihar
c. Eka movement	3. Bengal
d. Birsa Munda revolt	4. Awadh

	A	B	C	D
(a)	1	3	4	2
(b)	2	3	4	1
(c)	1	2	3	4
(d)	3	4	1	2

3. Which one of the following upheavals took place in Bengal immediately after the Revolt of 1857? (1994)

(a) Sanyasi Rebellion

(b) Santhal Rebellion

(c) Indigo disturbances

(d) Pabna disturbances

Previous Year's Answer (Prelims)

1. (d) 2. (a) 3. (c)

The Early Nationalists: Moderates and Extremists

6

The early years of the Indian National Congress (INC) saw the evolution of two different styles of politics and ideologies along with adoption of different political methods of agitation by each to oppose the colonial rule. The first two decades of the INC, that is, 1885–1905 were marked by **Moderate** politics, as during this period, the Congress was dominated by moderate leaders who had implicit faith in the providential nature of British rule and strongly believed in the efficacy of peaceful and constitutional agitation. However, by the end of the 19th century, the failure of moderate politics became quite apparent, and gradually a section emerged within the Congress referred to as the **Extremists** who criticised the Moderates for being too cautious and denounced their style of politics as being *politics of mendicancy*, and instead advocated for more direct confrontation with the colonial rule. Their differences eventually led to the **split in Congress** in 1907. In this chapter we will be studying these developments and how they affected the early national movement.

The Moderates (1885–1905)

The Congress phase from 1885 to 1905 is generally known as the Moderate phase, mostly owing to the fact that during this phase not only its demands were modest but the political activity undertaken by its leaders involving constitutional agitation was also moderate and well within the confines of law along with the loyalty to the crown and British empire. The leadership during this era was dominated by moderate politicians who shared an intrinsic faith in the essential sense of justice and goodness of the English democratic liberal political tradition and worked under the misplaced belief that if they could acquaint the liberal political opinion in England with the true miserable state of affairs in India, that is, the 'un-British rule' perpetrated by the Viceroy, his executive council and the Anglo-Indian bureaucracy, then the wrongs and imperfections will be rectified and they would be recognised as partners and not subordinates in the affairs of the government. The Moderates were also referred to as the ***Early Nationalists***.

Some of the prominent Moderate leaders were Dadabhai Naoroji, Pherozeshah Mehta, Surendranath Banerjee, G. K. Gokhale, G. Subramania Iyer, W. C. Banerjee, Badruddin Tyabji, R. C. Dutt, Rash Behari Ghosh, M. G. Ranade, William Wedderburn, Madan Mohan Malaviya and Ananda Charlu.

Leader	Remarks
• Dadabhai Naoroji (1825–1917)	• Famously called The Grand Old Man of India. • Was the **first Indian** to become a member of the House of Commons in Britain as a member of the Liberal Party (1892–95). • Wrote the seminal text, *Poverty and Un-British Rule in India* (1901), which focused on the economic drain of India because of British policies. • Started a fortnightly publication in Gujarati, *Rast Goftar* (1851), to promote the message of social reforms, equality and fraternity of the Parsi sect. • Founded the London Indian Society (1865) and East India Association (1867). • Served as the President of the INC in the years 1886, 1893 and 1906. • Was also the first moderate leader to demand ***Swaraj*** in the year 1904.
• Sir Pherozeshah Mehta (1845–1915)	• Famously called the *father of municipal government in Bombay* for both his involvement in and advocacy for local self-governance in Bombay. He not only helped in drafting the Bombay Municipal Act in 1872 but also served as Municipal Commissioner in 1873 and the Chairman in 1884–85 and again in 1905. Later, he also became a member of the Bombay Legislative Council in 1893. • He was also the founder of the Bombay Presidency Association and later presided over the sixth session of the INC in 1890. • He was knighted in 1904 by the British Government, and in 1910 he was also appointed as vice chancellor of the University of Bombay. • In 1910, he founded the newspaper *Bombay Chronicle*, and in 1911, he was instrumental in the establishment of the Central Bank of India.
• Sir Surendranath Banerjee (1848–1925)	• Also known as the *Rashtraguru* and *Indian Burke*. • Founded the Indian National Association (1876), which later merged with the INC. • Served as the President of the INC in the years 1895 and 1902. • Second Indian to clear the Indian Civil Service but was dismissed for a minor and apparently inadvertent procedural error. • Founded the newspaper *The Bengalee*. • Was knighted in 1921.
• Gopal Krishna Gokhale (1866–1915)  Gopal Krishna Gokhale	• Revered by Mahatma Gandhi as his political guru who also wrote a memoir on him in Gujarati, *Dharmatma Gokhale*. • Served as the President of the INC in 1905 (the youngest leader ever elected as President at the Benaras Session). • Founded the **Servants of India Society** (1905). • He had extensive experience of working in legislatures. Was a member of the Bombay Legislative Council (1899 and 1902) and Imperial Legislative Council (1902–15). • Was associated with the *Sarvajanik Sabha* journal started by M. G. Ranade. • Started the English weekly newspaper, the ***Hitavada*** (people's paper).

Leader	Remarks
• G. Subramania Iyer (1855–1916)	• Founded the newspaper *The Hindu* and a Tamil daily called *Swadesamitran*. • Co-founded the *Madras Mahajana Sabha* (1884). • Was a staunch supporter of **widow remarriage** (remarried his own widowed daughter) and was vehemently opposed to untouchability and child marriage.
• Womesh Chandra Bonnerjee (1844–1906)	• First President of the Bombay session of INC in 1885, who again presided over the Allahabad session of INC in 1892. • Lawyer by profession, he became the first Indian to be appointed as a **Standing Counsel** in 1882, and he officiated in this capacity thrice in 1884, 1886 and 1887. • He was also famous for defending **Surendranath Banerjee** in a contempt of court case in the High Court of Calcutta. • He also became the first Indian to stand for election for the British Parliament (although he was defeated).
• Badruddin Tyabji (1844–1906)	• He along with Pherozeshah Mehta and K. T. Telang formed the *Bombay Presidency Association* (1885). • He was the first Muslim President of the INC (third session, 1887). • He was the first Indian barrister in the High Court of Bombay and was also the first Muslim and third Indian to be elevated as judge of the Bombay High Court in 1895.

• R. C. Dutt (1848–1909)	• He joined the Indian Civil Service and belonged to the famous batch of 1869, which produced four Indians in the Indian Civil Service, including R. C. Dutt, Bihari Lal Gupta, Surendranath Banerjee and Sripad Babaji Thakur.
	• He became President of the INC in 1899.
	• After his retirement from the Civil Service, Dutt was appointed a Lecturer in Indian History in the University of London. He, however, returned to India in 1904 and served as Revenue Minister in the State of Baroda.
	• He also served as a member of the Decentralisation Commission (1908).
	• Is widely regarded as an economic historian of India. Famous books include:
	  • ***Economic History of India in the Victorian Age*** (1902)
	  • *India under Early British Rule*, 1757–1837 (1901)
	  • *Famines in India* (1900)
	  • *Peasantry of Bengal* (1875).

• Sir Rash Behari Ghosh (1845–1921)	• He was the President of two sessions of INC, in Surat (1907) and in Madras (1908). • He also served as a member of the Bengal Legislative Council between 1891 and 1894 (during which he also served as member of the Secretary of State's Council of India in 1891 and in 1893) and then again between 1906 and 1909. • He was knighted in 1915.

Leader	Remarks
• M. G. Ranade (1842–1901)	• He was a noted historian, social reformer and also a judge who fought tirelessly against child marriage and worked for **widow remarriage** and **upliftment of women** through education. • Regarded as the 'father of Indian economics', he believed that India's excessive reliance on agriculture was the root cause of its economic problems, and in order to achieve economic development, it is very crucial to prioritise industry and commerce over agriculture. • Authored famous books like *the publication of Rise of the Maratha Power* (1900).
• William Wedderburn (1838–1918)	• He was Scottish in origin and an accomplished civil servant who was supportive of the aspirations of Indians. • He presided over the fourth INC session held in Bombay in 1889 and later also entered Parliament in 1893 as a Liberal member and through that platform tried to voice India's grievances in the House. • He remained the Chairman of the British Committee of the Congress from 1889 until his death.

• Madan Mohan Malaviya (1861–1946)	• Was given the title of ***Mahamana*** by Rabindranath Tagore while Dr. S. Radhakrishna (the second President of India) bestowed on him the status of a ***Karmayogi***.
	• He popularised the term *Satyamev Jayate* (which originally belongs to the Mundaka Upanishad and is now is the national motto of India).
	• He is also remembered for his prominent role in ending the **Indian indenture system**, that is, recruitment of Indian indentured labour, especially in the Caribbean (one of the British colonies), and the nationalisation of railways.
	• One of his other great achievements was the introduction of the *Devnagri* in the British Indian courts.
	• He was elected President of Congress in 1909 (Lahore), in 1918 (Delhi), in 1930 (Delhi) and in 1932 (Calcutta).
	• He also served on the Imperial Legislative Council for 11 years (1909–20).
	• He helped establish the **Hindu Mahasabha** ('Great Society of Hindus') in 1906 and Banaras Hindu University in Varanasi in 1916. He also served as its Vice Chancellor for about two decades (1919–38).
	• He was also associated with certain dailies such as:
	  • the *Abhyudaya*, a Hindi-language weekly (1907)
	  • the *Leader of Allahabad*, an English-language daily (1909) and
	  • the *Maryada,* a Hindi-language monthly (1910).

• Ananda Charlu (1843–1908)	• Founded the Madras Mahajan Sabha (1884). • He was one of the founding members of INC and later in 1891, he also served as its President at the Nagpur session. • He was a member of the Madras Legislative Council (1903–05).

Nature and Character of the Moderates

- The Moderates were staunch believers in **liberalism** and **moderate politics**. They were cautious and modest in their demands, and elements of radicalism were absent in their attitude and activities. Not only the goals were modest but even the means by which such goals were pursued were also exceedingly moderate. The same is clearly evident from the language of the Congress resolutions adopted under Moderate leadership, wherein the opposing government action or inaction was never 'condemned' but rather 'regretted' and resolutions proposing some course of action or remedy to the government also never 'demanded' but rather 'suggested' or at the most 'urged'.

"The object of the Indian National Congress shall be to promote by constitutional means the interests and well being of the people of the Indian Empire and the provincial units of the Congress were to engage in political activity on the lines of general appreciation of British rule and of constitutional action for the removal of its defects"

First[1] Constitution adopted by Congress in 1899

"The general timidity of the Congress, its glossing over of hard names ... its fear of too deeply displeasing our masters"

Aurobindo Ghose, one of the Extremist critics of the INC

- The Moderates had absolute faith in the **providential nature** of British rule and its role in bringing modernisation in India. So, if modesty of goals and moderation in aims were two factors constitutive of the Moderates' 'moderation', an **active loyalism** was a third characteristic feature and one that underwrote the other two. Loyalty was frequently invoked by Moderate leaders to answer or preempt British accusations of disloyalty.

"If we do honestly expect the English nation will do its duty towards us, we must prove ourselves worthy by showing that we are never unreasonable, never violent, never uncharitable. We must show that we are earnest, but temperate, cognisant of our rights, but respectful of those of others."

Dadabhai Naoroji, 1886.

"Who ... will better appreciate advantages of good roads, railways, telegraphs and post offices, schools, colleges and universities, hospitals, good laws and impartial courts of justice?"

– the educated natives or the ignorant peasants of this country? Badruddin Tyabji in his 1887 presidential address to the Madras Congress speaking against the British charge that the Congress represented a small and unrepresentative elite that had become disaffected with British rule.

"Thanks to British rule that I could attend the Congress session with the help of railways and without the least fear that my children might be robbed and killed in my absence."

Dadabhai Naoroji pointing out the blessings of British rule.

"It was not 'a nest of conspirators and disloyalists'; they were thoroughly loyal and consistent well-wishers of the British Government."

W. C. Bonnerji, the President of the first Congress.

[1] Also one of the short-lived.

> *"The National Congress is the outcome of those civilising influences which Macaulay and his co-aujutors were instrumental in planning in the government of this country."*
>
> Surendranath Banerjee justifying the beneficial effect of British rule and declaring that INC was far from being a source of sedition and was itself the product of British rule.

- However, the Moderates did criticise British rule for failing to live up to its own promises, but their complaint was only against **un-British rule** in India which according to them was mostly perpetrated by the bureaucracy – an imperfection that they believed the British Parliament was not much aware of and, thus, in order to sensitise them about the Indian opinion and the problems faced by the Indians, they repeatedly sent resolutions, petitions and prayers to the English liberal democratic leaders, made speeches and published articles. By using these constitutional tools, they tried to prepare a convincing 'logical case' aimed at persuading the liberal political opinion in England to gradually grant 'self-government' to India. In fact, a great deal of Congress activity in the initial years was centred in England and directed at persuading the English. Deputations of leading Indians were sent to Britain to present the Indian viewpoint and to further the agenda, even a **British Committee of Indian National Congress**[2] was founded in 1889, which through its organ *India* presented the Indian opinion to the British authorities. Also, the Congress speeches, even when addressed to an Indian audience, seemed to address a second, English audience as one can witness in the speeches of many Moderate leaders, wherein support of any argument, English and Anglo-Indians officials were extensively quoted by them as if they were seeking the necessary validation from the English people.
- The Moderate leaders were **nationalist**, **liberal** and **modernising** in their orientation since the goals sought by the Moderate leaders were sought in the name of India and the Indian people, and the national aspirations were expected to be expressed through liberal and representative institutions based on the firm foundation of a modern and industrialised economy. They were **progressive** in their outlook as they tried to adopt positive elements from every possible source, including the west.
- The Moderates were primarily influenced by the western ideas of **Enlightenment**[3] and **Utilitarian thinkers** such as John Stuart Mill, Edmund Burke and John Morley, who believed that the government needs to be guided by expediency and not by any moral or ethical laws along with the firm belief in the **inviolability of the constitution**. Hence, they not only repeatedly appealed to the British parliament complaining about the Government of India subverting the constitution but also regularly employed the constitutional methods of agitation to fight for their demands. For instance, the Moderates frequently referred to the 1833 Government of India Act and the Royal proclamation of 1858 – both of which had stated that *natives would not be debarred from holding office in the bureaucracy*, thus always professing to desire nothing more than what was promised in those documents but had not in fact been granted. The Moderate leaders reiterated and prided themselves at every opportunity on the constitutionalist and gradualist nature of their political activity.
- Quite interestingly, even though the Moderates were conscious of the exploitative nature of British rule, they only wanted its **reform** and **not expulsion**. Also, since the Moderates equated liberty with class privilege, they never demanded equality but only gradual or piecemeal reforms. For instance, in terms of constitution, they only wanted a **limited self-government** within the imperial framework and, thus, never

---

[2] Dadabhai Naoroji was a prominent member of the British Committee of the Indian National Congress, and as a result he spent a major part of his life in England and even got elected to the British House of Commons and formed a strong Indian lobby in that House. Also, it was decided in 1890 to hold a session of the Indian National Congress in London in 1892, but owing to the British elections of 1891, the proposal was postponed and never revived later.

[3] Since most of them had received a western education.

visualised a clinical separation from the British empire. The immediate demand of Moderates was not democracy or full 'self-government', they demanded democratic rights only for the educated members of Indian society who would substitute for the masses. The expectation of the Moderate politicians was that full political freedom would come gradually and India would be ultimately given the self-governing right like those enjoyed by the other colonies such as Canada or Australia. With an intrinsic faith in the providential nature of British rule in India, they hoped that one day they would be recognised as partners and not subordinates in the affairs of the empire and be given the rights of full British citizenship. They demanded Indian control over the public purse and raised the slogan that had earlier been raised by the Americans during their War of Independence, *No taxation without representation*. Gradually, the scope of constitutional demands was widened and **Dadabhai Naoroji** (1904), **Gopal Krishna Gokhale** (1905) and **Lokmanya Tilak** (1906) demanded 'self-government' like the self-governing colonies of Canada and Australia.

"In my belief a greater calamity would not befall India than for England to go away and leave her to herself"

Dadabhai Naoroji, 1871.

"We have not asked for Parliamentary institutions which England has got after many centuries of discipline. We have not asked for the power of the purse, and we have not asked that the British Executive should be brought under subjugation to us."

K. T. Telang, speaking at the fourth annual session of Congress at Allahabad in 1888.

"The people of India are, at present, neither asking for, nor thinking of, representative government, but what they do insist on is, that an appreciable portion of the advisers of Government should be their elected representatives."

Surendranath Banerjee, 1888.

"We do not think India is ripe for it yet, nor do we want Home Rule ... we only press for the reform of the legislative councils which impose taxes and make the laws."

Surendranath Banerjee, April 1890.

"I can never think, that England will ever retrace her steps or forget her duty to India. She came not as a conqueror but as a deliverer with the ready acquiescence of the people, to heal and settle, to substitute order and good government for disorder and anarchy. ... That task has now been accomplished ... and it only remains for England now to fit us gradually for that autonomy which she has granted to her colonies."

Rash Behari Ghosh

"If we do honestly expect the English nation will do its duty towards us, we must prove ourselves worthy by showing that we are never unreasonable, never violent, never uncharitable. We must show that we are earnest, but temperate, cognisant of our rights, but respectful of those of others."

Dadabhai Nairobi, 1886

- The Moderate leaders raised very **modest demands**. They mostly demanded moderate constitutional reforms, reallocation of military charges, reformation of administrative system, adoption of protectionist policy to protect Indian industries and reduction of land revenue assessment.

Field	Major Demands
• **Within Constitutional Field**	• Broaden Indian participation in legislatures through an expansion of the central and provincial legislatures by introducing 50 per cent elected representation from local bodies, chambers of commerce, universities and so forth. • Two Indian members in the Viceroy's Executive Council and one such member in each of the executive councils of Bombay and Madras. • New councils for the North-Western Provinces and Punjab. • Right of reference of the budget to the legislature, which should have the right to discuss and vote on it, including the right of interpellation. • Provision of a right to appeal to the Standing Committee of the House of Commons against the Government of India. • Abolition or reconstitution of the India Council.
• **Reformation of the Administrative System**	• Indianisation of the services. • Simultaneous civil service examination both in India and London and the raising of the age limit for appearing in such examinations from 19 to 23.
• **Military Reforms**	• Reduction of military expenditure. • Even sharing of military expenditure by the British Government. • More intake of Indians into the army as volunteers. • The appointment of Indians to the commissioned higher ranks in the Army.
• **Other Administrative Demands**	• The separation of the judiciary from the executive. • Extension of trial by jury. • Repeal of the Arms Act. • No over-assessment of land revenue. • Extension of the Permanent Settlement to other parts of India. • Abolition of salt tax. • Prevention of exploitation of the indentured labour at the Assam tea gardens.

- But there was hardly any response from the Government, and none of the demands were ever fulfilled by the colonial administration. For instance, in terms of constitution, the British Government passed the Indian Councils Amendment[4] Act of 1892, which provided for only marginal expansion of the legislative councils both at the centre and the provinces, and even these councils were to be constituted through selection[5] rather than election. The budget could also not be voted on but only discussed in the legislatures, and neither could the members bring in any resolution nor demand a vote on any resolution proposed by the government.

[4] The Indian Councils Act of 1892 was an amending Act as the basic constitutional provisions introduced under the Act of 1861 remained the same but two types of prominent changes were introduced: (a) Changes in the composition of legislative bodies and (b) Enlargement of functions.

[5] The local bodies would send their nominees from among whom the viceroy at the centre and the governors at the provinces would select the members of the legislative councils.

The Indian Councils Act of 1892
• The Act increased the number of additional or non-official members in both Central and Provincial legislative councils though the official majority was maintained since the Act recommended for the strength of the non-officials at two-fifths of the additional members. For instance, the maximum number of non-officials was fixed at: • Central Legislative Council: 10–16 members (to be read as not less than 10 and not more than 16) • Madras: 8–20 members • Bombay: 8–20 members • Bengal: 20 members • Oudh: 15 members • North Western Province: 15 members. In 1892, out of 24 members, only 5 were Indians.
• The Act enlarged the functions of the Legislative Councils as besides discussing legislative proposals, they were authorised to discuss and ask questions about the annual financial statement, that is, Budget under certain conditions and restrictions (which was otherwise barred in the Indian Councils Act, 1861). Supplementary questions were, however, not allowed.
• The Councils' members were also given the right to ask questions to the Government of India on matters of public interest; however, the same was allowed on providing a previous notice of 6 days to the Government, and the President of the Council had the authority to disallow any questions without giving any reason.
• Though the word 'election' was not used in the Act, it did make a **limited and indirect provision for election** in filling up some of the non-official seats both in the Central and provincial legislative councils. Thus, instead of election, it did provide for the nomination by the Viceroy on recommendation of the provincial legislative councils and the Bengal Chamber of Commerce in the Central Legislative Council and by the Governors in case of provincial legislative councils based on the recommendation by certain bodies like the district boards, universities, municipalities, chambers of commerce and zamindars. So, in a way, a process of representation was initiated.

Thus, the legislative councils were at best only recommendatory and did not have any authority in the real sense, while incongruously the Government of India had the power to legislate even without referring to the legislatures. Similarly, the sorry state of affairs was regarding reformation of the administrative system. Though a resolution[6] was passed for simultaneous examination in the House of Commons, the same could not be effected until 1922[7] due to resistance by the Government of India. More ironically, instead of raising the age limit, the maximum age for examination was further lowered to the disadvantage of the Indians. Similarly, in terms of military reforms and other administrative demands, most of the demands were rejected. The Government of India only agreed to share a small fraction of the military expenditure[8] and, thus, the burden on the Indian finances more or less remained the same.

Moderates and Economic Nationalism

However, despite all these setbacks, the most significant historical contribution of the Moderates was that they offered an economic critique of colonialism that is often referred to as **economic nationalism** and which was based on the realisation that the British rule was inherently inimical to the economic interests of India. During the years 1870–1905, the economic analysis of British rule was done primarily by Dadabhai Naoroji, Justice

[6] In 1892–93 under the initiative of William Gladstone.

[7] When finally the demand of simultaneous exams was materialised and the exams for the Covenanted Services were first held in India.

[8] Less than £1 million in all, which was even further reduced by the higher exchange rates.

Mahadev Govind Ranade[9], Romesh Chander Dutt[10], G. Subramania Iyer, Gopal Krishna Gokhale, G. V. Joshi, Bal Gangadhar Tilak, Prithwas Chandra Ray and Surendranath Banerjee. These leaders along with hundreds of other political workers and journalists not only subjected the colonial economic policies to minute scrutiny but also raised basic questions about the process of the colonialisation of the Indian economy. Eventually, they delineated the colonial structure in all its aspects of domination and were able to clearly establish that colonialism no longer functioned through the crude, older and direct modes of extraction like tribute, plunder and mercantilism but operated through the more sophisticated and disguised mechanism of exploitation through free trade and foreign capital investment and in the process, India was intentionally reduced to the status of a dependent agrarian economy and a field for the investment of British capital.

The main thrust of this economic nationalism was on the following important themes:

- **The Drain of Wealth**: One of the key themes of economic nationalism was the 'drain of wealth', the theory put forward by the venerated nationalist Dadabhai Naoroji,[11] who argued that the colonial rulers were unilaterally transferring resources from India to Britain without any corresponding economic and commercial gain to India, thus leading to the country's impoverishment. The direct drainage of Indian capital and wealth[12] took place through **military charges**[13], **home charges**[14], **interests on loans** taken by the Indian Government, **profits of British capitalists** in India and **guaranteed interest payment** on railway investments. In Naoroji's own calculation, this huge drainage amounted to about £12 million per year, while William Digby who wrote the famous book *Prosperous British India* calculated it to be £30 million. On average, this amounted to at least half of the total revenue income of the British Indian Government, more than the entire land revenue collection, and over one-third of India's total savings[15], which thus directly impoverished India and stultified the process of capital formation. For nearly half a century, Dadabhai carried on his struggle against drain and declared that the drain was the basic cause of India's poverty. His book *Poverty and Un-British Rule in India* (1901) still remains a significant milestone in the formulation of the nationalist political economy. Dadabhai's work was further supplemented by several other nationalist leaders and journalists like William Digby, G. S. Iyer[16] and R. C. Dutt who made drain the major theme of his iconic book *Economic History of India* (1901–03).

> *"Britain was siphoning off India's wealth which amounted to about 25 per cent of country's revenue which was added to the resources of England."*
>
> Excerpts from Dadabhai Naoroji's speech, May 1867.
>
> *"How can Britain ignore India's interests, and make it the drudge for the benefit of England. This was unnatural and a monstrous evil and thus to stop the bleeding drain from India was the most important question of the day and I therefore exhort all my countrymen to summon all their energies to solve this problem."*
>
> Excerpts from Dadabhai Naoroji's speech, 1873.

---

[9] Who taught an entire generation of Indians the value of modern industrial development.

[10] A retired ICS officer who published *The Economic History of India* in which he examined in minute detail the entire economic record of colonial rule since 1757.

[11] In fact, cognition of the negative economic consequences of British colonial rule in India can be traced back to the early years of the 1830s in the writings of Raja Rammohan Roy who complained against the 'tribute' paid to Britain and showed his concern for the plight of the self-cultivating peasants.

[12] And the burden became heavier because of the falling exchange rates of the rupee in the 1890s, which was further compounded by budget deficits, higher taxes and military expenditure.

[13] Salaries and pensions of British military officials and costs of wars waged by the British on behalf of India.

[14] The payment of expenses of the Indian Government in Britain.

[15] In today's terms, this would amount to 8 per cent of India's national income.

[16] Wrote *Some Economic Aspects of British Rule in India (1903)*.

> *"It is not the pitiless operations of economic laws, but it is the thoughtless and pitiless action of the British policy; it is the pitiless eating of India's substance in India, and the further pitiless drain to England; in short, it is the pitiless perversion of economic laws by the sad bleeding to which India is subjected, that is destroying India."*
>
> Excerpts from Dadabhai Naoroji's speech, 1880.
>
> *"The present policy of the British has been rigorous in regard to draining India of its wealth and reducing it to poverty. The destruction of the indigenous industry in Maharashtra, as in India as a whole, resulted in poverty and misery of the artisans. Moreover, the siphoning of India's wealth between the battle of Plassey in 1757 and 1815 amounted to about 1,000 million pounds."*
>
> Bhaskar Tarkhadkar

With the drain theory, the exploitative character of British rule was made visible, and the nationalist leaders were able to call into question the economic essence of imperialism. Indeed, the drain theory was the high watermark of the economic analysis of the colonial situation, and the idea was quickly and easily grasped by a nation of peasants who understood the underlying economic exploitation as he could relate the same to his own daily life where he underwent the same experiences vis-à-vis the landlords, moneylenders, priests and state, and thus subsequently the drain analogy became the main staple of nationalist political agitation.

- **Poverty of Indian people**: Another popular sentiment in the anti-colonial nationalist narrative was that of 'poverty'. The nationalist intellectuals argued that India was one of the poorest countries in the world despite more than a century of British rule, and what was even worse was that this poverty was growing. They underlined that the all-encompassing poverty was not inherent or unavoidable but was in fact man-made due to the exploitative colonial policies and imperialist character of the colonial regime meant only to serve the British interests. They asserted that the poverty in India was created by the application of the classical economic theory of free trade as India was intentionally turned into a supplier of agricultural raw materials for Britain and a consumer of its manufactured goods, thereby reducing it to the status of a **dependent agrarian economy** which coupled with the drain of wealth resulted in impoverishment of India. Also, high land revenue demands resulted in **impoverishment** of the peasantry while the absence of protective tariff in the interest of the British manufacturers further hindered the industrialisation of India along with **destruction of the native handicraft industry**. This again led to the overburdening of agriculture and further impoverishment of the general masses, thereby creating a vicious cycle from which the common man could never come out of unscathed. This discussion made poverty a broad national issue and helped to unite different regions and sections of Indian society. The debate on the 'poverty problem' was raised to such a pitch that the British officials who initially denied the existence of poverty and instead tried to paint a rosy picture of colonial rule were forced to respond to them. But, the figures given by the nationalists, quoting mostly from the official sources, required something more than flat denial. Naoroji calculated the per capita income of the Indians to be ₹20, while Digby's calculation was ₹18 for 1899. The government did not accept this calculation and in 1882, Ripon's finance secretary calculated it to be ₹27, while Lord Curzon in 1901 calculated it to be ₹30; however, the famines and epidemics of this period told a different story.

> *"Materially British rule caused only 'impoverishment'; it was like 'the knife of sugar', that is to say there is no oppression, it is all smooth and sweet, but it is the knife, notwithstanding"*
>
> Dadabhai Naoroji
>
> *"If India is poor today, it is through the operation of economic causes."*
>
> R. C. Dutt
>
> *"Full fifty millions of the population, a number yearly increasing, are dragging out a miserable existence on the verge of starvation, and that, in every decade, several millions actually perish by starvation."*
>
> The Indian National Congress, 1891
>
> *"We are standing on the edge of a precipice, and the slightest push down will drive us into the abyss below of unmixed and absolute helplessness."*
>
> M. G. Ranade

- **Underdevelopment of Industry**: The early nationalists were of the firm opinion that under the colonial rule, India was going through a process of industrial underdevelopment which was caused by basically **three reasons**, all closely related to colonial policies:
    - progressive decline and ruin of India's indigenous industries like traditional handicrafts,
    - the failure to quickly develop the modern industry in India and
    - forcing the infant and underdeveloped native industries into a premature, unequal[17] and **unfair competition** with the highly developed and organised industries of the West.

    All of these reasons were responsible for the poverty of the Indian people as while the jobs in one sector were being lost, the same was not being compensated by the rapid growth of the modern industries. The Moderates regularly pointed out that India was once a great manufacturing country that exported its goods to all parts of Asia and Europe but now due to colonial policies, the pattern had undergone drastic changes as India **from being a net exporter of finished goods** was reduced[18] to an **exporter of raw materials** and **net importer of manufactured goods from Britain**. The Moderates argued that India was being integrated within global capitalism in a subordinate position which Ranade defined as 'dependent colonial economy'. All of this resulted in net decline in India's net wealth and employment opportunities while leading to increase in poverty, ruralisation and de-industrialisation, putting further pressure on agriculture which itself was in a precarious situation.

[17] The abolition of tariff on British goods adversely affected the native industries as cheap foreign goods were allowed to penetrate the country's markets, which not only limited the possibility of the growth of modern industry in India but also destroyed the indigenous handicrafts industry.

[18] Until 1813, India had been primarily an exporter of manufactured goods, particularly cotton and silk textiles, and an importer of precious metals such as gold and silver. However, in the 19th century, it became an exporter of primary products such as raw cotton, jute, other industrial raw materials such as tea, coffee and food grains, and an importer of manufactured goods.

> *"The country was being transformed into a plantation, growing raw produce to be shipped by British Agents in British ships, to be worked into Fabrics by British skill and capital, and to be re-exported to the Dependency by British merchants to their corresponding British firms."*
>
> M. G. Ranade
>
> *"It had been the settled policy of England in India ever since her rise in political power, to convert India into a land of raw produce for the benefit of the manufacturers and operatives of England."*
>
> Surendranath Banerjee

The nationalists, therefore, demanded that such policies which obstructed the growth of Indian industries be removed and emphasis be laid on speedy industrialisation of the country initiated by Indian capital itself and not foreign capital. Foreign capital, as Dadabhai puts it, represented *the despoilation* and *exploitation* of Indian resources, further leading to *political subjugation* since foreign capital investment created vested interests which demanded security for investors and, therefore, perpetuated foreign rule. The Moderates considered foreign capital as an unmitigated evil that did not develop a country but exploited and impoverished it, as foreign capital not only suppressed the Indian capital but also led to the drain of capital from India and further strengthened the British hold over the Indian economy.

> *"Where foreign capital has been sunk in a country, the administration of that country becomes at once the concern of the bondholders. If the influence of foreign capitalists in the land is allowed to increase, then adieu to all chances of success of the Indian National Congress whose voice will be drowned in the tremendous uproar of the empire in danger that will surely be raised by the foreign capitalists."*
>
> *The Hindu* in its issue dated 23 September 1889
>
> *"The introduction of foreign, and mostly British, capital for working out the natural resources of the Country, instead of being a help, is, in fact, the greatest of hindrances to all real improvements in the economic condition of the people. It is as much a political, as it is an economic danger. And the future of New India absolutely depends upon as early and radical remedy of this two-edged evil."*
>
> Bipin Chandra Pal

Similarly, the early nationalists pointed out that the railways, which the British often portrayed as an instrument of India's development and proof of its growing prosperity, had also not been coordinated with India's industrial needs since it was primarily utilised for importing foreign goods to undersell domestic industrial products. Also, the nationalists regularly argued that both backward and forward linkages pertaining to the benefits of railway construction in terms of encouragement to the steel and machine industry and to capital investment had been reaped by Britain and not India. Thus, according to them, railways ushered in a commercial revolution in India and not an industrial revolution.

> *"The expenditure on railways should be seen as Indian subsidy to British industries."*
>
> G. V. Joshi
>
> *"The expenditure spent on railways was like 'decorating another's wife."*
>
> Tilak

- **Public Finance**: The early nationalists strongly criticised the colonial pattern of finance and all aspects pertaining to it: **how much revenue was collected, from whom** and **how it was spent**. Taking the amount of collection as a proportion of the income of each individual, Naoroji argued that the taxes in India were 16 per cent while in England it was only 8 per cent. Also, the taxes so raised were by overburdening the poor while letting the rich, especially the foreign capitalists and bureaucrats, go scot-free. To address these concerns, the nationalists demanded the reduction of land revenue and abolition of the salt tax while extending support for the imposition of income tax and import duties on products which the rich and the middle classes consumed.

> *"The colonial rulers were screwing out more and more taxes, like squeezing a squeezed orange – inflicting suffering and distress."*
>
> Dadabhai Naoroji
>
> *"No article in India has escaped taxation. Even the foliage of trees has been taxed. There are, however, some things which are yet to be taxed, so that the triumph of the English may be complete. Among such things may be mentioned the skin of the Indian people and their atmosphere."*
>
> Tilak excerpts from his Marathi journal *Kesari*
>
> *"Any further increase of taxation must be adjured as political insanity."*
>
> M. G. Ranade, 1880

Even more important than the amount of taxes, from the nationalist point of view, was the manner of its expenditure. They pointed out that a large part of this tax collection was spent on serving Britain's imperial needs while the developmental and welfare departments of India were being starved. In particular, they condemned the high expenditure on the military, which was used by the British to conquer and maintain imperialist control over large parts of Asia and Africa.

> *"It is not the incidence of taxation that is India's evil ... The evil is the drain of a portion of the revenue out of the country."*
>
> Dadabhai Naoroji

"Taxation raised by a king, says the Indian poet, is like the moisture sucked up by the sun, to be returned to the earth as fertilizing rain; but the moisture raised from the Indian soil now descends as fertilizing rain largely on other lands, not on India. . . . So great an economic Drain out of the resources of a land would impoverish the most prosperous countries on earth; it has reduced India to a land of famines more frequent, more widespread, and more fatal, than any known before in the history of India, or of the world."

R. C. Dutt

"The utility of taxation in any country was decided by the purposes for which the increase has been incurred and the results produced by such outlay of public money. In the European countries and independent nations, the high level of taxation had resulted in increased strength and security to the nations, and increased enlightenment and prosperity to the people. But in India, constantly increasing taxation and its irrational expenditure under autocratic management, defective constitutional control, and the inherent defects of alien domination, only helped to bring about a constantly increasing exploitation of our resources, has retarded our material progress, weakened our natural defences, and burdened us with undefined and indefinite financial liabilities."

G. K. Gokhale, 1897

So, to rectify this situation what the Moderates wanted was a change in economic policies. Their recommendations included reduction of expenditure and taxes, a reallocation of military charges, a responsive Indianised civil service, a protectionist policy to protect Indian industries, reduction of land revenue assessment, extension of Permanent Settlement to *ryotwari* and *mahalwari* areas and encouragement of cottage industries and handicrafts. But none of these demands were fulfilled, and the moderate economic agenda, like its constitutional or administrative agenda, thus remained largely unrealised. However, the economic critique of colonialism at this historical juncture was not a complete failure since it had its own political and ethical significance.

Significance of Economic Nationalism and Moderates

The 'Economic Nationalism' agitation not only greatly contributed in the corrosion of the moral authority of colonial rule but also helped in challenging the whole concept of paternalistic British benevolence. It helped in undermining the ideological hegemony of the colonial rule, as by linking Indian poverty to colonialism, the moderate politicians not only generated anger against British rule but also created an awareness among the masses that India was economically backward because the British were ruling it in the interests of British trade, industry and capital, and thus poverty and backwardness were almost inevitable. The Moderates through their brilliant analysis of the complex economic nationalism could, thus, establish the chief contradiction between the interests of the Indian people and British rule, and over this strong foundation of discursive field laid down by them, the subsequent attacks on colonialism were launched by later nationalists.

"While India is safe-guarded against foreign inroads by the strong arm of the British power, she is defenceless in matters where the English and Indian interests clash and where (as a Tamil saying puts it) the very fence begins to feed on the crop."

P. Ananda Charlu's statement in the Legislative Council

"Surely India is treated as a vast pasture for the Europeans to feed upon."

Tilak's excerpts from his Marathi journal *Kesari*, 1896

"Under the present evil and unrighteous administration of Indian expenditure, the romance is the beneficence of the British Rule, the reality is the bleeding of the British Rule. The romance is that there is security of life and property in India; the reality is that there is no such thing. There is security of life and property in one sense or way, that is, the people are secure from any violence from each other or from Native despots . . . But from England's own grasp there is no security of property at all, and, as a consequence, no security for life . . . What is secure, and well secure, is that England is perfectly safe and secure . . . to carry away from India, and to eat up in India, her property at the present rate of 3,00,00,000 or 4,00,00,000 £ a year . . . To millions in India life is simply 'half- feeding,' or starvation, or famine and disease."

Dadabhai Naoroji

"The face of beneficence was a mask behind which the exploitation of the country was carried on by the British though unaccompanied with any open compulsion or violence to person or property which the world can see and be horrified with."

Dadabhai Naoroji

"With regard to the benefits of law and order there is an Indian saying: 'Pray strike on the back, but don't strike on the belly.' Under the native despot the people keep and enjoy what they produce, though at times they suffer some violence on the back. Under the British Indian despot the man is at peace, there is no violence; his substance is drained away, unseen, peaceably and subtly – he starves in peace, and peaceably perishes in peace, with law and order."

Dadabhai Naoroji

Eventually, the nationalist leaders linked nearly every important economic question with the politically subordinated status of the country. They could gradually establish that development and prosperity in the country could only be brought by a regime in which Indians had control over political power. While minds were being prepared and the goal was being formed, the Moderates cut at the political roots of the British empire and sowed in the hearts of the masses the seeds of disaffection and disloyalty and even sedition for the colonial rule. Thus, the period from 1875 to 1905 became a period of intellectual unrest and of spreading national consciousness, rightly called by Bipin Chandra as *the seedtime of the modern Indian national movement* when the Moderates sowed the seeds of nationalism well and deep which could later serve as strong and enduring foundations for the mass national movement to grow upon and based on this firm foundation, the later nationalists went on to stage powerful mass agitations and mass movements. Even though often accused of being limited elitist politics for limited reforms, nevertheless, the Moderates created a political context which later aided in the development of a unified national movement, eventually raising a very important political demand in the minds of Indian people: *that the basis of the government should be widened and the common masses should have their proper and legitimate share in it.*

Limitations of the Moderates

The Moderate politics, however, suffered from certain limitations in terms of its nature, goals, participation, programmes and achievements:

- The Moderate politics suffered from the lacunae that it was **mostly limited** and **simultaneously alienated** from the greater mass of the Indian population. One of the most probable reasons behind the same was the social background of the moderate politicians, as most of them belonged to the propertied classes. For instance, from the delegates who attended the Congress sessions between 1892 and 1909, about 18.99 per cent of them were landlords, 39.32 per cent of them were lawyers, 15.10 per cent of them were traders, 3.18 per cent were journalists, 2.94 per cent were doctors, 3.16 per cent were teachers and 17.31 per cent were other professionals, and among all segments, most of them were related to landlord families or had landed interests or belonged to commercial classes, which consequently prevented Congress in its initial years from **taking a pro-peasant** or **pro-working class position**. For instance, the early nationalists opposed cadastral survey in 1893–94, though it was meant to protect the peasants from the manipulations of the zamindars and their intriguing *amlas*. Similarly, they were opposed to factory reforms like the Mining Bill, which proposed to improve the living conditions of women and children and restrict their employment under a certain age. It was, thus, the **pro-landlord** and **pro-bourgeois policies** of the early Congress politicians that alienated it from the poor masses. It is also pertinent to note that Congress at that time was hardly a full-fledged political party and was more in the nature of an annual conference whose members were mostly part-time politicians, belonging to the anglicised upper class who had little time and commitment for full-time politics and even their politics was much limited in terms of goals and methods.
- Another limitation of the Moderate politics was its **social composition**, which inevitably resulted in social orthodoxy as social questions were not raised in the Congress sessions until 1907. The early Moderate politicians were mainly Hindus[19], mostly upper caste, and sadly after 1893, whatever little participation of Muslims was there, that too began to decline and there was no major effort on the part of Congress to bring the Muslims back into its fold. For instance, between 1892 and 1909, nearly 90 per cent of the delegates who attended the Congress sessions were Hindus, and only 6.5 per cent were Muslims and among the Hindus again nearly 40 per cent were Brahmans and the rest were upper-caste Hindus. Lord Dufferin, therefore, could easily get away with his remark at the St. Andrew's Day dinner in Calcutta in November 1888 that Congress represented only a *microscopic minority* of the Indian people.
- The Moderate politicians could not organise a successful agitation against British rule, may be more because of the reason that most of them still shared an intrinsic faith in the English liberal political tradition, and thus their methods were limited in approach and their political strategy was at most **the strategy of mendicancy** mostly using three P's – Prayers, Petition and Protest – as described in later years by the more Extremist elements in the Congress, which despite its high ideals failed to achieve its goals. It was because of the failures of the moderate politics that Extremist elements began to emerge within the Congress and the national movement soon changed its course.

The Extremists

By the end of the 19th century, the failure of Moderate politics became quite apparent and gradually the leadership within the Congress passed on to a group of individuals commonly referred to as the *Extremists* or *Radical Nationalists* or *Assertive Nationalists* or *Militant Nationalists*, who were **less conciliatory** than

[19] Barring the notable exception of the Bombay politician, Badruddin Tyabji.

the Moderates towards colonial rule and wanted to **employ extreme methods** in place of petition and resolutions to secure further constitutional progress and to realise their ultimate nationalist goals. It is, however, pertinent to note that even though the Extremists criticised the Moderates for being too cautious and stereotyped their politics as *the politics of mendicancy*, at the same time, they too believed in **non-violent peaceful agitation** against the British though with varying degrees of consistency. The extremism developed primarily from 1905 onwards and was majorly concentrated in three[20] regions under the leadership of **Bipin Chandra Pal** and **Aurobindo Ghosh**[21] in Bengal, **Bal Gangadhar Tilak** in Maharashtra and **Lala Lajpat Rai** in Punjab.

Leader	Remarks
• Bipin Chandra Pal (1858–1932)	• Was one of the key Extremist leaders of Bengal who along with Lala Lajpat Rai and Tilak was known as the famous trio of *Lal-Bal-Pal*, who participated in the *Swadeshi Movement* (exclusive use of Indian-made goods) and *Swaraj* (independence) and the Non-Cooperation Movement. • Edited the journals *The Democrat* and *The Independent* and also started many newspapers such as *Bande Mataram*, *Paridarsak*, *Swaraj* and *New India*. • Was a fierce critic of Mahatma Gandhi and his pacifist ways. • Was sent to jail for six months for refusing to give evidence against Aurobindo Ghosh in the Bande Mataram sedition case.
• Lala Lajpat Rai (1865–1928)	• Affectionately called ***Punjab Kesari***, Rai is remembered for his role during the *Swadeshi Movement* and for his lifelong commitment to education. • He was an ardent follower of Dayanand Saraswati, the founder of the Arya *Samaj*, and later in 1885, Rai established the Dayanand Anglo-Vedic School (DAV) in Lahore. • Founded the *Indian Home Rule League of America* in New York City in 1917. • Presided the special session of the INC in 1920 in Kolkata during which the Non-Cooperation Movement was launched. • Was imprisoned from 1921 to 1923, and later on his release was elected to the legislative assembly. • Introduced the legislative assembly resolution for the boycott of the Simon Commission on constitutional reform in 1928 but unfortunately died in Lahore, after being attacked by police during a protest rally against the Simon Commission. • Wrote biographies of Mazzini, Garibaldi, Shivaji and Shrikrishna. His important works include: *Young India*, *The Arya Samaj*, *England's Debt to India*, *India's Will to Freedom*, *Evolution of Japan*, *Political Future of India*, *Message of the Bhagwad Gita*, *Problem of National Education in India*, *The Depressed Classes* and the travelogue, *United States of America.*

[20] Though in other areas it was not totally absent but was comparatively less influential.

[21] In 1893–94, he gave the first systematic critique of moderate politics in a series of articles entitled 'New Lamps for Old' wherein he attacked Congress mendicancy and Moderates' satisfaction at slow constitutional progress.

Leader	Remarks
• Bal Gangadhar Tilak (1856–1920)  Bal Gangadhar Tilak	• Also known as ***Lokmanya Tilak***. • Founded the Deccan Education Society (1884) and Fergusson College (1885) in Pune. • Joined INC in 1890 and was part of the Extremist group who propagated boycott and Swadeshi movements. He along with Jamshedji Tata established the Bombay Swadeshi Stores. • Was one of the earliest and vocal proponents of *Swaraj* who gave the famous slogan *Swaraj is my birthright and I shall have it.* • Was a devout Hindu and used Hindu scriptures to arouse people to fight oppression. He often quoted the Bhagavad Gita, asserting that *killers of oppressors could not be blamed*. Spent 6 years in Mandalay Prison (1908–14) for defending the actions of revolutionaries Khudiram Bose and Prafulla Chaki. • In 1916, he along with Annie Besant and Muhammad Ali Jinnah founded the 'All India Home Rule League', which worked in Maharashtra (except Bombay), the Central Provinces, Karnataka and Berar. In the same year, he led INC in signing a pact with the All-India Muslim League led by Jinnah popularly known as the 'Lucknow Pact', which emphasised Hindu–Muslim unity in the nationalist struggle. • Emphasised the importance of cultural and religious festivals in creating awareness about the political movements. Popularised the Ganesh Chaturthi festival and celebration of Shiv Jayanti (birth anniversary of Shivaji) in the Maharashtra region. • Published two papers: ***Kesari*** in Marathi and ***Mahratta*** in English. • Wrote two books, *Srimad Bhagvat Gita Rhasya* and *Arctic Home of the Vedas*. • Despite being a nationalist radical leader, his social views were conservative and he was against Hindu women getting modern education.
• Aurobindo Ghosh (1872–1950)	• Passed the ICS examination securing the 11th rank out of 250 candidates and joined King's College for training but gradually lost interest in the ICS and thus he had himself disqualified for an exam by arriving deliberately late. Subsequently, he returned to India and secured employment in the Baroda State Service. • Was influenced by the American Revolution, revolts in Italy and the medieval French revolts against England and gradually developed interest in Indian politics. Interestingly, although in public, he favoured passive non-cooperation, in private, he supported violent revolutionaries in case the passive revolt did not yield results. • Was co-founder of the *Anushilan Samiti* in Calcutta in 1902 and started an English newspaper called ***Bande Mataram*** in 1905. He along with his brother Barindra Kumar Ghosh contributed articles to a Bengali weekly *Jugantar*, which inspired many young people to take up revolutionary work.

Leader	Remarks
	• Was arrested in connection with the *Alipore Conspiracy Case*, which was primarily the assassination attempt on the Chief Presidency Magistrate Douglas Kingford by Khudiram Bose and Prafulla Chaki. • Though Aurobindo was released just after a year of solitary confinement, in prison he underwent a profound and life-changing spiritual experience and started withdrawing from political life and instead started devoting his life to spirituality. • In 1910, he moved to the French colony of Pondicherry where he began to practise meditation and Yoga. He developed a kind of Yoga called *Integral Yoga* and also started a monthly journal *Anya* in which he discussed about the divine destiny of humankind, unification of the human race and the significance of Indian civilisation and culture. Later, in 1926, he founded the **Sri Aurobindo Ashram** and attracted followers from both India and abroad. • He wrote one of the longest poems in the English language known as the *Savitri*, an epic poem of about 23,813 lines of blank verse.
• Ashwini Kumar Dutt (1856–1923)	• Under his leadership, Barisal was turned into a strong centre of the Swadeshi Movement when he established the ***Swadesh Bandhab Samiti*** organised for this purpose and which had over 160 branches spread all over the district. In order to propagate his ideas he brought out the journal *Barisal Hitaisi*. • Was also actively associated with Swadeshi financial enterprises like the *Swadeshi Bank*, *Hindustan Cooperative Insurance* and *Cooperative Navigation Ltd.* • As a Congressman, he distanced himself from the Moderate–Extremist rivalry and attempted a reconciliation between the Moderates and the Extremists after the Surat split. • Became famous for his philanthropy, commitment to education and community welfare he founded the *Brajamohan Vidyalaya* (1884), Girls school in Barisal (1887) and the *Brajamohan College* (1889).
• V. O. Chidambaram Pillai (VOC) (1872–1936)	• Was an ardent follower of Tilak and important leader of the Swadeshi Movement in Tuticorin (then Madras State) who not only challenged the British shipping interests by launching **Swadeshi Steam Navigation Company** (a *swadesi* enterprise in shipping) but also successfully organised a worker's strike in the port city of Tuticorin and earned the epithet of *Kappalotiya Tamizhan* (the Tamil who steered the ship). He was subsequently sentenced to a double life imprisonment by the British for sedition in 1908 (which was later reduced to a 4-year imprisonment); however, he was admired more for his gesture of refusal to avail bail for himself without his fellow workers and other leaders of the strike. • Was also a Tamil scholar and prolific writer who penned commentaries on *Tirukkural* and *Sivagnana Potham*.

Nature and Characteristics of the Extremists

- **The goal of the Extremists was** *Swaraj*: The Extremist leaders were committed to a path of more direct and belligerent confrontation with colonial rule and explicitly wanted ***Swaraj***, which different leaders interpreted differently. For instance, for Bipin Chandra Pal and Aurobindo Ghosh, *Swaraj* meant 'complete autonomy' or 'absolute political independence', completely free of British control in all respects, while for Tilak, *Swaraj* meant Indian control over the administration, but not a total severance of relations with Great Britain. However, for most others, *Swaraj* still meant 'self-rule' within the parameters of British imperial structure.
- **Methods of agitation**: The Extremists were radical in their approach and the radicalisation was actually visible in their method of agitation, as they moved from the old methods of prayers and petition to that of '**passive resistance**', which meant opposition to colonial rule through violation of its unjust laws, boycott of its goods and institutions, and development of their indigenous alternatives, that is, Swadeshi and National Education.
- **Ideological inspiration**: Since the main focus of Extremists was to oppose the colonial rule in its all aspects, they tried to define Indian nation in terms of a non-western paradigm that was thus based on distinctly Indian cultural idioms. The Extremists derived the intellectual and ideological inspiration from India's rich and distinct spiritual and cultural heritage, which they tactfully also utilised in inculcating the spirit of nationalism among the masses. For instilling a sense of pride in the minds of Indians and to arouse nationalist passions, along with countering the colonial argument that British rule was an act of providence to prepare Indians for self-government, the Extremists tried to invoke the 'glorious golden past' and educated the masses about the ancient Indo-Aryan political republican traditions of the ***Yaudheyas*** and ***Lichchhavis*** that were clearly testimony to the fact that Indian people already had a strong tradition of self-rule, which apart from being better than the Anglo-Saxon political systems was also based on the concept of *dharma* and village self-government, thereby being democratic in approach and having due checks on the arbitrary powers of the king. Emphasis was also laid by thinkers like Vivekananda and Swami Dayanand on India's 'spiritual power' and 'self-discipline' to claim superiority over the 'body' that was dominant in the western idea of masculinity to counter the gendered discourse of colonialism that had established a teleological connection between masculinity and political domination, thereby stereotyping the colonised society as 'effeminate' and therefore unfit to rule. The new regional literature further provided a discursive field for defining the Indian nation in terms of its national heroes being *the martyrs of freedom*, the historical figures who were idolised as champions of national glory and who had demonstrated considerable valour and prowess to fight for their freedom like *Shivaji*, *Ranjit Singh* and even *Siraj-ud-daula*. Tilak started the Shivaji and Ganpati festival in Maharashtra and soon these ideas became popular all over the country. Efforts were also made by the assertive leaders to place the hitherto stereotyped martial races of colonial ethnography, that is, *Marathas*, *Rajputs* and *Sikhs*, in an Aryan tradition and appropriate them as national heroes. Religious revivalism was also a prominent feature of this new politics of mass mobilisation. Hindu religious symbols, usually imageries of Hindu mythological goddesses like Kali or Durga, were frequently used for mobilising the masses and for invoking strength and for arousing passion for fighting for the motherland. It is, however, pertinent to **note** that, though there was much focus on the Hinduism, its symbols and constructs, the Extremist ideology was **surely not defined by any definite religious attributes** and was merely a **political construct to reach the masses** and mobilise them in support of their politics.

> *"This political programme obviously required mass mobilisation and religion was one of the best means to reach the masses."*
>
> Aurobindo Ghosh

Causes behind the Rise of Extremism

- **Frustration with Moderate Politics**: One of the major reasons behind the rise of Extremist reaction was the fact that moderate politics had reached a dead end and Congress under moderate leadership could not achieve anything substantial since most of the demands raised by them remained unfulfilled. All of this produced disillusionment against the principles and methods of moderate leadership, thereby demanding more vigorous political action.
- **Recognition of the True Nature of British Rule**: The early nationalists through their scholarly writings and elaborate statistical studies exposed the true nature of British rule and conclusively proved that British rule was primarily responsible for the economic ruin of India and her deepening poverty. The day-to-day economic miseries of the common masses coupled with the terrible famines of 1896–97 and 1899–1900 along with the bubonic plague[22], which took a toll of over 90 lakh lives, further revealed to the masses their plight of utter helplessness and eventually provided a congenial atmosphere for the growth of extremism.
- **Disappointment with Political Events**: The political events of the years 1892–1905 further disappointed the nationalists as it was appearing from the British actions that even the few existing political rights of the people were under threat. For instance, the Indian Councils Act of 1892 was a complete disappointment; in 1898, a law was passed making it an offence to excite 'feelings of disaffection' towards the foreign government; and in 1899, the number of Indian members in the Calcutta corporation instead of being increased was further reduced, while in 1897, the Natu brothers were deported not only without being tried, but rather the charges against them were also not even made public and in the same year, Tilak and some other newspaper editors were sentenced to long terms of imprisonment for arousing the people against the foreign government.
- **Factionalism**: According to some historians, factionalism was also an important reason behind the emergence of Extremism at the turn of the century as around that time a good deal of faction fighting at almost every level of organised public life was observed in India. For instance, in Bengal, there was not only division within the two branches of Brahmo Samaj but also existent was bitter journalistic rivalry between the two newspaper groups, the *Bengalee* edited by moderate leader Surendranath Banerjee and the *Amrit Bazar Patrika* edited by the more radical Motilal Ghosh. Similar faction fighting can be witnessed in Maharashtra where there was competition between the moderate Gokhale[23] and radical Tilak for controlling the Poona Sarvajanik Sabha. In Punjab too, the Arya Samaj was divided after the death of Dayanand Saraswati, between the more moderate College group and the radical revivalist group as was the situation in Madras where there were three factions, the Mylapur clique, the Egmore clique and the suburban elites who regularly had issues with each other and therefore, the division in Congress between the Moderates and the Extremists around this time was just faction fighting that plagued organised public life in India.
- **Contemporary International Influences**: Several events outside India also exercised a powerful influence on the younger generation and encouraged the growth of extremism. The Abyssinia's repulsion of the Italian army in 1896 and Japan's thumping victory over Russia in 1905 further exploded the myth of European superiority. Indians found new hopes and new aspirations in the nationalist movements of Egypt, Turkey and Russia. Also, the humiliating treatment meted out to Indians in British colonies, especially in South Africa, aided in development of an anti-British atmosphere.

[22] Which broke out in Maharashtra.

[23] However, in 1895, Tilak captured the organisation, subsequently forcing Gokhale to start his rival organisation, 'the Deccan Sabha' in 1896.

"It was up to this time supposed that the Asiatics lacked the sentiment of nationality and were, therefore, unable to hold their own before the European nations in spite of their individual courage and heroism. It was further believed that the continents of Asia, Africa, and America were created by Providence to be dominated by European nations. The Russo-Japanese War has given a rude shock to these beliefs, and those who hold them are now beginning to see that, there is nothing inherently improbable in the Asiatics forming themselves into independent nations and taking rank with their European rivals."

Excerpts from *Kesari*, edited by Tilak in the issue dated December 1904

"What one Asiatic has done others can do . . . If Japan can drub Russia, India can drub England with equal ease . . . Let us drive the British into the sea and take our place side by side with Japan among the great powers of the world."

Karachi Chronicle issue dated June 1905

- **The Unpopular Administration of Curzon (1899–1905)**: During Lord Curzon's seven-year rule, a number of unpopular legislative and administrative measures such as the Calcutta Municipal[24] Amendment Act of 1899, the Indian Universities[25] Act of 1904, the Indian Official Secrets[26] Amendment Act of 1904 and above all, the partition of Bengal in 1905 were initiated, which not only hurt the susceptibilities of the educated Indians but also further magnified the nationalist angst against the British rule. His habit of regularly speaking derogatorily of India as a nation and Indian character in general and his intolerance of Indian political aspirations surely hurt the pride of the Indian nationalists and intelligentsia.

"Indians are having extraordinary inferiority in character, honesty and capacity."

Lord Curzon's statement in 1901

"It is often said why not make some prominent native a member of the Viceroy's Executive Council? The answer is that in the whole continent there is not an Indian fit for the post."

Lord Curzon

"(The Indian National) Congress is tottering to its fall, and one of my greatest ambitions while in India is to assist it to a peaceful demise."

Lord Curzon in a letter to the British Secretary of State in 1900

- **The Partition of Bengal (1905)**: There is hardly any doubt that the Bengal Presidency with a population of 78 million[27] as an administrative unit was indeed of an unwieldy size and therefore the necessity

[24] Through which the Calcutta Corporation was reconstituted and the number of elected representatives in it were reduced.

[25] Which placed Calcutta University under the most complete governmental control.

[26] Which further restricted press freedom.

[27] About a quarter of the population of British India.

to partition Bengal was being discussed in official circles since the 1860s[28]. However, equally true was the fact that the real motive behind the partition of Bengal was not administrative convenience but political considerations since at that time, Bengal was perceived as the nerve centre of Indian nationalism, and thus one of the key agendas behind the partition was to divide and weaken this politically articulate community.

"The attempt at that time was to 'dethrone Calcutta' from its position as the centre from which the Congress Party is manipulated. ... the centre of successful intrigue and divide. The best guarantee of the political advantage of our proposal is its dislike by the Congress."

Lord Curzon

"Bengal united, is power, Bengal divided, will pull several different ways. That is what the Congress leaders feel: their apprehensions are perfectly correct and they form one of the great merits of the scheme ... in this scheme ... one of our main objects is to split up and thereby weaken a solid body of opponents to our rule."

Home Secretary Herbert Risley's statement in 1904.

"If we are weak enough to yield to their clamour now, we shall not be able to dismember or reduce Bengal again: and you will be cementing and solidifying a force already formidable and certain to be a source of increasing trouble in the future."

Curzon in a letter to the British Secretary of State

"From a political point of view alone, putting aside the administrative difficulties of the old province, I believe partition to have been very necessary."

Lord Minto[29]

The partition was meant to foster two kinds of divisions, first on the basis of language as they intended to curb Bengali influence by reducing them to a linguistic minority in Bengal itself as according to the partition proposal, the old Bengal province, that is, western Bengal, would contain large numbers of Hindi- and Oriya-speaking population,[30] and second on the basis of religion, as in the new proposed province, that is, eastern Bengal, the Bengali Hindus would be outnumbered by the Muslims[31].

---

[28] More precisely since the time of the Orissa famine of 1866. Later in 1874, Assam was separated from Sylhet, and thereafter there was growing interest among the British to make Assam a viable administrative unit. In 1892, a proposal was laid to transfer the entire Chittagong division to Assam and in 1896, the then Chief Commissioner of Assam William Ward again proposed the transfer of the districts of Dacca and Mymensingh, so that Assam could become a Lieutenant Governor's province with a separate civil service cadre and the Assam planters could have cheaper maritime outlet through the port of Chittagong, but the scheme was not favoured at that time and only the *Lushai* Hills were transferred in 1897 and the rest of the scheme was shelved. However, in March 1900, Lord Curzon resurrected the scheme again.

[29] Who had succeeded Curzon as the new viceroy and even though he was critical of the way in which partition was imposed disregarding public opinion he still felt that it was good political strategy.

[30] The old province of Bengal was to have 17 million Bengali- and 37 million Oriya- and Hindi-speaking people.

[31] The new province would contain a population of 31 million, of which 18 million would be Muslims and 12 million Hindus.

"With partition, Dacca could become the capital of the new Muslim majority province (with eighteen million Muslims and twelve million Hindus) which would invest the Mohammedans in Eastern Bengal with a unity which they have not enjoyed since the days of the old Mussulman Viceroys and Kings. The Muslims would thus get a better deal and the eastern districts would be freed of the pernicious influence of Calcutta"

Lord Curzon

"This will destroy the virtual class rule by the Bengali bhadralok, or the landowning, moneylending, professional and clerical classes, belonging mostly to the three Hindu upper castes of Brahman, Kayastha and Baidya who had monopolised education and employment to the virtual exclusion of all other communities and this was the main source of their political power. So the antidote to bhadralok power was to encourage the development of other communities, perhaps the Muslims."

Indication derived from the Memorandum of Lord Minto and Resolution of October 1906 of Sir Lancelot Hare, the second Lt. Governor of East Bengal and Assam

But the partition instead of dividing and weakening the morale of the nationalists, further united them through an anti-partition agitation and laid the foundation for the **Swadeshi Movement**.

Swadeshi Movement (1903–08)

The agitation against the partition had started in 1903, but became stronger and more organised after the scheme was finally announced and implemented in 1905. Though the initial focus was to secure the annulment of partition, it soon enlarged into a more broad-based movement, known as the Swadeshi Movement, touching upon wider political and social issues. As rightly pointed out by **Sumit Sarkar**, four major trends[32] can be identified in the Bengal Swadeshi Movement:

- **The Moderate trend** (1903–05)
- **Constructive Swadeshi** (1905–06)
- **Political Extremism** (1906–08)
- **Revolutionary Terrorism**[33] (1908 onwards).

- **The Moderate trend** (1903–05): Ever since the partition scheme was announced in December 1903, assuming that the British would be amenable to arguments, the **Moderates** through their conventional methods of prayers, petitions, memoranda, speeches, public meetings and press campaigns sought to create public opinion in both India and England against the partition proposal. They hoped that by preparing a foolproof case against the scheme and creating sufficient pressure, they may be successful in preventing this injustice to happen and can get the British to revise the scheme in its formative stage. For instance, Surendranath Banerjee, Prithwishchandra Ray, Krishna Kumar Mitra and other prominent nationalist leaders through different journals and newspapers like the *Bengalee, Sanjibani* and *Hitabadi* launched a powerful press campaign against the partition proposal. Simultaneously, numerous petitions signed by a large number of people were sent to the Government of India and the Secretary of State to exert sufficient pressure on them for preventing this unjust partition. From March 1904 till January 1905, vast protest meetings were held in Calcutta as well as in small towns all over Bengal to protest against the proposed scheme.

[32] It is pertinent to note that exact periodisation of these trends is not possible since all the trends were present more or less simultaneously throughout the period but still broader categorisation has been done on the basis of a prominent trend.

[33] Though it is more appropriate to call it Revolutionary Nationalism.

But, despite the widespread protest voiced against the partition proposals, the **partition** was still announced by the British Government on 19 July 1905 and the Moderates for the first time went beyond their conventional political methods and took the initiative of transforming the narrow agitation into a wider Swadeshi Movement. On 7 August 1905, with the passing of a **formal boycott resolution** at a meeting at Calcutta Town Hall giving a call for the boycott of British goods and institutions, the formal proclamation of the Swadeshi Movement was made. **The day of partition**, that is, 16 October 1905, was observed as a day of mourning throughout Bengal and people fasted, bathed in the Ganges and then walked barefoot in the processions singing ***Bande Mataram***, tied *rakhis* on each other's hands as a symbol of the unity of the two halves of Bengal. Later, two huge mass meetings that drew crowds of 50,000 to 75,000 people perhaps, the largest mass meetings ever to be held under the nationalist banner, were organised and within a few hours, a sum of ₹50,000 was raised for the movement. It was, thus, apparent that the character of the movement in terms of both its goals and social base had begun to expand rapidly.

> *"What we could not have accomplished in 50 or 100 years, the great disaster, the partition of Bengal, has done for us in six months. Its fruits have been the great national movement known as the Swadeshi movement."*
>
> Abdul Rasul, President of Barisal Conference, April 1906

The Moderate leaders started touring the country and tried to mobilise even people other than the literate section of the population, urging them to boycott Manchester cloth and Liverpool salt. Some of them also participated in the national education movement, while others even got involved in labour strikes. It is, however, pertinent to **note** here that even though **Moderates** for the first time went beyond their conventional political methods, their political philosophy remained the same, since they only sought to pressurise the British parliament to secure an annulment of partition. They were neither in favour of a full-scale passive resistance nor could they conceptualise boycott as a step towards the regeneration of national economy. As a reaction, gradually a new trend developed having emphasis on ***Constructive Swadeshi***, basically an effort on the part of nationalist leaders to promote development of indigenous or *swadeshi* alternatives for foreign goods and institutions having focus on self-reliance or *atmashakti*.

- **Constructive Swadeshi** (1905–06): By 1905, as Sarkar demonstrates, two main trends were simultaneously visible in the course of the Swadeshi Movement, the first one was the **non-political 'Constructive Swadeshi'** trend with strong emphasis on self-reliance, while the other trend related to **political extremism** with its emphasis on passive resistance. Constructive Swadeshi or as referred by Rabindranath as ***atmashakti*** (self-help or self-reliance) can be understood as the non-political constructive programme aimed at re-assertion of national dignity, honour and confidence along with social and economic regeneration and integration of villages. The basic premise behind the notion of *atmashakti* was to make Indians aware of their innate capabilities, strength and to regain their lost confidence along with becoming self-reliant in the production of local goods and services. Some of the means adopted to achieve *atmashakti* were as follows:
    - **Establishment of Swadeshi or indigenous enterprises**: These attempted to manufacture daily necessities like textile mills and handlooms, soap and match factories, tanneries, insurance companies, shops etc. For instance, **the Bengal Chemicals Factory** was started by **Acharya Prafulla Chandra Ray** as a swadeshi enterprise and then another factory was started to manufacture porcelain.
    - **Setting up 'Swadeshi' national schools and colleges**: These were set upto impart education in vernacular along with establishment of National Council of Education in 1906 to organise a system of education on national lines and under national control. Some of the notable examples of national schools were

Tagore's Shantiniketan, the **Bengal National College** with Aurobindo as principal (1906), the **Bengal Technical Institute**, the **Saraswat Ayatan** of Brahmabandab Upadhyay[34].

- **Village upliftment societies and *samitis***: (corps of volunteers) These had the agenda of both social reform and development. These *samitis* proved to be effective tool of mass mobilisation and were able to spread the message of *Swadeshi* through regional swadeshi songs along with creating awareness through magic lantern lectures about the various social evils present at the village level such as early marriage, lack of education, dowry system, caste oppression, consumption of alcohol etc. These *samitis* also provided physical and moral training to the members in swadeshi craft, organised schools, did commendable philanthropic social work during famines and epidemics. One of the most well-known *samitis* was the one set up by Ashwini Kumar Dutt, a school teacher, in Barisal known as the ***Swadesh Bandhab Samiti***. The *samiti* through its 159 branches reached out to the remotest corners of the Barisal district and was able to generate an unparalleled mass following among the predominantly Muslim peasantry of the region so much so that even the British officialdom was alarmed at their growing popularity with the rural masses and feared that arresting Ashwini Kumar Dutt would trigger a public rebellion against the British.
- **Arbitration courts**: For example, the *Swadesh Bandhab Samiti* of Barisal reportedly settled 523 disputes through 89 arbitration committees.
- **Creative use of traditional popular festivals**[35]: Festivals like *Ganpati* and *Shivaji,* **traditional folk theatre forms** such as *jatras* and **traditional fairs commonly** called *melas* as a means of reaching out to the hitherto untouched masses who were being introduced to the modern political ideas of *Swaraj* and *Swadeshi* for the first time.
- **Exploration of new indigenous avenues in cultural and scientific spheres**: For instance, in the field of arts, Indian Society of Oriental Art was founded in 1907 and one of the first recipient of its scholarship was Nandalal Bose who later left an indelible imprint on Indian art while Abanindranath Tagore broke the domination of Victorian naturalism over Indian art and sought inspiration from the rich indigenous traditions of Mughal, Ajanta and Rajput paintings. *Bande Mataram* written by Bankim Chandra Chatterjee spontaneously became the **theme song** of the Swadeshi Movement while Rabindranath's ***Amar Sonar Bangla***[36], written at that time along with many other songs composed during that period by eminent writers like Mukunda Das, Rajani Kanta Sen, Syed Abu Mohammed and Dwijendralal Ray became the moving spirit for nationalists of all hues in the times to come. New literary milestones were created in the spread and growth of regional literature like that of Daksinaranjan Mitra Majumdar's ***Thakurmar Jhuli***[37], which delights the Bengali children even today. Similar progress was achieved in the field of science wherein **Jagdish Chandra Bose** and **Prafulla Chandra Ray** pioneered original research and garnered accolades worldwide.

  At the same time backed up by the *atmashakti*, that is, the positive development of Swadeshi industries, schools and arbitration courts, another trend was making its presence felt across the political spectrum of the Swadeshi Movement and that was the trend of '**political extremism**', which was gradually gaining momentum and emerging as 'the trend' holding a much wider appeal.

- **Political Extremism** (1906–08): After 1905 and particularly around mid-1906, the trend of political extremism acquired a dominant influence over the Swadeshi Movement. The political extremism was based on the '**Doctrine of Passive Resistance**' wherein the stress was on primarily four things:
  - **The relentless and organised boycott of British goods, institutions and its administration**[38]
  - **Development of their indigenous alternatives**

[34] Edited popular journal *Sandhya*.
[35] Popularised by Tilak.
[36] It was adopted as the national anthem of Bangladesh in 1971.
[37] Meaning grandmother's tales.
[38] Even including social boycott of its loyalists.

- **Violation of unjust laws and organisation of strikes**
- **Violent agitation**, if necessitated by British repression

The message of passive resistance was spread across the country under the able leadership of political Extremists like Bipin Chandra Pal and Aurobindo Ghosh who popularised it across Bengal; Lokmanya Tilak[39] who took the movement to Poona and Bombay; Lala Lajpat Rai and Ajit Singh who spread the message in Punjab and other parts of northern India like Rawalpindi, Kangra, Jammu, Multan and Haridwar; Syed Haidar Raza who led the movement in Delhi and Chidambaram Pillai who took the movement to the Madras presidency. Through these measures of boycott and organised non-cooperation, the Extremists intended to make the administration under colonial rule not only difficult but impossible.

> *"The aim was to make the administration under present conditions impossible by an organized refusal to do anything which shall help either the British Commerce in the exploitation of the country or British officialdom in the administration of it - unless and until the conditions are changed in the manner and to extent demanded by the people ... If the Chowkidar, the constable; the deputy and the munsif and the clerk, not to speak of the sepoy all resign their respective functions, feringhee rule in the country may come to an end in a moment.No powder and shot will be needed, no sepoys will have to be trained ..."*
>
> Aurobindo Ghosh

It is noteworthy to add that among the several forms of struggle thrown up by the movement, it was primarily **'the boycott of foreign goods'**[40] which met the greatest visible success at the practical and popular level. The boycott and public burning of foreign cloth and picketing of shops selling foreign goods not only became common in remote corners of Bengal but also in many important towns and cities throughout the country. The movement innovated boycott of all types and had participation from all sections of society, for instance, women refused to wear foreign bangles or use foreign utensils while washermen refused to wash foreign clothes and even priests declined offerings that contained foreign sugar. Different forms of mass mobilisation like public meetings and processions now started emerging having outreach at not only city and town levels but also at district, *taluqa* and village levels. Strikes were organised by Swadeshi leaders in foreign-managed enterprises like Eastern India Railway and Clive Jute Mills. At its Banaras Session of 1905, presided over by **G. K. Gokhale**, the INC also formally extended its support to the Swadeshi and Boycott Movement.

> *"Swadeshism during the days of its potency coloured the entire texture of our social and domestic life. Marriage presents that included foreign goods, the like of which could be manufactured at home, were returned. Priests would often decline to officiate at ceremonies where foreign articles were offered as oblations to the gods. Guests would refuse to participate in festivities where foreign salt or foreign sugar was used."*
>
> Surendranath Banerjee
>
> *"Curzon had hoped ... to bind India permanently to the Raj. Ironically, his partition of Bengal, and the bitter controversy that followed, did much to revitalize Congress. Curzon, typically, had dismissed the Congress in 1900 as 'tottering to its fall'. But he left India with Congress more active and effective than at any time in its history."*
>
> Denis Judd wrote in *Lion and the Tiger: The Rise and Fall of the British Raj*, 1600–1947

[39] Tilak called this movement *Bahishkar Yoga*.

[40] Boycott of foreign goods was first suggested by Krishna Kumar Mitra through his journal *Sanjivani*.

Emboldened by the positive response of the masses and gradually realising the fact that *without freedom, no real regeneration of national life is possible*, the Extremists now wanted to extend the movement to the rest of India and carry it beyond the programme of just *Swadeshi* or 'mere abrogation of the partition' to a **full-fledged political mass struggle** for complete independence or ***Swaraj***.

> *"The aim was now Swaraj and the abrogation of partition had become the pettiest and narrowest of all political objects."*
>
> Bipan Chandra
>
> *"Political freedom is the life breath of a nation."*
>
> Aurobindo Ghosh
>
> *"From 1907 onwards for several years, India was seething with unrest and trouble. For the first time since the Revolt of 1857, India was showing fight and not submitting tamely to foreign rule. News of Tilak's activities and his conviction, of Aurobindo Ghosh and the way the masses of Bengal were taking the swadeshi and boycott pledge stirred all of us Indians in England. Almost without an exception we were Tilakites or Extremists, as the new party was called in India."*
>
> An excerpt from Jawaharlal Nehru's autobiography describing the reaction of India during 1907

However, the Moderates, by and large, were not as yet willing to go that far. Still, in 1906, the INC at its Calcutta Session, presided over by Dadabhai Naoroji, took a major step forward and passed four resolutions in favour of boycott, swadeshi, national education and *Swaraj*. In his presidential address, **Naoroji** declared for the first time, from the platform of the INC that *the ultimate goal of the INC was Swaraj or self-government like that of the United Kingdom or the Colonies*. From hereafter, the movement took a giant leap and the Extremist party was born with Tilak as its leader and their main goal was to keep intact the four Calcutta resolutions. But, just a year later in 1907, the differences between the Moderates and the Extremists, especially regarding the pace of the movement and the techniques of struggle to be adopted, came to a head at the **Surat session** of the Congress where subsequently the party split with serious consequences for the Swadeshi Movement.

- **Revolutionary Terrorism** (1908 onwards): By 1908, the political extremism was on the decline and was taken over by another trend, that is, the rise of Revolutionary Terrorism or more appropriately Revolutionary Nationalism, a violent mode of political protest that was manifested through individual attacks against British officials and their Indian collaborators. This signified a major shift from non-violence to violence and also from mass action to elite action, necessitated primarily by the failure of the mass mobilisation efforts. We would be discussing in detail about both the Split in Congress and the rise of Revolutionary Nationalism in just a while but first let's cover all aspects related to the Swadeshi Movement.

Reasons Responsible for the Decline in Political Extremism

- **First** reason was **high-handedness of the Government** and **severe repression** faced by the Movement. The Government realising the revolutionary potential of the movement came down with a heavy hand and put all forms of controls and checks on the processions, public meetings and the press. The student participants were not only expelled from Government schools and colleges but were also fined, debarred from Government service and at times beaten up by the police. The notorious ***Carlyle Circular***, which threatened withdrawal of grants and scholarships including disaffiliation of such institutions that failed to prevent students participation in politics was a clear testimony to British brutality. The case of the **1906 Barisal Conference**, where the police forcibly dispersed the conference and brutally beat up a large number of the participants, is a telling example of the government's attitude and policy. Between 1907 and 1908, nine major leaders in Bengal including Ashwini Kumar Dutt and Krishna Kumar Mitra along with Ajit Singh and Lajpat Rai of Punjab were deported, Tilak was given a sentence of 6 years' imprisonment while Madras's Chidambaram Pillai and Andhra's Harisarvottam Rao were arrested. It is hardly a secret that the repressive measures of the government was a prominent factor behind Bipin Chandra Pal and Aurobindo Ghosh's decision to retire from active politics, and thus with most leaders either deported, arrested or retired, the movement was subsequently rendered leaderless.
- **Second**, the movement was weakened by the **internal squabbles** between the **different factions**, and especially, the Congress split of 1907 left a major dent. Also, though the Swadeshi Movement had spread outside Bengal, the rest of the country was not as yet fully prepared to adopt the new style and technique of politics.
- **Third**, the Swadeshi Movement lacked an **effective organisation** and **party structure**. Though the movement had thrown up programmatically the entire gamut of Gandhian techniques such as passive resistance, non-violent non-cooperation, the call to fill the British jails, social reform, constructive work, etc., however, no leader was able to give these techniques a centralised disciplined focus and convert these techniques into actual practical politics, as Gandhiji was able to do later.
- **Fourth**, the movement declined partially because of the **very logic of mass movements itself** – they cannot be sustained endlessly at the same pitch of militancy and self-sacrifice, especially when faced with severe repression.

Limitations of the Swadeshi Movement

- One of the major limitations of the Swadeshi Movement was that the Swadeshi Movement was **largely confined to the ranks of educated upper** and **middle classes** mostly *zamindars* and **lacked having a large mass base** specially low-caste peasantry or labour force. The Swadeshi *samitis* membership did not extend much beyond the ranks of educated *bhadralok* high-caste Hindu gentry, and thus the mass mobilisation efforts of the Swadeshi Movement ultimately failed. The grievances of the peasants were not at all taken up by the Swadeshi Movement, and thus because of the divergence of interests with those of the leaders who claimed to represent them, the peasants did not become a part of the Swadeshi Movement. Also, the vast body of Hindustani labour force as well as the plantation labour too remained untouched from the nationalist efforts of the *swadeshis* who could only primarily organise labour strikes in the foreign-owned companies and that too only among the ranks of white-collar workers. In fact, primarily because of this **failure of mass mobilisation**, the boycott movement failed to affect British imports into India.

- Another limitation of the Swadeshi Movement was that it was **not able to garner the support of the mass of Muslims** and especially of the Muslim peasantry. Some of the forms of mobilisation adopted by the Swadeshi Movement like the use of traditional popular customs, festivals and institutions led to certain unintended negative communal consequences as they were misinterpreted and distorted by the communalists backed by the colonial state and eventually all of this resulted in the **alienation of the Muslims** from the Swadeshi Movement. The Government was also helped in its communal designs by the peculiar situation present in large parts of Bengal where Hindus and Muslims were divided along class lines with the former being the landlords and the latter constituting the peasantry. People like Nawab Salimullah of Dacca were pressed into service by the Government to mobilise the Muslims on the basis of religion and eventually the All-India Muslim League was set up with the active guidance and support of the Government to be used as a counter[41] against the Swadeshi Movement.

> *"The use of traditional popular customs, festivals and institutions for mobilizing the masses—a technique used widely in most parts of world to generate mass movements, especially in the initial stages. ... The communal forces saw narrow religious identities in the traditional forms utilized by the Swadeshi movements whereas in fact these forms generally reflected common popular cultural traditions which had evolved as a synthesis of different religious prevalent among the people."*
>
> Bipan Chandra

- The Swadeshi Movement even though aroused the people **could not effectively channelise the newly released energy** or provide expression to popular resentment. In the absence of an effective organisation, party structure or centralised disciplined focus, the Movement was not able to effectively convert the great ideas of non-cooperation and passive resistance into actual practical politics as done by Gandhiji later.
- The 'Constructive Swadeshi' programme too **could not survive or sustain for long** as the promoters of the indigenous enterprises were more endowed with patriotic zeal than with business acumen and the Swadeshi alternatives were often more expensive than British goods. The national schools were also not adequate in number and, thus, not much in terms of financial independence was achieved by the *atmashakti* campaign.

Achievements of the Swadeshi Movement

Though the Swadeshi Movement subsided after mid-1908, it would be wrong, however, to see the movement as a failure. On the contrary, the Swadeshi Movement not only left a great imprint on Indian nationalism but also helped the Indian National Movement to take a major leap forward.

- The Swadeshi Movement was largely **responsible for broadening the base of the 'idea of nationalism'** and took this idea, in a truly creative manner, to hitherto untouched sections of the population like women

[41] Unsurprisingly, at the height of the Swadeshi Movement communal riots broke out in Bengal.

and students who became actively involved in politics for the first time. Almost **all the major political trends** of the Indian National Movement ranging from conservative moderation to political extremism, from revolutionary nationalism to incipient socialism, from petitioning and public speeches to passive resistance and boycott, had their **genesis in the Swadeshi Movement** itself. In fact, the Non-cooperation Movement and the Civil Disobedience Movement of the later years was just an extension of 'constructive boycott' of the Swadeshi Movement. Thus, the legacy the Swadeshi Movement bequeathed was the one on which the later National Movement drew heavily.

> *"The Swadeshi Movement brought the realm of the national movement from theory to absolute practicality."*
>
> R. C. Majumdar

- The movement **evolved several new methods and techniques of mass mobilisation**[42] and was able to draw for the first time large sections of society into the ambit of modern political ideas. During the course of the Swadeshi Movement, the social base of the participants was further enlarged to include a certain section of zamindars, the lower middle class in the cities and small towns, the school and college students[43] and also for the first time women, peasants and working class though they were largely confined to specific pockets. It is pertinent to note here that even though the movement was unable to make much headway in mobilising the peasantry especially its lower rungs[44] to actively join in certain forms of struggle such as boycott or passive resistance or to organise them around peasant demands, still the mobilisation of the peasantry on a limited scale count for a lot since it marked the very beginnings of modern mass politics in India and through these new mass mobilisation techniques of meetings, *jatras, melas* and so forth, the peasants were exposed for the first time to modern nationalist ideas and politics.
- The richness of the Swadeshi Movement was not confined to politics alone and the Swadeshi phase **expanding the creativity of the people in every direction** thereby influenced a **breakthrough in the realm of Indian art**, **culture**, **literature**, **music**, **science and industry**. The *atmashakti* programme not only eroded the hegemony of colonial ideas and institutions but also helped the masses to discover their innate potential, confidence and self-worth.

Thus, the Swadeshi Movement proved to be one of the crucial battles in the long-drawn-out complex war for Indian independence.

[42] Though it was not able to put them all into practice successfully.

[43] On a massive scale.

[44] Except in certain areas, such as the district of Barisal.

Analysis of Differences Between the Moderates and Extremists

Criterion	Moderates	Extremists

Ideology	• The Moderates shared an intrinsic faith in the **English liberal political tradition** and in the **efficacy of peaceful and constitutional agitation.**
	• They were influenced by the western ideas of enlightenment, constitutionalism and Utilitarian thinkers like Burke, Mill, Bentham and Morley.
	• Even though the Moderates were conscious of the exploitative nature of British rule, they only wanted its reform and not expulsion. They never visualised a clinical separation from the British empire and believed that political connections with Britain to be in India's social, political and cultural interests.
	• They professed loyalty to the British Crown.
		• The Extremists derived the intellectual and ideological inspiration from **India's rich and distinct spiritual and cultural heritage**, which they tactfully also utilised in inculcating the spirit of nationalism among the masses.
		• They had no faith in the 'politics of mendicancy' and were strongly critical of the three P's – prayers, petitions and protest – methodology of the Moderates.
		• They were primarily guided by four principles:
		  • swarajya
		  • *swadeshi*
		  • boycott of foreign goods
		  • national education
		• They believed that the British Crown was unworthy of claiming Indian loyalty.

Methods	• The Moderates were cautious and modest in their demands and elements of radicalism were absent in their attitude and activities. They primarily insisted on the use of constitutional methods only.	• The Extremists were radical in their approach and believed in extra constitutional methods like boycott and passive resistance to achieve their objectives. However, it is pertinent to note that even the Extremists believed in non-violent peaceful agitation against the British.
Aim	• they only wanted a limited self-government within the imperial framework.	• They explicitly wanted *Swaraj*.
Mass Base	• It was highly elitist and its social base included upper middle classes mostly coming from urban background and landed aristocrats like zamindars. • They believed that the movement should be limited to middle-class intelligentsia as according to them masses were not yet ready for participation in political work.	• It was mainly urban based educated middle and lower middle classes. • They had **immense faith in the capacity of masses** to participate and to make sacrifices.
Prominent Leaders	• Dadabhai Naoroji, Gopal Krishna Gokhale, Badruddin Tyabji, Pherozeshah Mehta, Surendranath Banerjee	• Bipin Chandra Pal, Aurobindo Ghosh, Ashwini Kumar Dutta, Bal Gangadhar Tilak and Lala Lajpat Rai

Criterion	Moderates	Extremists
Contributions	• Economic critique of British colonialism. • Constitutional reforms and propaganda in legislature. • Campaign for general administrative reforms.	• Broadened the base of the 'idea of nationalism' and took this idea, in a truly creative manner, to hitherto untouched sections of the population like women and students. • Raised the demand of 'Swaraj' and successfully organised Boycott and Swadeshi Movement. • Evolved several new methods and techniques of mass mobilisation. • Contributed in the spread of nationalist education.

The Split in the Congress and the Rise of Revolutionary Nationalism

The Surat Split

During the years 1905–07, even when the Moderates and the Extremists were working together against the partitioning of Bengal, there was still a great deal of public debate and disagreement among them. The real issue between the two factions was **how far the radicalism** generated by the Swadeshi Movement in Bengal **was to be incorporated into the future politics** of the Congress on an all-India level. The **Extremists** wanted to extend the Swadeshi and the Boycott Movement from Bengal to the rest of the country along with the gradual extension of the boycott movement from foreign goods to every form of association[45] with the colonial government. On the contrary, the **Moderates** wanted to confine the boycott part of the movement to Bengal and were totally opposed to its extension to other forms of association with the government. The matters nearly came to a head at the Calcutta session of Congress in **1906** over the question of its presidentship. However, a split was avoided by choosing **Dadabhai Naoroji** as the President, who was widely respected by all the nationalists and as a concession to the Extremists along with general statement on the condemnation of the partition, four compromise resolutions were passed in favour of **boycott**, **Swadeshi**, **national education** and ***Swaraj***[46]. Throughout 1907, the two factions fought over differing interpretations of the four resolutions and by the end of the year, serious trust issues had developed between the two.

Most of the Moderates, led by **Pherozeshah Mehta**, felt that any kind of association with the Extremists is not safe and it could shatter the Congress organisation built carefully over the last 20 years. They were afraid that the radical measures and large-scale anti-imperialist movement proposed by the Extremists would invite severe governmental repression and could damage the prospects of future devolution of power. Slowly, they began to distance themselves from the rising militant nationalist tendencies of the Extremists. Whereas, on the other hand, the Extremists felt that the moderate style of politics was fast becoming obsolete and the time had come for the big push to drive the British out. They considered Moderates to be a drag on the growing nationalist movement and, thus, were no less willing than Moderates to part ways with them.

[45] Such as legislative councils, government service, government institutions like schools, colleges, law courts and so forth.

[46] Dadabhai declared for the first time from the platform of the Indian National Congress that the ultimate goal of the Congress is Swaraj or self-government like the United Kingdom or the colonies.

"You (the Extremists) do not realize the enormous reserve of power behind the Government, if the Congress were to do anything such as you suggest, the Government would have no difficulty in throttling it in five minutes."

Gokhale's statement in 1907.

"The Extremists are the worst enemies of our cause. The union of these men with the Congress is the union of a diseased limb to a healthy body, and the only remedy is surgical severance, if the Congress is to be saved from death by blood poisoning."

H. A. Wadya, an ardent follower of Pherozeshah Mehta, wrote in an article in 1907.

"The battle for freedom had begun as the people had been roused and it was time for the big push. However, the Moderates were a big drag on the movement and the time had come to part company with the Moderates, push them out of the leadership of the Congress, and split the organisation if the Moderates could not be deposed."

Views articulated by Aurobindo Ghosh.

The **1907** session of the Congress was scheduled to take place in Poona, which was an Extremist stronghold. The Moderates, therefore, shifted the venue to **Surat** and proposed Rash Behari Ghosh as their president candidate while the Extremists' nominated candidate was Lala Lajpat Rai. But, Lalaji did not want a split and therefore he refused to accept the nomination, and thus the ultimate fight between the two contending groups rested on the question of either retention or rejection of the four Calcutta resolutions. The Bombay group led by Pherozeshah Mehta made every effort to keep the resolutions out of the Congress agenda while forcing the Moderates for retention of the resolutions; the Extremists decided to object to the nomination of Rash Behari Ghosh[47]. Eventually, the open session of the Congress in Surat, on the banks of the river Tapti thus ended in pandemonium with incessant shouting, shoes flying, hurling of chairs and men running for cover, thus disruptively ending the Congress session with the only victorious party, the colonial rulers.

"The 'Congress collapse' at Surat was a great triumph for us."

Viceroy Minto's immediate response to Secretary of State Morley after the Surat split.

It is pertinent to note here that even after this incident, Tilak was willing to reunite the Congress but Pherozeshah Mehta and his supporters seemed intransigent as they sought to reconstitute the Congress party by purging the Extremist elements, a task which he successfully accomplished at the Allahabad Session of 1908, which was attended only by Moderates and who reiterated their loyalty to the British Raj. But, the Mehta Congress of 1908 was surely a weak body where even the Extremists could not organise an effective alternative party to sustain the movement as Tilak, their main leader, was sent to Mandalay jail for 6 years and he died soon after while Aurobindo Ghosh became more spiritually oriented and retired from active politics. B.C. Pal too temporarily retired from politics and Lala Lajpat Rai, who had been a helpless onlooker at Surat, left for Britain

[47] Who was otherwise certainly going to be the duly elected president for the year in absence of any other contender.

in 1908 to come back for a short period in 1909 and then again left for the United States for an extended stay. Thus, after 1908, the nationalist movement as a whole declined by this unfortunate divide.

> *"When I went to jail the whole country was alive with the cry of Bande Mataram, alive with the hope of a nation, the hope of millions of men who had newly risen out of degradation. When I came out of jail I listened for that cry, but there was instead a silence. A hush had fallen on the country."*
>
> Aurobindo Ghosh's statement in 1909.

Analysis of the Surat Split

The Surat split proved to be a disaster for both the **Moderates** and the **Extremists** from both a nationalist point of view as well as their own factional point of view. The Moderates did not realise that the colonial state was negotiating with them not because of their inherent political strength but because of the fear of the Extremists, whereas the Extremists could not see that the Moderates were their natural outer defence line. Neither side realised that in a vast country like India, only a broad-based united movement could have any chance of success and the political demands could be successfully pressed on the rulers only with the united support of different political trends, and thus as a whole, the nationalist movement was weakened.

The Government Strategy Vis-à-Vis Congress

The Government had been suspicious of the INC from its inception though in the first few years of its existence, they had not been overtly hostile as they believed that its activities would remain academic and confined to a handful of intellectuals. However, as soon as it became apparent that the Congress would not remain so narrowly confined, and that it was gradually becoming a focus of Indian nationalism, the officials turned openly critical of the Congress and began to brand its leaders as *disloyal babus, seditious Brahmins* and *violent villains*. The Congress was described as *a factory of sedition* and Congressmen as *disappointed candidates for office and discontented lawyers who represent no one but themselves*.

> *"The Indian National Congress represents only the elite a microscopic minority."*
>
> The Viceroy, Lord Dufferin, ridiculing Congress in a public speech in 1888.
>
> *"The Congress leaders possess seditious and double sided character."*
>
> George Hamilton, Secretary of State for India

This hostility did not abate even when the Moderates, who then dominated the Congress, began to distance themselves from the rising militant nationalist tendencies of Extremists. On the contrary, the British appeared even more eager to attack and finish the Congress since the Government felt that the Moderates even though were moderate and loyal in their political perception were still nationalists and propagators of anti-colonialist politics and ideas.

> *"Gokhale either does not see where he is going, or if he does see it, then he is dishonest or his pretensions. You Cannot awaken and appeal to the spirit of nationality in India and at the same time, profess loyal acceptance of British rule."*
>
> Lord Curzon, statement in 1905.

> *"You announce yourself as a sincere supporter of British rule; you vehemently denounce the condition, and consequences which are it inseparable from the maintenance of that rule."*
>
> George Hamilton, Secretary of State for India, complained to Dadabhai Naoroji in 1900.

However, with the beginning of the powerful Swadeshi and Boycott Movement, the Government modified its strategy towards the nationalists to weaken the nationalist movement. They adopted the new policy of **the carrot and the stick**, a three-pronged approach of **repression-conciliation-suppression**. As a part of the strategy, in the first stage, instead of sneering at the Moderates, the policy was to be that of **rallying**[48] them and simultaneously **repressing** the Extremists, though mildly, mainly for **frightening** the Moderates. Then, as a part of the second stage, the Moderates were to be **placated** through some **concessions** and in order to **isolate** them further from Extremists, **promises** and **hints** were to be **dropped** to them that further concessions and reforms would be forthcoming if they disassociated themselves from the Extremists. Once the Moderates fell into the trap, the final third stage of the strategy was played out by **suppressing** the Extremists through the use of the full might of the state and the Moderates, could then be easily **ignored** for they had outgrown their utility. Unfortunately, neither the Moderates nor the Extremists were able to grasp the underlying machinations of the official strategy and consequently suffered a number of reverses that eventually weakened the nationalist movement. But while the upsurge was gone, the aroused nationalist sentiments did not disappear completely, thereby resulting in the emergence of another trend – Revolutionary Nationalism.

Revolutionary Nationalism

As we have discussed above that, with the decline of the Swadeshi Movement around mid-1908, another trend emerged, that is, revolutionary nationalism. The youth of the country, who had been part of the mass movement, now found themselves unable to disappear tamely into the background once the movement itself grew moribund and Government repression was stepped up. Frustrated, some among them opted for **individual heroism** as distinct from the earlier attempts at mass action.

Causes for the Rise of Revolutionary Nationalism

- **Growing awareness regarding national issues among youth along with lack of avenues for expression of their patriotism**: With growing awareness about the economic exploitation by the British Government, Extremist's critique of Moderate style of politics and by active participation in the Swadeshi and Boycott movement, the youth of the country were not only much more aware about the varied national issues but were also highly motivated to bring in a difference to the status quo. However, their creative energies and their patriotism failed to find expression within the existing political trends, which further led to a growing sense of impatience and frustration among the youth who began to feel that perhaps something even more dramatic was needed to arouse the people.
- **Disillusionment with both Moderate and Extremist leadership**: The youth of the country were mostly convinced of the futility of both the Moderate methodology of constitutional agitation as well as the Extremist agitation tools of passive resistance and boycott. Having been active participants in the Swadeshi and Boycott movements, they were greatly disheartened by the fallout of these movements and the consequent inability of the Extremists to either extract immediate concessions from the government or to achieve

[48] As John Morley, the new Secretary of State for India, put it in 1907.

a full-scale mobilisation of the masses. All of this further hardened their belief that nationalist aims could not be achieved by non-violent passive resistance methods.

- **Failure on part of Extremist leadership to tap revolutionary energies of the youth**: After the decline of the open mass movement, the younger nationalists who had participated in the movement were not ready to retreat and just disappear into the background. The Extremist leaders had often spoken about direct action and had called upon the youth to make sacrifices for the motherland. But, despite their best efforts, the Extremist leadership could neither create a viable effective organisation to provide practical expression to these ideas and nor could put forward a plan of action that could go beyond vigorous agitation and could actually achieve meaningful results. In absence of thus, an effective leadership for channeling their revolutionary energies and to educate them on the political difference between a revolution based on the activity of the masses and one based on individual violent activity, the youth were unfortunately drawn to '**the politics of the bomb**'. The inability of the Extremist leadership to either adequately analyse the weaknesses of the movement or to suggest new ways out of the impasse further strengthened this violent trend. In fact, some sections of the Extremist leadership, such as Aurobindo Ghosh, supported this new trend. It is pertinent to reiterate here that, this failure to politically and ideologically oppose the young revolutionaries proved a grievous error, for it enabled the individualistic and terrorist conception of revolution to take root among the youth who decided to take recourse to physical force to achieve their nationalist aims.
- **Government repression**: Another factor that helped in the growth of the trend of revolutionary nationalism was the brutal repression carried out by the British Government during and after the Swadeshi Movement. An apt example of police high-handedness would be the unprovoked assault by the police on the peaceful crowd at the Barisal Political Conference in 1906. The repressive Government tactics considerably increased after the Surat Split of 1907, as the government proceeded to launch an all-out attack on the Extremists. It was no coincidence that between 1907 and 1911, five[49] repressive laws were passed by the colonial government to check anti-government activity. The youth angered by this repression and realising that all avenues of peaceful political protest were closed to them under this repressive government, thought that if nationalist goals of independence were to be met, the British must be expelled physically by force.

> *"The remedy lies with the people themselves. The thirty crores of people inhabiting India must raise their sixty crores of hands to stop this curse of oppression. Force must be stopped by force."*
>
> A statement in the newspaper *Yugantar* in April 1906, after the police assault on the peaceful Barisal Conference.

- **Ideological appeal**: The writings of Bankim Chandra, the rituals of the Shivaji festival and Ganesh Puja, the inspiring exploits of the Irish and Russian secret societies, the electrifying effect of the Japanese victory over the Russians in 1904–05 (that marked the defeat of an European power by an Asian country) cumulatively created the **ideological atmosphere** for the development of revolutionary nationalism. This was further aided by the cultural regeneration and *atmashakti* campaign which produced a psyche of an aggressive nationalist posture vis-à-vis British colonial rule. With the development of a growing spirit of self-assertion and self-identity among the youth, the individual heroic acts of the revolutionaries came to be looked upon as the manifestations of Indian vigour and manhood in thought and deed. This latent sense of heroism and the revolutionary spirit of nationalism was further boosted by the vernacular press and organs like *Sandhya* and *Jugantar* in Bengal, and *Kal* in Maharashtra, which helped a great deal in spreading the message of radicalism among the young masses along with initiating among them a nationalist spirit.

[49] The important legislations passed during 1907–1911 were: (a) 1907 – Seditious Meetings Act; (b) 1908 – Indian Newspapers (incitement to offences) Act; (c) 1908 – Criminal Law Amendment Act and (d) 1910 – Indian Press Act.

- **Official arrogance and false promises of the government**: The youth were not only angered by official arrogance of the rulers but were also fed up with the false promises of the Government regarding devolution of power to the Indians. With the announcement of the Indian Council Act of 1909* popularly known as the Morley–Minto reforms, even their little hopes and expectations were belied and thus, finding all avenues of political action blocked, they desperately sought violent means to achieve their goals.

> *"If it could be said that this chapter of reforms led directly or necessarily up to the establishment of a Parliamentary system in India, I, for one, would have nothing at all to do with it."*
>
> Morley's statement on the Indian Council Act of 1909 in British Parliament.

The Revolutionary Programme

The revolutionaries considered, but did not find it practical at that stage, to either organise a popular mass uprising throughout the country or to subvert the loyalty of the Army. Instead, they opted to follow in the footsteps of the Irish nationalists and the Russian nihilists and drawing inspiration from them, the Indian revolutionaries started **organising assassinations** of **unpopular officials**, of **traitors** and of **informers** from their own ranks; conducted **swadeshi dacoities** to raise funds for revolutionary activities; and during the First World War even tried to organise **military conspiracies** with expectation of help from the enemies of Britain. The basic idea behind all these actions of revolutionaries was to inspire people by appealing to their patriotic instincts, arousing their latent sense of heroism, removing the fear of authority from their minds and simultaneously striking terror in the hearts of the colonial rulers. According to the revolutionaries, each assassination, and if the assassins were caught, the consequent trial would act as **propaganda by deed** inspiring more for this path of supreme sacrifice and individual heroic action.

A Brief Timeline[50] of Important Revolutionary Activities

Year	Remarks
1876–79	The first of the revolutionary activities took place in Maharashtra, under the organisation of the Ramosi Peasant Force by **Wasudeo Balwant Phadke** in 1876–77. The peasant force and other backward classes gathered together instigating an armed revolt by disrupting communication lines and planned to raise funds for its activities through dacoities. However, it could not stand against the mighty British Government and was, thus, suppressed prematurely. Wasudeo was caught in 1879 and was deported to Aden where he later died a lonely death.
1897	Two of Tilak's disciples – the Chapekar brothers of Poona-**Damodar** and **Balkrishna** – assassinated two notorious British officers, the Plague Commissioner of Poona, **Rand**, and **Lt. Ayerst**, in 1897. Rand was responsible for the atrocities perpetrated by the soldiers during their house searches to identify plague victims.

[50] Though the trend of revolutionary terrorism acquired a real force only around 1907–08, there had been earlier examples as well dating back to 1879.

Year	Remarks
1899	The repression by the British triggered the formation of secret societies. **V. D. Savarkar** and his brother organised *Mitra Mela*, a secret society, in 1899 that later merged in 1904 with Savarkar's ***Abhinav Bharat*** (after Mazzinni's 'Young Italy'). Around the same time, Nasik, Poona and Bombay emerged as centres of bomb manufacture.
1902	The first revolutionary groups in Bengal were organised in 1902 in Midnapore district under the guidance of Jnanendranath Basu and in Calcutta under the guidance of Promotha Mitter, Jatindranath Banerjee or Bagha Jatin, Barindra Kumar Ghosh and others popularly known as the ***Anushilan Samiti***. However, it is pertinent to note that these groups remained insignificant till 1907–08 and their activities were mostly limited to giving physical and moral training to the members.
1905	Around 1905, in search of safe havens, arms and ammunition and to bring out revolutionary literature that would be immune from the Press Acts, certain revolutionaries initiated activities abroad. For instance, **Shyamji Krishnavarma** started in London in 1905, an Indian Home Rule Society popularly known as the **India House**, which emerged as a centre for facilitating entry of radical young Indian students from India. **Hemachandra Kanungo** went abroad for military and political training. Prominent revolutionaries like Savarkar and Hardayal were the key members of this house. The 'India House' also started a journal *The Indian Sociologist*. Also after 1905, several newspapers openly (and a few leaders secretly) began to advocate revolutionary terrorism.
1906	• In April 1906, an inner circle within *Anushilan* group, that is, Barindra Kumar Ghosh (Aurobindo's brother), Hemchandra Qanungo, Prafulla Chaki and Bhupendranath Dutta started the weekly ***Yugantar*** and conducted a few abortive 'actions'. • The first swadeshi dacoity or robbery to raise funds was organised in Rangpur in August 1906 and a bomb manufacturing unit was set up at Maniktala in Calcutta. • Around the same time, Rash Behari Bose and Sachin Sanyal organised a secret society covering far-flung areas of Punjab, Delhi and United Provinces while in Punjab taking inspiration from the events in Bengal, the extremism was fuelled by issues such as frequent famines coupled with rise in land revenue and irrigation tax, practice of 'begar' by zamindars under the active guidance of Lala Lajpat Rai who brought out *Punjabee* (with its motto of self-help at any cost) and Ajit Singh (Bhagat Singh's uncle) who organised the Extremist *Anjuman-i-Mohisban-i-Watan* in Lahore with its journal, *Bharat Mata*. Other prominent radical leaders were Aga Haidar, Syed Haider Raza, Bhai Parmanand and the radical Urdu poet, Lalchand 'Falak'. • However, extremism in Punjab died down quickly around 1907 when due to severe government repression and a ban on political meetings along with the deportation of Lajpat Rai and Ajit Singh, the movement was rendered more or less leaderless. Subsequently, Ajit Singh and a few other associates like Sufi Ambaprasad, Lalchand, Bhai Parmanand, Lala Hardayal all gradually developed into full-scale revolutionaries.
1907	In 1907, there was an attempt, though unsuccessful, on the life of a very unpopular British official, Sir Fuller (the first Lt. Governor of the new province of Eastern Bengal and Assam though he had just retired a year before). Shortly after, in December 1907, there were attempts to derail the train on which the Lt. Governor Sri Andrew Fraser was travelling.

Year	Remarks
1908	• In April 1908, **Prafulla Chaki** and **Khudiram Bose** threw a bomb on a carriage which they believed was occupied by **Kingsford**, the unpopular district judge of Muzzafarpur. But, unfortunately, the carriage was carrying two British ladies who were thus inadvertently killed. Prafulla Chaki shot himself dead while Khudiram Bose was arrested and later hanged. • The Government used this opportunity to arrest the whole Anushilan group including the Ghosh brothers, Aurobindo and Barindra, who were tried in the **Alipore conspiracy case**, also called the **Manicktolla bomb conspiracy** or **Muraripukur conspiracy**, since Barindra Ghosh's house was on Muraripukur Road in the Manicktolla suburb of Calcutta. • The Ghosh brothers were charged with *conspiracy for waging war against the King* – one of the severest charges equivalent to high treason and punishable with death by hanging. Chittaranjan Das defended Aurobindo and eventually he was acquitted of all charges, but his brother Barindra Ghosh and many others were sentenced to deportation and harsh prison terms. • During the trial, Narendra Gosain (or Goswami), who had turned approver and Crown witness, was shot dead by two co-accused, Satyendranath Bose and Kanailal Dutta, in jail and in February 1909, the public prosecutor was shot dead in Calcutta while in February 1910, a deputy superintendent of police met the same fate while leaving the Calcutta High Court. • **Barrah dacoity** was organised by Dacca Anushilan under Pulin Das to raise funds for revolutionary activities.
1909	• In 1909, **A. M. T. Jackson**, the Collector of Nasik, who was also a well-known Indologist, was assassinated by a member of Savarkar's Abhinav Bharat group **Anant Lakshman Kanhere**. It was alleged by the police that the killing was part of a conspiracy by Savarkar and his two brothers to overthrow the British Government in India by means of armed revolution. Thirty-eight people were arrested in the **Nasik conspiracy case** and at the trial, Savarkar was sentenced to transportation for life and all his property was forfeited. • In London, **Madan Lal Dhingra** killed **Curzon Wylie**, an Indian Office official, in 1909. • Soon, London became too dangerous for the revolutionaries, particularly after the Savarkar extradition in 1910, and as a consequence new centres like Paris, Berlin and Geneva emerged. • **Madame Bhikaji Cama**, a Parsi revolutionary who brought out the journal *Bande Mataram*, and **Ajit Singh** operated out of Paris while **Virendranath Chattopadhyaya** chose Berlin as his base.
1912	• On 23 December, 1912, under the leadership of **Rash Behari Bose** and **Sachin Sanyal**, a daring attempt to kill the Viceroy, **Lord Hardinge**, was organised who was wounded by the bomb thrown at him as he was making his official entry into the new capital of Delhi in a procession through Chandni Chowk. • Investigations following the assassination attempt led to the **Delhi Conspiracy trial** and at the end of the trial, Basant Kumar Biswas, Amir Chand and Avadh Behari were convicted and executed for their roles in the conspiracy. Rash Behari Bose, however, escaped his arrest.

Year	Remarks
First World War (1914–19)	• During the First World War, the *Yugantar* party also known as ***Jugantar*** under the able leadership of Bagha Jatin arranged to import German arms and ammunition through sympathisers and revolutionaries abroad. At the close of 1913, Jatin asked Rash Behari Bose to take charge of Punjab and the upper provinces, aiming to extend the Bengal plan of bringing about an all-India insurrection in what has come to be called the **German Plot** or the **Zimmerman Plan** or the **Indo-German conspiracy**. • The *Jugantar* party raised funds through a series of dacoities and planned for a guerrilla force to start an uprising in the country, with a seizure of Fort William and a mutiny by armed forces. Unfortunately, the plot was leaked out by a traitor informer and Jatin and his associates were located by the police in Balasore on the Orissa coast in September 1915 where the revolutionaries were waiting for the delivery of German arms. Most of the revolutionaries were either killed or arrested. The plan ultimately failed with the heroic death of Jatin Mukherjee. • Rash Behari Bose escaped to **Japan** in 1915 and though during the First World War, he was also prominently involved in the Ghadar Revolution but not much could be achieved on that front too. It was only years later that he could bring some substantial difference by playing an important part in the founding of the Indian National Army.

"Neither rich nor able, a poor son like myself can offer nothing but his blood on the altar of mother's deliverance ... may I be reborn of the same mother and may I redie in the same sacred cause, till my mission is done and she stands free for the good of humanity and to the glory of God."

Madan Lal Dhingra

"We shall die to awaken the nation."

Bagha Jatin

"The ultimate object of the revolutionaries is not terrorism but revolution and the purpose of the revolution is to install a national government."

Subhash Chandra Bose

Analysis of Revolutionary Nationalism

Revolutionary nationalism gradually petered out mostly owing to the stern repression facilitated by a series of draconian laws such as the new wartime Defence of India Act (1915) by the colonial government. In all, it is an estimation that 186 revolutionaries were either killed or convicted between the years 1908–18. **Lacking a mass support base**, despite remarkable heroism, the individual revolutionaries, organised in small secret groups, **could not withstand suppression** by the still strong colonial state. It is also pertinent to note the fact that by its very nature only, this form of political action could only be emulated by a few individuals, and not by the mass of people, who still awaited a movement that could accommodate their weaknesses and make effective use of their strengths.

In terms of direct gains, it may be thus argued that the revolutionaries achieved very little as most of their attempts were either aborted or failed. **But** despite their small numbers, limited and symbolic role, they still achieved a lot and made a valuable contribution to the growth of nationalism in India as they succeeded in some ways to shake the very foundations of the British Raj in India. Even Gandhiji himself was forced to acknowledge the sincerity of revolutionary nationalists. He claimed to admire the patriotism of the revolutionaries[51]. It is often argued by historians that the Morley–Minto reforms of 1909 were announced more because of fear generated by revolutionary activities and even the appointment of Lord S. P. Sinha as the law member in the viceroy's executive council was surely the result of pressures generated by violent activities. The activities of the revolutionary groups were, thus, not contrary but supplementary to the independence-oriented broad-based mass movements. The individual heroic action of revolutionaries undoubtedly ignited the spark of latent patriotism among the masses, eventually making many of the revolutionaries like Khudiram Bose and Prafulla Chaki folk heroes. As a historian has rightly put, *they gave us back the pride of our manhood.*

The Indian Councils Act of 1909/Morley–Minto Reforms

As the part of the British Government strategy of repression-conciliation-suppression, though the British intensified their policy of suppressing the Extremists and the Revolutionaries, simultaneously they also tried to placate the Moderates by announcing certain political concessions. The Secretary of State for India, John Morley,[52] and the Viceroy, Lord Minto, thus worked out a set of measures that came to be popularly known as the **Morley–Minto Reforms** or the **Indian Councils Act of 1909**. It is pertinent to note here that prior to the Morley–Minto reforms, in 1906, a group of elite Muslims led by **Aga Khan** famously known as the **Shimla Deputation** met Lord Minto and placed their demand for a separate electoratefor the Muslims, a demand which proved to be historic in the sense that it was not only agreed upon completely by the Government but it emerged to be one of the poisonous trees which was to yield a bitter harvest in later years.

The Indian Councils Act of 1909

- The Act considerably increased the number of elected or non-official members in both Central and Provincial legislative councils. The number of members in the Central/Imperial legislative Council was raised from 16 to 60 members while in the legislative Councils of major provinces such as Bengal, Madras, Bombay and United Provinces, it was raised to 50 and in the legislative Councils of minor provinces of Punjab, Burma and Assam, it was raised to 30.
- It retained official majority in the Imperial legislative Council popularly known as the Governor-General Council but in the provincial councils, **non-official majority was introduced**; however, since some of these non-officials were nominated and not elected, a non-elected majority remained.
- The legislative councils at both Centre and the provinces were to have four categories of members:
  - Ex Officio Members: Governor-General and members of his executive council.
  - Nominated Official Members: Government officials who were nominated by the Governor-General.
  - Nominated Non-Official Members: Members nominated by the Governor-General but were not government officials
  - Elected Members: The elected members were elected indirectly as the local bodies elected an electoral college who would elect members of the provincial legislative councils and these members would, in turn, elect the members of the Imperial legislative council. Thus, the elective principle was recognised for the non-official membership of the councils in India and Indians were allowed to participate in the election of various legislative councils, though on the basis of class and community. For instance, the elected members were from the trader communities, zamindars, local bodies, the chambers of commerce, universities and Muslims.

[51] Though 'he had no faith whatsoever in their methods'.

[52] John Morley was a member of the Liberal Government, and he wanted to make positive changes in India's governance.

The Indian Councils Act of 1909—Cont'd

- Indians were provided membership to the executive Councils of the Viceroy and Governors for the first time. **Satyendra Prasad Sinha** became the first Indian to become member of the Viceroy's Executive Council as Law Member. Similarly, two Indians were nominated to the Council of the Secretary of State for Indian affairs.
- It introduced one of the most detrimental steps for Indian politics, the system of communal representation. Under the provision of **separate electorates** for the Muslims, some constituencies were earmarked for Muslims and only Muslims could vote for their representatives. Thus, the Muslim members were to be elected only by Muslim voters and Lord Minto came to be known as the **Father of Communal Electorate.**
- The Act also provided for the separate representation of presidency corporations, chambers of commerce, universities and zamindars.
- Under the Act of 1909, the deliberative functions of the legislative councils at both levels were enlarged and following important changes were introduced: The restriction on the right to propose resolutions or to divide the Council on the budget was removed.
  - Members were given the right to discuss on matters of general public importance, and to propose resolutions and also divide the Council on them.

    So, now apart from discussing budget, the members could move resolutions, ask supplementary questions and also discuss matters of public interest. They could also vote separate items in the budget though the budget as a whole could not be voted upon and certain heads of revenue and expenditure were expressly stated to be not open for discussion. The resolutions were to take the form of recommendations to the Government, but the Government was not bound to act upon them. Likewise, the members were also not permitted to discuss on foreign policy or on relations with the princely states.

Analysis of Morley–Minto Reforms

The Extremists, even the Moderates leading the Congress and the country as a whole, were quite disappointed by the 'constitutional' reforms of 1909 since the reforms could not address the expectations of the Indians in terms of self-governance.

- The Indian Councils Act of 1909, even though increased the number of elected members in the Imperial Legislative Council and the provincial legislative councils, most of the elected members were being elected indirectly. Also, the system of election was too indirect, which at times gave the impression of 'infiltration of legislators through a number of sieves'. And, while parliamentary forms were introduced, along with certain new changes like permitting the members to introduce resolutions, enhancing their power to ask questions, allowing of voting on separate budget items, still, these reformed councils did not enjoy any real power and remained mere advisory bodies. The position of the Governor-General remained unchanged and his veto power remained undiluted, thereby failing to fulfil the aspirations of Indians who were now vociferously demanding self-government.

> *"Colonial Self-government (as demanded by the Congress) was not suitable for India, and I am against the introduction of parliamentary or responsible government in India."*
>
> Lord Morley's statement on the Indian Council Act of 1909.

> *"What the reforms of 1909 gave to the people of the country was a shadow rather than substance. The people had demanded self-government but what they were given was 'benevolent despotism'."*
>
> Bipan Chandra

- The Act introduced **communal representation** in Indian politics by introducing the system of separate electorates for Muslims, a regressive step aimed at dividing the nationalist ranks and to weaken the growing tide of nationalism by encouraging the notion that the political, economic and cultural interests of Hindus and Muslims were separate and not common. The ill effects of this differential treatment ultimately resulted in the partition of the country along religious lines.
- However, to say that the Act of 1909 was a complete disaster is also wrong since it was crucial in the sense that it did increase Indian participation in the legislative councils, especially at the provincial levels and with the introduction of the electoral principles, a basic groundwork for a parliamentary system was laid even though that was contrary to the intent of Lord Morley. Also for the first time, 'elective principle' was being recognised as the basis of the composition of legislative council. The Act by increasing the participation of the Indians and by enhancing the deliberative functions of the Councils further provided avenues to the Indians to constructively use the councils for not only ventilating their grievances but to also make suggestions for better administration. For instance, some members like **G. K. Gokhale** put to constructive use the opportunity to debate in the councils by demanding universal primary education, attacking repressive policies and drawing attention to the plight of indentured labour and Indian workers in South Africa. Thus, it would not be wrong to state that the Indian Councils Act of 1909 was yet another step forward towards a representative form of government.

Previous Year's Questions (Prelims)

1. The 'Swadeshi' and 'Boycott' were adopted as methods of struggle for the first time during the....? (2016)

(a) Agitation against the partition of Bengal
(b) Home Rule Movement
(c) Non-Cooperation Movement
(d) Visit of the Simon Commission to India

2. What was the main reason for the split in Indian National Congress at Surat in 1907? (2016)

(a) Introduction of communalism into Indian politics by Lord Minto
(b) Extremists lack of faith in the Capacity of the moderates to negotiate with the British government
(c) Foundation of Muslim League
(d) Aurobindo Ghosh's inability to be elected as President of Indian National Congress

3. Which one of the following movements has contributed to a split in the Indian National Congress resulting in the emergence of Moderates and Extremists'? (2015)

(a) Swadeshi Movement
(b) Quit India Movement
(c) Non-Cooperation Movement
(d) Civil Disobedience Movement

4. Who out of the following was/were economic critic(s) of colonialism in India? (2015, 2012)

1. Dadabhai Naoroji
2. G. Subramaniam Iyer
3. R. C. Dutt

Select the correct answer from the following options:

(a) Only 1
(b) 1 and 2

(c) 2 and 3
(d) 1, 2 and 3

5. The partition of Bengal made by Lord Curzon in 1905 lasted until? (2014)
(a) The first World War when Indian troops were needed by the British and partition was ended
(b) King George V. abrogates Curzon's Act at the Royal Darbar in Delhi in 1911
(c) Gandhiji launched his Civil Disobedience Movement
(d) The partition of India in 1947 when East Bengal became East Pakistan

6. Consider the following statements: (2012)

The most effective contribution made by Dadabhai Naoroji to the cause of Indian National Movement was that he

1. exposed the economic exploitation of India by the British
2. interpreted the ancient Indian texts and restored the self confidence of Indians
3. stressed the need for eradication of all the social evils before anything else

Which of the statement(s) given above is/are correct? Select the correct answer from the following options:

(a) 1 only
(b) 2 and 3
(c) 1 and 3
(d) 1, 2 and 3

7. What was the immediate cause for the launch of the Swadeshi Movement? (2010)
(a) The partition of Bengal done by Lord Curzon
(b) A sentence of 18 months rigorous imprisonment imposed on Lokmanya Tilak
(c) The arrest and deportation of Lala Lajpat Rai and Ajit Singh; and passing of the Punjab colonisation bill
(d) Death sentence pronounced on the Chapekar brothers

8. Four resolutions were passed at the famous Calcutta session of Indian National Congress in 1906.

The question of either retention or of rejection of these four resolutions became the cause of split in Congress at the next congress session held in Surat in 1907.

Which of the following was not one of those resolutions? (2010)

(a) Annulment of partition of Bengal
(b) Boycott
(c) National Education
(d) Swadeshi

9. In the context of the Indian freedom struggle, 16 October 1905 is well known for which of the following reasons? (2009)
(a) The formal proclamation of Swadeshi movement was made in Calcutta Town Hall
(b) Partition of Bengal took effect
(c) Dadabhai Naoroji declared that the goal of Indian National Congress was Swaraj
(d) Lokmanaya Tilak stated swadeshi movement in Poona.

10. Who among the following used the phrase 'Un-British' to criticise the English colonial control of India? (2008)
(a) Anand Mohan Bose
(b) Badruddin Tyabji
(c) Dadabhai Naoroji
(d) Pherozeshah Mehta

11. Who among the following rejected the title of knighthood and refused to accept a position in the council of the Secretary of State for India? (2008)
(a) Motilal Nehru
(b) M. G. Ranade
(c) G. K. Gokhale
(d) B. G. Tilak

12. Who among the following gave a systematic critique of the moderate politics of the Indian National Congress in a series of articles entitled 'New Lamps for Old'? (2008)

(a) Aurobindo Ghosh
(b) R. C. Dutt
(c) Syed Ahmed Khan
(d) Viraghavachariar

13. The song 'Amar Sonar Bangla' written during the Swadeshi movement of India inspired the liberation struggle of Bangladesh and was adopted as the National Anthem of Bangladesh. Who wrote this song? (2007)

(a) Rajni Kanta Sen
(b) Dwijendra lal Ray
(c) Mukunda Das
(d) Rabindra Nath Tagore

14. With reference to the period of extremist nationalist movement in India with its spirit of Swadeshi, which one of the following statements is not correct? (2002)

(a) Liaqat Hossian led the Muslim peasants of Barisal in their agitations
(b) In 1898, the scheme of national education was formulated by Satish Chandra Mukherjee
(c) The Bengal National College was founded in 1906 with Aurobindo as the principal
(d) Tagore preached the cult of Atmashakti, the main plan of which was social and economic regeneration of the villages.

15. That the per capita income in India was `20 in 1867-68, was ascertained for the first time by: (2000)

(a) M. G. Ranade
(b) Sir W. Hunter
(c) R. C. Dutta
(d) Dadabhai Naoroji

16. Who organised the 'Abhinav Bharat' a secret society of revolutionaries? (1999)

(a) Khudiram Bose
(b) V. D. Savarkar
(c) Prafulla Chaki
(d) Bhagat Singh

17. Which among the following was the most short-lived of all the Britain's constitutional experiments in India? (1999)

(a) Indian Council Act of 1861
(b) Indian Council Act of 1892
(c) Indian Council Act of 1909
(d) Government of India Act of 1919

18. The paintings of Abanindranath Tagore are classified as (1999)

(a) Realistic
(b) Socialistic
(c) Revivalistic
(d) Impressionistic

19. Which one of the following Indian leaders was dismissed by the British from the Indian Civil Service? (1999)

(a) Satyendranath Tagore
(b) Surendranath Banerjee
(c) R. C. Dutt
(d) Subhash Chandra Bose

20. "The Congress is tottering to its fall and one of my great ambitions while in India, is to assist it to a peaceful demise. The statement is attributed to (1998)

(a) Lord Dufferin
(b) Lord Curzon
(c) Lord Lytton
(d) None of these

21. Assertion (A): Partition of Bengal in 1905 brought an end to the Moderates role in the Indian freedom movement.

Reason (R): The Surat session of Indian National Congress separated the extremists from the Moderates. (1998)

(a) Both A and R are true and R is the correct explanation of A.
(b) Both A and R are true but R is not the correct explanation of A.
(c) A is true but R is false.
(d) A is false but R is true.

22. The Indian Muslims in general, were not attracted to the extremist movement because of the (1998)
   (a) Influence of Sir Syed Ahmad Khan
   (b) Anti-Muslim attitude of Extremist leaders
   (c) Indifference shown to Muslim aspirations
   (d) Extremists policy of harping on Hindu past

23. Which one of the following defines the extremist ideology during the early phase of Indian Freedom movement? (1998)
   (a) Stimulating the production of indigenous articles by giving them preference over imported commodities
   (b) Obtaining self-government by aggressive means in place of petitions and constitutional ways
   (c) Providing national education according to the requirements of the country
   (d) Organising coups against the British Empire through military revolt

Previous Year's Answers (Prelims)

1. (a)	2. (b)	3. (a)	4. (d)	5. (b)	6. (a)	7. (a)	8. (a)
9. (b)	10. (c)	11. (c)	12. (a)	13. (d)	14. (a)	15. (d)	16. (b)
17. (c)	18. (c)	19. (b)	20. (b)	21. (d)	22. (d)	23. (b)	

First World War and Indian Politics

7

The First World War[1] (1914–18) was not merely behind various changes in Europe's politico-social atmosphere, but was also a significant factor for bringing crucial changes in the socio-economic conditions and political life of India, and thus resulted in varying reactions among the different nationalists across India. While both the **Moderates** and the **Extremists** extended their support[2] to the British in their war efforts, it was, however, the **revolutionaries** who looked upon the War as a heaven-sent opportunity for a successful ***coup d' etat*** for achieving immediate and complete independence from the British rule as it was felt that being embroiled in the War, Britain was not in a position to effectively answer a nationalist challenge since not only the troops stationed in India were at their lowest[3], but the War also brought the possibility of financial and military help from Germany and Turky, the enemies of Britain.

The challenge was thus thrown by the violent group of nationalists, that is, the revolutionaries, who decided to take advantage of Britain's difficulty and attempted at a violent overthrow of British rule such as the **Ghadar group** based in North America. During the same period, this opportunity was also seized in a different way by **Lokamanya Tilak**, **Annie Besant** and their Home Rule Leagues in India who launched a nation-wide agitation for securing **Home Rule** or *Swaraj*. In this chapter, we will discuss all about these important political events surrounding the First World War: the **Ghadar Movement**, the **Home Rule Leagues**, the **Lucknow Pact** and the **Montague Declaration**.

The Ghadar Movement

The *Ghadar* – also written as *Ghadr* in English – is an Urdu word for rebellion. It was initiated in 1913 by a coalition of Punjabi immigrants, mostly Sikhs, small and middle peasants at home, working as labourers in farms and factories on the Pacific Coast that is, the west coast of the United States of America (USA) and Canada. The Movement having **shared leadership** from Sikhs, Hindus and Muslims was dedicated to raising money and support for the overthrow of British rule in India.

Background of the Movement

The West Coast of North America had, since 1904, become home to a steadily increasing number of Punjabi[4] immigrants, many of whom had served in the British Indian Army and because of their service in the Army and their travel to distant lands owing to the service, they were better aware of the overseas

[1] In the First World War, Britain allied with France, Russia, USA, Italy and Japan against Germany, Austria-Hungary and Turkey.

[2] Though both had different reasons as the Moderates felt it was a matter of duty for them while the Extremists believed that Britain would repay India's loyalty with gratitude in the form of self-government after the War.

[3] At one point, the number of white soldiers went down to only 15,000.

[4] Mostly were from the Jullundur and Hoshiarpur districts of Punjab.

opportunities and had also acquired the confidence and the means necessary for emigration. Thus, their **emigration** was both a response to economic frustration and oppression at home combined with search for livelihood along with building a new and prosperous life for themselves and their kin in these promised lands. However, coming to these strange lands, they were confronted with racial hostility, fear and a sense of alienation due to the restrictive immigration laws[5] and other disabilities, such as those imposed by the **Alien Land law** which practically prohibited Indians from owning land in the United States. These discriminatory policies and their inability to get the Government of India or the British Government to intercede on their behalf regarding immigration restrictions and other disabilities soon resulted in a flurry of political activity among the Indian immigrants.

As early as 1907, a ***Circular-e-Azadi*** (Circular of Liberty) was brought out by Ramnath Puri, a political exile living on the West Coast, in which he also pledged support to the **Swadeshi Movement**. Tarak Nath Das, an Indian student in Vancouver, Canada, started a paper called ***Free Hindustan*** and generating awareness about the hypocrisy of British Government pointed to their partisan approach wherein they were keen on sending Indians to Fiji to work as labourers for British planters, but were against their immigration to the North America where the British feared that these opportunities of close familiarity with Whites of North America might infect them with ideas of liberty. G. D. Kumar set up a **Swadesh Sevak Home** in Vancouver on the lines of the India House in London and also brought out a Gurmukhi paper ***Swadesh Sevak*** advocating both social reform and open revolt against the British by Indian troops.

In 1910, **Tarak Nath Das** and **G. D. Kumar**, by now forced out of Vancouver, set up the United India House in Seattle in the United States, where every Saturday they lectured to a group of Indian labourers and gradually also developed close links with the Khalsa Diwan Society, which resulted in 1913 in a decision to send a deputation to meet the **Colonial Secretary** in London and the **Viceroy** and other officials in India. Though they failed to meet the Colonial Secretary in London even after waiting for a whole month, in India they succeeded in meeting the Viceroy and the Lieutenant Governor of the Punjab, and, more importantly, their visit to Punjab became the occasion for a series of public meetings in different Punjab towns[6] and they received enthusiastic support from the Press and the general public. Meanwhile, in early 1913, **Bhagwan Singh**, a Sikh priest who had earlier worked in Hong Kong and the Malay states, visited Vancouver and started preaching openly about the violent overthrow of British rule and urged the people to adopt ***Bande Mataram*** as a revolutionary salute. Bhagwan Singh was swiftly externed from Canada after a stay of three months and soon due to relatively free political atmosphere the centre of revolutionary activity was shifted to the United States.

As a result of this sustained political agitation both in Canada and the United States, and convinced that their inferior status in foreign lands was a consequence of their being citizens of an enslaved country, a feeling of solidarity and nationalist consciousness was formed among immigrant Indians and this mood of discontent and impatience quickly blossomed into a revolutionary movement wherein they tried to analyse both fundamental reasons of their oppression on one hand and political mobilisation and organisation on the other. The task of mobilisation was undertaken by middle-class intellectuals among the Indian community in North America such as **Lala Har Dayal**[7] who in his sharp anti-British diatribe explained to the fellow immigrants that the basic reason for all their oppression and misery was the British rule in India as due to the

[5] The British through their Secretary of State also urged for restrictions on immigration of Indians since they felt that the terms of close familiarity of Indians with Whites which would inevitably take place in America was not good for British prestige as it was by prestige alone that India was held and not by force.

[6] Towns like Lahore, Ludhiana, Ambala, Ferozepur, Jullundur, Amritsar, Lyallpur, Gujranwala, Sialkot and Shimla.

[7] Lala Har Dayal was a political exile from India, who had arrived in California, USA, in 1911 and had been lecturing at Stanford University as well as to various American groups of intellectuals, radicals and workers on the anarchist and syndicalist movements but had not shown much interest in the affairs of Indian immigrants. But, the bomb attack on the Viceroy in Delhi in December 1912 changed his attitude and roused his dormant Indian revolutionary who issued a *Yugantar* Circular praising the attack on the Viceroy.

ruin of the country's economy, thousands had to leave the country in search of livelihood, and in these foreign lands they were hated and ridiculed because they were 'slaves' of the British and thus there was the need to overthrow the British rule through armed revolt.

Towards Organisation

Lala Har Dayal soon assumed leadership of the immigrant Indian community and, in May 1913, the need for a central organisation was met with the setting up of the Hindi Association in Portland, which later changed its name to Hindustan Ghadar Party. Baba **Sohan Singh Bhakna** was elected its President, while **Lala Har Dayal** was chosen as its General Secretary and **Pandit Kanshi Ram** as the Treasurer at its first meeting which was also attended by others including **Bhai Parmanand** and **Harnam Singh 'Tundilat'**. A sum of $10,000 was collected on the spot and a Working Committee was set up to oversee the establishment of headquarters of the Association by the name of *Yugantar Ashram* in San Francisco and it was also decided to start a weekly paper, the ***Ghadar***, for free circulation. The Ghadar Movement had begun.

> *"Do not fight the Americans, but use the freedom that is available in the US to fight the British; you will never be treated as equals by the Americans until you are free in your own land, the root cause of Indian poverty and degradation is British rule and it must be overthrown, not by petitions but by aimed revolt; carry this message to the masses and to the soldiers in the Indian Army; go to India in large numbers and enlist their support."*
>
> –Lala Har Dayal

Strategy and Action

The plans of political action outlined by Lala Har Dayal and accepted by the Hindi Association were based on the understanding that British rule could only be overthrown by armed revolt and that for this to happen it was necessary that Indian immigrants go to India in large numbers and carry this message to the masses and the soldiers of the Indian army. Basing themselves on this understanding, the militant nationalists launched an extensive propaganda campaign, touring factories and farms where Indian immigrants worked.

The paper *Ghadar* was launched on 1 November 1913, the first issue was in Urdu followed a month later with the Gurmukhi version. The format of the paper was designed to convey the message of nationalism in simple and bold terms. Its very name meant 'revolt', thereby leaving no doubts about its intentions. And if any doubts remained, they were to be dispelled by the captions on the masthead: ***Angrezi Raj ka Dushman*** meaning 'An Enemy of British Rule'.

> *"Today there begins in foreign lands ... a war against English rule ... a cannonade with the strength of a pen, and the time is soon to come when rifle and blood will be used for pen and ink."*
>
> –Excerpts from the first issue of *Ghadar.*

Besides that the front page of each issue carried the *Angrezi Raj Ka Kacha Chittha* or 'An Expose of British Rule', which consisted of 14 points enumerating the negative effects of British rule, more precisely a summary of the entire nationalist critique of British rule on the issues of drain of wealth, the destruction of Indian handicrafts and traditional industries, the low per capita income, high land revenue, the recurrence of famines and plague that killed millions of Indians, the contrast between the low expenditure on health and the high expenditure on the military, the use of Indian tax payers' money for wars in Afghanistan, Burma, Egypt, Persia and China, the British policy of promoting discord in the Indian States to extend their own influence and the British policy of Divide and Rule to create enmity between Hindus and Muslims. The last two points of the *Chittha* also suggested the solution by highlighting the small number of Englishmen present in India as compared to the crores of Indians and by further pointing to the fact that the time had come for another revolt as 56 years had lapsed since the last Revolt of 1857. The *Ghadar* also exhorted the Punjabi community to atone for their pro-British role in the Revolt of 1857 by changing their self-image from that of a loyal soldier to that of a rebel whose only aim was freedom.

"Why do you disgrace the name of Singhs?

How come! you have forgotten the majesty of 'Lions' Had the like of Dip Singh been alive today

How could the Singhs have been taunted?

People say that the Singhs are no good

Why did you turn the tides during the Delhi mutiny? Cry aloud. 'Let us kill the Whites'

Why do you sit quiet, shamelessly

Let the earth give way so we may drown

To what good were these thirty crores born."

The *Ghadar* also contained references from the **Savarkar's** *The Indian War of independence – 1857* along with contributions of **Sri Aurobindo**, **Lokamanya Tilak**, **Madame Cama**, **Shyamji Krishna Varma**, **Ajit Singh** as well as highlights of the daring deeds of the ***Anushilan Samiti***, the ***Yugantar group*** and the **Russian secret societies**. In no time, the *Ghadar* was circulated widely among Indian immigrants in North America, and soon reached the immigrants in the Philippines, Hong Kong, China, Malay states, Singapore, Trinidad and the Honduras as well as Indian regiments stationed in many of these centres along with reaching the readers in India itself and evoking an unprecedented response among the immigrant communities slowly becoming the subject of lively discussion and debate. But, perhaps, the most powerful impact was made by the poems that appeared in the *Ghadar*, soon collected and published as ***Ghadar di Goonj*** (Echo of Ghadar) and distributed free of cost. The poems were marked by a revolutionary spirit and a strongly secular tone, as the following extract shows:

"Hindus, Sikhs, Pathans and Muslims,

Pay attention ye all people in the army.

Our country has been plundered by the British, We have to wage a war against them.

We do not need pandits and quazis,

We do not want to get our ship sunk.

The time of worship is over now,

It is time to take up the sword."

The message of the *Ghadar* went home with a swift pace, and ardent young militants soon became impatient for action. Lala Har Dayal himself was surprised by the intensity of the response and 10 years as expected by him to organise the revolution[8] in India now seemed a long time.

The Main Events

The subsequent course of the Ghadar Movement was, however, determined by three major events in 1914: the arrest, jumping of bail and flight to Switzerland of **Lala Har Dayal**, the fateful voyage of the ship ***Komagata Maru***, and the beginning of the **First World War**.

- In March, 1914, Lala Har Dayal was arrested on the stated reason of his anarchist activities but the most likely reason was the pressure exerted by the British Government who for obvious reasons wanted him to be removed. However, released on bail, he used the opportunity to slip out of the United States and went to Switzerland.
- Meanwhile, in an attempt to defy the Canadian immigration laws which forbade entry to all except those who made a *direct and continuous journey from India* and encouraged by the decision of the Supreme Court that allowed entry to 35 Indians who had not made a continuous journey, **Gurdit Singh**, an Indian contractor living in Singapore, chartered a ship named ***Komagata Maru*** and with 376 Indian passengers, mainly Sikh and Punjabi Muslim would-be immigrants originating from various places in East and South East Asia, set sail for Vancouver, Canada. On the way in **Yokohama**, Japan, Ghadar activists visited the ship, gave lectures and distributed revolutionary and anti-imperialist literature. The Canadian Government authorities as well as the Press in Canada took a very negative view about the intended immigration and labelled it as the '**Mounting Oriental Invasion**'. In the meantime, the Canadian Government prepared to meet the challenge posed by the Supreme Court judgement and plugged all the leftover legal loopholes while ensuring that no incoming passenger of *Komagata Maru* is allowed entry on Canadian soil.

  Thus, on arrival in **Vancouver** on 29 September 1914, the ship was not allowed into the port and was cordoned off by the police. Despite the strenuous efforts of the '**Shore Committee**' set up for fighting for the rights of the passengers under the leadership of **Balwant Singh**, **Husain Rahim** and **Sohan Lal Pathak** and a powerful campaign launched by Ghadar leaders of the United States such as **Bhagwan Singh**, **Mohammed Barkatullah**, **Sohan Singh Bhakna** and **Ram Chandra**, the *Komagata Maru* was eventually forced out of Canadian waters after two months of privation and uncertainty. As luck would have it, before the ship reached Yokohama, the First World War broke out and the British Government passed orders that *no passenger was to be allowed to disembark anywhere*[9] *on the way till it reached Calcutta*. Thus, the return journey of the ship triggered a wave of resentment at every port of call among the communities of immigrant Indians and eventually increased anti-British hostility. When the ship finally reached Budge Budge near **Calcutta**, the irate and the harassed passengers, provoked by the hostile attitude of the authorities, clashed with the police, which resulted in the death of 18 passengers and the arrest of 202 passengers.
- The third and most important event that brought about a dramatic change in the situation and made the Ghadar revolution imminent was the outbreak of the **First World War.** This was the opportunity of Britain's difficulty that the Ghadarites had been long waiting for to seize, and even though it had come earlier than they had expected and their preparations were still in a rudimentary stage, they couldn't muster either the courage or the foresight to let it pass by so easily. Hence, within no time, a special meeting of the leading activists of the Ghadar Movement was convened and it was decided unanimously that the

[8] Earlier on one occasion, Lala Hardayal had spoken in terms of '10 years' when asked about how long it would take to organise the revolution in India.

[9] Not even at the places from where they had joined the ship.

time had come for action and it was better to die than to do nothing at all. Regarding their major weakness of lack of arms, it was assumed that it could be made good by winning over the Indian soldiers to their cause and by persuading them to revolt against the British. The Ghadar party accordingly issued its *Ailan-e-Jung* or 'Proclamation of War', which was widely circulated among Indians living abroad. The leading Ghadar activists also started organising and addressing a series of public meetings and tours across Canada, the United States, Japan, Philippines, China, Hong Kong, Malay states, Singapore and Burma, exhorting people to return home and organise an armed revolt. The response was tremendous, with large numbers of immigrant Indians offering themselves and their entire belongings to the cause of the nation. Some of the activists like **Kartar Singh Sarabha** and **Raghubar Dayal** immediately left for India. Encouraged by this, the Ghadar party began the exodus to India, and batches of revolutionaries began to arrive in India by different routes in the latter half of 1914.

> *"O warriors! the opportunity that you have been looking for has come ... Don't delay a moment ... This is the right moment to start a war of independence. You can very soon expel the British from India. Go to India and incite the native troops. Preach mutiny openly. Take arms from the troops of the native states and wherever you see the British, kill them. If you do your work quickly and intelligently, there is hope that Germany will help you. Get help from Nepal and Afghanistan. Start the War quick."*
>
> An article entitled 'the Trumpet of War' in the *Ghadar* issue of 4 August 1914.

The Last Phases of the Ghadar Movement

The *Ghadar* plans were hardly a secret and even the Government of India was fully informed of them and thus was much well prepared to deal with any type of threat posed by the Ghadarites. The Government keeping a close watch over the events armed itself with the Ingress into India Ordinance and started careful scrutiny of the returning emigrants, thereby allowing only the 'safe' ones to proceed home and arresting the more 'dangerous' ones while ordering the 'less dangerous' ones to not to leave their home villages. It is roughly estimated that of the 8,000 emigrants who returned to India during that time, 5,000 were considered 'safe' and allowed to go unhindered, while precautionary measures were taken for roughly 1,500 men and up to February 1915, 189 were interned and 704 were restricted to their villages. Nevertheless, some of 'the dangerous' ones still escaped British detection and succeeded in reaching Punjab to foment rebellion.

One of the first to reach Punjab safely among the hard-core Ghadar core activists was **Kartar Singh Sarabha**, who immediately started mobilising the returning emigrants, organising and holding meetings to formulate a plan of action for the intended Ghadar Movement. The Ghadar activists soon started touring villages, cyclostyled and distributed party publications, addressed gatherings at *melas* and made every effort to persuade the people to rise in revolt. But, to their dismay, the Punjab in 1914 was very different from what the Ghadarites had expected, and the people were in no mood to embark upon their romantic Ghadar adventure. Also present were active **British loyal elements** like the Chief Khalsa Diwan who declared them to be 'apostates' or 'fallen Sikhs' and criminals and cooperated fully in the government's efforts to crush them.

Frustrated and disappointed with the attitude of the civilian population, the Ghadarites next attempted to spread their message among the soldiers and engineer a mutiny in the Army. However, all their naive efforts of mutiny in the Army in November 1914 too failed for lack of proper organisation and centralised leadership. Further disillusioned with the futile events, the Ghadarites made an attempt to find a leader and in February 1915 through the efforts of Bengali revolutionaries **Sachindranath Sanyal** and **Vishnu Ganesh Pingley**, contacted **Rash Behari Bose**[10], and entrusted the task of leadership and organisation of Ghadar revolution in India to him. Though Rash Behari Bose arrived in Punjab to assume leadership of the revolt and sent out men to contact army units in different centres, (from Bannu in the North-West Frontier to Faizabad and Lucknow in UP) and fixed the date for the mutiny first for 21 February 1915 and then for 19 February, soon he had to flee from Punjab to Japan, and the whole scheme of things proved abortive as the government in the meantime succeeded in penetrating the organisation, and taking pre-emptive measures arrested most of the Ghadar leaders and crushed the Ghadar Movement even before its start on Indian soil. In one of the most repressive actions carried out by the British Government, the conspiracy trials were held in both Punjab and Mandalay, and 45 revolutionaries were sentenced to death and over 200 to long terms of imprisonment.

> *"An entire generation of the nationalist leadership of Punjab was, thus, politically beheaded."*
>
> Bipan Chandra
>
> *"If I had to live more lives than one, I would sacrifice each of them for my country's sake."*
>
> The final words of Kartar Singh Sarabha just before his death, a 19-year-old organizer of mutiny among Punjab garrisons.

Nevertheless, some Indian revolutionaries like those operating from Berlin such as the **Indian Independence Committee** set up in 1915 under Virendranath Chattopadhyay, Bhupen Dutta and Har Dayal who were working in close collaboration with the German foreign office under the so-called '**Zimmerman Plan**' and having links with the Ghadar leader Ram Chandra in America still attempted to organise a mutiny among Indian troops stationed abroad, but these and all other attempts failed to record any significant success. For instance, though funds were channelled through German embassies in the Far East, and from Japan Rash behari Bose and Abani Mukherji made several efforts to send arms after 1915 but nothing much was achieved. Similarly, in December 1915, **Raja Mahendra Pratap** and **Barkatullah** and **Obeidullah Sindhi** tried to enlist the help of the Amir of Afghanistan, **Amanullah**, to set up a *Provisional Government of Free India* in Kabul, but none of this resulted in any major success. Another notable mutiny held abroad was in **Singapore** on 15 February 1915, of the Punjabi Muslim 5th Light Infantry, and the 36th Sikh battalion under the leadership of Jamadar **Chisti Khan**, Jamadar **Abdul Ghani** and Subedar **Daud Khan** was brutally suppressed and around 37 of the soldiers were executed and 41 transported for life. The '**Hindu Conspiracy trial**' in San Francisco in 1918 after US entry into the war further jolted the revolutionary network of Ghadarites in the United States and ended anti-British activities carried on in the United States, and thus on the whole, the Ghadar Movement to overthrow British rule failed on all fronts, both domestic and abroad.

The Critical Analysis of the Ghadar Movement

Though politically and militarily the Ghadar Movement failed to achieve much and did not succeed in its stated objective of organising a successful armed revolt against British rule, it would be wrong to conclude that the Movement was a complete failure since the success or failure of a political movement is not always

[10] The Bengali revolutionary who had become famous by his daring attack on Hardinge, the Viceroy.

measured in terms of its achievement of stated objectives. If we go by that measure, then all the major national struggles of 1920–22, 1930–34, or 1942 would have to be termed as failures, since none of them resulted in achieving immediate independence. But if the yardstick of success is measured in terms of the deepening of nationalist consciousness, creation of traditions of resistance, the evolution and testing of new strategies and methods of struggle, the spread of progressive ideas of secularism, democracy and egalitarianism, then the Ghadar Movement surely occupies a very prominent place in India's journey of struggle for freedom.

Achievements of the Ghadar Movement

- One of the major achievements of the Ghadar Movement lay in the realm of its **progressive ideology**, which was strongly secular, democratic and egalitarian in its approach. Though the vast majority of Ghadarites were recruited from amongst Punjabi Sikh immigrants, they preached militant nationalism with a completely secular approach. They freely accepted non-Sikhs and non-Punjabis as leaders, for instance, Lala Har Dayal along with Ram Chandra and many others were Hindus, Barkatullah was a Muslim while Rash Behari Bose was a Bengali Hindu, and the masthead of all *Ghadar* publications bore the names *Ram, Allah and Nanak.* Their philosophy was based on the premise that 'any type of concern with religion is petty and narrow-minded, and unworthy of revolutionaries'. Another testimony to their secular outlook was the fact that instead of any religious greeting such as *Sat Sri Akal*, the Ghadarites popularised the **nationalist salute** *Bande Mantram* as the rallying cry of their movement.

> *"We were not Sikhs or Punjabis, our religion was patriotism."*
>
> Sohan Singh Bhakna, a prominent Ghadarite who later became a major peasant and Communist leader.

It is, however, pertinent here to note that some of the ambiguities that are at times reported as a limitation of the *Ghadar* ideological discourse, such as those evidenced by Har Dayal's advocacy of Khilafat as a religious cause of the Muslims, or when the British policy of not allowing Sikhs to carry arms was criticised, and others, were not necessarily an aspect of communal ideology or consciousness. They were more a product of the transitional stage in the evolution of a secular nationalist ideology since the defence of religious interests needs to be seen as part of the whole aspect of cultural defence against colonialism and not just from a narrow prism of communalism.

- The Ghadarites were also not tied to any particular regional affiliations or narrow regional loyalties. They revered leaders from all over India – be it **Lokamanya Tilak**, **Savarkar** from Maharastra or **Khudi Ram Bose** and **Aurobindo Ghosh** from Bengal. It is a hard fact that Ghadarites chose and accepted Rash Behari Bose as their leader of the abortive *Ghadar* revolt in 1915. Instead of dwelling on the greatness of the Sikhs or the Punjabis, the *Ghadarites* constantly criticized them for betraying their motherland in the 1857 revolt by siding with the British and therefore urged them regularly to make amends to *Bharat Mata,* by fighting for her honour. Similarly, they condemned the presence of Sikhs in large numbers in the British Indian Army and negated the British ideology of the Sikhs being a 'martial race' as just a colonial propaganda meant to preserve them as loyal soldiers. Instead, the Ghadarites saw it all as a matter of shame and asked the Sikh soldiers to revolt against the British.
- Another prominent feature of *Ghadar* ideology was its strong **democratic** and **egalitarian character**. The ultimate aim of the Ghadarites was the establishment of an independent republic of India. The constant

references to the Irish, Mexican and Russian revolutionaries not only imparted an **inter-nationalist character** to the movement but also saved the movement from becoming a chauvinist nationalist propanganda. The deep roots of socialist and egalitarian ideology among the Ghadarites further facilitated many of them to eventually emerge as prominent peasant and Communist leaders in the 1920s and 1930s.

- The Ghadar Movement through its popular propaganda ***Ghadar ki Goonj*** and other in-house publications helped in educating an entire generation of Indian immigrants in a powerful and simple form about the national issues concerning India, specially the critique of colonialism and the understanding that Indian poverty and backwardness was a consequence of British rule. Through the various meetings, gatherings and awareness campaigns, the Ghadarites gradually succeeded in creating a cadre of highly motivated nationalists who later played an important role in building up the communist and peasant movements in Punjab and other parts of India for many decades to follow.

This does not, however, mean that the *Ghadar* Movement did not suffer from any limitations.

Limitations of the Ghadar Movement

- The Ghadar Movement inevitably had its share of limitations as well, the major one being the total underestimation of the extent and amount of preparation required at every level, be it **organisational**, **ideological**, **strategic**, **tactical** or **financial**, for a successful rebellion. The sudden outbreak of the war along with the *Komagata Maru* episode hastened the Ghadarite actions and perhaps, they sounded the bugles of war without examining the state of their army. They were misled into thinking that the vast mass of Indians in India were in the same state of readiness as were the immigrant Indian community who were not only highly emotionally charged but whose nationalist consciousness was also aroused by daily experiences of racial insult and alienation produced by living in unfamiliar surroundings. Besides that, they made the mistake of overlooking the simple fact that mobilising and organising a few thousand discontented immigrant Indians was much easy than motivating lakhs of peasants and soldiers in India along with completely underestimating the strength and might of the British power in India.
- The Ghadar Movement also failed to generate an effective and sustained central leadership that was capable of integrating the various aspects of the movement. Lala Har Dayal did try to fill in for some time but even he was not much suited for the role as he was more of an inspirer, a propagandist and ideologue whose own ideas did not form a structured whole but remained a shifting amalgam of various theories that attracted him from time to time. Further, his departure from the United States at a critical stage left his compatriots floundering and leaderless.
- Another major weakness of the Ghadar Movement was its almost non-existent organisational structure, which ultimately led to the February 19 planned uprising ending in a tragic fiasco. The emergent pattern of authority, the way members were recruited and the manner in which coordination of efforts was sought to be achieved by the Ghadarites, all point to a great degree of spontaneity and lack of efficient preparedness. The statements of Ghadarites in the conspiracy trials too point out to the basic organisational weaknesses and ambiguities surrounding different organisational positions. There have been instances which clearly establishes that the Ghadar Movement did not possess a recognised hierarchy of leadership and not much significance was given to planning, coordination or collective organisation under one leader. For example, Sachin Sanyal, who came to Punjab to make an assessment of the situation on behalf of Rash Bihari Bose, related an incident wherein at a meeting with some of the important Ghadar leaders, he expressed his desire to talk to their chief and then Amar Singh told him frankly that they do not have a real leader and that's why they needed Rash Bihari Bose.
- These weaknesses of leadership, of understanding and of organisation all resulted in a tremendous waste of valuable human resources. The brute repression by the authorities resulted in the **beheading of an entire generation of secular nationalist leadership**. The heavy cost that had to be paid for all these weaknesses

was not only borne by the Ghadar Movement but also by the entire national movement, as had the major part of the Ghadar leadership remained politically effective, the political atmosphere of the national movement, certainly in Punjab, would have been very different since the Ghadarites with their committed nationalist and secular ideology would inevitably have played a critical role in checking the communal tendencies that were to raise their head in later years.

The spectre of revolutionary violence, however, did not disappear at all with the Ghadar Movement. and it made a reappearance at the stage of the Indian National Movement again, a development which we are going to study in later chapters. The British, too, again came out with more draconian laws such as the Rowlatt bills of 1918, which eventually inflamed Mahatma Gandhi into action and a new phase in Indian politics was thus initiated, where the central focus shifted from violence to non-violence and from elite action to mass agitation, all of which we will be studying in the next chapter. Meanwhile, let's discuss about another less dramatic but more effective response to the situation arising out of the First World War – the **Home Rule Leagues**.

Home Rule Leagues

In 1915–16, **two** Home Rule Leagues were started in India, one under the leadership of Lokmanya Tilak and another under Annie Besant and S. Subramaniya Iyer with the common purpose of educative propaganda in favour of the demand for the grant of Home Rule or 'self-government' to India after the First World War. However, the two Leagues demarcated their areas of operation: **Tilak's League** was to work in Maharashtra (excluding Bombay city), Karnataka, the Central Provinces and Berar, while **Annie Besant's League** was having the rest of India under its domain.

Background of the Leagues

When Tilak returned to India in June 1914 after serving a long sentence of 6 years in Mandalay in Burma, he made **conciliatory gestures** both to the government reassuring it of his loyalty and to the Moderates that he wanted, like the Irish Home Rulers, a reform of the administration and not an overthrow of the Government.

"I may state once for all that we are trying in India, as the Irish Home-rulers have been doing in Ireland, for a reform of the system of administration and not for the overthrow of Government; and I have no hesitation in saying that the acts of violence which had been committed in the different Parts of India are not only repugnant to me, but have, in my opinion, only unfortunately retarded to a great extent, the pace of our political progress."

Tilak's public declaration in order to conciliate the Moderates and convince them of his bonafides, as well as to express his loyalty to the Government to stave off any possible government repression.

Thus, initially he concentrated all his attention on securing the readmission of himself and other Extremists into the Indian National Congress from which they had been banished in 1907 in Surat. We have already discussed in the last chapter that even in 1907, Tilak had been very upset with the split, and now after all these years he was even more convinced that unity of both Moderates and Extremists is very crucial to bring any meaningful change in the country. Besides that, he was also aware of the fact that gradually the Congress had come to symbolise the national movement and therefore, its sanction was a necessary pre-condition for the success of any political action. Further, the almost inactivity on the part of Congress since the split of Surat made many Moderate leaders realise the futility of the Surat split, and thus now many of them were more favourably disposed towards the question of the return of the Extremists to the fold. They were also under considerable pressure from Annie Besant, who wanted to build up a movement in India on the lines of the Irish Home Rule League and was urging them to accept the Extremists back into the Congress.

The Extremists, however, were not allowed re-entry into the Congress at its session in December 1914, more because of opposition put forward by Pherozeshah Mehta and his Bombay Moderate group, but consistent efforts throughout 1915, including the campaigns launched separately by Annie Besant through her two papers ***New India*** and ***Commonweal*** and Tilak through his newspapers ***Kesari*** and local associations, secured them their re-entry[11] in December 1915. However, Annie Besant did not succeed in getting the Congress to set up Home Rule Leagues but she did manage to persuade the Congress to commit itself to a programme of educative propaganda and to revival of the local-level Congress committees by September 1916, failing which she would be free to set up her own league. **Tilak** was, however, not bound by any such commitment and having gained the right of readmission, now took the lead, and in April 1916, set up the Home Rule League at the Bombay Provincial Conference in Belgaum. The Congress, still dominated as it was by the Moderates, however, failed to keep its promise of reviving local-level Congress Committees and beginning a programme of educative propaganda by September 1916, and thus eventually in September 1916, **Annie Besant** too launched her own Home Rule League, with George Arundale as the Organising Secretary.

Annie Besant

- Annie Besant, aged 66 in 1914, had come to India from England in 1893 to work for the Theosophical Society, and had earlier been an exponent of Free Thought, Radicalism and Fabianism.
- She had set up her headquarters in Adyar near Madras and developed a large network of followers of the Theosophical Society from among those educated Indians.
- In 1914, she decided to start a political movement on agitational lines for Home Rule on the lines of the Irish Home Rule League.

Tilak's Home Rule League

Tilak set up his Home Rule League in April 1916, and it was restricted to Maharashtra (excluding Bombay city), Karnataka, Central Provinces and Berar. It was organised into six branches and the demands included *Swarajya*, formation of linguistic states and education in the vernacular. It published 6 pamphlets in Marathi and 2 in English, of which 47,000 copies were sold. Pamphlets were also brought out in Kannada and Gujarati. Apart from these, the most crucial role was played by Tilak's tours during which he lectured and explained to the common folk about the demand for Home Rule.

> *"India was like a son who had grown up and attained maturity and it was right now that the trustee or the father should give him what was his due. The people of India must get this effected. They have a right to do so."*
>
> Excerpt from Tilak's speeches of Maharashtra tours.

[11] The opposition to the Extremists was also considerably whittled down by the death of Pherozeshah Mehta who had been the most recalcitrant in his opposition.

He also linked up the question of *Swaraj* with the demand for the formation of linguistic states and education in the vernacular and extended support for all the regional languages.

> *"Form one separate state each for Marathi, Telugu and Kanarese provinces . . . The principle that education should be given through the vernaculars is self-evident and clear. Do the English educate their people through the French language? Do Germans do it through English or the Turks through French?"*
>
> Excerpt from Tilak's speeches of Maharashtra tours.
>
> *"Speak in Kannada to establish the right of Kannada language."*
>
> Tilak's advice to V. B. Alur at the Bombay Provincial Conference in 1915, when he got up to support his condolence resolution on Gokhale's death.

Tilak's demand for Home Rule was made on a wholly secular basis as evident from his speeches of this period where one cannot discern any trace of religious appeal. He considered the British as aliens for the simple reason that they did not act in the Indian interest and not because they belonged to another religion.

> *"He who does what is beneficial to the people of this country, be he a Muhammedan or an Englishman, is not alien. 'Alienness' has to do with interests. Alienness is certainly not concerned with white or black skin . . . or religion."*
>
> Excerpt from Tilak's speeches of Maharashtra tours.

Nor did his ideas reflect any sort of caste bias as he openly urged Brahmins to be tolerant of the non-Brahmin demands and not oppose them, and simultaneously urged non-Brahmins to not see their problems of lack of jobs, and others in terms of Brahmin vs. non-Brahmin, but to understand it in terms of educated and non-educated, as it was the greater spread of education among Brahmins that gave them greater access to jobs.

> *"If we can prove to the non-Brahmins, by example, that we are wholly on their side in their demands from the Government, I am sure that in times to come; their agitation, now based on social inequality, will merge into our struggle."*
>
> Excerpt from Tilak's speeches of Maharashtra tours.
>
> *"If a god were to tolerate untouchability, I would not recognise him as God at all."*
>
> Bal Gangadhar Tilak's views on untouchability.

As soon as Tilak's movement began to gain ground, the government decided to strike a blow, causing him to furnish security of ₹60,000 along with binding him for good behaviour for a period of 1 year. Tilak was defended by a team of lawyers led by Mohammed Ali Jinnah, but he lost the case in the lower court and was later exonerated by the High Court in November 1916. The government's attempt to silence him and its subsequent failure gave a big fillip to the movement, and Tilak pushed home the advantage by declaring that Home Rule now had the sanction of the Government. Within no time, Tilak's league had enlisted 14,000 members.

"The Lord is with us, Home Rule will now spread like wildfire."

Tilak's statement after Government repression on his Home League.

"Thus, a great victory has been won for the cause of Home Rule which has, thus, been freed from the chains that were sought to be put upon it."

Gandhiji's statement in his journal *Young India* after Tilak's exoneration by High Court.

Annie Besant's Home Rule League[12]

Annie Besant set up her league in September 1916 in Madras and covered the rest of India (including Bombay city). It had 200 branches and was loosely organised[13] as compared to Tilak's League. Besides **Arundale**, the main work was done by **B. W. Wadia** and **C. P. Ramaswamy Aiyar**, and apart from the existing Theosophical Society members, many new members, including **Jawaharlal Nehru** in Allahabad, **B. Chakravarti** and **J. Banerjee** in Calcutta joined her League.

Agenda of the Leagues

The major agenda of the Leagues was to build a robust agitation for Home Rule, which was achieved by promoting political education and political discussions among people to join the movement, organising classes for students on politics, arranging political meetings and lectures, establishing libraries containing material on national politics, printing and circulating pamphlets in favour of Home Rule, organising social work and taking part in local government activities. The immensity of the propaganda effort can be gauged from the fact that even before the Besant League was formally inaugurated in September 1916, the Propaganda Fund started earlier in the year had already sold 3,00,000 copies of 26 English pamphlets discussing mainly the system of government existing in India and the reasons for the demand for self-government. More pamphlets in Indian languages were gradually brought out and the local branches organised lectures and discussions

[12] In 1922, it was renamed the Commonwealth of India League and tried to lobby British MPs in support of self-government for India within the empire, or dominion status along the lines of Canada and Australia. It was soon transformed by Krishna Menon into the India League in 1928.

[13] In case of Besant's League, three members could form a branch while in case of Tilak's League, each of the six branches had clearly defined areas and activities. Nor was there any organised method for passing on instructions as these were conveyed mostly through individual members and through Arundale's column on Home Rule in New India. Also, the membership of Annie Besant's League increased at a rate slower than that of Tilak's, as by March 1917, her league had 7,000 members while Tilak's League had grown to 14,000.

and set up libraries. The branches of both the Leagues also responded when a nation-wide call was given for protest on any specific issue. For instance, when Annie Besant was externed from the Central Provinces and Berar in November 1916, most of the branches held meetings and sent resolutions of protest to the Viceroy and the Secretary of State. A similar response was elicited at Tilak's externment from Punjab and Delhi in February 1917.

The Leagues also succeeded in enlisting the support of many Moderate Congressmen who were dissatisfied with the lack of activity by the Congress. For instance, the members of Gokhale's Servants of India Society though not permitted to become members of the League still toured and lectured in UP and brought out pamphlets supporting the demand for Home Rule along with organising meetings explaining to the masses the drain of wealth from the country and contrasting India's current poverty with her glorious past. The annual session of the Congress in December 1916 at Lucknow also provided the Home Rule Leaguers with an opportunity of demonstrating their strength and they turned up at this Congress in large numbers. Eventually, Tilak and his extremist friends were welcomed back into the Congress.

> *"After nearly 10 years of painful separation and wanderings through the wilderness of misunderstandings and the mazes of unpleasant controversies ... both the wings of the Indian Nationalist party have come to realize the fact that united they stand, but divided they fall, and brothers have at last met brothers ..."*
>
> Congress President of the 1916 Session, Ambika Charan Mazumdar's statement after readmission of Extremists to Congress.

The Lucknow session was also significant for the historic **Lucknow Pact** between the Congress and the Muslim League. Both Tilak and Annie Besant had played a leading role in bringing about this agreement,[14] which proposed separate electorates and proportional representation for minorities, especially Muslims, at the provincial and federal legislatures. We will also be studying in detail about the historic Lucknow session but let's complete all aspects related to Home League first. At the end of the session, the two Home Rule Leagues held a joint meeting attended by more than 1,000 delegates and addressed by Besant and Tilak hailed the Congress League Pact. Subsequently, on their return journeys, both the leaders toured extensively through various parts of North, Central and Eastern India.

The increasing popularity of the Home Rule Leagues soon attracted the Government's wrath which came down with severe repression, especially in Madras where the students were prohibited from attending political meetings.

> *"The Government is fully aware that the wave of patriotism strikes the students most, and if at all a nation is to prosper, it is through an energetic new generation."*
>
> Comments of Tilak condemning the Madras Government Order.

The turning point in the Home Rule Movement came with the decision of the Government of Madras in June 1917 to place Annie Besant and her associates, B. P. Wadia and George Arundale, under arrest

[14] Much against the wishes of many important leaders, including Madan Mohan Malaviya.

which sparked nation-wide protests. Condemning the Government's action, in a dramatic gesture, Sir S. Subramaniya Aiyar renounced his knighthood, and many Moderate leaders like Madan Mohan Malaviya, Surendranath Banerjee and M. A. Jinnah who had earlier stayed away now started enlisting themselves as members of the Home Rule Leagues to record their solidarity with the internees. Tilak proposed the use of 'passive resistance' or civil disobedience at the AICC meeting in July 1917, in case of Government refusal to release the internees. At Gandhiji's insistence, Shankerlal Banker and Jamnadas Dwarkadas collected signatures of a million peasants and workers on a petition for Home Rule and also collected signatures of 1,000 men willing to defy the internment orders and march to Besant's place of detention. Thus, the repression only served to harden the attitude of the agitators and strengthen their resolve to resist the Government.

> *"Shiva ... cut his wife into fifty-two pieces only to discover that he had fifty-two wives. This is what happens to the Government of India when it interns Annie Besant."*
>
> Montague, the Secretary of State for India.

Faced with this growing agitation, the Government in Britain decided to adopt a conciliatory stance, and as a part of the reconciliatory gesture the new Secretary of State for India, **Montague** on 20 August 1917 stated in the British House of Commons that, *The policy of His Majesty's government. ... is that of increasing association of Indians in every branch of the administration and the gradual development of self-governing institutions with a view to the progressive realisation of responsible government in India as an integral part of the British Empire*. This statement was a clear advance on the position taken in 1909 when Morley while introducing the constitutional reforms had categorically stated that they were not intended to lead to any kind of self-government. After Montague's declaration, the demand for self-government or 'Home Rule' could no longer be treated as seditious, and this was surely an important achievement. However, it is pertinent to note that in spite of this statement the British Government was not immediately granting self-government to India as the accompanying clause in the statement clarified that the nature and timing of the reforms would be decided by the government alone, thus giving enough leeway to the Government for continual postponement of transfer of any real power to Indians. One of the immediate gains of the conciliatory posture was that in September 1917, Annie Besant was released. She was at that time at the height of her popularity and on Tilak's insistence was elected as the President[15] of the annual session of the Congress in December 1917. However, quite surprisingly, instead of going forward after its great advance in 1917, the Home Rule Movement gradually dissolved.

Reasons for the Decline of the Home Rule Movement

During 1918, a lot of factors combined resulted in the decline of the Home Rule Movement.

- One of the major factors behind the decline of the Home Rule Movement was the pacification of the League leaders and Moderates[16] by the promise of reforms[17] and by Besant's release. The interest of Moderates in the Home Rule Movement was further diffused by Tilak's proposal of passive resistance or civil disobedience and subsequently from September 1918 onwards, they stopped attending the Congress.

[15] Became the first woman President of the Congress.

[16] Had joined the movement after Besant's arrest.

[17] Contained in Montague's statement of August 1917 which held self-government as the long-term goal of the British rule in India.

- The division and vacillation in the nationalist ranks after the **Montague Declaration** (1917) and publication of the scheme of Government reforms in July 1918 further jolted the movement. Some leaders wanted to accept the Government recommendations in total while some others wanted to reject it outrightly while many others felt that, though inadequate, they should be given a trial. Annie Besant herself indulged in a lot of vacillation on this issue as well as on the proposal of civil disobedience as initially, along with Tilak she considered the reforms unworthy of Britain to offer and India to accept, but later on she argued in favour of their acceptance. Similarly, at times she would disavow civil disobedience, and at other times, under pressure from her younger followers, would advocate it. As rightly pointed out by Bipan Chandra that *though Tilak was more consistent in his approach, but given Besant's vacillations, and the change in the Moderate stance, there was little that he could do to sustain the movement on his own*.
- After 1918, the movement was left practically leaderless as towards the end of 1918, **Tilak** was away in England to pursue the libel case that he had filed against Valentine Chirol[18]. His departure from the national scene for many critical months along with the inability of **Annie Besant** to give a firm lead in his absence thus practically left the movement leaderless.
- The Movement also suffered from the lacuna that most of the Muslims, Anglo-Indians and non-brahmins from the South did not join the Movement as they felt Home Rule would mean the rule of the Hindu majority, and that too mainly by the high caste.
- The Home Rule League leaders also failed to show the way forward to the new generation of nationalists awakened to politics by the Home Rule Movement. This new generation was frustrated and impatient with the slow pace of change and thus was looking for some alternate means of effective political expression.

The stage was thus set for the entry of **Mohandas Karamchand Gandhi**, a man who soon became the rallying point for mass agitation in India and was responsible for changing the dynamics of mass struggle in time to come with a totally different methodology of *Satyagraha*. In the next chapter we are going to study in detail about his leadership of the struggle of Indians in South Africa and his leadership of the struggles of Indian peasants and workers in Champaran, Ahmedabad and Kheda along with his Satyagraha against the obnoxious 'Rowlatt' Act.

Achievements of the Home Rule Movement

- One of the major achievements of the Home Rule Movement and its legacy was that it created a generation of ardent nationalists who in the later years became the backbone of the National Movement.
- The Home Rule Leagues through its various branches created organisational links between towns and villages, which in later years proved to be an invaluable foundation for mass agitation and prepared the masses for politics of the Gandhian style.
- Another crucial contribution of the Home Rule Movement was popularisation and making of the idea of Home Rule or self-government a commonplace thing, which immensely helped in expanding the political awareness in the country. It is a well-accepted fact that Montague's August 1917 declaration and the subsequent Montford reforms were greatly influenced by the Home Rule agitation.
- The Home Rule Movement also carried a much wider appeal than the earlier mobilisations and attracted the hitherto 'politically backward' regions of Gujarat and Sindh.
- Also, the Home Rule Movement by working towards the Moderate–Extremist reunion indirectly contributed in the revival of the Congress as an effective instrument of Indian nationalism.

---

[18] The author of *Indian Unrest*.

- It is true that the leaders of the Home Rule Movement were themselves unable to show the way forward and translate the growing consciousness into a mass struggle, but it is also an established fact that they did prepare the ground for the next stage of mass politics – a stage that was later utilised by **Mahatma Gandhi**. In this regard, it is pertinent to note that at the Lucknow session of 1916, Tilak proposed for a very significant reform for transforming the Congress from a deliberative body into one capable of leading a sustained movement, that is, appointment of 'Working Committee' – a small and cohesive group of Congress workers that would carry on the day-to-day affairs of the Congress and would be responsible for implementing the resolutions passed at the annual sessions. However, the proposal was unfortunately quashed by Moderate opposition, but the significance of the Tilak proposal can be gauged by the fact that just 4 years later, in 1920, when Mahatma Gandhi prepared a reformed 'constitution for the Congress', the same proposal was accepted by the Congress with full support.

Lucknow Pact and the Readmission of Extremists to Congress

The Lucknow session of the Indian National Congress, presided over by Ambika Charan Majumdar, was **historic** due to two reasons:

- First, for the readmission of Extremists led by Tilak to the Congress fold.
- Second, for the union of Muslim League and the Congress and the presentation of common demands by them to the Government.

List of Factors Facilitating the Reunion of the Extremists and the Moderates

- Both the Moderates and the Extremists had eventually realised that the split had led to political inactivity and had not turned out to be beneficial for either side. Also, they realised that over time the old controversies had become relatively meaningless and for the sake of the National Movement both sides need to work together as a team.
- The vigorous efforts of Annie Besant and Tilak facilitated a lot in the reunion. Also, Tilak's assurances regarding adoption of the Moderate path denouncing his earlier acts of violence further convinced the Moderates of his bonafides and aided in the reunion.
- The death of Pherozeshah Mehta, who had led the forefront against the reunion of Extremists, further weakened the opposition from the Bombay group and eased the process of reunion.

Lucknow Pact between the Congress and Muslim League

Another important event in the course of the Nationalist Movement was the 'Lucknow Pact' between the Congress and the Muslim League which prepared the way for Hindu–Muslim cooperation in agitational politics[19] and their presentation of common demands to the Government. The barriers between the Congress and the Muslim League were surmounted first as a result of a number of political developments in India between 1909 and 1916 and second, through the efforts of leading personalities on both the sides of the Congress and of the Muslim League, most notably being Gokhale, Annie Besant, Jinnah and Wazir Hasan.

[19] Specifically from 1919 to 1922.

Reasons for Change in the League's Attitude

Hugh F. Owen in his seminal paper '*Negotiating the Lucknow Pact*[20]' has discussed in detail about different reasons responsible for the change in the League's Attitude:

- **Increasing Influence of Nationalist Muslims within the Muslim League**: From 1912 onwards, the Muslim League was dominated by the younger nationalists, who were influenced more by the bold politics of the day and were constantly trying to come out of the shadow of the limited political outlook of the Aligarh School. In fact, at the Calcutta session of the Muslim League in 1912, under the influence of the Nationalist Muslims[21], the League committed itself for *working with other groups for a system of self-government suitable to India, provided it did not come in conflict with its basic objective of protection of interests of the Indian Muslims*. Thus, over time the League turned increasingly anti-imperialist and linked hands with Congress towards the achievement of the goal of 'self-government'.
- **A series of actions on the part of the British which alienated Muslims and in particular provoked the antagonism of Muslim communalists**: The British alienated the Muslims in a series of episodes between 1911 and 1914:
    - Annulment of the partition of Bengal in 1911 annoyed those sections of the Muslims who had supported the partition in the hope that in the new districts of East Bengal and Assam due to their pre-dominance, the Muslim prospects could prosper.
    - The Britain Government further alienated the Muslims by its refusal to help Turkey[22] in its wars with Italy (during 1911) and with the Balkans (1912–13) and by the speeches of British ministers, making it clear that they approved of the dismemberment of the Ottoman Empire by Christian states. All this brought the Hindu nationalists and militant Muslim pan-Islamists[23] closer and a feeling of mutual cooperation and common enemy developed between the two.
    - The refusal of the British Government in India to set up a university in Aligarh with powers to affiliate colleges all over India further angered the Muslims.
    - The severe repression by the Government during the First World War also acted as a contributing factor towards the growing understanding between the Congress and the Muslim League. The younger Muslims were greatly upset by the suppression faced by Maulana Azad's ***Al Hilal*** in Calcutta, Mohammad Ali's ***Comrade*** in Delhi and Zafar Ali Khan's ***Zamindar*** in Lahore, who through their various columns denounced the British Government and proposed rapprochement between the Muslim League and the

---

[20] Published in the *Journal of Asian Studies*, 1972.

[21] The Muslim elite of the 20th century was a differentiated lot and was divided into three major types of groupings:

- **The Conservatives**: The Conservatives held in the tradition of Sir Saiyid that Muslims should rely on the British to protect and advance the Muslim community and, conversely, should avoid political collaboration with Indian nationalism, which would alienate the British. This style came naturally to the aristocratic, landholding elements among the Muslims – the Aga Khan, the great taluqdars and Khwaja Salimullah, the Nawab of Dacca.
- **The Nationalists**: The Nationalist Muslims saw themselves as Indians first and Muslims second. They looked forward to 'self-government' for India, based on secular, democratic institutions, and to this end they sought to cooperate with Hindus and Parsis in Congress. Most of the prominent Nationalists were Western-educated Muslims, especially those living in the Westernised port cities – Mohammad Ali Jinnah, brought up in Karachi and Bombay, the Tyabjis in Bombay, A. Rasul in Chittagong and Calcutta and Syed Nawab Muhammad in Madras and also some Western-educated Muslims brought up in Hindustani traditions of the old Mughal provincial capitals, such as Wazir Hasan and Samiullah Beg in Lucknow, Fazl-i-Husain in Punjab and Mazharul Haque and Hasan Imam in Bihar.
- **The Communalists**: The Communalists put advancement of the Muslim community above all else, above loyalty to the British or to India. It is pertinent to note that the even nationalist Muslims might swing towards communalism if sufficiently convinced that their community was threatened, but the communalists tended to be found more among the Conservatives.

[22] The seat of the Khalifa who claimed religio-political leadership of all Muslims.

[23] The Pan-Islamism Movement was introduced in India around the 1880s and aimed to rehabilitate Islamic brotherhood on an international scale as a means of arresting the decline of Islam due to Western Imperialism. Some of the leading Pan-Islamists were Abul Kalam Azad, Dr M. A. Ansari, Mohamed and Shaukat Ali and S Kitchlew, who after embracing Pan-Islamism rejected loyalty to the British and sought allies among other Indian communities.

Congress. The younger elements were also upset with the internment of the Muslim leaders like Ali brothers, Maulana Azad and Hasrat Mohani, who thus sought coordination between the Congress and the League believing that the interests of the Muslim community were better off by possible alliance with the Congress Nationalists.

- **A stepping up in the overtures for rapprochement from Congress**: Certain policies of the Congress helped the Muslim League to look more favourably on the Congress:
  - The rebuffing of the attempts of the Extremists to take control of Congress in 1907 at Surat, along with the subsequent aversion of the identification of Congress with Hindu revivalism helped in creating a positive image of Congress in the minds of Muslims.
  - Though most of the Congress Moderates working for the development of a secular democracy opposed the separate representation granted to Muslims under the Morley–Minto reforms, some among them such as **Gokhale** recognising the insecurities of the Muslims felt in the face of the Hindu majority, gradually came around to publicly accept[24] the separate electorates primarily to remove *the feeling of soreness in the minds of minorities*.
  - Organisation of a Hindu–Muslim conference in Allahabad in 1910 by **Gokhale** and Sir **William Wedderburn**[25], to compose differences between the two communities did help in preparing the ground for future rapprochement.
  - Over later years, a series of conciliatory gestures were made to the League by the Congress. For instance, in 1912, when Congress met in Bihar, nearly half the Congressmen were Muslims, and the President *recognised the expediency of adopting … communal representation for Muslims*. In a similar vein, the following Congress session was held in the conspicuously Muslim city of Karachi, with its president a Muslim, Nawab Syed Muhammad of Madras, who was soon elected one of the general secretaries of Congress and later in 1914, the Moderate leaders succeeded in having Bhupendranath Basu as President of the Congress in lieu of Lala Lajpat Rai more because of the acceptability of the former among the Muslims.
- During 1915, the **movement for rapprochement was further accelerated** due to certain other factors:
  - First, due to very determined and successful efforts on the part of **Jinnah**, **Wazir Hasan** and other nationalist Muslims to bring the League together with Congress.
  - Second, due to **Annie Besant's** persistent advocacy of the need to draw up a scheme of reforms on the side of the Congress and her initiatives in bringing congressmen and members of the League together in planning for a program of agitation for self-government.
  - Third, due to a constitutional issue which brought Hindus and Muslims together. The issue pertained to the British rejection of an Executive Council, containing at least one Indian member, to advise the lieutenant governor of the United Provinces. The Indian and British Governments endorsed Indian demands for such a Council, but the House of lords, Lord Curzon at their head, rejected it in March 1915, and thus both Hindus and Muslims came in support of the same.
- **The gaining of safeguards for the Muslim community in the Morley–Minto reforms of 1909**: The grant of special electorates in the Morley–Minto reforms resulted in an immediate increase in Muslim confidence.

> *"Now that we have secured [separate electorates], I hope it will result in a permanent political sympathy and a genuine working entente cordiale between the members of the two great sister communities."*
>
> Aga Khan's statement at the January 1910 session of the Muslim League.

[24] Though he could not even brought himself to accept the 'weightage' of extra seats for Muslims.

[25] The then President of the Congress.

The Nature of the Pact

While the **League** agreed to present joint constitutional demands with the Congress to the government, the **Congress** accepted the Muslim League's position on **separate electorate** apart from granting a fixed proportion of seats in the legislatures at all-India and provincial levels. The basic terms of the **Lucknow Pact** included the clauses that:

- Muslims, who comprised a minority of some 21 per cent in the overall population of the subcontinent would have constitutional safeguards in the form of **separate electorates**, with a weightage of seats in excess of their proportion of the population in areas[26] where they were in a minority.
- Both Congress and the League postulated self-government as India's goal, and their joint scheme demanded:
  - Government should declare that it would confer self-government on Indians at an early date.
  - An elected majority in the central and provincial legislatures with more powers given to them such as the control of all-India's internal affairs by these legislatures through the power of the purse.
  - Half the positions on the Viceroy's and provincial governors' **executive councils** should be for Indians.
  - The term of the legislative council should be 5 years.
  - The salaries of the Secretary of State for India should be paid by the British treasury and not drawn from Indian funds along with the abolishment of the office of Council of the Secretary of State.
  - Ban on the members of the Indian Civil Service from occupying political positions in government.

Notable Aspects of the Lucknow Pact

- The document was organised around seven parts; four dealt with the composition and functioning of the legislature and executive at the provincial and federal levels. The other three were titled: *Secretary of State*, *India and the Empire*, and *Military and Other Matters*.
- The main feature of the Pact was the demand for an **expansion of the representative assemblies**, both at the all-India and provincial levels on a **broad franchise**, and **appointment of Indians** to the central executive councils of the Viceroy and the Provincial governors.
- The Muslims would have **one-third representation** in the Imperial Legislative Council, and they will be elected by **separate Muslim electorates** while the Provincial Legislative Councils shall consist of **4/5th elected** and **1/5th nominated** members.
- The Muslims were given **over-representation** in the provincial legislatures of Bihar, Bombay, Madras and the Central Provinces.
  - In Bihar (where they were 13 per cent of the population), Muslims were to have 25 per cent of the seats
  - In Bombay (where they were 20 per cent of the population), Muslims were to have 33.33 per cent of the seats
  - In Madras (where they were 7 per cent of the population), Muslims were to have 15 per cent of the seats
  - In Central Provinces (where they were 4 per cent of the population), Muslims were to have 10 per cent of the seats.

  In return for these concessions, the League agreed to reduce Muslim representation in Punjab from the 55 per cent indicated by their population to 50 per cent.
- The Muslims were **represented** in the other Provincial Legislative Councils in the following proportions:
  - Punjab: One-half, that is, 50 per cent of the elected members
  - United Provinces: 30 per cent of the elected members
  - Bengal: 40 per cent of the elected members
  - Central Provinces: 15 per cent of the elected members.

[26] Except the area of Punjab and Bengal, where they gave some ground to the Hindu and Sikh minority.

It is pertinent to note that except for the provision for the central executive, most of the proposals were largely embodied in the **Government of India Act, 1919** (popularly known as the Montague–Chelmsford reforms).

Critical Analysis of the Lucknow Pact

The Lucknow Pact of 1916 between the Congress and the Muslim League can be justly considered an important landmark event in the history of the National Movement. As rightly pointed out by **Hugh Owen**,[27] the fact that *the Lucknow Pact was successfully negotiated is perhaps more striking than the fact it should later break down.* For one thing, the two bodies who made the Pact were quite fundamentally arrayed against each other in their notions of their identity. The Congress claimed to speak for all Indians, including Muslims, whereas the Muslim League claimed to speak for the Indian Muslims, and had in fact spoken with some success for them in the years preceding the Pact. In terms of the objects of these two organisations, Congress under moderate leadership had worked for a secular India and had repeatedly deplored recognition of communal or religious distinctions in political matters, whereas the Muslim League asserted that Indian Muslims must work as members of the Muslim Community for representation and safeguards for that community as such.

That the Pact was achieved in the face of great obstacles and difficulties by sacrifices in varying degrees on each side for the sake of nationalist goals demonstrated that leading figures in Indian politics – both in the Congress and the Muslim League – were willing to rethink their positions and the positions taken up by the organisations to which they belonged in order to find some workable solution to the great political problems confronting India. If one attempts to draw up a balance sheet of this compromise in terms of the gains and losses of both Congress and the Muslim League, one sees that both sides made concessions in order to win what they wanted.

Some of the Muslim League's gains were obvious:

- Congress had accepted its demands for electorates in which the Muslims should vote separately from other Indians and further had agreed to join in demanding weightage for Muslims in all those provinces where the Muslims are in minority.
- Since the percentage of Muslim representation in every provincial legislature in 1917 was less than that conceded in the Pact, so in that sense the Pact marked a gain for the Muslims.
- Once arrived at in the Lucknow Pact, the mutual acceptance of separate electorates became the basis for future dialogue upto 1940; the Nehru Report tried to do away with them in 1928, but most Muslims insisted on treating them as a benchmark in any negotiations.

On the other hand, the **League** had given up its claim to legislative majorities in the two major provinces where it had a majority of the population, Bengal and the Punjab.

It is pertinent to note here that with the Lucknow Pact, not only had the Congress abandoned its opposition to separate electorates and weightage for religious communities, it somehow had also accepted the right of the League to speak for the Muslims, and this was later taken as a surrender by the Congress of its claim to speak for the Muslims, and even implying recognition of the Muslim League as an equal partner in working to shape India's future and later its role in the evolution of the two-nation theory. However, in the immediate sense, the Congress won the confidence and cooperation of many Muslims in return.

> *"I am sure I represent the sense of the community all over India when I say that we would not care if the rights of self-government are granted to the Mohammedan community only ... I would not care if these rights are granted to any section of the Indian community. When you have to fight against a third party, it is a very important thing that we stand on this platform united, united in race, united in religion and united as regards all shades of different political opinion."*
>
> Tilak's answer to the criticism that the Hindus had been too generous to the Muslims.

[27] In his paper 'Negotiating the Lucknow Pact'.

> *"India's real progress can only be achieved by a true understanding and harmonious relations between the two great communities. With regard to our own affairs, we can depend upon nobody but ourselves."*
>
> M. A. Jinnah in his presidential speech in Lucknow.

Achievements of the Pact

- The Pact ushered in a period of Hindu–Muslim cooperation and helped in creating an atmosphere of mutual trust in which Hindus and Muslims could join together against the British in the later agitations of the **Rowlatt** and the **Khilafat movement**.
- The concurrent sessions of the Congress and the Muslim League held as a part of the preparation for the Pact became a convention over the next 5 years and provided Gandhi and Pan-Islamic leaders with an enlarged arena for mounting their campaigns.
- The Pact constituted a statesmanlike attempt marked by a willingness on the part of the participants to compromise and even to sacrifice their interests or principles in the short run for the sake of working in a united fashion for the larger goal of self-government.
- The Pact also represented a serious desire on the part of the Congress to allay minority fears of majority domination.

> *"A considerable section of the educated Mohammedans have begun to perceive.... the necessity of political agitation on the Congress lines and it would be a fault of the Congress if it does not meet them halfway ... suitable concessions[must be] made."*
>
> Tilak's views in an article in *Mahratta* in 1914.

- The Pact also marked a readiness to face facts, and in particular a readiness on the part of both nationalist Muslims and Congressmen to recognise that separate electorates and weightage for Muslims had been introduced into the legislatures by the Morley–Minto reforms, and that continued opposition to them in these circumstances would seem all the more unfriendly and menacing to Muslims.

Limitations of the Lucknow Pact

- Though the Pact helped to clear the way for Hindu–Muslim cooperation, simultaneously it did aggravate some of the fears and resentments which played a damaging role in the politics of the following decades. The negotiations and the terms of the Pact in themselves provoked objections and opposition, both among Muslims and Hindus inside and outside Congress, which pointed towards some aspects of the later breakdown in Hindu–Muslim relations.
- The increasing willingness of Congress during 1910–13 to come to terms with Muslim League and a growing conviction that Congress was making *the Hindu forget that he is a Hindu* encouraged the formation of Hindu Sabhas, the forerunners of the assertive Hindu communal organisations of the 1920s and later notably the formation of the **Hindu Mahasabha**. There was also considerable dissatisfaction among some Hindus, especially in the United provinces and the Punjab on the issue of concessions accorded to Muslims at the expense of Hindus, thereby stimulating the Punjab Hindu Sabha to increased action and according to Gokhale led to the formation of new *Hindu Leagues*. Hindu criticism, veiled and overt, of the weightage

granted to Muslims in the Pact continued to sour Hindu–Muslim relations in the United Provinces in the following years.

- The Muslim masses were also not all happy, and there was considerable Muslim opposition to the Lucknow Pact which may be classified into basically two types, though these both often overlapped in practice.
    - First, there was a considerable amount of communal opposition, in the sense of aversion to cooperation with non-Muslims. Such aversion was promoted and reinforced by the hue and cry raised over separate representation by Hindu communalists in 1916 and 1917, especially in the United Provinces.
    - Second, some of the Muslim opposition to the Pact was a fundamental conservatism, a continuing reliance on collaboration with the British and the fear of change and its implications for Muslims. As early as 1913 with the change in the League's aims to include self-government, some muslims had deserted the League in Bihar, Bengal and elsewhere, and it seems that a number of more conservative members of the League stayed away from the Lucknow sessions which sealed the Pact. Probably most important of the strands in Muslim opposition to the Pact was that of the regional leaders in the two provinces where Muslims had sacrificed their majorities, the Punjab and Bengal.
- Since the Pact was negotiated by relatively small groups in both the League and the Congress so with time as larger groups became involved in nationalist politics, issues other than the electoral arrangements agreed upon in the Pact became the **foci of tension** and **conflict** – notably religious revivalism, appeals to group pride and group interest, proselytise and counter-proselytise. The agitation over the United Provinces Municipalities Bill in 1916 indicated that there were potential points of tension over constitutional arrangements that were not covered by the terms of the Lucknow Pact.
- In the terms of balance sheet of gains and losses, some groups on either side were asked to give up considerably more than others as evidenced in the case of Muslims of Punjab and Bengal and Hindus of United Provinces and Punjab. Thus, the Pact alienated certain important groups and encouraged Hindu and Muslim communalists to build up communal organisations asserting and working for the separate interests of their respective communities, thus preparing the way for the communal clashes in the 1920s.
- The Congress leaders agreed to the pact in the expectation that the executive–legislature relationship in the package of constitutional reforms would essentially be a continuation of the Morley–Minto reforms, but the Montague–Chelmsford reforms, when announced, revealed that the nature of this relationship would be significantly different, leading the Congress leaders to oppose the pact and accept communal electorates for the Muslims that it entailed, before the Southborough Committee.
- The pact also contained significant omissions and ambiguities which led to divergent interpretations on crucial provisions. Also, while the leaders of the two groups came together, efforts to bring together the masses from the two communities were never much considered and eventually the Pact was not equipped to deal with organised communal rioting combined with other forms of communal assertiveness.

Montague Declaration (1917)

On 20 August 1917, the Secretary of State for India, Edwin Samuel Montague, made a **historic** statement in the British House of Commons which later came to be known as the 'August Declaration of 1917', which stated that *The policy of His Majesty's Government . . . is that of an* ***increasing participation of Indians*** *in every branch of administration and gradual* ***development of self-governing institutions*** *with a view to the progressive realisation of responsible government in India as an integral part of the British Empire.* As discussed earlier, with this statement the demand for self-government or 'Home Rule' could no longer be treated as seditious and that was a very important milestone in the journey of the national movement. Also, by using the term 'responsible government', it was implied that the rulers were to be answerable to the elected representatives, and not merely to the imperial government in London.

Objections Raised by the Indian Leaders

- No specific time frame for delegation of power was given. There was no provision in the statement for immediate grant of self-government to India as the British Government would alone decide the nature and the timing of advance towards a responsible Government, thus keeping enough leeway with them for continual postponement of transfer of any real power to Indians.
- Some leaders also considered the reforms unworthy of Britain to offer and India to accept as they were resentful of how the British could decide what was good and what was bad for Indians.

In this chapter, we have discussed about the *Ghadar* Movement and Home Rule Movement in detail along with the landmark Lucknow Pact of 1916 and how all of these movements created the necessary political atmosphere for Gandhiji to initiate the phase of mass politics in India. In the next chapter, we will be studying in detail about the man who took over the reins of the Indian National Movement at the most crucial juncture and guided its destinies through its most climactic years.

Previous Year's Questions (Prelims)

1. In the context of Indian history the principle of 'Dyarchy refers to which of the following(2017)
   (a) Division the central legislature into two houses.
   (b) Introduction of double government that is central and state government.
   (c) Having two sets of rulers one in London and another in Delhi.
   (d) Division of the subjects delegated to the provinces into two categories.

2. The Montague-Chelmsford proposals were related to which of the following? (2016)
   (a) Social reforms
   (b) Educational reforms
   (c) Reforms in public administration
   (d) Constitutional reforms

3. The Ghadr(Ghadar) was a (2014)
   (a) revolutionary association of Indians with headquarters at San Francisco.
   (b) nationalist organisation operating from Singapore.
   (c) militant organisation with headquarters at Berlin.
   (d) communist movement for India's freedom with headquarters at Tashkent.

4. Annie Besant was (2013)
   1. responsible for starting Home Rule Movement.
   2. the founder the Theosophical society.
   3. the president of the Indian National Congress.

   Select the correct answer from the following options:
   (a) Only 1
   (b) 2 and 3
   (c) 1 and 3
   (d) All of these

5. Which of the following is/are the principal feature(s) of the Government of India Act, 1919? (2012)
   1. Introduction of diarchy in the executive government of the provinces.
   2. Introduction of separate communal electorates for Muslims.
   3. Devolution of Legislative authority by the centre to the provinces.

Choose the correct answer from the following options:

(a) 1 only
(b) 2 and 3 only
(c) 1 and 3 only
(d) 1, 2 and 3

6. Where were the Ghadar revolutionaries, who became active during the outbreak of the World war I based (2005)

(a) Central America
(b) North America
(c) West America
(d) South America

7. The Montague-Chelmsford Report formed the basis of which of the following (2004)

(a) Indian Council Act of 1909
(b) Government of India Act of 1919
(c) Indian Council Act of 1935
(d) Indian Council Act of 1947

Previous Year's Answers (Prelims)

1. (d)	2. (d)	3. (a)	4. (c)	5. (c)	6. (b)	7. (b)

The Emergence of Mahatma Gandhi

8

Mohandas Karamchand Gandhi[1] (also known as **Mahatma**[2] **Gandhi**), the father of the nation[3], undoubtedly played the most pivotal and unparallelled role in transforming the ideology, content, reach and range of Indian politics during the course of national movement. His entry into nationalist politics shifted the focus from the 'classes' to the 'masses' and elevated it to a whole new level. It was due to him that the hitherto untouched masses were brought into the national movement, and the movement itself was revolutionised to such an extent that after Gandhi's emergence, it never remained the same. It was under his towering leadership that India achieved her independence from the British rule and that too, by the successful use of and adherence to his innovative techniques of ***Satyagraha*** and ***Ahimsa***. Gandhi has left a much wider and deeper imprint on not only the national movement but also on all aspects of Indian life and is thought so much so that one can find a 'Gandhi' in almost everything, and internationally too people still identify 'India' with 'Gandhi'. In this chapter, we will discuss about Gandhi's early struggles in South Africa and political activities in India till 1922, along with his ideology and philosophy.

"Gandhi's novel political ideology appealed to a few wholly, but to many partially as everyone could find in it something to identify with."

Judith Brown

"There is something in Mahatma Gandhi which appeals to the mass of the Indian people … Wherever he may go, even the poorest of the poor feels he is the product of Indian soil - bone of his bone, flesh of his flesh … when he talks to them about Swaraj, he does not dilate upon the virtues of provincial autonomy or federation, he reminds them of the glories of Ram Rajya and they understand. And when he talks of conquering through love and ahimsa, they are reminded of Buddha and Mahavira and they accept them."

Subhash Chandra Bose

Early Struggles of Mahatma Gandhiji in South Africa

The broad details of Gandhiji's eventful life are fairly well known. He was born in a well-to-do Hindu traditional family of Porbandar[4] on 2 October 1869. His father, Karamchand Gandhi, was a leading

[1] 1869–1948.

[2] Meaning 'gareat soul'; was first called 'Mahatma' by Rabindranath Tagore.

[3] First addressed as the 'Father of Nation' by Subhash Chandra Bose.

[4] In Kathiawar, Gujarat.

court official in a small princely state, and his mother, Putlibai, was a very devout and pious lady in her religious inclinations and practices, and according to Gandhiji's own admission had a great influence in shaping his personality and character. Gandhiji had his school education in Porbander, Rajkot and Ahmedabad before he left for England in 1888 to qualify as a 'barrister at Law'. He returned to India in 1891 and began practising first in the Bombay High Court and then at Rajkot[5]. Two years later, that is, in 1893, he went to South Africa to argue a legal case for an Indian[6] client and went on to live there[7] for 21 years, that is, till 1914. It would not be wrong to say that his South African experience[8] eventually contributed in a number of different ways to his foundation of ideology and methods, as well as to his later achievements in India.

> *"She would not think of taking her meals without her daily prayers ... she would take the hardest vows and keep them without flinching. To keep two or three consecutive fasts was nothing to her."*
>
> Gandhiji's views on his mother Putlibai.

Gandhiji's experience and experiments in South Africa not only shaped his ideology but also evolved his different protest policies and methods apart from preparing him for taking the reins of Indian National Movement in years to come. In fact, Gandhiji himself as an individual was transformed by the struggles he faced in South Africa, and from being a timid and modest man, he gradually became a defender of the rights of the oppressed and downtrodden. His first battles for the rights of a small group of Indians in South Africa eventually broadened his outlook into a more universal struggle for peace, human dignity, justice, equality and human rights.

Gandhiji's Initial Encounters with Prevalent Racism in South Africa

In May 1893, when Gandhiji had arrived[9] in Durban[10], it had a sizeable Indian population divided mostly into three categories: **indentured labourers** who were under a labour contract,[11] **ex-indentured labourers** who had settled down in South Africa after the expiry of their contract and **passenger Indians**[12] were the mostly wealthy *Meman* Muslims merchants, who had trade interests in the province. However, none of these groups of Indians had much access to either education, particularly English education, or basic amenities and were regularly subjected to various racial disabilities by the White settlers with regards to rights of trade, citizenship and ownership of property.

---

[5] Where petition-writing brought him a monthly income of about ₹300.

[6] Dada Abdulla and Co., an Indian firm, doing trade in South Africa. The case involved a trade rivalry and a family feud between two big merchants – Abdullah of Natal and Tyeb Sheth of the Transvaal. Because the local traders were deficient in English and inexperienced in legal matters, they needed somebody to carry on the legal correspondence and represent them in the courts, and for this purpose Gandhiji was sent to South Africa.

[7] With two breaks in between.

[8] From 1893 to 1914.

[9] Only 8 years after Africa, south of the Sahara was parcelled out by the European powers among themselves under the arrangements of the 1884–85 Berlin conference.

[10] Natal province, South Africa.

[11] Mostly a 5-year contract to work as labourer in sugar plantations of Natal province. Sadly, most of them were illiterate and quite ignorant of the terms of the labour contracts.

[12] Mainly *traders* who were called so because they had paid for their passage in the ships.

Various Racial Disabilities Faced by the Indians

- Every Indian, without any distinction, was contemptuously called a '***coolie***', which basically meant 'a **labourer**'. The condition of indentured labourers was much worse and they were treated as semi-slaves by the White planters.
- The Indians were prohibited to travel in first- and second-class railway compartments, and were forced at times to travel on the footboard of trains, despite having first- or second-class tickets.
- The Indians were denied the **right to vote** and had to register and pay a poll tax.
- The Indians were not permitted to enter hotels exclusively reserved for Europeans and in certain places were prohibited to walk on footpaths or to be out at night without a permit.
- The Indians could not reside except in prescribed locations, which mostly were insanitary, unhygienic and congested.

Gandhiji himself had a firsthand account of racial discrimination immediately after reaching South Africa. At **Durban**, in the court, the European magistrate ordered Gandhiji to remove his turban, and when Gandhiji refused to do so, he was asked to leave the court room, which he did under protest. Later, within a week, he experienced a series of racial humiliations while on his journey to Pretoria from Durban. **Despite** having a first-class ticket, he was thrown out of the first-class compartment by a White man and was made to spend the night shivering in a cold waiting room. In addition, he was not only made to travel in the driver's box in a coach when he had again bought a first-class ticket but was also soundly thrashed when he ignored the coach leader's order to vacate even that seat and was made to sit on the footboard. He faced similar racial insults on reaching Johannesburg, as the moment he asked for a room to stay the night, he found that all the hotels became full up despite having a vacancy. Again on his return journey from Johannesburg to Pretoria, after strenuous efforts[13] of securing a first-class train ticket, he was again almost[14] pushed out from his railway compartment. He was more dismayed to witness that the Indians had sadly come to accept the racial discrimination[15] and segregation to which they were subjected as a way of life, and were clueless in terms of a solution even if they resented it.

> *"I was afraid for my very life. I entered the dark waiting-room. There was a white man in the room, I was afraid of him. What was my duty? I asked myself. Should I go back to India, or should I go forward, with God as my helper and face whatever was in store for me? I decided to stay and suffer. My active non-violence began from that date."*
>
> Gandhiji's views on his forcible eviction from a Whites-only carriage on a train in Pietermaritzburg[16] in 1893 and him spending the rest of the night in a cold waiting room.

So, immediately on his return to Pretoria, he convened a meeting of the Indians and offered to teach English to anybody who wanted to learn. He also tried his best to hold discussions and meetings with the

[13] Of quoting extensively from railway regulations.

[14] Was somehow saved by the humiliation on the intervention of a wise European passenger.

[15] It was a part of their daily existence. Gandhiji by virtue of being a British-educated barrister demanded many things as a matter of right, such as first-class train tickets and rooms in hotels, which other Indians before him had never probably even had the courage to ask for. Perhaps, they believed that they were discriminated against because they were not 'civilized', that is, 'westernised.' However, Gandhiji's experience, the first of a westernised Indian in South Africa, demonstrated clearly, to him and to them, that the real cause lay elsewhere, in the assumption of racial superiority by the White rulers.

[16] Pietermaritzburg was the capital of the Natal province.

fellow Indians to arouse a sense of their own dignity as human beings and to further persuade them to resist all types of racial disabilities. He also urged them to organise themselves in protest against the racial discrimination and oppression, and to further his cause of creating awareness against the racial discrimination, he started contributing articles on the issue of racial discrimination in different leading newspapers.

> *"Is this Christian-like, is this fair play, is this justice, is this civilisation? I pause for a reply."*
>
> Gandhiji's questions in an indignant letter to the *Natal Advertiser*, a popular newspaper of that time.

A year later, in 1894, having settled the law suit for which he had come, and having no further concrete plans of staying in South Africa at that stage, Gandhiji eventually prepared to leave for India. However, as fate would have it, on the eve of his departure from Durban at a farewell party being given in his honour, he raised the issue of a proposed bill, which was in the process of being passed by the Natal legislature and aimed at disenfranchising Indians. The bill known as the **Franchise Amendment Bill** was introduced in April 1894 by Natal province's first legislative assembly under responsible government and stated that '*no person belonging to Asiatic races not accustomed to the exercise of franchise rights under parliamentary institutions could in future qualify for the vote.*' The bill was further troubling for the Indians in the sense that in the recent past, the Indian traders were herded out of the neighbouring Orange Free State in a similar way, and now Natal was out to introduce a racial measure, which carried serious implications for the future of Indians in South Africa.

To understand properly the agitation against the bill, let us first understand the background of the introduction of the bill. The Natal province was granted self-governance in 1893, and the grant of a responsible government to White settlers united the White community against immigrant Indians as the former perceived the increasing[17] numbers of Indians as a threat to their existence and felt that Indians would soon become rivals for political power in Natal. In fact, the Wragg Commission of 1885–87 stated in its report that '*Indian traders were responsible for much of the irritation existing in the minds of European Colonists*'. Therefore, in the background of this growing anti-Indian sentiment throughout the province, the White settlers tried to pass a **series of laws discriminating against Indians** such as not to permit voting rights to natal Indians, to stop all future immigration of Indians, to compulsorily repatriate Indians on the termination of their indentured contracts, requiring them to undergo literacy tests, keep accounts in English and introducing a system of licencing of Indians to conduct business.

Since the bill was clearly against the Indian community in South Africa, which comprised mostly of either plantation workers or immigrants who were engaged in the small '*dukan*' trading with a few relatively large merchant traders and who were not knowing even enough English to draft petitions against the proposed legislation or understand the intricacies of the complex law machinery, they requested **Gandhiji to stay** on for a month[18] to guide them in organising the protest against the discriminatory legislation. Not surprisingly, after he himself experienced what colour prejudice meant in South Africa, Gandhiji agreed and plunged himself in the struggle of Indians based in South Africa which, as if, awaited his arrival, and his path hereafter changed forever.

---

[17] According to an estimate, between 1860 (when the Indians had first arrived in South Africa as indentured labourers) and 1911, around 1,52,000 Indians had come to work in the sugar estates in Natal. The increasing number of Indians was also slowly creating their hold in the province and were visible everywhere in a short span of 30 years, be it sugar estates or railways or coal mines.

[18] Interestingly, Gandhiji agreed to stay on for a month but got so involved in the South African political affairs that he eventually stayed here for the next 20 years. He was then only 25 when he came and was 45 when he left.

Moderate Phase of Gandhiji's Struggle (1894–1906)

Gandhiji's political activities from 1894 to 1906 may be best classified as the **Moderate phase** of his struggle in South Africa, as during this phase, he concentrated primarily on petitioning and sending memorials to the South African legislatures, the Colonial Secretary in London and the British Parliament. Having an implicit faith in the British Government, he felt that '*if all the facts of the case were presented to the Imperial Government, the British sense of justice and fair play would be aroused and the Imperial Government would intervene on behalf of Indians who were, after all, British subjects*'. He had utmost respect for **Queen Victoria's 1858 declaration** and considered it to be as a promissory note for equitable treatment of Indians as partners in a multi-racial empire and, thus, regularly referred to this document in his appeals to the British Government. Gandhiji's loyalty to the British Government is also attested by his explicit support for the British Crown in the **Anglo-Boer War**[19] of 1899–1902. Gandhiji, on this occasion, convinced his fellow Indians that being British subjects, they should join the war on the Natal British settler side. In his autobiography also Gandhiji notes that '*during the Boer War though he had a great deal of personal sympathy for the plight of Boers but his feelings for and support of the British Crown – in spite of the fact that India was a colony – resulted in him volunteering to lead an ambulance corps of Indians to assist the British army*'. Gandhiji interpreted his service in the ambulance units as a means of showing the loyalty of his people and improving their bargaining position.

"The South African Indians probably identified more with the pastoral ways of the Boers than with the industrial capitalism of the British, but most of them had no wish to take sides in the war, for fear of reprisals. Gandhiji, however, felt so much loyalty to the British Crown that he wanted the Indians to go to war alongside the British."

Ved Mehta

"Gandhiji's outlook until 1906–09 centred on his conviction that the Victorian and Edwardian Empire had a civilising mission to perform and its defects can be remedied. Because England would deliver India from servitude, he wrote in an 1895 appeal, Indians were proud to be under British crown. As to the racial matters, he cited Cecil Rhodes and Lord Milner idea of 'equal rights for civilised men' as a promise of fair play for non-indentured Indians."

Excerpts from the famous article '*Gandhiji in South Africa*' written by Paul F. Power in the *Journal of Modern African Studies*.

"What we (Indians) want is not political power; but we do wish to live side by side with other British subjects in peace and with dignity and self-respect."

Gandhiji's statement to the British High Commissioner in South Africa.

[19] The Boers and the British, although both were White settlers, were sworn rivals often prone to fight to finish to establish their unquestioned supremacy in South Africa.

Thus, within a month of deciding to stay back in South Africa, Gandhiji, through a series of meetings and discussions, arrived at a common ground with other immigrant Indian community members that, to have their views and commercial interests represented, they needed to create pressure on the local electorate, and so by August 1894, Gandhiji established the **Natal Indian Congress**, a permanent organisation to look after the interests of South African Indians. To create awareness, activate political consciousness among immigrants, mobilise popular support about the Indian demands, infuse a strong sense of solidarity among the heterogenous sections of the Indian community of Natal along with the purpose of enlightening Europeans about their obligations towards Asians, Gandhiji also started a newspaper in 1903 – **The *Indian Opinion***, which was published in three major languages – Gujarati, Tamil[20] and English.

"I believe that a struggle which chiefly relies upon internal strength cannot be wholly carried on without a newspaper – it is also my experience that we could not perhaps have educated the local Indian community, nor kept Indians all over the world in touch with the course of events in South Africa in any other way, with the same ease and success as through the Indian opinion which therefore was certainly a most useful and potent weapon in our struggle."

An extract from Gandhiji's book *Satyagraha in South Africa.*

Further realising that one of the probable reasons behind the low leverage of Indians with the Natal and Transvaal regime was probably the modest social and economic standing of the community, since part of it was still indentured, Gandhiji tried to improve the bargaining strength of Indians by making appeals to **emerging Indian Nationalists** and **British Liberals** to persuade the imperial authorities to bring pressure on the South African governments, and pursuing the same, he twice went to India[21], and twice travelled to London[22]. During this phase, he effectively utilised his abilities as an organiser, as a journalist, as a propagandist and as a fund-raiser. As a result of his efforts, the *London Times* carried as many as eight leading articles on the problem of South African Indians, and the Indian National Congress in its December 1894 annual session recorded its protest against the Natal disenfranchising bill, and at its annual session at Calcutta, a resolution condemning the condition of Indians in South Africa was passed.

The next 9 years, however, witnessed the reactions to the failure of their attempts and actions to mitigate the effects of laws passed in 1897, especially the **Franchise Amendment** and the **Immigration Restriction Acts**[23]. Initially, on Gandhiji's insistence, about 500 Indians living in Natal submitted[24] a petition against the bill, but it was still passed by the Natal legislature and even the Governor gave his assent to it. Gandhiji then appealed to the Queen[25] for not approving the bill by means of a long petition[26] signed by 9,000 Indians[27] and eventually in view of the strong opposition, the colonial office in London vetoed the bill on the ground that it discriminated against the inhabitants of another part of the British Empire. However, later bowing to the pressures of the Natal legislators,

[20] Tamils were a predominant component of Indian indentured labour (in some estimates even over 60 per cent).

[21] 1896 and 1899.

[22] 1906 and 1909.

[23] The Act required that the indentured labourers who had already served for 5 years to either return to India or serve under the same terms and conditions. Furthermore, those among them who were illiterate or did not know any of the European languages were to be sent back with or without consent.

[24] On 28 June 1894.

[25] Through the office of British Secretary of State for Colonies in England in July 1894.

[26] Stating that 'the bill was a direct affront to India, as a part of the British Empire and a clear violation of the Queen's post 1857 proclamation'.

[27] Almost the entire adult population of Free Indians in Natal. It is interesting to note that nothing on this scale has happened before and the petition was termed by some as 'Monster Petition'.

the Queen subsequently approved the bill in an amended form which stated that '*No native of countries (not of European origin) which had not hitherto possessed elective institutions founded on parliamentary franchise were to be placed on voters list unless they obtained exception from Governor-General'.*

Disheartened at these developments and having fully tried the 'Moderate' method of struggle, Gandhiji now adopted the method of passive resistance or ***Satyagraha***.

Passive Resistance Phase of Gandhiji's Struggle (1906 Onwards)

During the passive resistance phase of Gandhiji's struggle in South Africa, his agitation style evolved from a scrupulous adherence to colonial forms, in particular that of the petition, to the use of extra legal devices such as designing and sharpening of his main fighting weapon – the **Satyagraha**[28], meaning soul force, an instrument to fight the might of the White settlers through peaceful resolution. The departure from the old moderate traditions began with the three campaigns of passive resistance[29] of 1907–08, 1908–11 and 1913–14, which involved basically four issues:

- **The Transvaal Ordinance on Compulsory Registration and Passes for Indians** (1906)
- **The Immigration Restrictions Act**
- **The abolition of £3 poll tax on ex-indentured labourers**
- **The de-recognition of non-Christian Indian marriages** (1913)

- **The Transvaal Ordinance on Compulsory Registration and Passes for Indians** (1906): It was the 'Transvaal Asiatic Registration Law' in 1906 that initiated the phase of Gandhiji's first passive resistance or civil disobedience campaign in South Africa. It was during the struggle against this law that Gandhiji first used the term 'Satyagraha' for non-violent resistance. The Transvaal Government tried to enact an ordinance on the re-registration of Asians thereby making the registration of Asians compulsory along with defining the Asians residents through **registration**, **fingerprinting** and **passes**. The new law, thus, meant that it was both compulsory for Indians[30] to have their certificates of registration[31] and along with that it was also essential on their part to carry these on person at all times. Indians saw these rules to be more restrictive than the procedure for Africans, and in the absence of any distinction between the Indians and other Asians, the self-pride of the Indians was hurt and, thus, within no time, strong opposition developed against the Act, and the rule about carrying a 'pass' at all times became a burning issue, both literally and figuratively in the South African Struggle, as the burning of these hated passes became a signifier of the Gandhian passive resistance movement.

"Whether old or young, whether man or woman, whether at day time or at night, anyone found without a pass can be arbitrarily arrested and detained. ..."

An extract from the Transvaal Asiatic Registration Act.

"The law would spell absolute ruin for the Indians of South Africa and it's better to die than submit to such a law."

Gandhiji views on Transvaal Asiatic Registration Act.

---

[28] Satyagraha basically originated from 'Sadagraha' (Sat=truth, Agraha=firmness) meaning 'firmness in a good cause'. The term 'Sadagraha' was coined by Maganlal Gandhiji, a relative of Mahatma Gandhiji, but for more clarity Gandhiji changed it to 'Satyagraha'.

[29] Soon redefined as '*Satyagraha*' in 1907.

[30] Every Indian man, woman or child above eight was required to register and to give finger and thumb impressions on the registration form, and whoever failed to register before a certain date would be guilty of an offence for which he could be punished or deported.

[31] Which also held their finger prints.

On 11 September 1906, to raise a voice against this proposed ordinance, a huge public meeting was organised under the leadership of Gandhiji at the **Empire Theatre** in Johannesburg, where the Indians resolved that they would refuse to submit to this law and would rather face the consequences. On 20 September 1906, the British government passed the Asiatic Law Amendment Ordinance No. 29, which became to be known as the **Black Act**. Meanwhile, despite vehement opposition by the Indians, the Transvaal legislature passed the Asiatic Registration Bill, and even Gandhiji's efforts[32] of getting the bill vetoed did not yield much results, and it was announced that the new law would take effect from 1 July 1907. Gandhiji then formed the **Passive Resistance Association** to conduct the campaign, and with his novel technique of 'Satyagraha' he urged his fellow Indians to passively and non-violently resist the implementation of what they considered an intolerable law. Despite all best efforts of the Transvaal Government to exhort Indians to get themselves registered, by 30 November 1907 only some 500 took the registration forms, leaving more than 9,000 unregistered[33], and with the last date for registration being over, the Government then initiated proceedings against Gandhiji and 26 others. Gandhiji and his passive resisters all pleaded guilty and were ordered to leave the country and, on refusing to do so, were sent to jail. Soon others followed them in jail[34], and their numbers swelled to 155.

> *"There is only one course open to those like me to die but not to submit to the law. It is unlikely, but even if everyone flinched, leaving me alone to face the music, I am confident that I would not violate the pledge."*
>
> An extract from Gandhiji's speech at the Empire Theatre Meeting.

While in prison, Gandhiji had discussions in January 1908, through an intermediary with Transvaal authorities about a compromise settlement. Gandhiji's later understanding was that in return for voluntary registration, the Act would be repealed. Immediately upon his release at the end of the month, to pacify the matters, Transvaal Colonial Secretary **General Jan Smuts**[35] called Gandhiji for talks and gained the impression that the compromise had been confirmed. Gandhiji accepted the proposal and was the first to register and persuaded some 2,000 compatriots to do the same, despite facing opposition from many Indians[36] for accepting this agreement, for they did not expect any justice from General Smuts.

---

[32] In October, Gandhiji went to London to appeal to the British government for abolition of this Black Act, and met with the Secretary of State for the Colonies, Lord Elgin, and the Secretary of State for India Sir John Morley. Subsequently, in December 1906, while Gandhiji was on a ship returning to South Africa, the British government vetoed the law. However, the British government granted the Transvaal province right of self-governance from 1 January 1907, leaving the new administration under Prime Minister General Louis Botha free to re-enact the law, this time as the Transvaal Registration Act.

[33] Who should have been registered according to the new Act.

[34] The fear of jail had disappeared, and it was popularly called King Edward's Hotel.

[35] General Smuts was the English-educated Boer politician and military leader who became an architect of the modern British Commonwealth. During his stay in South Africa, Gandhiji indulged in long-term negotiation with the Colonial Secretary of Transvaal, Jan Smuts, first on behalf of Indians in that province and later, after the establishment of the Union in 1910, on behalf of all South African Indians. The Gandhiji Smuts encounters began a series of personality and political struggles involving Gandhiji and other opponents like Lord Irwin and Mohammad Ali Jinnah. It is often argued that Smuts, the anglo Boer leader, somehow helped to educate Gandhiji in the skills and pitfalls of 'summitry'.

[36] One Pathan even assaulted him for backsliding.

> *"A Satyagrahi bids goodbye to fear. He is therefore never afraid of trusting the opponent. Even if the opponent plays him false twenty times, the Satyagrahi is ready to trust him for the 21st time – for an implicit trust in human nature is the very essence of his creed."*
>
> Gandhiji's statement addressing the criticism to his agreement with Smuts since his fellow passive resisters wanted the Act itself to be repealed before they would register while Gandhiji saw the move as the way of the Satyagrahi

As expected, Smuts soon backed out from his words and denied[37] that he had agreed to have the basic law repealed if voluntary registration takes place and instead ordered that the voluntary registrations be ratified under the law. Negotiations between the Indians and the Transvaal Government broke down in May 1908, and angered by the betrayal of Smuts and retaliating against the same, Gandhiji restarted his **Satyagraha movement** and a large number of Indians under the leadership of Gandhiji consigned their registration certificates to flames. Gandhiji's strategy of consigning registration certificates to the flames was compared by *Daily Mail*, with the historic political protest of 'Boston Tea Party' and the 'Satyagraha' soon gathered an authentic stamp of 'mass movement'.

> *"A large three legged pot was filled with the registration certificates, about 1,000 in all, and about 500 trading licenses. Paraffin was then poured in, and the certificates set on fire amid a scene of wildest enthusiasm. The crowd hurrahed and shouted themselves hoarse; hats were thrown in the air, and whistles brown. One Indian .... walked on to the platform and setting alight his certificate held it aloft."*
>
> As reported by the Transvaal leader

- **The Immigration Restrictions Act**: The Transvaal government, in the meantime, enacted another legislation, **The Immigration Restrictions Act**[38] aimed at restricting Indian immigration and enacted a ban on interprovincial travel by Asians. The *Satyagraha* movement was widened to oppose the new legislation and thus, consequently in August 1908 a number of prominent Indians from Natal defying the new immigration laws crossed the frontier into Transvaal and were arrested. The passive resistance was expressed by certain other Indians from Transvaal by hawking without a licence, while some traders who had licences refused to produce them before authorities. Gandhiji[39] along with all of the *Satyagrahis* was eventually jailed and was sentenced to a prison term involving hard physical labour and miserable conditions. The Government with the motive of demoralising the masses started

[37] Causing a controversy between the camps of Gandhiji and Smuts that persist to even this date.

[38] Primarily aimed at excluding new immigrants from Asia, particularly India, chiefly through introducing varied tests like European language test, confining Indians to only certain 'locations'.

[39] In October 1908.

pressurising the rich merchants by threatening their economic interests and also resorted to deportation to India, especially of the poorer Indians, and at this stage, the movement reached an impasse.

A small band of committed Satyagrahis still continued to go in and out of jail, but the majority of masses were showing signs of fatigue while the struggle was appearing to be a protracted one as the Government was in no mood to relent and even Gandhiji's visit to London in 1909 to meet the authorities yielded almost no fruitful result. Meanwhile, the funds for supporting the families of the Satyagrahis and for running Indian Opinion were fast running out and at this point, Gandhiji set up the **Tolstoy Farm** through the generosity of his German architect friend, Kallenbach, to house the families of the Satyagrahis and give them a way to sustain themselves. A **Satyagraha Association** funded by the Indian National Congress, the Muslim League and other prominent rich people from India like Sir Ratan Tata and Nizam of Hyderabad was also formed, which provided financial support to the Satyagrahis.

Finally, breaking the impasse in 1911, an agreement[40] was reached between the Government and the Indians which, however, lasted only till the end of 1912. In the meantime, Gokhale paid a visit[41] to South Africa and was made a promise by the Government that all discriminatory laws against Indians would be removed. However, the promise was never kept, and the Satyagraha was resumed in 1913.

- **The abolition of £3 poll tax on ex-indentured labourers**: After the resumption of the *Satyagraha*, the movement was widened further to include demand for the abolition of the poll tax of three pounds[42] that was imposed on all ex-indentured Indians. With the inclusion of this demand, the indentured and ex-indentured labourers were immediately drawn into the struggle, and *Satyagraha* took a truly mass character.
- **The derecognition of non-Christian Indian marriages**: Further fuel was added to the already raging fire in 1913 by a judgement of the Supreme Court[43] which invalidated all marriages not conducted according to Christian rites and registered by the Registrar of Marriages. This judgement implicated that all Hindu, Muslim and Parsi marriages were illegal and the children born through these marriages were illegitimate. Gandhiji made a strong representation against the implications of the judgement and exhorted his fellow Indians to oppose the legislation in every way. Indians too were aroused passionately against the judgement as they considered it as an insult to the honour of their women and children. The movement was also significant from the point of view of extensive **participation of Indian women**[44] who saw it as a direct attack on their dignity and actively participated in the movement.

Gandhiji's strong and persistent protest in this case did not, however, yield any immediate positive result, and realising that time has now come for the final push, he intensified his struggle against the proposed legislation. In November[45] 1913, Gandhiji launched his **final civil disobedience campaign** with a march of around 2,000 Indians into the Transvaal state from Natal, combined with a strike of mine and plantation workers. Arrests and temporary imprisonments were followed by the appointment of a government commission, headed by Sir William H. Solomon[46].

---

[40] Coinciding with the coronation of King George V.

[41] Was treated as a guest of the Government.

[42] A particularly heavy charge on poor labourers whose wages hardly averaged ten shillings a month. The tax was levied even on the unemployed children of the labourers.

[43] Cape Colony Supreme Court Judgement more popularly known as Justice Searle decision of March 1913.

[44] Probably for the first time in such large numbers in South Africa.

[45] On 6 November 1913.

[46] Indians boycotted this commission for lack of Indian membership.

"The campaign was launched by the illegal crossing of the border by a group of sixteen Satyagrahis, including Kasturba, Gandhiji's wife, who marched from Phoenix Settlement in Natal to Transvaal, and were immediately arrested. A group of eleven women then marched from Tolstoy Farm in Transvaal and crossed the border into Natal without a permit, and reached New Castle, a mining town. Here, they talked to the Indian mine workers, mostly Tamils, and before being arrested persuaded them to go on strike."

Extract from India's Struggle for freedom, Bipan Chandra.

"I never dreamt that 20,000 poor Indians would arise and make their own and their country's name immortal ... This fight was joined by women and many young boys of 16, so that the campaign became much more of a moral struggle. South Africa Indians became the talk of the world."

An extract from Gandhiji's essay of 23 July 1913.

The use of brutal force on unarmed and peaceful men and women aroused widespread indignation and condemnation, but all of this failed to weaken Gandhiji's resolve or crush the spirit of the resisters. In India, Gopal Krishna Gokhale toured throughout India to mobilise support for Gandhiji's movement, while Lord Harding, the Viceroy of India, demanded an impartial enquiry into the charges of atrocities levelled against the South African government.

"The repression inflicted on Indians in South Africa is one that would not be tolerated by any country that calls itself civilised."

Viceroy Lord Harding

Eventually, through a series of negotiations involving Gandhiji, the Viceroy, **Lord Harding**, **C. F. Andrews** and **General Smuts**[47], an agreement was reached by which the Government of South Africa passed the **Indian Relief Act of 1914** conceding to the major Indian demands. According to provisions of this Act, the principle of voluntary registration was accepted, the term 'Asiatic' from immigration laws was removed, some educated Indians were allowed to enter South Africa, the poll tax of £3 on non-indentured labourers was abolished, the marriages solemnised according to Indian rites was legitimised, and it was promised to consider the question of Indian immigration in a sympathetic manner. The following month Gandhiji, accompanied by Kasturba, visited England just as the World War started[48] and then returned to India to confront the British rule there.

---

[47] Smuts, who now represented the Union of four colonies: Transvaal, Natal, Orange Free State and Cape Colony.

[48] During the First World War, Gandhiji considered it to be his duty to support the British government who decided to organise an Ambulance Corps of the Indians. For the same, he was awarded *Kaiser-i-Hind* Gold Medal in 1915. However, after some time, due to differences with the British officials, Gandhiji dissociated himself from it.

> *"The saint has left our shores, I sincerely hope for ever."*
>
> General Smuts reaction on Gandhiji's departure from South Africa.

Critical Analysis of Gandhiji's Struggle in South Africa

The struggle in South Africa had a lasting influence on Gandhiji, who during his stay of 21 years not only developed his own philosophy but also the operational mode[49] accompanying that philosophy. It would not be wrong to state that though all of the Gandhian ideas and techniques may have been developed in India, they were clearly formulated in South Africa only. As rightly stated by Bipan Chandra, '*South Africa provided Gandhiji with an opportunity for evolving his own style of politics and leadership, for trying out new techniques of struggle, on a limited scale, untrammelled by the opposition of contending political currents*'.

> *"Gandhiji received his political baptism in South Africa."*
>
> Bridglal Pichai comment on influence of South Africa on Gandhiji.
>
> *"Though I was born in India but was made in South Africa."*
>
> M. K. Gandhi

Significance of South Africa's Experience

- The South African experiment prepared Gandhiji for the leadership of the Indian national struggle. At South Africa, he not only gained the invaluable experience of leading poor Indian labourers but also got the opportunity of leading Indians belonging to different religions (Hindus, Muslims, Christians and Parsis), regions (Gujarat or Tamil Nadu) and even different social classes (rich merchants along with poor indentured labourers, women along with the men). All of these experiences enriched him to understand the different expectations of different groups along with learning the process of taking them all together. The South African experiment not only built up his faith in the capacity of the Indian masses to participate in and sacrifice for a cause that moved them, but with it, he also gained valuable insight about the capacity of the poor masses for sacrifice and for bearing hardship and their morale in the face of repression.
- Gandhiji himself was transformed by the struggles he waged at South Africa as evident from the fact that his early battles for the rights of a small group of Indians in South Africa eventually matured in years to come into the struggle for the rights of the oppressed and downtrodden, and by his own admission even subsequently broadened his outlook towards a more universal struggle for basic human rights.

---

[49] For instance, the Tolstoy Farm near Johannesburg was the precursor of the later Gandhian ashrams that were to play so important a role in the Indian national movement. The Tolstoy Farm was established in May 1910 as a retreat for Satyagrahis, a place where their families could live while they were in prison. The farm was bought by Kallenbach, one of the German friends of Gandhiji who later donated it to the *Satyagrahis*. At farm, Gandhiji and other residents engaged in various self-help activities such as farming, carpentry, tannery and making stuffs like bread, sandals and so forth.

- Gandhiji learnt a lot from his South African experiments and experiences. One of the crucial learnings he derived from the South African experience[50] was the hard fact that leadership involves facing the ire of not only of the enemy but also of one's followers. For instance, there were two occasions in South Africa when Gandhiji faced serious threats to his life: one incident of assault carried out by his so-called enemies and another one by one of his ardent followers. The first instance was of 1896, when a White mob offended by Gandhiji's work chased him down a street in Durban and surrounded his house where he was staying asking for his blood. The second instance pertains to the incident of assault on Gandhiji in 1908 by an Indian Pathan, who felt betrayed because of his agreement with General Smuts. It was, thus, the harder way that Gandhiji learnt that leaders often have to take hard decisions that are unpopular with enthusiastic followers.

Limitations of South Africa's Experience

However, one of the major limitations and tragic legacies of Gandhiji's time in South Africa was the failure on his part to expand the passive resistance struggle to a larger issue of racial abuse of the indigenous Africans and his lack of concern for the nation-building exercise or national liberation. It is unfortunate that Gandhiji while in South Africa sought at least a notional equality for Indians and Europeans, but felt no compulsion to demand the same for the native indigenous Africans. There have been certain reports to suggest that Gandhiji advised Indians to keep their issues distinct from those of other non-White groups and focussed primarily on the 'Indian question'.

One of the probable explanations for this is that Gandhiji had just started his Satyagraha experiment and maybe it was relatively easier for him to awaken the conscience of his own countrymen who were settlers, just like the Whites. In addition, it would be fair to assume that at that stage Gandhiji was yet unfamiliar with the earlier civilisational thrust of the 'native' Africans and so could not take up their cause with that much zeal as he took the Indian cause. However, Gandhiji's philosophy of non-violent passive resistance had a strong influence on the later freedom struggle of South Africa, a fact attested by almost all the leaders of African national movement.

"Mahatma Gandhiji had exerted an incalculable influence in the history of the people of … South Africa. His legacy is writ large in the political, religious, and social realms of South Africa's past, present, and future."

Nelson Mandela

"It is not hard to see a residue of Gandhijism when a man who was prosecuted, banned, insulted, and jailed on Robben Island for 27 years emerges and asks South Africa to look to the future and not the past, to work together for the country, to forgive the oppressors."

Brian M. Du Toit on Gandhiji's influence on Nelson Mandela.

"Generations to come, it may be, will scarcely believe that such a one as this ever in flesh and blood walked upon this earth."

Great scientist Alfred Einstein's statement in July 1944 on Gandhiji.

[50] Which also helped him in his future campaigns

Thus, Mohandas Karamchand Gandhi, though arrived in South Africa as an inexperienced young barrister, in due course of time the passive resistance campaigns initiated by him in South Africa changed the course of history and a new form of struggle against oppression emerged that gradually became a model for political and ethical struggles in other parts of the world be it India[51] or the United States[52].

Gandhiji's Arrival in India

On **9 January 1915**, Gandhiji returned[53] to India and was warmly welcomed for his partial victory in South Africa. However, unlike South Africa where at times Gandhiji could occasionally seek support from the British Government of India, and even the Imperial Government of London, in India he was now in direct confrontation with the British authority and its exploitative rule. In India, the moderate leader **Gopal Krishan Gokhale** was his political Guru, who advised him not to express any opinion on political matters for a year and instead observe the situation in the country for himself to grasp the basic understanding of India's social, economic and political reality. On Gokhale's advice and in keeping with his own style of never intervening in a situation without first studying it with great care, Gandhiji spent 1915, and most of 1916, travelling around the country, and visiting places as far as Sindh, Rangoon, Banaras and Madras seeing things for himself while maintaining his distance from the political affairs of the country, including the Home Rule Movement that was gathering momentum at that time in the country. At meetings, he mostly spoke on his experiences in South Africa and the ideas he had formulated there. In the meantime, Gandhiji organised his ashram at Ahmedabad[54] where he and his devoted band of followers who had come with him from South Africa started leading a community life. During the same period, he also visited Rabindranath Tagore's Shantiniketan and the *Kumbh Mela* at Hardwar. Interestingly, by his own admission Gandhiji was surprised to learn that his work in South Africa was well known at that time, not only to educated Indians but even to the masses who flocked to him for his '*darshan*' as he discovered on his visit to the *Kumbh Mela* at Hardwar.

"He is without doubt made of the stuff of which heroes and martyrs are made and more importantly he has in him the marvellous spiritual power to turn ordinary men around him into heroes and martyrs."

G. K. Gokhale views on Gandhiji.

As rightly said by Bipin Chandra that one of the probable reasons behind Gandhiji's distance from political affairs of the day was that his own political understanding did not coincide with any of the political currents that were active in India then, since his faith in 'Moderate' methods was long eroded, and neither did he agree with the Home Rule League leaders that the best time to agitate for Home Rule was when the British were in difficulty because of the First World War. Furthermore, he was deeply convinced that none of these methods of political struggle were really viable in the long term and that he could only join an organisation or a movement that adopted non-violent *Satyagraha* as its method of struggle.

---

[51] The struggle for independence.

[52] The civil rights campaign of the 1960s.

[53] The day is now celebrated every year as *Pravasi Bharatiya Divas*.

[54] On the banks of the Sabarmati river.

> *"At my time of life and with views firmly formed on several matters, I could only join an organisation to affect its policy and not be affected by it. This does not mean that I would not now have an open mind to receive new light. I simply wish to emphasise the fact that the new light will have to be specially dazzling in order to entrance me."*
>
> Gandhiji's own admission explaining the reason for not joining the existing political organisations.

However, that did not mean that Gandhiji remained politically idle for the complete period. Rather, as a matter of fact, during the course of 1917 and early 1918, his formative years in India, he was involved in three significant **struggles**: in **Champaran**, Bihar, in **Ahmedabad** and in **Kheda**, Gujarat. All of these struggles were related to specific local issues[55] and were fought for the economic demands of the masses wherein he experimented with his innovative technique of Satyagraha, Non-Cooperation and Civil Disobedience.

The Champaran Movement	1917	First Civil Disobedience Movement
The Ahmedabad Mill Strike	1918	First Hunger Strike
The Kheda Movement	1918	First Non-Cooperation Movement
The Rowlatt Satyagraha	1919	First All India Satyagraha

Gandhiji's Entry into Indian Politics

Gandhiji's entry into Indian politics was initiated by his involvement in the issue of Champaran Indigo farmers who were forced by the European planters to cultivate indigo on 3/20th of their holdings[56] (known as the ***tinkathia*** system).

The Champaran Movement (1917)

The Champaran[57], as we had discussed earlier, had been seething with peasant discontent against the European planters since the early 19th century. However, towards the end of the 19th century, a completely new dimension was added to the discontent as owing to the popularity of German synthetic dyes, the Indian indigo was forced out of the market and the European planters had no option but to release the tenant cultivators from their obligation of cultivating indigo. They, however, now tried to turn their necessity to their advantage by demanding **enhanced rents** and other illegal dues from the cultivators as a price for the release of their obligation resulting in agrarian unrest led by local middle and rich peasant leaders[58]. The resistance against the same issue had surfaced in 1908 as well, but the exactions of the planters continued unabated till

[55] Two of these struggles, Champaran and Kheda, involved the cause of peasants, while the Ahmedabad one involved the cause of industrial workers.

[56] Which generally constituted the best portion of the land.

[57] In the Tirhut division of North Bihar.

[58] Such as Rajkumar Shukla, Sant Raut, Khendar Rai and was also led by local maharanis and traders who resented planter competition in moneylending and trade, and a few village *mukhtars* (attorneys) and school teachers (Pir Muhammad, Harbans Sahai).

1916 when a local peasant leader **Raj Kumar Shukla** met[59] Gandhiji at Lucknow session of Congress and persuaded him to visit Champaran to investigate the issue.

However, on reaching Champaran, Gandhiji was ordered by the Commissioner to immediately leave the district, which he flatly refused and rather offered to serve the punishment for this defiance. Gandhiji's civil disobedience or passive resistance to an unjust order was, thus, both unusual and novel for those times in India as mostly leaders, even the likes of Tilak and Annie Besant, when externed from a particular province obeyed the orders and would only indulge in organised protests against the unjust orders. Gandhiji was then immediately arrested and tried in the district court, but the Government of India ordered[60] the local Government to retreat and allow Gandhiji to proceed with his enquiry.

Gandhiji and his colleagues such as Brij Kishore, Rajendra Prasad, Mahadev Desai, Narhari Parikh and J. B. Kripalani started touring the villages of the district and recorded the statements of about 8,000 peasants to ascertain the true nature of grievances. Meanwhile, the Government appointed a **Commission of Inquiry**[61] about the whole issue, and nominated **Gandhiji** as one of its members. The Commission unanimously recommended the abolition of *tinkathia* system, reduction of enhanced rents and compensation for illegal recoveries, to the tune of 25 per cent refund against illegal enhancements.

It is pertinent to note here that in case of Champaran, the local educated Congress leaders like Rajendra Prasad or J. B. Kriplani played a little role in mobilising the peasants, and rather the peasant masses spontaneously rallied to the call of Gandhiji, who they believed to be their divinely ordained deliverer. His intervention, accompanied by telling rumours, broke the barrier of fear in the minds of poor peasants, who now dared to defy the authority of the British Raj and the European planters.

> *"Gandhiji is daily transfiguring the imaginations of masses of ignorant men with visions of an early millennium."*
>
> Statement by the Bettiah SDO on 29 April 1917.
>
> *"Tenants would not fear the rakhshasa planters now that Gandhiji was there."*
>
> A declaration by a raiyat before the enquiry committee comparing Gandhiji to Ramchandra.

The Ahmedabad Mill Strike (February–March 1918)

The next intervention done by Gandhiji was about the internal conflict between the mill owners at Ahmedabad and their workers. The dispute between the workers and the owners was over the withdrawal of the 'plague bonus'[62] and subsequent demand of workers for a 50 per cent wage hike in lieu of the plague bonus, while owners were offering only 20 per cent. Gandhiji persuaded the mill owners and the workers to agree to

[59] Raj Kumar Shukla's decision to get Gandhiji to Champaran is indicative of the image he had acquired by then in India as the one who fought for the rights of the exploited and the poor.

[60] Not willing to make an issue of it and not yet used to treating Gandhiji as a rebel.

[61] The major recommendations of the Commission were included in the Champaran Agrarian Act of 1918.

[62] The owners withdrew the bonus after the epidemic had passed and the workers opposed the withdrawal since the enhancement hardly compensated for the rise in the cost of living during the War.

arbitration by a tribunal, but the mill owners, taking advantage of a stray strike, withdrew from the agreement and instead offered a 20 per cent bonus while threatened dismissal to those workers those who would not comply to the said condition. Gandhiji was greatly offended by this breach of agreement and advised the workers to go on strike. He further suggested, on the basis of a thorough study of the production costs, profits of the industry as well as the cost of living, that instead of 50 per cent, they would be justified in demanding a 35 per cent increase in wages.

The strike began and Gandhiji assisted by **Anasuya Sarabhai**[63] organised daily mass meetings of workers, in which he delivered lectures and issued a series of leaflets urging the workers to be peaceful and non-violent in their protest against the employers. However, after some days when Gandhiji noticed that the workers were slowly losing their morale and were exhibiting signs of weariness, on 15 March, he decided to go on a **hunger strike** to not only rally the tired workers but to also strengthen their resolve for continuation. As expected by Gandhiji, the hunger strike had the tremendous effect of putting pressure on the mill owners and they soon agreed to submit the whole issue to a tribunal, which later awarded the increase of 35 per cent to the workers.

The Kheda Satyagraha (March–June 1918)

The dispute in Ahmedabad was still going on when Gandhiji learnt that the peasants[64] of Kheda district, Gujarat, were in extreme distress due to the failure of their crops[65] owing to late rains combined with high rate of inflation, sudden rise in agricultural wages and outbreak of bubonic plague. Their hardship was further compounded by subsequent dismissal of their appeals for the remission of land revenue by the Government. Enquiries by the members of the Servants of India Society, Vithalbhai Patel and the *Gujarat Sabha*, of which Gandhiji was the President, confirmed the validity of the peasants case as according to the prevalent revenue code, the peasants were entitled to a total remission of the land revenue as a legal right[66] **if** the crops were less than 25 per cent of the normal yield.

With the failure of subsequent appeals and petitions, Gandhiji advised the withholding of land revenue and inaugurated the Satyagraha at a meeting in Nadiad. It is pertinent to note here that the initiative for no-revenue actually came in November 1917 from two local village leaders **Mohanlal Pandya** and **Shankarlal Parikh** with a demand for revenue remission, and it was through the Gujarat Sabha that they got in touch with Gandhiji, but it was not until 22 March 1918 that Gandhiji decided[67] to launch Satyagraha in their support. He along with Vallabhbhai Patel, Indulal Yajnik and Anasuya Behan started touring villages and exhorted peasants to take a solemn pledge for not paying revenue and resisting Government repression, which at times included the seizing of cattle and household goods of helpless peasants and even included the attachment of their standing crops.

---

[63] She was the sister of Ambalal Sarabhai, one of the leading mill owners who was also a friend of Gandhiji and had recently given a liberal donation to the Sabarmati Ashram, thereby saving it from near extinction.

[64] Who were mostly belonging to Kanbi-Patidar castes and were also relatively prosperous than the extremely impoverished petty tenants of Champaran.

[65] Mostly food grains, cotton and tobacco.

[66] And not as a concession by grace.

[67] The delay proved unwise, as by that time the poorer peasants had already been coerced to pay up revenue, and a good rabi crop had weakened the case for remissions. Even then, it was a 'patchy campaign', as it affected only a few villages as evidenced by the fact that only 70 villages out of 559 in Kheda were actually involved in it. Often the peasants capitulated to Government pressure and crossed the boundaries of Gandhian politics of non-violence.

> *"Fight unto death against such a spirit of vindictiveness and tyranny and show that it is impossible to govern men without their consent."*
>
> Gandhiji statement at a village meeting

Eventually, the Satyagraha reached at its peak by 21 April when about 2,337 peasants pledged not to pay revenue and even the cultivators who could afford to pay took a vow that they would not pay in the interests of the poorer *ryots* who would otherwise panic and sell off their belongings or incur debts to pay the revenue. It was however consensually decided that, if the Government agreed to suspend collection of land revenue, the ones who could afford to do so could pay the whole amount. Soon, the Bombay government partially fulfilled the peasants' demands by not confiscating the properties of defaulting peasants who could not pay, and subsequently Gandhiji withdrew[68] the movement in June after this token concession.

Critical Analysis of Champaran, Ahmedabad and Kheda Movement

By championing these localised causes, not only did **Gandhiji** gain nationwide popularity and reputation of a man who could take up local wrongs and can manage to do something concrete about them but as a result of these struggles he also gained a surer understanding of the problems of ordinary Indians, the strengths and weaknesses of the **Indian masses**, as well as of the viability of his own political style and methodology of non-violent satyagraha. He could eventually find his feet among the people of India and earned the respect and commitment of many political workers, especially the younger ones, like **Rajendra Prasad**, **J. B. Kripalani**, **Vallabhbhai Patel**, **Mahadev Desai**, **Indulal Yajnik** and **Shankarlal Banker,** who later served as his life-long trusted lieutenants[69] in his future struggles. Along with leaders, he could also form a solid political base among these localised rural areas, be it Champaran or Kheda, which later proved to be strongholds of political support for future Gandhian movements, and people from these regions responded eloquently to his later calls for political action. Through these movements, Gandhiji also exhibited his special talent for reconciling apparently opposed interests, as evident in the case of Ahmedabad Mill Strike, wherein he was able to keep his friendship with the mill owners intact along with gaining the trust of the workers at the same time. However, if we look closely at these movements, we also identify certain **unique aspects** related to these movements:

- In each movement, Gandhiji was invited to provide leadership where considerable mass mobilisation had already taken place under local initiative, and the intervention of the educated Congress leaders like Vallabhbhai Patel, Rajendra Prasad or J. B. Kriplani was of little direct consequence. For instance, the Kheda movement was started and subsequently sustained by the local leaders, like Mohanlal Pandya and Shankarlal Parikh, and similarly in the Champaran Satyagraha, the major role was played by local middle and rich peasant leaders like Rajkumar Shukla, Sant Raut and Khendar Rai.
- The masses interpreted Gandhiji's message in their own terms, and everywhere the masses pushed their own agendas, much to the dislike of the elite nationalist leaders in the regions, and often their activism followed trajectories that were vastly divergent from the one desired by Gandhiji. For instance, during Champaran movement, the rich local peasant leaders would often organise the lesser peasantry into violent actions, without Gandhiji's knowledge or his approval. Similarly in Kheda district, Gandhiji and his followers received an extremely poor response for their recruitment campaign for World War I in the summer

[68] Gandhiji later recalled that by this time 'the people were exhausted', and he was actually 'casting about for some graceful way of terminating the struggle'.

[69] Also termed as 'sub-contractors' by Judith Brown.

of 1918 as the peasants rejected the request with contempt, and surprisingly those who had met them previously during Kheda peasant agitation with garlands now refused them even food.

The same phenomenon, that is, overwhelming mass support for Gandhiji but for reasons and considerations that were quite different from those of the leader, was witnessed in another significant movement in 1919: the **Rowlatt Satyagraha**, the first all India movement of Gandhiji against the provocative unpopular legislation – the Rowlatt Act.

The Rowlatt Satyagraha (1919)

The Rowlatt Satyagraha was aimed against two repressive bills popularly known as **Rowlatt Bills**[70] severely curbing the civil liberty of Indians through a system of special courts and arbitrary detention without trial for a maximum of 2 years. Ever since the content of the bill was published, Gandhiji registered his opposition against the same as he felt that not only the spirit of the bill primarily echoed distrust for the common men but also the reluctance on the part of government to part with arbitrary powers made a mockery of the progress achieved so far in case of democratic constitutional reforms. In fact, almost all the Indian political leaders were greatly disappointed by this act of the Government and considered it to be their insult, since it came at a time when around the end of the War they were expecting substantial constitutional concessions and a greater control over their own affairs, but instead one of the repressive bills was passed in the Imperial Legislative Assembly[71] even after the unanimous protests of the elected Indian members.

Having witnessed the futility of the protests from the Council members and others, Gandhiji launched 'Satyagraha' against the legislation and a 'Satyagraha Sabha' was formed on 24 February 1919 in Bombay to publish propaganda literature, collection of signatures to a satyagraha pledge and to disobey this and similar other unjust laws, while Gandhiji himself embarked on a tour visiting Bombay, Delhi, Allahabad, Lucknow and a number of South Indian cities between March and early April. Although a group of liberals like Sir D. E. Wacha, Surendranath Banerjee, T. B. Sapru and Srinivas Sastri, along with some Home League leaders, like Annie Besant, opposed Gandhiji's Satyagraha on the ground that it would hamper the Montford Reforms, the main cadre of Satyagraha Sabha came mostly from the younger and radical elements of Home Rule League like **Jamnadas Dwarkadas**, **Shankerlal Banker**, **Umar Sobhani** and **B. G. Horniman**, along with certain Pan-Islamic leaders, like **Abdul Bari**[72] of Lucknow, and some radical members of the Muslim League like Ansari and M. A. Jinnah.

> *"It is my firm belief that we shall obtain salvation only through suffering and not by reforms dropping on us from the English – they use brute force, we soul force."*
>
> Gandhiji statement while launching the Satyagraha agitation against the Rowlatt Bill
>
> *"The growing generation will not be satisfied with petitions, etc.... Satyagraha is the only way, it seems to me, to stop terrorism...."*
>
> Gandhiji's letter dated 25 February 1919 urging the old Moderate leader Dinshaw Wacha to accept his programme of Satyagraha

[70] Prepared on the recommendations of a Sedition Committee of 1918 under Justice S. A. T. Rowlatt and were proposed to provide the government with additional coercive power to deal with revolutionary terrorism.

[71] On 18 March 1919 while the Viceroy gave assent to the bill on 21 March 1919.

[72] Was the Muslim religious leader of the Firangi Mahal ulema, the religious preceptor of the Ali brothers who were still interned.

On 26 February, Gandhiji issued an 'open letter' to all the Indians urging them to join the Satyagraha, and it was then decided to launch a nationwide movement, starting with a general strike or *hartal* on 30 March, which was later postponed to 6 April. However, because of some confusion, Delhi and some parts of the country observed the *hartal* on 30 March, but the movement soon lapsed into violence, when the government fearing mass protests arrested Gandhiji on 9 April, thereby provoking unprecedented mob fury and considerable violence and disorder in areas like Delhi, Bombay, Ahmedabad and Punjab.

Events in **Punjab** were rather moving in a particularly tragic direction as Punjab, which was suffering from the after effects of severe war-time repression, forcible recruitment and the ravages of disease, reacted particularly strongly to Gandhiji's Satyagraha call. Gandhiji had earlier tried to go to Punjab to pacify the people, but the Government deported him to Bombay, and as Bombay and Ahmedabad were also experiencing disturbances at that time, he decided to stay and control the violence there. Meanwhile, on 10 April, the news of Gandhiji's arrest coincided with the arrest of two local leaders, **Dr Saifuddin Kitchlew** and **Dr Satyapal**, and the situation particularly at both Amritsar and Lahore went out of control especially after the firing on a peaceful demonstration near Hall Bridge in Amritsar leading to mob violence and attack on the symbols of British authority like post offices, banks, railway station and the town hall along with murder of five Englishmen and assault on an English woman. It was appearing as if the civil authority had almost lost its control, and in these circumstances the army was called in and Lieutenant-Governor **M O'Dwyer** handed over the command from **Miles Irving**, the Deputy Commissioner in charge of Amritsar district to General **Reginald Dyer**[73], and immediately issued an order prohibiting public meetings and assemblies.

On the fateful day of **13 April 1919**, a large crowd of people, many of whom were innocent visitors from neighbouring villages, had assembled in the **Jallianwala Bagh**, Amritsar, to attend the Baisakhi celebrations along with a public meeting of some *satyagrahis* condemning the arrest of its leaders. Incensed that the orders of assembly were disobeyed, and in a bid to break the morale of the *Satyagrahis*, **General Dyer** ordered his troops of 50 soldiers to fire upon the unarmed peaceful crowd, killing **379** people[74] and wounding about 1,200 people. What was even more disturbing was the way the brutal orders were executed, as most of the people assembled in the park were not aware of the ban on meetings, and no prior warning was issued to the people before the shots were fired and nor there was any escape for the hapless victims other than the narrow pathway where Dyer's men stood with their guns as the Jallianwalla Bagh was totally hemmed in by high walls from all sides leaving little chance for escape.

> *"My only regret is that my ammunition ran out and the narrow lanes prevented me for bringing in an armoured car – for it was no longer a question of merely dispersing the crowd, but one of 'producing a moral effect'."*
>
> General Dyer statement before the Hunter Committee[75] constituted for investigating the Jallianwala Bagh tragedy, which held him guilty and forced him to resign.
>
> *"Plassey laid the foundation of the British Empire, Amritsar had shaken it."*
>
> Statement of an eminent historian.

---

[73] Who was General Officer Commanding of the 45th Infantry Brigade at Jullundur (now Jalandhar).

[74] According to official estimate, but the unofficial accounts gave much higher figures, almost three times of the official figures. It was reported that the shooting continued for ten minutes and the soldiers had fired about 5,000 shots and did stop only when their ammunition was finished.

[75] After the name of chairman, Lord William Hunter, and was officially named as the Disorders Inquiry Committee. It should also be noted that earlier in 1882 also, a Hunter Commission was constituted to look into different aspects of education in India, particularly primary education.

In Punjab, this brutal incident was followed by even more violent, brutal and ruthless repression, as Punjab was placed under **martial law**[76], and General Dyer with the full backing of the Lieutenant-Governor M O'Dwyer[77] unleashed a reign of terror on the residents of Punjab province, especially Amritsar through indiscriminate arrests, public flogging, torture, special tribunals, forced indignities on the people such as rubbing noses on the ground and crawling on their bellies before Europeans. The Congress Committee Report brought out certain facts that clearly showed the total disproportion between popular and government violence during the aftermath of Jallianwala Bagh as in the whole of the Punjab only 4 Whites were killed, while Indian casualties were at least 1,200 dead and 3,600 wounded. The brutality at Jallianwala Bagh and harsh repression of innocent people in Punjab stunned the entire nation so much so that **Rabindranath Tagore** voiced his agony and anger against this brutality by renouncing his knighthood stating that '*such mass murderers aren't worthy of giving any title to anyone*', while Gandhiji overwhelmed by the total atmosphere of violence not only gave up the title of Kaiser-i-Hind[78] but also withdrew the movement on 18 April.

Critical Analysis of Rowlatt Satyagraha

The significance of the **Rowlatt Satyagraha** lies in the fact that it is often claimed in the national historiography as the first nationwide mass agitation under the leadership of Gandhiji, which also marked the beginning of the transformation of Indian nationalist politics from being the politics of some restricted classes to becoming the politics of the masses. Nevertheless, it did suffer from some serious **limitations**:

- The Rowlatt Satyagraha as a political campaign was a manifest failure, since it failed to secure its only aim, that is, the repeal of the Rowlatt Act. Although meant to be non-violent, the campaign also lapsed into violence defeating the Gandhian ideology and methodology. Even Gandhiji admitted to have committed a 'Himalayan blunder' by offering the weapon of Satyagraha to people insufficiently trained in the discipline of non-violence.
- The Gandhian mass movement also suffered from the limitation that in terms of reach and scope, the whole of India literally was not affected and the movement was more effective in the cities than in the rural areas. And here too, the strength of the movement was more due to the local social and economic grievances against the British rule, like war-time inflation or scarcity of basic commodities, than against the Rowlatt bills, about which there was very little popular public awareness. Nor many local leaders could effectively sensitise the public relating the local grievances to the national issue of the Rowlatt Act.
- Another lacunae was that the whole agitation against the Rowlatt Act was not properly organised, and the Satyagraha Sabha set up for organising the movement concentrated mainly on just publishing propaganda literature and collecting signatures on the Satyagraha pledge. In fact, the failure of Rowlatt Satyagraha made Gandhiji realise the need for an impersonal political organisation such as the Congress.

[76] On April 16, which was back-dated to March 30. Under Martial Law, the officers of the Crown had absolute powers that could be exercised by military force. They could exert any amount of physical force, extending to the destruction of life and property to any extent and in any manner. They were indemnified from legal action for any act of rights violation by them when Martial Law was in force and no legal action could be taken against the military personnel for the atrocities.

[77] Often there is great confusion between the roles of Lieutenant-Governor of Punjab M O'Dwyer and General R Dyer regarding Jallianwala Massacre. Mostly, historians now affirm that though General Dyer was the man on the spot, it was M O'Dwyer who ordered the Jallianwala Massacre. According to Indu Banga, a specialist in history of Punjab: '*Dwyer was an arch imperialist who was responsible for this massacre. Dyer was merely following his orders*'. While Dwyer was shot dead by Indian revolutionary Udham Singh in London's Caxton Hall on 13 March 1940, Dyer died of cerebral haemorrhage and arteriosclerosis in 1927.

[78] Bestowed by the British for his work during the Boer War.

That, however, did not mean that Gandhiji had lost faith either in his non-violent *Satyagraha* or in the capacity of the Indian masses to adopt this non-violent approach and, thus, just a year later in 1920, he launched two nation-wide mass struggles, **Khilafat** and **Non-Cooperation** on a scale much bigger than that of the Rowlatt Satyagraha.

Khilafat and Non-Cooperation Movement (1920–22)

Since the beginning of the First World War till 1920, the developments within the country as a whole such as wartime hardships[79], the repressive Rowlatt Act, the unsatisfactory Montford Reforms, the Jallianwala Bagh massacre and the subsequent martial law atrocities in Punjab combined with the disillusionment generated by the Hunter Committee Report along with the widespread hurt caused to the Muslims by the humiliating terms dictated to Turkey[80] followed by the dismemberment of the Turkish Empire greatly discontented the Indian people thereby dramatically **widening the mass base** of the agitation against the Government which was tending to be now more and more outspoken and firm in its opposition to all forms of colonial domination, and it was under these circumstances that Gandhiji assumed the leadership of the Khilafat and Non-Cooperation Movement.

> *My blood is boiling over since I read the summaries (of the Hunter Report) you have sent. We must hold a Special Congress now and raise a veritable hell for the rascals.*
>
> Motilal Nehru's statement to Jawaharlal Nehru on 27 June 1920.

Background of the Khilafat and Non-Cooperation Movement

During the First World War, **Turkey** allied with Germany and Austria against the British and since the Indian Muslims regarded the Sultan of Turkey that is, the Ottoman Emperor as their spiritual leader ***Khalifa***, so naturally their sympathies were with Turkey. However, with the defeat of Turkey, a spectre of **Islam in danger** was created in the minds of the Indian Muslims who now launched the Khilafat movement in India by forming a Khilafat Committee at Bombay in March 1919 which raised primarily three demands:

- The Khalifa's control should be retained over the Muslim holy places.
- In territorial adjustments, the ***Khalifa*** should be left with sufficient pre-war territories so that he could maintain his position as the head of the Islamic world.
- The *jazirat-ul-Arab* (Arabia, Syria, Iraq and Palestine) must remain under Muslim sovereignty.

It was thus a pan-Islamic movement in all its appearance, but as rightly pointed out by **Gail Minault** that this pan-Islamic movement had the potential to utilise '*Khalifa*' as a symbol that could unite the Indian Muslim community divided along many fault-lines, such as regional, linguistic, class and sectarian and could result in anti-British pan-Indian Islamic political mobilisation. Thus, eventually the Khilafat movement emerged as the first mass agitation to forge political unity among a divided Indian Muslim community aroused now by the common '*Khilafat*' issue. In addition, being anti-British in character and having the tremendous potential of bringing the

[79] In the towns, the workers and artisans, the lower middle class and the middle class had been hit by high prices, and shortage of food and essential commodities while the rural poor and peasants were in addition victims of widespread drought and epidemics.
[80] By the Treaty of Sevres signed in May 1920.

Muslims into the mainstream of Indian nationalism along with a splendid opportunity to unite the Hindus and the Muslims in a common struggle against the British, Gandhiji was also inspired to support *Khilafat* cause.

Initially, the Khilafat movement had two broad trends: a moderate trend headed by the prosperous Bombay merchants like **Chotani**, who preferred to confine the agitation to familiar moderate methodology of meetings, memorials and sending delegations to the Viceroy or ensuring Muslim representation in the Paris Peace Conference, and on the other hand a radical trend led by the younger Muslim leaders, like **Ali brothers**[81], **Maulana Azad**, **Hasrat Mohani** and the ***ulama***[82], who wanted a mass agitation against the British on the basis of unity with the Hindus, and it was from this group that the call for **Non-Cooperation** with the British Government first came at the **All India Khilafat Conference** in Delhi (22–23 November 1919) and Hasrat Mohani made a call for the boycott of British goods. The radical leaders clearly spelt out that in case the peace terms after the war were unfavourable to Muslims, they would stop all cooperation with the Government.

> *In case, the Government fails to pacify Indian Muslims, we would start a joint Hindu-Muslim movement of non-cooperation under the guidance of Mahatma Gandhiji, a man who commands the respect of both Hindus and Muslims.*
>
> Shaukat Ali's statement in April 1920

Gandhiji initially played a mediating role between the moderates and the radicals group and in fact till May 1920, sided more with the Bombay group[83], opposing, for instance, Hasrat Mohani's call for boycott of British goods. However, the turning point came soon after the publication of the terms of the **Treaty of Sevres**[84] with Turkey on 14 May 1920 followed by the publication of the Hunter Committee Report on 28 May, which as described by Gandhiji was just thinly disguised official eyewash[85] and Gandhiji now took an open position and backed the radicals. The Indians were further infuriated to learn that the House of Lords had voted in favour of General Dyer's action and had acquitted O'Dwyer of any blame while the British public had also demonstrated its support by helping the *Morning Post* collect 30,000 pounds for General Dyer. Thus eventually, the moderate trend began to lose ground and the radicals now took charge of the movement and at the Allahabad conference of the **Central Khilafat Committee**, held from 1 to 3 June 1920, a four-stage **non-cooperation programme** was announced:

- boycott of titles
- boycott of civil services
- boycott of police and army
- non-payment of taxes

Gandhiji was requested by the committee members to lead the movement and to begin the whole movement with a hartal on 1 August. Because the Muslim and Congress opinion on non-cooperation was still divided, throughout the summer of 1920, Gandhiji and Shaukat Ali toured extensively mobilising popular support for the programme. Gandhiji now also pressed the **Congress** to adopt a similar plan of campaign on three issues: Punjab wrong, Khilafat wrong and Swaraj[86].

---

[81] Shaukat Ali and Muhammad Ali Jauhar.

[82] Having a considerable influence over small towns and villages, particularly in the United Provinces, Bengal, Sind and Malabar.

[83] The bulk of Bombay Muslim merchants were importers and retailers of such goods.

[84] Which made it amply clear that the dismemberment of the Turkish Empire was complete.

[85] Since it did not strongly condemn General Dyer's role in the Jallianwala Bagh massacre.

[86] Gandhiji quite deliberately never defined what this swaraj would actually mean, and although he said that it was '*Parliamentary Swaraj in accordance with the wishes of the people of India*' Jawaharlal Nehru did admit that it was a '*vague swaraj with no clear ideology behind it*'.

Towards Non-Cooperation: Calcutta to Nagpur

However, it was not an easy task for Gandhiji to get the entire Congress to approve his programme of political action as the established Congress politicians like Lala Lajpat Rai, C. R. Das, Bipin Chandra Pal, Lokmanya Tilak[87] and Motilal Nehru still had their doubts about a non-cooperation programme along with a strong opposition for Gandhian idea of boycotting council elections (scheduled for November 1920). In fact, the opposition to Council boycott was, conversely, strongest in **Bengal** and **Maharashtra**, the old extremist strongholds where electoral chances were relatively bright, while on the other hand, the politically backward provinces and groups like **Gujarat** and **Bihar**, which were not hitherto involved in Congress politics, greatly supported the Gandhiji's proposals.

> *Almost the entire old Guard of the Congress opposed Gandhiji's resolution of non-cooperation.*
>
> Jawaharlal Nehru wrote in his autobiography.

The All India Congress Committee, therefore, met in May 1920 and decided to convene a **special session** in September to enable the Congress to decide on its course of action and in the meanwhile also placed the programme of non-cooperation and boycott before the Provincial Congress Committees (PCC) for their opinions.

PCC	Opinion
• The PCC of the United Provinces	• After prolonged debate, it approved the principle of non-cooperation, gradual boycott of government schools, colleges and offices and British good but expressed reservations about the boycott of the legislative councils.
• The Bombay PCC	• It approved 'non-cooperation' as the legitimate method of agitation, but objected to boycott of council and only recommended boycott of British goods as a first stage.
• The Bengal PCC	• It readily accepted the principle of non-cooperation but disagreed with the idea of council boycott.
• The Madras PCC	• It approved the policies of non-cooperation but rejected Gandhiji's programme.
• The Andhra PCC	• It approved the non-cooperation but deferred a decision on Gandhiji's programme until the special Congress session.
• The Punjab PCC	• It approved the non-cooperation but deferred a decision on Gandhiji's programme until the special Congress session.

Meanwhile, as declared earlier by the Khilafat Committee, the hartal on 1 August[88] was a grand success, and from then on the support for non-cooperation began to rise. It was under these circumstances that a special session of the All India Congress Committee was held at Calcutta from 4 to 9 September 1920 with

[87] It is pertinent to note here that Tilak was not in favour of having an alliance with Muslim leaders over a religious issue as he felt that the basis of cooperation between Hindus and Muslims should be a secular one just like the Lucknow Pact (1916) and a lot depended on Tilak's attitude whether hostile or neutral – but unfortunately he passed away on 1 August 1920.

[88] Incidentally also coinciding with the death of Tilak.

Lala Lajpat Rai as its president where to everyone's surprise Gandhiji's resolution on non-cooperation programme was approved[89] despite stiff opposition from the old guards, such as C. R. Das, Pandit Madan Mohan Malaviya, Annie Besant, M. A. Jinnah or Bipin Chandra Pal.

The non-cooperation programme provided for surrender of government titles, boycott of schools, courts and councils, boycott of foreign goods, encouragement of national schools, arbitration courts and ***khadi*** (homespun cloth). No mention was made here, however, of resignations from services, police or the army, or of no-tax. In November 1920, all the Congress candidates boycotted[90] the council elections. The programme was then endorsed at the regular session of the Congress at Nagpur in December 1920, which saw the dramatic change of stance[91] of C. R. Das from being a critic of Gandhiji's programme to the mover of the non-cooperation resolution. The resolution accepted all the parts of the non-cooperation programme which primarily focussed on following two aspects[92]:

Constructive	Non-Constructive
• Setting up of national schools, colleges and arbitration courts	• Boycott of Government-affiliated educational institutions
• Promotion of indigenous goods	• Boycott of law courts
• Popularisation of *Charkha* and Khadi	• Boycott of elections to the legislature and official functions
• Enrolment of volunteer corps	• Surrender of honours and titles conferred by the British
• Maintenance of Hindu–Muslim unity and giving up of untouchability	• Public bonfire of foreign clothes and other goods

Gandhiji assured that the Non-Cooperation Movement would bring Swaraj within 1 year and if that did not happen or if government resorted to repression, then a civil disobedience campaign would be launched, involving **non-payment of taxes**. The **Nagpur session** is also famous for initiating radical restructuring in the Congress to transform the party into a true mass organisation like:

- Constitution of district and village level units
- Formation of a working committee[93] of 15 members as the real executive head
- Reorganisation of Provincial Congress Committees on a linguistic basis
- Fixing of the number of delegates in proportion to population
- Opening of Congress membership to all men and women of the age of 21 or more on payment of 4 annas as annual subscription.

This was rather one of the first positive moves on the part of the Congress to make it a real mass-based political party, and during this phase a fundamental change in the social composition of the party as well as

[89] Among Gandhiji's supporters were Motilal Nehru, Saifuddin Kitchlew, Jitendralal Banerjee, Shaukat Ali, Yakub Hasan and Dr M. A. Ansari.

[90] The dramatic conversion of the established leaders to Gandhiji's programme between September and December 1920 has been explained by Gordon and Brown largely in terms of political calculation of election prospects.

[91] There is still a great deal of conjecture and controversy regarding this change as certain historians have conflicting views about the same. While Judith Brown considers that the Nagpur resolution was a victory for Gandhiji as he made 'no concessions of principle', on the other hand Richard Gordon and Rajat Ray consider that it was Gandhiji who captivated to Das and accepted many of his proposals.

[92] To be implemented in stages, as directed by the All India Congress Committee.

[93] A demand first raised by Tilak in 1916.

in its outlook and policies was also witnessed with the emergence of a centrist leadership within the pluralist structure of political India. The creed of Congress was modified[94] from '*attainment of self-government through constitutional means*' to '*the attainment of Swaraj by all legitimate and peaceful means*'. Eventually, in the whole process Gandhiji emerged as the mass Congress leader, whose potential as a political organiser got firmly established along with the fact that he enjoyed access to new areas of political support from backward classes and backward regions along with Muslim *Khilafatists*, which were earlier beyond the reach of the older Congress leaders.

Main Phases of the Non-Cooperation Movement

The Non-Cooperation Movement started with great enthusiasm from January 1921 with initial emphasis on gradual withdrawal by the Indian people from all forms of cooperation with the British Government like boycott of schools, colleges, law courts and so forth. The movement can be identified through **four phases**:

- **Phase 1 (January–March 1921)**: During the first phase, the emphasis was laid on **educational boycott** that is, students leaving government affiliated schools and colleges, **boycott of law courts**[95] by lawyers, development of national schools[96] and arbitration courts. The educational boycott was particularly successful in **Bengal** and **Punjab**, where with massive student strikes at Calcutta and Lahore, the students even forced the managements of their institutions to disaffiliate themselves from the Government and according to one estimate around 90,000 students left schools and colleges and joined more than 800 national schools and colleges. **Subhash Bose**[97] and **Lala Lajpat Rai** both played a prominent role in promoting the movement during this phase, which was further strengthened by support from many leading lawyers of the country, like Motilal Nehru, C. R. Das, Saifuddin Kitchlew, Asaf Ali, M. R. Jayakar, C. Rajagopalachari, Vallabhbhai Patel and T. Prakasam, who gave up their lucrative practices and joined the movement.
- **Phase 2 (April–June 1921)**: During the second phase, the initial emphasis was laid on raising a **Tilak Swaraj Fund** of ₹1,00,00,000, recruiting an equal number of volunteers and installing ₹20,00,000 Charkhas[98] by 30 June. Because of the vigorous drive, the Tilak Swaraj Fund was oversubscribed and *Charkhas* were popularised on a wide scale, while *khadi*[99] became the uniform of the national movement though the Congress membership target of one crore members was not achieved, but it still managed to reach roughly ₹50,00,000.
- **Phase 3 (July–November 1921)**: In the third phase, the stress was on boycott of foreign cloth with the organisation of public bonfires of foreign cloth, further **popularisation of *Charkha***[100] and ***khadi*** along with ***Jail Bharo*** campaign of Congress volunteers and boycott of the forthcoming November visit of the Prince of Wales.

---

[94] At this stage some leaders like Mohammad Ali Jinnah Annie Besant and B. C. Pal left the Congress as they believed in constitutional struggle, while some others like Surendernath Banerjee, popularly known as *Rashtraguru*, founded the Indian National Liberation Foundation and played a minor role in national politics henceforth.

[95] though not as successful and effective as the educational boycott.

[96] It was during NCM that certain new national institutions like the Kashi Vidyapeeth, the Gujarat Vidyapeeth and the Jamia Millia Islamia were started.

[97] who became the principal of the National Congress in Calcutta.

[98] It is pertinent to note here that the *Charkha* programme initially had a strong intelligentsia orientation, with students and educated urban people in general being urged to take up spinning on a voluntary basis, as a symbol of identification with the rural masses.

[99] Interestingly at one of the meetings held in Madurai, Gandhiji received a complaint from the students that *khadi* was around 30–40 per cent more expensive than mill cloth. Gandhiji retorted that the answer lay in wearing less clothes and, from that day, discarded his *dhoti* and *kurta* in favour of a *langot* and for the rest of his life, he then remained a 'half-naked fakir'.

[100] Though Rabindranath Tagore appreciated the movement for bringing to the masses a new consciousness, yet simultaneously, he attacked the movement's 'narrowness, obscurantism and *Charkha*'.

> *"Our triumph consists in thousands being led to prisons like lambs to the slaughter-house."*
>
> Gandhiji giving a call for flooding the prisons with volunteers in 1921

- **Phase 4 (November 1921–February 1922)**: In the last phase of the movement, a clear shift towards radicalism was visible and with government policy of large-scale arrests and ban on meetings and volunteer groups, it was appearing as if the whole country was on the verge of a revolt. The situation was further aggravated by the speeches of Khilafat leaders like **Hasrat Mohani**[101], who had earlier in July at the Karachi Khilafat Conference asked all Muslims to resign from the army, and later at the Ahmedabad Congress in December raised the demand for complete independence and giving-up of the non-violence dogma. A nationwide strike was observed on 17 November, the day of arrival of the Prince of Wales and Bombay witnessed the outbreak of the first violent riot of the movement, targeting the **Europeans**, **Anglo-Indians** and the **Parsis** in the city, leaving Gandhiji furious who postponed the full-scale civil disobedience or a no-tax campaign and instead decided that an experimental no-revenue campaign would be launched on the issue of infringed liberties of speech, press and association at a later date to begin from the second week of February 1922 from Bardoli[102] in Gujarat.

But this never happened, as with the unfortunate attack on a local police station by angry peasants at **Chauri Chaura**, in Gorakhpur district of Uttar Pradesh on 5 February 1922, the whole situation just changed and Gandhiji immediately withdrew the **Non-Cooperation Movement**. Many Congressmen were shocked, and surprised by Gandhiji's decision they vehemently protested against the movement's abrupt end. **Subhas Chandra Bose** called it a 'national calamity', while **Jawaharlal Nehru** expressed his 'amazement and consternation' at the decision. However, Gandhiji did not relent and also persuaded the Congress Working Committee to ratify his decision and, thus, on 12 February 1922, while condemning the Chauri Chaura incident, Congress immediately withdrew the Non-Cooperation Movement and instead passed the Bardoli resolution, which emphasised the need for constructive work before beginning any political agitation. Gandhiji was arrested on 10 March 1922 and was sentenced to 6 years imprisonment.

> *"I would suffer every humiliation, every torture, absolute ostracism and death itself to prevent the movement from becoming violent."*
>
> Gandhiji's statement on the withdrawal.
>
> *"The movement had unconsciously drifted from the right path. We have come back to our moorings, and we can again go straight ahead."*
>
> Gandhiji explaining his position to Jawaharlal Nehru.

Soon after, the Khilafat movement too lost its relevance, as in 1924 a nationalist revolution in Turkey under Kemal Pasha abolished the office of *caliphate* and stripped the Sultan of Turkey of all political power making it a secular state.

---

[101] Angered by the jailing of the Ali brothers in November.

[102] The venue was carefully chosen by Gandhiji, as it was a ryotwari area, with no zamindars, and therefore no danger of a no-revenue campaign snowballing into a no-rent campaign tearing apart the fragile coalition of classes.

Critical Analysis of the Movement

Participation

In terms of participation in the Non-Cooperation Movement, it was marked by the involvement of regions and classes that did not participate in the past in any other movement initiated by the Congress, for instance, the **peasant** and **working class participation**, which was far more impressive than the middle class participation. In fact, the centres of elite political leaders like Calcutta, Bombay and Madras responded on a very limited level to Gandhiji's movement, while there was significant peasant participation[103] in Rajasthan, Sind, Gujarat, Awadh, Assam and Maharashtra. Similarly, the lower-caste non-Brahman participation was witnessed more in **Madras** and **Maharashtra** as compared to other areas, and out of the four linguistic regions in South India, three were effectively brought into the movement except Karnataka, which remained unaffected. In addition, besides the elite politicians, a lot of new comers in Indian politics like **Rajendra Prasad** in Bihar and **Sardar Vallabhbhai Patel** in Gujarat found expression of their interests and aspirations in the Non-Cooperation Movement. The students and women also came forward in large numbers and became active volunteers of the movement.

Boycott

Similarly, in terms of boycott, the educational boycott was far more effective than boycott of legal courts, as revealed in the figures, for instance, till March 1921, out of 5,186 only 24 titles were surrendered and only 180 lawyers gave up their practice, whereas in terms of educational boycott about 20 headmasters or teachers were resigning per month till April 1921. The boycott of council election was also effectively successful with the polling average of 5–8 per cent in most districts except in Madras. The economic boycott was also more intense and successful, as the value of imports of foreign cloth dropped from ₹1,020 million in 1920–21 to ₹570 million in 1921–22 while during the same period the import of British cotton piece goods also declined[104] from 1,292 million to 955 million yards. Interestingly, during 1918–22, fearing the labour unrest and other economic motives **while** the large industrialists remained pro-government and anti-Non-Cooperation Movement, the smaller traders and merchants remained consistently pro-nationalist. Although the production of the handloom increased and the textile industry benefited from the nationalists emphasis on the use of ***Swadeshi***, no definite statistics are available for the same.

Success of Other Related Social Movements

During 1920–22, certain other associated Gandhian social movements also achieved some success along with the Non-Cooperation Movement, for instance the **anti-liquor campaign** resulted in significant drop in liquor excise revenue in Punjab, Madras, Bihar and Orissa. Another significant milestone achieved during the Non-Cooperation Movement was on the front of **untouchability campaign** as by inserting in the historic 1920 resolution an appeal '*to rid Hinduism of the reproach of untouchability*' Gandhiji succeeded in bringing the anti-untouchability campaign for the first time to the forefront of nationalist politics. The emphasis of the movement was clearly on unification and reconciliation of class and communal disjunctions as evident by the fact that the Hindu–Muslim alliance too remained unshaken throughout the period, except in the Malabar region.

---

[103] Although in some cases such peasant movements were autonomous of any Congress organisational intervention.

[104] Partly responsible for this success was trader participation, as the businessmen pledged not to indent foreign cloth for specific periods. However, their refusal to import foreign cloth might have also been due to a sudden fall in rupee-sterling exchange rates that made import extremely unprofitable.

Spread of the Movement: Local Variations

Another significant aspect of the Non-Cooperation Movement was its uneven geographical spread and wide regional variations, since some areas were more active than others, while at most places, the movement was shaped according to local conditions and often the local grievances of the people found expression through this movement though at times the principle of non-violence was not always strictly followed. For instance, in Gujarat, mobilisation depended on local issues, like temple politics, control over municipalities or control over educational institutions, while in the southern towns of India mobilisation was centred on the local issue of rising municipal taxes or the income tax. Similarly, each movement was having a different emphasis as for instance in Andhra delta the movement witnessed powerful tribal movements, while the focus was on forest Satyagraha in Bengal.

Region	Remarks
Punjab	In Punjab, already irritated by the administration of martial law and the Jallianwala Bagh, the powerful Akali movement for reform and control of the *Gurudwaras* got closely identified with Non-Cooperation Movement and with the support of Gandhiji and the Congress the Government was eventually forced to surrender the keys and administration of the temple to the Akalis.
Bengal	In Bengal, the mass participation in the Non-Cooperation Movement was comparatively less enthusiastic than the Swadeshi movement and mass mobilisation for Non-Cooperation depended more on personal influence of local leaders, such as C. R. Das, whose act of giving up a lucrative legal practice, inspired the younger generation and when he was arrested followed by his wife Basanti debi in May 1921, thousands of Bengal youth courted arrest.
UP	The Non-Cooperation Movement was most effective in United Provinces where it got entangled with the *kisan* movement specially in the Awadh district of U.P. where a radical peasant movement was being organised since 1918–19 against the oppressive *taluqdars* primarily centred on following demands: • No *nazarana* (extra premium on rent) • No eviction from holdings • No *begar* (forced labour) • No *rasad* (forced supplies). Between January and March 1921, the districts of Rae Bareli, Pratapgarh, Faizabad and Sultanpur witnessed widespread agrarian riots under the leadership of local leader Baba Ramchandra. This peasant militancy organised at the grassroots level was also harnessed by the U.P. Kisan Sabha, which gradually had 450 branches in U.P. Later in 1921, another strong peasant agitation popularly known as the *'Eka'* movement emerged under the leadership of radical tribal leader Madari Pasi, demanding the conversion of produce rents into cash. Another significant event in U.P. was the destruction of thousands of acres of reserved forests in the Kumaon Division in July 1921 by the hill-tribes as they disliked the forest regulations.
Bihar	In north Bihar, especially Champaran, Saran, Muzaffarpur and Purnia districts, which had earlier witnessed the previous anti-planter agitation, Swami Viswananda's campaign and Kisan Sabha activities, the Non-Cooperation Movement proved to be most effective in these areas.
Rajasthan	The peasant movements protesting against cesses and begar in the princely states of Rajasthan strengthened the Non-Cooperation Movement, as they did in Bihar and U.P. In fact, the Bijolia Movement in Mewar and the Bhil Movement under Motilal Tejawat acquired great impetus from the Non-Cooperation Movement.

Region	Remarks
Maharashtra	The Non-Cooperation Movement was relatively weak in Maharashtra because the Tilakites were unenthusiastic about Gandhiji while the higher castes disliked Gandhiji's emphasis on the elevation of the depressed classes and their participation in the Non-Cooperation Movement and, on the other hand, the Non-Brahmins felt that the Congress was a Chitpavan-led affair.
Assam	Non-Cooperation Movement received massive support in the distant province of Assam wherein in the tea plantations, seeking Gandhiji's blessings the labourers rose in revolt for higher wages and better condition of work.
Andhra	In the Gudem Hills of Andhra, another local leader, Alluri Sitaram Raju, organised the tribals against forest laws and linked their campaign with the Non-Cooperation Movement.
Madras	In Madras, from the very beginning the movement witnessed a Brahman-non-Brahman conflict, as the Justice Party launched an active campaign against the 'Brahman' Congress and its non-cooperation programme and rallied in support of the Montagu-Chelmsford Reforms. Because of this resistance, the boycott of foreign cloth was also much weaker in the Tamil regions than in other provinces of India.

Significance

- The Non-Cooperation Movement commanded the support of vast sections of the Indian people such as peasants, workers, artisans, shopkeepers, traders, professionals and White-collar employees. In fact, the image of Congress as an national organisation received a significant boost after Non-Cooperation Movement, as now the charge of being just a representative of a 'microscopic minority'[105] could never again be hurled at the Indian National Congress.
- The Non-Cooperation Movement clearly demonstrated the strength and ability to face repression and suffering of the Indian masses. By their undying courage, sacrifice and fortitude in the face of adversity and repression, thousands of poor Indians dispelled the notion that the desire for national freedom was just the preserve of the educated and the rich. Rather their behaviour amplified the notion that it was an elemental urge common to all members of a subject nation. The movement gave a new confidence to the masses and taught them to be fearless in their political pursuit.
- The Movement was also significant in the sense that it was for the first time that peasants and working classes, nationalists from the small towns made the first serious attempt to adopt the Gandhian Ideology. Although they may not have fully comprehended all its implications or observed all the discipline that the non-violent movement demanded for its successful conduct, still for many of them it was their first contact with the modern world of nationalist politics and the modern ideology of nationalism.
- The tremendous participation of Muslims, and the maintenance of Hindu–Muslim unity, despite the Malabar developments, was in itself no mean achievement and it was rather unfortunate that this positive feature of communal unity was not repeated in later years.

Limitation

The Movement, however, did suffer from certain limitations:

- The masses even though participated in large numbers more often also crossed the limits of non-violent Satyagraha. On many occasions, for instance, Gandhiji himself condemned the unruly mob, but even he failed to restrain them, and this was probably the main reason why he hesitated to begin a full-fledged civil

[105] As hurled by the Viceroy, Lord Dufferin, in 1888.

disobedience or a no-revenue campaign. The unfortunate incident at Chauri Chaura somehow eclipsed the entire movement.

- Another limitation of the movement was that by bringing in the *ulama* and by overtly using a religious symbol during the Khilafat movement, even though unintentionally but religious emotions were evoked among the Muslim masses and as a result, violent tendencies soon appeared in the Khilafat movement. The worst-case scenario was the 1921 Moplah uprising in **Malabar**, where the Moplah peasants, emboldened by the Khilafat spirit, rose against the Hindu moneylenders and the state, followed by other communal riots in various parts of the subcontinent in 1922–23, wherein there was a visible breach of the Hindu–Muslim solidarity. Therefore, it would not be wrong to deduce that though the Khilafat movement died down after some time, the religious emotions articulated as a result of it continued to persist for much longer time, unfortunately matched by an equally militant Hindu radicalism.
- Although vast sections of the masses joined the movement, a lot many people remained outside the ambit of the new awakening. However, this was just the beginning and more serious and consistent efforts were yet in the offing.
- The Non-Cooperation Movement did not achieve its stated aims and its sudden retreat provided a big jolt to the national movement.

However, Gandhiji later clarified that '*may be the battle was over, but the war would continue*'.

> *"It is high time that the British people were made to realise that the fight that was commenced in 1920 is a fight to the finish, whether it lasts 1 month or 1 year or many months or many years and whether the representatives of Britain re-enact all the indescribable orgies of the Mutiny days with redoubled force or whether they do not."*
>
> Gandhiji's statement in an article written in *Young India* on 23 February 1922 after the withdrawal of the movement.

The Gandhian Ideology

An integration and synthesis of a number of diverse social, intellectual and political influences along with certain personal experiences helped in the evolution of **Gandhiji philosophy** and **ideology**. According to Gandhiji's own admission, the outlook of his parents and the socio-religious millieu of his native place along with the values of **Vaishnavism** and, in particular, the tradition of **Jainism** shaped his early thoughts. He was also profoundly influenced by certain religious texts such as the ***Bhagavad Gita***, ***the Gospels in Brief*** (especially the Sermon on the Mount[106]), Washington Irving's ***Life of Mohammed and His Successors*** and ***the Sayings of Zarathustra.*** A number of other basic influences also stimulated the development of Gandhiji's beliefs and ideas, notably **John Ruskin**, **Tolstoy** and the **South African** experience. In his autobiography, Gandhiji asserts that reading Tolstoy's *The Kingdom of God Is Within You* (1894) left an abiding impression on him and taught him that man's highest duty was to love his fellow man and resist evil and violence. His beliefs were further enriched by Ruskin's *Unto This Last* (1860) which laid emphasis on manual work as the 'joy of exercise'. In fact, being particularly impressed with the theories of love for fellow humans and the renunciation of urban comforts, Gandhiji established communal settlement at **Phoenix** in 1904 and gradually matured unto profound worldliness when lure of money had lost all charm for him and service had become the sole goal of his life.

[106] Which preached that renunciation was the highest form of religion.

"I could not get any sleep that night. I determined to change my life in accordance with the ideals of the book. After reading of this book I came to the conclusion that the true basis of society was not wealth but human relationships. The reading of Ruskin can be summarised in three basic prepositions: (i) The good of the individual is contained in the good of the groups; (ii) the labourers work has equal value to that of the lawyer since both have the right to earn a living; and (iii) a life of labour that is, tilling the soil or working as a handicraftsman, is the life worth living. Unto This Last made it clear as daylight for me that the second and the third were contained in the first. I arose with the dawn, ready to reduce these principles to practice."

Gandhiji's self-attested testimony for Ruskin's *Unto This Last* (1860).

"It was the New Testament which really awakened me to the rightness and value of passive Resistance. When I read in the 'Sermon on the Mount' such passages as 'resist not him that is evil but whosoever smitten thee on thy right cheek turn to him the other also, and Love your enemies and pray for them that prosecute you, that ye may be sons of your Father which is in heaven', I was simply overjoyed, and found my own opinion confirmed where I least expected it. The Bhagavad Gita deepened the impression, and Tolstoy's 'The Kingdom of God is Within You' gave it permanent form."

Mahatma Gandhi

"I should have more and more occasions for service of the kind I was rendering, and that I should find myself unequal to my task if I were engaged in the pleasures of family life and in the propagation and rearing of children."

The process of renunciation of worldly life in Gandhiji's own words.

The experience of collecting and caring for the wound in the **Anglo-Boer War** and the **Zulu rebellion** also left an indelible imprint on Gandhiji, and eventually in 1906, he took the ancient Jain commandant of *ahimsa* or non-violence to all things, and Satyagraha, the force of truth and love.

"The Zulu rebellion was full of new experiences and gave me much food for thought. The Boer War had not brought home to me the horrors of war with anything vividness that the rebellion did."

Gandhiji

Satyagraha

One of the chief aspects of Gandhiji's ideology was *Satyagraha*, which basically originated from '***Sadagraha***' (*Sat*-truth, *Agraha*-firmness) meaning 'firmness in a good cause'. It, thus, signifies non-violent active resistance against those who hinder the realisation of the goal of truth and justice and is undertaken not against evil doer but against his evil policies and actions. Gandhiji considered *Satyagraha* to effect a moral transformation in his constituents, to change them from passive objects of someone's else will to free and independent moral agents, masters of their own destiny. He further believed that it was not by violence but through self-suffering that the *Satyagrahis* convert the enemy into one's own view. In words of Gandhiji, '*the appeal is never to his fear, but always to his heart. The object is not to coerce but to convert the evil doer to the cause of justice through persuasion and appeal.*'

"It involves self-chosen suffering and humiliation for the resisters. If it is effective, it is so by working on the conscience of those against whom it is being used, sapping their confidence in the exclusive rightness of their cause making their physical strength important, and weakening their resolution by insinuating a sense of guilt for the suffering they have part in causing."

Satyagraha aptly explained by P. Sitaramayya.

"No matter how often a Satyagrahi is betrayed, he will repose his trust in the adversary so long as there are no cogent grounds for distrust. Pain to a Satyagrahi is the same as pleasure."

Gandhiji's

In fact, for Gandhiji, *Satyagraha* was not merely a political tactic but part of a total philosophy of life and ideology of action, as he believed that since the realisation of Truth was the ultimate goal of human life, therefore, devotion to truth and Justice through both moral ends and pure means was essentially crucial. Gandhiji also clarified that in practice, Satyagraha could assume various forms such as **fasting**, **non-violent picketing**, different types of **non-cooperation** and **civil disobedience** in willing anticipation of the legal penalty.

"Satyagraha means to be strong not with the strength of the brute but with the strength of the spark of God. In fact Satyagraha is the vindication of truth not by infliction of suffering on the opponent but on one's self and the intention is to convince the opponent and not to crush him, to convert the opponent, who must be 'weaned from error by patience and sympathy."

Gandhiji's views on Satyagraha.

Gandhiji also made a clear distinction between the ***Satyagraha*** and **passive resistance** as passive resistance does not exclude the use of physical force or violence for the purpose of gaining one's end and is thus a weapon of the weak, whereas the former that is, Satyagraha is the weapon of the strongest since it excludes the use of violence in any form or way.

Truth and Non-Violence (*Ahimsa*)

According to Gandhiji, Truth means '***Satya***' that 'which is or exists' thereby meaning 'reality' and is identical with God who is known as *Sat–Chit–Ananda*, one who combines in himself truth, knowledge and bliss. For Gandhiji, the individual ought to strive for realisation of truth through right means and, therefore, he asserts, '*devotion to truth is the sole justification of our existence*'.

"The golden rule of conduct is mutual toleration seeking that we will never all think alike and we shall see truth in fragments and from different angles of vision. There is nothing wrong in everyone following truth according to his light."

Mahatma Gandhi

Regarding non-violence or **Ahimsa** Gandhiji meant avoiding injury to anything on earth in thought, word or deed and implies uttermost selflessness, which forms a strong foundation for Satyagraha. Ahimsa basically encompasses both positive and negative aspects: as in its **negative sense**, it meant non-killings as well as avoidance of ill-will, anger, spite, cruelty, the torture of men and animals, humiliation and oppression of the weak and so forth, while in its **positive sense** it meant benevolence or love for whole creation and the mankind even the evil-doer. It, thus, meant an **indomitable moral courage** on the part of its practitioner to be prepared to suffer in the cause of truth and to not to resort to any sort of violence when provoked. Gandhiji repeatedly emphasised that one must '*hate the sin and not the sinner' and 'ahimsa paramadharma'* meaning non-violence is the supreme virtue.

"When a person claims to be non-violent, he is expected not to be angry with one who has injured him. He will not wish him harm; he will wish him well; he will not swear at him; he will not cause him any physical hurt. He will put up with all the injury to which he is subjected by the wrong doer. Thus, non-violence is complete innocence. Complete Non-Violence is complete absence of ill will against all that lives."

Mahatma Gandhi

However, it is interesting to note[107] here that Gandhiji was totally against a cowardly surrender to injustice, and at times even he emphasised that violence is still preferable to a cowardly surrender.

"I saw non-violence in the Gandhian model not as an inviolable principle but as a tactic to be used as the situation demanded. The principle was not so important that the strategy should be used even when it was self-defeating, as Gandhiji himself believed. I called for non-violent protest for as long as it was effective."

Excerpt from Nelson Mandela's autobiography which mentions the influence of the Mahatma on the Defiance Campaign during the 1950s and 1960s.

Religion

Another important aspect of Gandhian ideology was his attitude towards religion. For Gandhiji, religion was not a doctrinal formulation of any religious system but a **basic truth underlying all formal religions.** He was convinced that the religion could not be relegated to the realm of private opinion and it must influence and permeate all activities of men. He was also convinced that religion provided the fundamental basis for

[107] In fact, this point of view of his sometimes does create a delicate problem of interpretation regarding his principle of non-violence.

political action in India and probably this was the reason behind his usage of religious idioms[108] like '*Ram raj*'[109] to mobilise people in the national movement. He repeatedly emphasised that every truly religious man must be active in politics and every political actor must be genuinely imbued with ethical and spiritual values of the true religion. In fact, the spiritualisation of politics and of the political man is indeed a novel contribution of Gandhiji to mankind. He was also indefatigable not only in insisting on '***sarvadharma sambhav***' that is, interfaith harmony but also on the fact that India was a nation composed of many religious groups and each has its own relevance. He also seemed to view religions not so much in terms of its formal practices but as a kind of service to humanity. For him, service to mankind is service to God and an individual's religion is expressed in his 'Service to the helpless'.

> *"My religion has no geographical limit and is based on truth and non-violence. My religion forbids me to hate anybody. Religion is not for separating people but for binding them."*
>
> Gandhiji's opinion expressed in an article published in *Young India* in 1920.
>
> *"True religion is based on justice and makes the individual conscious of the spiritual unity of all human beings and their dignity and equality and to strive for the establishment of justice and harmony among human beings in the society. As true religion does not permit toleration of exploitation and injustice in social relationships but encourages to fight against them non violently."*
>
> M. K. Gandhi

Hind Swaraj

The other important feature of Gandhian thought was the body of ideas, which he illustrated in his book *Hind Swaraj* (1909). In this work, Gandhiji pointed out that Indians were themselves responsible for their colonial plight as the British hold is strengthened due to internal quarrels of the Indians. He further stated that the real enemy was not the British political domination but the modem western civilisation, which was luring India into its stranglehold. He was severely critical of the Indians educated in western style, particularly lawyers, doctors, teachers and industrialists, who were undermining India's ancient heritage by insidiously spreading modern ways. As a counter to all this, he suggested **Swaraja** or 'self-rule', wherein Indians would follow their traditional traditions uncorrupted by modern civilisation.

> *"Indian's salvation consists in unlearning what she has learnt during the past 50 years or so. The Railways, telegraphs, hospitals, lawyers, doctors and such like have to go and the so-called upper classes have to learn to live consciously and religiously and deliberately the simple life of peasant."*
>
> M. K. Gandhi

[108] However, it cannot be denied that this use of religious idiom prevented Gandhiji and the national movement under his leadership from giving effective challenge to a major category of division among the Indian people, which later caused a fissure in our national unity in periods of crisis and strain, and tended to push into the background their internal differences and conflict.

[109] An ideal political state, a stateless Republic which represents the maximum consummation of the values of Truth, Justice, Non-violence, Freedom and Equality.

"I am not opposed to modern industry but what I object to is the craze of machinery, not machinery as such. The character of production should be determined by social necessity and not by selfish interest. Modern industrial capitalism had two defects that requires urgent remedies. The first was the damage it was doing to nature, the urban areas, and the countryside and the second was its inability either to satiate the greed of the rich or to alleviate the misery of the poor."

M. K. Gandhi

"My problem is not with modern science or technology but with the ideology of science that asserted that scientific truths and spiritual truths were incompatible. I intend to reconcile aspects of modernity with spirituality, science with religion, rational knowledge with spiritual experience."

M. K. Gandhi

Even though these ideas certainly look regressive and obscurantist in the context of the early 20th century, still benefit of doubt can be accorded to Gandhiji as it seems that his ideas originated more because of adverse effects of 'modernisation' under the colonial rule on the artisans and poor peasantry and for its continued dependence on foreign capital and investment. In fact to address these issues, Gandhiji advocated **Swadeshi** stressing on use of things belonging to one's own country, particularly focussing on the replacement of foreign machine-made goods with Indian handmade cloth. According to him, *Swadeshi* not only held the solution to the poverty of peasants who could spin at home to supplement their income, but with it, the problem of the drain of wealth could also be addressed. He was perhaps anxious to protect the modern Indian civilisation from the onslaught of modern materialism. It is, however, pertinent to note here that despite his pronounced opposition to the influences of Western Industrial civilisation, Gandhiji never adopted a hostile attitude towards emerging modern industries in India and rather advocated the **concept of trusteeship** wherein the capitalists were held as 'trustees' for the workers. In the later years, Gandhiji did try to give concrete shape to his social and economic ideas by taking up the programme of *Khadi*, village reconstruction, welfare of Harijans, specially focussing on the abolition of evil practice of untouchability. In fact, when he assumed national leadership, he made it amply clear that he was not concerned with just **national liberation** but the larger issue of **social liberation**, without which independence even if achieved could not be sustained.

Individual

Gandhiji had profound faith in personal ethics, self-discipline and self-reliance. According to Gandhiji, an individual should strictly adhere to **five moral vows** such as ***satya***, (truth), ***ahimsa*** (non-violence), ***brahmacharya*** (celibacy), ***asteya*** (non-stealing) and ***aprigraha*** (non-possession) to lead a disciplined moral life which will purify his soul and will help him to realise his ultimate goal of self-realisation and realisation of ultimate Truth. Gandhiji was strong supporter of the belief that every individual should reduce his wants and possessions to the minimum as the desire for material possessions beyond the necessity would not only involve him in violence and exploitation but will also distract him from his spiritual quest for truth. Gandhiji prescribes the institution of **trusteeship** for possessions beyond the minimum requirement.

"God alone is the sovereign of the material world. Humans may enjoy it as its trustees, renouncing any claim to absolute ownership."

M. K. Gandhi

Education

Gandhiji believed that every individual is an integral part of the society and his performance of roles is greatly influenced by the education he receives during the formative years of his life and, therefore, he prescribes for a scheme of education known as the ***nayi talim*** (New Education or Basic Education) in which every child needs to be educated and trained for the realisation of his ethical goal in life and also the goal of a just social order. Education, according to Gandhiji, should aim at a balanced and harmonious development of the body, mind and soul along with development of character of an individual. In fact, he was also a great supporter of **vocational education**.

Although there may have been strong differences of opinion on the utility of Gandhian ideology, but the fact remains that his ideas deeply influenced the course of our struggle against the British rule and determined its major thrust and direction.

Relevance of Gandhiji in Contemporary Times

Gandhiji's ideology, teachings and principles still have great relevance in socio-economic and political life of both the Indians and people across the globe by virtue of their **universality** and **concern for the entire humanity**. As contemporary society is a fragmented and polarised society with an absence of a basic consensus, in such scenario Gandhiji's prescription of tolerance and mutual respect is just more than relevant in today times. Today, when the whole world is facing crisis in terms of social, economic and environmental challenges such as poverty, racial discrimination, social disharmony, violence, terrorism, conflict, crime, religious bigotry, ethnic discord, communal frenzy, environmental degradation, pollution, global warming, and so forth, **Gandhian philosophy** can emerge as a game changer to provide **equitable solution** to all these issues and help in the providing an effective panacea for eliminating and eradicating the ills and evils of all these social and economic challenges that afflict contemporary societies and politics throughout the world. Through Gandhian techniques of ***sarvodaya***[110] and **decentralisation**, the moral compass of today's degenerated politics can be effectively shifted back in the righteous direction of equitable and sustainable development along with good governance. It, therefore, seems that Gandhian philosophy is **more relevant today** than yesterday and will continue to have relevance throughout the coming ages.

> *"Perhaps Gandhi's most important legacy was in creating a culture of peace, in proving the effectiveness of non-violent non-cooperation, and drawing the world's attention to the gap between what we do, and what we are capable of doing. Gandhi's ideas drive the work of the United Nations for equality, empowerment and global citizenship every day and give a beacon of hope that the world can still become a better place to live in."*
>
> Excerpts from UN Secretary General António Guterres' speech on relevance of Mahatma Gandhi in the Contemporary World.

---

[110] Meaning 'Progress of All'.

Previous Year's Questions (Prelims)

1. With reference to Rowlatt Satyagraha, which of the following statements is/are correct? (2015)
   1. The Rowlatt Act was based on the recommendations of the Sedition Committee.
   2. In Rowlatt Satyagraha, Gandhiji tried to utilise the Home Rule League
   3. Demonstrations against the arrival of Simon Commission coincided with Rowlatt Satyagraha.

   Choose the correct answer from the following options.
   (a) 1 only
   (b) 1 and 2
   (c) 2 and 3
   (d) 1, 2 and 3

2. What was the aim of Rowlatt Act? (2012)
   (a) Compulsory economic support to war efforts
   (b) Imprisonment without trial and summary procedures for trial
   (c) Suppression of the Khilafat movement
   (d) Imposition of restrictions on freedom of the press

3. What was the reason for Mahatma Gandhi to organise a Satyagraha on behalf of the peasants of Kheda? (2011)
   1. The administration did not suspend the land revenue collection in spite of a drought.
   2. The administration proposed to introduce Permanent Settlement in Gujarat.

   Which of the statements given above is/are correct?
   (a) 1 only
   (b) 2 only
   (c) Both 1 and 2
   (d) Neither 1 nor 2

4. Mahatma Gandhi said that some of his deepest convictions were reflected in a book titled," Unto the Last" and the book transformed his life. What was the message from the book that transformed Mahatma Gandhi? (2011)
   (a) Uplifting the oppressed and poor is the moral responsibility of an educated
   (b) The good of individual is contained in the good of all
   (c) The life of celibacy and spiritual pursuit are essential for a noble life
   (d) All the statements (a), (b) and (c) are correct in this context

5. Consider the following statements: (2010)
   1. Dr Rajendra Prasad persuaded Mahatma Gandhi to come to Champaran to investigate the problem of peasants
   2. Acharya J. B. Kriplani was one of Mahatma Gandhi's colleagues in his Champaran investigation. Which of the statements given above is/are correct?

   Choose the correct answer from the following options:
   (a) 1 only
   (b) 2 only
   (c) Both 1 and 2
   (d) Neither 1 nor 2

6. During the Indian freedom struggle, why did Rowlatt Act arouse popular indignation? (2009)
   (a) It curtailed the freedom of religion
   (b) It suppressed the Indian traditional education
   (c) It authorised the government to imprison people without trial
   (d) It curbed the trade union activities

7. Who among the following founded the Ahmedabad Textile Labour Association? (2009)
   (a) Mahatma Gandhi
   (b) Sardar Vallabhbhai Patel
   (c) N. M. Joshi
   (d) J. B. Kriplanians

8. Who was the Viceroy of India when the Rowlatt Act was passed? (2008)
   (a) Lord Irwin
   (b) Lord Reading
   (c) Lord Chelmsford
   (d) Lord Wavell

9. Which one of the following aroused a wave of popular indignation that led to the massacre by the British at Jallianwala Bagh? (2007)
   (a) The Arms Act
   (b) The Public Safety Act
   (c) The Rowlatt Act
   (d) The Vernacular Press Act

10. At which one of the following places did Mahatma Gandhi first start his Satyagraha in India? (2007)
   (a) Ahmedabad
   (b) Bardoli
   (c) Champaran
   (d) Kheda

11. Which of the following pairs are correctly matched? (2005)

	Person actively Movement/ Satyagraha	**Person actively associated with**
1.	Champaran	Rajendra Prasad
2.	Ahmedabad mill workers	Morarji Desai
3.	Kheda	Vallabhbhai Patel

   Choose the correct answer from the following options.
   (a) 1 and 2
   (b) 2 and 3
   (c) 1 and 3
   (d) 1, 2 and 3

12. What was the name of the famous person of India who returned the Knighthood conferred on him by the British government as a token of protest against atrocities in Punjab in 1919? (2004)
   (a) Tej Bahadur Sapru
   (b) Ashutosh Mukherjee
   (c) Rabindranath Tagore
   (d) Syed Ahmed Khan

13. The Hunter Commission was appointed after the (2001)
   (a) Black hole incident
   (b) Jallianwala Bagh massacre
   (c) Uprising of 1857
   (d) Partition of Bengal

14. Where did Gandhiji launch his first successful Satyagraha after returning from South Africa? (2000)
   (a) Chauri Chaura
   (b) Dandi
   (c) Champaran
   (d) Bardoli

15. Which one of the following events was characterised by Montague as preventive Murder? (1998)
   (a) Killing of INA activists
   (b) Massacre of Jallianwala Bagh
   (c) Shooting of the Mahatma
   (d) Shooting of Curzon willy

Previous Year's Answers (Prelims)

1. (b)	2. (b)	3. (a)	4. (d)	5. (b)	6. (c)	7. (a)	8. (c)
9. (c)	10. (c)	11. (c)	12. (c)	13. (b)	14. (c)	15. (b)	

The Rise of the New Forces: 1922–27

9

After the withdrawal of the Non-Cooperation Movement in 1922, there was considerable demoralisation, disorganisation and disintegration among nationalist ranks, resulting in the quick breakdown of the national consensus constructed a few years ago, thereby eventually leading to a *crisis of unity*. The Congress was divided among the – '**no-changers**' and '**pro-changers**', with the latter preferring to revert to constitutional politics and the former opposing council entry and wanting to stick to Gandhian ways. The position of the 'pro-changers' or the Swarajists had weakened by 1924 and an internal split on communal lines further divided them into **Responsivists** and **non-Responsivists**.

However, despite such fissures in organised political life, there were also significant events during the period 1922–27 which brought to the fore certain underlying political currents and varied contradictions of Indian society, thereby resulting in the emergence of new forces which eventually found expression at the level of mass action and brought considerable ideological transformation in the national movement of 1920s lending it a **socialist orientation** in terms of organising the peasants in *Kisan Sabhas*, workers in trade unions, youth in student unions and backward classes in terms of caste associations. There was also a resurgence of the revolutionary nationalism with greater mass orientation, and a good number of young men who had earlier left the 'revolutionary' path to take part in the movements under the Congress went back to their old ways. In this chapter, we will be discussing in detail about the divisions in the nationalist ranks along with the emergent new forces[1].

Pro-Changers and No-Changers

Two main trends were apparent in the national movement by December 1922:

- **Pro-changers**: This section of leaders such as C. R. Das, Motilal Nehru and Hakim Ajmal Khan openly **advocated** entry into the legislative councils with focus on the aggressive form of non-cooperation based upon the sole premise of obstructing the councils, exposing them as *sham parliaments* and to ultimately use them as an arena of political struggle to arouse popular enthusiasm. They were popularly known later as the **Swarajists**.
- **No-changers**: The second section headed by Vallabhbhai Patel, Rajendra Prasad, M. A. Ansari, K. Iyengar and C. Rajagopalachari **opposed** council entry and instead advocated the constructive programme laid down by Gandhiji.

At the Gaya session of the Congress in December 1922, **C. R. Das** as the President of the Congress and **Motilal Nehru** as its Secretary put forward the programme of *either mending or ending*[2] the

[1] Kindly note that for the sake of conceptual and comprehensive understanding, the time line of study of these events may at times exceed the duration of 1922–27.

[2] Signifying that the Councils set up by the British had to be mended in a manner suitable to the attainment of Swaraj or to be ended completely.

councils. Another section of the Congress under the guidance of Rajendra Prasad, Vallabhbhai Patel and C. Rajagopalachari opposed the new proposal, which was consequently defeated by 1748 to 890 votes. Consequently, C. R. Das and Motilal Nehru resigned from their respective offices in the Congress and in March 1923 formed the Congress-Khilafat *Swaraj* Party better known later as the ***Swaraj* Party** with Das as its President and Motilal as one of its Secretaries to contest the coming elections in November. The *Swaraj* Party declared that it would put forth the national demand for self-government in the councils and in case of its rejection its elected members would adopt *a policy of uniform, continuous and consistent obstruction within the councils, with a view to make the Government through the councils impossible.*

> *"The Congress should enter the Councils to wreck them from within by total obstruction of their proceedings, creating a deadlock which would force the British to concede further reforms. The Swaraj must be for the 'masses' and not for the 'classes' alone."*
>
> C. R. Das

Programme of the Swaraj Party	
Inside the Councils	**Outside the Councils**
• Attaining Swarajya (self-rule) and dominion status	• Engaging in the constructive programmes of the Congress with special focus on Swadeshi, *Khadi*, National Education, Prohibition and Arbitration boards
• Obtaining the right to frame a constitution and obtaining full provincial autonomy	• Inter-communal unity
• Establishment of nationalists control over the bureaucracy and government administration	• Removal of untouchability and raising the status of the depressed classes
• Establishment of control of nationalists over local and municipal bodies	• Organisation of industrial and agricultural labour including village organisation
• Acquisition of economic control of the country to prevent the drain of public wealth from India along with the development of commerce and industry	• Creating an agency for propaganda outside the country and of national work enlisting sympathy and support of foreign countries in the struggle for Swaraj along with establishment of a federation of Asian countries to secure Asian solidarity and mutual help in trade and commerce

On the other hand, the **no-changers**[3] insisted on total boycott and non-cooperation, along with focus on the constructive programme like establishment of Ashrams, popularisation of *Charkha* and *Khadi*, setting up of schools and colleges and working towards the prohibition and abolition of untouchability along with quiet preparations for the resumption of the suspended Civil Disobedience Movement (CDM).

Differences soon increased among the two sections but drawing lessons from the disastrous split of 1907 and understanding the strong need for unity, leaders from both the groups moved towards mutual accommodation, and at the special session of the Congress held in **Delhi**[4] (September 1923) and the

[3] Whose effective head was Gandhiji even though he was in jail.

[4] Under the presidentship of Maulana Azad.

regular **Kakinada** session (December 1923), a compromise was struck between the two as the **Congress** suspended all propaganda against council entry and permitted Congressmen to stand as candidates and exercise their franchise in forthcoming elections while the **pro-changers** reiterated their faith in the constructive programme.

Swarajist Performance at the Polls

In November 1923, elections[5] to the legislative councils were held, and despite the fact that the *Swarajists* got only a few weeks to prepare for the elections and the franchise was also extremely narrow[6], they managed to do quite well as they won 42 out of 101 elected seats in the **Central Legislative Assembly** and got a clear majority in the **Central Provinces** along with emerging as the single largest party in **Bengal** and **Bombay**. They fared also quite well in Uttar Pradesh, however not so in Madras and Punjab. The victory of the *Swarajists* at the polls strengthened their position within the Congress and they came to be now recognised as the parliamentary wing of the Congress.

Swarajist Work in the Legislatures

In the Central Legislative Assembly, since the *Swarajists* were not in majority, they sought support from other groups and subsequently succeeded in building a common political front known as the **Nationalist Coalition**[7] with the Liberals[8], the Independents[9] and individuals such as Madan Mohan Malaviya to effectively implement the policy of obstruction against the Government. In fact, at the centre as well as in many of the provinces, the *Swarajists* repeatedly intervened on every issue and in their zeal to wreck the reforms from within often outvoted and humiliated the Government by rejecting and blocking the passage of the Government's legislations including budgetary grants. It eventually forced the government to resort to **certifying**,[10] thus exposing the true sham character of the reformed councils. Also, in order to expose the misdeeds of the imperial Government, they often passed adjournment motions and asked inconvenient questions.

> *"We want you to carry on the administration of this country by veto and by certification. We want you to treat the Government of India Act as a scrap of paper which I am sure it has proved to be."*
>
> Vithalbhai Patel's comments on the Government on one such occasion.
>
> *"We feel that we have no further use for these sham institutions and the least we can do to vindicate the honour and self-respect of the nation is to get out of them. We will try to device those sanctions which alone can compel any government to grant the demand of a nation."*
>
> Motilal Nehru's observations while staging a walkout of his party.

---

[5] There were altogether three elections held under the provisions of the Act of 1919: in 1920, 1923 and 1926. In 1920, owing to the Non-Cooperation Movement, the Congress had boycotted the elections leaving the field for the liberals and others while in 1926 polls, the Swarajists did not fare well.

[6] Only about 6.2 million or less than 3 per cent had the right to vote.

[7] Though not all its constituents and members share the radicalism of the Swarajists.

[8] Some of the prominent liberals were Surendra Nath Banarjee, Tej Bahadur Sapru, V. S. Srinivasa Sastri and M. R. Jayakar.

[9] Led by M. A. Jinnah.

[10] If the legislation was rejected in the legislature, the Viceroy or the Governor had power to certify the legislation to get it passed.

Primarily, the *Swarajists* concentrated their energies on three major sets of issues:

- The issue of constitutional advance leading to **self-government**[11]
- The issue of civil liberties, release of political prisoners and repeal of repressive laws
- The issue of the development of indigenous industries

On all these issues, they regularly raised concerns, delivered powerful speeches which were fully reported in the Press and followed avidly every morning by the readers across the country helping them to develop political awareness and interest. In fact, in February 1924, on the initiative of the Swarajists, a resolution was passed in the Central Assembly demanding a **Round Table Conference** to discuss reforms leading up to responsible government while it was again on the behest of the Swarajists that protection[12] was granted to the Tata Steel industry by the government in 1924.

Meanwhile, the **no-changers** too proactively joined the Swarajists in contesting the election of the municipalities and other local bodies and emerged victorious arousing further popular enthusiasm. For instance, **C. R. Das** became the Mayor of Calcutta[13], **Vithalbhai Patel**, the President of Bombay Corporation, **Vallabhbhai Patel** of Ahmedabad Municipality, **Rajendra Prasad** of Patna Municipality and **Jawaharlal Nehru** of Allahabad Municipality and despite their circumscribed powers, they did excellent work in the fields of sanitation, education, health, anti-untouchability and *khadi* promotion. In fact, through their keen efforts in March 1925, they got **Vithalbhai Patel**, a leading Swarajist, elected as the President of the Central Legislative Assembly.

The Swarajist activities, thus, produced a stir in the country and enlivened an otherwise dull political atmosphere. Their tactics of obstruction not only embarrassed the Government, but also the parliamentary duels of the period did constitute a brilliant page in the annals of parliamentary politics.

Gandhi and Swarajists

However, in February 1924, with the release of Gandhiji from jail, the old conflict was again revived since the balance seemed to tilt again in favour of the 'no-changers' and a split seemed imminent in Congress. But, contrary to the government's expectation, Gandhiji moved towards an **accommodation** with the Swarajists as even though he was completely opposed to council entry and had no faith in the Swarajists' programme, yet he never expressed his adverse opinion publicly, and in fact sensing that the public opposition to the 'settled fact' of council entry would be counterproductive for the national movement, he refrained others also to express any negative views about the same.

> *"The council entry had already occurred and now to withdraw would be 'disastrous' and would be 'misunderstood' by the Government and the people as a rout and weakness. This would further embolden the Government in its autocratic behaviour and repressive policy and add to the state of political depression among the people."*
>
> M. K. Gandhi

Moreover, the courageous and uncompromising manner in which the Swarajists had functioned in the councils eventually convinced Gandhiji that *however politically wrong, they were certainly not becoming a*

[11] In the very first session, Motilal Nehru put forward the national demand for the framing of a new constitution, which would transfer real power to India. This demand was passed by 64 votes to 48. It was reiterated and passed in September 1925 by 72 votes to 45.

[12] Under the policy of 'discriminating protection' enunciated by the Fiscal Commission of 1921.

[13] With Subhas Chandra Bose as his Chief Executive Officer.

limb of imperial administration and rather they have shown determination, grit, discipline and cohesion and have not feared to carry their policy to the point of defiance while introducing a new spirit into the Indian Legislatures. In fact, when the Government promulgated an ordinance[14] in the name of fighting terrorism and conducted raids on Congress offices while arresting a large number of revolutionary nationalists and *Swarajists*[15] and other Congressmen including Subhas Chandra Bose, Gandhiji expressed his solidarity with the *Swarajists* and brought the strife between the *Swarajists* and no-changers to an end by getting both Congress and Swarajists sign a joint statement declaring that the *Swarajist* Party was an integral part of the Congress which would carry on work in the legislatures on behalf of the Congress. This decision was later endorsed in December 1924 at the Belgaum[16] session of the Congress.

> *"I would have been false to the country if I had not stood by the Swaraj Party in the hour of its need. . . . I must stand by it even though I do not believe in the efficacy of Council-entry or even some of the methods of conducting Council Warfare and again Though an uncompromising No-changer, I must not only tolerate their attitude and work with them, but I must even strengthen them wherever I can."*
>
> Gandhiji wrote in *Young India*.

Gradual Decline of the Swarajists

Gradually, the enthusiasm of 1924 began to wane, and during the period 1925–27, there was considerable demoralisation and subsequent decline of the Swarajists. The probable causes behind the gradual decline of the Swarajists were:

- The parliamentary politics of Swarajists suffered from the inherent weakness of reaching the **limits of politics of obstruction**, since having repeatedly outvoting the Government and forcing it to often certify its legislation, the Swarajists were left with no other novel method to escalate the politics of confrontation. Gradually, even the policy of unqualified obstruction too lost its appeal and the party showed signs of disintegration.
- The Swarajists also were not able to carry their coalition partners for ever and in every respect, as the grant of immediate constitutional advance as a pre-condition for cooperation was too limited a goal to hold together men of diverse thinking and independent views. The liberals and the independents did not subscribe fully to the Swarajists' tactic of '*uniform, continuous and consistent obstruction*' and expectedly, differences emerged among them which subsequently led to their withdrawal from the coalition and from the Swarajists agenda of obstructionism. In fact, before the elections of 1926, the erstwhile Nationalist Party was split into three clear-cut groups:
  - The Swarajist or the Congress Party
  - The responsive cooperators, which included the Hindu Mahasabha and Independent Congressmen who together formed the Nationalist Party under the leadership of Lajpat Rai and Madan Mohan Malaviya
  - The Independent Party[17] headed by Jinnah.
- The Swarajists could neither initiate nor sustain a mass movement on their own since they lacked any concrete policy to coordinate their militancy inside legislatures with the mass struggle outside. They also

[14] On 25 October 1924.
[15] Swarajist members of the Bengal legislature, Anil Baran Roy and S. C. Mitra.
[16] Presided over by Gandhiji who also gave the Swarajists a majority of seats on his Working Committee.
[17] Jinnah seceded from the National Coalition and formed a separate party, the Independent Party.

failed to resist the pulls of parliamentary perquisites and positions of status and patronage as well. Also, at times they could not grab the opportunity of supporting the right causes at right time as evident in the case of Bengal where the majority of the leaders of the *Swaraj* Party failed to support the tenants cause against the *zamindars*, and in the process, thus, eventually lost the support of its pro-tenant, mostly Muslim members.

- Another probable cause was regarding the internal cohesion of the *Swaraj* Party, as with passing time, the protracted Hindu-Muslim tension, presence of reactionary elements[18] of both the communities within the party really created a difficult situation, and even the Swarajists could not avoid the intrusion of communal discord in their own ranks and were subsequently divided among the **Responsivists** and **non-Responsivists**. The **Responsivists** led by Madan Mohan Malaviya, Lala Lajpat Rai, M. R. Jayakar and N. C. Kelkar were of the opinion that opposition to the Government injured the interests of the Hindus and, thus, they wanted to cooperate with the government and hold offices wherever possible[19], whereas the **non-Responsivists** led by Motilal Nehru were in favour of non-cooperation inside the councils. The Muslims on the other hand were so much alienated from the Congress that its erstwhile Muslim members fought elections as Muslims, not as Swarajists. The emotional appeal of religion thereby emerged dominant, and in the process, secularism became the casualty. Also subsequently, the Government too succeeded in cajoling the Swarajists[20] into some kind of cooperation, and a substantial section emerged even among the hardcore Swarajists like C. R. Das[21] who were gradually becoming opposed to the destructive opposition to all government measures and instead wanted to focus on 'responsive cooperation' and, thus, by the end of 1925, the Swaraj Party was a house divided against itself and its credibility was at its all-time low owing to the mutual bickerings, internal dissension, distrust and desertions.

> *"My only hope therefore lies in prayer and answer to prayer."*
>
> Gandhiji wrote in May 1927 on the simultaneously prevailed virulent factionalism and indiscipline in both the camps of Swarajists and the Gandhian constructive workers.

However, in order to prevent further dissolution and disintegration of the party along with further weakening of the moral fibre of its members, the main leadership of the party reiterated their faith in mass civil disobedience and decided to withdraw from the legislatures in March 1926. But, the damage already done to the Swarajists prospects could not be undone as revealed by the election results of November 1926, in which they suffered heavy losses everywhere[22] with their strength going down in the legislative bodies of all provinces especially in United Provinces, Central Provinces and Punjab, where they were completely routed while both Hindu and Muslim communalists increased their representation in the councils. Their tally came down to 35 from earlier 42 in the Central Legislative Assembly and they could not form a nationalist coalition as they had done in 1923. Eventually, by 1929 they proved to be undeniably a spent force.

---

[18] Which ostensibly professed secularism.

[19] As they did in the Central Provinces.

[20] For instance, Motilal Nehru, who had earlier declined a seat on the Muddimen Committee, now accepted one of the Skeen Committee while Vithalbhai Patel became President of the Assembly and A. Ramaswamy Iyengar was a member of the Public Accounts Committee. Similarly, in the Central Provinces, the two Swarajist stalwarts B. Tambe and Raghavendra Rao were converted by the Government to its side as they accepted the membership of the Governor's Executive Council.

[21] Presiding over the Bengal Provincial Conference at Faridpur on 2 May 1925, he appealed to effect a reasonable settlement and said that 'cooperation with the Government was possible if some real responsibility was transformed to the people' and in return assured the government that the Swarajists would do everything to discourage 'revolutionary propaganda'. In fact, the Faridpur declaration accelerated the drift towards constitutional opposition and cooperation with the Government.

[22] Except Madras where it won half the seats and registered substantial gains compared to its earlier position of 1923.

Significance of Swarajists

One of the greatest significance of the Swarajists lies in the fact that they were able to fill the political void at a time when the national movement was recouping its strength. While it is indeed true that some of the Swarajists could not[23] resist the perks and privileges of their office, still the overwhelming majority of the Swarajist leaders did prove their mettle and stood their ground by working in the legislatures in an orderly disciplined manner conforming to their real aim of politics of obstruction. They not only outvoted the Government several times, but through their powerful speeches on self-government, civil liberties and industrialisation, they effectively utilised the legislatures in a creative manner to highlight the shortfalls of the imperial government along with exposing the hollowness of the constitutional reforms of 1919.

> *"The only really well organised and disciplined party with a definite programme (though, it is true, a negative one) is that of the Swarajists. Only in Bengal and the Central Provinces did they, even temporarily, achieve their initial object of making dyarchy unworkable and in the provinces they have tended everywhere, in varying degrees to be transformed into an opposition of a more constitutional kind, and have not infrequently played a useful part as keen and vigilant critics."*
>
> The success of the Swarajists admitted although somewhat grudgingly even by Indian Statutory Commission, popularly known as the Simon Commission (1927).

Merger of the Swarajists with Congress (1930)

The announcement of Simon Commission in the closing months of 1927 and Lord Birkenhead's challenge to Indians to produce a constitution acceptable to all sections of society opened new political vistas in the country. Eventually, the council entry programme was pushed to a back seat and it also lost its relevance, thereby bringing the Swarajists and the no-changers closer to one another. While the Simon Commission evoked universal boycott on the one hand, on the other hand, taking up the challenge of Birkenhead, Motilal Nehru prepared a constitution known as **Nehru Report** for which the Calcutta Congress of 1928 resolved that in case the British Government did not accept the Nehru Report by 31 December 1929, it would declare 'Complete Independence' as its goal. Thus, in this changed political scenario wherein the country began to prepare for the second round of direct mass action to achieve complete independence, the Swaraj Party merged with its parent body, that is, the Congress.

Constructive Work

In the meantime, both no-changers and Swarajists carried on the grassroots focussed constructive work with its emphasis on the promotion of *Swadeshi*, national education, *khadi*, spinning using *Charkha*, Hindu-Muslim unity, prohibition, the removal of untouchability and the boycott of foreign cloth. In fact, during the 1920s, hundreds of ashrams came up all over the country where political cadres got practical training in spinning *khadi* and understanding of the ways to ameliorate the life of the lower castes and tribal people. For instance, at the **Vedchi Ashram** in Bardoli *taluqa*, Gujarat, Chimanlal Mehta, Jugatram Dave and Chimanlal Bhatt devoted their entire lives to the spread of education among the *kaliparaj* or adivasis while Ravishankar Maharaj carried on the similar work among the lower caste *Baralyas* of Kheda district.

---

[23] Which was also inevitable in the parliamentary framework.

Constructive Work Field	Approach of No-Changers and Swarajists
Charkha, *Khadi* and spinning	• The Swarajists lent support to the Constructive Programme but at times they did not share Gandhi's passion and idealism in same measure in certain fields. For instance, though the Swarajists regarded *charkha* (spinning wheel), *khadi* (coarse cloth) and spinning instrumental in improving the economic life of Indian people, they, however, did not subscribe to the orthodox Gandhian and no-changers ideology that *khadi*, *charkha* and indigenous industries alone would make India independent and would bring *Swaraj*. • The Swarajists exhorted the people to wear *khadi* and also issued instructions to all its members to attend the meetings of the Central Assembly and Provincial Councils dressed in pure *khadi*, but at the same time Gandhi's resolution making Charka spinning the basis for Congress membership and his proposal to make spinning obligatory for members of all elected organisations of the Congress drew strong disapproval from the Swarajists.
Swadeshi	• The concept of ***Swadeshi*** occupied a very prominent role in Gandhian constructive programme. Gandhi's definition of *Swadeshi* was comprehensive as it included not only *charkha* and *khadi* but also all other forms of indigenous industries and to him *Swadeshi* meant a wholesome *Swadeshi* mentality, a determination to find all the necessities of life in India and that too through the labour and intellect of the villagers. • The Swarajists also espoused the programme of *Swadeshi* but again their passion for Swadeshi was not as strong and as deep as that of Gandhi or no-changers.
Untouchability	• The Swarajists were in full agreement with Gandhiji and no-changers on the issue of untouchability and they extended full support to both Nagpur Congress resolution (1920) and Belgaum Congress resolution (1924) condemning untouchability in all forms and worked towards the elevation of the depressed classes. • Both Swarajists and no-changers worked sincerely to remove the discrimination in the matter of religious worship in temples as evident by their tireless work in the **Vaikom Satyagraha**, Travancore, also popularly known as the first Temple Entry movement. In Vaikom, the reformers satyagraha to secure for untouchables the right to use a public road leading to a Hindu temple received full support from both no-changers and the Swarajists, who not only passed a resolution favouring the reformers cause but also the Belgaum Congress (1924) exhorted the Travancore Government to recognise the justice of the Satyagrahis claim and grant speedy relief, and consequently yielding to the all-round pressure, the government of Travancore removed barricades and supported the cause. • Similarly in Tarakeshwar, Bengal, the no-changers and the Swarajists especially C. R. Das supported the struggle of two religious reformers Swami Viswanand and Swami Sachidanand against the autocracy of a corrupt Mahant. The temple was eventually declared a public property and its doors were opened for worship to all including the depressed classes. • On many occasions, both the Swarajists and no-changers also organised inter-caste dinners to break down caste prejudices while the Swarajists also took every opportunity to vindicate the rights of the depressed classes in the Central Legislative Assembly and the provincial councils.

Constructive Work Field	Approach of No-Changers and Swarajists
Prohibition	• On the issue of prohibition too, the Swarajists and the no-changers were on the same page as both proclaimed their full faith in the policy of prohibition and in fact the Swarajists included 'the enforcement of temperance' as a key agenda in their programme too.
Hindu-Muslim Unity	• Both the no-changers and the Swarajists regarded Hindu-Muslim unity and political education of the masses as *sine qua non* for the attainment of *Swaraj*. As a matter of fact, the Congress resolved in 1926 for the establishment of a permanent publicity bureau for educating the masses on communal amity, and Maulana Azad, Motilal Nehru and Sarojini Naidu were authorised to take necessary steps in this direction.

"It is stated that Khadi alone will, I ask my countrymen in what way is it possible for Khadi to lead us to Swaraj. The Swarajists have no objection to spin and they have over and over again declared their faith in the constructive programme but we strongly resent anything being forced upon us, and we think making hand spinning mandatory for membership is an attempt to exclude us unconstitutionally from the congress executive."

C. R. Das's statement on Gandhi's proposal[24] pressing for a minimum spinning qualification for Congress membership.

"Non-cooperation is a plea, for a change of heart, not merely in the English but in ourselves and therefore it is necessary to revive hand-spinning and hand-weaving on a large scale as it would benefit millions of weavers-pariahs of Indian society."

Gandhiji's views on hand-spinning and hand-weaving.

Significance of Constructive Work

- The constructive work had multi-faceted significance as it not only brought much-needed relief to the poor but also helped in forging a stable bond between the two hitherto unconnected sections, that is, the urban-based upper caste cadres and the rural-based lower caste cadres. Due to the constructive work, the urban-based upper caste cadres became familiar with the conditions of villages and lower castes and the hitherto untouched villagers and lower castes in turn became aware of the national movement and Congress style of politics increasing their faith in organising capacity and self-reliance.

[24] The proposal was defeated at the AICC session at Ahmedabad in 1924 and Gandhiji declared himself to be 'defeated and humbled', and later in November 1924, he came to an agreement with C. R. Das and Motilal Nehru regarding the spinning qualification for Congress membership, which could be fulfilled either personally or by asking a substitute to spin the required 2000 yard and the PCCs were authorised to take proper action against the defaulters. Later, facing huge resistance from the Swarajists, the penalty clause was removed.

- The constructive programme not only provided Congress new political workers or cadres but also provided the Congress organisation effective work during the passive phases of the national movement and helped it increase its base and influence with the hitherto untouched masses.

> *"The constructive work was a major channel for the recruitment of the soldiers of freedom and their political training – as also for the choosing and testing of their 'officers' and 'leaders'. Constructive workers were to act as the steelframe of the nationalist movement in its active Satyagraha phase. It was, therefore, not accidental that khadi bhandar workers, students and teachers of national schools and colleges, and Gandhian ashrams inmates served as the backbone of the civil disobedience movements both as organisers and as active Satyagrahis."*
>
> Bipan Chandra

Emergence of the Socialist and Left Ideas

During the 1920s, owing to the impact of the **Soviet Revolution**[25] of 1917 combined with the growing **dissatisfaction** and **disillusionment** among the younger cadre of nationalists regarding the failure to achieve any substantial gains either by Gandhian ideas and political programme or by Swarajists and no-changers, there was a considerable spread of **Socialist** and **Left**.[26] Ideas inspired many socialist and communist groups to come into existence, thereby resulting in the rise of a socialist orientation and Left wing within the Congress, represented primarily by two young nationalists[27] **Jawaharlal Nehru** and **Subhash Chandra Bose**. In fact, the election of Jawaharlal Nehru as president for 1936 and 1937 sessions of INC and of Subhas Bose for 1938 and 1939 sessions points out to the inclination for the Left-wing tendency within the Congress.

Nehru Versus Bose

Similarities	Differences
• Both were intellectuals by their own rights, coming from an upper middle class background, having also received education abroad. Both were totally committed to the cause of Indian Nationalism and were Socialist in orientation.	• Subhash did not share Nehru's steadfast commitment to Gandhi's leadership of the Congress nor his belief in the usefulness of non-violence as a technique in anti-imperialist struggles.

[25] On 7 November 1917, the Bolshevik (Communist) party, led by V. I. Lenin, overthrew the despotic Czarist regime and declared the formation of the first socialist state which unilaterally also renounced its imperialist rights in China and other parts of Asia. The revolution in which the workers, peasants and the intelligentsia united together overthrew the mighty Czarist empire and established a social order where there was no exploitation of one human being by another instantly attracted the people across Asia as it strengthened their belief in the power of the masses and socialist doctrines, like Marxism the guiding theory of the Bolshevik Party, acquired a sudden attraction.

[26] There is a history associated with the origin of the term 'Left' which also clarifies its meaning. During the period of French Revolution, in the National Assembly of France, there were distinct three groups:

- **The Rightists**: The conservative group who used to sit on the right side of the speaker and who supported the monarch and nobility and did not want to reduce their powers. Later, signified those groups which are opposed to any change in the existing socio-economic order.
- **The Centrists**: The liberals who sat in the centre and who wanted limited reforms of the government. Later, signified those groups who stand for limited changes in the socio-economic order.
- **The Leftists**: The radicals who used to sit on the left side of the speaker and who wanted drastic changes in the system of government. Later, signified those groups which stand for radical reforms in the socio-economic order.

[27] Interestingly, both of these nationalists, that is, Nehru and Bose, never joined the Communist Party of India or Congress Socialist Party.

These young nationalists stressing on the need to combine nationalism and anti-imperialism with **social justice** wanted a more consistent anti-imperialist approach to attain ***purna swarajya***, that is, complete independence. Gradually, workers and peasants parties (WPPs) were organised all over the country and along with them two powerful parties subscribing to Left ideology, the **Communist Party of India** (CPI) and the **Congress Socialist Party** (CSP)[28] emerged which worked alongside the Congress taking up the issues of workers and peasants. A similar inclination towards Socialism was found among the 'revolutionaries' as evident by their rechristening of their organisation as the Hindustan Socialist Republican Association (HSRA) and some other individuals like **Swami Sahajanand Saraswati**, Professor **N. G. Ranga** and **Indulal Yagnik** who worked outside the framework of any organised Left-wing party. The trade unions and peasant movements grew rapidly throughout the 1920s and the socialist ideas became even more popular during the 1930s as the world was engulfed by the great economic depression.

"The Revolution in Russia and its beginning was regarded in India as a triumph over despotism. It had given an impetus to Indian political aspirations."

Impact of the October Revolution on the Indian political atmosphere was admitted even by the official Report on Indian Constitutional Reform (1918).

"It was salvoes fired in revolutionary Russia that brought the message of Communism to India."

Mao Se Dong, the chairman of the Chinese Communist Party and founding father of the People's Republic of China.

Crucial Milestones in the Journey of the Indian Communists

Formation of the Communist Party of India at Tashkent (1920)

- The CPI was formed in October 1920 at Tashkent[29] by M. N. Roy[30], Abani Mukherji and others after the second Congress of Communist International[31].
- In 1922, Roy published his own journal, *The Vanguard*, which later became the mouth piece of the CPI.

Peshawar Conspiracy Case (1922–23)

- Thousands of Muslim *mujahirs* disappointed with British government's attitude towards the Sultan of Turkey, joined M. N. Roy military school at Tashkent. However, immediately upon their return to India, they were caught by the police and tried at Peshawar and were sentenced to rigorous imprisonment.

[28] It was a part of Congress party only and functioned as its Left wing.
[29] Now, the capital of Uzbekistan.
[30] Manabendra Nath Roy whose original name was Narendranath Bhattacharya. He joined the Anushilan Samiti after his expulsion from the high school for participating in the anti-partition movement. Escaping from British authorities, he travelled to many countries including the United States and Mexico and later went to Russia on the invitation of Russian leader Lenin where he helped him evolve the Communist International's policy towards the colonies.
[31] Also called Comintern held in July–August 1920.

Kanpur Bolshevik Conspiracy Case (1924)

- In 1924, a trial of conspiracy case involving four prominent communists – **S. A. Dange**, **Muzaffar Ahmed**, **Shaukat Usmani** and **Nalini Gupta** – was held at Kanpur on the charges of seditious activity against the British authorities and all four accused were sentenced to 4 years of rigorous imprisonment.

Formation of the Communist Party of India at Kanpur (1925)

- In 1925, a number of Left-wing and communist groups came together at **All India Conference of the Communists** held under the presidentship of Singarvelu Chettiar at Kanpur in December 1925 and founded an All India Organisation under the name **CPI**. Thus, the Communist Party was formally constituted on Indian soil and S. V. Ghate was chosen as its general secretary.
- The CPI urged all its members to enrol themselves as members of the Congress and form a strong left-wing within the Congress.

Formation of the Workers and Peasants Party (1928)

- The different provincial organisations of the CPI were renamed as the WPP in 1928:
  - **Labour Swaraj Party** (Bengal, 1925–26): Organised by Muzaffar Ahmed[32], Qazi Nazrul Islam and Hemanta Kumar Sarkar[33];
  - **Congress Labour Party** (Bombay, 1926): Its main organ was Kranti which was published in Marathi.
  - **Kirti Kisan Party** (Punjab, 1926): Included any Ghadar members of 1914 and was headed by Sohan Singh Josh. It brought out two popular journals *Kirti* and *Mihnatkash.*
  - **WPP** (Meerut, October 1928)
- The basic objective of the WPPs was to work within the Congress, to radicalise its program and make it a true '*party of the people*'.
- However, with WPP's pre-occupation with the trade unionism, the agrarian questions did not garner that much attention.

Meerut Conspiracy Case (1929)

- In March 1929, 31 leading communists, trade unionists and Left-wing leaders, including three British Communists[34] – Philip Spratt, Ben Bradley and Lester Hutchinson – were arrested in different parts of the country and brought to Meerut to stand trial for entering into a conspiracy against the British State. Two more were added later to be arrested and tried.
- The Meerut trial went on for 4 years and harsh judgements were pronounced while the trial proved to be a **turning point** in the Indian **communist movement** as the Government could axe the left-wing activity to a considerable extent.
- Congress set up a Central Defence Committee comprising Jawaharlal Nehru, K. N. Katju, M. C. Chagla and M. A. Ansari while Gandhiji visited the prisoners in jail and expressed his solidarity[35] with the communist leaders.
- On contrary to the British expectation of isolating the Communists from the mainstream of national movement, though the Meerut Conspiracy Case did just opposite and familiarised the masses for the first time with communist ideas, it did, however, result in the deprivation of leadership at a crucial juncture of the left movement which suffered an irreplaceable loss.

---

[32] Who brought out a popular magazine Navayug.

[33] Who later gained popularity as a Bengali poet.

[34] Who had come to India to help organise the trade union movement.

[35] However, the Congress enthusiasm on their behalf soon waned after especially the Round Table Conferences, the Delhi statement of 2 November 1929 issued in praise of Lord Irwin and signed by Gandhiji and other Congress leaders including both Nehrus. Ironically, neither Meerut accused nor Bhagat Singh and his comrades figured in the ambit of Gandhi-Irwin Agreement of 1931. In fact, bitterness against Gandhiji went so far that in Calcutta in 1934, the Communists helped to organise a 'League against Gandhism'.

Leftist Deviation (1929)

- After the severe Government repression, the Communists inflicted more deadly blow on themselves by suddenly shifting their political position often termed as 'leftist deviation'.
- Guided by the resolutions of the Sixth Congress of the Communist International, the Communists broke their connection with the National Congress and declared it to be a class party of the bourgeoisie.
- The Communists also dissolved the WPP and instead concentrated their energies on forming of an '*independent and centralised*' communist party.
- As a result of this sudden shift in the Communists political position, they were isolated from the national movement at a very crucial juncture when it was gearing up for its greatest mass struggle and conditions were otherwise ripe for massive growth in the influence of the Left over it. Also, the Communists split into several splinter groups.

Banning of CPI (1934)

- Taking advantage of this situation, the Government declared the CPI as illegal in 1934, thereby forcing the Communists to function underground or under the guise of the Congress and the newly formed **CSP**.
- However, the Communist movement was saved from complete disaster by the active participation of some of its members in the CDM, which aided in the spread of the socialist and communist ideas in the country.

Reorganisation of CPI (1935) and formation of National Front (1935–37)

- Under the guidance of the Seventh Congress[36] of the Communist International and the Dutt-Bradley thesis[37], the Communist Party was reorganised in 1935 under the leadership of **P. C. Joshi**.
- The Communist Party while making a U-turn now radically changed its earlier position of boycotting Congress and instead again decided participate in the activities of the mainstream of the national movement led by the INC forming an anti-imperialist National Front.
- The Communist Party now again began to call upon its members to join the Congress and enrol the masses under their influence to the Congress while many Communists occupied important official positions inside the Congress district and provincial committees. During 1936–42, they built up powerful peasant movements in Kerala, Andhra, Bengal and Punjab and once again recovered their popular image of being the most militant of anti-imperialists.

> *"The greatest class struggle today is our national struggle of which Congress was the main organ."*
>
> P. C. Joshi

> *"Some people think that the participation of the Communist Party in the anti-imperialist united front signifies a weakening of its struggle for the hegemony of the proletariat. This of course, is absolutely incorrect."*
>
> Wang Ming's Report on the Revolutionary Movement in the Colonial Countries (1935).

---

[36] Faced with the threat of fascism, the Seventh Congress of the Communist International meeting at Moscow in August 1935, radically changed its earlier position and advocated the formation of a united front with socialists and other anti-fascists in the capitalist countries and with bourgeois-led nationalist movements in colonial countries.

[37] The theoretical and political basis for the change in communist politics in India was laid in early 1936 by a document popularly known as the Dutt-Bradley Thesis, framed by R. Palme Dutt and Ben Bradley of the British Communist Party. According to this thesis, the INC could play a great part and a foremost part in the work of realising the anti-imperialist people's front. The thesis laid focus on the United Front Strategy, which required the consolidation of the left wing comprising Congress Socialists, Trade Unionists, Communists and Left Congressmen. The document was later supplemented by a direct appeal by Dutt and Bradley in an 'open letter to Indian Patriots'.

The National Front in Crisis (1938–39)

- The growth in the mass influence of the Left proved to be short-lived as once the ministries began to function, the tension between them and the Right wing became increasingly sharper. For instance, in Bihar, the famous Left peasant leader Sahajanand resigned from the working committee of Bihar PCC to free himself for leading peasants struggle against a government which was so openly supportive of the landlords, while even Nehru joined Gandhiji in expressing suspicions that the Kisan Sabhas were undermining the Congress organisation.
- Similarly, in 1938, Gandhiji proposed 'purge' of the Congress, clearly aimed at the Left, and the Delhi AICC asked the Congress ministries to be strong against those who pursed 'class war by violent means'. About the same time, acting under the influence of the mill owners, the Bombay Government introduced the Bombay Industries Disputes Bill against which the trade unions unitedly organised a general strike on 7 November 1938.
- These conflicts led to increasingly strained relations between the Left and the Right, which went for a further toss during the tense re-election of **Subhash Chandra Bose** in Tripuri (1936). But, the Communists as well as the Socialists were not prepared for a total break with the right, for such a break would have meant the end of the National Front, and thus, when the right moved the **Pant Resolution** at Tripuri binding Bose to the 'wishes' of Gandhiji, CSP and the communists tried to avoid a split by not opposing the resolution. However, this episode did disrupt not only the unity of Congress but also the Socialist unity as the Left wing supported by Communists challenged the leadership of Gandhiji while the Gandhi Socialists like Jai Prakash Narayan and Narender Dev affirmed their faith in the Congress and Gandhiji. Similarly, the Communists having distrust in CSP started resigning from it while the CSP leadership being afraid of suffering the fate of Bose's followers began a purge of the Communists. Gradually, the Communists gained control of the leadership of the major mass organisations, the AITUC, AIKS and the All India Students Federation hitherto regarded as being under CSP influence.
- Thus, though the Communist Party now enmeshed as the major force among all the groups of the Left, the anti-imperialist national front was certainly gravely weakened by the dissensions.

Stagnation Years and Substantial Shift (1939–45)

- With the start of World War II and resignation of the Congress ministries[38] along with the imposition of direct British rule, the 1934 ban was imposed more stringently on Communists and their hide and seek with arrests and imprisonments began once again. The result was that by May 1941, almost the entire communist leadership was in jail and the plight was well described by general secretary P. C. Joshi in 1942 that though '*the National Front remained intact ... it did not move forward*'.
- Also with the attack on Soviet Union by Nazi Germany[39] on 22 June 1941, the Communist's characterisation of war changed from that of an '**imperialist war**' **to** '**people's war**'. They quickly made a considerable shift in its long established hostile position against British from a position of confrontationist policy against British Imperialism to treat the British as an ally in the 'People's War'.
- However, interestingly in an ironical twist to the events when the Congress leadership shifted to a policy of confrontation with the British government, leading to the 'Quit India' Resolution, the

[38] On the issue of making India a belligerent country in the World War without consulting the representatives of the Indian people.

[39] Despite Germany's non-aggression pact with Soviet Union.

Communist did not support the resolution resting their case on the call of internationalism, since they felt that the primary need of the world at that hour was defeat of Fascism and not opposition to British.

Anti-Imperialist and Anti-Communal struggle (1945–47)

- As the World War II drew to a close and fall of the Axis power became a matter of time, the communist again shifted back from the strategy of people's war to the strategy of anti-imperialist struggle and thus in December 1945, the CPI Central Committee described the post war period in India as '*the period of unprecedented opportunity to make a final bid for power*'.
- The Communists Party now putting aside its opposition to the INA during the people's war period, treated INA men as fighters of freedom in line with the general national sentiment and in February 1946 organised student strikes combined with industrial strikes while fully supporting the RIN mutiny at Bombay. In May 1946, they also participated in the 'Quit Kashmir' movement of Shaikh Abdullah's National Conference.
- Meanwhile, the Communist-led economic struggle was also intensified and the Tebhaga movement in Bengal initiated in 1944 to reduce the rent to a third of the produce spread to many parts of Bengal during the subsequent 3 years. Similarly, during 1944–46, there were also strikes by the tribal Warlis in Maharashtra against forced labour, high rents and usury. The Communist also provided their support to the uprising of the Telangana peasants against the Nizam and the landlords.
- However, the communists' fight against communalism during this period deserves the special mention as they were clearly the forerunners in denouncing communal hatred and riots. In fact, the Communist Party was perhaps the first political party of any significance to exclude persons belonging to communal organisations and so strong was their communal sentiments that the slightest concessions to communal feelings by a member of the party invited immediate expulsion[40]. The Communists through their periodicals **Langal** and **Ganavani** regularly denounced communal antagonism and during the period of the rising communal tide and the growing strength of the right wing, the CPI gave its support to Nehru and expressed their solidarity with him to build the Indian Republic on secular and democratic foundations.

Congress and Socialism

The seeds of Socialism were sowed in INC by certain Indian intellectuals and militants, who were drawn towards Socialist ideology and had some amount of foreign exposure on account of living in the Western countries like Madame Cama, Shyamji Krishan Verma, Virendra Nath Chattopadhyay, Shapurji Sakhlatvala, Bhupendra Nath Dutta, Lala Hardayal, M. N. Roy and others. But, none of these eminent persons functioned within the framework of the main nationalist organisation of India, that is, the INC, and this explains the absence of any major influence of Socialism on the political behaviour of the Congress till the end of First World War. It was only after the **Non-Cooperation Movement** (1920–22) in the post-World War years that Socialist ideas started influencing Congress policies and played an important role in Indian politics. In fact, only a few early Congress leaders were favourably disposed towards the Socialism, for instance, **Dadabhai Naoroji** was one among such few who had close contact with British Socialists like H. M. Hyndman and who had also attended the **International Socialist Conference** in Amsterdam (August 1904). Similarly, leaders like Bal Gangadhar Tilak and Lala Lajpat Rai were also reported to have maintained some Socialist connections who at times did discuss about the evils of the private property and felt the need for providing equal opportunities for all. But, on a whole the early nationalists did not seriously concern themselves with

[40] Communism: Final stage of history in Marx analysis, which visualises a class less society Socialism: A stage in transition to communism which calls for the dictatorship of the proletariat under whose control resources and wealth can be equitably distributed.

the Socialist ideology probably more because of the fact that Socialism mostly encourages the resistance of the exploited against the exploiters and sets up peasants against landlords, workers against industrialists and thus had the potential to weaken the national unity the Congress was trying to build up in the initial phases. The suspicion against the Socialism was further understandable due to another key fact that most of the early INC leaders came from the upper strata of the Indian society – the Western educated middle class, which included rentiers, professionals and entrepreneurs who could sympathise with the misfortunes of the common man from a distance and that too to the extent their own interests were not threatened. Furthermore, up to the First World War, the INC was engaged primarily in winning concessions from the British authorities through resolutions and representations and had hardly attempted to reach out to the Indian masses[41].

The change came during the post-World War years of economic recession and emergence of Gandhiji who brought the national movement to the masses and enlisted the hitherto neglected categories – the tribals, the peasants, the workers and the women. However, the sudden withdrawal of the NCM resulted in deep frustration and compelled some thoughtful Congressmen, particularly who did not join either the camp of 'no-changers' or the 'pro-changers' to search for an appropriate ideology that could help in the upliftment of the masses along with the attainment of Swaraj. Socialism within the Congress was, thus, born out of this intense intellectual and political exercise.

Formation of the Independence of India League within the Congress (1928)

- In August 1928, Jawaharlal Nehru launched the **Independence for India League**[42] as a pressure group within the Congress with the aim of:
  - Countering the concept of dominion Status[43]
  - Pleading for complete independence of India from the British
  - Working for the establishment of an Indian republic on Socialist lines

Congress Adopts 'Complete Independence' as the Goal (1929)

- At Lahore session of Congress under the presidentship of Jawaharlal Nehru, Congress replaced its earlier goal of 'dominion status' by 'Complete Independence'[44].
- At Lahore only, a tri-coloured flag of independence was hoisted by Nehru on the midnight of 31 December 1929 and nationwide Independence day was subsequently observed on 26 January 1930, but still the content of kind of independence the people would enjoy was not adequately defined.

Congress Resolution on Fundamental Rights and the National Economic Programme (March 1931)

- In March 1931, at the Karachi session of the Congress, an important step in the march towards Congress Socialism was taken with adoption of the Fundamental Rights and the National Economic Program, an answer to the kind of independence Congress would stand for.
- The resolution clearly stated that '*in order to end the exploitation of the masses, the political freedom must include real economic freedom of the starving millions*' and certain crucial demands were raised such as:
  - living wages for workers
  - special taxes on property
  - the state control and ownership of key industries, mineral resources, railways, waterways, shipping and other means of transport

[41] With the solitary exception of the Swadeshi movement (1905–08).

[42] Nehru and Bose were its Secretaries and S. Srinivas Iyengar was its President.

[43] Self-government under the formal supervision of the colonial power.

[44] It is pertinent to note here that just a year before in December 1928, at the Calcutta session, Jawaharlal Nehru and Subhash Chandra Bose had jointly moved a resolution to replace the Congress goal of 'dominion status' by 'Complete Independence'.

Formation of the Congress Socialist Party (October 1934)

- The CSP was an organised group within the Congress party, which aimed at spreading the socialist ideology and strived to give socialist content to the objectives of the Congress.
- It was formed primarily from the sense of despondency generated by the vacuum created by the decline of the CDM when in Nasik Jail (1932–33), the convicts of the CDM like Jaya Prakash Narayan, Achyut Patwardhan, Yusuf Meharally, Ashok Mehta, N. G. Gore, S. M. Joshi and others disenchanted by the Gandhian strategy and leadership as well as by the Communists and attracted by socialist ideology projected the idea of creating a national **CSP** intended to develop as the nucleus of the alternative socialist leadership of the Congress.
- These Congress Socialists were opposed to the willingness of the Congress to participate in legislative Councils and instead wanted Congress to pursue a more revolutionary and a more radical pro-labour and pro-peasant socialist policy in the economic field.
- Eventually, in May 1934, at Patna, the **First All India Conference of Socialists** was convened by Jayaprakash Narayan[45], which was held under the chairmanship of Acharya Narendra Dev and another Conference was held at Bombay in October 1934 where the **CSP** was formally established[46] under the leadership of Jayaprakash Narayan, Acharya Narendra Dev and Minoo Masani to both transform the Congress (at the ideological and organisational level) and to strengthen the Congress (at the mass people level).
- Interestingly, the initial attitude of the CPI towards the newly formed CSP was one of the unreserved hostility and it branded CSP as Social Fascist Party while the CSP was equally disapproving of CPI and was not in favour of the admission of the communists into the CSP.

> *"The Complete independence of India is our goal and by complete independence we mean, India's liberation from British Imperialism and establishment of a Socialist Society with all power to the toiling masses, focus on economic planning, nationalisation of key industries, government's control over foreign trade, abolition of feudalism and landlordism without compensation, redistribution of land and cooperative and collective farming."*
>
> Objective of the Congress Socialist Party.

The Meerut Thesis of the CSP and the CSP-CPI Agreement (1936)

- The Meerut Thesis emphasised on the possibility of a united socialist-communist leadership for attaining socialist unity and for bringing all anti-imperialist forces under one umbrella. Following its Meerut Conference, the CSP revised its Bombay decision of 1934 and invited members from CPI to join the CSP. As a result in no time, both at the central and state levels, prominent communist became office bearers of the CSP. For instance, two communists EMS Namboodiripad and Z. A. Ahmed became All India Joint Secretaries of CSP while in Kerala and Orissa, communists won control over CSP.
- The idea of *an all embracing united front against imperialism with the consolidated forces of the left* was further strengthened at the third Conference of the CSP held at Faizpur and Lucknow Congress held under presidentship of Jawaharlal Nehru in 1936 which ultimately resulted in CSP-CPI Agreement[47] that played a major role in the anti-imperialist upsurge immediately preceding the outbreak of the Second World War.

---

45 There was a Marxist trend led by J. P. Narayan and Narender Dev, the Fabian socialist trend led by Minoo Masani and Ashok Mehta and a Gandhian socialist trend led by Ram Manohar Lohia and Achyut Patwardhan.

46 Interestingly, the initial attitude of the CPI towards the newly formed CSP was one of the unreserved hostilities.

47 The CPI-CSP Agreement, more popularly known as the Lucknow Agreement, also received impetus from the Dutt-Bradley thesis, which had also advocated for a united anti-imperialist front.

- The Agreement helped in the unification of the trade union movement as well as in the development of the Kisan and student movement, both oriented towards the unity of all anti-imperialist forces. Simultaneously, it helped in the emergence of a well-organised left in the Congress organisation and weakening of the hold of the right-wing leadership of INC. In fact, the electoral defeat of Gandhiji's candidate for Congress presidentship, characterised by Gandhiji as his own defeat, was the high water-mark of this developing unity of the left.

"The immediate task before us is to develop the national movement into a real anti-imperialist movement– a movement aiming at freedom from the foreign power and the native system of exploitation. For this it is necessary to wean the anti-imperialist elements in the Congress away from its present bourgeois leadership and to bring them under the leadership of revolutionary socialism. This task can be accomplished only if there is within the Congress an organised body of Marxian Socialists and all other anti-imperialist forces in the country are brought together."

Excerpts from the document adopted at the second national conference of the CSP held in Meerut in January 1936, popularly known as the Meerut thesis.

The Battle Between the Right and the Left in Congress (1939)

- The consolidation of the Leftists and their strength in the wake of the united anti-imperialist front naturally unnerved the right wing, and in 1939, a fierce battle was fought between Right and Left for the post of Congress presidentship in which for a brief period the left emerged successful with the re-election of Subhash Chandra Bose.
- However, the epic battle was soon followed by a still more fierce battle in which the right succeeded in manoeuvring the elected Congress President out of office and cracks started appearing in the anti-imperialist front formed 3 years earlier. So in a way, if the Lucknow congress of 1936 marked the beginning of the united anti-imperialist front in which the Communists and Congress Socialists cooperated with leftist Congressmen, the Tripuri Congress of 1939 was its end.

"We Socialists do not want to create factions in the Congress nor do we desire to displace the old leadership of the Congress and to establish rival leadership. We are only concerned with the policy and programme of the Congress. We only want to influence the Congress decisions. Whatever our differences with the old leaders, we do not want to quarrel with them. We all want to march shoulder to shoulder in our common fight against imperialism."

Jayaprakash Narayan's statement in 1939 after Tripuri.

The Break-Up of United Front (1940–45)

- The months preceding the outbreak of the Second World War and the first years of the War, therefore led to a breakup of the relations between the CSP[48] and the CPI.

Thus, it cannot be denied that during 1920–47, the Congress imbibed a large dose of socialist doctrine, however, the Socialism which emerged in the Congress due to an attempt of a mix up of seemingly different

[48] In fact, at many instances, the CSP proved to be more firmly grounded in the reality of the Indian situation as compared with the Communists as it never carried its opposition to the existing leadership of the Congress to breaking point.

ideologies like **Gandhism**, **Marxism** and **Democratic Socialism** was not as radical as militant Socialists wanted it but it was certainly socialistic in essence.

Congress Socialists	Communists
• Believed in the ideology of Democratic Socialism	• Believed only in Marxist Ideology and Communism and derived inspiration from the Bolshevik revolution of Russia
• Allegiance to Indian National Congress	• Allegiance to the Communist International
• Wanted more radical and egalitarian nature of Congress along with establishment of a socialist state focussing on equality of opportunity	• Wanted establishment of a just state focussing on equality of outcome and advocated radical solutions of political, economic and social crisis while seeking social transformation through a violent struggle against imperialist forces

Nehru and Socialism

Jawaharlal Nehru was the focus of socialist ideas in India particularly after 1929 and it was he who imparted a socialist vision to the national movement along with the notion that political freedom would become meaningful only if it led to the socio-economic emancipation of the masses. His early contact with Socialism was initiated when he came in touch with the peasant's cause in **eastern UP's** Eka movement in 1920–21 and then during 1922–23, when he utilised his jail time to read widely on the history of the Russian and other revolutions. However, opportunity to explore new world views regarding Socialism and its relevance in struggle against a colonial power was better understood by him only in 1926 when he got an opportunity to go to Europe[49].

During his one and a half years sojourn there, he got a splendid opportunity to interact with best exponents of the European radical tradition, as well as leading Socialist political thinkers, and eventually by all these interactions and exchange of views, he could appreciate the essence of Socialism in a much better way. In 1927, he was invited to participate as the representative of the INC in the International Congress against Colonial Oppression and Imperialism, held at **Brussels**, and was later appointed as a member of the Executive Committee of the League Against Imperialism and for National Independence, an organisation set up by the Brussels Conference. The same year, on an official invitation, he visited the Soviet Union and was greatly impressed by the novel experiments in governance and the new socialist society. By now, he had begun to accept Marxism in its broad contours and by the time he returned to India in December 1927, he had for all practical purposes turned into a Socialist as described in the words of his biographer S. Gopal, 'a self-conscious revolutionary radical'.

"I must frankly confess that I am a Socialist and a republican and am no believer in kings and princes or in an order which produces modern kings of industries .... the philosophy of Socialism has permeated the entire structure of society the world over, and almost the only points in dispute are the pace and the methods of advance to its full realisation. India will have to go that way too, if she seeks to end her poverty and inequality, though she may evolve her own methods."

Jawaharlal Nehru's presidential address at the Lahore Session of the Congress (December 1929).

[49] Though primarily for obtaining medical relief for his ailing wife, Kamala, in Switzerland.

Later, in 1928, Nehru joined hands with Subhash Chandra Bose to organise the **Independence of India League** for achieving the twin aims of achieving complete independence and 'a socialist revision of the economic structure of society'. In fact, in his presidential addresses at the Lahore Session of the Congress (1929), Nehru reiterated his belief in Socialism and asked his fellow Congressmen to accept[50] it with open hands. It would not be an exaggeration to assume that it was mainly due to Nehru's persuasive delineation of the theme of Socialism that AICC adopted a landmark[51] resolution regarding Socialism in 1929 clearly stating that '*the great poverty and misery of the Indian people was not only due to the foreign exploitation but also due to the prevalent economic structure of the society and thus in order to remove poverty and gross inequalities, it was essential to make revolutionary change in the present social and economic structure of society*', while at the Karachi session in 1931, it was mostly on Nehru's insistence only that an important resolution focussing on fundamental rights and economic programme was passed by the Congress. His commitment to Socialism found a much clearer and sharper expression during 1933–36 when during his presidential address at Lucknow Session[52] (June 1936) or Faizpur Session (December 1936), he defined his admiration to Socialism in clear, unequivocal and passionate words. At Faizpur session, he inducted three key Congress Socialists: J. P. Narayan, Narender Dev and Achyut Patwardhan into the **Congress Working Committee** and under socialist orientation led Congress to adopt agrarian programme that included reduction of rent and revenue, lowering of canal irrigation rates, abolition of feudal dues and levies, fixing of tenure, moratorium on debts and provision of cheap credit facilities, statutory provision for ensuring living wage and suitable working conditions for the agricultural labourers.

> *"I am convinced that the only key to the solution of the world's problems and of India's problems lies in socialism, and when I use this world I do so not in a vague humanitarian way but in the scientific, economic sense. ... I see no way of ending the poverty, the vast unemployment, the degradation, and the subjection of the Indian people except through socialism. That involves vast and revolutionary changes in our political and social structure. That means the ending of private property, except in a restricted sense, and the replacement of the present profit system by a higher ideal of cooperative service."*
>
> Jawaharlal Nehru's presidential address at the Lucknow Congress.

However, during the World War II, the political movement to win freedom assumed greater importance, and Nehru's attention, time and energy were devoted more to the cause of political freedom and, after the war, to the negotiations for Independence, which testifies that for Nehru, the cause of the national independence was far superior to the cause of socialist movement. It is, therefore, pertinent to note that Nehru's commitment to Socialism was given within a framework that recognised the primacy of the political, anti-imperialist struggle over the socialist revolution. He wanted to influence and transform the Congress as a whole in a socialist

[50] Though the Right-wing members of the Congress Working Committee resigned in protest against Nehru's support for the cause of Socialism. It is often alleged that it was wealthy industrialists who had engineered the revolt of the working committee with an intent to control and check Nehru whose socialist inclination was posing a threat of class struggle by the working class.

[51] It was landmark in the sense as till now, the Congress leaders believed that the pathetic condition of the masses was due to foreign rule but, henceforth, they could understand and appreciate that the gross inequalities and economic structure of the society also adds to the great poverty and misery of Indian masses, which are also supported by the alien rulers in a bid for continuation of their exploitative rule.

[52] Just a few days after the Lucknow Congress, A. D. Shroff of Tatas fired off a refutation of Nehru's speech and three weeks later, on 18 May 1936, 21 leading Bombay businessmen issued what came to be known as the '***Bombay Manifesto***' against Nehru. Among the signatories were Sir N. Saklatvala, Sir Purshottamdas Thakurdas, Sir Chimanlal Setalvad, Sir Pheroze Sethna, Sir Cowasji Jehangir, Walchand Hirachand, Dharamsey Khatau and A. D. Shroff. The '***Bombay Manifesto***' openly opposed the preaching of socialist ideals. It is pertinent to note here that Bombay Manifesto was different from Bombay Plan, which was actually formulated during World War II, when in January 1944, a small group of influential business leaders in Bombay drew up a plan for the economic development of India.

direction but in spite of the fact that he had basic differences with the majority of congress leadership[53] including Gandhiji, he never entertained the idea of leaving the Congress. One of the probable reasons behind this was the fact that he was convinced that splits and factions would weaken the national movement (that is, Congress) and thereby needs to be avoided at all costs.

"I felt it would be injurious in the interests of India and our cause for me or you to create this definite split."

Excerpts from Jawaharlal Nehru's letter which he wrote to Subhash Chandra Bose when differences between Subhash and Gandhiji were deepening after the Tripuri Session.

"I have been and am a convinced socialist and believer in democracy, and have at the same time accepted whole heartedly the peaceful technique of non-violent action which Gandhiji has practised so successfully during the past 20 years. I am convinced that the strength can only come from the masses but that strength, either for struggle or for the great work of building a new world, must be disciplined and orderly. It is not out of chaos or the encouragement of chaotic forces that we can fashion the India of our dreams."

Nehru's declaration in February 1938.

Also, though Nehru differed[54] with Gandhiji on multiple issues and often described him as an '*extraordinary paradox*', still at many instances it is evident that his loyalty and devotion[55] to Gandhiji led him to surrender his intellectual convictions. His concept of Socialism was diluted under the impact of Gandhi's ideas of class harmony and collaboration, trusteeship of property and peaceful methods of social change. Thus, even though he accepted the essentials of Marxism and appreciated Soviet Russia and its system of economic planning, under Gandhian impact he did not accept Communist methods and even gave secondary position to the concept of class struggle. Deeply convinced that '*Socialism without democracy would mean tyranny in India*', Nehru was clearly devoted towards evolving a set of principles and ideas to achieve a socialist reconstruction of society with democratic means rather than a violent revolution. Furthermore, in his assessment of the existing Indian situation, any radical transformation was not easily possible because of the compulsions of the objective situation since the Indian masses at that time were deep rooted in superstition, religion fanaticism and ignorance while class distinctions had not yet been crystallised in India as industrial labour or the proletariat was confined to a few industrial centres only and peasantry was conservative lacking even social consciousness. Thus, it would not be wrong to assume that Nehru essentially remained a socialist at the intellectual level but under influence of his liberal outlook, belief in democracy and faith in non-violence along with his loyalty towards Gandhiji, he could never reconcile his philosophy with

[53] Specifically the Right-wing of the Congress.

[54] He criticised Gandhiji for refusing to recognise the conflict of classes, for preaching harmony among the exploiters and the exploited and for putting forward the theories of trusteeship and conversion of the capitalists and landlords.

[55] At multiple occasions, Nehru defended Gandhiji against his Left-wing critics. He contended in an article written in January 1936 that '*Gandhiji has played a revolutionary role in India of the greatest importance because he knew how to make the most of the objective conditions and could reach the heart of the masses, while groups with a more advanced ideology functioned largely in the air. At the same time, he fully appreciated the radical role that Gandhiji had played and was playing in Indian society as Gandhiji's actions and teachings had inevitably raised mass consciousness tremendously and made social issues vital*'.

the total philosophy of Socialism. Nevertheless, Nehru did succeed in making following significant advances on socialist front:

- On the **agrarian question** (by contributing to the formulation of a liberal Faizpur Congress Agrarian Programme, which included items such as the reduction of rent and revenue, introduction of cooperative farming, provision of cheap credit, abolition of feudal dues and levies and living wages for agrarian labourers)
- On the issue of **Constitution** (by highlighting the demand for an elected Constituent Assembly)
- On the question of **civil liberties** (by ordering the Congress provincial ministries to release all political prisoners)
- On **responsible government** (by championing the cause of the Praja Mandal[56] movement in the Indian States against the tyranny of their rulers)
- On the worldwide campaign against Fascism, the worst form of imperialism (by taking the side of '*forces of progress*' in the Spanish Civil War, by protesting against the Italian attack on Ethiopia and by organising relief for China when it was attacked by Japan).

Nehru did try to inject Socialism in the innermost core of the Congress and tried to bridge the gap between village-oriented, humanitarian, non-violent creed of Gandhism and the industry-oriented scientific notions of Socialism.

Subhash Chandra Bose and Socialism

Subhash Chandra Bose was a dynamic socialist leader and a true champion for the cause of Left unity. From the late 1920s, he tried to unite the forces of the Left within the Congress consisting of the organised sections of the students, youth, peasants, workers and the socialists. In fact, in 1928 in collaboration with Nehru and S. Iyengar, he founded the **Independence of India League**, which for the first time made a declaration for reconstruction of Indian society on the basis of economic equality. The League served as a pressure group and created awareness about the socio-economic issues among the other Congress leaders and made them realise that the creed of nationalism by itself was inadequate and the Congress should give due emphasis to socio-economic requirements of the masses.

> *"We can no longer make any progress by the cry of Swaraj only. We must make it clear that we aim at economic and social swaraj as well as political and for this purpose we must lay down a definite economic and social programme."*
>
> Independence for India League.

At the Calcutta session of the Congress in 1928, he along with Nehru fought against the move for dominion status as the goal of the Congress and moved amendment to the official resolution for complete independence. Though the resolution in 1928 was defeated, but just a year later, with the complete support of Subhash and under the presidentship of Nehru, the resolution for complete independence was passed at the 1929 Lahore session of the Congress. In the meantime, true to his Left credentials, Bose also became the leader of the trade unions, particularly the Tata Workers Union at Jamshedpur and was elected as the President of the All India Trade Union Congress (AITUC). Later, in July 1931, he presided over its All India Conference in Calcutta.

[56] Peoples movement in Princely Indian States demanding democratic setup.

In fact, it was because of the left support that Bose could win the Presidential election for Congress twice – Haripura (1938) and Tripuri[57] (1939) – and it was at Tripuri he reiterated his proposal[58] of the Jalpaiguri Session of the Bengal Provincial Congress Committee, wherein he had suggested that an ultimatum of six months be given to the British Government, and if after the expiry of this period, the British Government did not leave India, the final struggle by the people of India would start in all places.

> *"I must give clear and unequivocal expression to what I have been feeling for some time past, namely that the time has come for us to raise the issue of Swaraj and submit our national demand to the British Government in the form of ultimatum and give a certain time limit; if no reply is received within this period, or if an unsatisfactory reply is received, we should resort to sanctions like mass civil disobedience or Satyagraha and the British Government today is not in a position to face a major conflict like an all India Satyagraha for a long period."*
>
> Excerpts from Subhash Chandra Bose's presidential address at Tripuri (1939).

However, Bose's suggestion was not approved by the majority of the delegates at Tripuri who did not consider that the time was ripe for giving a call for the struggle. Further deadlock was created by the Pant Resolution[59] and Subhash now cornered by the Congress Working Committee and having failed in his efforts for a compromise with Gandhiji ultimately resigned from the presidentship of the Congress on 29 April 1939. He then formed a separate party, the **Forward Block**, a platform for all the leftists in the Congress who were willing to join him for preparation for an anti-imperialist struggle and undertook an extensive tour of the country with the clarion call to the people to get themselves ready for the struggle. With the outbreak of the Second World War on 3 September 1939, Bose immediately convened an Anti-Imperialist Conference at Nagpur and gave a call 'to utilise the situation'. In addition to the Forward Bloc, he also formed the Left Consolidation Committee[60] to rally all left forces behind his programme for the struggle.

> *"The Forward Bloc stands for uncompromising national struggle, for the attainment of Independence and for the post struggle period, socialist reconstruction."*
>
> Subhash Chandra Bose

Subhash left his Socialistic mark on the Congress by laying emphasis on the industrialisation of India and planned economic growth on the Soviet pattern. It was in fact only Bose only who in 1938 as the president of

[57] The election at Tripuri was a keenly contested one between Subhash Chandra Bose and Pattabhi Sitaramayya. The Congress rightists backed by Gandhiji were not in favour of Bose and instead wanted Sitaramayya to win, but with support from Left and CSP leaders Bose could defeat Sitaramayya by securing 1580 votes as compared to 1375 got by Sitaramayya.

[58] It is pertinent to note here that the Quit India resolution passed by the AICC at its session on 8 August 1942 in Bombay under Gandhi's direction was nothing but the same resolution of 6 months ultimatum passed at Jalpaiguri Session of the BPCC in February 1939 under the leadership of Bose and reiterated later by him in his Tripuri speech.

[59] The re-election of Bose as the President of the Congress in 1939 was never accepted by the Right-wing leaders with grace who were determined not to accept him for the second term. Just after the results of the re-election, the AICC Working Committee resigned including Nehru who though actively tried to bring about a rapprochement between the two factions and it was owing to his efforts that the Pandit Govind Ballabh Pant Resolution was passed which aimed at a reconciliation and acceptance of Gandhiji leadership. As per the terms of this resolution, Subhash was directed to form the Congress Working Committee on the advice of Gandhi.

[60] Having Forward Bloc, CSP, CPI, Kisan Sabha, Labour party, Radical Democratic Party of M. N. Roy.

the Congress set up the National Planning Committee with Nehru as its Chairman and initiated the beginning of economic planning in India.

> *"Industrialisation is necessary for solving the problem of unemployment. Though scientific agriculture will increase the production of land, if food is to be given to every man and woman, a good portion of the population will have to be transferred from land to industry. Secondly, the rising generation is now thinking in terms of socialism as the basis of national reconstruction, and socialism presupposes industrialisation. Thirdly, industrialisation is necessary if we have to compete with foreign industries. Lastly, industrialisation is necessary for improving the standard of living of the people at large."*
>
> Reply of Subhash Chandra Bose when asked about his views on industrialisation

Important Socialist Book/Journal/Pamphlet	Author
• *Why Socialism*	Jaya Prakash Narayan
• *Gandhi and Lenin*	S. A. Dange
• *The Socialist*	S. A. Dange
• *Navayuga*	Muzaffar Ahmed
• *Langal*	Nazrul Islam and Muzaffar Ahmed
• *Inquilab*	Ghulam Hussain
• *Labour Kisan Gazette*	M. Singaravelu

Critical Analysis of the Left and Socialist Movement

Leftism in India, thus, developed along two main streams of ideologies: Communism and Democratic Socialism. Communism was the projection of Communist International movements, whereas Democratic Socialism represents the tradition of Fabian Socialism[61]. The effect of this synthesis was that the Left movement in India over time evolved a broad common political programme comprising of:

- consistent policy of anti-imperialism and anti-landlordism
- acceptance of a socialist programme for the economic and social transformation of society
- organisation of workers and peasants in trade unions and Kisan Sabhas.

Significance of the Left and Socialist Movement

The Left and Socialist Movement did succeed in leaving a basic imprint on the Indian society and politics.

- Under the influence of Left, the Congress as a whole[62] received a strong Left orientation, which resulted in the reframing of its strategy regarding freedom, equality and justice. Due to the Socialist influence, the Congress, including its Right-wing, accepted that the poverty and misery of the Indian people was the result not only of colonial domination but also of the internal socio-economic structure of Indian society

[61] According to tenants of Fabian Socialism, Socialism was not an alternative to the present socio-economic system but was necessary to make society more liberal for which they laid emphasis on peaceful means.

[62] That is, both on political and ideological levels.

which had, therefore, to be drastically transformed. The impact of the Left on the national movement can clearly be ascertained by the passage of the resolution on **Fundamental Rights and Economic Policy** by the Karachi session of the Congress in 1931, the resolutions on **economic policy** at the Faizpur session in 1936, the **Election Manifesto** of the Congress in 1936 and the setting up of a **National Planning Committee** in 1938.

> *"Indian nationalism was powerfully pushed towards vital social changes, and today it hovers, somewhat undecided, on the brink of a new social ideology."*
>
> Jawaharlal Nehru

- Another significant achievement of the Left and Socialist Movement was in terms of giving voice and platform to hitherto politically backward classes such as peasants and workers. The Left provided immense support in the foundation and organisation of the WPPs, the All-India Students Federation, the Progressive Writers Association along with convening the first All-India States People's Conference in 1936.
- Another key achievement of the Left and Socialist Movement was that they were firm secularists, who repeatedly denounced communalism in every form and underlined at multiple occasions that they prefer the economic basis of the class identity[63] instead of any other social basis of the identities while aspiring to transcend communal divisions through class solidarity. Perhaps, both CPI and CSP were the first political parties of any significance to exclude membership to persons belonging to any communal organisation as evident by the restriction imposed on Hasrat Mohani and S. D. Hasan to quit the Muslim League in 1927, characterising the dual association as splintered consciousnesses and treating the case of K. N. Joglekar for having association with Brahmin Sabha in the same way.

However, while it can be argued that the ideology of Leftism and Socialism made a major impact over the Congress and its other affiliated organisations like the CSP, the Left movement in India did suffer from certain limitations.

Limitations of the Left and the Socialist Movement

The Left and Socialist Movement failed in the most basic task it had taken upon itself, that is, to establish the dominance of socialist ideas and parties over the national movement. Several reasons can be attributed for the same:

- **Alien Loyalty** and **Isolation from the mass anti-imperialist struggle**: The Left did the mistake of according more importance to their ties with Comintern than the public sentiment while their isolation from the mass anti-imperialist struggle can be attributed to primarily three factors:
    - First, they suffered for a long time from Left sectarian errors and were unable to understand the reality of the Indian scenario in totality as they took recourse to a simplistic model of analysing Indian social classes and their political behaviour. The Left considered the dominant Congress leadership as bourgeois and its policy of negotiations with British Government as merely working towards a compromise with imperialism, and due to their this misconception, they could not participate in the mass demonstrations organised by the Congress which proved to be a grave mistake on their part.

[63] However, 1945 onwards, the Adhikari thesis and subsequent position of CPI regarding its support to the question of right to self-determination for nationalities created serious confusion regarding its communalist stance. Having insisted on class identity, the CPI was questioned for having taken this kind of position, which *prima facie* contradicted the economic basis of class identity.

- Second, the Left living in their illusionary world instead of concentrating on the nature of mass involvement and mobilisation and ideology constantly counterposed the armed struggle to non-violence as a superior form and method of struggle.
- Third, the Left did not possess sufficient forces independently to organise a powerful anti-imperialist movement.

- **Erratic strategy and dogmatic policy**: Another limitation of the Left parties was its erratic strategy of invariably fighting with the dominant Congress leadership on wrong issues and failure on its part to show ideological and tactical flexibility. For instance, its most serious charge against the Congress Right-wing was that it was frightened of mass struggle and its anti-imperialism was not wholehearted because of bourgeois influence over it. The right-wing had little difficulty in disposing of such charges and the people rightly believed it and not the Left.
- **Lack of unified leadership and factional struggle**: Another major weakness of the Left was the failure of the different Left parties, groups and individuals to work unitedly except for short periods. All efforts at forging a united front of left-wing elements ended in frustration as evident by the lack of coordination among CSP and CPI along with drifting apart of Nehru and Bose after a few years of togetherness. The inevitable result was a long-term schism between the Socialists who suffered from an anti-Communist phobia and Communists who saw every Socialist leader as a potential bourgeois ultimately leading to serious trust issues among them.

The Peasant Movements During the 1920s

The period between 1920 and 1946 witnessed the emergence of several peasant organisations and peasant movements that were both deeply influenced by the national movement and in their turn also had a marked impact on the ongoing struggle for national freedom. At times, the political liberalism of the INC and particularly Gandhiji's methodology of passive resistance formed the basis of these movements while some peasant organisations emerged out of the growing Left and Socialist ideology. In general, the peasants movements and organisations of this era tried to address the following grievances of the peasants:

- In many regions, the peasants had no occupancy rights on the lands tilled by them while on the contrary, the landlords were having the absolute power to evict their tenants and arbitrary ejectments or *bedakhali* were clearly norm of the day for a majority of the cultivators.
- Besides the regular exorbitant taxes payable to the landlords, the tenants were compelled by the landlords to pay illegal levies like 'nazranas[64]', 'adwabs' and other gifts on different pretexts.
- The heavy burden of the land revenue made the peasantry heavily indebted to the village landlords and moneylenders who charged heavy interest rates, which often made it difficult for the poor peasants to get out of the debt trap.

It is pertinent to note here that in almost all the peasants movements, the peasants themselves were not demanding abolition of rent or landlordism, instead what they only wanted was an end to illegal levies, ejectments and exorbitant rents – the demands that were widely supported by the national leadership. During the 1920s and 1930s, primarily three important peasant struggles can be recounted: the ***Kisan Sabha*** and **Eka** movements of Avadh in Uttar Pradesh, the **Mappila** rebellion of Malabar, the **Bardoli** *Satyagraha* of Gujarat and the Formation of **All India Kisan Sabha** (AIKS).

[64] A sort of renewal fee charged illegally by the landlords. According to the provisions of the Awadh Rent Act XXII of 1886, there was a check on the power of landlord to enhance the rent, that is, not to enhance the rent by more than 6.25 per cent after the expiry of the statutory period. However, to defeat the main provisions of the Act, the landlords started the practice of '*nazrana*', that is, after the expiry of 7 years, before a fresh lease could be granted by the landlord, the tenant was required to pay heavy *nazrana* for his fresh entry else the land was leased out to a new tenant who was willing to meet the landlord's demands.

The Kisan Sabha and Eka Movement of Avadh, UP

The history of the peasant movement in the province may be traced back to 1920–21 when the first expressions of peasants discontent with the existing legal framework and the oppressions from the taluqdars and zamindars in the form of exorbitant rents, illegal levies like *nazrana, hari or begar*[65] and arbitrary ejectments or *bedakhli* were witnessed during the course of the Non-Cooperation Movement of the INC leading even the nationalists to take note of the problems faced by the peasantry. The high price of food and other necessities that accompanied and followed World War I made the oppression all the more difficult to bear, and the tenants of Avadh started demanding greater **tenurial security** and **fair rents**.

The initial credit for initiating the process of the organisation of the peasants of the province on modern lines into *Kisan Sabhas* goes to members of the Home Rule League in UP and through the efforts of more active members like **Gauri Shankar Misra**, **Indra Narain Dwivedi** and **Madan Mohan Malaviya**, the UP *Kisan Sabha* was set up in February 1918, and its popularity can be gauged by the fact that by June 1919 it had established at least 450 branches in 173 tehsils of the province. The UP *Kisan Sabha* also demonstrated its capability of generating political awareness among the peasants as evident by the fact that a large number of *Kisan* delegates from UP attended the Delhi and Amritsar sessions of the INC in December 1918 and 1919.

In the middle of 1920, **Baba Ramchandra**[66] demonstrating considerable leadership and organisational skills emerged as the leader of the peasants of Avadh and played pivotal role in establishment of **Oudh *Kisan Sabha***[67] at Pratapgarh on 17 October 1920. He attempted a systematic organisation of the Kisan Sabha and took the lead in expanding the base of the *Kisan Sabha* movement while incorporating Kisans belonging to both high and low castes in its ranks along with sensitising the influential political leaders of Allahabad Gauri Shankar Misra and Jawaharlal Nehru about the miserable conditions of the tenants. As a result of Baba's efforts, both Nehru and Misra made several visits to the rural areas and developed close contacts with the *Kisan Sabha* movement. They along with a conscientious Deputy Commissioner[68] of Pratapgarh district started motivating the peasants to file complaints regarding illegal levies like '*nazrana' and* '*bedakhli*', and were able to eventually thwart the evil intentions of landowners by adopting a pro-tenant stance. This easy victory, however, gave a new confidence to the movement and it burgeoned forth while the popularity of Baba Ramchandra reached new heights[69]. In fact, in their first big show of strength, roughly 1,00,000 peasants attended a rally held at Ayodhya on 20 and 21 December, and to symbolise the oppression of the Kisans, Baba Ramchandra turned up bound in ropes. Emboldened by the enthusiastic response of the peasants, the Oudh *Kisan Sabha* urged the *Kisans* to refuse to till *bedakhli* land or to offer *hari* and *begar*, to boycott those who did not accept these conditions and to solve their disputes through panchayats.

However, the peasant movement of 1920–21, which began as a pacific movement, underwent a marked change and burst into agrarian riots in early 1921. The centres of militant activity, which included the looting of bazaars, houses, granaries, raiding of houses of the landlords and the moneylenders, along with the clashes with the police were primarily located in the Central UP comprising of the districts of Rae Bareli, Faizabad and Sultanpur. The Government, however, had little difficulty in suppressing these outbreaks of violence, and

---

[65] Forms of unpaid labour.

[66] Baba Ramchandra was a Maharashtrian Brahmin, who was a wanderer and had left home at the age of 13, done a stint as an indentured labourer in Fiji and finally turned up in Faizabad in Uttar Pradesh in 1909. Till 1920, he had wandered around as a *sadhu*, carrying a copy of Tulsidas *Ramcharitmanas*, from which he would often recite verses to rural audiences and utilised the same for awakening and mobilising peasants against the exploitation of *taluqdars* and the British authorities.

[67] Which basically emerged as an alternative to the UP Kisan Sabha. This new body succeeded in integrating under its banner all the grassroots *Kisan Sabhas* that had emerged in the districts of Avadh in the past few months and through the efforts of Misra, Jawaharlal Nehru, Mata Badal Pande, Baba Ramchandra, Deo Narayan Pande and Kedar Nath, the new organisation brought under its wing, by the end of October, over 330 *Kisan Sabhas*.

[68] Mr Mehta.

[69] In fact, when Baba Ramchandra was arrested by the British government in August 1920, numerous peasants, almost about 60,000, flocked to the court compound demanding his release.

the movement faded out by mid-1921 due to the repressive policy[70] of the Government. In the meanwhile, to contain the agrarian unrest and redress the immediate grievances of the peasants, the Government came forth with the **Oudh Rent (Amendment) Act[71] of 1921**, and though it brought little relief to the tenants, it did rouse the hopes of the tenants and in its own way assisted in the decline of the movement.

However, in late 1921 and early 1922, the peasant discontent[72] re-surfaced in Avadh, but this time the centres were located in the northern part of the province mainly involving the districts of Hardoi, Bahraich and Sitapur where serious challenges were posed to the authority of landlords and the administration. The movement grew under the name of the **Eka**[73] or **Unity** where the initial thrust was provided by Congress and Khilafat leaders. Later, the movement came under the influence of radical peasant leader **Madari Pasi** and some other low-caste leaders who were not particularly inclined to accept the discipline of non-violence urged by the Congress and Khilafat leaders. Consequently, the movement's contact with the nationalists gradually decreased and after some time it went its own way. By March 1922, however, owing to severe repression on the part of the British authorities, the Eka Movement was brought to its end. It is pertinent to note here that unlike the earlier ***Kisan Sabha* movement** that was based almost solely on tenants, the **Eka Movement** included in its ranks many small zamindars who found themselves disenchanted with the Government because of its heavy land revenue demand.

The UP peasants became active again around 1928 when on an extensive scale Kisan sabhas begin to be formed and no-tax campaign was launched during the CDM.

The Mappila Rebellion of the Malabar Region (1921)

As you may recall, we have earlier discussed about the Mappila uprising of the 19th century wherein the **Mappilas**[74] have registered their protest and resistance against the acts of oppression and exploitation by both *Jenmis*[75] and British officials. The Mappila rebellion was, thus, peculiar from the point of view of a resistance movement having its genesis due to the intermingling of religion and economic grievances. Equally interesting is the fact about Mappila rebellion that despite brutal suppression in 19th century, there were as many as **25** unorganised, isolated and sporadic instances of Mappila resistances occurring on same common issues of agrarian discontent till 1921 but what erupted in 1921 was on a different scale together.

The 1921 Mappila peasant rebellion in the Malabar region[76] basically revolved around three key issues: the long pending grievances of Mappila peasants related to agrarian economic oppression such as high rents, lack of security of tenure, renewal fees and other oppressive landlord exactions along with assertions by the

---

[70] The crowds were fired upon and dispersed, leaders and activists arrested and cases were filed against them.

[71] The main provisions of the Act were:

- The statutory period of tenancy was raised from 7 to 10 years and every resident tenant was given a life tenure, subject to revision of rent after the period of 10 years, either by a written agreement between the landlord or the tenant as sanctioned by the settlement officer,
- A roaster year system was evolved for the determination and sanction of fair and equitable rent rates for each district by a special officer every tenth year,
- The payments under 'nazrana' were illegal and the tenant was entitled to compensation and
- The landlord was given extensive powers for the acquisition of holdings from his tenant for the purpose of his own cultivation and for agricultural development.

[72] The main grievance of the peasants was related to the extraction of a rent that was generally 50 per cent higher than the recorded rent, the oppression of *thekedars* to whom the work of rent collection was farmed out and the practice of share rents.

[73] All the Eka meetings were marked by a specific religious ritual in which a hole that represented the river Ganges was dug in the ground and filled with water, a priest was brought in to preside and the assembled peasants 'owed that they would pay only the recorded rent but pay it on time, would not leave when ejected, would refuse to do forced labour, would give no help to criminals and abide by the panchayat decisions'.

[74] The Muslims of the Malabar Coast are called Mappilas in local dialect.

[75] The big Hindu landowners.

[76] The northern Kerala.

Mappila peasants regarding their tenacy rights[77] culminating ultimately in rebellion against the *jenmis*, the anti-colonial and anti-imperialist struggle and the support extended to the defence of the Turkish *Caliphate* by the Mappila under the sway[78] of the Khilafat movement.

> *"'The Mappila rebellion was complicated by the fact that religion played abiding role in mobilising Mappila pesantry and the religious idiom expressed the anti-landlord and anti-British sentiments."*
>
> K. M. Pannikar's views in his book *Against Lord and State: Religion and Peasant Uprisings in Malabar.*

The impetus for resistance first came from the Malabar District Congress Conference held at Manjeri in April 1920. This conference along with adopting a policy of progressive Non-Cooperation Movement with the Government also extended its support to the tenant's cause and demanded legislation[79] to regulate landlord-tenant relations. The Manjeri conference was followed by the formation of a **tenant's association** at Kozhikode and soon tenant's associations were set up in other parts of the district.

Simultaneously, the Khilafat Movement influence was also on rise in Malabar region and local Khilafat committees were formed in various parts of Malabar. Disturbed by the growing popularity of the tenant-cum-Khilafat agitation, which had received considerable impetus from the visits of Gandhiji, Shaukat Ali and Maulana Azad, the Government issued prohibitory notices on all Khilafat meetings on 5 February 1921, and subsequently on 18 February, all the prominent Khilafat and Congress leaders like Yakub Hasan, P. Moideen Koya, U. Gopala Menon and K. Madhavan Nair were arrested, which immediately resulted in the leadership passing into the hands of the local Mappila leaders who were not wholly committed to the cause of non-violence while the movement now spread to grassroot levels and drew greater support for the cause of non-cooperation.

The Mappilas angered by the repression and emboldened by the rumours that the British[80] were no longer in a position to take strong military action began to exhibit increasing signs of turbulence and defiance of authority. However, the things went from bad to worse on 20 August 1921 when the District Magistrate of Eranad *taluq*. E. F. Thomas accompanied by a contingent of police and troops raided the mosque at Tirurangadi to arrest **Ali Musaliar**, a highly respected priest and a local popular Khilafat leader. Though the police found and arrested only three fairly insignificant Khilafat volunteers from the premises, within no time rumour spread that the famous Mambrath mosque had been raided and destroyed by the British authorities. This was enough to provoke a rebellion and soon Mappilas from Tanur, Kottakkal and Parappanagadi converged at Tirurangadi to secure the release of the arrested volunteers. A clash ensued between the people and the authorities and many Mappila peasants were killed leading to the rebellion turning violent and its further spread to the Mappila strongholds, the *taluqs* of Eranad, Walluvanad and Ponnani.

In the first stage of the rebellion, the targets of attack were the **unpopular *jenmies*** and the **symbols of Government authority** such as the treasuries, offices, courts, police stations and estates of British planters. However, at this stage though the relations between the two communities were strained, the rebellion did

[77] Apart from a very high revenue demand, the Mappilas had to contend with rapacious *jenmies* whom, contrary to customary practices, the British had recognised as the sole proprietors of land, with the right to evict tenants, thereby clearly upsetting the traditional tenurial relations existing between the landlords, that is, the *jenmies*; intermediary tenant, that is, the *Kanakkaran*, and the actual cultivator, the *verumpattakaran*.

[78] The Mappilas belonging to the Muslim community had a stronger reason to rally round the Khilafat issue than the Hindus.

[79] This change was significant because earlier the Congress had rarely taken such a pro-tenant stand and till now the lobby of landlords had successfully prevented it from committing itself to the tenants cause.

[80] Weakened as a result of the World War.

not have communal overtone, as the lenient Hindu *jenmies* and poor Hindu peasants were rarely touched by the Mappila rebels. Eventually, there was utter disorder and chaos across Malabar district and realising the collapse of civil authority, British proclaimed Martial law in the district. But, with the increasing brutal repression by the government authorities, the character of the rebellion underwent a significant change and hostile communal passions were roused resulting in increased incidents of attacks on Hindu population, forcible conversions and destruction of life and property. Thus, what had started largely as an anti-government and anti-landlord affair acquired strong communal overtones and created not only a wedge between the two communities but also distanced it from Congress. The recourse to violence and communalisation by the peasants created a wide gap distance between them and the national movement.

"Although the rebellion was not intrinsically communal, its consequences were decidedly so."

K. M. Pannikar views in his book *Against Lord and State: Religion and Peasant Uprisings in Malabar.*

The official reaction of the Congress was not in favour of the rebels as after the violent and communal rebellion, the Congress Working Committee in a formal resolution expressed its sense of deep regrets over the acts of violence committed by the Mappilas in certain areas of Malabar though it also condemned the repressive actions of the Government in the name of maintaining peace and order. The AICC also expressed its firm conviction that the Non-Cooperation and Khilafat movements was in no way responsible for the violent outbreak. With the isolation of Mappilas, it did not take long for British to suppress the rebellion and by December 1921, all resistance by Mappilas had come to a halt. However, the repression that followed the suppression was very brutal. According to official estimates alone, around 3989 Mappila rebels had lost their lives, though the real figures were much higher[81]. Some died in hellish torture as the 70 who suffocated to death in a closed wagon in which they were transported. More than 40,000 were arrested and imprisoned for long periods. In fact, due to this ferocious repression, the Mappilas were so completely demoralised and crushed that till independence their participation in any form of politics was almost nil as they neither joined the national movement nor the peasant movement that was to grow in Kerala in later years under the Left leadership.

Bardoli Satyagraha (1928)

As you may recall, during the Non-Cooperation Movement, the Bardoli *taluq* of Surat district in Gujarat was meant to be the site of the launching of the CDM with the initiation of a no-tax campaign but events in Chauri Chaura changed all that and the campaign never took off as the movement was withdrawn. However, due to the preparations for the CDM and intense constructive work[82] carried on by the local leaders **Kunverji Mehta**[83], **Kalyanji Mehta** among the Patidars community and **Dayalji Nanubhai Desai** among the Anavils community, a distinctive change regarding increased political awareness among the local population was

[81] According to some unofficial estimates the figures were placed around 10,000.

[82] In 1922, Gandhiji rebuked the local leaders of Bardoli that they had done nothing for the upliftment of the low-caste untouchable tribal inhabitants popularly known as the *Kaliparaj* (meaning dark people) who mostly provided agricultural labour. Taking the Gandhian criticism to heart, the local leaders started constructive work among the *Kaliparaj*. In fact, for the education of the tribals, Kunverji Mehta and Keshavji Ganeshji learnt the tribal dialect and developed a '*Kaliparaj* literature', which contained poems and prose that aroused the *Kaliparaj* against the exploitative *Hali* system under which they were laboured as hereditary labourers for upper-caste landowners popularly known as *Ujaliparaj* (fair people). The local leaders also exhorted the tribals to abjure intoxicating drinks and high marriage expenses which led to financial ruin.

[83] Founded Patidar Yuvak Mandal in 1908 to raise the educational level of the Patidars and to discourage social evils like child marriage and dowries.

witnessed. So in January 1926, when the *taluq* revenue official[84] recommended a 30 per cent increase over the existing assessment hardest hitting the landed class or *Khatedars* as they were called consisting of Patidars, Anavil Brahmins and Baniyas, a good deal of social mobilisation against the proposed enhancement had already taken place. The Congress leaders sensing the mood of the people were quick to protest against the increase and set up the **Bardoli Inquiry Committee** which after a through enquiry concluded that the increase was unjustified. The sensitisation against the proposed increase was followed by an intensive campaign in the Press, with the lead taken by the journals *Young India* and *Navjivan* edited by none other than Gandhiji. The issue was also taken up with the Government by the members of the Legislative Council and thus eventually in July 1927, the Bombay Government reduced the enhancement to 21.97 per cent.

But the concessions announced were too meagre to satisfy anybody and the stage was set for the starting of a no-revenue campaign. A meeting of representatives of 60 villages was convened at Bamni in Kadod division which formally invited **Vallabhbhai Patel**, the president of the Gujarat Congress Committee to lead the campaign. The Bardoli Satyagraha was thus launched on 4 February 1928 by Sardar[85] Vallabhbhai Patel, with the blessings of Gandhiji. Patel immediately set up an effective and highly efficient organisational machinery and had a series of meetings with the local leaders, following which a resolution was passed advising all peasants to not pay the revised land revenue until the Government appointed an independent tribunal or accepted the current amount as full payment.

Known for his impeccable organisation skills, Sardar Patel divided the *taluq* into 13 workers camps or *Chhavanis* each under the charge of an experienced leader. The top leadership consisted of about 150 trained political workers drawn from all over the province, assisted by 1,500 volunteers recruited from the peasantry, many of whom were students. For the mobilisation of the peasants, extensive propaganda via meetings, speeches, pamphlets and door-to-door persuasion was carried out. Also, the *Kaliparaj* community extended their full support to the Satyagraha mostly owing to the work done by the local leaders among the *Kaliparaj* people which paid rich dividends during this movement and the Government was totally unsuccessful in its attempts to use them against the upper caste peasants.

To establish communication with every stratum of society, a publications bureau was set up which brought out the daily Bardoli Satyagraha *Patrika*. This Patrika which was distributed to the farthest corners of the *taluq* by the army of volunteers updated the masses about the latest reports about the Satyagraha, speeches of the leaders along with the pictures of the *jabti* or confiscation proceedings. Interestingly, the organisational machinery also had its own intelligence wing, whose job was to find out about the indecisive peasants[86] and secure information about Government moves, especially of the likelihood of *jabti* (confiscation) to warn the villagers to lock up their houses or flee to neighbouring Baroda.

To galvanise the peasant masses into militant action groups, Sardar Patel also made effective use of caste councils[87] and caste symbols by appealing to their caste pride and traditional value systems. Special emphasis was also placed on the mobilisation of women, who often outnumbered men at the meetings and stood firm in their resolve not to submit to Government threats. In fact, Bardoli Satyagraha did provide many women activists like **Mithuben Petit**, a Parsi lady from Bombay, **Bhaktiba**, the wife of Darbar Gopaldas, **Maniben Patel**, the Sardar's daughter, **Shardaben Shah** and **Sharda Mehta** finest opportunity to be in contact with the political momentum of the day and later many of these activists proved their worth in the struggle for independence and attained new heights of popularity.

---

[84] Mr Jayakar, the officer charged with the duty of reassessment of the land revenue.

[85] It was the women of Bardoli who gave him the title of *Sardar*.

[86] The members of the intelligence wing would shadow them night and day to see that they did not pay their dues. Also, those who showed signs of weakness were brought into line by means of social pressure and threats of social boycott.

[87] Those who opposed the movement had to face the prospect of being refused essential services from sweepers, barbers, washermen and agricultural labourers and of being socially boycotted by their kinsmen and neighbours while the Government officials faced the worst of this form of pressure as they were refused supplies, services and transport and found it almost impossible to carry out their official duties.

Sardar Patel also made constant efforts to take along both the moderate leadership and the public opinion with the Satyagrahis on all important issues. Consequently, the Government soon found even its supporters and sympathisers, as well as impartial men, deserting its side. For instance, showing their solidarity for the Satyagrahis, the representatives of the Indian Merchants Chamber and Bombay Legislative Council members **K. M. Munshi** and **Lalji Naran** resigned their seats. In fact, by July 1928, the Viceroy, Lord Irwin, himself casted doubts about the correctness of the Bombay Government's stand and started putting pressure on Governor Wilson to find a graceful way out since uncomfortable questions had started appearing in the British Parliament as well.

A judicial enquiry was initiated under judicial officer, **Broomfield**, and a revenue officer, **Maxwell** who both concluded that the increase was indeed unjustified and reduced the enhancement to 6.03 per cent. Later, owing to public pressure, the confiscated lands were returned and for some time being, the revenue revisions were abandoned.

"The report of the Committee constitutes the worst rebuff which any local government in India has received for many years and may have far-reaching results... It would be difficult to find an incident quite comparable with this in the long and controversial annals of Indian Land Revenue."

Excerpts from an article in *The New Statesman* of London published on 5 May 1929.

"Whatever the Bardoli struggle may be, it clearly is not a struggle for the direct attainment of Swaraj. That every such awakening, every such effort as that of Bardoli will bring Swaraj nearer and may bring it nearer even than any direct effort is undoubtedly true."

Gandhiji's statement on Bardoli Satyagraha.

Formation of All India Kisan Sabha (1936)

The second phase of the peasant movement was initiated again with the revival of No-Rent Campaign as a part of CDM in the 1930s and with the increasing influence of **Socialist** and **Communist** ideas among the peasantry. By 1920s already provincial Kisan Sabhas were formed in different regions. However, a strong need was felt for a central organisation of the peasants dedicated towards their economic and political empowerment which ultimately culminated in the formation of **AIKS**[88] at Lucknow in April 1936. **Swami Sahajanand Saraswati**, who was the founder of Bihar Provincial Kisan Sabha (BPKS) and pioneer of Bihar Kisan Sabha Movement, was the first President of the AIKS while **N. G. Ranga** who was the founder of the Andhra Provincial Riots Association was its General Secretary. Some other prominent leaders of the AIKS were **Narendra Dev**, **Indulal Yagnik**[89], **Ram Manohar Lohia**, **Jaya Prakash Narayan**, **Sohan Singh Josh** and **Bankim Mukherjee**. Subsequent noteworthy sessions of the AIKS were held at Faizpur[90] in December 1936, Comilla in May 1938, Gaya in April 1939, Bakhna Kalan in 1943 and Bezwada in March 1944. It is also pertinent to note that till 1941, AIKS included all sections of the agrarian population (except landlords) in its conception of 'peasant' and strongly emphasised for peasant unity, but from 1942, due to the dominance of Communists influence in AIKS, the problems of rural proletariat[91] acquired more significance than those of rich and middle peasants.

[88] Was earlier known as All India Kisan Congress.

[89] Edited a periodic bulletin of AIKS.

[90] Interestingly, first two sessions of AIKS were held at the same place as that of INC, that is, 49th session of INC held in June 1936 at Lucknow and 50th session of INC held in December 1936 at Faizpur, under the presidentship of Nehru where efforts were done by the Congress to adopt the agrarian programme on the basis of a Kisan Manifesto finalised at the All India Kisan Committee, which also became the part of Congress Manifesto for the 1937 elections.

[91] Proletariat is Karl Marx's defined social class signifying the people who live by their labour and are often exploited by the *bourgeoisie* (the capital owners).

Objectives of the Kisan Sabha
• Agrarian reform and the protection of the peasants from economic exploitation • The abolition of landlordism, such as Zamindari, Taluqdari and Jenmi systems • Reduction of revenue, rent and taxes • Moratorium on debts • Licensing of moneylenders • Minimum wages for agricultural labourers • Fair price for commercial crops • Irrigation facilities

Like the glorious tradition of AIKS, other provincial peasant organisations under able leadership of AIKS conducted a relentless struggle against feudal oppression and played a leading role in the freedom movement. Some of the prominent provincial peasant organisations are as follows:

Provincial Peasant Organisation	Achievements
Bihar Provincial Kisan Sabha (BPKS)	• One of the significant regional peasant organisations was BPKS which was started under the able leadership of Swami Sahajanand around 1928–29 when the economy was heading towards the depression and the political ferment, which finally led to the nationwide Civil Disobedience Movement that had just begun. • With the reluctance on part of Bihar Congress to start a 'no-rent campaign' or to demand rent remissions for tenants, BPKS parted company with the Bihar Congress in 1932 and got engaged in a fervent campaign against landlordism, against landlord tenant compromises and in defence of the occupancy rights of tenants. • In 1934, many Congress socialists joined BPKS, which gave the organisation a more socialist orientation while from 1941 onwards with the increasing influence of CPI, the organisation became more radical and the Gandhian techniques of non-violent resistance were discarded to be too inefficient to attain radical changes in the agrarian structure. • One of the successful agitation launched by BPKS was the ***Bakasht* Movement** in 1937–39 and again in 1946–47 in South Bihar which was mainly against the landlords and the forced eviction of tenants by them. '**Bakasht**' meant 'self-cultivated' and referred to those lands which formerly belonged to the tenants but were grabbed by the landlords for arrears of rent during the bleak years of depression (1929–34). However, even after eviction, the tenants were allowed to till the lands as share croppers. The issue started when during their term in office the Congress Government passed restoration of Bakasht Land Act 1938 which restored these lands to their former owners if it was proved that they still tilled the land. Fearing that this would provide permanent rights to the tenants, the landlords began to evict their tenants, and to protest against the same, the BPKS initiated the *Bakasht* agitation which spread to many villages in Monghyr (under the leadership of **Karyanand Sharma**), Gaya (under the leadership of **Yadunandan Sharma**), Saran (under the leadership of **Jamuna Karjee**) and Sahabad districts.

Provincial Peasant Organisation	Achievements
Bengal Provincial Kisan Sabha	• Like BPKS, Bengal Provincial unit also exercised considerable influence in the region and perhaps was one of the most successful provincial peasant organisations in terms of mobilising the peasantry right from the days of WPPs. • In Burdwan district, Kisan Sabha organised a satyagraha movement for the reduction of Canal Tax which was imposed on the peasants after the construction of the Damodar Canal. As a result of their agitation, the Government was forced to partly accept the demands and the movement was thus withdrawn. • In north Bengal district, Kisan Sabha launched the ***hat tola*** movement which was basically aimed against landlords collecting a levy from the peasants who sold rice, vegetables, cattle in fairs and hats (weekly markets). • In 1946–47, the **Tebhaga struggle** was launched under the guidance of the Kisan Sabha by the share-croppers locally called '*Bargadars*' to retain a two-thirds share of the produce from land for themselves and to store the crop in their own *khamars* (godowns), also recommended by the Bengal Land Revenue Commission, popularly known as the Floud Commission. The movement meant to reduce the amount of rent the share-croppers paid to the class of rich peasants popularly called '*Jotedars*' unlike the other Indian peasant movements marked by dominant Gandhian passive resistance that was radical in approach and reflective of the outgrowth of Left orientation on rural masses.
Andhra Provincial Kisan Sabha (APKS)	• As the BPKS, the mobilisation of peasantry in Andhra began in 1928–29 and gathered momentum during the years of economic depression and nationwide campaign for the Civil Disobedience. • The 'Andhra Provincial Ryots Association' was first founded by **N. G. Ranga** and **M. B. Naidu** in 1928 at Guntur which primarily aimed at preventing revenue enhancements, promoting revenue remissions, famine relief and agricultural credit on liberal terms. • The APKS also organised frequent long peasant marches to raise awareness about the agrarian issues.
Telangana	• **Telangana Movement** (1946–51) signified the peasant movement under a princely state and was directed by the Telangana tribal peasants against the Nizam of Hyderabad officials, jagirdars, that is, big landlords and moneylenders who exploited the tribal peasants by charging high rents, indulging in forced evictions and coercing them to do Vethi (forced labour). The movement which received enormous support from Praja Mandal Organisation and Communist party was also classified as the biggest peasant guerrilla war in modern Indian history.

Kerala	• In Malabar, *Karshaka Sanghams*, that is, peasant associations were established which mainly demanded:
	  • Abolition of feudal levies or *akramapirivukal* and renewal fees or the practice of *policceluthu* and Advance rent
	  • No eviction of the tenants by landlords
	  • Reduction in the tax, rent and debt burden
	  • Use of proper measures by landlords to measure grain rent
	  • End to the corrupt practices of the landlords managers
	  • Amendment of the Malabar Tenancy Act of 1929.

Provincial Peasant Organisation	Achievements
Punjab	• In the princely state of Punjab, one of the most powerful movement emerged in Patiala wherein the peasants demanded restoration of the lands to the peasants illegally seized by a landlord-official nexus through various forms of deceit and intimidation. The muzaras (tenants) refused to pay the batai (share rent) to their biswedars (landlords). This struggle continued intermittently till 1953 when legislation enabling the tenants to become owners of their land was passed. • The peasants were led by Left leaders like Bhagwan Singh Longowalia and Jagir Singh Joga and in later years by Teja Singh Swatantar.

The Congress and the Peasantry

Although, the whole history of the peasant movement has been strongly nationalist in outlook and the peasants and the Congress have frequently worked together in struggle against the colonial rule while the Congress was equally concerned about the peasant issues and the grievances of the peasantry, the relations between the two have not always been uniform and harmonious.

> *"The outstanding problem of India is the peasant problem. All else is secondary."*
>
> Jawaharlal Nehru

During the formative years of the peasant movement, the Congress leaders realising the importance and strength of the peasantry as a collective group did embark on political awakening of the peasants and worked towards peasant mobilisation in most of the provinces notably Bihar, Bengal, Gujarat, United Provinces, Central Provinces and Madras. However, they were not in favour of a separate organisation and urged them to work through Congress but the peasant leaders while eager to work with the Congress felt that certain sections within the Congress notably the right-wing leaders who represented the dominant social groups and were afraid of the growing class consciousness of the Indian peasant and of the demand of the Kisan Sabha for the abolition of the landlordism were intentionally neglecting peasants' problems taking the side of rich peasants and were thus not effectively working towards the peasants' cause. Consequently, the peasant bodies demanded a separate organisation for addressing their grievances on their own and it was precisely for this reason that the Kisan Sabha stated that '*though it could work with Congress on specific issues it could not endorse every action of Congress*'. The formation of the AIKS further increased the discord between the peasant leaders and the conservative or right elements in the Congress party who viewed the formation of AIKS as a challenge to the Congress organisation. Meanwhile, the peasant leaders were equally critical of the Congress Ministries failure to take a positive stand on questions of agrarian reform and gradually the peasant movement drifted towards the Communist ideology. Nevertheless, the Congress and the peasantry did work together on agrarian issues and for the cause of India's freedom.

Comparative Analysis of the Peasant Movements of 19th and 20th Century

The nature of peasant movements between the 19th century and the 20th century did change and evolve due to the natural progression emerging between the movements on account of increased political awareness among the peasants, the emergence of Congress as a mass-based political organisation and the spread of the socialist and communist ideas.

Characteristics of 19th Century Peasant Movements	Characteristics of 20th Century Peasant Movements
• The 19th century movements were directed towards specific and limited objectives and redressal of particular grievances related to local economic issues. The immediate target of the movement was not Colonialism and the struggles were mostly directed against the foreign planters, zamindars and moneylenders. The movements were comparatively less organised and less diverse in terms of participation.	• The 20th century peasant movements combined the local issues with the national ones and brought the peasants into the broader struggle against colonialism beginning with **Champaran**, **Kheda** and later **Bardoli** movement. The peasant movements not only became more organised and diverse in their participation but there was also an emergence of anti-colonialism consciousness among peasant.
• The leadership in these movements were from the peasantry itself as in the case of the Indigo Revolt (1859–60), Pabna agrarian disturbances in the 1860s and 1870s and Deccan Riots.	• The peasant movements during this period were led by Congress, Socialist and Communist leaders who came from either well-to-do middle peasant families or the urban middle class professionals and intelligentsia.
• The territorial reach was limited to a particular local region and the movements lacked the intensive mobilisation carried out in the later movements.	• The territorial reach of the peasant movements was widened to an all India level, specifically after the emergence of AIKS. Extensive mobilisation was carried out through holding Kisan conferences and meetings where demands were raised and resolutions were passed.
• The peasant movements during this period lacked any formal organisation which actually inhibited the formation and continuity of long-term strategy.	• The peasants during this period were organised in different organisations like WPPs, Provincial Kisan Sabhas and AIKS.
• The peasant movements during this period lacked any coherent ideology and there was absence of any alternative ideas about the future of these movements since most of the movements were just spontaneous reaction of the exploited peasantry.	• The peasant movements during this period were based on the ideology of nationalism and generally vacillated between the polarities of Gandhism on the one hand and Marxism-Leninism on the other. However, after 1941, the peasant organisations moved gradually away from Gandhian approach and came near to Marxism.

Significance of the Peasant Movements

- While it is true that the peasant movements did not register immediate successes but still one of the most significant contribution of the peasant movements was that they **created the climate** which **necessitated the post-Independence agrarian reforms**, for instance, *zamindari* abolition did not come about as a direct culmination of any particular struggle, but the AIKS certainly contributed to its achievement by intense popularisation of this demand among the masses.

- It is another crucial achievement of the peasant movements that the struggles based on the demands raised by these organisations did corrode the power of the landed classes in many ways and thus prepared the ground for the transformation of the structure itself, although it is also pertinent to note here that the peasant movements were clearly not aimed at the overthrow of the existing agrarian structure but towards alleviating its most oppressive aspects.
- Another significant factor about the growth and development of the peasant movement was that they were indissolubly linked with the freedom struggle and often occupied common ground complementing each other as the areas where the peasant movement was most active like Uttar Pradesh, Bihar, Andhra, Punjab and Kerala were usually the ones that had been drawn into the earlier national struggles while the politicised and conscious peasantry formed the backbone for the national movement. The peasant movements across diverse regions were based on the common ideology of nationalism and its cadres and leaders not only promoted the organisation of the peasantry but also tenants of national freedom.

Working Class Movements

With the slow beginnings of modern industry and the growth of utilities like the post and the telegraph network along with the railways, the **working class** gradually registered its appearance on the national scene in the second half of the 19th century in terms of spontaneous, sporadic and unorganised collective action[92]. However, in the initial stages, the collective action was more on the account of workers seeking redressal towards immediate economic grievances, oppression and exploitation than having any wider political implications. But, gradually with time the process of the disparate groups of workers emerging as an organised, self-conscious class got inextricably linked with the growth of the Indian National Movement. The growth of the working class movements vis a vis the national movement can be traced primarily in six phases:

Phase I: Initial Phase of Lukewarm Response by the Early Nationalists (1870s–1900)

In the initial phase, there were mostly sporadic attempts on the part of few philanthropist individuals who being moved by the miserable condition of the workers tried to improve their working conditions. For example, **Sasipada Banerjee**, a Brahmo Social reformer in Bengal, founded the Workingmen's Club in 1870 and brought out a monthly journal called Bharat Sramjeebi (Indian Labour) in 1874 and organised night schools for educating the jute mill workers. Similarly, at Bombay **N. M. Lokhanday** brought out an Anglo-Marathi weekly called Dina Bandhu[93] in 1880 and founded the Bombay Millhands Association in 1890 which took the initiative of forwarding some minimum workers' demands to the Bombay Factory Commission such as reduction in working hours, a weekly holiday and adequate compensation for injuries suffered by the workers during work at the factories. Similarly, in 1878, **Sorabjee Shapoorji Bengalee** tried unsuccessfully to introduce a Bill in the Bombay Legislative Council to limit the working hours for labour.

However, it is pertinent to note here that all these efforts were admittedly of a philanthropic nature by certain individuals who did not belong to the mainstream contemporary national movement and by no means represented the beginnings of an organised working class movement. The **mainstream nationalist movement** was still largely indifferent to the question of labour as the early nationalists paid relatively little attention to the wretched conditions of the workers, and quite strikingly[94], the early nationalists adopted a

---

[92] Which included agitations and strikes by workers in the textile mills of Bombay, Calcutta, Ahmedabad, Surat, Madras, Coimbatore, Wardha and in the Railways and in the Plantations.

[93] Meaning Friend of the Poor.

[94] Though perhaps understandably.

differential attitude towards the workers employed in Europeans enterprises and those employed in Indian enterprises. Also, at this stage most of the nationalist newspapers except *Mahratta*[95] protested against any sort of Government legislation for regulating the working conditions and actively opposed the passing of Factories Act of 1881 and 1891.

One of the probable reasons for the relatively lukewarm attitude of early nationalists towards labour issues in the initial years was due to fact that the anti-imperialist movement was still in its infant stage and the early nationalists were apprehensive that any divisions within the ranks of the Indian people on the basis of classes would ultimately weaken the common struggle against colonial rule. Thus, unfortunately in the name of an anti-imperialist united front, the unity was sought at the unilateral cost of the workers while not much effort was undertaken to secure concessions from the powerful propertied class.

> *"The Congress must confine itself to questions in which the entire nation has a direct participation, and it must leave the adjustment of social reforms and other class questions to class Congresses."*
>
> Dadabhai Naoroji's statement at the second session of the INC (1886).

Gradually, with the national movement gaining in strength and with the emergence of pro-labour ideological trends within the nationalist ranks, certain efforts were now being made to organise labour and secure for them a better bargaining position vis-a-vis the more powerful propertied classes. However, still at this stage, the nationalists were unwilling to take up the question of labour vis a vis the indigenous employer and the strikes in their enterprises generally did not elicit same kind of support that was extended in case of strikes by Indian labour employed in European enterprises[96].

> *"This differential attitude was partially because the employer and the employed were not part and parcel of the same nation."*
>
> Statement of P. Ananda Charlu, Congress president in 1891.

Phase II: Swadeshi Upsurge and Initiation of Political Involvement (1900–08)

The Swadeshi upsurge of 1903–08 was a distinct landmark in the history of the working class movement as not only the various segments of workers classes recognised the 'power of organisation' but even nationalists specifically Swadeshi leaders like B. C. Pal, C. R. Das, Liaqat Hussain and G. Subramania Iyer strongly acknowledged and promoted the ideology of **unions** and **strikes** to protect the workers' interests against the powerful employers. Four Swadeshi leaders, however, stand out in terms of their dedication towards the cause of the working class movement: **Ashwini Kumar Banerjee**, **Prabhat Kumar Roy**, **Chowdhuri**,

[95] Then under the influence of the radical thinker, G. S. Agarkar, which even at this stage supported the workers cause and asked the mill owners to make concessions to them.

[96] It was not fortuitous, then, that perhaps the first organised strike by any section of the working class occurred in British-owned and managed railway, the signallers strike in May 1899 in the Great Indian Peninsular (GIP) Railway wherein the demands were raised related to wages, hours of work and other conditions of service and it received support from prominent nationalists like Pherozeshah Mehta, D. E. Wacha and Surendranath Tagore and almost all nationalist newspapers.

Premtosh Bose and **Apurba Kumar Ghose**, who all enthusiastically threw themselves into the tasks of organising trade unions, a number of strikes and fund collection drives to support the labour movement.

Though the first tentative attempts to form all-India unions were also made at this time but these attempts were unsuccessful, however, during the Swadeshi days, there was a considerable shift in terms of the nature of the working class movement from being relatively unorganised and spontaneous strikes on economic issues to organised strikes on economic issues with greater involvement of the working class with the wider political issues of the day along with enhanced support from the nationalists. For instance, on the day the partition of Bengal came into effect, that is, on 16 October 1905 there was numerous working class strikes and hartals across Bengal. Similarly, when the famous Swadeshi leader Chidambaram Pillai and Subramania Siva were arrested, there were widespread strikes and riots in Tuticorin and Tirunelveli in Tamil Nadu. Likewise, in Punjab as a part of the 1907 upsurge, the arsenal and railway engineering workers went on strike while in Maharashtra one of the perhaps biggest political demonstration by the working class happened during the famous Tilak's trial and his subsequent conviction.

During the Swadeshi period, due to the exposure to the contemporary Marxist and social democratic forces and working class movement in Russia, there was also faint beginnings of a **socialist orientation** among some of the radical nationalist leaders and workers; however, the differential attitude towards workers employed in European enterprises and those in Indian ones still persisted throughout this period. Gradually with the decline in the nationalist mass upsurge after 1908, the labour movement also suffered an eclipse and it was only after post World War I years that the working class movement regained its élan, though now on a qualitatively higher plane.

Phase III: Formation of AITUC

Post World War I, there was a resurgence of working class activity mostly on account of the momentum generated by the Home Rule Leagues, Rowlatt *Satyagraha* and the Non-Cooperation and Khilafat Movement of 1920. The working class now started getting involved in the mainstream of nationalist politics to a significant extent[97] while also gearing towards establishing its own national level organisation for taking forward the workers cause. Two events in 1918, however, had special significance in terms of working class movement: the first was the **formation of the 'Madras Labour Union'** in April 1918 by B. P. Wadia[98], which in effect was the first trade union in India, which even though was regional in character did galvanise the imagination of labour leaders across country, while the second event was the strike of the Ahmedabad textile workers under the able leadership of Gandhiji[99]. Simultaneously, during 1919–20, there was a wave of strikes in many industrial centres such as Calcutta, Bombay, Madras, Kanpur, Jamshedpur and Ahmedabad. Thus, with the basic groundwork laid out for the establishment of a national organisation, the **AITUC**[100] was formed in 1920 at Bombay with Lala Lajpat Rai as its first President and Dewan Chaman Lal as its General Secretary. The inaugural session was attended by several prominent leaders[101] and trade unionists like **Joseph Baptista**, **B. P. Wadia**, **B. G. Tilak**, **C. R. Das**, **Subhas Bose**, **C. F. Andrews**, **J. M. Sengupta**, **Satyamurti**, **Annie Besant**, **M. L. Nehru**, **Jawaharlal Nehru** and **N. M. Joshi**.

[97] For instance, in April 1919, following the repression in Punjab and Gandhiji's arrest, the working class in Ahmedabad and other parts of Gujarat resorted to strikes, agitations and demonstrations while waves of working class protest rocked Bombay and Calcutta.

[98] A close associate of Annie Besant.

[99] It also led to the formation of a trade union, the Ahmedabad Textile Labour Association (ATLA), which was founded on the Gandhian principles of trusteeship, cooperation between labour and management, conciliation and arbitration.

[100] The formation of AITUC was further hastened due to the founding of the International Labour Organisation (ILO) in 1919 and due to the provision in ILO Constitution which required workers delegates to be chosen from the most representative labour organisation in member countries.

[101] Interestingly, Gandhiji was averse to the formation of AITUC and even asked the ATLA members also to not join AITUC.

"Indian labour should lose no time to organise itself on a national scale... the greatest need in this Country is to organise, agitate, and educate. We must organise our workers, make them class conscious...."

Excerpts from Lala Lajpat Rai's presidential address to the first AITUC.

"It was to be a Swaraj, not for the capitalists but for the workers."

Dewan Chaman Lal

"India ... has ... been bled by the forces of organised capital and is today lying prostrate at its feet. Militarism and Imperialism are the twin-children of capitalism; they are one in three and three in one. Their shadow, their fruit and their bark all are poisonous. It is only lately that an antidote has been discovered and that antidote is organised labour."

Lala Lajpat Rai's statement linking capitalism with imperialism.

Also, a marked change was emerging in the nationalist attitude towards labour employed in Indian enterprises, and reflecting the same, the INC at its Gaya session in 1922 welcomed the formation of the AITUC and also formed a committee consisting of prominent Congressmen to assist in its work while on the other hand the workers too were getting involved in the national movement in big numbers. It is noteworthy to add here that although strikes became frequent in the 1920s, growth of trade unionism among the workers was rather slow[102]. However, after 1922, again there was a lull in the working class movement as evident by the workers' reversion to purely economic struggles and it was only towards the end of the 1920s that the next wave of working class activity registered its presence under the significant influence of Left movement.

Phase IV: Influence of Left Wing on Working Class Movements (1927–29)

Since 1922 with the spread of the Communist and Socialist ideas, the working class gradually came under the influence of radical ideology and the workers participated in a large number of strikes and demonstrations all over the country between 1922 and 1929. By early 1927, under communist influence, various **WPPs** were organised in different parts of the country led by Left leaning people like **S. A. Dange**, **P. C. Joshi**, **Muzaffar Ahmed** and **Sohan Singh Josh**. Eventually, the Communist influence on the working class movement, which was only marginal till early 1927, had become very strong by the end of 1928. The historic 6-month-long general strike by the textile workers in Bombay from April–September 1928 under the command of the Communist led Girni Kamgar Union (GKU) clearly establishes the strong hold of left ideology over the trade union movement. On the same lines, numerous workers meetings were also organised on May Day, Lenin Day and the anniversary of the Russian Revolution.

[102] The Royal Commission on Labour gave two probable reasons for the same:

- Differences of language and community were factors that stood in the way of workers unity. For instance, in Bengal Jute Mills, the majority of the workers came from Bihar and Uttar Pradesh and Bengali workers were in minority.
- The Employers and the Jobbers (also known as *Sardars* in eastern and western India who generally do recruitment of the labour) were opposed to the growth of trade unions.

> *"There was hardly a single public utility service or industry which had not been affected in whole or in part, by the wave of communism which swept the country."*
>
> Excerpts from Government Report in 1928.

Due to this coming together of the nationalist and the Left trends and increased political involvement of the working class, the Government came down with a heavy hand on the Communists and enacted repressive laws like the Public Safety Act and Trade Disputes Acts along with arresting in one swoop virtually the entire radical leadership of the working class movement in the famous **Meerut Conspiracy Case**. Meanwhile, from the end of 1928, the Communists reversed their policy of aligning themselves with and working within the mainstream of the national movement and thus due to both the Government offensive and the shift in the stance of the Communists, the working class movement suffered a major setback and due to their hold over, the working class was greatly reduced. In fact, the reduction in the membership of the GKU from 54,000 in December 1928 to about 800 by the end of 1929 speaks for itself.

Phase V: Split in the AITUC (1929–35)

During the Great Depression period, when hundreds of factories closed down and thousands of workers lost their jobs, there was also a considerable decrease in the number of trade unions. The working class movement was further weakened by the two splits within the AITUC which took place during the same period. The first split happened in 1929 on the issue of boycott of the Royal Commission on Labour between the moderate faction of AITUC and the extremist faction. The moderate section led by V. V. Giri wanted to join the Commission while the extremists wanted to boycott the same. Finally, the moderates left the AITUC and formed the **ITUF** (Indian Trade Union Federation). The second split took place in 1931, when the communists left the AITUC and formed the **Red Trade Union Congress** resulting in further dip in the working class movement between 1931 and 1936 when neither did the workers take an active part in the CDM of 1932–34 nor any worthwhile strike was organised by them.

Phase VI: Restoration of Unity and Resurgence of Left Ideology

Meanwhile, the Communists abandoned their suicidal sectarian policies and re-enacted the mainstream of nationalist politics since 1934 and, subsequently, the unity in the AITUC was restored in 1935. The Left influence in nationalist politics and the trade union movement once again began to grow rapidly, and the Communists, the Congress Socialists and the Left nationalists led by Jawaharlal Nehru and Subhas Bose now formed a powerful Left consolidation within the Congress and other mass organisations.

The next wave of working class activity came with provincial autonomy and the formation of Congress ministries during 1937–39 when a phenomenal rise was noticed in the **trade union movement** owing to increased civil liberties and the pro-labour attitude of the Congress Governments. For instance, between 1937 and 1939, the number of trade unions increased from 271 to 362 and the total membership of these unions increased from 2,61,047 to 3,99,159 while there was a considerable increase in the number of strikes too. Even during the World War II, several strikes on economic issues were organised across the country but with the Nazi attack on the Soviet Union in 1941, the Communists again changed their stance and dissociated itself from both from the Quit India Movement[103] launched by Gandhiji and any strikes or hartals to render complete support to the British Government during the War. However, it is pertinent to note here that despite the Communist indifference or opposition, the working class still participated in the Quit India Movement

[103] In August 1942.

and strikes and *hartals* were organised by workers in major towns all across the country like Delhi, Lucknow, Kanpur, Bombay, Nagpur, Ahmedabad, Jamshedpur, Madras, Indore and Bangalore.

Between 1945 and 1947, there was again a resurgence in working class activity and the workers participated in large numbers in the post-war political upsurge as evident by the strikes and *hartals* organised by the workers in solidarity with the INA trials as well as the mutiny of the naval ratings in 1946.

Revolutionary Nationalism in the 1920s

When Gandhiji launched the Non-Cooperation Movement, then most of the revolutionaries either joined the movement or suspended their own activities in order to give the Gandhian mass movement a chance[104]. However, after the sudden suspension of the Non-Cooperation Movement in 1922, the revolutionaries' high hopes were shattered and disenchanted with the Gandhian leadership, they began to question the very basic strategy of non-violent struggle. The government repression further alienated them from the 'passive resistance' politics and they were again attracted towards the path of 'violent revolution' to free India from the colonial rule. The Russian Revolution of 1917 and the consequent rise of the Soviet Republic along with the revolutionary movements and uprisings of Ireland, Turkey, Egypt and China also greatly influenced their thinking, and under the influence of the emergent Socialist and Communist ideology, the revolutionaries now wanted both political freedom and freedom from economic exploitation and misery. Eventually, two separate strands of revolutionary nationalism emerged in India: one in Punjab, UP, Bihar and Madhya Pradesh (old central provinces) and the second one in Bengal. However, as we are going to discuss subsequently, in both the regions, the revolutionary movement did try to move away from individual heroic action to a mass-based movement and from religious nationalism to secular patriotism.

Revolutionaries in Northern India

The revolutionaries in northern India were the first to emerge out of the mood of frustration and reorganise under the leadership of **Sachindranath Sanyal**[105], **Ramprasad Bismil** and **Jogesh Chatterjee**.

Formation of the Hindustan Republican Association (HRA) (1924)

- The revolutionaries met in Kanpur in October 1924 and founded the **Hindustan Republican Association** (HRA) (or Army) to organise an armed revolution to overthrow colonial rule and establish in its place a 'Federal Republic of the United States of India' with a government elected on the basis of adult franchise. To recruit men, provide training to them, to procure arms, to organise propaganda and to finance their organisation, the HRA deduced to organise dacoities against the Government.

Kakori Conspiracy Case (1925)

- On 9 August 1925, ten revolutionaries held up the 8-Down train from Saharanpur to Lucknow at Kakori, a small village station near Lucknow, and looted its official railway cash.
- The Government, however, succeeded in arresting a large number of HRA members and leaders involved in the dacoity who were tried in the Kakori Conspiracy Case. **Ashfaqulla Khan**, **Ramprasad Bismil**, **Roshan Singh** and **Rajendra Lahiri** were hanged, 4 others were sent to the Andamans for life and 17 others were sentenced to long terms of imprisonment. Only Chandrashekhar Azad remained at large though he was declared absconder.

[104] It is not accidental that nearly all the major new leaders of the revolutionary nationalist politics, for example, Jogesh Chandra Chatterjee, Surya Sen, Jatin Das, Chandrashekhar Azad, Bhagat Singh, Sukhdev, Shiv Varma, Bhagwati Charan Vohra and Jaidev Kapur, had been enthusiastic participants in the non-violent Non-Cooperation Movement.

[105] Whose *Bandi Jiwan* served as a textbook to the revolutionary movement.

"We shall be born again, shall meet again and shall jointly fight once again for the cause of the motherland as comrades in arms."

Ram Prasad Bismil's statement before his martyrdom.

"You must remember that the Hindu community has dedicated great souls like Khudi Ram and Kanailal. To me, this is a good fortune that, belonging to the Muslim community, I have acquired the privilege of following in the footsteps of those great martyrs."

Ashfaqullah's words to his nephew just a day before his martyrdom.

Formation of the Hindustan Socialist Republican Association (HSRA) (1928)

- After the Kakori case, new batch of revolutionaries such as **Bejoy Kumar Sinha**, **Shiv Verma** and **Jaidev Kapoor** in UP and **Bhagat Singh**, **Bhagwati Charan Vohra** and **Sukhdev** in Punjab started the reorganisation of the HRA under the overall leadership of Chandrashekhar Azad.
- On 9 and 10 September, 1928, nearly all the major representative revolutionaries of northern India met at Ferozeshah Kotla Ground, Delhi, and being highly motivated by the socialist ideas adopted Socialism as their official goal and also changed the name of the party to **HSRA** (Army).

Saunders Murder or Lahore Conspiracy Case (December 1928)

- Even though the HSRA was rapidly moving away from individual heroic action and towards the ideology of mass-based armed struggle, yet when **Lala Lajpat Rai**, one of the most revered nationalist leaders, died as a result of a brutal lathi charge while leading an anti-Simon Commission demonstration in Lahore on 30 October 1928, the angry revolutionaries felt it necessary to avenge the grave insult to the nation and under these circumstances, they were compelled to take recourse once again to the earlier practice of the individual assassination. And so, on 17 December 1928, in Lahore, **Bhagat Singh**, **Azad** and **Rajguru** assassinated **Saunders**, a police official involved in the lathi charge of Lala Lajpat Rai.

"The murder of a leader respected by millions of people at the unworthy hands of an ordinary police official ... was an insult to the nation. It was the bounden duty of young men of India to efface it. ... We regret to have had to kill a person but he was part and parcel of that inhuman and unjust order which has to be destroyed."

Poster justifying the assassination put up by the HSRA after the assassination.

Central Legislative Assembly Bomb Case (April 1929)

- The HSRA leadership now decided to let the people know about its changed objectives and the need for a revolution by the masses. As a part of this propaganda, **Bhagat Singh** and **B. K. Dutt** were deputed to throw bombs in the Central Legislative Assembly on 8 April 1929 against the passage of the **Public Safety Bill and the Trade Disputes Bill**, which would reduce the civil liberties of citizens in general and workers in particular.

- The aim of the revolutionaries was not to kill[106], as the bombs were relatively harmless, but, as the leaflet they threw into the Assembly proclaimed, '**to make the deaf hear**'[107]. The intention was to arrest[108] and to use the trial court as a forum for propaganda so that people would become familiar with the programme and ideology of HSRA.
- Bhagat Singh and B. K. Dutt were tried in the Assembly Bomb Case. Later, the police was able to uncover the details of the Saunders assassination and thus Bhagat Singh, Sukhdev, Rajguru and several other revolutionaries were tried in the Lahore Conspiracy Case.
- As per their plan, Bhagat Singh and his comrades turned the court into a forum of propaganda as their courageous and defiant conduct[109] in the courts was reported in newspapers and widely discussed among the people and won them the support and sympathy of people all over the country including those who had complete faith in non-violence.

> *"Our protest was against the institution, which since its birth, has eminently helped to display not only its worthlessness but its far reaching power for mischief ... Time and again the national demand has been pressed by the people's representatives only to find the waste paper basket as its final destination."*
>
> Bhagat Singh and B. K. Dutt's joint statement on 6 June 1929.

Hunger Strike in the Jail (1929)

- The country was also stirred by the prolonged hunger strike, the revolutionary under-trials undertook as a protest against the horrible conditions in jails. They also demanded that they be treated not as criminals but as political prisoners.
- On 13 September 1929, **Jatin Das**, a frail young man possessing an extraordinary iron will, died on the 64th day of the epic fast. The entire nation was massively stirred and as the train carrying his body from Lahore to Calcutta passed from each station, thousands came to pay him homage at every station. At Calcutta, a two-mile-long procession of more than six lakh people carried his coffin to the cremation ground.

> *"If ever a man died a hero and martyr to a noble cause, that man is Jatindra Nath Dass and the blood of martyrs has in all ages and countries been the seed of higher and nobler life, better social and political order."*
>
> The excerpts on Jatin Dass's death from *The Tribune* of Lahore.
>
> *"No Indian can refrain from admiring their great courage and our hearts must go to them now in their great and voluntary suffering. They are fasting not for any selfish ends but to improve the lot of all political prisoners."*
>
> Jawaharlal Nehru

---

[106] Even Lord Irwin, the then Viceroy, accepted that the bombs were not aimed at individuals but against the institution itself.

[107] Quotation from the Grench Revolutionary Valiant who said that *It takes a loud voice to make the deaf hear*.

[108] In fact, Bhagat Singh and Dutt made no attempt to escape.

[109] Every day they entered the courtroom shouting slogans *Inquilab Zindabad, Down, Down with Imperialism, Long Live the Proletariat* and singing songs such as *Sarfaroshi ki tamanna ab hamare dil mei hai* (our heart is filled with the desire for martyrdom) and *Mera rang de basanti chola* (dye my clothes in saffron colour, the colour of courage and sacrifice).

Eventually, a large number of revolutionaries were convicted in the Lahore Conspiracy Case and other similar cases and sentenced to long terms of imprisonment while Bhagat Singh, Sukhdev and Rajguru were sentenced to be hanged. The sentence was carried out on 23 March 1931 and as the news of their hanging spread, a death like silence engulfed the entire country. All over the country, millions of people wept and refused to eat food, attend schools or carry on their daily work. Bhagat Singh soon became a legend in the country and his popularity rivalled that of Gandhiji. Chandrashekhar Azad also died in a shooting encounter in a public park in Allahabad in February 1931, and thus subsequently, the revolutionary movement virtually came to an end in Punjab, Uttar Pradesh and Bihar.

"Stepping upon the path of revolution, I had thought that if I could spread the slogan of "Inquilab Zindabad" throughout the country, by giving away my life, I would feel that I have received the full value of my life. Today sitting behind the bars of the execution barracks, I hear the sound of the slogan from crores of people. I believe that this slogan of mine would attack imperialism as the driving force of the freedom struggle till the end ... What more value can be of such a small life?."

Bhagat Singh's reply to Jaidev Kapoor on being asked if he regretted dying so young.

The Revolutionary Ideology of the HRA and HSRA

During the 1920s, a major shift was witnessed in the ideological development of the new generation revolutionaries like **Bhagat Singh**, **Bejoy Kumar Sinha**, **Chandra Shekhar Azad**, **Shiv Verma**, **Sukhdev** and **Bhagwati Charan Vohra** who under the influence of Socialism and Marxism were primarily interested in not only achieving freedom from the exploitative British Raj but were also keen in the reorganisation of the society on a socialistic basis. Being greatly influenced with the Soviet Revolution, Communism and the upsurge of the working class after the First World War, the revolutionaries desired to harness the potentialities into a nationalist revolution. In fact, the HRA itself decided in its founding council meeting in October 1924 *to preach social revolutionary and communistic principles*, while its manifesto ***The Revolutionary*** in 1925 clearly spelt out its ideological commitments ranging from the nationalisation of the major public works and industries to abolition of all systems which make the exploitation of man by man possible. The HRA also tried to condemn the mischievous propaganda against the revolutionaries for being terrorists and anarchists.

"The Indian revolutionaries are neither terrorists nor anarchists. They never aim at spreading anarchy in the land, and therefore they can never properly be called anarchists. Terrorism is never their object and they cannot be called terrorists ... The HRA will try incessantly to organise a band of selfless and devoted workers who will devote their best energies towards the political and social emancipation of their country."

Statements from a pamphlet of HRA.

However, a real breakthrough in terms of revolutionary ideology, the goals of revolution and the forms of revolutionary struggle was made by **Bhagat Singh** and his comrades who were able to convince his fellow revolutionaries that the salvation of India lay not merely in political independence but in economic freedom and not in individual heroic action but popular mass-based movements. Believing that revolution could only be achieved *by the masses for the masses* and to carry out open political work among the youth, peasants and workers, Bhagat Singh founded the **Punjab Naujawan Bharat Sabha**[110] in 1926 and also organised the Lahore Students Union in partnership with Sukhdev for open political work among the students. Bhagat Singh and his comrades also redefined and broadened the scope and meaning of term 'Revolution' as according to them *Revolution was much more than mere militancy or violence and its first objective was national liberation and then the building of a new socialist society.*

"Revolution is independence; social, political and economic aimed at establishing a new order of society in which political and economic exploitation will be an impossibility. Definition of Revolution as provided in The Philosophy of the Bomb,"

Written by Bhagwati Charan Vohra, Azad and Yashpal.

"Revolution does not necessarily involve sanguinary strife, nor is there any place in it for individual vendetta. It is not the cult of the bomb and the pistol. By Revolution we mean that the present order of things, which is based on manifest injustice must change."

Bhagat Singh's statement before the court during the trial proceedings of the Assembly Bomb Case.

"The struggle in India would continue so long as a handful of exploiters go on exploiting the labour of common people for their own ends. It matters little whether these exploiters are purely British capitalism, or British and Indians in alliance, or even purely Indians. The peasants have to liberate themselves not only from foreign yoke bum also from the yoke of landlords and capitalists."

Excerpts from Bhagat Singh's letter from jail.

"I see myself above all as a precursor and not maker of the revolution, as a propagator of the ideas of socialism and communism, as a humble initiator of the socialist movement in India."

Bhagat Singh

Another distinctive ideological aspect of the revolutionaries was the fact that they were not only fully secular in their approach but were also acutely conscious of the growing menace of communalism in the 1920s. They understood more clearly than many other contemporary leaders about the danger that communalism posed to the socio-political environment of the nation and the national movement. In fact, Bhagat Singh often told his audience that *communalism was as big an enemy as colonialism*. The revolutionaries did not hesitate to sharply criticise[111] even Lala Lajpat Rai when he took a turn towards communal politics after 1924. On the similar lines, at the conference of youth organised by the Naujawan Bharat Sabha in April 1928, Bhagat Singh and his comrades openly opposed the membership option to the youth belonging to religious-communal organisations. Significantly, two of the six rules of the Naujawan Bharat Sabha, drafted by Bhagat Singh himself, were *to have nothing to do with communal bodies or other parties which disseminate communal ideas*' and '*to create the spirit of general toleration among the public considering religion as a matter of personal belief of man and to act upon the same fully.*

[110] Bhagat Singh was its general secretary and Bhagwati Charan Vohra was propaganda secretary. Among other activities, NBS worked to organise lantern shows of patriot's pictures. And at all their public meetings, they used to garland Kartar Singh Sarabha's picture, a Ghadar revolutionary who was executed at the young age of 19 in 1915 at Lahore. Interestingly, Bhagat Singh always kept Sarabha's photo in his pocket.

[111] The method of criticism of Lala Lajpat Rai was also innovative in its approach as instead of using harsh words of criticism against the respected leader, a pamphlet was printed having photograph of Lala Lajpat Rai's on the front cover. The pamphlet contained Robert Browning's famous poem *The Lost Leader*, in which Browning criticises Wordsworth for turning against liberty. The poem begins with the line 'Just for a handful of silver he left us'. A few more of the poem's lines were: 'We shall march prospering,—not thro his presence; Songs may inspirit us,—not from his lyre', and 'Blot out his name, then, record one lost soul more'.

Remembering a Radical: Bhagat Singh (September 1907–23 March 1931)

Bhagat Singh is among the most celebrated martyrs of the Indian freedom struggle who at a young age of 23 left behind an unparallelled legacy of courage, intellect and sacrifice. When most senior leaders of the country had only one immediate goal – the attainment of freedom, Bhagat Singh had the prescience to look beyond the immediate and have aspirations for transforming India into a secular, socialist and egalitarian society. Bhagat Singh was born into a Sikh family to Sardar Kisan Singh Sandhu and Vidyavati in 1907 in Lyallpur, Punjab (now in Pakistan). He was the nephew of the famous revolutionary Ajit Singh and thus, the spirit of patriotism was in his blood. At the age of 12, he visited Jallianwala Bagh[112] and this visit deeply affect his child heart. In early days of youth, he also got inspired from the revolutionary movement of 'Babbar Akalies' and 'Ghadrites' and their heroic sacrifices. He also joined the Non-Cooperation Movement but became disappointed with the sudden withdrawal of the movement. Gradually, he joined HRA in 1923 after informing his father in letter that he had dedicated his life to the nation and hence he could not think of marrying, as desired by him.

Very early in life, Bhagat Singh had inculcated the habit of reading, and being a voracious reader, he was one of the most well read of political leaders of the time whose shirt pockets were always bulged with books which he constantly offered to lend to his associates. He had, in fact, devoured books in the Dwarkadas Library in Lahore on Socialism, the Soviet Union and revolutionary movements, especially those of Russia, Ireland and Italy. At Lahore, he organised several study circles with the help of Sukhdev and others and carried on intensive political discussions, while during his prison time of 2 years, he read a wide range of authors including Marx, Engels, Bertrand Russell, T. Paine, Sinclair, Lenin, William Wordsworth, Tennyson, Rabindranath Tagore, Trotsky, among others. He was also able to articulate quite maturely on varied themes such as universal brotherhood and religion though at times he wrote under the pseudonym of Balwant Singh.

"The sword of revolution is sharpened on the whetting-stone of ideas."

Bhagat Singh emphasizing on the role of ideas in the making of revolution.

Bhagat Singh was a Socialist but with humanist and scientific outlook fully believing that Socialism stands for the state of abolition of capitalism and class domination. He accepted Marxism and was determined to bring revolution through mass movement of the exploited and suppressed sections of society.

"Force when aggressively applied is 'violence' and is therefore morally unjustifiable, but when it is used in the furtherance of a legitimate cause, it has its moral justification."

Bhagat Singh

"Apparently, I have acted like a terrorist. But I am not a terrorist. … Let me announce with all the strength at my command, that I am not a terrorist and I never was, except perhaps in the beginning of my revolutionary career. And I am convinced that we cannot gain anything through those methods."

Bhagat Singh

[112] While it is said that from Jallianwala Bagh, he brought home 'blood soaked sand'.

Bhagat Singh was in complete favour of separation of religion and politics. For him, religion was a private affair of a person, which had nothing to do with his political activities. He strongly also felt the importance of freeing the people from the mental bondage of religion and superstition. One of the profound articles written by him just a few weeks before his death was '**Why I am an Atheist**,[113], a strong rebuttal of blind faith and a zealous defence of reason. In the article, he traced his own path to atheism, how he first gave up belief 'in the mythology and doctrines of Sikhism or any other religion', and in the end lost faith in the existence of God. He was convinced that religion is a tool in the hands of the exploiters who keep the masses in constant fear of God for their own interests.

"In the struggle for self-emancipation, humanity had to struggle against the narrow conception of religion as also against the belief in God. To be a revolutionary, one required immense moral strength, but one also required criticism and independent thinking. Any man who stands for progress has to criticise, disbelieve and challenge every item of the old faith. Item by item he has to reason out every nook and corner of the prevailing faith."

Excerpts from *Why I am an Atheist*, by Bhagat Singh

"This is the highest award for patriots and I am proud that I am going to get it ... They may kill me, but they will not be able to crush my spirits. My ideas will haunt the British like a curse till they are forced to run away from here. Bhagat Singh dead will be more dangerous to the British enslavers than Bhagat Singh alive. After I am hanged, the fragrance of my revolutionary ideas will permeate the atmosphere of this beautiful land of ours. It will intoxicate the youth and prepare them for freedom and revolution."

Bhagat Singh

Revolutionaries in Bengal

In Bengal too, after 1922, the revolutionary nationalists started reorganising and developing their underground activities. However, unlike the revolutionaries of northern India, the Bengal revolutionaries were also quite active in the Congress organisation and cooperated with **C. R. Das** in his *Swarajist* work. However, after his death in 1925, the Congress leadership in Bengal divided into two wings, one led by **Subhas Chandra Bose** and the other by **J. M. Sengupta**. Consequently, the revolutionaries belonging to **Yugantar** group joined forces with the Bose wing while the **Anushilan** group went with the Sengupta wing.

Assassination Attempt on Charles Tegart, Police Commissioner of Calcutta (1924)

- Among the several 'actions' of the reorganised groups was the attempt to assassinate Charles Tegart, the hated Police Commissioner of Calcutta, by **Gopinath Saha** in January 1924.
- However, by an error, another Englishman named Day was killed.
- The Government initiated large-scale repression and arrested a large number of people, suspected of being terrorists or their supporters, under a newly promulgated ordinance. These also included Subhas Chandra Bose and many other Congressmen. Despite massive popular protest, Saha was hanged on 1 March 1924 while the revolutionary activity suffered a severe setback.

[113] The article was primarily written as a reply to one of his co-prisoners Randhir Singh's accusations that since he had earned so much fame, he had become egoistic and his disbelief in God was born out of this sense of vanity.

The Chittagong Armoury Raid Led by Surya Sen (1930)

- Surya Sen[114] had actively participated in the Non-Cooperation Movement and had become a teacher in a national school in Chittagong, which led to his being popularly known as Masterda. He was arrested in 1926 for revolutionary activity and till 1928, he remained in prison. He and his group were also closely associated with the Congress work[115] in Chittagong.
- Surya Sen soon gathered around himself a large band of revolutionary youth including Anant Singh, Ganesh Ghosh, Ambika Chakravarty and Loknath Paul. In early 1929, they formed a plan to organise an armed rebellion, on however small a scale, to demonstrate that it was possible to challenge the armed might of the British Empire in India.
- Their action plan included the occupation of the two main armouries in Chittagong and the arming of a large band of revolutionaries with the seized arms; the destruction of the telephone and telegraph systems of the city; and the dislocation of the railway communication system between Chittagong and the rest of Bengal. The young band of revolutionaries was carefully selected and trained with great care.
- The plan was put into execution at 10 o'clock on the night of 18 April 1930 in the name of the **Indian Republican Army**, Chittagong Branch by a total 65 revolutionaries.
- Initially, six revolutionaries led by Ganesh Ghosh captured the **police armoury**, shouting slogans like *inquilab zindabad, down with imperialism* and Gandhiji*'s raj has been established.* Meanwhile, the other revolutionaries succeeded in dislocating telephone and telegraph communications and disrupting movement by train.
- Another group of ten revolutionaries, led by Loknath Paul, captured the **Auxiliary Force Armoury**. However, unfortunately they could not locate the ammunition which proved to be a very disastrous setback for the overall plans.
- All the revolutionary groups then gathered outside the Police Armoury where Surya Sen was formally declared as the President of the Provisional Revolutionary Government and he hoisted the National Flag among slogans of *Bande Mataram* and *Inquilab Zindabad.*
- Since it was not possible for the band of revolutionaries to put up a fight against the British forces which were expected to arrive soon, the revolutionaries therefore left Chittagong before dawn and marched towards the Chittagong hill ranges, looking for a safe place.
- On 22 April, they were surrounded by several thousand troops on the Jalalabad hill, and after a fierce fight in which over 80 British troops and 12 revolutionaries died, Surya Sen decided to abandon frontal warfare and instead launch guerrilla warfare from the neighbouring villages.
- Despite several repressive measures and combing operations by the authorities, the revolutionaries survived for nearly 3 years owing to the shelter and support provided to them by the villagers, most of them Muslims.
- Surya Sen was finally arrested on 16 February 1933, tried and hanged on 12 January 1934 while many of his co-fighters were caught and sentenced to long terms of imprisonment.

The **Chittagong Armoury Raid** had an immense impact on the people of Bengal, a fact even acknowledged by an official report which stated that *it fired the imagination of revolutionary-minded youth and recruits poured into the various terrorist groups in a steady stream.* Even the sections of the bureaucracy, police

[114] Surya Sen, a brilliant and inspiring organiser, was an unpretentious, soft-spoken and transparently sincere person. Possessed with immense personal courage, he was deeply humane in his approach. He was fond of saying: 'Humanism is a special virtue of a revolutionary'. He was also very fond of poetry, being a great admirer of Rabindranath Tagore and Kazi Nazrul Islam.

[115] In fact, Surya Sen was the Secretary, and five of his associates were members of the Chittagong District Congress Committee in 1929.

and army exhibited sympathy[116] towards the cause of the revolutionaries. There was a major revival of revolutionary activity, and in Midnapore district alone, three British magistrates and two Inspectors-General of Police were assassinated, while attempts were made on the lives of two Governors. In this span of a 3-year period, around 22 officials and 20 non-officials were killed.

"A dedicated band of youth must show the path of organized armed struggle in place of individual terrorism. Most of us will have to die in the process but our sacrifice for such a noble cause will not go in vain."

Surya Sen

"The plan – was that when, after the Chittagong rebellion, the Government would bring in troops to take back Chittagong they (the terrorists) would die fighting – thus creating a legend and setting an example before their countrymen to emulate."

Kalpana Joshi (Dutt)

The Government response to the Armoury Raid and the revival of revolutionary terrorist activity was initially one of panic and then of brutal reprisals. It armed itself with 20 repressive Acts and indiscriminately arrested nationalists. In Chittagong alone, it burnt several villages and imposed punitive fine on many others while in general it established a reign of terror. For instance, in 1933, it arrested and sentenced Jawaharlal Nehru to a 2-year term in jail for sedition when he in a speech in Calcutta condemned imperialism, police repression and praised the heroism of revolutionary youth (even while criticising the policy of terrorism as futile and out-of-date).

One of the remarkable aspects of this new phase of the revolutionary movement in Bengal was the large-scale participation of young women. Under Surya Sen's leadership, they not only provided shelter, acted as messengers and custodians of arms but also fought hand in hand with men. Some striking examples were:

- **Pritilata Waddedar**, who died while conducting a raid.
- **Kalpana Dutt**, who was arrested and tried along with Surya Sen and given a life sentence.
- **Santi Ghosh** and **Suniti Chowdhury**, two school girls of Comilla who shot the District Magistrate in December 1931.
- **Bina Das**, who fired point blank at the Governor while receiving her degree at the Convocation in February 1932.

Also, unlike the northern India revolutionaries and the older Bengal revolutionaries, the Chittagong rebels successfully exhibited the group action aimed at the different organs of the colonial state instead of an individual's act of heroism or the assassination of an individual. Also, the Bengal revolutionaries groups of the 1920s and 1930s successfully shed some of their earlier Hindu religiosity as they no longer took religious oaths and vows and also no longer excluded Muslims. For instance, the Chittagong group included many Muslims like **Sattar**, **Mir Ahmad**, **Fakir Ahmad Mian** and **Tunu Mian**, and most of these groups also received massive support from the Muslim villagers around Chittagong who enabled them to avoid detection and resist arrest for nearly 3 years. However, unlike Bhagat Singh and his comrades, the Bengal

[116] An interesting incident in this regard was narrated by Kalpana Dutt, one of the revolutionaries of the Chittagong Armoury Raid. When she surrendered after a bitter fight in 1933, a Subedar of the Jat Regiment slapped her. Immediately, she was surrounded by other soldiers who warned the Subedar that 'She is not to be touched. If you raise your hand once again, we will not obey you'.

revolutionaries failed to evolve a broader radical socio-economic programme and most of the revolutionaries working in the Swaraj Party failed to support the cause of peasantry against the *zamindars*.

Gradual Decline of the Revolutionary Nationalist Movement

The revolutionary nationalist movement gradually declined in the 1930s owing to both opposition to violence in the ranks of mainstream national movement led by Gandhiji even while the Congress leaders admired the heroism of the young revolutionaries and condemned the police repression directed against them along with defending them in the courts. Second, the Government's strong repressive action also gradually decimated the revolutionary ranks and initiated a process of rethinking in a large number of the revolutionaries who turned to Marxism and Socialism and joined the Communist Party, the Revolutionary Socialist Party and other Left parties along with Gandhian wing of the Congress.

Even though the revolutionary nationalists of the 1920s and 1930s failed in their stated objective of leading a mass-based armed struggle, they made an abiding contribution to the national freedom movement. Their deep patriotism, courage and determination and sense of sacrifice stirred the Indian people and gave them pride and self-confidence. In north India, the spread of socialist consciousness owed a lot to them.

Caste Movement

- Caste Movements: As in earlier periods, the varied contradictions of the Indian society found expression in caste associations and movements. These movements could be divisive, conservative and at times potentially radical, and included the following:
  - Justice Party (Madras)
  - Self-Respect Movement (1925) under 'Periyar': E. V. Ramaswamy Naicker (Madras)
  - Satyashodhak activists in Satara (Maharashtra)
  - Bhaskar Rao Jadhav (Maharashtra)
  - Mahars under Ambedkar (Maharashtra)
  - Radical Ezhavas under K. Aiyappan and C. Kesavan in Kerala
  - Yadavs in Bihar for improvement in social status
  - Unionist Party under Fazl-i-Hussain (Punjab).

Previous Year's Questions (Prelims)

1. The demand for the Tebhaga Peasant Movement in Bengal was for, (2013)
   (a) the reduction of the share of the landlords from one-half of the crop to one-third.
   (b) the grant of own ownership of land to peasants as they were the actual cultivator of the land.
   (c) the uprooting of zamindari system and the end of serfdom.
   (d) writing of all peasant debts.

2. Who among the following was not associated with the formation of UP Kisan Sabha in February 1918? (2005)
   (a) Indra Narayan Dwivedi
   (b) Gauri Shankar Misra
   (c) Jawaharlal Nehru
   (d) Madan Mohan Malviya

3. Which party was founded by Subhash Chandra Bose in the year 1939 after he broke away from the Congress? (2005)

(a) Indian Freedom Party
(b) Azad Hind Fauj
(c) Revolutionary Front
(d) Forward Block

4. When Congress leaders condemned the Montagu-Chelmsford Report, many moderates left the party to form which of the following (2003)

(a) Swaraj Party
(b) Indian Freedom Party
(c) Independence Federation of India
(d) Indian Liberal Federation

5. With reference to Indian freedom struggle, which one of the following statements is not correct? (2003)

(a) The Rowlatt Act aroused a wave of popular Indian on and led to the Jallianwala Bagh massacre.
(b) Subhash Chandra Bose formed the Forward Bloc.
(c) Bhagat Singh was one of the founders of Hindustan Republican Socialist Association.
(d) In 1931, the congress session at Karachi opposed Gandhi Irwin pact.

6. The radical wing of the congress party with Jawaharlal Nehru as one of its main leaders founded the Independence for India League in opposition to which one of following? (1995)

(a) The Gandhi Irwin Pact
(b) The Home Rule movement
(c) The Nehru Report
(d) The Montford Reforms

Previous Year's Answers (Prelims)

1. (a) 2. (c) 3. (d) 4. (d) 5. (d) 6. (c)

The Nationalist Advance: 1927–37

10

The decade between the appointment of the Simon Commission in November 1927 and the formation of the Congress ministries in the provinces in July 1937 was full of complex and often contradictory political developments. We have already discussed about some of these developments like the emergence of the Socialist and Left Ideology, Working Class Movements, Peasants Organisations along with resurgence in the Revolutionary Nationalism in the previous chapters. However, despite the varied ups and downs, the national movement did register a remarkable advance during this period. For instance, being deliberately and insultingly ignored through the setting up of an **all-white Commission** to consider the next scheme of constitutional changes, the nationalists fought their way through the **Civil Disobedience Movement** to a position of near-equality with the **Gandhi–Irwin Pact** of March 1931. Similarly, after the major British counter-offensive under Viceroy Willingdon and Prime Minister Ramsay Macdonald's Government resulting in sharp decline in the national movement during 1933–34, the Congress and the nationalist movement did rebound swiftly as evident by its sweeping electoral triumph in March 1937, which for the first time gave the national movement some real, though very partial, control over the state machinery at the provincial level. In this chapter, we will be discussing in detail about all these developments which helped in the nationalist advance during the decade of 1927–37.

Anti-Simon Commission Upsurge and Nehru Report (1927–29)

The mass anti-imperialist upsurge began to take a marked upward turn from the latter part of 1927, with the announcement of formation of an all-White Indian Statutory Commission, popularly known as the **Simon Commission** after its Chairman, Sir John Simon, on 8 November 1927 by the Conservative[1] Government of Britain to review the operation of constitutional system in India, to decide the course of further constitutional progress and the lines on which it needed to be further evolved.

> *"The act of appointment (of the Simon Commission) needs for an answer, not speeches, however heroic they may be, not declarations, however brave they may be, but corresponding action …."*
>
> Excerpts from Gandhiji's article in the issue of *Young India* of 12 January 1928.

[1] Although the constitutional reforms were due only in 1929, the Conservatives or the Tory government faced with the prospect of electoral defeat at the hands of the Labour Party, and scared to leave the future of the British Empire in the irresponsible hands of an inexperienced Labour Government, decided for an early appointment of the Statutory Commission in 1927.

Anti-Simon Protests (1927–28)

- The non-inclusion of Indians in the Commission and the British attitude of not considering any Indian fit enough to serve on a body that claimed the right to decide the political future of India was taken as a grave insult by most of the political groups,[2] thereby resulting in immediate protests across India and a successful nation-wide boycott – organised by **Congress**[3], **Liberal Federation**[4], the **Indian Industrial and Commercial Congress**, as well as **Hindu Mahasabha** and the **Muslim League**.
- When the Simon Commission arrived in the country on 3 February 1928, all the major cities and towns observed a complete *hartal,* and there were black flag demonstrations greeting it with slogans like **Go Back Simon** all along the route of the Simon Commission. New ways of defiance and protest were being constantly invented by the people, for instance, in Lucknow, Khaliquzzaman floated kites and balloons imprinted with the popular slogan *Go Back Simon.*
- However, the police came down heavily on demonstrators not sparing even the respected and senior leaders. In Lucknow, for example, Jawaharlal and Govind Ballabh Pant were beaten up by the police while at Lahore, **Lala Lajpat Rai**, one of the most revered extremist leaders, was brutally lathi-charged on 30 October who later succumbed to his injuries on 17 November 1928.
- The Simon boycott movement proved to be quite significant as:
  - It provided the first taste of political action to a new generation of youth who not only played the most active role in this protest but with their participation in the Simon agitation, a real fillip was provided to the formation of youth leagues and associations all over the country with **Jawaharlal Nehru** and **Subhas Bose** emerging as their leaders.
  - The Anti-Simon upsurge also gave a stimulus to the radical forces demanding not just complete independence but major socio-economic reforms based on socialist pattern.

> *"A constitutional war has been declared on Great Britain. Negotiations are not to come from our side. Let the Government sue for peace. We are denied equal partnership. we will resist the new doctrine to the best of our power. Jallianwala Bagh was a physical butchery, the Simon Commission is a butchery of our souls. By appointing an exclusively white Commission, Lord Birkenhead has declared our unfitness for self-government …."*
>
> Mohammad Ali Jinnah declaring support for the national boycott of the Simon Commission.

Nehru Report (1928)

- Meanwhile, responding to Lord Birkenhead[5] challenge of formulating a concrete scheme of constitutional reforms having the support of wide sections of Indian political opinion, **Motilal Nehru** started negotiating for constitutional scheme at an all parties conference[6] in Lucknow. The scheme was finalised in August 1928 by a committee having eminent members such as Tej Bahadur Sapru, Subhash

[2] The Unionists in Punjab, the All India Achut Federation and the Justice Party in the South decided not to boycott the Simon Commission.

[3] The INC meeting under the presidency of Dr. M. A. Ansari in December 1927 at Madras resolved to boycott the Commission *at every stage and in every form*. During this prevailing excitable atmosphere, Jawaharlal Nehru even succeeded in getting passed a snap resolution declaring complete independence as the goal of the Congress.

[4] Led by Tej Bahadur Sapru.

[5] The then Secretary of State appointed by the conservative government.

[6] The All parties conference was held in February 1928 and was presided by Dr M. A. Ansari.

Chandra Bose, Jawahar Lal Nehru, Ali Imam, Shuab Qureshi, M. S. Aney and later came to be known as the Nehru Report[7] after Motilal Nehru, its principal negotiator.

Main Recommendations of the Nehru Report

- Dominion status for India within the British Commonwealth on the lines of self-governing dominions like Canada, Australia, and others. (This issue became a huge point of disagreement with the younger generation of leaders like **Jawaharlal Nehru** and **Subhas Chandra Bose** who favoured complete independence and regarded the idea of dominion status as a step in backward direction. Later, both of these leaders set up the **Independence for India League** for demanding complete independence.)
- A federal form of government with residual powers with the centre and provision for a bicameral legislature at the centre. The Report favoured responsible government at the Centre and in the province:
  - The Indian Parliament at the Centre to consist of a 500-member House of Representatives elected on the basis of adult suffrage, a 200-member Senate to be elected by provincial councils.
  - The House of Representatives to have a tenure of 5 years and the Senate to have a tenure of 7 years.
  - The central government to be headed by a governor general, appointed by the British government but paid out of Indian revenues, who would act on the advice of the Central Executive Council responsible to the Parliament while the Provincial councils to have a 5-year tenure, headed by a governor acting on the advice of the provincial executive council.
- The Report **rejected** the principle of separate electorates which had been the basis of constitutional reforms so far. Instead, the Nehru Report recommended for joint electorates with reservation of seats for Muslims at the Centre and in provinces where they were in minority, but not in those where they had a numerical majority such as Punjab and Bengal. On the similar limes, it provided for reservation for non-Muslims in the NWFP.
- Nineteen fundamental rights including equal rights for women, right to form unions, and universal adult suffrage, that is, the right to vote for men and women above 21 years of age, unless disqualified.
- The creation of the Linguistic provinces and the language of the country would be Indian, written either in Devanagari (Sanskrit/Hindi), Telugu, Tamil, Kannada, Bengali, Marathi or Gujarati in character. Usage of English was permitted.
- Full protection to cultural and religious interests of Muslims.
- Complete dissociation of State from religion.

It is pertinent to note here that the issue of separate electorates was a bone of contention between the communal leaders. In December 1927, a section of the **Muslim League** leaders met Motilal Nehru in Delhi and suggested a few proposals better known as the **Delhi Proposals** which were accepted by Congress at its Madras session. These proposals were:

- one-third representation of Muslims in the Central Legislature
- representation to Muslims in Punjab and Bengal in proportion to their populations
- formation of three new provinces with a Muslim majority – Sindh, Baluchistan and North-West Frontier Province (NWFP)
- residual powers to be vested with the provinces and not the centre

[7] This was the first major attempt by Indians to draft a constitution for themselves.

Fourteen Points Proposed by Jinnah (March 1929)

- Federal constitution with residual powers with the provinces.
- Provincial autonomy.
- No constitutional amendment without the agreement of the states.
- All legislatures and elected bodies to have adequate Muslim representation without reducing Muslim majority in a province to minority or equality.
- Adequate Muslim representation of Muslims in the services and in self-governing bodies.
- 1/3rd representation of Muslims in the Central Legislature.
- 1/3rd Muslim members in the central and state cabinets.
- Separate electorates.
- No bill to be passed in any legislature if 3/4th of a minority community considers it against its interests.
- Any reorganisation of territories not to affect the Muslim majority in Bengal, Punjab and the NWFP.
- Separation of Sindh from Bombay Presidency.
- Constitutional reforms in the NWFP and Baluchistan.
- Full religious freedom for all communities.
- Protection of the religious, cultural, educational and language rights of Muslims.

However, the **Hindu Mahasabha** registered its opposition to the formation of the new provinces and the communal representation being demanded in Bengal and Punjab while also expressing its desire for a strong unitary centre. Motilal Nehru and other secular leaders facing a tough dilemma[8] still tried to accommodate both groups and thus advocated for joint electorates with reservation of seats for Muslims only where they were in a minority and accepted the demand of creation of Sindh into a new province but with the qualifying condition that the same would be done only after the grant of dominion status and in accordance with safeguarding the interests of the Hindu minority in the province. But despite all these accommodations, both parties were unsatisfied. The Muslim League led by Jinnah was not in the mood of giving up the demand for reservation of seats for Muslims even in Muslim majority provinces and thus at the all-party conference held in Calcutta in 1928 to discuss the report, a deadlock was created and Jinnah led the Muslim League and withdrew its support to the Nehru report and instead went ahead to propose his famous **Fourteen Points** in March 1929 which were not only a reiteration of his objections to the Nehru Report but which became the basis of all future agenda of the Muslim League.

Preparation for the Civil Disobedience Movement (1928–30)

Calcutta Session of the INC (1928)

- At the Calcutta session of the INC (1928), the opposition to the Nehru Report had become stronger and was led not only by the groups headed by Jinnah and Aga Khan but also by the younger group of Congressmen led by Jawaharlal Nehru and Subhas Chandra Bose who were dead against the proposed dominion status and instead wanted complete independence. So, Gandhiji proposed a **compromise resolution**, which adopted the Nehru Report, but laid the condition[9] that if the government did not accept the Report by 31

[8] If they conceded more to Muslim communal opinion, then Hindu communalists would withdraw support to the Report and if they satisfied the latter, then Muslim leaders would be estranged.

[9] Gandhiji, Motilal Nehru and many other older leaders felt that the national consensus achieved with such great difficulty on Dominion Status should not be abandoned in such haste and a period of 2 years be given to the Government for accepting this.

December 1930, the Congress would go in for a civil disobedience movement to achieve complete independence. However, under pressure from the younger radical leaders, the grace period for the Government was reduced to a year, that is, to 1929.

- At the same session, a second resolution was also passed which contained a detailed programme of **constructive work** involving revival of organisational work, spread of khadi, boycott of foreign cloth, removal of untouchability, village reconstruction, temperance and removal of disabilities of women. Thus, Gandhiji undertook extensive mass contact tours to mobilise the masses for the future struggle. For instance, by the beginning of 1929, he had already toured Kutch, Central Provinces, United Provinces, Kathiawad, Bengal, Bihar, Assam, Orissa, Travancore, Maharashtra, Malabar, Tamil Nadu, Karnataka, Sind, Delhi and Andhra Pradesh urging people to be ready for direct political action and organising constructive work among them.

Irwin Offer (31 October 1929)

- The then viceroy, Lord Irwin, in consultation with the newly elected Labour government hinted towards a **reconciliation** with his offer of introducing a constitutional scheme with a dominion status as the ultimate goal and proposed a Round Table Conference to settle the issue once the Simon Commission submits its report.

> *"In view of the doubts which have been expressed both in Great Britain and in India regarding the interpretations to be placed on the intentions of the British government in enacting the statute of 1919, I am authorised on behalf of His Majesty's Government to state clearly that in their judgement it is implicit in the Declaration of 1917 that the natural issue of India's progress as there contemplated, is the attainment of dominion status."*
>
> Lord Irwin Announcement on 31 October 1929.

Delhi Declaration (2 November 1929)

- At a conference of prominent national leaders, the Irwin's offer was discussed in detail and responding to the same, the leaders issued a **Delhi Declaration** which basically demanded the details of the dominion status to be discussed, and not just the principle. Through the Delhi Declaration, the Congress leaders also laid down certain conditions for attending the Round Table Conference:
  - The basic principle of dominion status should be immediately accepted and the purpose of the Round Table Conference should be not to determine whether or when dominion status was to be granted but to formulate a constitution[10] for implementation of the dominion status
  - The Congress should have majority representation at the conference
  - A policy of conciliation needs to be followed by the Government and there should be a general amnesty for political prisoners
- However, on 23 December 1929, the negotiations finally broke down when Lord Irwin stated that he was in no position to give the assurance demanded by the INC. Thus, the stage was set for the confrontation.

[10] Thus acting as a constituent assembly.

Lahore Session of Congress (December 1929)

- Meanwhile, the public attention shifted to Lahore where the INC session begin under the presidentship[11] of **Jawaharlal Nehru** under whose command, the historic resolution of complete independence or *Purna Swaraj* as Congress' ultimate goal was passed.
- At the Lahore session, the following key decisions were also taken:
  - The Round Table Conference was to be boycotted.
  - The Congress Working Committee was authorised to launch a programme of civil disobedience including non-payment of taxes and as a preliminary to the same, a boycott of legislature[12] was proposed to be effective immediately and thus all members of legislatures were asked to resign from their seats.
  - **26 January 1930** was fixed as the first Independence *(Swarajya)* Day, to be celebrated everywhere.
- On 31 December 1929, at midnight, on the banks of the river Ravi, the tricolour flag of Indian independence was unfurled amidst cheers and jubilation.

"Remember once again, now that this flag is unfurled, it must not be lowered as long as single Indian, man, woman, or child lives in India."

Jawaharlal Nehru's message[13] while unfurling the national flag at Lahore in December 1929.

"We have now an open conspiracy to free this country from foreign rule and you, comrades, and all our countrymen and countrywomen are invited to join it. Any great movement for liberation today must necessarily be a mass movement, and mass movements must essentially be peaceful …."

Excerpts from Jawaharlal Nehru's Presidential Address at the Lahore Session.

---

[11] Nehru got the presidentship due to Gandhi's backing since only 3 out of 18 Provincial Congress Committees had wanted Jawaharlal, but recognising the appositeness of the occasion, and the upsurge of the youth who had made such a glorious success of the Simon Boycott, Gandhiji insisted on Nehru's name. *Older men have had their innings. The battle of the future has to be fought by younger men and women. And it is but meet that they are led by one of themselves . . . Responsibility will mellow and sober the youth, and prepare them for the burden they must discharge* – Gandhiji's famous statement while backing J L Nehru for presidentship.

[12] The call for the boycott of legislatures evoked only limited response, and the Muslim Conference and the Muslim League condemned the movement as a devise to establish Hindu Raj. Similarly, Sikh support also seemed to have shifted away from Congress whereas non-Congress Hindus, like the Hindu Mahasabha and the Justice Party in Madras declared their opposition to civil disobedience.

[13] Nehru's message was taken to heart by many Indians and their attempts to defend the honour of the national flag in the face of severe brutalities often turned into heroism of the most spectacular variety. For instance, at Bundur on the Andhra Coast, Tota Narasaiah Naidu preferred to be beaten unconscious by a fifteen-member police force rather than give up the national flag. Similarly, in Calicut, P. Krishna Pillai, who later became a major Communist leader, suffered lathi blows with the same determination. In Surat, even a group of children used their little ingenuity to defy the police and frustrated by the repeated snatching of the national flag from their hands, they came up with the idea of stitching khadi dresses in the three colours of the national flag, and thereafter these little 'living flags' triumphantly paraded the streets and defied the police to take away the national flag.

Observation of the Independence Day (26 January 1930)

- On January 26, as per the resolution adopted at the Lahore session of the Congress, public meetings were organised all over the country and the Independence Pledge drafted by Gandhiji which contained the summary of major grievances of the Indian people against British rule was read out in local languages with the hoisting of the national flag.

> *"We believe that it is the inalienable right of the Indian people, as of any other people, to have freedom and to enjoy the fruits of their toil and have the necessities of life, so that they may have full opportunities of growth. We believe also that if any government deprives a people of these rights and oppresses them, the people have a further right to alter it or to abolish it. The British Government in India has not only deprived the Indian people of their freedom but has based itself on the exploitation of the masses, and has ruined India economically, politically, culturally and spiritually. We believe, therefore, that India must sever the British connection and attain Purna Swaraj or Complete Independence …."*
>
> Excerpts from the Independence Pledge.

Gandhiji's Eleven-Point Ultimatum (31 January 1930)

- On 31 January 1930, to carry forward the mandate given by the Lahore Congress and to appeal to a wide cross section of political opinions, Gandhiji announced an eleven-point ultimatum[14] for Lord Irwin relating the abstract concept of independence to certain specific demands, a compromise formula which included, according to Sumit Sarkar's classification:
    - Six **issues of general interest**:
        - Reduction of military expenditure and civil service salaries
        - Total prohibition
        - Discharge of political prisoners not convicted of murder
        - Reform of the CID and its popular control and changes in the Arms Act
    - Three **specific bourgeois demands**:
        - Lowering of the rupee-sterling exchange rate to 1s 4d
        - Protective tariff on foreign cloth
        - Reservation of coastal traffic for Indian shipping companies
    - Two basically **peasant themes**:
        - 50 per cent reduction of land revenue and its subjection to legislative control
        - Abolition of salt tax and government salt monopoly
- However, many Congress leaders considered this charter of demands as a climb down from the goal of *Purna Swaraj* and registered their protest against the same.

> *"What is the point of making a list of our political and social reforms when we were talking in terms of Independence. Did Gandhiji mean the same thing when he used this term as we did or did we speak a different language."*
>
> Excerpts from Jawaharlal Nehru's Autobiography.

[14] Gandhiji stated that if these eleven demands of administrative reform were accepted by Lord Irwin, then there would be no civil disobedience and the Congress would participate in any conference.

Congress Working Committee Meeting (mid-February 1930)

- With the Government paying no heed to Gandhi's proposal, the Congress Working Committee met at Sabarmati Ashram and invested Gandhiji with full powers to launch the Civil Disobedience Movement at a time and place of his choice.

> *"On bended knees, I asked for bread and received a stone instead. The English nation responds only to force and I am not surprised by the Viceregal reply."*
>
> Gandhiji

Civil Disobedience Movement (1930–34)

Out of all the demands raised, Gandhiji chose to start the Civil Disobedience Movement with the violation of the salt tax. The selection of the issue of the salt tax was done after careful scrutiny by Gandhiji since salt being the part of food habits of people was a daily necessity for the masses and apart from affecting all sections of the population, it also had a far-reaching emotional content since in common folklore, it carried with it the implications of trust, hospitality and mutual obligations. Moreover, the violation of the salt tax did not have any socially divisive implications unlike a no-rent campaign and it also did not threaten government finances or any vested interests and therefore had minimal possibility of alienating any of the non-Congress political elements, or provoking severe government repression. Gandhiji also probably felt that the salt *satyagraha* could be made into a highly emotive issue and had potential for great publicity value which could be effectively utilised to politically mobilise the masses and thus, he formally launched the movement by his historic **Dandi March**.

Dandi March (12 March 1930 – 6 April 1930)

Gandhiji accompanied by 78 of his followers started his famous Dandi March from the Sabarmati Ashram at Ahmedabad to Dandi on the Gujarat Coast. As the 241-mile-long [15] march proceeded, the number of *satyagrahis* grew and finally on 6 April, reaching the coast at Dandi Gandhiji and his companions defiantly broke the law by picking up a handful of salt from the sea and inaugurated the Civil Disobedience Movement. The violation of the Salt Law symbolised the resolve of Indian people to not live under the British-made laws and rule along with also signifying a rejection of the Government's claims on the allegiance of the people.

> *"There is no article like salt outside water by taxing which the State can reach even the starving millions, the sick, the maimed and the utterly helpless. The tax constitutes therefore the most inhuman poll tax the ingenuity of man can devise."*
>
> Gandhiji

[15] Which is 385 Kms.

Spread of the Salt Satyagraha (1930)

- The March attracted enormous publicity both in India and overseas, and was followed by wholesale illegal manufacture and sale of salt, accompanied by boycott of foreign cloth and liquor all over the country. For instance:
  - In Tamil Nadu, **C. Rajagopalachari**, led a salt march from Trichinopoly to Vedaranniyam on the Tanjore coast.
  - In Malabar, **K. Kelappan**, the hero of the Vaikom *Satyagraha,* walked from Calicut to Payannur to break the salt law.
  - A band of *satyagrahis* walked all the way from Sylhet in Assam to Noakhali on the Bengal coast to make salt.
  - In Andhra, a number of sibirams (military style camps) were set up in different districts to serve as the headquarters of the salt *satyagraha,* and bands of *satyagrahis* marched through villages on their way to the coastal centres to defy the law.
- However, things began to take an abrupt turn towards the end of April, as violent revolutionary activities and less disciplined mass upsurge began to take place in different parts of the country. It is during this time that the **armoury raid** was conducted by Surya Sen and his team at Chittagong in Bengal while in Peshawar, the masses became unruly after the arrest[16] of **Khan Abdul Ghaffar Khan** (Badsha Khan), the local charismatic leader. The Peshawar demonstrations were also significant and **historic** in itself as it was at Peshawar that the soldiers of the Garhwali regiments refused to fire on the unarmed crowd. Then, around early May, Gandhiji himself was arrested resulting in a spontaneous textile strike in Sholapur, where the workers went around rampaging government buildings and other official targets in the city.
- Another memorable non-violent heroic event happened on May 21 at **Dharasana Salt Works** where Sarojini Naidu[17], Imam Saheb[18] and Gandhiji's son, Mani Lal leading a band of 2000 volunteers took up the unfinished[19] task of Bapu and raided the sealed Dharasana Salt Works. The unarmed and peaceful *satyagrahis* were met with a brutal lathicharge which left 2 dead and 320 injured yet none of the volunteers raised a finger.

> *"Suddenly at a word of command, scores of native policemen rushed upon the advancing marchers and rained blows on their head with their steel-shod lathis. Not one of the marchers even raised an arm to fend off the blows ... Those struck down fell sprawling unconscious or writhing with fractured skulls or broken shoulders. The survivors, without breaking ranks, silently and doggedly marched on until struck down. In 18 years of my reporting in twenty countries, during which I have witnessed innumerable civil disturbances, riots, street fights and rebellions, I have never witnessed such harrowing scenes as at Dharasana."*
>
> Excerpts from the article written by American journalist Webb Miller.[20]

---

[16] On 23 April 1930, Khan Abdul Gaffar Khan also known as Frontier Gandhi was arrested in the North West Frontier Province which led to a mass demonstration of unprecedented magnitude in Peshawar. Popularly known as Badsha Khan, it was more because of his mass work that led to the formation of the band of non-violent revolutionaries, the Khudai Khidmatgars, popularly known as the Red Shirts, who played an active role in the Civil Disobedience Movement. The atmosphere created by their political work contributed to the mass upsurge in Peshawar during which the city was virtually in the hands of the crowd for more than a week.

[17] The first Indian woman to become President of the Congress.

[18] Gandhiji's comrade of the South African struggle.

[19] Before his arrest, Gandhiji was planning a *satyagraha* at the Dharsana Salt Works in Gujarat.

[20] Whose account of the Dharasana *satyagraha* carried the flavour of Indian nationalism to many distant lands, and whose description of the resolute heroism of the *satyagrahis* demonstrated effectively that non-violent resistance was no meek affair.

- The salt *satyagraha* in the meantime grew almost spontaneously into a mass satyagraha and was eagerly adopted by people in Wadala (Bombay), Karnataka (Sanikatta Salt Works), Andhra Pradesh, Midnapore, Balasore, Puri and Cuttack.

Other Forms of Mass Struggle (1930)

- Meanwhile, with the onset of monsoon which made the manufacture of salt difficult, the Congress Working Committee switching off to other forms of mass struggle now urged the people for non-payment of revenue in the Ryotwari areas, non-payment of Chaukidari taxes in the zamindari areas and violation of forest laws in Maharashtra, Karnataka and the Central Provinces.
- Gradually, the movement also included the social boycott of police and lower level administrative officials. Everywhere merchants and shopkeepers dealing in foreign cloth had to face picketing and social boycott.
- The Government too retaliated through large-scale confiscations of property, yet thousands of peasants heroically stood their ground, at times migrating *en masse* to neighbouring princely states. For instance, the peasants in Gujarat, starting from Bardoli, refused to pay revenue, braving the seizure of their crops and lands moved to Baroda and stayed there in the open fields.
- Similarly, in Monghyr, Saran and Bhagalpur districts of **Bihar**, in Midnapore district of **Bengal**, peasant defiance took the form of refusal to pay chowkidar tax[21] as with the case of **UP**, where a no-revenue and no-rent campaign was launched specifically in the districts of Agra and Rae-Bareli.
- In **Assam**, a powerful agitation was launched against the infamous 'Cunningham circular' by students which forced students and their guardians to furnish assurances of good behaviour, whereas in **Nagaland**, Rani Gaidinliu[22], at a mere age of 13 years, urged her community to reject the British rule and ignited the flame of nationalism in the hearts of the people of North East. She was arrested when she was merely 16 years old in 1932 and was put on trial and sentenced to life imprisonment in 1933.
- The movement also popularised a variety of other forms of mobilisation like **Prabhatpheris,** in which bands of men, women and children went around at dawn singing nationalist songs, utilisation of magic lanterns lectures to spread the nationalist message across the villages and towns and even organisation of Children into vanar senas or monkey armies thereby initiating the young brains to the nationalist fold. Strategic efforts were also undertaken to defy the ban under the hated Press Act and hence secret *Patrikas* or illegal news-sheets, sometimes written by hand and sometimes cyclostyled were utilised to spread the awareness about the movement.
- All of these encouraged in nearly all parts of India, a mass movement that did not merely involve non-cooperation with a foreign government, but actual violation of its laws to achieve complete independence.

---

[21] *Chowkidar* tax was levied specially on the villages for maintaining the guards who supplemented the small police force in the rural areas.

[22] Gaidinliu was just 13 when she joined her cousin, Haipou Jadonang's, Heraka movement, a spiritual movement dedicated to reviving the ancient Naga tribal religion which soon evolved into a political movement fighting the British to establish a Naga Raj in the area. When Haipou was executed in 1931 by the British, Gaidinliu took over the leadership of the Heraka movement and successfully mobilised her people (including young girls and women) to wage guerrilla warfare against the British. She proclaimed, '*We are free people, the white men should not rule over us....*' After getting arrested in 1932 by the British authorities, she could be freed only in 1947 after India won independence when Nehru bestowed on her the title of 'Rani'. She was probably the only woman freedom fighter who was imprisoned for such a long period, of almost 15 years. After release from prison, she worked for the development of the Zeliangrong tribal people (which comprised the Rongmei, Zeme and the Liangmai tribes).

Government's Confusion (1930)

- However, the Government's attitude throughout 1930 was ambivalent and full of confusion. It faced the classic dilemma of *damned if you do, damned if you don't*, that is, if it did not suppress a movement that brazenly defied its laws, its administrative authority would be seen to be undermined and Congress will cry 'victory', but on the other hand if it did suppress it, it would be seen as a brutal administration that used violence on non-violent agitators and Congress will cry 'repression'. Either way, it led to the erosion of the hegemony of the British government.
- Even Gandhiji's arrest came after much vacillation and thereafter adopting a strict demeanour, the government issued certain ordinances curbing the civil liberties of the people along with giving a free hand to the provincial governments to ban the civil disobedience organisations. From September 1930 onwards, the movement also began to decline. In the urban areas, the enthusiasm of the mercantile classes were dampened by the financial losses while the educated youth felt more attracted towards revolutionary nationalism. In the countryside too, the enthusiasm of the richer peasantry, such as the Patidars of Gujarat or the Jats of UP dissipated due to confiscation and sale of properties. But, still the strategy-wise confusion persisted among government ranks and till the end of June, the Congress Working Committee was not declared unlawful while neither the functioning Congress President, Motilal Nehru, put behind bars and nor the local Congress Committees were banned till August.
- Meanwhile, in May 1930, the report of the Simon Commission was published which surprisingly contained no mention of 'Dominion Status' upsetting even the moderate political opinion. In fact, registering their protest against the same, Madan Mohan Malaviya and M.S. Aney courted arrest.

Efforts for Truce (July–August 1930)

- Thereafter, on 9 July, as a conciliatory gesture, the **Viceroy Irwin** suggested a Round Table Conference and reiterated the goal of Dominion Status. He also accepted the suggestion made by 40 members of the Central Legislature that Tej Bahadur Sapru and M. R. Jayakar be allowed to explore the possibilities of peace between the Congress and the Government.
- Later in August, as the part of the strategy to convince the Congress to take part in the First Round Table Conference, Motilal and Jawaharlal Nehru were taken from Naini Jail to Yervada Jail to meet Gandhiji and discuss the possibilities of a settlement. However, the Congress leaders unequivocally reiterated the acceptance of the following demands for taking the things forward:
  - Right of secession from Britain
  - Complete National government with control over defence and finance
  - An independent tribunal to settle Britain's financial claims
- The British government outrightly rejected these demands and thus talks broke down at this point and as a result, Congress refused to participate in the First Round Table Conference.

First Round Table Conference (12 November 1930–19 January 1931)

- The first ever conference conducted between the **British** and **Indians** as equals was held in London and was attended by the Liberals, the Muslim League, the Hindu Mahasabha and the princes, representatives[23]. For instance:
  - Tej Bahadur Sapru and C. Y. Chintamani represented **Liberals**
  - M. R. Jayakar and B. S. Moonje represented **Hindu Mahasabha**
  - Agha Khan, Mohammed Ali Jinnah, Fazlul Haq represented **Muslim opinion**

[23] Alwar, Baroda, Bhopal, Bikaner, Kashmir, Patiala, Hyderabad, Mysore and Gwalior.

- Sardar Sampuran Singh as a spokesman of the **Sikhs**
- B. R. Ambedkar as representative of the **depressed classes** and K. T. Paul of the **Indian Christians**.

- However, it resulted in nothing substantial, partly because these groups could not agree among themselves on any point, and, partly, because they did not command that kind of influence over the Indian opinion as Congress and, thus, their agreement was politically worthless. Still, two noteworthy takeaways from the Conference were:
  - It recommended the formation of an All India Federation of the British Indian provinces and the Indian States.
  - It also proposed to establish a responsible government at the centre with certain safeguards for the transitional period; however, the period of transition was not clearly specified.
- In fact, accepting the reality, virtually every delegate of the conference reiterated that a constitutional discussion to which the Congress was not a party was a meaningless exercise, thereby making it very clear to the British government that if the Government's strategy of survival was to be based on constitutional advance, then an olive branch to the Congress was imperative.
- And therefore, on the closing day of the conference, even the British Prime Minister Ramsay MacDonald hinted in his statement on the possibility of Congress joining in the next round of deliberations to be held later in the year and, thus, adopting a conciliatory posture, on 17 January 1931, **Lord Irwin** invited Gandhiji and Congress to participate in the Second Round Table Conference. Taking the things further forward, the government unconditionally released all members of the Congress Working Committee, including Gandhiji and Jawaharlal Nehru, on 26 January 1931, the very first anniversary of Independence Day.

The Delhi Pact/Gandhi–Irwin Pact (5 March 1931)

- The Congress Working Committee after deliberating amongst itself for close to 3 weeks, and later having long conversations with delegates who had returned from London, and with other leaders representing a cross section of political opinion, authorised **Gandhiji** to initiate discussions with the Viceroy.
- The fortnight-long discussions which began on 27 February culminated on 5 March 1931 in the form of the Gandhi–Irwin Pact, which being held at Delhi was also known as the Delhi Pact. The Pact was signed by Gandhiji on behalf of the Congress and by Lord Irwin on behalf of the Government, and was historic in the sense that it placed the Congress on an equal footing with the Government.
- The terms of the agreement included acceptance from the British Government for:
  - the immediate release of all political prisoners not convicted for violence
  - the remission of all fines not yet collected
  - the return of confiscated lands not yet sold to third parties
  - lenient treatment for those government employees who had resigned
  - right to make salt for personal consumption to villages along the coast
  - right to peaceful and non-aggressive picketing
  - withdrawal of emergency ordinances[24]
- The **Congress**, on its part, agreed to:
  - discontinue the Civil Disobedience Movement
  - participate in the next Round Table Conference

[24] Like the Prevention of Intimidation Ordinance and the Unlawful Instigation Ordinance both promulgated on 30 May, along with the News Sheets and Newspaper Ordinance (promulgated on 20 July), followed by the Unlawful Association Ordinance of 10 October.

- However, the Congress demands for commutation of Bhagat Singh and his comrades' death sentence to life sentence and a public enquiry into police excesses[25] were not accepted.
- The Pact was later presented to the Congress meeting in Karachi, held in the last week of March 1931, and despite some public demonstrations against Gandhiji by groups of radical youth, the Congress passed a resolution on 29 March approving the terms of 'the provisional settlement', but also asserted that the Congress goal of *Purna Swaraj* remains intact. Thus, phase I of the Civil Disobedience Movement was brought to an end.

Critical Analysis of the Civil Disobedience Movement (Phase-I)

The Civil Disobedience Movement of 1930–31 marked a significant impact on the nationalist movement and proved to be an important stage in the progress of the anti-imperialist struggle.

Significance and Impact

- The movement was significant from the point of view that it widened the base of the freedom struggle and garnered remarkable support from the hitherto untouched sections. The overall strong middle class support to the movement reflected in the election data wherein the Congress imposed boycott in the limited electorates forced a fall from a poll percentage of 48.07 in the previous elections (1926) to a mere 26.1 in the elections held in September 1930 for the central legislative assembly. A similar trend was noticeable in all provinces with the sharpest fall observed in Bombay, from 48.2 in 1926 to 16.5 in 1930.
  - One of the unique features of the movement was that it received massive support from the business community that provided the finance during the initial days and supported the boycott movement, particularly that of foreign cloth. For instance, the value of imported cloth declined from £26 million in 1929 to £13.7 million in 1930. Though depression partly contributed to this fallout, it was also partly on account of the merchants' refusal to indent foreign cloth for a specific period.
  - The other most important feature of the Civil Disobedience Movement was large-scale women's participation. Once the movement was launched, the women belonging to all sections of society were fully incorporated into the struggle and they participated enthusiastically in large numbers in the picketing of shops dealing in foreign cloth and liquor, at times astonishing the whole country and bewildering the authorities. The Civil Disobedience Movement surely marked their entry into the public spaces and is believed to be one of the most liberating experiences for them till date.
  - A vast variety of social groups were also politicised though regional variations were noticed. For instance, if the urban elements like merchants and shopkeepers and students were more active in Tamil Nadu and Punjab, and in cities in general, the peasants had come to the forefront in Gujarat, UP, Bengal, Andhra and Bihar, while the tribals held the fort in the Central Provinces, Maharashtra, Karnataka and Bengal. The workers also joined numerous mass demonstrations in Bombay, Calcutta and Madras and were in the forefront in Sholapur.
  - Though the participation of Muslims in the Civil Disobedience Movement was certainly nowhere[26] near that in 1920–22, still the participation of Muslims was not insignificant. There was an overwhelming participation in the North-West Frontier Province as well in Bengal where the enthusiastic middle-class Muslim participated in large numbers in the Senhatta, Tripura, Gaibandha, Bagura and Noakhali districts while the Muslim weaving community of Bihar, Delhi and Lucknow also supported the movement.

---

[25] But Gandhiji's insistent request for an enquiry was recorded in the agreement.

[26] Partly due to the appeals of communal leaders to stay away and partly because of the active Government encouragement of communal dissension to counter the forces of nationalism.

- In terms of radicalism as Sumit Sarkar (1983) has argued, the Civil Disobedience movement witnessed a definite advance over the 1920 movement. In Civil Disobedience Movement, the number of people who went to jail were estimated at over 90,000, more than three times the figure for the Non-Cooperation Movement of 1920–22. Similarly, during the Civil Disobedience Movement, the imports of cloth from Britain decreased by half, while other imports like *cigarettes* suffered a similar fate, and there was a substantial decrease in the Government income from liquor excise and land revenue.
- Above all, with the Gandhi–Irwin pact, the mighty British Government was forced to treat the movement and their leader as an equal for the first time, which greatly boosted the morale of the masses and added to the prestige and strength of the Congress who portrayed the pact as a trophy of victory over the Government. Indeed, the severe repression exhibited during the 1932–33 period was much to retaliate the earlier embarrassment faced by the Government due to the countryside celebrations of triumph.

Limitations of the Civil Disobedience Movement

- The Civil Disobedience Movement was, however, not an unqualified success as there was a discernible absence of Hindu–Muslim unity, and unlike the past movements it did suffer from the absence of major participation on account of the intelligentsia and labour class.
- A certain section of people, especially the youth of the country and young leaders like Jawaharlal Nehru and Subhash Chandra Bose, who had considered the movement as an uncompromising struggle for complete independence, were greatly disappointed with the withdrawal of the movement and were left to wonder if all the sound and fury had not ended in 'a whimper'. Similar dismay was expressed by the peasants of Gujarat who were not happy that some of their lands did not come back to them immediately[27].
- Another major limitation was on account of the discontinuation of the Civil Disobedience Movement on account of the **controversial**[28] Gandhi–Irwin pact. Many historians like R. J. Moore (1974) and Sumit Sarkar (1976) proposed the theory that the compromise of 1931 and the subsequent withdrawal of the movement was more **on account of bourgeois pressure**. The same position was also widely accepted by other historians too across the ideological spectrum, like Judith Brown (1977), Claude Markovits (1985) and Basudev Chatterji (1992), who all argued that the alliance between Congress and the Capitalists was uneasy and vulnerable from the very beginning, and with the uncontrolled mass movement, the business classes got unnerved and wanted to give peace a chance. Hence, they built up the pressure on Gandhiji to return to constitutional politics, which ultimately culminated in the Gandhi–Irwin Pact.

> *"The enthusiasm of the industrialists was dampened by the depression, boycott, hartals and the social disruptions, and they wanted either to destroy civil disobedience or broker a peace between Congress and the government."*
>
> A. D. D. Gordon

However, the ground level position was not that much simplistic as explained by the critics of this theory who pointed out to the fact that the business communities were never entirely in a position[29] to pressurise Gandhiji to withdraw the movement. Also, the business groups hardly represented a homogeneous class in 1931 and did not speak with one voice and probably one of the most weighty **reasons for withdrawal** of the

[27] They were returned after the Congress Ministry assumed office in Bombay in 1937.

[28] The terms on which the Pact was signed, its timing, the motives of Gandhiji in signing the Pact, his refusal to make the Pact conditional on the commutation of the death sentences of Bhagat Singh and his comrades have generated considerable controversy and debate among contemporaries and historians alike.

[29] Although they supported the movement and could partly claim credit for its early success.

movement was appearance of radicalism and violence among certain groups of people who refused to remain under the control of local Congress leaders. Since the movement was moving against the Gandhian creed of non-violence, Gandhiji settled for compromise and withdrawal. More significantly, these perceptions are based on an understanding that fails to grasp the basic strategy and character of the Indian national movement. For one, this understanding ignores the fact which has been stressed earlier that the mass movements are necessarily short-lived as they cannot go on forever, since the people's capacity to sacrifice, unlike that of the activists, is not endless, and specifically after September, 1930, there were certainly signs of exhaustion in large and important sectors of the movement. For instance, in the towns, the shopkeepers and merchants were finding it difficult to bear any more losses, and the support from these sections, so crucial in making the boycott a success, had begun to gradually decline. Similarly, in rural India those areas that had begun their resistance early in the year were fairly quiet in the second half of the year.

The Truce Months (March–December 1931)

- During the truce months, as per the Delhi Pact, Congress restrained **no-tax** and **no-rent movements**, which surely resulted in the loss of some crucial months precisely when rural discontent was at its height, with the Depression having its initial impact, and when sheer economic distress had not yet ruined the potential for large-scale struggle. Ironically, later when the Congress did give the call for no-tax again, in January 1932, precious time had lapsed. Even Gandhiji's entry into the Second Round Table Conference ended in a virtual fiasco.

Second Round Table Conference (7 September 1931–1 December 1931)

- The Second Round Table was attended by the British Prime Minister, **Ramsay Macdonald**[30] and **Gandhiji** (represented the INC), Sarojini Naidu (represented the Indian women), Madan Mohan Malaviya, M. R. Jayakar, Dr B. R. Ambedkar (represented the depressed classes), Ghanshyam Das Birla, Tej Bahadur Sapru, Mohammad Ali Jinnah, Aga Khan III, Muhammad Iqbal, Sir Mirza Ismail Diwan of Mysore, S. K. Dutta and Sir Syed Ali Imam along with further representation from Liberals, Justice Party, Sikhs, Indian Christians, Parsis, Europeans, Anglo-Indians, big landlords and the princes.
- The conference recommended on the matters of:
  - the composition of the Indian federation
  - structure of the federal judiciary
  - the mode of accession of states to the federation
  - distribution of financial resources
- However, it was deemed a failure because of the many disagreements among the participants regarding separate electorates,[31] and while the INC claimed to speak for the entire nation, the claim was strongly contested by the other participants resulting in further chaos.
- The session ended with **MacDonald's announcement** of:
  - Two Muslim majority provinces – North-West Frontier Province (NWFP) and Sindh
  - The prospect of a unilateral British Communal Award if Indians failed to agree.
- Eventually, the British Government refused to concede the basic Indian demand for independence and Gandhiji came back disappointed from the Conference to a changed political situation.

[30] However, unlike the previous time, British PM Macdonald was heading not a Labour government, but a coalition National government dominated by Conservative Cabinet with Samuel Hoare as the Secretary of State for India.

[31] Gandhiji and Ambedkar differed on the issue of separate electorates for the depressed classes or untouchables as Gandhjii was strongly against treating untouchables as separate from the Hindu community, and this issue was later resolved through the Poona Pact (1932). Similarly, there were differences regarding providing separate electorates to the Minorities, and except Sikhs, the gap between the Congress and all of the minorities (including Dalits) was increased.

Pre-Emptive Strike Against the Congress (1931 Onwards)

- Meanwhile, the new British dispensation as well as the new Viceroy **Lord Willingdon** drawing their own inferences from the political impact of the Delhi Pact and believing that the earlier Government had made a major error in negotiating and signing a truce with the Congress thereby doing the blunder of raising the political prestige of the **Congress** along with undermining and lowering the **British prestige** were now determined to reverse the process and, thus, the higher British officials in India decided to launch a pre-emptive strike against the Congress, and in the coming months followed the Government policy of *No pact, no truce, no Gandhi-Viceroy meetings, no quarter for the enemy.*
- The new British policy was described as one of **Civil Martial Law** and was dominated by three major considerations:
  - Gandhiji must not be permitted to build up the tempo for a massive and protracted mass movement, as he had done in 1919, 1920–21 and 1930.
  - The Government functionaries, that is, the village officials, police and higher bureaucrats and the loyalists must not feel disheartened that Gandhiji was being 'resurrected as a rival authority to the Government of India', and that the Government was losing the will to rule.
  - In particular, the nationalist movement must not be permitted to gather force and consolidate itself in rural areas, as it was doing all over India, especially in UP, Gujarat, Andhra, Bihar, Bengal and NWFP.
- While Gandhiji was in London, the Government of India through carefully drafted series of ordinances decided to launch 'a hard and immediate blow' against any revival of the movement and, thereby, ushered a virtual civil martial law in certain areas in the name of establishing law and order. For instance:
  - In UP, during the truce period, when the Congress was leading a campaign for reduction of rent, remission of arrears of rent and prevention of eviction of tenants for non-payment of rents, the Government defying the truce behaviour arrested many prominent leaders like **Jawaharlal Nehru** and confiscated the lands, houses, cattle, agricultural implements and other property of the protesters.
  - Similarly, in the North-Western Frontier Province (NWFP), the Government continued its severe repression against the non-violent Khudai Khidmatgars and arrested their leader **Abdul Ghaffar Khan** again on 24 December along with putting Peshawar district under martial law.
  - The same situation prevailed in Bengal where the Government ruled through draconian ordinances and detained thousands of political workers in the name of fighting terrorism. In September, the police even fired upon political prisoners in Hijli jail, killing two.

Resumption of the Civil Disobedience Movement (December 1931–April 1934)

- With nothing concrete or useful coming out of the Second Round Table Conference along with taking cognisance of the harsh pre-emptive strike against the national movement, the Congress Working Committee decided to resume the **Civil Disobedience Movement** after the immediate return of Gandhiji from London on 28 December. However, still trying to explore the possibilities of a truce, Gandhiji requested the Viceroy for a meeting on 31 December and offered to suspend the decision on civil disobedience till the conclusion of the meeting but the **Viceroy** bluntly refused[32] to meet Gandhiji. Rather on the contrary, **Gandhiji** was arrested on 4 January 1932, and within a week, all other leading Congressmen across the country were put behind bars.

[32] The first of many such refusals during the next 5 years.

- The **Congress** and its allied organisations were declared illegal and their offices and funds were seized. Even the Gandhi Ashrams were not spared and nearly all of them were occupied by the police. Peaceful picketers, *satyagrahis* and non-violent processionists were subjected to relentless repression and were lathi-charged, brutally beaten and often awarded rigorous imprisonment and heavy fines, which were at times realised by selling their lands and property at throwaway prices. Severe restrictions were also imposed on the freedom of the press to report or comment on the disobedience movement, or even to print pictures of *satyagrahis* along with large-scale ban on all forms of Nationalist literature. Thus, within the first 6 months of 1932, action was taken against 109 journalists and 98 printing presses.
- Outmanoeuvred and facing severe repression on an unprecedented scale, the Indian masses still fought valiantly for about a year and half. Around 80,000 *satyagrahis* were jailed in the first 3 months while lakhs took to the picketing of shops selling liquor and foreign cloth. Unbaffled by the Government harassment, even a small village like Ras in Kheda withheld revenue despite confiscation of 2,000 acres, public whipping and electric shocks in 1933.

However, as with mass movements that they cannot sustain at the same pace for quite long and also due to the added factors of ruthless repression, political realism combined with economic calculations of certain sections of Indians[33] and due to absence of sufficient time and momentum to build up the tempo of the movement, it gradually started declining. In fact, by August 1933 only *4,500 satyagrahis* were in jail. Thus, even though the movement was renewed with greater vigour, it had evoked less enthusiasm as compared to phase I of the movement. Still, the movement continued to linger till early **April 1934** when the inevitable decision to withdraw it was taken by Gandhiji. The nationalists were clearly frustrated and despaired at the turn of events and many started raising questions over Gandhiji's leadership and strategy. On the other hand, the British were gloating over their sense of victory.

"Mr. Gandhi as a political leader has failed and thus there is need for a radical reorganisation of the Congress on a new principle with a new method, for which a new leader is essential."

Statement of Subhas Chandra Bose and Vithalbhai Patel, 1933.

"The Congress is in a definitely less favourable position than in 1930, and has lost its hold on the public."

Viceroy Willingdon declared in early 1933.

Though it is true that people were cowed down by superior force, they had not lost faith in the Congress. The Civil Disobedience Movement may not have succeeded in its goal of achieving independence and may had been temporarily crushed, but coming in contact with the process of the movement, the Indian people had been further transformed and their will to fight against the unjust British rule had been further strengthened. The left alternatives emerged from the aftermath of civil disobedience only. And, as with other movements, this hiatus too was primarily to rest and regroup. And this became evident to all, when the Congress captured a majority in six out of eleven provinces in the elections in 1937, despite the restricted nature of the franchise (to be discussed in detail shortly).

---

[33] Specifically the big business houses who now collaborated with the British like the Bombay mill owners who concluded the Lees Mody Pact in October 1933, aligning with Lancashire out of fear of Japanese competition and businessmen like G. D. Birla and Thakurdas who were pressing the Congress for a compromise since as early as 1932 when Thakurdas had warned Motilal Nehru that *the capacity of the commercial community for endurance has reached its limits* and industrialists like Homi Body who had denounced that the *frequent hartals dislocated trade and industry*.

"Withdrawal of the movement did not mean defeat or loss of mass support; rather it only meant having fought long enough, we prepare to rest, to fight another day a bigger battle with greater and better organised force."

Dr. M. A. Ansari

"I have no sense of defeat in me and the hope in me that this country of ours is fast marching towards its goal is burning as bright as it did in 1920 …. I feel no despondency in me … I am not feeling helpless … The nation has got energy of which you have no conception but I have."

Gandhiji

Communal Award and Poona Pact (1932)

In pursuance of the old colonial policy of 'Divide and Rule', the British Prime Minister, **Ramsay MacDonald**, announced on August 16 1932, the proposal on minority representation, better known as the **Communal Award**,[34] which provided for separate electorates for the Muslims, the Europeans, the Sikhs, the Anglo-Indians, the Indian-based Christians and the **depressed classes**. Under the separate electorates system, each minority community was allocated a number of seats in the legislatures, and only the members from these communities were eligible to vote to elect a representative, that is, Muslims would be elected only by Muslims and Sikhs only by Sikhs and so on. The Award declared the depressed classes[35] also to be a minority community entitled to separate electorate and, thus, separated them from the rest of the Hindus.

Though the Congress was in principle strongly opposed to the system of separate electorates as it encouraged the communal notion that each minority community was a separate group having interests different from the general body of Indians which inevitably led to the division of the Indian people thereby hampering the growth of a common national consciousness and consequently weakening of the national movement, **yet** the idea of a separate electorate for other minorities had been accepted by the Congress as far back as 1916 (Lucknow Pact) and, thus, the Congress was now not in favour of changing the Communal Award without the consent of the minorities and, hence, decided neither to accept the Communal Award nor to reject it. However, the provision of according separate electorates to the depressed classes by treating them as separate political entities was vehemently opposed by all the nationalists, especially by Gandhiji who argued that separate electorates would ensure that *untouchables remain untouchables in perpetuity*.

"The Award was an attack on Indian unity and nationalism, harmful to both Hinduism and the Depressed Classes, for it provided no answers to the socially degraded position of the latter. Whatever harm separate electorates might do to Muslims or Sikhs, it did not affect the fact that they would remain Muslims or Sikhs. But, once the Depressed Classes were treated as a separate community, the question of abolishing untouchability would not arise, and the work of Hindu social reform in this respect would come to a halt."

Gandhiji's strong reaction from Yeravada jail on the issue of separate electorates to the Depressed Classes.

[34] The Communal Award was based on the findings of the Indian Franchise Committee, called the Lothian Committee.

[35] Which is the Scheduled Castes.

Emphasising further on addressing the root cause of the problem, **Gandhiji** advocated for total eradication of untouchability, and instead of separate electorates, he demanded that the representatives of the depressed classes be elected by the general electorate through universal common franchise and even larger number of the seats can be reserved for the depressed classes. To enforce his demand and persuade the recalcitrant B. R. Ambedkar to accept his view point on this issue, he resorted to a fast unto death on 20 September 1932.

> *"My life, I count of no consequence. One hundred lives given for this noble cause would, in my opinion, be poor penance done by Hindus for the atrocious wrongs they have heaped upon helpless men and women of their own faith …."*
>
> Gandhiji's statement to the Press.

As expected, to placate **Gandhiji**, the political leaders of different political persuasions, such as Madan Mohan Malaviya, M. C. Rajah and B. R. Ambedkar, initiated discussions and subsequently on 25 September 1932, arrived at an agreement, known as the **Poona Pact**[36], according to which the idea of separate electorates for the depressed classes was abandoned and instead the principle of joint electorates with increased number of reserved seats for depressed classes was accepted. The specific clauses of the Poona Pact included:

- As against 71 allotted seats promised to the depressed classes in the provincial legislatures by the Communal Award, they were increased to 148 (later to 151) while in the Central Legislature they were fixed to 18 per cent of the total seats.
- Apart from that, it was also promised to reserve a certain percentage of seats for the depressed classes allowed to the general non-Muslim electorate.
- Adequate representation to be provided to the depressed classes in the civil services.

> *"I would like to assure my Harijan friends … that they may hold my life as a hostage for its due fulfilment."*
>
> Gandhiji's declaration regarding the Poona agreement just immediately after his breaking of fast.

As true to his words, for the next nearly 2 years, Gandhiji gave up all other pre-occupations and initiated a whirlwind campaign against untouchability, first from Yeravada jail and after his release from his ashram at **Wardha**[37]. In fact, for the next nearly 9 months, starting from Wardha, he undertook an intensive 'Harijan Campaign' covering almost 20,000 kms across the country sensitising the people against different forms and practices of untouchability. He also founded the **Harijan Sewak Sangh** and urged the social workers to go to the villages for the social, cultural, economic and political uplift of the Harijans[38]. As a matter of fact, it was Gandhiji who made untouchability one of the crucial questions of Indian politics, necessary to achieve Swaraj.

Gandhiji's Harijan Campaign (7 November 1933–29 July 1934)

During the course of his Harijan campaign, Gandhiji devoted himself in convincing both his followers as well as the general masses about his concern regarding the **removal of the untouchability**. In fact, for expressing his seriousness

[36] Madan Mohan Malaviya signed it on behalf of Gandhiji. The Pact was later ratified by the British Government and became the basis of Dalit representation to provincial assemblies in the Government of India Act, 1935. However, neither the Pact was able to satisfy the depressed classes fully nor was it liked by the caste Hindus. As rightly summed up by Ambedkar, '*Disliked by the Hindus and disfavoured by the untouchables, though the Poona Pact was given recognition by both parties and today the untouchables have a few more seats than were given by the Communal Award yet, this is all that they have. Every other member is indifferent, if not hostile. If the Communal Award with its system of double voting had remained, the untouchables would have had a few seats less but every other member would have been a member for the untouchables.*'

[37] Interestingly, Gandhiji had vowed in 1930 not to return to Sabarmati till *Swaraj* was won.

[38] His name for the depressed classes meaning *Children of the God*. In fact, he also renamed his journal *Young India* as Harijan in 1934.

towards the cause and creating public opinion in favour of equal access of all public places and institutions, particularly the entry of *harijans* to public temples, he undertook two major fasts on 8 May and 16 August 1933. Gandhiji's entire campaign was based on the grounds of humanism and reason. He tried to tackle the problem of untouchability at two levels, at one level, affirming faith in the moral and spiritual force of the human mind, he laid emphasis on the change of heart among the upper castes, calling upon them to become sensitive to the extreme wretchedness of the victims of untouchability, to atone for the centuries-long misery that Hindu custom had heaped and imposed upon great part of its adherents, while at the religious level, he strongly repudiated the belief that untouchability was sanctified by original Hinduism in the first place and urged the people to ignore the *shastras* if they went against human dignity.

> *"They must either remove untouchability or remove me from their midst…. As a Savarna Hindu, when I see that there are some Hindus called avarnas, it offends my sense of justice and truth and if I discover that Hindu shastras really countenance untouchability as it is seen today, I will renounce and denounce Hinduism."*
>
> Gandhiji's ultimatum, 2 February 1934.

> *"Hinduism dies if untouchability lives, and untouchability has to die if Hinduism is to live."*
>
> Gandhiji

Simultaneously, to integrate the Harijans into the mainstream of the Hindu society, he also suggested a programme of internal reform among Harijans and exhorted them to become aware, conscious of their rights, acquire education and dignity with their own efforts, maintain cleanliness and hygiene among them while uniting and organising among themselves till the rest of the society treated them with the respect due to them. Gandhiji also pointed towards the positive impact that the struggles against untouchability would have on the communal and other questions. For instance, drawing an analogy between the treatment of the non-Hindus by Hindus as untouchables 'in some way or the other', especially in the matters of food and drink, Gandhiji asserted that *if untouchability is removed, it must result in bringing all Indians together.* He also repeatedly pointed out to the fact that the movement had innate potential to produce great political consequences since **untouchability** poisoned the entire social and political fabric and hampered the nation's growth. In fact, during its non-mass movement phases, the Harijan work along with other items of constructive work not only enabled the Congress cadre to be busy but also gradually carried the message of nationalism to the Harijans, who also happened to be agricultural labourers in most parts of the country, leading to their increasing participation in the national as well as peasant movements.

As expected, throughout Gandhiji's Harijan campaign, he was attacked by orthodox and social reactionaries who disrupted his meetings and met him with black flag demonstrations. They publicly burnt his portraits, accused him of attacking Hinduism and also brought out scurrilous and inflammatory leaflets against him. Even a bomb was thrown on a car believed to be carrying Gandhiji, injuring its seven occupants at Poona on 25 June 1934.

However, there were certain controversial issues pertaining to Gandhiji's Harijan Campaign. For instance, though he was an ardent supporter of the removal of untouchability, he was initially not at all in favour of mixing up this issue with the issues of inter-dining and inter-marriage. Rather, on the contrary, he supported the restrictions on the same[39]. Similarly, he distinguished between the abolition of the caste system and the abolition of untouchability. While being in favour of the latter, he believed in the continuity of the caste system. Also, in keeping with his basic philosophy of non-violence, Gandhiji was completely opposed to exercise compulsion even on the orthodox supporters of untouchability and rather insisted on the approach of persuasion even for adamant orthodox Hindus.

---

[39] Gandhiji's reasoning for the logic was that they were also practised by caste Hindus among themselves as also the Harijans among themselves. The present All-India campaign, he said, had to be directed against the disabilities which were specific to the Harijans.

> *"Whatever the limitations and defects of the Varnashram, there is nothing sinful about it, as there is about untouchability."*
>
> Gandhiji's views on the Caste System.

His campaign was, thus, not a clear success, though not much owing to Gandhiji's fault but on account of failure of Indian people, rather of Hindu society which failed to overcome the forces of inertia, orthodoxy, retrogression and the vested interests to remove the blot of untouchability.

Gandhi versus Ambedkar

Though both the leaders were critical of ills pertaining to the caste system and were committed to the upliftment of depressed classes, both differed greatly in their belief system and approach.

Difference	Gandhiji	B. R. Ambedkar
Belief System	• Gandhiji was a staunch follower of Hinduism, and for the most part of his life he never decisively and categorically renounced his belief in Chaturvarna, that is, *Varnashrama* system. In fact, he took a very long time to acknowledge that the roots of untouchability lay deep within the caste system. However, quite interestingly, though Gandhiji reposed faith in Varnashram, his conception of the Chaturvarna system was quite different than the prevalent hierarchical model as in terms of Gandhiji's version, the 'varna' system was not hierarchical and all the four varnas were equal in status and functional to the society. In his Chaturvarna model, the four varnas were placed horizontally and were mutually replaceable. Also, Gandhiji considered Caste and Varna to be different. • Gandhiji had basic faith in the Vedas and Hindu scriptures like Gita. • Gandhi believed caste-based discrimination to be only a social and moral concern. • Gandhiji never approved of a separation of State and religion. • Gandhiji was immensely proud of the Indian villages and had great faith in the self-sufficiency of villages and for him *Gramrajya* meant *Ramrajya*.	• Ambedkar disregarded Hinduism and regarded it just a prototype of Brahmanism meant for perpetual subjugation of the Dalits. He used to often say that *he wouldn't die a Hindu though he was born one* and eventually having lost all hopes of reform in Hinduism, he converted to Buddhism in the latter phase of his life. Also, Ambedkar held that Varna system was fundamentally opposed to the notion of equality and could not be rationally defended in any form. He denounced the caste system in every way and demanded the complete abolition of the Chaturvarna system. *There cannot be a more degrading system of social organisation than the chaturvarna. It is the system that deadens, paralyses and cripples the people.* –Ambedkar's views • Ambedkar also used to denounce the Vedas and other Hindu scriptures since he believed that the Hindu scriptures do not provide a unified and coherent understanding, and the caste system and untouchability were the manifestations of the Hindu religious scriptures only. • Ambedkar considered caste-based discrimination to be emanating from the ideological, economic and political factors. • Ambedkar believed in the separation of State and Religion. • Ambedkar, on the other hand viewed villages as the scourge of casteism and untouchability and considered them to be status-quoist.

Difference	Gandhiji	B. R. Ambedkar
Difference of Approach and Mode of Action	• Gandhiji was not in favour of the abolition of the caste system or Varnashrama order. Instead, he was in favour ofbringing behavioural changes in the society regarding the ills of the caste system and wanted to reform it bychanging the hearts and minds of people. • Gandhi's approach for the upliftment of the 'Harijans' was through faith and spirituality. In fact, the name given by Gandhiji to the depressed classes was *Harijan*, to primarily sensitise the upper castes Hindus to the plight of the depressed classes by invoking spirituality. • Gandhiji insisted on the importance of changing the moral culture of the wider society to address the grievances of the Harijans. • Gandhiji believed that upper class and Dalits must resolve their differences through peace process without any violence or fights.	• Ambedkar was in favour of annihilation of the caste system and transformation of the Hindu society into casteless society since according to him it was beyond reforms. *There will be outcastes as long as there are castes. Nothing can emancipate the outcaste except the destruction of the caste system.* –Excerpts from Ambedkar's *Annihilation of the Caste* (1936). • On the contrary, regarding the upliftment of the Dalits, Ambedkar preferred a rights-based approach as Ambedkar's referred depressed classes as Dalits to give them a political identity. • While Ambedkar relied much on institutional mechanisms to protect and promote the interests of the untouchables. • Ambedkar insisted that Dalits must use aggressive means to snatch their rights from what he termed as 'oppression' by upper castes.

Critical Analysis of Gandhiji's Approach to Caste and Untouchability

Gandhiji's approach towards caste system has created much misunderstanding in scholarly circles, and till date, he has been accused of excessive deference to Hindu orthodoxy while his approach regarding caste system has been often subjected to numerous attacks by a number of critics for its ambiguity and inconsistency. One of the charges levelled against Gandhiji is that he acted as an apologist for the caste system. Much of the basis for this charge is primarily drawn from the statements of Gandhiji during the 1920s when he considered ***Varnashram*** and the caste system to be an essential form of social organisation, a practicable system of social division of labour, which had in ancient India served Hindu society well to integrate a wide range of ethno-entities.

"If the Hindu society has been able to stand, it is because it is founded on the caste system …. I believe that inter-dining or inter marriage is not necessary for promoting national unity … To destroy caste system and adopt Western European social system means that Hindus must give up the principle of hereditary occupation, which is the soul of the caste system. Hereditary principle is an eternal principle. To change it is to create disorder."

Gandhiji's views as elaborated by him in a Gujarati journal called *Navajivan* in 1921–22.

However, such interpretations regarding Gandhiji's approach towards caste system reflect an oversimplified understanding of a complex phenomenon. Gandhiji's position on caste system cannot be fully understood just from one vantage point as pointed out by **Louis Fischer** and some other sympathetic interpreters who argue that Gandhiji's ideas on caste system evolved from a simplistic understanding to a rational outlook over time, ranging from an all-out orthodox stance in the early years to a liberal one by the 1930s and 1940s. For instance, in the

1920s, Gandhiji defended caste restrictions and stated that he considered the four divisions to be fundamental, natural and essential. This was according to Fischer, the '**orthodox**' Gandhi, but by 1932, Gandhiji moved to a more liberal phase of thought as he began to understand that restrictions on inter-caste dining and marriages were weakening the Hindu society as evident by his article on this issue titled **Caste Must Go**, published in 1935 in which Gandhiji insisted that in *Varnashrama* there was and should be no prohibition of inter-marriage and inter-dining. In the later years, he began to move further away from the orthodox tradition and by 1946 there was the emergence of a 'radical' Gandhi who would approve not only inter caste marriages but also encouraged them as evident in his declaration, '*I therefore tell all my boys and girls who want to marry that they cannot be married at Sevagram Ashram unless one of the parties is a Harijan.*'

Another two important points to be noted before arriving at any conclusive statement regarding Gandhiji's approach towards caste system are:

- Even in early years when he defended the four-fold varna order, Gandhiji **did not observe it in his own circle**. In fact, Gandhiji's beliefs were backed by the force of a lifetime of action. At the age of 12, he had disregarded his mother's warning not to touch Uka, an untouchable who came to clean toilets in his house and challenged his mother that Hinduism did not sanction untouchability. At the age of 18, he defied caste to go abroad, thereafter facing the wrath of his brother who admonished him. In South Africa, persons of all castes, communities, religions and races were welcomed in his house and stayed as members of his family. In 1915, while in India, he accepted the first 'Untouchable' family in the Kocharb Ashram and adopted **Lakshmi,** an untouchable as a daughter and subsequently took the risk of social boycott for accepting untouchables in his ashram on equal terms, performed unclean tasks himself and vowed and worked to eradicate untouchability.
- Certain historians like **Anthony J. Parel** have also pointed out to the fact that Gandhiji's understanding of the caste system was based on the egalitarian principle as sanctioned in the Rig Veda and the Gita, where all the four castes were equal in dignity. In fact, as early as 1934 Gandhiji had declared that the caste ideal as envisaged in the scriptures and as it was practised today was a *hideous travesty* of the original idea and it existed only in distorted form. Later, in a 16 November 1935 article in *Harijan* titled 'Caste has to Go' Gandhiji wrote '*the sooner public opinion abolishes caste the better*', and in his 1936 debate with Ambedkar, Gandhiji reiterated his rejection of caste and claimed it to be harmful both to spiritual and national growth and publicly affirmed his acceptance of inter-dining and intermarriage, which he had thus far hesitated to do, especially after learning of the discrimination faced personally by Ambedkar.

Thus, it would not be wrong to assume that though there was no element of compromise in Gandhiji's attitude towards untouchability, yet his approach towards caste and varna **evolved over time** as he moved from a position of being a cautious reformer to a bolder revolutionary in the later stages of his life.

"When Gandhi first undertook to remove untouchability, the problem of varna dharma was also there. It was easy to see intellectually, even then, that caste ought to go root and branch if untouchability was to be completely eradicated. But as a practical proposition, caste was not the immediate problem then. The problem was only the removal of untouchability. So, he allowed caste to continue, though personally he observed no caste even then. Thus, the work of the removal of untouchability progressed through the early stages, leaving the contradictions of the caste system untouched, and, therefore, without the complication of opposition from those who would resist the abolition of caste. When the stage had come where he found caste ought to go root and branch he proposed not only inter-dining but inter-marriages as well. A mere intellectual might read inconsistency in Gandhi's tolerance of caste earlier and his denunciation of it later. But, to a practical man of non-violent creed these are stages of progress and not principles of contradiction."

Explanation of Gandhiji's approach and method by famous Indian social reformer G. Ramachandra Rao.

"I asked Gandhiji repeatedly why don't u hit out at the caste system directly? He said that he did not believe in the caste system except in some idealised form of occupations and all that; but that the present system was thoroughly bad and must go. I am undermining it completely, he said, by my tackling untouchability ... if untouchability goes ... caste system goes. So I am concentrating on that ... So, he made untouchability the one thing on which he concentrated, which ultimately affected the whole caste system."

Jawahar Lal Nehru's statement clearly pointing out that his concentration on 'untouchability' made him favour abolition of caste-based discrimination more than the caste itself.

The Strategic Debate (1934–37)

Following the withdrawal of the Civil Disobedience Movement, a major debate occurred among the nationalists regarding the future strategy to be followed by them, particularly at two stages:

- **The First-Stage Debate** (1934–35): The first-stage debate happened just immediately after the suspension of the second phase of the Civil Disobedience Movement, that is, during the phase of non-mass struggle when certain disagreements arose between the nationalists about the immediate future course of action.
- **The Second-Stage Debate** (1937): The second-stage debate happened around the question of office acceptance in the context of provincial elections held under the autonomy provisions of the Government of India Act, 1935.

The First-Stage Debate (1934–35)

Immediately after the end of the Civil Disobedience Movement, basically three broad trends emerged regarding the future course of action:

- **Gandhian Trend**: The emphasis was laid on constructive work in the villages, especially the revival of the village crafts and upliftment of the downtrodden Harijans through the special campaign.
- '**New Swarajists' Trend**: A section of Congressmen advocated the revival of the constitutional method of struggle and participation in the elections to the Central Legislative Assembly due for 1934. Popularly known as the New Swarajists, they included the prominent leaders like **Asaf Ali**, Dr. **M. A. Ansari**, **Satyamurthy**, **Bhulabhai Desai** and **B. C. Roy** who argued that:
    - in a period of political apathy, when the Congress was no longer in a position to sustain a mass movement, it was necessary to utilise the opportunity of elections and work in the legislative councils to keep up the political interest and morale of the people.
    - participation in elections and council work did not amount to faith in constitutional politics, rather it only meant opening up another political front, which would help build up the Congress, organisationally extend its influence and prepare the people for the next mass struggle.
- **Strong Leftist Trend**: A strong leftist trend also emerged within the Congress, represented by young radical leaders like **Nehru** and **Bose** who were critical of both constructive work and council entry. Instead, this section favoured resumption or continuation of non-constitutionalist mass struggle and adoption of **Struggle-Victory (SV) strategy** instead of the regular Congress strategy of **Struggle-Truce-Struggle (STS)**.

Struggle-Truce-Struggle Versus Struggle-Victory Strategy

Struggle-Truce-Struggle	Struggle-Victory Strategy
Under STS strategy, a mass phase of movement (struggle phase) had to be followed by a phase of reprieve (truce phase) before the next stage of mass struggle could be taken up. The truce period, it was argued, would enable the masses to recoup their strength to fight and also give the government a chance to respond to the demands of the nationalists.	Under S-V strategy, Nehru suggested a continuous confrontation and conflict with imperial forces till they were overthrown, that is, maintenance of an aggressive direct action policy focusing on 'continuous permanent hostility and non-cooperation' by the Congress, without any interposition of a constitutionalist phase.

With these three diverging trends, a split in the Congress on Surat lines sooner or later was being speculated, but **Gandhiji** conciliated the proponents of council entry by acceding to their basic demand of permission to enter the legislatures and, thus, subsequently in May 1934, the All India Congress Committee (AICC) met in Patna to set up a Parliamentary Board to fight elections[40] under the aegis of the Congress itself, while he placated the Left by strongly backing Nehru for the Presidentship of the Lucknow Congress despite contrary pressure from C. Rajagopalachari and other right-wing leaders.

> *"Parliamentary politics cannot lead to freedom but those Congressmen who could not, for some reason, offer satyagraha or devote themselves to constructive work should not remain unoccupied and could express their patriotic energies through council work provided they are not sucked into constitutionalism or self-serving."*
>
> Gandhiji defending the New Swarajists from the accusations of being lesser patriots.

> *"The withdrawal of the Civil Disobedience Movement did not mean bowing down before the opportunists or compromising with imperialism .... Only civil disobedience had been discontinued, the war continued."*
>
> Gandhiji's statement assuring the leftists.

However, during the same time, Gandhiji realising that he was out of tune with all the powerful trends in the Congress, announced his resignation from the Congress in October 1934 to serve it better in thought, word and deed.

The Government of India Act, 1935

After the Third Round Table Conference[41], a white paper on the new constitution of India was prepared which contained three major proposals, namely **Federation**, **Provincial Autonomy** and **Safeguards**, which vested special powers in the central and provincial executives. Even though the White paper was criticised

[40] Eventually, in the elections held in November 1934 to the Central Legislative Assembly, the Congress captured 45 out of 75 seats reserved for Indians.

[41] Took place between 17 November 1932 and 24 December 1932 without Congress participation (actually INC was not invited). Only 46 delegates in total took part in this conference.

and rejected by all the political parties of India, as it fell far short of complete independence, yet the same formed the basis of the **Government of India Act, 1935**. Some of its main provisions were as follows:

- **Creation of an All India Federation**: The Act prescribed federal structure, comprising all the British Indian provinces and the Indian states (princely states). The British India provinces had to mandatorily join the federation, but this was not compulsory for the princely states. Interestingly, the federation never came into being as the princely states did not join it and the central government carried on up to 1946 as per the provisions of Government of India Act, 1919.
- **Provincial Autonomy**: The Act for the first time recognised provinces as having separate legal entity and introduced **provincial autonomy** while abolishing the system of dyarchy in the provinces.
  - The provinces were provided more autonomy and were allowed to act as autonomous units of administration in their defined spheres. The Governor was the head of the executive and there was a Council of Ministers to advise him. However, the governors still retained special reserve powers. The British authorities could still suspend a provincial government.
  - The Act introduced responsible Government in the provinces, that is, the Governor was required to act with the advice of ministers responsible to the provincial legislatures.
  - The Provinces were freed from the superintendence and direction of the Secretary of the State and Governor-General, and henceforth, derived their legal authority directly from the British Crown.
  - The Provinces were given independent financial powers and resources and they could also borrow money on their own security.

  This, however, does not mean that the Act of 1935 established a full-fledged responsible Government in the Provinces as the Ministers were not absolutely free in matter of running their departments while the Governors still continued to possess a set of overriding powers like power to refuse assent to a bill, promulgate ordinances and were also invested with special executive powers like they could exercise discretion in matters like law and order, interests of minorities and the people of the backward areas, the protection of the British commercial interests and those of the rulers of the states.
- **Division of Powers**: The Act divided the powers between the **Centre** and the **Provinces** in terms of three lists:
  - Federal List (for Centre, with 59 items)
  - Provincial List (for provinces, with 54 items)
  - Concurrent List (for both, with 36 items).

  Residuary powers were given to the Viceroy who could:
  - restore cuts in grants,
  - certify bills rejected by the legislature,
  - issue ordinances,
  - exercise his veto.
- **Dyarchy at the Centre**: The Act abolished dyarchy at the provincial level, but introduced it at the Centre. Consequently, the federal subjects were divided into two categories:
  - Reserved subjects: The mentioned subjects in this category such as external affairs, religious affairs, defence, administration of tribal areas were to be exclusively administered by the Governor-General on the advice of the executive councillors who were not responsible to the central legislature.
  - Transferred subjects: Transferred subjects included all other subjects which were to be administered by the Governor-General on the advice of ministers elected by the legislature.
- **Bicameral Legislature**: The Act introduced bicameralism in the Central Legislature, consisting of an upper house (Council of States) and a lower house (Federal Assembly). Interestingly, the election to the Council of States was direct and that to the Federal Assembly was indirect.

- The Council of States was to be a 260-member house, partly directly elected from British Indian provinces and partly (40 per cent) nominated by the princes, whereas the Federal Assembly was to be a 375-member house, partly indirectly elected from British Indian provinces and partly (one-third) nominated by the princes.
- Council of States was to be a permanent body with one-third members retiring every third year while the term of the Federal Assembly was 5 years but it could be dissolved earlier also.
- Members of Federal Assembly could move a vote of no-confidence against ministers, while the Council of States could not move a vote of no-confidence.
- It also introduced bicameralism in six out of eleven provinces. Thus, the legislatures of Bengal, Bombay, Madras, Bihar, Assam and the United Provinces was made bicameral.

- **Extension of Principle of Communal Representation**: The Act further extended the principle of communal representation by providing separate electorates for the depressed classes (Scheduled Castes[42]), women and labour (workers).
- **Abolition of Council of India**: The new Act abolished the Council of India[43] and instead provided for the appointment of a team of 3-6 advisors for the Secretary of State. It is pertinent to note here that with the introduction of Provincial Autonomy, the control of Secretary of State over the transferred subjects was greatly diminished; however, his control remained intact over the discretionary powers of the Governor-General and the Governors.
- **Extension of Franchise**: Another highlight of the Act was the extension of franchise and nearly 10 per cent of the total population got the right to vote. For the first time, the direct election was introduced in India with the help of this Act though the franchise was based on the criterion of property qualifications.
- **Establishment of New Institutions**: The Act provided for the establishment of a Federal Court, Reserve Bank of India, Federal Public Service Commission, Provincial Public Service Commission, Joint Public Service Commission, Federal Railway Authority[44].
- **Separation of Burma** from India and **Creation of two new provinces** of Sindh and Orissa.

Critical Analysis of Government of India Act, 1935

The Government of India Act, 1935,[45] was an important milestone in the development of a responsible constitutional government as it introduced several new features which later formed the nucleus of our Constitution. Although the Act faced a lot of criticism, there is no denying the fact that the Act did provide the basis for negotiation between the British and Indians for getting independence and was a pioneer in terms of according provisional autonomy.

Significance of the Act

- The Government of India Act, 1935, curtailed the power concentrated in the hands of the Central Government and distributed it among the decentralised form of government and appeared to be the first attempt on part of the Government to give the provinces an autonomous status.
- The Act provided voting rights to more number of people and the introduction of separate electorates for women and workers was surely a welcome step.

[42] A new term introduced by the Act for the depressed classes or untouchables.

[43] Established by the Government of India Act, 1858.

[44] The Act gave the command of the railway in the hands of a new authority called Federal Railway authority, which directly reported to the Governor-General and whose members were free from the control of councillors and ministers. The main idea behind the establishment of this authority was to confirm the British stakeholder that the investment they have done in the railway was safe.

[45] This was the longest Act passed by the British government with 321 sections and 10 schedules. The Act had drawn its content from four sources: Report of the Simon Commission, Discussions and deliberations at the Third Round Table Conference, the White Paper of 1933 and the reports of the Joint select committees.

Criticism of the Act

- The Act of 1935 was condemned by nearly all sections of Indian opinion and was unanimously rejected by the Congress and other political leaders as in spite of its recognition of the aspirations of the Indians to have a responsible government, the Act of 1935 did nothing to fulfil those aspirations and they did not receive anything substantial to feel contented from the Act. Instead, it disappointed them for not providing any assurance about granting Dominion Status, let alone complete independence. The Congress at that stage was, however, demanding the convening of a constituent assembly elected on the basis of adult franchise to frame a constitution for an independent India.
- The Act was criticised and rejected by the Congress also on the ground that in formulating it, the people of India were never consulted, and as such it did not represent their will. Congress charged the government of formulating the Act in such a way as to stall the introduction of responsible government, perpetuate their rule and exploit the Indian masses. The Act was, therefore, denounced as undemocratic in spirit, offensive to people's sovereignty and institutionally unworkable.

> *"A slave constitution that attempted to strengthen and perpetuate the economic bondage of India."*
>
> Indian National Congress statement on Government of India Act, 1935.

> *"The Act had so much to promise to the people for their welfare but was not able to deliver anything that could turn out in its implementation. The Act for Indians seems like driving a car with all breaks but with no engine."*
>
> Jawaharlal Nehru

> *"The Act is thoroughly rotten, fundamentally bad and totally unacceptable."*
>
> M. A. Jinnah

> *"After all, we framed the constitution ... of 1935 because we thought it the best way ... to hold India to the empire."*
>
> Confession of Viceroy Lord Linlithgow.

- Though provisional autonomy was the right step in the right direction, yet with tremendous discretionary overriding powers with the Governors even the provincial autonomy was reduced to a farce. Also, in terms of the net effect, not much gain was achieved as while the Congress' attention was diverted to the provinces, strong imperial control was maintained at the centre. As rightly pointed out by **B. R. Tomlinson**, '*in terms of any change that happened, the apex of the system of imperial control moved from London to*

Delhi'. The Viceroy was now to enjoy many of the powers previously exercised by the Secretary of State but still the relationship was meant to protect imperial interests only.

- The Act also failed to provide a proper federal structure, as the majority of the power was with the Governor General who was not at all responsible for the central legislature which meant that the legislature was basically toothless. Even, the proposed formation of the federation was also fundamentally defective since the entry into the federation was compulsory for the provinces but voluntary for the princely states. Besides it, the princely states were to be represented in the federal legislature not by the elected representatives of the states but by the nominees of the native rulers. Still after all that, the federation scheme ultimately failed as the princes eventually did not join it[46].
- The Act did not concede the right to vote to all the adults. The property qualifications, the system of separate electorates and the provisions of safeguards were violative of democratic rights of the people. The Act not only retained the system of communal electorate but also extended it, thus, poisoning the political atmosphere with the evil of casteism and sectionalism.

Government of India Act, 1935 and the Constitution of India

The drafters of the Constitution of India borrowed a lot of features from the Government of India Act, 1935. For instance:

- Features of Federal Legislature
- Provincial autonomy
- Division of powers between the Centre and the Province
- Establishment of a Federal Court in 1937 later known as the Supreme Court and Public Service Commission (as defined in Article 315)
- Provision of post of Governor duly elected by the Union Government
- Emergency provisions
- Administrative details

The Second-Stage Debate (1937)

Immediately after the notification of the Act of 1935, the British Government announced the holding of elections to provincial legislatures in early 1937, thereby initiating the second stage of debate over strategy among the Congress leaders. Though all of the Congressmen agreed that they should fight the coming elections on the basis of a detailed political and economic programme, there was no consensus among the Congress leaders over the question of office acceptance and ways to combat the Act of 1935. Gradually, the two sides to the debate also got identified with the emerging ideological divide along **Left** and **Right** lines. For instance, Jawaharlal Nehru, Subhas Bose, the Congress Socialists and the Communists were totally opposed to office acceptance and working on the 1935 Act while the **Right-Wing leaders** though equally committed to combating the 1935 Act, favoured office acceptance and felt that due to non-availability of option of a mass movement, the objective political situation made it necessary to go through a constitutional phase.

[46] The princes' reluctance was primarily due to their main objection that the Act did not resolve the issue of paramountcy and the Government of India as a paramount power still enjoyed the right to intervene in the affairs of their states or even overthrow them if necessary. Their other concern was about joining a democratised federal central government, where the elected political leaders of British India would have little sympathy for their autocratic rules and would provide encouragement to the democratic movements in their territories.

"Firstly, to accept office, was to negate our rejection of it (the 1935 Act) and to stand self-condemned. It would mean assuming responsibility without power, since the basic state structure would remain the same .... Secondly, office acceptance would take away the revolutionary character of the movement imbibed since 1919. Behind this issue lay the question whether we seek revolutionary changes in India or (whether we) are working for petty reforms under the aegis of British imperialism. Office acceptance would mean, in practice, 'a surrender' before imperialism. The Congress would get sucked into parliamentary activity within the colonial framework and would forget the main issues of freedom, economic and social justice, and removal of poverty. It would be co-opted and deradicalized. It would fall into a pit from which it would be difficult for us to come out."

Jawaharlal Nehru's passionate address presenting the Left case at the Lucknow Session in early 1936.

"So far as I can judge, no one wants to accept offices for their own sake. No one wants to work the constitution as the Government would like it to be worked. The questions for us are altogether different. What are we to do with this Constitution? Are we to ignore it altogether and go our way? Is it possible to do so? Are we to capture it and use it as we would like to use it and to the extent it lends itself to be used in that way. . . . It is not a question to be answered a priori on the basis of pre-conceived notions of a so-called pro-changer or no-changer, cooperator or obstructionist."

The case of the right-wing elaborated by Rajendra Prasad in a letter to Nehru in December 1935.

However, the **leftists** recommended an older counter-strategy, the one used by the *Swarajists,* that is, to enter the assemblies with an intention of creating deadlocks and making the working of the Act impossible while in the long term increasing reliance on workers and peasants and their class organisations and integrating them with the Congress, thereby imparting it a socialist direction along with preparing for the resumption of a mass movement. On the other hand, the **right wing** or pro-office acceptance leaders insisting on the practical reality that even if the Congress rejected office, there were other groups and parties who would readily form ministries and use them to weaken nationalism and encourage reactionary and communal policies and politics and so it was not in anybody's interest to leave the administrative field unchallenged to pro-Government forces. They felt that despite their limited powers, the provincial ministries could be used to promote constructive work, especially in respect of education, village and Harijan uplift, *khadi,* prohibition and reduction of burden of debt, taxes and rent on the peasants. In other words, what was involved was not a choice between principles but a choice between the two alternative strategies of STS and S-V.

"To my socialist comrades, I would say, capture or rejection of office is not a matter of socialism. I would ask them to realise that it is a matter of strategy. There is no office and there is no acceptance. . . . Do not look upon ministries as offices, but as centres and fortresses from which British imperialism is radiated . . . The Councils cannot lead us to constitutionalism, for we are not babies; we will lead the Councils and use them for Revolution."

T. Vishwanathan of Andhra

As the overwhelming mood of the Congress party favoured the option of acceptance of office, even Gandhiji after his initial reluctance agreed to support the decision and, thus, the Congress decided at Lucknow in early 1936 and in Faizpur in late 1936 to fight the elections while postponing the decision on office acceptance to the post-election period.

1937 Elections and 28 Months of Congress Rule in Provinces

The elections to the provincial assemblies were held in February 1937, and despite narrow franchise, **Congress** won a massive mandate at the polls. Not only did it won 716 out of 1,161 seats contested by it, but it also succeeded in forming Ministries[47] in **six** provinces: UP, Central Provinces, Madras, Orissa, Bombay and Bihar and emerged as single largest party in Bengal, Assam and the North-West Frontier Province,[48] thereby greatly increasing the prestige of the Congress as an alternative power that would look after the interests of the Indian masses. Interestingly, with the forming of Congress Ministries, also began a novel unique experiment in the political history of India as the Congress was now to function both as a government in the provinces and also as the opposition vis-à-vis the Central Government. The Congress party though took charge of administration in the provinces, yet it was still committed to carry on the struggle for independence and prepare the people for the next phase of mass struggle. Also, as a part of the office acceptance strategy, Congress did try to utilise the administration and legislature to coordinate with the outside political work and promote the mass political activity.

"These offices have to be held lightly, not tightly. They are or should be crowns of thorns, never of renown. Offices have been taken in order to see if they enable us to quicken the pace at which we are moving towards our goal. Use the Act of 1935 in a manner not expected by them (the British) and by refraining from using it in the way intended by them."

Gandhiji's advice to the Congress leaders on the issue of office acceptance in Harijan on 7 August 1937.

"Organisational and other work outside the legislature was to remain the major occupation of the Congress for without it, the legislative activity would have little value and that the two forms of activity must be coordinated together and the masses should be kept in touch with whatever we do and consulted about it."

A circular dated 10 July 1937 sent by Jawaharlal Nehru as the president of the Congress to all Congressmen.

The formation of the Congress Ministries boosted the confidence of the masses and provided them with a sense of ownership regarding the government. In fact, Congress also got an opportunity to demonstrate that apart from leading the people in mass struggles, it was equally capable of administering the state power

[47] After a few months tussle with the Government, the Congress Working Committee eventually decided to accept office under the Act of 1935.

[48] Later, Congress Ministries were also formed in the North-West Frontier Province and Assam.

for their benefit, though there were certain **limitations** on them regarding the basic imperialist character of the administration and lack of financial resources at their disposal. Still, within the narrow limits of their powers, and the time[49] available to them, they did try to change the face of governance by introducing certain key reforms in the domain of civil liberties, to the cause of peasants and workers, along with passing some ameliorative legislation focusing on social reforms and welfare, thereby trying to fulfil many of the promises made by them in their election manifesto[50].

- **In the domain of Civil Liberties**: The Congress Ministries registered major achievements in their efforts to defend and extend the domain of civil liberties. For instance:
  - All the emergency powers acquired by the provincial governments during 1932, through Public Safety Acts and the like, were repealed.
  - The ban on illegal political organisations[51] such as the Hindustan Seva Dal and Youth Leagues and on political books and journals were lifted.
  - All restrictions on the press were removed and the securities taken from newspapers and presses were refunded while all the pending prosecutions were withdrawn. The act of blacklisting of newspapers for purposes of government advertising was also abandoned.
  - All the confiscated arms were returned and forfeited arms licenses were restored.
  - The police arbitrary powers were curbed and the reporting of public speeches and the shadowing of political workers by CID (Central Investigation Department) agents in the Congress ruled provinces was mostly stopped.
  - Thousands of political prisoners and *detenus* were released and the internment and deportation orders of political workers were cancelled. In most[52] of the Congress-ruled provinces, many of the revolutionaries involved in the Kakori and other conspiracy cases were also released. In fact, the difference of approach was clearly visible between the **Congress ruled provinces** and the **non-Congress ruled provinces** of Bengal and Punjab as in the latter, especially in Bengal, civil liberties continued to be curbed and revolutionary prisoners and *detenus* continued to be in prison without trial for years, and were not released despite popular movements demanding their release or on account of repeated hunger strikes by the prisoners.
  - In Bombay[53], the lands confiscated[54] by the Government were restored to the original owners while the pensions of officials dismissed during 1930 and 1932 for sympathising with the movement were also restored.
- **In the domain of Agrarian and Labour Reforms**: Within their limited powers, the Congress Ministries also tried to provide much needed economic relief to the peasants and the workers. For instance:

---

[49] Their tenure lasted only 2 years and 4 months.

[50] In its election manifesto, Congress had promised the restoration of civil liberties, the release of political prisoners, the removal of disabilities on grounds of sex and untouchability, the radical transformation of the agrarian system, substantial reduction in rent and revenue, scaling down of the rural debts, provision of cheap credit, the right to form trade unions and the right to strike.

[51] Though the ban on the Communist Party remained, since it was imposed by the Central Government and could only be lifted on its orders, the Communists could in effect now function freely and openly in the Congress provinces. The Communist Party was able to bring out its weekly organ, *The National Front,* from Bombay. Another interesting example is *of Kirti Lehar*, which the Kirti Communists of Punjab brought out from Meerut, UP, because they could not do so in Unionist-ruled Punjab.

[52] However, problems persisted in UP and Bihar, where several revolutionaries convicted of crimes involving violence remained in jails. In February 1938, there were 15 such prisoners in UP and 23 in Bihar. Their release required consent by the Governors, which was refused. But, the Congress Ministries determined to release them, put forward their resignations on this issue on 15 February forcing the Governors to come to the negotiating table. The problem was finally resolved through negotiations, and all the prisoners in both provinces were released by the end of March.

[53] Here too, the Congress ministries had to threaten resignation before it could persuade the Governor to agree.

[54] As a result of the no-tax campaign during the Civil Disobedience Movement in 1930.

- Agrarian Reforms: Committed by its election manifesto of agrarian reform, the Congress Ministries did try to bring in an agrarian policy[55] keeping the interests of the peasantry in mind and focused on the reform of the system of land tenures such as tenancy rights, security of tenure along with addressing the key issues of reduction of rent, land revenue, the burden of debt and the problem of rural indebtedness.
- The Congress Government[56] also passed a series of stringent debtors relief acts, which provided for the regulation of the moneylender's business, such as the cancellation or drastic reduction of accumulated interest ranging from 6.25 per cent in Madras to 9 per cent in Bombay and Bihar.
- Various rural reconstruction programmes were also undertaken by the Congress Ministries as in case of Bombay where 40,000 *dublas* or tied serfs were liberated along with the abolishing of the grazing fees in the forests.
- Labour Reforms: Adopting a pro-labour stance, the Congress Ministries tried to advance workers interests while promoting industrial peace. They specifically urged for:
    - Reduction in the number of strikes and creation of a goodwill between labour and capitalists, along with the establishment of a conciliation machinery for compulsory arbitration. The **Industrial Disputes Act**[57] was based on the same philosophy of *class collaboration and not class conflict*, and focused on conciliation, arbitration and negotiations in place of direct action.
    - Improvement in the conditions of the workers and secure wage increases. For instance, immediately after assuming office, the Bombay Ministry appointed a Textile Enquiry Committee, which recommended, among other improvements, the increase of wages amounting to a crore of rupees, and despite mill owners protesting against the recommendations, they were implemented by the government.

- **In the domain of Social Reform and Welfare**: The Congress Ministries also undertook certain other measures of social reform and welfare, such as:
    - Introduction of measures for the upliftment of untouchables including the passing of laws enabling them to enter temples and to get access to public office, public sources of water such as wells and ponds, roads, means of transport, hospitals, educational and other similar institutions maintained out of public funds, and restaurants and hotels. The number of scholarships and freeships for *Harijan* students was increased and efforts were made to increase the number of *Harijans* in police and other government services.
    - A lot of attention was paid by the Congress Ministries in the field of primary, technical and higher education and public health and sanitation. Special efforts were undertaken to expand the education for girls, *Harijans* along with organisation of literacy campaigns among adults.
    - Prohibition was introduced in selected areas in different states while different schemes of prison reforms were also taken up under the command of the Ministries.
    - The Congress Ministries also tried to remove the impediments in the path of indigenous industrial expansion and, in fact, actively attempted to promote several modern industrial ventures such as automobile manufacture while providing support and subsidies to *khadi,* spinning and village industries.

---

[55] It is pertinent to note here that the agrarian legislation brought by the Congress Ministries differed from province to province depending on differing agrarian relations, the mass base of the Congress, the class composition and the outlook of the provincial Congress organisation and leadership and the nature and extent of peasant mobilisation. For instance, in UP, a tenancy act was passed in October 1939, which gave all statutory tenants both in Agra and Awadh full hereditary rights in their holdings while taking away the landlord's right to prevent the growth of occupancy while in Bihar in 1937 itself, much early than UP, a much more radical tenancy legislation was passed greatly reducing the landlord's power to realise rent while granting protection to the tenant who could no longer be arrested or imprisoned, nor could his immovable property be sold without his consent. In fact, the only right that the landlord retained after passing of this legislation was the right to get his rent, which was also reduced significantly. Similarly, in Orissa, a tenancy bill was passed in May 1938 granting the right of free transfer of occupancy holdings, reducing the interest on arrears of rent from 12.5 to 6 per cent and abolishing all illegal levies on tenants. The measures of tenancy reform, usually extending security of tenure to tenants in landlord areas, were also carried in the legislatures of Bombay, the Central Provinces and the North-West Frontier Province.

[56] Except for UP and Assam.

[57] Passed in November 1938.

Critical Analysis of the 28-Month Rule of the Congress Ministries

The Congress Ministries resigned in October 1939 because of the political crisis brought about by World War II. The 28 months of Congress rule was a mix of both positives and negatives.

Positive Aspects of the 28 Months of the Congress Ministries

- With the establishment of Congress rule in provinces, not only a considerable advance[58] was noticed in Congress as an organisation but even the confidence of the general masses was at an all-time high as the Ministries could showcase the governance capability of Indians to the world along with shattering the British-created myth *that Indians were not fit to rule*. The formation of Congress Ministries and the vast extension of civil liberties unleashed popular energies and gave a major thrust to the *kisan sabhas,* trade unions, student and youth movements and state people's movement all across the country.
- The Ministries were not only easily accessible to the common people but even their legislative and administrative record was mostly positive, including their firm handling of the communal riots.

> *"Looking back, I am surprised at their achievements during a brief period of 2 years and a quarter, despite the innumerable difficulties that surrounded them."*
>
> Jawaharlal Nehru's statement in 1944.

- The Congress leadership was also able to successfully foil the imperialist design of using constitutional reforms to weaken the national movement and, instead, demonstrated to the British their ability of using the constitutional structure for furthering their welfare oriented approach without getting co-opted. Even though, the leaders were engaged in day-to-day administration, still the national movement was never diverted from its main task of fighting for self-government, and the Congress was successfully able to utilise the offices for enhancing the national consciousness and increasing the area of nationalist influence, thereby strengthening the movement's capacity to wage a mass struggle in the future and extend its influence among otherwise hostile elements, such as landlords and bureaucrats, who came to now believe that the British departure from India was only a matter of time and in the near future, there is a high possibility that Congress might again assume power.
- The Ministries also successfully belied the British hopes of growth of provincialism and instead presented a common front before the Government of India. Though, some sort of factionalism, particularly at the top, was noticed yet the Congress organisation as a whole remained disciplined as evident by the prompt resignations of the Ministries when the same was demanded by the central Congress leadership. The Congress also successfully avoided the British plan of split[59] between its Left and Right wings, and despite being strong critiques of each other, they not only remained united but tended to come closer to each other, as the crisis at Tripuri unravelled.

> *"The resignations of the ministries demonstrated to all those who had any doubts that Congress was not out for power and office but for the emancipation of the people of India from the foreign yoke."*
>
> Statement of Congress General Secretary in 1939.

---

[58] It emerged stronger after the period of office acceptance.

[59] A split which the British were trying to actively promote since 1934.

Negative Aspects of the 28 Months of the Congress Ministries

There were, however, certain blemishes on the Congress ministerial record of 28 months:

- In case of the domain of Civil Liberties, for instance, on the directions of some right-wing Congress ministers, certain Left and Socialist ideology inclined Congress leaders were prosecuted such as **Yusuf Meherally**, a Socialist leader, who was prosecuted by the Madras Government for making an inflammatory speech in Malabar in July 1937 and **S. S. Batliwala**, who was prosecuted by the Madras Government for making a seditious speech and was sentenced to 6 months imprisonment in October 1937, resulting in a big furore[60] in the Congress ranks led by none other than Jawaharlal Nehru. The use of state apparatus in a politically repressive manner was another cause of concern which resulted in increasing the rift between the right and the left wing leaders. For instance, the act of maliciously using CID to watch the Communists and other left-wing Congressmen by K. M. Munshi, the Home Minister of Bombay, earned him a rebuke from mature Congress leaders.
- Similarly, on the issue of **agrarian reforms**, it was noticed that the crucial benefits of the tenancy acts were reaped by the statutory and occupancy tenants while the interests of the sub-tenants of the occupancy tenants and the agricultural labourers were still overlooked[61]. The same state of affairs was evident in case of the **Industrial Disputes Act**, which was facing strong opposition from the Left Congressmen, including Communists and Congress Socialists, for restricting the freedom to strike and for laying down a new complicated procedure for registration of trade unions, which according to them encouraged unions promoted by employers only.
- Another issue of concern was the inability on the part of Congress Ministries to deal with situations where their own mass base was affected. Though they often tried to play a mediatory role, which sometimes proved successful in UP and Bihar and to a certain extent in Madras, it was clearly a failure in Bombay. The Congress Ministries also faced the charges of treating all radical protests, especially peasants and trade union struggles, as a law and order problem, resulting in their adoption of the same approach as the colonial state, thereby increasing their clashes with the popular movements and leading to further widening of their differences with the agitating workers, peasant and trade union leaders. For instance, the *Kisan Sabha* movement, in Bihar, often resulted in frontal confrontation[62] with the provincial Congress Ministry, which consequently led to a breach of relations between the two, that is, the Bihar *kisan sabha* and the provincial Congress leadership.

> *"The political work outside the legislatures often involved organisation of popular protest and the Congress was confused regarding its approach towards the same. It faced the classic questions as how far could a movement go in organising protests and agitations against itself? Could a party which ran a government be simultaneously the organiser of popular movements and enforcer of law and order? And what if some of the protests took a violent or extra- legal form? Could civil liberties have their excess? How should the governmental wing of the movement then respond, since it is one of the functions of any government – colonial or nationalist, leftist or rightist or centrist – to see that the existing laws are observed."*
>
> Dilemma of Congress beautifully elaborated by Bipan Chandra.

---

[60] Since this action was in complete contrast to the well-established Congress position that nobody should be prosecuted for making a speech and least of all for a speech against colonial rule.

[61] This was partially because these two sections had not yet been mobilised by the *kisan sabhas,* nor had they become voters because of the restricted franchise under the Act of 1935. Consequently, they could not exert pressure on the Ministries through either elections or the peasant movement.

[62] Especially when the *kisan sabha* under Swami Sahajanand asked the peasants not to pay rent or to forcibly occupy landlord's lands.

- The period of Congress Ministries also witnessed the emergence of serious weaknesses in the Congress party as there was a great deal of factional strife and bickering both on ideological and personal levels for jobs and positions of advantage, eventually leading to a great amount of indiscipline among the Congressmen.

> *"I feel strongly that the Congress ministries are working inefficiently and not doing much that they could do. They are adapting themselves far too much to the old order and trying to justify it.....What is far worse is that we are losing the high position that we have built up, with so much labour, in the hearts of the people. We are sinking to the level of ordinary politicians who have no principles to stand by and whose work is governed by a day to day opportunism. .. I think there are enough men of goodwill in the Congress. But their minds are full of party conflicts and the desire to crush this individual or that group."*
>
> Excerpts from Jawaharlal Nehru's letter dated 28 April 1938 to Gandhiji expressing his frustration at the lack of positive role played by the Ministries in the later years.

- The Congress Ministries had to also regularly face the **criticism of the radical parties** like the Left and the Socialist parties who often accused them of trying to suppress peasants and workers movements and also of **senior leaders** like Gandhiji who felt that the decision of ministry formation was not good and leading to a crisis and began to question the efficacy of continuing with the policy of office acceptance, though his point of consternation was completely different from that of the Communists. He was against the frequent recourse by the Congress Ministries to colonial laws for dealing with the popular agitations and could see the immense harm that the Congress party would suffer in terms of erosion of popular support, especially of the workers and peasants because of the repeated use of law and order machinery to deal with their agitations. Instead, Gandhiji emphasised on the political education of the masses against the use of violence and repeatedly lashed out in the columns of *Harijan* against the growing misuse of office and creeping corruption in Congress ranks.

> *"We seem to be weakening from within. I would go to the length of giving the whole Congress organisation a decent burial, rather than put up with the corruption that is rampant. If the Congress is not purged of illegalities and irregularities, it will cease to be the power it is today and will fail to fulfil expectations when the real struggle faces the country."*
>
> Gandhiji's views as expressed in his journal *Harijan*.

Previous Year's Questions (Prelims)

1. Who among the following organised a march on the Tanjore coast to break the Salt law in April,1930? (2015)

(a) V. Chidambaram Pillai

(b) C. Rajagopalachari

(c) K. Kamaraj

(d) Annie Besant

2. Why is the 1929 session of Indian National congress of significance in the history of the freedom movement? (2014)

(a) Attainment of self government was declared as the objective of the Congress

(b) Attainment of *purna swaraj* was adopted as the goal of the Congress
(c) Non-cooperation movement was launched
(d) Decision to participate in the round table conference in London was taken

3. The people of India agitated against the arrival of Simon Commission because (2013)
(a) Indians never wanted the review of the working of the Act of 1919
(b) Simon Commission recommended the abolition of Dyarchy in the province
(c) There was no Indian member in the Simon Commission
(d) The Simon Commission suggested the partition of the country

4. The Lahore Session of the Indian National Congress (1929) is very important in history, because (2012)
1. The Congress passed a resolution demanding complete Independence
2. The rift between the extremists and moderates was resolved in that session
3. A resolution was passed rejecting the two Nation theory in that session

Which of the statements given above is/are correct? Choose the correct answer from the following options:
(a) 1 only
(b) 2 and 3
(c) 1 and 3
(d) None of the above

5. Why did Mahatma Gandhi undertake the fast unto death in 1932. (2012)
(a) Round table conference failed to satisfy Indian political aspirations
(b) Congress and Muslim League had differences of opinion
(c) Ramsay MacDonald announced the Communal Award
(d) None of the statements (a), (b) and (c) given above is correct in this context

6. The distribution of powers between the Centre and the States in the Indian Constitution is based on the scheme provided in which of the following? (2012)
(a) Morley Minto reforms 1909
(b) Montague Chelmsford Act 1919
(c) Government of India Act 1935
(d) Indian independence Act 1947

7. With reference to the period of freedom struggle, which of the following was/were recommended by the Nehru report? (2011)
1. Complete Independence for India
2. Joint electorates for reservation of seats for minorities
3. Provision of fundamental rights for the people of India in the constitution

Choose the correct answer from the following options:
(a) 1 only
(b) 2 and 3 only
(c) 1 and 3 only
(d) 1, 2 and 3

8. With reference to Simon Commission's recommendations, which one of the following statements is correct? (2010)
(a) It recommends the replacement of Dyarchy with responsible government in the provinces.
(b) It proposed the setting up of inter provincial council under the Home Department.
(c) It suggested the abolition of bicameral Legislature at the centre.
(d) It recommended the creation of Indian Police Service with the provision for increased pay and allowances for British recruits as compared to Indian recruits.

9. For the Karachi session of Indian National Congress in 1931 presided over by Sardar Patel, who drafted the resolution on Fundamental Rights and economics Programme? (2010)
(a) Mahatma Gandhi
(b) Pandit Jawaharlal Nehru

(c) Dr Rajendra Prasad

(d) Dr B. R. Ambedkar

10. Which one of the following began with the Dandi March? (2009)

(a) Home Rule Movement

(b) Non-Cooperation Movement

(c) Civil Disobedience Movement

(d) Quit India Movement

11. Consider the following statements: (2009)

1. The discussions in the Third Round Table Conference eventually lead to the passing of the Government of India Act of 1935.
2. The Government of India Act of 1935 provided for the establishment of an all India Federation to be based on Union of the provinces of British India and the Princely States.

Which of the statement(s) given above is are correct? Choose the correct answer from the following options:

(a) 1 only

(b) 2 only

(c) Both 1 and 2

(d) Neither 1 nor 2

12. Under whose Presidency was the Lahore Session of the Indian National Congress held in the year 1929 wherein a resolution was adopted to gain complete Independence from the British? (2006)

(a) Bal Gangadhar Tilak

(b) Gopal Krishna Gokhale

(c) Jawaharlal Nehru

(d) Motilal Nehru

13. At which Congress Session was the Working Committee authorised to launch a programme of Civil Disobedience? (2005)

(a) Bombay

(b) Lahore

(c) Lucknow

(d) Tripuri

14. Consider the following statements: (2005)

1. In the first Round Table Conference, Dr Ambedkar demanded separate electorates for the depressed classes.
2. In the Poona Pact, special provisions for representation of the depressed class people in the local bodies and civil services were made.
3. The Indian National Congress did not take part in the Third Round Table Conference.

Which of the statements given above are correct? Choose the correct answer from the following options:

(a) 1 and 2

(b) 2 and 3

(c) 1 and 3

(d) 1, 2 and 3

15. Who among the following drafted the resolution on Fundamental Rights for the Karachi session of Congress in 1931? (2005)

(a) Dr B. R. Ambedkar

(b) Jawaharlal Nehru

(c) Dr Rajendra Prasad

(d) Sardar Vallabhbhai Patel

16. Consider the following statements, The Government of India Act., 1935 provided for (2005)

1. The Provincial Autonomy
2. The establishment of Federal Court
3. All India Federation at the centre

Which of the following statements given above are correct? Choose the correct answer from the following options:

(a) 1 and 2

(b) 2 and 3

(c) 1 and 3

(d) 1, 2 and 3

17. Consider the following statements: (2004)

Some of the main features of the Government of India Act, 1935 were the

1. Abolition of Dyarchy in the Governor's Provinces
2. Power of the Governors to Veto legislative action and to legislate on their own
3. Abolition of the Principle of Communal Representation

Which of the statements given above is/are correct? Choose the correct answer from the following options:

(a) 1 only
(b) 1 and 2
(c) 2 and 3
(d) 1, 2 and 3

18. What was the real intention of the British to include the princely states in the Federal Union proposed by the India Act of 1935? (2002)

(a) Exercise more and direct political and administrative control over the princely states
(b) Involve the Princes activity in the administration of the colony
(c) Finally effect the complete political and administrative takeover of all the princely states by the British
(d) Use the princes to balance the anti-imperialist doctrines of the nationalist leaders

19. Which one of the following is not a feature of the Government of India Act of 1935? (2000)

(a) Dyarchy at the Centre as well as in the Provinces
(b) A Bicameral Legislature
(c) Provincial Autonomy
(d) An All India federation

20. Why was the Simon commission of 1927 boycotted? (1998)

(a) There was no Indian member in the Commission
(b) It supported the Muslim League
(c) Congress felt that the people of India are entitled to Swaraj
(d) There were differences among the members

21. At the time of India's Independence what was Mahatma Gandhi was (1998)

(a) A member of Committee Congress Working
(b) Not a member of the Congress
(c) The President of Congress
(d) The General Secretary of the Congress

22. The Poona pact which was signed between the British government and Mahatma Gandhi in 1932 provided for (1997)

(a) The creation of Dominion status for India
(b) Separate electorates for the Muslim
(c) Separate electorates for the Harijans
(d) Joint electorates with reservation of Harijans

Previous Year's Answers (Prelims)

1. (b)	2. (b)	3. (c)	4. (a)	5. (c)	6. (c)	7. (b)	8. (a)
9. (b)	10. (c)	11. (c)	12. (c)	13. (b)	14. (c)	15. (b)	16. (d)
17. (a)	18. (d)	19. (a)	20. (a)	21. (b)	22. (d)		

The Evolution of Communalism

11

Communalism can be simply understood as the development of a communal ideology which perpetuates the notion that religion forms the basic unit of division in society and all those who have a common religion also have common social, political, cultural and economic interests. Communal ideology, thus, prescribes the superimposition of the religious identity over all other identities[1] of an individual and is often seen not to be an instant development. Rather, as rightly pointed out by Bipan Chandra, communal ideology evolves gradually in three stages[2]:

- **The First Stage of Identity Consciousness**: At this stage, a gradual consciousness emerges among the people following the same religion that they have common political, economic, social and cultural interests. This stage generally forms the bedrock of communal ideology, which subsequently creates a belief system among the different religious communities that they can protect their collective non-individual secular interests[3] only as being members of these religion-based communities. For instance, at this stage, a consciousness develops among a Muslim *zamindar* and a Muslim peasant that they have similar interests as both of them are Muslims. The same is the case with Hindus or Sikhs.
- **The Second Stage of Mutual Divergence or the Liberal Communalism or Moderate Communalism**: In this stage of propagation of the communal ideology, gradually the followers of one religion realise that their secular interests are **dissimilar** and **divergent** from the interests of the followers of another religion, though they still upheld certain liberal, democratic, humanist and nationalist values along with believing that the different communal interests could be gradually accommodated and brought into harmony within the overall national interests. So, at this stage a realisation emerges among the Hindus that they had different interests from all Muslims and vice versa. Most of the communalists before 1937 were liberal communalists such as the Muslim League, the Hindu Mahasabha, the Ali Brothers (after 1925), M. A. Jinnah, Lala Lajpat Rai, Madan Mohan Malaviya and N. C. Kelkar (after 1922).
- **The Third Stage of Mutual Exclusion or the Extreme Communalism or Fascist Communalism**: The third stage of communalism is reached when the interests of the followers of different religious communities are seen to be mutually incompatible, antagonistic and hostile. The extreme communalism at this stage is typically based on fear and hatred, and uses the language of war and enmity against political opponents. Thus, at this stage the Hindus and Muslims had arrived at a conclusion that their interests are conflicting to each other's. In terms of Indian historiography of communalism, this stage particularly arrived after 1937 in communal politics, and the activities of Muslim League, the Hindu Mahasabha and the Rashtriya Swayamsevak Sangh (RSS) specifically after 1937 increasingly shifted towards extreme communalism.

---

[1] His other identities can be based on his country, region, gender, occupation, position within the family or caste.

[2] Though the three stages of communalism are generally different from one another, they also interacted with each other and provided a certain continuum.

[3] Like the social, cultural, economic and political interests.

In India, the trajectory of evolution of communalism nearly followed the same path. Thus, at first, a communal consciousness emerged among the Hindus and Muslims, particularly till the **end of the 1860s**, which subsequently resulted in the second stage of liberal communalism which lasted **till 1937**, wherein the communalists gradually started asserting that Hindus and Muslims can never have common secular interests, thereby eventually evolving in the final stage of communal politics or extreme communalism, specifically **after 1937** wherein it was reinforced among the two communities that their secular interests are completely opposed to each other and fulfilment of one negates the other. Needless to say, all of these arguments were based on a wrong understanding of interests. But, the communal forces did not let people differentiate between the right and wrong, which eventually led to the partition of the country. In this chapter, we are going to study in detail about the different factors responsible for the growth and emergence of communalism, the trajectory of its evolution and different events responsible for the same.

Factors Responsible for Growth and Emergence of Communalism

There are multiple factors responsible for the genesis and growth of communalism:

- **Politics of Communal Identity**: Owing to certain colonial policies and some other indigenous factors, a construct of communal identity based on the premise of separate interests of each community was created:
    - Construction of a construct of a homogenous religious identity on account of British policies: Though both Hindus and Muslims were by no means homogenous communities in themselves and a lot of dissimilarities[4] existed in terms of not only demographic characteristics but also in terms of differences in the position and composition of the communities, yet owing to certain British policies, such as the various official ethnographic studies and the Indian colonial census, the religion was made a fundamental ethnographic category[5] of division, which further gave a concrete and recognisable shape to the religious communities resulting in the reconstitution of relationships between them in the late 19th century. So, on the one hand, it resulted in Hindu mobilisation, while on the other hand, it contributed to the unification of Muslims under a common allegiance to the essentials of the Islamic faith. The colonial authorities, thus, conveniently ignoring the demographic incongruities and diversity of status while defining the Indian society, caused the creation of a myth of the homogeneous religious construct that was unified, cohesive and segregated from the other religious communities.

[4] Significant regional variations were present in terms of Muslim distribution as in the case of United Provinces, where the Muslims constituted a minority, being slightly more than 13 per cent of the population, while in Punjab, they were a majority, accounting for slightly more than 51 per cent of the population and the same was the case with Bengal, wherein Muslims represented nearly half of the population (49.2 per cent), but not only all these dissimilarities in demographic characteristics were conveniently ignored for defining the communities but apart from them even other important differences in terms of the position and composition of the Muslim community, such as the sectarian differences (Shia-Sunni), the linguistic barriers and economic disparities were also downplayed. The same state of affairs was in the case of Hindus who were also not homogenous in any respect. In fact, in the late 19th century, an upper-class Muslim had far more in common, even culturally, with an upper-class Hindu than with a lower-class Muslim. Similarly, a Punjabi Hindu stood closer culturally to a Punjabi Muslim than to a Bengali Hindu. The unreal communal division, thus, obscured the real division of the Indian people into linguistic-cultural regions and social classes as well as their real, emerging and growing unity into a nation.

[5] Each census report discussed the numerical size of each community, their percentage to the whole population, relative or absolute decline and geographic distribution, indicating their majority or minority status in each region and in the country as a whole. The break-up of literacy and occupational statistics according to religion provided an apparently objective picture of the relative or comparative material and social conditions of each religious community. This colonial knowledge was later incorporated into every structure that the state created, every opportunity that it offered to the colonial subjects – from educational facilities, public employment, representation in local self-governing bodies to entry into the expanded legislative councils.

> *"Religion did no longer mean just a set of ideas, but came to be identified with an aggregate of individuals united by formal official definition, sharing supposedly the same characteristics, and conscious of their comparative demographic as well as socio-economic position vis-à-vis other communities. It was this universalised knowledge which made a difference between pre colonial localised relations between religious groups and colonial competition and conflict among subcontinental religious communities."*
>
> Shekhar Bandopadhyay

- Colonial stereotyping: The colonial stereotyping of a *homogenous community* was further propounded through books like W. W. Hunter's *The Indian Musalmans* (1871), which mistakenly presented the image of a homogeneous community, suffering from 'backwardness' in terms of education and employment. Further, in his book he put forth the faulty thesis that it was on account of the exclusion of the Muslims from the government-sponsored education system and civil employment that the anti-British Wahabi and Faraizi movements were gaining popularity, and thus, advocated a policy of special government favour for Muslims in matters of education and employment, which was gradually adopted by the colonial government.
- A distorted communal and unscientific view of Indian history: The spread of communal consciousness can also be attributed to the wrong communal interpretations of history, especially of its ancient and medieval periods, by imperialist historians like James Mill, who described the ancient period of Indian history as the Hindu period and the medieval period as the Muslim period[6]. His approach was soon adopted by other British and Indian historians who repeated the same mistake of interpreting the history, polity, culture and society of an era in terms of only religion. For instance, during medieval period, though the Muslim masses were as poor, exploited and oppressed as the Hindu masses, and there were both Hindu nobles and rulers along with Muslim ones, these writers declared that in medieval India, all Muslims were rulers while all Hindus were the ruled. All these contributed to the rise of communal passions on both sides as communalists on both sides readily adopted the imperialist view. Hindu communalists on the one hand started propagating that the medieval period was not only a period of anti-Hindu foreign rule but was also the period of *thousand years of slavery* and forceful conversions. They further perpetuated the myth that the Indian society and culture had reached great heights in the ancient period from which they fell into permanent and continuous decay during the medieval period because of 'Muslim' rule and domination. Muslim communalists on the other hand tried to defend and glorify all Muslim rulers, including religious bigots like Aurangzeb. The communal view of history was further propagated among the masses through poetry, short stories, drama, historical novels, pamphlets, newspapers, popular magazines and, above all, orally through the public platform, private discussions and conversations.

> *"Communal harmony could not be permanently established in our country so long as highly distorted versions of history were being taught in her schools and colleges, through the history textbooks."*
>
> Gandhiji

[6] Though he failed to characterise the modern period as the Christian period.

- **Colonial Character of the Economy**: Communalism was also one of the by-products of the colonial character of the Indian economy, colonial underdevelopment and incapacity of colonialism to develop the Indian economy, which ultimately resulted in economic stagnation and produced conditions[7] that were conducive to division and antagonism within the Indian society, thereby adversely impacting the lives of the Indian people, especially the middle classes, who in an attempt to get a larger share of the existing limited economic opportunities tried to use freely all the means at their disposal, even group identities such as caste, province and religion to enhance their capacity to compete. All of this eventually resulted in the emergence of a system of communal reservations and nominations, which further gave a certain aura of validity to communal politics[8]. Communalism, hence, emerged as an expression of the interests and aspirations of the middle classes in a social situation in which opportunities for them were grossly inadequate.

> *"History of the communal representation is the history of British policy in India, also one of the growth and diversity of middle class consciousness in India and the demand of the middle class for political powers. But British imperialism is one aspect of the problem. The social economy of the country another."*
>
> Analysis presented by historian K. B. Krishna[9] in his book *Problems of Minorities* (1939)

> *"The political policy of the government would have been less successful than it was, had there not been powerful economic factors operating to re-inforce it. Communalism could not have proved so effective a divisive force, nor could the upper class Muslims have been so effectively repressed, had the Hindu and the Muslim sections of the class concerned been of the same economic level. But they were not."*
>
> W. C. Smith (*Modern Islam in India*, 1946)

- **Socio-Economic Power Factors**: Communalism was also brought into existence and sustained by the then socio-economic-power structure. The colonial conquest brought about a change in the conventional power structure and marked the decadence of the upper class Muslims, who gradually lost their semi-monopoly in employment in the upper posts of army, administration and judiciary, while being slowly evicted from their dominant position in land-holding as well. As it happened, owing to the uniqueness of the Indian situation, the loss of the Muslims invariably went in favour of the Hindus who had responded more positively to education and other modernising forces than the Muslims who remained largely backward. For instance, if we compare the two prominent provinces of Bengal and United Provinces (UP), both having sizeable Muslim population and had witnessed the good old days of glory, we will notice that in both the provinces, the Muslims gradually lost their predominance owing to their backward position in educational status both in absolute numbers as well as in relative terms vis-à-vis the Hindus.
  - In case of Bengal: In 1874–75, Muslims constituted only 29 per cent of the school-going population as against 70.1 per cent Hindus. They had even lesser share at the higher levels of education: in 1875, Muslims represented 5.4 per cent of the college students, as against 93.9 per cent Hindus; and only 1.50

---

[7] Because of economic stagnation, there was intense competition among individuals for government jobs, in professions like law and medicine, and in business for customers and markets.

[8] Communal politics was thus used to put pressure on the Government to reserve and allocate its jobs and also seats in professional colleges on communal and caste lines. Consequently, communal politics till 1937 was organised around government jobs, educational concessions, and political positions such as seats in legislative councils and municipal bodies.

[9] Who was probably one of the earliest scholars to work on the communal problem.

per cent of Muslim literates were English-knowing, compared with 4.40 per cent among the Hindus. Not surprisingly, the poor representation in education was reflected also in the employment situation: in 1871, the Muslims constituted only 5.9 per cent of the government officials in Bengal proper, while the Hindus accounted for 41 per cent.

- In case of United Provinces and Northern India: The situation in north India was slightly different from Bengal since it was the centre of Mughal rule and the Muslim elites here constituted a privileged minority who were well represented in high administrative jobs during the early British period, but even they gradually lost ground to the Hindus. For instance, Muslims as late as 1882 held as much as 35 per cent of government jobs in UP, with a fair share of high and influential positions as well, but their position in the subordinate executive and judicial services declined from 63.9 per cent in 1857 to 45.1 per cent in 1886–87 and to 34.7 per cent in 1913, whereas Hindus improved their representation in these services from 24.1 per cent to 50.3 per cent to 60 per cent during the same time span. In other words, in course of a little more than half a century, the relative position of the two communities in the public services had just been reversed.

Many reasons have been offered to explain the backwardness of Muslim and their eventual loss of position of power and influence to the Hindus, such as the **supersession of Persian by English** as the official language in 1837, **quick adaptation on part of Hindus** to the new official environment, **economic decline** of the *ashraf*[10] **Muslims** following the Permanent Settlement, the **religious aversion on part of Muslims** particularly the *ajlaf* Muslims to an **un-Islamic education** along with a **general apathy** towards **western education** while having **strong preference** for the **indigenous**, less expensive traditional **institutions**, like the *maktabs* and *madrassas*. Many historians also point out the *Lag Theory* which basically postulates that there was a considerable time lag between **Ram Mohan Roy** and **Syed Ahmed Khan** or the Hindus and Muslims in responding to the forces of modernisation, re-assessment of the old beliefs, customs and values and socio-economic development in the 19th century, which eventually resulted in relative backwardness of Muslims.

> *"Economic development within the British imperialist system benefited a group of Indians of whom a far larger proportion were Hindus than Muslims."*
>
> Excerpts from W. C. Smith's book *Modern Islam in India* (1946)

> *"The Hindus took to English education which led to state services much more than the Muslims. The Hindus also took the professions and to industry in large numbers. Among the Muslims, the reactionary elements, prevented the spread of modem education as well as industry. The Hindus developed a new middle class during this period, while the Muslims still continued to remains largely feudal. A conflict arose between the various middle class elements for state services and this was the beginning of the communal problem in its modem phase."*
>
> Excerpts from a letter written by Jawaharlal Nehru to his friend in 1939, aptly summing up the relationship of the Lag Theory with communalism

[10] *Ashraf* basically represented the Muslim elites and landlords who generally spoke in Urdu and Hindustani, boasted of foreign racial origin and tried to preserve Delhi or Lucknow court culture and were averse to manual labour as the Hindu bhadralok while *ajlaf* or *atrap* represented the rural Muslim gentry who were closer to peasantry in their language, manners and customs.

Thus, across regions, Muslims suffered from a sense of relative deprivation in comparison with Hindus, and gradually when the political mobilisation of the Muslims began, their leaders asked them to organise themselves as a political pressure group to demand their just share of the institutional opportunities created by colonial rule. In fact, one of the first Muslim organisations in Bengal was the Mohammedan Association or the *Anjuman-i-Islami*, established[11] in 1855, which in a petition to the Lieutenant Governor demanded *no exclusive privilege, but a fair field* to compete on equal terms with the Hindus. However, over time, encouraged by the colonial bureaucracy, the stance of *no exclusive privilege* was tactfully discarded and instead preferential treatment was routinely demanded by the Muslim groups, as early as 1882 when the Central National Mohammedan Association (CNMA) presented a memoranda to the Government demanding special favours and not just fair justice in matters of employment in government services. Communalism in India, thus, initially started as a struggle for jobs between various communities, unequal educationally, politically and economically. However, there did exist a socio-economic situation that was funnelling it and without which it could not have survived for long.

> *"Under the pressure of communal propaganda, the masses are unable to locate the real causes of their exploitation, oppression, and suffering and imagine a fictitious communal source of their origin."*
>
> C. G. Shah

- **Result of Provocative Colonial Policy**: British rule and the colonial policy of Divide and Rule bore special responsibility for the growth of communalism, **though** it is equally true that their policy of communalism could succeed only because of the internal social and political conditions. However, it is important to note here that the state, with its immense power, has the potential to promote either national integration or all kinds of divisive forces, and in case of India, the colonial state chose the latter course. It effectively used communalism[12] as a counter-strategy to weaken the growing national movement and the welding of the Indian people into a nation. The colonial rulers often presented communal deadlock, the worsening communal situation, the defence of the minorities and the need for protecting minorities from domination and suppression by the majority as the main **justification**[13] for the **continuation** of the **British rule**. In fact, communalism was the route through which colonialism was able to place the middle classes at the service of colonialism and could extend its narrow social base among the sections of workers, peasants, the middle classes and the bourgeoisie whose interests were otherwise in contradiction with colonialism. Following are the different ways and policies, or acts of omission and commission, through which the British encouraged and nurtured communalism:
    - First, by consistently treating **Hindus**, **Muslims** and **Sikhs** as separate communities and socio-political entities which had little in common. The colonial state always supported the notion that India was neither a nation or a nation-in-the-making, nor did it consist of nationalities or local societies, but consisted of structured, mutually exclusive and antagonistic religion-based communities. This was intentionally done to prevent the unity among the masses and also to negate the legitimacy and credibility of the nationalist demands, ideology and organisation.

---

[11] With two-fold objective of promoting the interests of the community and preaching loyalty to the British.

[12] Communalism was, of course, not the only constituent of the policy of Divide and Rule. Every existing division of Indian society was encouraged to prevent the emerging unity of the Indian people. An effort was made to set region against region, province against province, caste against caste, language against language, reformers against the orthodox, the moderate against the militant, leftist against rightist, and even class against class. It was, of course, the communal division that survived to the end and proved the most serviceable.

[13] Ever since, the other justifications like theories of civilising mission, white man's burden, welfare of the ruled, and so forth got increasingly discredited by the end of the 19th century.

- Second, by extending official favour and patronage to the communalists. For instance, the Government freely rewarded communal leaders, intellectuals and government servants with titles, positions of profit and high salaries.
- Third, by exhibiting extraordinary tolerance towards the communal press and persons and agitations. For instance, the Government refused to take action against the propagation of virulent communal ideas and communal hatred through the press, pamphlets, leaflets and literature which was otherwise in sharp contrast with the frequent suppression of the nationalist press and literature.
- Fourth, by readily accepting the communal demands, thereby politically strengthening the communal organisations and their hold over the people. For instance, while the Congress could get none of its demands accepted from 1885 to 1905, the Muslim communal demands were readily accepted in 1906 as soon as they were presented to the Viceroy. Similarly, in 1932, the Communal Award accepted all the major communal demands of the time and even during World War II, the Muslim communalists were given a complete veto on any political advance.
- Fifth, by readily accepting the communal organisations and leaders as the real spokesperson for their 'communities', while treating the nationalist leaders as representing a microscopic minority of the elite.
- Sixth, by according separate electorates which served as an important instrument for the development of communal politics.
- Last, by adopting a policy of not only non-action against the communal elements but on the contrary, following a policy of indirect encouragement towards communalism. For instance, the British administrators deliberately followed a policy of relative inactivity and irresponsibility in dealing with situations of communal tension like communal riots that were often not crushed energetically; however, the same careless approach was not adopted in case of the nationalist and other popular protest movements.

"After all a riot does not occur spontaneously. It's not a sub generic phenomenon, instead it's orchestrated into being. Year after year, there've have been games played with people's minds, poison has been brewed between the communities, fuelled by suspicion, distrust, greed and lust."

Manabendra Bandyopadhyay

- **Role Played by Revivalist and Communal Organisations**: A strong contributory factor in the growth of communalism was the various Hindu and Islamic reform-revivalist movements and organisations of the 19th century through which a distinct **Hindu** and **Muslim identity** started developing at the mass level. These revivalist movements **though** inculcated a sense of pride among Indians and attempted to restore self-respect of the Indians, which had been deeply injured by political subjugation also resulted in the imbalance of the prevalent syncretism between the two communities. While creating religious consciousness among the masses, the movements simultaneously ended up demarcating the boundaries between the two communities, resulting in further contestation between them over sacred public space or ceremonies, which eventually led to a number of communal riots between Hindus and Muslims – in Bareilly in the 1870s, in Agra in the 1880s and finally the cow protection riots in the 1890s. The role played by an aggressive Arya Samaj movement with its controversial *Shuddhi campaign* leading to the counter-mobilisation of the Muslims in urban Punjab has already been discussed in earlier chapters.

A pronounced Hindu tinge in much of the nationalist thought and propaganda in the beginning of the 20th century not only produced a retaliatory reaction in Muslims but also did great damage in the already fragile relationship of the two communities. Due to the introduction of a strong Hindu religious element in nationalist thought and propaganda by the Extremists, such as the utilisation of **Ganesh Puja** and the **Shivaji Festival** to propagate nationalism by Tilak, initiation of the anti-partition Bengal agitation by taking dips in the Ganges, use of Hindu symbols, idioms and myths like portraying of India nation as **Bharat Mata**, talking of bringing ***Ramarajya***, songs like ***Vande Mataram*** during the different phases of the nationalist agitation all helped in creating a vague Hindu aura that ultimately resulted in the **alienation** of **Muslims**. The situation was further deteriorated by certain conservative Hindu leaders and writers who tended to emphasise on ancient Indian culture as the golden ages while simultaneously condemning the medieval period as an age of barbarians along with referring to the Muslim rulers as foreign tyrants. This damage became clear in the 20th century when Mohammed Ali Jinnah, while formulating his two-nation theory (that is, India was not one nation, but two – Hindu and Muslim nations), declared that Hindus and Muslims were two nations also because they had a different history. All of this, ultimately, resulted in the carving of the ideological openings for Hindu communalism along with the opening of the vistas for the spread of a Muslim tinge among Muslim nationalists.

The colonial government and certain Muslim communalists further used this misunderstanding and alienation to keep large sections of Muslims away from the nationalist movement and to instil among them the feeling that the success of the movement would mean *Hindu supremacy* in the country. Also, all along, the leading communal organisations, Muslim League (1906), the Hindu Mahasabha (1915) along with the Rashtriya Swayamsevak Sangh (RSS) provided justification for each other's existence and increasingly made each other more communal. Through their political activities and propaganda, they not only prevented Hindus and Muslims from coming together but also made them distrust each other, thereby spreading communalism among the hearts of people.

> *"One must never forget that communalism in India is a latter-day phenomenon which has grown up before our eyes."*
>
> Jawaharlal Nehru (1936)

- **Political and Social Trends of the Late 19th Century**: The emergence of certain political and socio-economic trends in the late 19th century further complicated the communal atmosphere. Under the influence of communalism, the social tension and class conflict prevalent between the exploiters and the exploited belonging to different religions found a distorted expression in terms of **communal conflict**. While the discontent and clash of interests was real and was mostly due to non-religious factors, owing to regressive communal consciousness and given misunderstandings between the two communities, even a non-communal conflict was given the colour of communal conflict. However, it is pertinent to note here that the communal distortion was made possible on account of certain specific socio-economic trends present in several parts of the country during that time, wherein the religious distinction somehow **coincided** with social and class distinctions and most often the exploiting sections, that is, the landlords, merchants and moneylenders, were generally **upper caste Hindus** while the poor and exploited were **Muslims** and lower caste Hindus. Consequently, propaganda by the **Muslim communalists** that Hindus were exploiting Muslims or by the **Hindu communalists** that Muslims were threatening Hindu property or economic interests could succeed even while wholly incorrect. For instance, owing to this factor, the struggle between tenants and landlords in East Bengal and Malabar and the peasant-debtor and the merchant-moneylender in Punjab could be portrayed by the communalists as a struggle between Muslims and Hindus. Similarly, the landlord-moneylender oppression was represented as the oppression of Muslims by Hindus, and the attack by the rural poor on the rural rich as an attack by Muslims on Hindus. Unfortunately, both the communalists and the colonial administrators stressed the communal as against the class aspects of agrarian exploitation and oppression while creating a misconception among the masses that the Muslim peasants and debtors were being exploited not as peasants and debtors but because they were Muslims.

Also, in many instances, a communal form is given to the social conflict not by the participants but by the **observers**, that is, the officials, the journalists, the politicians, and, finally, the historians, all of whom did a disservice by providing a post facto communal explanation for the otherwise social conflict because of their own conscious or unconscious outlook. Another noteworthy point in this regard is that, the social, economic and political vested interests deliberately encouraged communalism because of its capacity to distort and divert popular struggles, to prevent the masses from understanding the real socio-economic and political forces responsible for their social condition and to prevent unity on national and class lines.

- **Weaknesses in the National Movement**: The growth of communal ideology could have been checked by the nationalist ideology, but despite being committed to secularism and desirous for a unity among the Indian people, the Congress, as a representative of the nationalist forces, failed to prevent the spread of communalism among its people. Two probable reasons can be attributed to this failure:
  - One of the probable reasons was that the Congress could neither comprehensively understand the nature of communalism and nor could keep pace with the fast changing character of communalism, thereby failing to evolve a key robust strategy to combat the menace of communalism. For instance, the Lucknow Pact of 1916 thereby according sanction to the separate electorates was surely a subject matter of strategic debate. So were its different decisions after 1937.
  - Also, at times, at the level of implementation, the Congress, sometimes, made wrong choices, while dealing with the communal forces. For instance, it often tried to offer concessions and made compromises with the communal groups eventually increasing their credibility while on certain other occasions, opportunities for a compromise were lost, thereby creating a deadlock.

> *"The fact is that communalism is basically an ideology which could not have been, and cannot be, appeared; it had to be confronted and opposed. ... The failure to do so was the real weakness of the Congress and the national movement."*
>
> Bipan Chandra

However, while pointing out the limitations, the complexity of the situation should not be ignored. Attention needs to be paid to the attitude of the British Government, who aggravated the difficulties for Congress as no matter what the Congress offered to the Muslims, the Government always offered them more, thereby making the proposal of Congress redundant in the eyes of Muslims.

Trajectory of Evolution of Communalism

Syed Ahmed Khan and His Modernisation Campaign (1875)

- Realising that Muslims have been lagging behind the Hindus in modern education and in government jobs, Sir Syed Ahmed Khan started a modernisation movement among Muslims, though without any communal bias, and founded the **Mohammedan Anglo-Oriental College** in Aligarh in 1875, which interestingly received financial support from many rich Hindus and had a large component of both Hindu faculty and students. In fact, in the initial stages till the founding of the Congress in 1885, Khan himself preached harmony between Hindus and Muslims.

> *"Do you not inhabit this land? Are you not buried in it or cremated on it? Surely you live and die on the same land. Remember that Hindus and Muslims are religious terms. Otherwise Hindus, Muslims and Christians who live in this country are by virtue of this fact one quam (nation or community)."*
>
> Syed Ahmed Khan (1884)

- However, his politics changed soon after the formation of the **anti-imperialist** Congress in 1885 as his political philosophy revolved round the idea that the Muslims' share in administrative posts and in profession could be increased only by professing and proving loyalty to the colonial rulers and since this was in absolute contradiction with the goals of the national movement initiated by the Congress, Syed Ahmed Khan voiced his disapproval towards the Congress. Gradually, in the process of launching frontal attack[14] on the Congress, Syed Ahmed Khan laid down the foundation of certain basic themes of **communal ideology**:
  - One such theme was that being a majority, **Hindus would dominate Muslims** and override their interests, if the British rule ended and the power was transferred to Indians and thus the British were needed to safeguard Muslims as a minority. It was majorly due to this premise that Syed Ahmed Khan was opposed to the establishment of representative democratic institutions, because according to him, *the democracy would only mean the power to the majority*[15].
  - The second theme of permanent **clash of Hindu and Muslim interests** was also brought forth into the public domain. Giving up his earlier views, he now declared that India could not be considered a nation and simultaneously, criticised and labelled the Congress to be only a Hindu body whose major objectives were 'against Muslim interests'. He, therefore, asked the Muslims to remain politically passive, that is, non-agitational, in their approach and to stay away from the agitational politics of Congress.
  - The theme for 'separate interests' was also incorporated in the communal dialogue by persistent raising of demands for safeguards for Muslims in Government jobs, legislative councils and district boards by Syed Ahmed Khan and his followers. Having strong belief that Muslims being an ex-ruling class were entitled to a special position of authority, he laid down the condition that irrespective of being a minority, the Muslims need to have a greater representation in the sharing of power and should enjoy special relationship with the political order.

> *"In the Indian context, the British were the best guardians of Muslim interests. Muslims must, therefore, remain loyal and oppose the National Congress. In case of democratic elections, the Muslims would not be able to guard their interests, for it would be like a game of dice in which one man had four dice and the other only one. Any system of elections, would put power into the hands of Bengalis or of Hindus of the Bengali type which would lead to Muslims falling into a condition of utmost degradation and the ring of slavery being put on them by Hindus."*
>
> Syed Ahmed Khan

[14] The attack was strongly supported by Theodore Beck, the Europffean principal of the Aligarh College, who in 1888 formed the Indian Patriotic Association to oppose Congress and to plead for government patronage for the Muslims. In 1893, the Mohammedan Anglo-Oriental Defence Association was also formed, once again with Beck's encouragement, to check the growing popularity of the Congress and to organise Muslim public opinion against it.

[15] However, it is equally pertinent to note here that this majority-phobia was increased further because of the cow-killing riots of 1893, the Hindi–Udru controversy, the Nagri Resolution of 1900 which recognised the Nagri script along with Persian for official use in the courts and the Hindu demand for legal ban on cow slaughter and Congress silence about it.

- Thus, quite ironically, the three major themes of communalism, that is, opposition to the nationalist forces, opposition to the democratic process and institutions, and loyalty to the British Government, could be traced back to the ideology of Syed Ahmed Khan and his followers in the 1880s. Eventually, under the influence of Syed Ahmed Khan who held that any kind of agitational politics would create suspicion and disloyalty among the rulers, the Muslim politics begin to drift away from the Congress and the mainstream nationalism[16], for instance between 1892 and 1909, only **6.59** per cent of the Congress delegates were Muslims.

Partition of Bengal and the Formation of the Muslim League (1906)

- However, after Sir Syed's death in 1898, even the younger generation at Aligarh became restless, as they began to feel that they were losing out because they were not properly organised and hence could not voice their demands effectively. As a result, they gradually began to deviate from the existing loyalist tradition of Aligarh politics and felt the urgent need for a political organisation for the Muslims.
- The events of 1906 further charged the atmosphere as in eastern Bengal, the resignation of Lt. Governor Bampfylde Fuller, known for his pro-partition and pro-Muslim sympathies, and the possibility of partition itself being rescinded under the nationalist pressure, made the Bengal Muslim leadership panicky. The anti-partition movement appeared in Muslim consciousness as an anti-Muslim campaign. And then, the Secretary of State **Morley's budget speech** of 1906 indicated that representative government was going to be introduced in India.
- This alarmed the Muslim leaders across the board, as they thought that in the new self-governing bodies they would be swayed by the Hindu majority who were now well organised under the Congress, which provided the context for the **Simla deputation** of 1 October 1906 to the Governor General Lord Minto. The deputation depicted the Muslims as a separate community with political interests different from those of the Hindus and therefore having legitimate claim to minority rights to proportional representation in the representative bodies and public employment. The Viceroy gave the deputation a patient hearing, and also assured them that their rights would not be jeopardised.
- The success of the deputation was a tremendous morale booster to Muslim politics, yet mere verbal assurances were hardly expected to satisfy the younger Muslims who had long been feeling the need for a separate political organisation for themselves, a religious orientation of the movement was also on their agenda, as there has now been, as **David Lelyveld** (1978) describes it, a clear shift of emphasis from *qaum* (community based on common descent) to *ummah* (community based on allegiance to a common faith). Also, over time a gradual Islamisation of Muslim politics was being observed as the earlier politicians of Sir Syed's generation had kept the *ulamas* at arm's length in favour of the Western-educated intelligentsia, but by contrast, the younger leaders like Muhammad Ali and Shaukat Ali were profoundly influenced by the *ulamas*, like Maulana Abdul Bari, and through their influence rediscovered the inspiration of Islam as a mobilising force.
- The 35 delegates at Simla, therefore, decided to organise the community for independent political action to secure for themselves a recognition from the government as *a nation within a nation*, to use the words of **Aga Khan**, the leader of the delegation. Since, the next annual Mohammedan Educational Conference was scheduled to be held in December 1906 in Dacca[17], it was decided that this opportunity would be taken to launch a new Muslim party and, thus, on 30 December 1906, a new

[16] However, it is equally pertinent to note that though it definitely affected in terms of absolute numbers, not all the attempts to keep the growing Muslim intelligentsia politically passive were wholly successful because many Muslim intellectuals from Bombay, Bengal and Northern India joined the Congress and their numbers increased in the succeeding years. For instance, Badruddin Tyabji presided over the Congress session in 1887 while a number of Muslim delegates like Mir Musharaff Hussain, R. M. Sayani, Hamid Ali Khan, A. Bhimji took active part in the agitational politics of Congress.

[17] The capital of the new province of Eastern Bengal and Assam, later known as Dhaka.

party named the **All India Muslim League** (AIML), popularly known as the Muslim League under the leadership of Nawab Salimullah[18] of Dacca, Aga Khan and Nawab Mohsin-ul-Mulk, was launched having professed goals of safeguarding the political rights and interests of the Muslims, to preach loyalty to the British and to further the cause of intra-communal amity. Other prominent leaders included a group of educated elite Muslims like big *zamindars*, ex-bureaucrats and other upper class Muslims like Viqar-ul-Mulk, Syed Amir Ali, Syed Nabiullah, Khan Bahadur Ghulam and Mustafa Chowdhury. However, it is important to note here that, at this stage, this was just the beginning of a search for distinctive political identity and not a quest for a separate homeland.

- Between 1907 and 1909, provincial Muslim Leagues were formed in all the major provinces and its London branch was inaugurated in May 1908, which under the leadership of Syed Amir Ali played a significant role in shaping the Morley–Minto Reforms, the constitutional reform of 1909.

> *"God forbid, if the British rule disappears from India, Hindus will lord over it and we will be in constant danger of our life, property and honour. The only way for the Muslims to escape this danger is to help in the continuance of the British rule."*
>
> Viqar-ul-Mulk

Separate Electorates (1909)

- Under the provisions of the **Morley–Minto Reforms** (1909), separate electorates[19] were provided for the Muslims along with reserved seats in imperial as well as provincial legislatures, in numbers much in excess of their numerical proportions, thereby providing official legitimacy to their minority status and to the separate political identity of the Indian Muslims and proved to be a major landmark in the evolution of communalism and contributed to the forging of an all-India Muslim political identity.

> *"The granting of this privilege of separate electorate by the colonial state in the Morley-Minto reforms of 1909 not only elevated them to the status of an all-India political category, but positioned them as a 'perpetual minority' in the Indian body politic. These structural imperatives of representative government henceforth began to influence the relationship between the Congress and the Muslim League."*
>
> Shekar Bandopadhyay

Growth of Hindu Communalism and Formation of All India Hindu Mahasabha (1915)

- Meanwhile, all along Hindu communalism was also slowly emerging, and specifically, from the 1870s, a section of Hindu *zamindars*, moneylenders and middle-class professionals began to arouse anti-Muslim sentiments and laid down the foundations of Hindu communal ideology and politics. Subscribing to the colonial view of Indian history, they propagated the ideology that medieval period

[18] The leader of the east Bengali Muslims.

[19] Separate electorates meant grouping of constituencies, voters and elected candidates on the basis of religion. In practical terms it meant introducing Muslim constituencies, Muslim voters and Muslim candidates. It also meant that non-Muslim voters could vote for a Muslim candidate. The election campaign and politicisation was, thus, strictly confined within the walls of each religion.

belonged to the 'tyrannical' Muslim rule and expressed gratitude towards the British for liberating and saving the Hindus from 'Muslim oppression'.

- A communal twist was also provided to the **Hindi–Urdu controversy**[20], more particularly in UP and Bihar while anti-cow slaughter propaganda was undertaken by them all over India[21] in the early 1890s and later in a more virulent form during the second decade of the 20th century, which many times took a communal turn, often resulting in communal riots. Like Muslim communalists, Hindu communalists also carried on a regular agitation for a 'Hindu' share of seats in legislatures and in government services.
- During the early 20th century, as a result of the growing communal consciousness among the Hindus, two prominent Hindu Communal Organisations were formed. In 1909, **Punjab Hindu Sabha** was founded under the leadership of U. N. Mukherji and Lal Chand, who accused the National Congress for 'sacrificing Hindu interests' to appease Muslims and for unnecessarily trying to unite Indians into a single nation. Later, under the presidentship of the Maharaja of Qasim Bazar, the first session of the **All-India Hindu Mahasabha** was held in April 1915.

"The Congress is the self-inflicted misfortune of Hindus. Hindus were moving towards extinction because of the poison imbibed for the last 25 years. They could be saved only if they were willing to purge the poison and get rid of the evil. The Congress is making impossible demands to the Government, leading to its justifiable anger against the Congress and Hindus. Instead, Hindus should try to neutralise the third party, the Government, in their fight against Muslims. It is also essential that Hindus abandon and end the Congress. A Hindu should not only believe but make it a part and parcel of his organism, of his life and of his conduct, that he is a Hindu first and an Indian after."

Excerpts from a booklet titled *Self-Abnegation in Politics* written by Lal Chand

- However, Hindu communalism was relatively weaker as compared to Muslim communalism due to the following reasons:
  - One of the broader social reasons was that the dominant hold of reactionary *zamindars,* aristocrats, ex-bureaucrats and conservative traditional religious priests like *mullahs* was **much more in case of Muslims** as compared to Hindus, and with time, even they were gradually losing positions of leadership or influence among the Hindus. Thus, the weak position of the middle class among Muslims and its social and ideological backwardness contributed more to the growth of Muslim communalism.
  - Also, another prominent reason was that since the Colonial Government was not in a position to simultaneously **placate** both types of communalisms, it banked heavily on Muslim communalism and, thus, due to little support and few concessions to Hindu communalism, it could not grow as much as the Muslim communalism.

Lucknow Pact (1916)

- A brief period of political unity was brought between the Muslim league and the Congress following the signing of the Lucknow Pact in 1916, which recognised the Muslim demand for **separate electorates**. However, this settlement later proved to be a disastrous step as not only it provided recognition

[20] Declaring that Urdu was the language of Muslims and Hindi of Hindus.

[21] Ironically, the campaign was primarily directed not against the British but against Muslims, because no objection was raised against the British cantonments that were left free to carry on cow slaughter on a large scale.

to the communal politics but the Pact also tacitly supported the assumption that India consisted of different communities with separate interests of their own and thus, way for future resurgence of communalism was opened.

- In fact, from 1912 to 1924, the young nationalists like M. A. Jinnah[22] began to overshadow the loyalists in the League and tried to move nearer to the policies of the Congress and adopted self-government as one of its objectives.

Khilafat Agitation and Non-Cooperation Movement (1920–22)

- Though an unprecedented Hindu–Muslim rapport[23] was produced during the agitation against the Rowlatt Acts, the Khilafat and the Non-Cooperation Movements, yet even the **Khilafat movement** itself contributed further to the strengthening of Muslim identity in different parts of the country, particularly in Punjab and Bengal. The frequent use of religious symbols, like fatwas[24] by the overzealous ulamas, not only highlighted the Islamic self of the Indian Muslims but also encouraged the trend of looking at political questions from the religious point of view, which at a later stage, aided in the development of communal ideology and politics.

> *"The Muslim mobilisation under the banner of Khilafat generated a sense of inferiority and insecurity among the Hindus, who in emulation of their aggressive Other now started counter-mobilisation."*
>
> Christophe Jaffrelot (1996)

Rise in Communal Tension (1922–27)

- During the period from 1922 to 1927, not only was there a rapid deterioration of Hindu–Muslim relations but also a considerable rise in the communal tension across the country resulting in the revival of the old communal organisations like **Muslim League** and **Hindu Mahasabha** while fresh ones like **Rastriya Swayam sevak Sangh** (RSS)[25], were being founded.
- Mobilisation along communal lines was the order of the day and both Hindu as well as Muslim communalists were indulged in *fear politics* trying their best to inculcate the psychology of fear[26] among both Hindus and Muslim masses. The communal atmosphere was further charged with the *Sangathan* and *Shuddhi* movements among Hindus and *Tanzeem* and *Tabligh* movements among Muslims, all working for communal consolidation and religious conversion. The inevitable result of such mobilisation along community lines was the outbreak of a **series of riots** between the Hindus and the Muslims in the 1920s, affecting practically all parts of India. For instance, according to the Simon Commission Report, nearly 112 major communal riots occurred between 1922 and 1927.
- This contestation made its presence felt in the arena of institutional politics too, as now even many nationalists started adopting communal or semi-communal positions and eventually not able to withstand the communal pressure, the Swarajists were split into the groups of ***Responsivists*** and ***Non-Responsivists***.

---

[22] He joined the League in 1912.

[23] For instance, Swami Shradhanand, a staunch Arya Samajist, was asked by Muslims to preach from the pulpit of the Jama Masjid in Delhi, while Dr. Saifuddin Kitchlu, a Muslim, was given the keys to the Golden Temple, the Sikh shrine in Amritsar. The atmosphere in the entire country was resounded to the cry of *Hindu–Muslim ki Jai*.

[24] Opinion or decision on a point of Islamic law given by a religious person of standing.

[25] An overtly aggressive Hindu organisation founded in 1925.

[26] The fear of being deprived, surpassed, threatened, dominated, suppressed, beaten down and exterminated.

Leaders like Lajpat Rai, Madan Mohan Malaviya and N. C. Kelkar increasingly became vocal for Hindu communal solidarity and joined the Hindu Mahasabha trying constantly to marginalise the secularists and destroy any possibility of an understanding with the Muslims, while on the Muslim side, leaders like Dr Kitchlew, Muhammed Ali and Shaukat Ali who were once staunchly in favour of Hindu–Muslim unity, now turned uncompromisingly against any communal reconciliation and accused the Congress of trying to establish a Hindu government and Hindus of wanting to dominate and suppress Muslims.

- The factor of communalism was also visible in the election results. For example, in 1923, at the municipal level elections in UP, the alliance between the Swarajists and the Khilafatists won most of the seats in 1923 on a note of communal harmony, but in the next municipal election of 1925, the Swarajists lost all seats to the Hindu Mahasabhites and their support base was systematically undercut by the Hindu Mahasabha under Madan Mohan Malaviya.
- Another reason for substantial dehyphenation of relationship between the Congress and Muslim League was the lack of consensus between the two regarding the **renegotiation[27] of the Lucknow Pact**. Although Swarajists were willing, the Mahasabhites like Malaviya, B. S. Moonje and Lala Lajpat Rai successfully torpedoed all efforts at reconciliation. Even the Bengal Pact, which C. R. Das had negotiated with the local Muslims, was rejected at the Kakinada Session of the Congress in December 1923 on the ground that a national issue could not be resolved on a provincial basis while a resolution condemning separate electorate for Muslims was prevented from being passed at the Guwahati Congress of 1926 by the timely intervention of Gandhi and Nehru.
- In the meanwhile, certain trivial issues were dampening the already fragile Hindu–Muslim unity and fast becoming the bone of communal contention. For example, like the mobilisation of Hindus around the claim of a **right to play music before mosques** was gathering momentum in various parts of the country along with the increased public contest for contending community rights became sharper such as the disputes over the route of a religious procession. Gradually, such non-essentials became non-negotiable demands for those wanting to mobilise communities along religious lines and the otherwise trivial issues like the 'music before mosque' not only sparked off a series of violent riots between 1923 and 1927, but also in the election of 1926, it became an emotive issue dividing the electorate along communal lines.

"The resolution of the problem of Hindu-Muslim relations was now beyond human control, and had passed on to the hands of God."

An exasperated Gandhi lamented in 1927

Opposition to Nehru Report and Jinnah's Fourteen Points (1928)

- The Muslim support for Congress further diminished when the process of renegotiating the Lucknow Pact was finally derailed by the Mahasabhites at the All Parties Conference at Delhi in January 1928, which was organised to settle communal issues and draw up an agreed constitution for India.

[27] At the Central Legislative Assembly, Mohammad Ali Jinnah, elected by the Bombay Muslims, appeared as the most prominent spokesman of the Muslims. Earlier, due to Jinnah's preference for constitutional methods and abhorrence for agitational politics, he was driven away from Gandhian Congress, but after the withdrawal of non-cooperation, when the Congress once again reverted to constitutionalism under the Swarajists, he co-operated with them and his 'Independent Party' formed an alliance with the Swarajists and together they came to be known as the Nationalist Party in the Assembly. Simultaneously, he focused on reviving the Muslim League at its Lahore Session in 1923 and decided to work on a new constitutional arrangement for India, and for that purpose, wanted to renegotiate the Lucknow Pact with the Congress.

- Background for the opposition of the Nehru Report: Even before the Congress of 1928, a large number of Muslim communal leaders had met at Delhi in December 1927 and evolved four basic demands known as the **Delhi Proposals**:
  - Sind should be made a separate province
  - the North-West Frontier Province should be treated constitutionally on the same footing as other provinces
  - Muslims should have 1/3rd representation in the central legislature
  - in Punjab and Bengal, the proportion of representation should be in accordance with the population, thus guaranteeing a Muslim majority, and in other provinces, where Muslims were a minority, the existing reservation of seats for Muslims should continue.
- However, the **Nehru Report** though accepted the first two demands, that is, the separation of Sind from Bombay and constitutional reform in the North-West Frontier Province, it did not accept the other two demands and instead recommended that:
  - India should be a federation on the basis of linguistic provinces and there should be provincial autonomy
  - Elections to be held on the basis of **joint electorates**
  - Seats in central and provincial legislatures be reserved for religious minorities in proportion to their population
- Though there were wide differences among Muslims communalists, a section of the Muslim League, under the leadership of Jinnah, were willing to give up separate electorates in favour of joint electorates, if three amendments were met:
  - Muslims should have 1/3rd representation in the central legislature
  - in Punjab and Bengal, the proportion of representation should be in accordance with the population, thus guaranteeing a Muslim majority, and in other provinces, where Muslims were a minority, the existing reservation of seats for Muslims should continue
  - residuary powers should be vested in the provinces
- Though even the Congress was positively contemplating Jinnah's offer because it opened up prospects for unity, its rejection in uncompromising terms by the Hindu Mahasabha and refusal on part of a large section of the League led by **Mohammed Shafi** and the **Aga Khan** and many other Muslim communal groups at the All Parties Conference (1928) complicated matters.
- The incompatibility between the League and Mahasabha frustrated all attempts at unity and further led to the estrangement of Jinnah who discarding his earlier secular approach moved more towards communalism and declared that the Nehru Report only represented Hindu interests and later described this phase as the ***Parting of the Ways*** with the Congress. He now went back to the demand of separate-electorates and consolidated[28] all the communal demands into a single document which came to be known as Jinnah's Fourteen Points.
- The Fourteen Points basically consisted of the four Delhi Proposals, the three amendments proposed and the demands for the continuation of separate electorates along with reservation of seats for Muslims in government services and self-governing bodies. The Fourteen Points later formed the **basis of all future communal propaganda** in the subsequent years.
- The events of 1928–29 thus resulted in drifting apart of the communal forces, and soon this drifting apart reached a point of no return. This also proved to be the starting point of communalism transforming into an irresistible mass force. Subsequently, the Muslims were further alienated from the Congress as evident from their large-scale abstention from the Civil Disobedience and the Quit India

[28] Made by different communal organisations at different times

Movement. Their frustration increased in the years after 1929, as depression constricted opportunities, leading to more tension, conflicts and violence.

The Round Table Conferences and the Communal Award (Early 1930s)

- The communal leaders again got a chance to come into the limelight during the Round Table Conferences. At these conferences, both the Muslim and Hindu communalists made strenuous efforts to win the support of British authorities to defend their so-called communal interests. For instance, in 1932, at a meeting in the House of Commons, Muslim communal leaders like Aga Khan, the poet Mohammed lqbal and the historian Shafaat Ahmad Khan stressed on *the inherent impossibility of securing any merger of Hindu and Muslim, political, or indeed social interests* and *the impracticability of ever governing India through anything but a British agency.* Similarly, in 1933, presiding over the Hindu Mahasabha session, prominent Hindu communal leader Bhai Parmanand made a plea for cooperation between Hindus and the British Government and said that *I feel an impulse in me that Hindus would willingly cooperate with Great Britain if their status and responsible position as the premier community in India is recognised in the political institutions of new India.*
- The British Government also did its best to patronise the communal trend, and in an effort to bolster the sagging Muslim communalism, it announced the **Communal Award** in 1932, which accepted virtually all the Muslim communal demands embodied in the Delhi Proposals of 1927 and Jinnah's Fourteen Points of 1929, resulting in both jubilation and confusion among the communal forces as they were now faced with an entirely new situation, that is, what more to achieve now and where should they go from here.

Provincial Elections Results and a Complete Ideological Shift (1937)

- The 1937 provincial election results were quite revealing as both the Congress and regional parties did well, while Muslim League had a dismal performance throughout India. For instance, on the one hand, Congress was in a position to form ministries in six provinces and was the largest single party in two other provinces, while the regional parties[29] also succeeded in forming the ministries in the crucial provinces of Bengal and Punjab where otherwise Muslims were in majority. On the other hand, ironically the Muslim League, claiming to be the representative of the Muslims, fared very badly[30] in all the provinces and was not in a position to form a ministry in even Muslim-dominated provinces. The Hindu Mahasabha fared even worse and it was, thus, a **battle of survival** for both Hindu and Muslim communalists who were on the verge of political extinction and were in desperate need for a new ideology and programme for their survival and growth.
- The election results, therefore, confronted the Muslim League and the Congress with different messages:
    - **For the Congress**, the message was loud and clear that it had a strong base among the Hindus but had yet to establish itself as a representative of the Muslims. However, they had the satisfaction that even their rival, the Muslim League, could not claim to represent the Muslims. The Congress, therefore, had to work among the Muslim masses and bring them into the Congress fold, and in 1937, this did

[29] Unionist Party led by Sikander Hayat Khan in Punjab and Praja Krishak Party led by Fazl ul-Haq in Bengal.

[30] The Muslim League, for example, won only 109 out of the 482 seats allotted to Muslims under separate electorates, securing only 4.8 per cent of the total Muslim votes. It could get only 2 seats out of 84 in Punjab and 3 out of 33 in Sind while could not win a single seat in the North-West Frontier Provinces.

not seem to be a difficult task as the Muslims were not a political community[31] yet, not even in the late 1930s. For this, the Congress under the leadership of Jawahar Lal Nehru decided to launch a *Muslim mass contact campaign*[32], an attempt to make a direct appeal to the Muslims to join the Congress. Also, the Congress was in position to comfortably ignore the League as the election results had demonstrated its unrepresentative character. Thus, not only did Congress refuse to enter into any coalition government in the minority provinces like UP to share power with the Muslim League, but Jawaharlal Nehru declared with supreme arrogance that there were now only two parties on the Indian political scene – the Raj and the Congress. Gradually, a steady propaganda against separate electorate and a constant vilification of the Muslim League as unpatriotic and reactionary was initiated.

- **Lessons for the Muslim League** were also very clear that it had absolutely no base among the masses and, thus, needed to discard its elitist character and expand its horizons among the masses to become a popular organisation, much like the Congress. In order to achieve this, Jinnah launched a massive campaign for the popularisation of the League and discarding its elitist character started mobilisation among the Muslim masses through reduction of membership fee, formation of provincial committees and transforming the party programme so as to acquire a socio-economic character. An equally strong campaign was launched to denounce and condemn the Congress ministries and to propagate the ideology that they were just edifices of Hindu-Raj and were inherently hostile to Muslim minorities. Gradually, all the divergent groups were brought together under the banner of a revived and revitalised Muslim League under the leadership of **Jinnah** who projected himself as the 'sole spokesman of Muslims'.

- As a result of all that, **communalism, after 1937,** increasingly acquired a popular base and began to emerge as a mass force while the liberal communalism transformed into the extreme communalism,[33] making the year 1937 a **turning point** in the communal history.

Postulation of Two-Nation Theory and Pakistan Resolution (24 March 1940)

- On 22 December 1939, when the Congress ministries resigned in protest against India being drawn into World War II without consultation, Jinnah decided to celebrate it as a 'Deliverance Day'[34] and within this political context of estrangement and distrust, another idea gradually germinated, and that was the notion of **Muslim nationhood**.

---

[31] As there had been positional differences and ideological contestation within Muslim politics and it remained caught in provincial dynamics, as their interests in Bengal and Punjab, where they were a majority, were different from those of others in the minority provinces. For instance, in Bengal, the Krishak Praja Party under A. K. Fazlul Huq mobilised both the Muslim and lower-caste Hindu peasants on class-based demands, and competed with the Muslim League, after its revival in 1936, for Muslim votes, whereas in Punjab, the Unionist Party led by Fazl-i-Husain, Sikandar Hayat Khan, as well as the Jat peasant leader Chhotu Ram, appealed to the composite constituency of Muslim, Hindu and Sikh rich landlords and peasant producers – who had benefited from the Punjab Land Alienation Act of 1900 – and had a complete control over rural politics while the Muslim League, on the other hand, was until 1937, as Ayesha Jalal puts it,' "*little more than a debating forum for a few articulate Muslims in the minority provinces and had made no impact on the majority provinces*'.

[32] Jinnah was, however, quite alarmed by this move and warned the Congress to stay away from the Muslims, as according to him, only the Muslim League could represent the Muslims.

[33] It is pertinent to note here that after 1937, even Hindu communalism entered into an extremist phase. Madan Mohan Malaviya's place was taken by leaders like V. D. Savarkar, M. S. Golwalker of the RSS who posing as the saviours of the Hindus continuously vilified the Muslims. They accused the nationalist Congress leaders of emasculating the Hindus by their talk of non-violence and communal unity and exhorted Hindus to retaliate and teach a lesson to the Muslims.

[34] In words of Jinnah, *a day of deliverance from the tyranny, oppression and injustice from which Muslim had suffered under the Congress Rule.*

- In 1930, Sir Mohammad Iqbal, as president of the Muslim League had proposed the constitution of a centralised territory for Islam within India, by uniting the four provinces of Punjab, North west Frontier Provinces, Sind and Baluchistan.
- The idea was further elaborated by the Cambridge student **Rahmat Ali**, who in 1933 vaguely talked about 'Pakistan' to be constituted of the four Muslim provinces and Kashmir. It was, however, at the Karachi meeting of the Sind branch of the Muslim League, presided over by Jinnah himself, that a resolution was passed that mentioned the need for *political self-determination of the two nations, known as Hindus and Muslims*, and asked the Muslim League to think of appropriate measures to realise it.
- Though it was the first declaration of the '**two nation**' theory, it was not separatism yet as the two federations of Hindus and Muslims were meant to be united through a common centre. Since then, public discussions went on about the practicality of a constitutional arrangement that could give shape to this abstract notion, with intellectual inputs coming from a variety of Muslim leaders, from the Sindhi leader Abdoola Harun, Dr Syed Abdul Latif, Abdul Bashir of the Pakistan Majlis in Lahore, to the prominent Aligarh scholars, Professor Syed Zafarul Hasan and Dr M. A. H. Qadri.
- Finally, the **Lahore resolution** of the Muslim League in March 1940 formally proclaimed the Muslims as a nation. The Resolution though did not mention partition or Pakistan, but only talked about **Independent states** to be constituted of the Muslim majority provinces in an unspecified 'future'.
- The resolution, in other words, only signalled the transformation of Indian Muslims from a *minority* to a *nation*, so that no future constitutional arrangement for India could any more be negotiated without their participation and consent. The central plank in Jinnah's politics henceforth was to be a demand for 'parity' between the Hindus and the Muslims in any such arrangement.
- Thus, from now onwards, recognition of national identity of the Muslims and their right to self-determination, as well as 'parity' of representation with the Hindus at the centre became the **non-negotiable demands** for Jinnah and the Muslim League. It was also a big development for Muslim leaders, who in the 1920s saw no conflict between their Indianness and Muslim identity, but now in the 1940s were asking nothing less than a separate Muslim nationhood.

Conciliatory Approach Adopted towards the League by British during World War II (1939–45)

- After the outbreak of World War II, the Muslim League was assiduously fostered by Viceroy Linlithgow and it was officially recognised as the representative voice[35] of Muslims. The British Government accorded a blanket veto to Jinnah and promised that no political settlement would be made unless it was acceptable to the League.
- The colonial masters tactfully utilised the League and its 'Pakistan demand' to counter the demand for complete independence raised by the Congress and regularly pointed out to them that Hindus and Muslims must come to an agreement first on how power was to be transferred before the process of devolution of power could actually begin.

> *"Hindu-Muslim feud is the bulwark of British rule in India."*
>
> Winston Churchill

[35] Even though its performance in the last elections hardly substantiated this claim.

Legitimacy to the Pakistan Demand by the Cripps Mission (March–April 1942)

- Though the Cripps Mission failed, its proposals provided a boost to the activities of the Muslim League and gave legitimacy to the Pakistan demand by accommodating it in their provision for provincial autonomy[36]. Thus, at a time when the 'Pakistan demand' had hardly been taken seriously by Indians, its sympathetic consideration by officialdom was a great boost to the communal forces.
- Later, as the Congress chose the collision course and launched the Quit India Movement, the British found useful allies in Jinnah and the Muslim League, and between 1942 and 1943, League ministries were installed in Assam, Sind, Bengal and the North-West Frontier Province through active manoeuvring by the British bureaucracy. Meanwhile, on **23 March 1943**, Pakistan day was observed.
- However, it is pertinent to note here that the demand for Pakistan was still not well defined as what Jinnah primarily wanted even at this juncture was autonomy for the Muslim majority provinces in a loose federal structure, with Hindu–Muslim parity at the central government, the minority Hindus in the Muslim majority provinces serving as security for the Muslim minorities elsewhere. Sensing the same, the Congress initiated top-level political negotiations in an effort to meet League demands.

Rajagopalachari Formula (1944)

- In April 1944, C. Rajagopalachari with the blessings of Gandhiji proposed a formula for Congress-League Cooperation:
    - Muslim League to endorse Congress demand for independence and to cooperate with Congress in forming a provisional government at the centre.
    - A post-war commission would be formed to demarcate the contiguous districts where the Muslims were in absolute majority, and there a plebiscite of the adult population would decide whether they would prefer a separate sovereign state, that is, Pakistan or not.
    - In case of a partition, there would be a mutual agreement to run certain essential services, like defence and communication.
    - The border districts could choose to join either of the two sovereign states.
    - The implementation of the scheme would wait till after full transfer of power.
- In July 1944, Gandhiji proposed talks with Jinnah on the basis of the *Rajaji formula*, which indeed amounted to an acceptance of Pakistan demand, but Jinnah did not agree to this proposal and Gandhi–Jinnah talks broke down in September 1944.
- In Gandhiji's view, the talks failed because of fundamental differences in perspectives, while he looked at separation as within the family and therefore preferred to retain some elements of partnership, Jinnah wanted complete dissolution with sovereignty as he wanted only the Muslims of North-West and North-East to vote in the plebiscite and not the entire population and was also completely opposed to the idea of a common centre.

[36] According to which the provinces were given the right to sign individual agreements with Britain about their future status should they choose to reject the new constitution that would be framed.

Desai–Liaqat Pact (1944)

- The efforts to end the deadlock still persisted by way of political negotiations, and thus, taking things forward, a proposal in the form of a pact between **Bhulabhai Desai**, the leader of the Congress Party in the Central Legislative Assembly and **Liaqat Ali Khan**, the deputy leader of the Muslim League in the Assembly.
- A draft proposal for the formation of an interim government at the centre was drawn:
  - an equal number of persons nominated by the Congress and the League in the central legislature.
  - 20 per cent reserved seats for minorities.
- However, no settlement could be reached between the Congress and the League on these lines, but the fact that a sort of parity between the Congress and the League was decided upon with the Desai–Liaqat Pact had again far-reaching consequences.

Simla Conference and Post-War Elections (1945–46)

- At the end of World War II, at the initiative of **Viceroy Wavell**, the Congress leaders were released from jail in mid-1945 and invited to Simla (25 June–14 July 1945) to work out an interim political agreement under which an entirely **Indian Executive Council**[37] was on the cards.
- The Simla Conference, however, crashed on the insistence of Jinnah's demand for parity. He claimed that the Muslim League alone had an exclusive right to nominate all the Muslim members to the Executive Council. Congress[38] refused to accept it, for that would reduce the Congress party to the status of only a Hindu caste party.
- Instead of bypassing the League, or making an effort to explore other possibilities, Wavell upholding the virtual veto provided to Jinnah, announced the breakdown of the Conference, thereby further strengthening the League's position.
- The post-war elections held in the winter of 1945–46 proved to be another watershed event in the communal politics as they were fought by the League purely on the basis of extreme communalism. The choice between Congress and the League was portrayed as a choice between the *Gita* and the *Quran*, mosques were used for elections meetings and *ulamas* and *maulvis* were pressed in service to issue *fatwas* directing Muslims to only vote for the League. The political campaign was further given religious legitimacy by different communal slogans like '*A vote for the League and Pakistan would be a vote for Islam*'. Not surprisingly, the League made a clean sweep of the Muslim seats.

> *"This was the inevitable result of an election campaign that had been turned into a religious crusade."*
>
> Maulana Azad

Cabinet Mission and Ambivalence Over Groupings (March 1946)

- In March 1946, the Cabinet Mission was sent to India to establish a national government and work out a constitutional arrangement for transfer of power. However, **reversing** their earlier strategy of

[37] With the exception of the viceroy and commander-in-chief as the only British members.

[38] Quite ironically, at that time, Maulana Abul Kalam Azad was the Congress president.

divided India[39] and due to the strong concern for imperial defence, along with having the implicit belief that Pakistan with six provinces would not be viable as a separate entity, a plan was drawn up by the Cabinet Mission to safeguard the interests of the Muslim minority within the overall framework of unity of the country.

> *"A minority will not be allowed to place a veto on the progress of the majority."*
>
> Statement of Attlee, British Prime Minister, on 15 March 1946

- After wide consultation across the political spectrum, the Cabinet Mission rejected the proposal of a sovereign Pakistan and offered instead, on 16 May:
  - A three-tier structure of a loose federal government for the Union of India, including both the provinces and the princely states.
  - There would be a union government at the top, in charge only of defence, foreign affairs and communications while all residual powers would be vested in the provincial governments, which would be free to form groups.
  - Each group could also have their own executives and legislatures and could decide what provincial subjects to take on.
  - A Constituent Assembly was to be elected by the recently constituted provincial assemblies to draft a constitution for the whole of India; it would first meet at the Union level and then split into three sections:
    - **Section A**: Containing **Hindu majority provinces** like Madras, Bombay, UP, Bihar, Central Provinces and Orissa;
    - **Section B**: Containing **Muslim majority provinces** in the north west like Punjab, NWFP and Sind;
    - **Section C**: Would Include **Bengal** and **Assam**.
  - After a constitution was finally settled for all the three levels (Province, Group and Union), the provinces would have the right to opt out of any particular group, but not from the Union, that is, after the first general elections. However, they could also reconsider the constitution after an interval of 10 years and could then demand the modification of both the group and union constitutions.
  - In the meanwhile, an interim government would look after the day-to-day administrative matters.
- Since the Cabinet Mission Plan was not clear about whether grouping was compulsory or optional, disagreement arose between the Congress and the League regarding their interpretation of the Plan over the issue of grouping. While **Congress**[40] demanded that provinces should have the option of not to join a group at a very beginning, rather than wait till general elections, the **League**, on the other hand, demanded that the right of provinces to modify the Union Constitution should be granted immediately without waiting for ten years. The Cabinet Mission, however, deliberately refused to clarify its stand, probably in the hope that their ambivalence might reconcile the irreconcilable position of the Congress and the League, but in effect, it only complicated matters.
- Both parties saw it as a confirmation of their stand. While Congress was drawing satisfaction from the fact that not only the League's power of veto had been withdrawn but with categorical rejection of the

[39] British officials now felt that the strategies in the Indian sub-continent after independence would be better served if India was united. It was believed that a united India, which was friendly with Britain, could be an active partner in the defence of the Commonwealth, whereas a divided India's defence potential would be weak and conflict between India and Pakistan would frustrate the joint defence plans.

[40] Keeping in mind the interests of NWFP and Assam, where it had won majorities in recent elections and which had been placed in sections B and C along with the Sikh majority areas of Punjab.

Pakistan demand in the Mission preamble, it was now also out of the picture. The League, however, reiterated in its 6 June 1946 statement that it accepted the Plan on the assumption that *the basis and the foundation of Pakistan* had been inherent in the plan itself on the grounds of compulsory grouping, which would ultimately lead to the *establishment of complete sovereign Pakistan*.

- Further increasing the anxiety, within a few days of the League stand, **Nehru** declared in a press conference on 10 July that Congress had *agreed to nothing else* other than participation in the Constituent Assembly and since the Assembly was a sovereign body, it would formulate the rules of procedure, implying that the rules laid down by the mission could be amended. He also raised doubts over the grouping system that it may collapse since the NWFP and Assam would not agree to it. Subsequently, the short-term plan to constitute an interim government also fell through on the sticky issue of parity, as Congress wanted to include a Muslim candidate among its nominees. **Jinnah** treated it all as the ultimate betrayal by the Congress and thus on 29 July 1946, the League Working Committee withdrew its earlier approval of the Mission's long-term plan and gave a call for ***direct action***.

Invitation for Formation of the Interim Government (1946)

- However, in sharp departure from earlier British practice, for the first time, the British without waiting for the League's cooperation and defying Jinnah's stand that no constitutional settlement be made unless it was acceptable to the League, invited the Congress to form an Interim Government,[41] which ultimately came into being on 2 September 1946 without the Muslim League.

> *"A surrender to the Congress by the British would compel the Muslims to shed their blood."*
>
> Jinnah's warning to the British Prime Minister, Attlee

Direct Action Day (16 August 1946)

- Enraged at being left out, Jinnah started popular agitation for Pakistan and gave a call for 'Direct Action'[42] to be commenced on **16 August 1946** with the slogan, *Lekar rahenge Partition, Larke Lenge Pakistan*, (we will fight and get Pakistan). The day was meant to be observed through nationwide hartal, protest meetings and demonstrations to explain the meaning of Pakistan and the reasons for rejecting the Cabinet Mission plan.

> *"The Muslims of India wouldn't rest contended with anything less than the immediate establishment of independent and fully Sovereign state of Pakistan ... now the time has come for the Muslim nation to resort to Direct Action. ... Never before in the whole history of the Muslim League did we do anything except by constitutional methods. Throughout the painful negotiations the two parties (Congress and the British) held a pistol at us. ... The situation must be met. We also have a pistol."*
>
> Jinnah giving a call for Direct Action

[41] With Jawaharlal Nehru functioning as its prime minister or *de facto* head.

[42] Quite ironically, this was in sharp contrast with the principles of *Qaid-i-Azam,* that is, Jinnah since almost all his life, he had expressed complete abhorrence for agitational politics and affirmed faith in the constitutional politics but now with direct action, the day finally arrived for him to bid goodbye to constitutional methods and prepare his Muslim followers for agitational politics.

- However, quite unfortunately with tacit support from League ministry in power under premier **H. S. Suhrawardy**[43], a communal frenzy was provoked by Muslim communal groups resulting in equal brutal retaliation by Hindu communal elements, in Calcutta, in what later came to be known as the ***Great Calcutta killings***. Around 5,000 people were killed and 10,000 were injured in this unfettered craziness for four days.
- As a 'chain reaction' to the Calcutta carnage, riots broke out in the districts of Chittagong, Dacca, Mymensingh, Barisal and Pabna. But, the worst came in October in the two southernmost districts of **Noakhali** and **Tippera**, where mostly the Hindus were on the receiving end, as Muslim peasants, in a very systematically orchestrated attacks, destroyed Hindu property, raped their women and killed thousands of them.
- Soon, the whole of subcontinent was engulfed in the communal fire as riots began in **Bombay** from 1 September, in **Bihar** from 25 October, and in **Garhmukteshwar** in UP from November and in all these places, under the growing[44] influence of Hindu communal forces like RSS and Hindu Mahasabha, now Hindus were primarily in the offensive.

"The non-Hindu peoples in Hindustan must either adopt the Hindu culture and language, must learn to respect and hold in reverence Hindu religion, must entertain no ideas but those of glorification of the Hindu race and culture, that is, they must not only give up their attitude of intolerance and ungratefulness towards this land and its age long traditions but must also cultivate the positive attitude of love and devotion instead – in one word, they must cease to be foreigners, or may stay in the country, wholly subordinated to the Hindu nation, claiming nothing, deserving no privileges, far less any preferential treatment – not even citizen's rights."

Statement of M. S. Golwalkar, head of the RSS

- Gradually, the **NWFP** was also engrossed in the communal polarisation as the Congress government in power there started facing a civil disobedience campaign by local Muslims who under the Pathan code of honour identified with the grievances of their community and initiated the cycle of vengeance for the wrongs done to Muslims in UP, Bihar and Bombay. Instigated by local *pirs*, the Pathan tribesmen began to attack local Hindus and Sikhs from December 1946 in Dera Ismail Khan and Tonk.

Joining of the Interim Government by the Muslim League (26 October 1946)

- Jinnah's ability to unleash civil war forced the British authorities back to their old policy of placating the Muslims and, thus, due to Lord Wavell's continuous efforts of persuading the League to join the Government, it joined the Interim Government on 26 October 1946, ironically without forsaking its idea of Pakistan or accepting the aspects of Cabinet Mission plan.

"The Interim Government was merely the continuation of civil war by other means and it is just a foothold which would help League to advance towards its goal of Pakistan."

Jinnah

---

[43] Who declared a public holiday on the day and addressing a public rally at the Ochterlony Monument in Calcutta gave a hint to the Muslim crowds that the army and police had been 'restrained'.

[44] For instance, the number of RSS *swayamsevaks* (volunteers) rose from 40,000 in 1938 to 7,600 in 1943 to 6,00,000 by the beginning of 1948.

Threat of Breakdown of the Interim Government (1946–47)

- However, the League's entry into the Interim Government did not end the conflict, rather it opened up another arena of struggle and a complete impasse. The League ministers disagreed on almost all the issues taken up by their Congress colleagues and boycotted often most of the consultative meetings. For instance, on 9, December, the League boycotted the Constituent Assembly meeting, for refusal on part of Congress to accommodate League's demand for sectional meetings drafting group constitutions.
- The breaking point came when the **League** demanded that the Constituent Assembly be dissolved since it was unrepresentative while the **Congress** members frustrated at the non-cooperation of League members at every juncture sent a letter to the Viceroy Wavell seeking resignation of the League ministers.

Fixing of a Time Limit for British Withdrawal (20 February 1947)

- Meanwhile, the diversion from the constitutional crisis was made by **Attlee**'s, 20 February announcement[45] in British Parliament stating that the British would withdraw from India by 30 June 1948 to such authority or in such a way as would seem most reasonable and be in the best interests of the Indian people. Since, this statement reaffirmed the British departure from India, Congress tried to extend a gesture of cooperation to the League.

"The British are fading out of the picture and the burden of this decision must rest on all of us here. It seems desirable that we should face this question squarely and not speak to each other from a distance."

Nehru appealed to Liaqat Ali Khan

- But, Jinah turned down the gesture, rather his reaction to the Attlee's statement was entirely different and taking cue from the declaration that the power would be transferred to more than one authority if the Constituent Assembly did not become a fully representative body, that is, if the Muslim majority provinces did not join it, he further became confident that now he only needed to stick firmly to his position in order to achieve his goal of Pakistan. Soon, he began a civil disobedience campaign[46] in Punjab, which brought out the collapse of the coalition ministry headed by Khizr Hayat Khan of the Unionist Party.
- Lord Wavell was also replaced by **Lord Mountbatten** who, on his arrival in India on 22 March, found a fairly intractable situation wherein it was virtually impossible to hand over power to a united India since the League was on the war path, as evident by its Punjab manoeuvre and Jinnah was obdurate that he would accept nothing less than a sovereign Pakistan.

"We would have preferred a united India. We couldn't get it, though we tried hard."

Attlee's statement some years later

[45] However, certain historians also feel that it was due to Attlee's 'forced march' to the demission of power that the communal tension was further heightened and the partition was made inevitable.

[46] Trouble started brewing when the Unionist ministry, on the advice of Governor Jenkins, banned the Muslim National Guard, a paramilitary organisation of Muslims, and also the RSS in January. This led to the launching of a civil disobedience movement by the League, which organised protest demonstrations and processions, participated by hundreds of thousands of ordinary Muslim men and also women. The ministry ultimately resigned on 2 March in the face of mounting discontent, plunging the region into chaos and disorder.

Rejection of 'Plan Balkan' by Both Congress and the League (April 1947)

- In the middle of April, Lord Mountbatten proposed a plan better known as 'Plan Balkan' since it proposed the partition of Punjab and Bengal and handing over power to the provinces and sub-provinces, which would be free to join one or more of group Constituent Assemblies on the basis of self-determination, while the Interim Government would remain until June 1948.
- Since the plan proposed demission of power to the provinces and in the absence of a strong centre would certainly lead to **balkanisation of India**, it was outrightly rejected by Nehru. Jinnah cast it aside too, as he was not yet prepared to accept the partition of Punjab and Bengal which would give him only a *truncated or mutilated, moth-eaten Pakistan.*

> *"Instead of producing any sense of certainty, security and stability, the plan would encourage disruptive tendencies everywhere and chaos and weakness."*
>
> Nehru

3 June Plan and Its Outcome (1947)

- On 3 June, Lord Mountbatten announced his new plan and proposed to transfer the power to two successor **dominion governments** of India and Pakistan, along with the advance of the date of transfer of power from June 1948 to 15 August 1947.
- The plan provided for:
  - the partition of Bengal and Punjab,
  - the Hindu majority provinces which had already accepted the existing Constituent Assembly would be given no choice,
  - the Muslim majority provinces, that is, Bengal, Punjab, Sind, North-West Frontier Province and Baluchistan, would decide[47] whether to join the existing or a new and separate Constituent Assembly for Pakistan.
- The following day **Nehru**, **Jinnah** and **Sardar Baldev Singh** on behalf of the Sikhs endorsed the plan and thus began the fast march to transfer of power.
- Consequently, the Bengal Assembly on 20 June and the Punjab Assembly on 23 June decided in favour of partition: West Punjab and East Bengal would go to Pakistan and the rest would remain in India. Shortly following this, Sind, Baluchistan and NWFP[48] opted to join Pakistan. Two Boundary Commissions – one for Bengal and one for Punjab – both under **Sir Cyril Radcliffe** were appointed with a mandate of delineating the international frontiers within a strict time frame of not more than six weeks. On 18 July, the India Independence Act was ratified by the Crown, which was eventually implemented[49] on 14/15 August 1947.

[47] This was to be decided by the provincial assemblies, and there would be a referendum in the North West Frontier Provinces, and in case of Baluchistan, the Querta municipality and the tribal representatives would be consulted.

[48] Against the wishes of the popular Gandhian leader Abdul Gaffar Khan.

[49] On 14 August at a brief ceremony in Karachi, the newly designated capital, Mountbatten handed over power to the newly created dominion of Pakistan and Jinnah took over as its first governor general. That night the Indian Constituent Assembly met in a special session, where at the stroke of midnight Nehru delivered his now famous 'Tryst with Destiny' speech and India became independent on 15 August 1947.

Partition and Communal Massacres (1947)

- Though the scheme of partition was announced, it was still a contentious and complicated issue. The speed with which the country was partitioned, without planning for the involved complicated processes, proved to be disastrous for the entire country. Neither was there any institutional structure to which the problems arising from the division could be referred and nor a clear-cut mechanism to address the worsening communal situation. The delay in announcement of the awards[50] of the Boundary Commission further aggravated the communal problem as migrations became a frenzied affair often culminating in massacres.

"Neither Jinnah nor Muslim League ever defined the rights of non-Muslims in future Pakistan, and this omission, proved to be a fatal defect of their scheme, causing anxieties in religious minorities in Punjab and Bengal."

Ayesha Jalal

- One of the worst communal infernos ravaged in Punjab where since the fall of the Unionist ministry in March 1947, the region had plunged into chaos and disorder. A mindless mayhem started in the wake of partition, with great loss of lives and property on both sides. According to an estimate, about 14 million people were displaced from their homes and around 2 million people were killed.

"It was learnt that in East Punjab, Hindu and Sikhs mobs attacked Muslim villages. They were burning houses and killing innocent men, women and children. Exactly the same reports came from West Punjab. Muslims were indiscriminately killing men, women and children of Hindu and Sikh communities. The whole of Punjab, east and west, was becoming a graveyard of destruction and death."

Maulana Abul Kalam Azad

Thus, as we witnessed in the above paragraphs, the **Muslim communalism** which manifested itself through the issue of Muslim identity from minority status to nationhood to the actual realisation of a separate sovereign state in 1947 took a long and tortuous trajectory and all along, the relationship between the League and the Indian National Congress went through a lot of ups and downs. The making of Pakistan which was the ultimate communal demand of Muslims was the result of the twin processes of gradual alienation of the Muslims as a group from the national mainstream of politics along with their consolidation, on a communal platform under a communal organisation. However, it is very important to note here that these twin processes became possible only because communalism in the 1940s began to attract the masses and became a mass force and ideology, a process which had begun in the 1920s, got accelerated in the 1930s and gathered a further momentum in the 1940s. The conceptualisation of a Muslim nation was, thus, not only on the basis of the imagining of Jinnah alone or of a select group of articulate Muslim intellectuals, rather the demand was legitimated by thousands of ordinary Muslims who joined the processions at Lahore, Patna or Karachi, participated in the hartals, organised demonstrations or even took part in riots between 1938 and 1948. At the same time, an extreme strand of Hindu

[50] It is often speculated that Mountbatten delayed the announcement of the Boundary Commission Award even though it was ready by 12 August 1947 to disown responsibility for further complications.

communalism, the British policy of using the communal card to counter the nationalist movement along with recognising the League as the sole representative of Muslims and giving it power to veto progress in political settlements and the inability on part of Congress to draw the Muslim masses into the national movement are equally responsible for the subsequent win of the communal forces.

Know the Person: Mohammed Ali Jinnah

It is indeed ironical and intriguing that a person who started as the **Ambassador of Hindu–Muslim Unity**[51] ended up leading the movement for demanding Pakistan, and eventually achieving it. The ideological shift in the case of Jinnah from being a secular nationalist to a communal secessionist is a classic case study for understanding the evil influence of communalism.

Year	Remarks
1906	• After becoming a Barrister, M. A. Jinnah came back to India from London as a secular, liberal nationalist and immediately joined the Congress. In fact, he was highly influenced by **Dadabhai Naoroji** and for a while also acted as his secretary at the Calcutta session of the Congress. • Interestingly, at the time of founding of the Muslim League, he expressed his strong resentment against the same, a fact even admitted by Aga Khan, the first president of the League, who wrote some years later that '*Jinnah was our toughest opponent in 1906 and he came out in bitter hostility toward all that I and my friends had done and were trying to do . . . He said that our principle of separate electorates was dividing the nation against itself*'.
1909	The first step towards communalism was taken without any desire of his own and perhaps against his own wishes when he entered the Central Legislative Council from Bombay as a Muslim member under the system of separate electorates.
1913	He remained in the Congress but joined the All India Muslim League in 1913 and gradually started assuming the role of a spokesperson of the Muslim 'community' as a whole. However, he still was in opposition to the principle of separate electorates and considered them to be divisive factor which would divide India into *two watertight compartments*. At this stage, he also refused the communal assumption that self-government in India would lead to Hindu rule; and instead argued that the real political issue in India was Home Rule or *transfer of power from bureaucracy to democracy*.
1916	It was due to his and Tilak's efforts that in 1916, the Lucknow Pact was signed between the Indian National Congress and the Muslim League. He also played a prominent role in the founding of All India Home Rule League in 1916.
1919	He resigned from the Legislative Council as a protest against the passing of the Rowlatt Bill.
1920	Being a hardcore believer in constitutional politics while being a firm opposer of agitational politics, he left the Congress when it took a turn towards mass politics under Gandhiji. But, at this stage, the logic of communalism had gradually started asserting itself over him and transformed him first from a nationalist to communal nationalist and then into a liberal communalist.

[51] The title given by Sarojini Naidu owing to Jinnah's continuous propagation of the theme of national unity in his addressed meetings.

Year	Remarks
1924	• He revived the otherwise redundant Muslim League in 1924 and started building it upon and around the demand for safeguarding *the interests and rights of the Muslims*. His politics was now based on the basic communal idea that *Muslims should organise themselves, stand united and should press every reasonable point for the protection of their community.* • At the same time, he still pleaded for Hindu–Muslim unity and when Congress once again reverted to constitutionalism under the Swarajists, his 'Independent Party' formed an alliance with the *Swarajists* in opposing Government policies and measures in the Central Legislative Assembly. In fact as late as 1925, he told a young Muslim, who said that he was a Muslim first that '*My boy, no, you are an Indian first and then a Muslim*'.
1927	He supported the boycott of the Simon Commission, though he did not join in the mass demonstrations against it.
1928–29	However, by 1928–29, he surrendered to the more reactionary communalists, led by the Aga Khan and M. *Shafi*, and in the end, became the leader of Muslim communalism as a whole. This became apparent during the discussions on the Nehru Report and his becoming the author of the famous fourteen Points, most reactionary demands of the Muslim communalism.
1930–34	• Jinnah was further alienated from the main currents of nationalism as the Congress organised the Civil Disobedience movement of 1930 and started moving towards a more radical socio-economic programme. Moreover, the Muslim masses especially the younger generation were also increasingly shifting to nationalist and left-wing politics and ideologies leaving Jinnah further disenchanted and thus, consequently from 1930 to 34 Jinnah returned to London on a self-imposed exile. • During his stay in England, though he took part in the first two Round-Table Conferences, for the most part, he remained aloof from the happenings of the sub-continent. Meanwhile, his health also started to deteriorate and he developed severe respiratory ailments and later tuberculosis.
1934–36	But Jinnah was too much of a man of action and of politics to stay aloof and, eventually, in 1934, he returned to India to once again revive the Muslim League. Still at this stage, he was inclined towards liberal communalism as evident in his speeches of this duration stressing on nationalism, desire for freedom and Hindu–Muslim cooperation. For instance, at a public event at Lahore in March 1936, Jinnah said that '*Whatever I have done let me assure you there has been no change in me, not the slightest, since the day when I joined the Indian National Congress. It may be I have been wrong on some occasions. But it has never been done in a partisan spirit. My sole and only object has been the welfare of my country. I assure you that India's interest is and will be sacred to me and nothing will make me budge an inch from that position* while exhorting his fellow co-religionists he asked them to *prove that their patriotism is unsullied and that their love of India and her progress is no less than that of any other community in the country*'.
1937	• Jinnah and the League fought the provincial elections of 1937 on a semi-nationalist type of programme as evident by their list of only 'Muslim' demands being *protection and promotion of the Urdu language and script, and adoption of measures for the amelioration of the general conditions of Muslims.* • But, the poor election results completely disheartened Jinnah and made him to shift his weight towards extreme communalism, which was primarily based on the themes of hate and fear, that is, *Islam in danger* and the *dominance of Hindu raj*. His change of stance was clearly visible in his speeches as in his presidential address to the League in 1938, Jinnah said, '*the High Command of the Congress is determined, absolutely determined to crush all other communities and cultures in this country and establish Hindu raj in this country*'. Similarly in his presidential address on April 1941, he declared that in a united India *the Muslims will be absolutely wiped out of existence.*

Year	Remarks
1939–47	• He now launched a vicious campaign against the Congress and taking his communal politics further, brought religion into the forefront of the League's propaganda by portraying the League's fight with the Congress as a fight between Islam and *Kufr (infidelity)*. Be it the celebration of **Deliverance Day** on the resignation of the Congress Ministries in December 1939, or proclaiming himself to be 'sole spokesman' of Muslims, or the Pakistan Resolution of March 1940 or the Direct Action Day of 1946, he used all tactics from his arsenal now to get Pakistan at all costs and eventually he did on 14 August 1947 and became its first Governor General.
1948	• However, quite ironically, once Pakistan was formed, Jinnah tried to go back to his old ways of secularism as evident in his Presidential address to the Constituent Assembly of Pakistan on 11 August 1947: '*You may belong to any religion or caste or creed – that has nothing to do with the business of the State . . . We are starting with this fundamental principle that we are all citizens and equal citizens of one State*'. • But, probably it was all too late, as was rightly said by Bipan Chandra, '*Jinnah had cynically spawned a monster which not only divided India, but would, in time, eat up his own concept of Pakistan and do more harm to Muslims of Pakistan than the most secular of persons could have predicted or even imagined*'.

Previous Year's Questions (Prelims)

1. Why was the Radcliffe Committee appointed? (2014)
   (a) Solve the problem of minorities in India
   (b) Give effect to the independence Bill
   (c) Delimit the boundaries between India and Pakistan
   (d) Enquire into the riots in East Bengal

2. Assertion (A): According to the Wavell plan the number of Hindu and Muslim members in the executive Council were to be equal. (2007)

   Reason (R): Wavell thought that this arrangement would have avoided the partition of India
   (a) Both A and R are true and R is the correct explanation of A.
   (b) Both A and R are true but R is not the correct explanation of A.
   (c) A is true but R is false.
   (d) A is false but R is true.

3. In which one of the following provinces was a Congress Ministry not formed under the Act of 1935? (2005)
   (a) Bihar
   (b) Madras
   (c) Orissa
   (d) Punjab

4. Who headed the interim Cabinet formed in the year 1946? (2003)
   (a) Rajendra Prasad
   (b) Jawaharlal Nehru
   (c) Sardar Vallabhbhai Patel
   (d) C. Rajagopalachari

5. The last opportunity to avoid the partition of India was lost with the rejection of which of the following? (2002)
   (a) Cripps Mission
   (b) Rajagopalachari formula
   (c) Cabinet Mission
   (d) Wavell Plan

6. Who was the brainchild of the Balkan plan for fragmentation of India? (2002)
   (a) Winston Churchill
   (b) M. A. Jinnah

(c) Lord Mountbatten
(d) V. P. Menon

7. Who was the President of Indian National Congress at the time of partition of India?(2002)
(a) C. Rajagopalachari
(b) J. B. Kripalani
(c) Jawaharlal Nehru
(d) Maulana Abul Kalam Azad

8. A London branch of the All India Muslim League was established in 1908 under the presidency of (2001)
(a) Aga Khan
(b) Ameer Ali
(c) Liyaqat Ali Khan
(d) M. A. Jinnah

9. As an alternative to the partition of India what had Gandhiji suggested to Mountbatten? (2000)
(a) Postpone granting of independence
(b) Invite Jinnah to form the government
(c) Invite Nehru and Jinnah to form the government together
(d) Invite the army to take over for some

10. At the time of partition of India, which one of the following provinces of British India came forward with a plan for a United and independent existence? (2000)
(a) Punjab
(b) Assam
(c) Bengal
(d) Bihar

11. Which one of the following leaders of the Congress was totally in favour of Cabinet Mission Plan? (1999)
(a) Mahatma Gandhi
(b) Jawaharlal Nehru
(c) Sardar Patel
(d) Maulana Abul Kalam Azad

12. 'It made its proposals in May. It still wanted a United India. There was to be a Federal Union composed of British provinces (1999)

The above question is related to
(a) Simon Commission
(b) Gandhi Irwin pact
(c) Cripps mission
(d) Cabinet mission

13. When the Indian Muslim League was inducted into the interim government 1946, Liaqat Ali Khan which assigned the portfolio which of the following? (1998)
(a) Foreign affairs
(b) Home
(c) Finance
(d) Defense

14. With what specific instruction did Lord Mountbatten come to India as Viceroy? (1998)
(a) Balkanise the Indian subcontinent
(b) Keep India united if possible
(c) Accept Jinnah's demand for Pakistan
(d) Persuade the Congress to accept partition

15. Why did the Indian National Congress mainly agree to the partition of the country in 1947? (1998)
(a) The principle of two Nation theory Was then acceptable to them
(b) It was imposed by the British government and the Congress was helpless in this regard
(c) They wanted to avoid large-scale communal riots
(d) India would have otherwise lost the opportunity to attain freedom

16. Which one of the following is not correct about the Cabinet Mission Plan? (1996)
(a) Provincial grouping
(b) Interim Cabinet of Indians
(c) Acceptance of Pakistan
(d) Constitution framing right

17. Who among the following leaders did not believe in the drain theory of Dadabhai Naoroji? (1996)
(a) B. G. Tilak
(b) R. C. Dutt
(c) M. G. Ranade
(d) Sir Syed Ahmed Khan

Previous Year's Answers (Prelims)

1. (c)	2. (c)	3. (d)	4. (b)	5. (c)	6. (c)	7. (b)	8. (b)
9. (b)	10. (a)	11. (c)	12. (d)	13. (c)	14. (b)	15. (c)	16. (c)
17. (d)							

Towards Independence and Partition

12

The period from 1939 to 1947 represents a climax to the political events of the preceding decades. The outbreak of World War II in **September 1939** brought in new variables in Indian politics, resulting in changes in both the Congress strategies as well as the British policies. Outrightly rejecting the Cripps Mission and its hollow promise of '*Indian self-government after the war*', the Indian nationalists organised the '*Quit India*' Movement to hasten the British departure. The **August Revolution** and later the heroic struggles waged by the INA and the subsequent RIN Mutiny made it amply clear to the British that it will be difficult for them to retain their hold in India for a long time, and hence a greater readiness emerged among the British political circles to accept a negotiated settlement for a respected and ordered **withdrawal**. In this chapter, we will be discussing in detail about all these events which ultimately took us towards the long cherished dream of Independence, which, however, came with a sense of loss caused by the Partition.

Indian Nationalism During World War II

On 1 September 1939, World War II broke out, when **Germany** invaded Poland and Britain, which had been following a policy of appeasement[1] towards Hitler till then, was now forced to go to Poland's aid and declare war on Germany on 3 September 1939. Viceroy Lord Linlithgow associated India with England's declaration of war against Germany without consulting any Indian opinion as neither the Congress or any other political party nor the elected members of the central legislature were consulted before making such a declaration.

However, different opinions were voiced on the question of Indian support to British war efforts and, initially, mixed reactions were evoked across politicians:

- **Taking Advantage of the Situation**: The Socialists and the Left-wing leaders[2] like Subhash Bose, Acharya Narendra Dev and Jayaprakash Narayan wanted to **seize the rare opportunity** of the empire's weakest moment and advocated for taking the advantage of the situation to wrest freedom from Britain by immediately starting a civil disobedience movement. They argued that because the War was an imperialist one as both the sides were fighting for gaining or defending colonial territories, therefore, the question of supporting either of the two sides did not arise at all.
- **Unconditional Support**: Some leaders like Gandhiji[3] having full sympathy with the Allied cause and total dislike for the fascist forces advocated an unconditional support to the British in their war efforts and were of the opinion that in the moment of crisis, the Indians should not seek advantage of Britain's

[1] Earlier, Nazi Germany had occupied Austria in March 1938 and Czechoslovakia in 1939 and Britain in false hopes that agreeing to limited German expansion would satisfy Hitler, avoided any confrontation with him.

[2] It is pertinent to note here that initially from start of War in 1939 till 1941, the Left leaders were against any cooperation with Britain. However, with Germany's attack on Soviet Union on 22 June 1941, for Leftist forces, the anti-imperialist character of the War was suddenly changed to People's War and, thus, from 1941, they expressed their full support with Britain.

[3] Gandhiji denounced the Japanese slogan of 'Asia for Asiatics'.

problems. They further hoped that after the war, the British would adopt a lenient view towards India in light of her services and would suitably reward her.

> *"I am not therefore thinking of India's deliverance. It will come, but what will it be worth if England and France fall."*
>
> Gandhiji's statement in his weekly *Harijan* on 9 September 1939.

- **Conditional Support**: There were, however, some other leaders like Nehru, who though considered Fascism as a greater threat to mankind were alive to the need of supporting the war against fascism but were in favour of only conditional support to the British war efforts. if some constitutional concessions were promised to them, since they were also convinced that even the Allied powers like Britain and France were imperialist countries and the War was the result of the inherent inner contradictions of imperialism only. They, therefore, argued that India should neither take advantage of Britain's difficulties by starting an immediate struggle nor join the War till she herself gained freedom.

Official Congress Stand (September 1939)

- To decide the official Congress stand, a meeting of the Congress Working Committee was held in Wardha from September 10 to 14 in which after much deliberation Nehru's position was adopted by the Working Committee and, thus, it made the support to the war efforts **conditional** on two key issues:
  - A post-war Independence Pledge and Convening of a Constituent Assembly to frame the constitution of free India
  - An immediate National Government at the Centre.

> *"While we unequivocally condemn the Nazi attack on Poland as well as Nazism and Fascism, at the same time, we declare that India could not be party to a war which was ostensibly being fought for democratic freedom while that freedom was being denied to her. If Britain was fighting for democracy and freedom, she should prove this in India. In particular, she should declare how her war aims would be implemented in India at the end of the War."*
>
> Congress Resolution passed at Wardha.

Linlithgow Statement (17 October 1939)

- However, the British Government's response was entirely negative. The Viceroy, Lord Linlithgow, issued a statement on 17 October 1939, which fell far short of Congress expectations. In his statement, harping on the differences among Indians, he tried to use the Muslim League and the Princes against the Congress, and refused to **define Britain's war aims** beyond stating that Britain was resisting aggression.
- As an immediate measure, he only offered to set up a consultative committee whose advice might be sought by the Government, whenever it felt the need and for the future prospects, he only promised that, at the end of the War, the British Government would enter into consultations with representatives of several communities, parties and interests in India and with the Indian princes as to how the Act of 1935 might be modified.

- Linlithgow's statement drew angry and sharp reactions from the Indian people and the national leadership, especifically from **Gandhiji** who had been advocating more or less unconditional support to Britain. The Congress Working Committee met on 23 October and rejected the Viceregal statement as a reiteration of the old imperialist policy, and decided not to support the War efforts, and called upon the Congress ministriesto resign as a protest, which they did[4] on 30 October, 1939.

"The Indian declaration (of the Viceroy) shows clearly that there is to be no democracy for India if Britain can prevent it . . . The Congress asked for bread and it has got a stone."

Gandhiji's angry reaction on Linlithgow's statement.

"The Congress will safeguard the rights of every minority so long as they do not advance claims inconsistent with India's independence. But, independent India will not tolerate any interests in conflict with the true interests of the masses."

Gandhiji's answering to the question of minorities and special interests such as those of the princes, foreign capitalists, zamindars raised by the Linlithgow's statement.

Debate on the Question of Immediate Mass Satyagraha (1939–40)

- Though there was an agreement among Congressmen on the question of attitude to the War and the resignation of the ministries, however, sharp differences did emerge among them over the question of the immediate starting of a mass Satyagraha. While **Gandhiji** and most of the dominant Congress leadership were not in favour for initiating an immediate movement, the **Left-wing groups** and its leaders like Subhash Chandra Bose, on the contrary, being convinced about the masses being fully ready for action urged the Congress leadership to adopt immediate measures to launch a mass struggle.
- Gandhiji and most of the dominant Congress leadership **instead** wanted to carry on intense political work among the people, to prepare them for future struggles, to tone up the Congress organisation and purge it of its weaknesses. The resistance on part of the leaders was primarily on account of three broad reasons:
  - **First**, they felt that since the cause of the Allied powers, that is, Britain and France was just, so they should not be embarrassed in the prosecution of the War.
  - **Second**, the lack of Hindu–Muslim unity was considered a big barrier to any kind of struggle by them as in the existing communal atmosphere, any civil disobedience movement had potential of degenerating easily into communal rioting or even civil war.
  - **Third**, and above all, they felt that there did not exist in the country an atmosphere for an immediate struggle as neither the masses were ready nor was the Congress organisationally[5] in a position to launch a struggle.

---

[4] Celebrated by Muslim League as a '*day of deliverance*'.

[5] According to Gandhiji, during 1938–39, Congress organisation was weak and had been corrupted. There was indiscipline and lack of cohesion within the Congress ranks and, thus, under these circumstances, a mass movement would not be able to withstand severe repressive measures by the Government.

- However, the Left-wing groups[6] such as Subhash Chandra Bose and his Forward Bloc, the Congress Socialist Party and the Communist Party posed an alternative to the position of the dominant leadership and asserted that the war crisis provided an excellent opportunity to achieve freedom through an all-out struggle against British imperialism. Although they accepted that obstacles, like the communal problem, and weaknesses in the Congress organisation did exist, they were fully convinced that these hurdles would be automatically swept away, once a mass struggle would begin.

"Organisational strength was not to be built up prior to a struggle but in the course of the struggle. The Congress leadership's policy of 'wait and see', is not yielding any fruitful results over the years and may be Congress is now afraid of the masses, have lost zest for struggle ....."

Criticism of the Congress by the Left groups

"I cannot and will not start mass civil disobedience so long as I am not convinced that there is enough discipline and enough non-violence in the Congress ranks."

Gandhiji

Ramgarh Congress (March 1940)

- It was in such an atmosphere that the Congress met in Ramgarh in March 1940 and passed a resolution reiterating the Congress position on the War and called upon the people to prepare themselves for participating in a **Satyagraha** to be soon launched under Gandhiji's leadership, the form and timing to be decided by him only.

"India cannot endure the prospect of Nazism and Fascism, but she is even more tired of British imperialism. Now, nothing short of complete independence can be accepted by the people and the Congress would resort to civil disobedience as soon as the Congress organisation is considered fit enough for the purpose, or in case circumstances so shape themselves as to precipitate a crisis."

Statement of Maulana Abul Kalam Azad, the President of Ramgarh Congress.

- However, unhappy and unsatisfied with the resolution, the Left-wing groups such as the Socialists, the Communists, the Kisan Sabhaites and those belonging to the Forward Bloc held an **anti-compromise** conference in Ramgarh, where Subhash Chandra Bose urged the people to resist compromise with imperialism and be ready for immediate action.

[6] While agreeing on the need for an immediate struggle, the Left was, however, internally divided both in its understanding of political forces, and on the course of political action in case the dominant leadership of the Congress did not accept the line of immediate struggle. For instance, Subhash Bose wanted the Left to split the Congress if it did not launch a struggle, to organise a parallel Congress and to start a struggle on its own. He was convinced that the masses and the overwhelming majority of Congress would support the Left-led parallel Congress and join the movement it would launch. The CSP and CPI, on the contrary, differed from this view and they were convinced that Bose was grossly overestimating the influence of the Left, and no struggle could be launched without the leadership of Gandhiji and the Congress. Therefore, an attempt should be made not to split the Congress and, thus, disrupt the national united fronts but persuade and pressurise its leadership to launch a struggle.

August Offer (8 August 1940)

- Meanwhile, as the war in Europe had undertaken a new turn with Hitler's astounding success and the fall of Belgium, Holland and France, the British Government being in a **conciliatory mood** to get the cooperation of India in the war efforts, came up with its own offer. The Viceroy Lord Linlithgow announced the **August Offer**, which proposed:
  - Dominion Status as the objective for India
  - Expansion of Governor General's Executive Council having **majority representation** of the Indians (who would be drawn from major political parties)
  - Establishment of a War Advisory Council, which would meet at regular intervals and would include representatives of the Indian States
  - Setting up of a Constituent Assembly after the war where mainly Indians would decide the constitution according to their social, economic and political conceptions, subject to fulfilment of the obligation of the government regarding defence, minority rights, treaties with States, all India services.
  - No future constitution to be adopted **without the consent of** minorities[7]
- **Significance** of the August Offer: The August Offer was significant as for the first time:
  - the inherent right of Indians to frame their constitution was recognised, and the Congress demand for a constituent assembly was conceded,
  - Dominion status was explicitly offered,
  - in July 1941, the Governor General's Executive Council was enlarged to give the Indians a majority of 8 out of 12,
  - a National Defence Council was set up with purely advisory functions.
- The **Congress**, however, rejected the **August Offer** at its meeting in Wardha in August 1940 having found no common ground between its demand for complete independence and the Viceroy's offer of an enlarged Executive Council, while the **Muslim League**, though welcomed the veto assurance, rejected the offer as it did not go far enough to meet the demand of the League for a separate nation and it reiterated its position of the Lahore Resolution, which declared that the Muslims of India were a nation by themselves and, thus, partition was the only solution to the deadlock.

> *"Dominion status concept is dead as a doornail."*
>
> Statement of Nehru on August Offer
>
> *"The declaration had widened the gulf between the Nationalists and the British rulers."*
>
> Statement of Gandhiji on August Offer
>
> *"The offer was ridiculously out of place in a country demanding complete independence."*
>
> Statement of Maulana Azad on August Offer

Individual Satyagraha (October 1940–December 1941)

- Frustrated at the Government's position that no constitutional advance could be made till the Congress came to an agreement with the Muslim communalists and angry at the high handedness of the colonial

[7] Thereby granting a virtual veto to the Muslim League and other minorities.

authorities who were systematically issuing ordinance after ordinance taking away the freedom of speech and expression and putting under preventative arrest many Nationalist workers, especially those belonging to the Left-wing, the patience of both the Congress leadership and the masses, was getting exhausted.

- Consequently, near the end of 1940, the Congress once again requested Gandhiji to take command who decided to now initiate a limited civil disobedience in the form of **individual Satyagraha**[8] by a few personally selected volunteers, who would only offer anti-war speeches. It was basically a symbolic satyagraha for asserting the right of free speech. The **first** designated chosen volunteer of the Individual Satyagraha was Acharya Vinoba Bhave who initiated the Satyagraha on 17 October 1940 by delivering an anti-war speech in Paunar, a village near Wardha while his other two nominees were Jawaharlal Nehru and Vallabhbhai Patel, who were arrested before they could offer Satyagraha.

"The British rulers believed that in this world of force, of bombing aeroplanes, tanks, and armed men how weak we are! Why trouble about us? But perhaps, even in this world of armed conflict, there is such a thing as the spirit of man, and the spirit of a nation, which is neither ignoble nor weak, and which may not be ignored, save at peril."

Excerpts from an article entitled 'The Parting of the Ways' (1940) written by Nehru.

"It is wrong to help the British war-effort with men or money. The only worthy effort is to resist all war with non-violent resistance."

Public declaration of the Satyagrahi

- The two fold aim of the anti-war speech of the *Satyagrahi* was to not only utilise the right of freedom of speech to give expression to the popular discontentment against participation in the War but also disprove the British claim of whole-hearted support of India towards the War efforts. Gandhiji elaborated in detail even the procedure to be adopted by the *Satyagrahi,* who was required to inform the district magistrate beforehand of the time and place where he or she was going to make the anti-war speech. And in case the Government did not arrest the *Satyagrahi*, then he or she was supposed to not only repeat the performance but move into the villages and start his or her journey towards Delhi, and thereafter the movement came to be popularly known as the ***Delhi Chalo*** movement.
- During the next 14 months, according to an official statement, around 25,000 *Satyagrahis* courted arrest, including 398 members of Provincial Legislative Assemblies, 31 ex-Ministers and 22 members of the Central Legislature.

"The Congress is as much opposed to victory for Nazism as any Britisher can be. But their objective cannot be carried to the extent of their participation in the war. And since you and the Secretary of State for India have declared that the whole of India is voluntarily helping the war effort, it becomes necessary to make clear that the vast majority of the people of India are not interested in it. They make no distinction between Nazism and the double autocracy that rules India."

Excerpts from a letter written by Gandhiji to the Viceroy.

[8] Because of their anti-Nazi and anti-fascist feelings, Gandhiji and the Congress were still reluctant to take advantage of the British predicament and embarrass her war effort by a mass upheaval in India.

- However, due to limited nature of participation and restrictions imposed on Congressmen by Gandhiji, the movement could not achieve much and, thus, eventually in December 1941, the Congress Working Committee decided to suspend the movement. Still, the movement helped to not only politically arouse, educate and mobilise the people for the future upcoming struggles but also put back the Congress organisation in shape.

Gandhiji Designates Jawaharlal Nehru as His Successor (December 1941)

- Meanwhile, the War had taken a new turn[9] and was brought to India's doorstep as the Japanese, after overrunning the Philippines, Indo-China, Indonesia, Malaysia and Burma, came closer to the borders of India. The Indian leaders, released from prisons in early December, were worried about the safety and defence of India and were eager to go to the aid of the Allies.
- The Congress Working Committee overrode the objections of **Gandhiji** and Nehru and passed a resolution at the end of December offering to fully cooperate in the defence of India and the Allies if:
  - Britain agreed to give full independence after the War,
  - The substance of power was transferred immediately.
- It was at this time that **Gandhiji** designated **Jawaharlal Nehru** as his successor.

"Somebody suggested that Pandit Jawaharlal and I were estranged. It will require much more than differences of opinion to estrange us. We have had differences from the moment we became co-workers, and yet I have said for some years and say now that not Rajaji (C. Rajagopalachari) but Jawaharlal will be my successor. He says that he does not understand my language, and that he speaks a language foreign to me. This may or may not be true. But language is no bar to union of hearts. And I know that when I am gone he will speak my language."

Excerpts from Gandhiji's speech before the AICC, 15 January 1941

Cripps Mission (March–April 1942)

- The fall of Rangoon and Andaman and Nicobar Islands in March 1942 to the Japanese further increased the possibility of a Japanese invasion and, thus, in view of the **unfavourable war situation** and **international pressures** on the British from Soviet Union, United States and China to reconsider their India policy, they were compelled to seek an amicable settlement with India and obtain her active cooperation in the War. The British Government, thus, sent to India in March 1942 a mission headed by a Cabinet Minister **Stafford Cripps**[10] with a set of constitutional proposals to seek Indian support for the war.
- The main proposals of the Cripps mission were as follows:
  - An Indian Union with a dominion status would be set up immediately after the War with the right to secede from the Commonwealth, that is, it would be free to decide its relations with the Commonwealth and free to participate in the United Nations and other international bodies.
  - Immediately after the cessation of hostilities, a constituent assembly would be convened to frame a new constitution, which will consist of members from British India as well as Native States who would be partly elected by the provincial assemblies through proportional representation and partly nominated by the princes.

[9] The Soviet Union had been attacked by the Nazis on 22 June 1941, while the United States was also dragged into the War when Japan launched a surprise attack on the American fleet in Pearl Harbour on 7 December, 1941.

[10] a Left-wing Labourite who had earlier been an active supporter of the Indian National Movement

- The British government would accept the new constitution subject to two conditions:
  - Any **province** not willing to join the Union could have a separate constitution and form a separate Union.
  - The new constitution-making body and the British government would negotiate a treaty to effect the transfer of power and to safeguard racial and religious minorities.
- In the meantime, defence of India would remain in British hands and the Governor General's powers would remain intact.

- **Difference from Past Proposals**: The Cripps Proposals was certainly a step ahead than the earlier proposals as:
  - The making of the constitution was to be solely in Indian hands now (and **not 'mainly'** in Indian hand, as proposed in the August Offer).
  - A concrete plan was provided for the Constituent Assembly.
  - An option was now available to any province which was not prepared to accept the new constitution to sign a separate agreement with Britain regarding its future status and have a separate constitution, implying that the **blueprint for India's partition** was ready.
- Even though Cripps Mission announced that the aim of British policy in India was '*the earliest possible realisation of self-government in India*' the draft declaration failed to satisfy the Indian nationalists and was rejected by almost all the Indian parties.
  - Objections raised by the Congress: **Nehru** and **Maulana Azad** were the official negotiators on behalf of the Congress, who basically objected to:
    - The offer of Dominion Status **instead of** complete Independence
    - Representation of the Princely States **by nominees** and not by elected representatives
    - Right to provinces to secede which went completely against the principle of national unity
    - Absence of any plan for immediate transfer of power and absence of any real share in defence
    - The retention of the supremacy of the Governor General's instead of accepting the nationalists demand of making the position only constitutional and ceremonial.

> *"The Cripps proposal is like a post-dated cheque on a crashing bank."*
>
> Gandhiji
>
> *"When I read those proposals for the first time I was profoundly depressed......The existing structure and autocratic powers would remain and a few of us will become the viceroy's liveried camp followers and look after canteens and the like."*
>
> Jawaharlal Nehru
>
> *"The Declaration is in essence a conservative, reactionary and limited offer."*
>
> Observations of Leopold Amery, the Secretary of State

  - Objections raised by the Muslim League: The Muslim League also registered its unhappiness over the declaration as:
    - It demanded a definite declaration by the British in favour of the creation of a separate state for the Muslims, and also seats for the Muslim League on a 50:50 basis with the Congress in the interim government.

- It criticised the idea of a single Indian Union and did not like the machinery for the creation of a constituent assembly and the procedure to decide on the accession of provinces to the Union.
- Objections raised by the other sections:
  - The Liberals and the Hindu Mahasabha criticised the basis of the right to secede and considered the secession proposals to be against the unity and security of India.
  - The Depressed Classes, the Sikhs, the Indian Christians and the Anglo Indians demanded more safeguards for their communities.

- An important **reason** for the failure of the negotiations was the incapacity of Cripps to bargain and negotiate as he did not have the mandate[11] to go beyond the Draft Declaration. Subsequently, in the middle of April, Stafford Cripps returned home leaving behind frustrated and embittered Indian masses, who though still sympathised with the anti-fascist forces, especially that of the Russian and Chinese, but now felt that since the Britain was unwilling to offer an honourable settlement, so any further silence on part of Indians would be tantamount to accepting the right of the British Government to decide India's fate without any reference to the wishes of her people and, thus, now the time had come for a final assault on colonialism.

"Leave India to God, if that is too much, then leave her to anarchy. This ordered disciplined anarchy should go, and if there is complete lawlessness, I would risk it."

Gandhiji

The Quit India Movement (August 1942–September 1944)

- A fortnight after Cripps departure, that is, in May 1942, **Gandhiji** drafted a resolution for the Congress Working Committee calling for Britain's withdrawal and the adoption of non-violent non-cooperation against any Japanese invasion. In fact, he briskly set aside all opposition against direct action, coming mainly from Nehru and Rajagopalachari, and prepared the party for the final struggle, '*the biggest fight in my life*' in his own words.
- As a result, in July, the Congress Working Committee approved of a draft resolution on mass civil disobedience later came to be known as **Quit India Resolution**, which was finally adopted by the All India Congress Committee in Bombay on 8 August 1942 which proposed to begin the mass civil disobedience under Gandhiji's direction, if power was not immediately handed over to the Indians.
- On this occasion, **Gandhiji** exhorted British to **quit India** and leave it in God's hands while delivering his famous 'Do or Die' speech, arguing that this was the final battle – a 'fight to the finish' – and so the Indians must win independence or give up their lives for it, which fired the imagination of an already rankled Indian population, expecting a breakdown of the established authority, and with this, the Quit India Movement was started.

[11] In addition, there are certain unofficial reports that Prime Minister Churchill, the Secretary of State, Amery, the Viceroy, Linlithgow and the Commander-in-Chief, Wavell, did not want Cripps to succeed and had merely taken up this exercise to demonstrate to the world that they cared about Indian sentiments, rather than to actually do something concrete. So, they constantly opposed and sabotaged Cripps efforts to accommodate Indian opinion.

> *"Here is a mantra, a short one, that I give you. You may imprint it on your hearts and let every breath of yours give expression to it. The mantra is: 'Do or Die.' We shall either free India or die in the attempt; we shall not live to see the perpetuation of our slavery. Every true Congressman or woman will join the struggle with an inflexible determination not to remain alive to see the country in bondage and slavery."*
>
> Excerpts from Gandhiji's speech at Gowalia Tank in Bombay on 8 August 1942
>
> *"Everyone is free to go the fullest length under Ahimsa to complete deadlock by strikes and other non-violent means. Satyagrahis must go out to die not to live. They must seek and face death. It is only when individuals go out to die that the nation will survive, Karenge Ya/Marenge (do or die)."*
>
> Gandhiji

- Though the Congress had given the call for ousting British, but it did not give any concrete line of action to be adopted by the people, yet taking no chances, the **Government** in the early hours of 9 August **arrested** all prominent Congress leaders, including Gandhiji in a single sweep. While the Congress as a whole was not outlawed, the national and provincial committees were banned and about 1,000 of their members were arrested within that week.
- The sudden arrests resulted in unprecedented popular outbursts in different parts of the country. Be it Bombay, Ahmedabad, Poona, Delhi, UP or Bihar, as soon as the news of arrests of Congress leaders spread, lakhs of people clashed with the authorities and there were *hartals,* public demonstrations and processions in defiance of the law.
- The spread of the movement can basically be traced in three phases, as delineated by **Sumit Sarkar**:
  - Phase I (**Urban Revolt**): The movement initially started as an urban revolt, marked by strikes, boycott and picketing, which were quickly suppressed.
  - Phase II (**Spread to the Countryside**): In the middle of August, the focus was shifted to the countryside, which witnessed a major peasant rebellion, marked by destruction of communication systems, such as railway tracks and stations, telegraph wires and poles, attacks on government buildings or any other visible symbol of colonial authority and finally, the formation of '**national governments**' in isolated pockets. This brought in severe government repression forcing the agitation to move underground.
  - Phase III (**Underground Activity**): The third and the final phase was characterised by underground activities, which primarily involved sabotaging of war efforts by dislocating communication systems and propaganda activities by using various means, including **clandestine radio stations**.
- The Government taking advantage of wartime emergency powers ruthlessly crushed the Movement. By the end of 1943, though, most of the movement had been thoroughly crushed, yet it lingered on as sporadic events across different parts of the country till September 1944.

Critical Analysis of the Quit India Movement

The Quit India Movement, popularly known as the **August Revolution,** surprised everyone with its unusual intensity. Even Viceroy Linlithgow described it as '*by far the most serious rebellion since 1857*'. Though the Movement eventually collapsed, but not without demonstrating the determination of the masses to do away with British rule.

> *"I am engaged here in meeting by far the most serious rebellion since that of 1857, the gravity and extent of which we have so far concealed from the world for reasons of military security."*
>
> Viceroy Linlithgow's Confidential telegram dated 31 August 1942 to Churchill.

Factors precipitating the start of the Quit India Movement

Besides the failure of Cripps Mission, a multiple set of factors were operational, which provided the required thrust for the start of the Movement.

- Economic Hardships and Scarcity Crisis on Account of War: Though the economic impact of War was initially beneficial to a certain lot of industrialists, merchants and rich peasants who were producing for the market, yet the overall effect of War resulted in **economic hardships** and **scarcity crisis**[12] for the general public. For instance, between April and August, the price index for food grains rose by 60 points in north India partly because of bad seasonal conditions and partly due to the stoppage in the supply of Burmese rice and the stringent procurement policy of the British, resulting in both high inflation and scarcity crisis. While the higher food prices hit the poor, the rich were hurt by excess profit tax, forcible collection of war funds and coercive sale of war bonds.
- Situation of Panic Created on Account of Abandonment of Indian Refugees: The horror stories shared by the streams of refugees coming back from Malay and Burma of not only Japanese atrocities but also of collapse of British power in Southeast Asia and the **abandonment** of the Indian refugees to their fate by the British authorities, forcing them to transverse hostile terrains on foot, enduring hunger, disease and pain, created a popular mentality of panic, as British power seemed to be on the verge of imminent collapse. There was also a widespread fear among the Indian masses that if Japan invaded, the British would do the same in India, and that seemed no longer a distant possibility, as the British initiated a harsh **denial policy** in coastal Bengal by destroying all means of communications, including boats and cycles, paying very little compensation.

The arrival of American and Australian soldiers from May 1942, and circulation of the stories of the racial harassment of civilian population and shameful incidents of rape by these forces further added to the anger and **disillusionment** of the masses. In addition, many leaders like Gandhiji were completely opposed to accept that the Japanese could be liberators in any way and instead believed that India in the hands of the Indians was the best guarantee against fascist aggression.

Thus, by the middle of the year, there was a widespread popular belief in India that British power was **going to collapse** soon, and therefore it was the opportune moment for a fight to the finish and to liberate India from nearly two hundred years of colonial rule.

Regional Variations of the Movement

As with other movements, even the intensity of the Quit India Movement varied from region to region, and the whole of India did not convulse in the same way. For instance, the movement was most powerful in terms of intensity and spontaneity in **Bihar** and **eastern UP**, while it was less instantaneous and intense, but more prolonged, in other regions of India like **Bengal**. On similar lines, although it received a **massive response** from the people of Bombay, Uttar Pradesh, Bihar, Maharashtra, Orissa, Assam, Bengal, the responses in Punjab, Sindh, NWFP and Madras presidency were **weak**.

[12] resulting from mainly a shortfall in the supply of rice

Region	Remarks
Bihar	• In Bihar, owing to the major preparatory organisational groundwork done by the **Kisan Sabha**, peasants revolts occurred in practically every district of Bihar. Under the initiative of students, thousands of ordinary peasants attacked and looted local treasury buildings and railway stations, killed unarmed European officers in public, thus ceremonially destroying the physical presence of colonial authority. In Bihar alone, around 72 police stations were attacked and 332 railway stations and 945 post offices damaged. • The Quit India Movement started with the conflagration in **Patna** city, where under the initiative of the students mammoth rally was mobilised at the Secretariat on 11 August and efforts were undertaken to hoist a Congress flag atop the Assembly building. The student initiative was soon appropriated by the masses, who burnt railway stations, municipal buildings and post offices. The situation seemed to be out of control of the local police in Patna and army was called out on the 12 August. Similarly, in **Jamshedpur**, the movement started with a strike of the local constabulary on the 9th, a strike in TISCO on the 10 and again on the 20, when about 30,000 workers took part. • The movement was covertly supported by the *zamindars* and merchants who supplied funding and maintained a stance of neutrality while refusing to assist the British in crushing the rebellion. For instance, the **Raja of Darbhanga**, one of the biggest zamindars, refused to let his armed retainers to be used by the Government and even instructed his managers to assist the tenants who had been arrested. • The participation in Bihar came from across caste barriers. One of the most significant example of lower caste participation was the formation of a parallel government in Barh by the *Gops* and *Dusadhs*, who formed their own 'Raj' and started levying taxes. • After the ruthless suppression by the British army, the movement thereafter went underground and was coordinated from around 1943 by a new organisational structure called the ***Azad Dastas*** or guerrilla bands, which operated mainly in south Bihar, conducting raids on ammunition depots, treasuries and other government offices. However, the *Dastas* soon developed links with the professional dacoit gangs of low caste landless peasants and indulged in some instances of social crime too. The movement was finally suppressed in Bihar in 1944.
Eastern UP	• The reaction to the arrests of the national leaders was also most intense in Eastern UP, where the movement attained the proportions of a rebellion. Emboldened and inspired by the student volunteers from the **Banaras Hindu University** (BHU) and **Allahabad University**, the local peasantry was also galvanised into action, who attacked and looted the railway stations and destroyed the railway tracks, particularly in the districts of Ghazipur and Azamgarh. • The mass insurrection was much more intense in the district of **Ballia**, where British rule ceased to exist for a few days and a parallel administration was established under the leadership of Gandhian leader **Chittu Pande** who proclaimed himself the *Swaraj Ziladhish* or Independent District Magistrate of the district. However, the parallel administration could not survive for long and just a week after when the army arrived, all the leaders fled and the whole town of Ballia lay deserted.

Region	**Remarks**
Bengal	• In Bengal, the movement took place in Calcutta and in the districts of Hugli, Bankura, Purulia, Birbhum and Dinajpur. However, it was undoubtedly the strongest in **Tamluk** and **Contai** (Kanthi) subdivisions of Midnapur district, where the peasants had already been mobilised by the *Krishak Sabhas* and Forward Bloc. One of the other precipitating factors behind their mobilisation was the fact that since April 1942, in the coastal areas of Midnapur, the government had destroyed nearly 18,000 boats in pursuance of its '***denial policy***', and this not only deprived the peasants of their vital means of communication and also severely impacted their local economy. The problem was further aggravated by the general price rise and stringent procurement policy. • The Quit India Movement started in Midnapur from around 8 September, with orchestrated attacks on several police stations by crowds ranging from 10,000 to 20,000. By the 30th, British administration almost collapsed in these two sub divisions and finally the army was called in to ruthlessly suppress the movement. The Congress now moved on to establish parallel national governments: In **Contai,** the *Swaraj Panchayat* was started in November, while in **Tamluk,** the *Tamralipta Jatiya Sarkar* was inaugurated on 17 December which also had a trained volunteer corps or *Bidyut Bhagini Sena or Vidyut Vahini*, and a mouthpiece, *Biplabi.* • Both of these parallel governments, organised cyclone relief work, settled 1681 cases in arbitration courts, ran the civil administration, clashed with powerful loyalist zamindars, merchants and local officials and despite ruthless repression, continued to function until August 1944 when following Gandhiji instructions of surrender, both the parallel governments were disbanded.
Orissa	• The movement was also strongest in Orissa, where under the influence of the *Kisan Sangha's* and the *Praja mandal's*, the peasantry was already mobilised. The movement started as usual in cities like Cuttack, with *hartals* and strikes in educational institutions and then spread to the countryside, mainly in the coastal districts of Cuttack, Balasore and Puri where the peasants in open defiance attacked all visible symbols of colonial authority like police stations, local cutcheries, district offices and so forth. • This rural revolt in districts, marked by the participation from across caste barriers, was, however, virtually over by October–November under the pressure of police repression. However, in the state of **Talcher**, the Quit India took a novel form as the local Praja mandal leaders, in a bid to end the rule of the local raja and his patron the British government, decided to establish a ***chasi-mulia raj*** on a programme of 'popular peasant utopia' with promises of food, shelter and clothes for everyone. By 6 September, the new raj had established its authority over most of the state and men from various directions now closed in towards the town of Talcher to destroy the centre of power. The following day, the demonstrators were mercilessly machine gunned from air using RAF planes followed by further ruthless repression but in spite of that, guerrilla warfare in region continued until about May 1943. • In Malkangiri and Nawrangpur, efforts were undertaken to establish an alternative raj under the charismatic leadership of **Laxman Naiko**, who assembled tribal and non-tribal peasants in his attacks on liquor and opium shops, and declared publicly in crowded meetings that British Raj had ended and had been replaced by Gandhi Raj which no longer required payment of '*shandy*' and forest dues. However, this movement too was crushed by the end of September by troops called in from the neighbouring states of Bastar.

Region	Remarks
Maharashtra	• The experiment to establish effective alternative national government was indeed most successful and long-lasting in Maharashtra, in the district of **Satara** where the *Prati Sarkar* (parallel government) emerged out of the organisational bases created by the non-Brahman movement, which had mobilised the *bahujan samaj* in anti-caste and anti-feudal agitation and in the 1930s had forged links with the nationalism and the Congress. Although dominated by middle ranking Kunbi peasants, it equally attracted because of its anti-feudal and anti-caste orientation, significant participation and support from poorer dalit peasants. • An interesting aspect about the *Prati Sarkar* was that, it was formally established between February and June 1943, by the young and educated members of the *bahujan samaj* in the Satara district, significantly, at a time around late 1942 when the initial outburst of violent sabotage activities subsided under pressure of army repression and the Quit India Movement had almost died down in other provinces. • The *Prati Sarkar* had elaborate organisational structures, with a **volunteer corps** or ***Seba Dal*** and village units or *Tufan Dal*, with **Nana Patil** and **Y. B. Chavan** handling the central commands. The parallel administration was involved in various activities and these included running the peoples courts or ***nyayadan mandals***, implementing constructive programmes and conducting armed sabotage activities. It is, however, pertinent to note here that in contrast to the *Azad Dastas* of Bihar, the *Prati Sarkar* volunteers fought hard battles to destroy local dacoit gangs in the rugged ravines of Satara to establish its own authority and legitimacy. • The parallel government continued to function until the election of 1946, despite various British attempts to repress it and even defying Gandhiji's call for surrender in August 1944.

Gujarat	• The Quit India Movement was most powerful in the districts of Kheda, Surat and Broach in Gujarat and in the princely state of Baroda. The movement started in the cities of Ahmedabad and Baroda, with labour strikes, hartals and rioting, using various community structures such as **exclusive caste enclaves** of *pols* and *mahajans* or unions of traders. A parallel 'Azad Government' was established in Ahmedabad.
	• One of the unique aspects in Ahmedabad was that in contrast to all other regions where the merchants and the industrialists did not extend much support to the movement, here, the industrialists expecting the Congress to become the party in power soon, expressed sympathy with the nationalist cause and did nothing to end the industrial strike, which went on for nearly three and a half months on purely political demands, rather on any economic claim for higher wages.
	• The revolt in the countryside, which went on from September to December, followed the usual pattern of sabotage activities as elsewhere. In Broach, Surat and Navsari districts, however, there was rural unity across caste and class lines and British rule almost disappeared, until it was recovered again through ruthless repression that made the Gandhian Congress rather more popular.
	• Two significant aspects of the Movement were:
	  ◦ Although Tribal peasants in many places participated in the movement, the dalit *Baraiya* and *Pattanvadiya* peasants dissatisfied with the Patidar dominated Congress ministry, actively opposed the **Quit India Movement** in Kheda and Mehsana districts.
	  ◦ One major dissimilarity with the past movements in this region was the **absence of any no-revenue campaign** this time, as the rich Patidar peasantry did not want to risk confiscation of their properties at a time when they had prospered due to recent price hikes.

Region	Remarks
Madras	• In the Madras Presidency, the movement was fairly moderate owing to the following factors: • Many leading figures of Madras politics like **Rajagopalachari** opposed the movement • Absence of the Socialists and opposition of the Kerala communists to the movement • Indifference of the non-Brahmans and a strong southern challenge to a political campaign dominated by the north.

Characteristics of the Quit India Movement

- **Spontaneous and Leaderless:** Though the movement is generally characterised as a 'spontaneous and leaderless revolution' as the element of spontaneity was certainly larger in Quit India Movement since the entire upper echelon of the Congress leadership was behind bars even before the movement could formally began and the leaders were not able to spelt out clearly even the broad programme of action **however**, it is equally important to note here that:
  - In a way, the degree of spontaneity and popular initiative that was actually exercised had been sanctioned by the leadership itself. As eminent historian Gyanendra Pandey puts it, Gandhji provided the Indian masses with a **psychological break**, by asserting that everyone should, henceforth, consider themselves as '*free man or woman*' and should choose their own course of action if the leaders were arrested.

> *"A time may come when it may not be possible to issue instructions to reach our people, and when no Congress committees can function. When this happens every man and woman who is participating in this movement must function for himself or herself within the four corners of the general instructions issued. Every Indian who desires freedom and strives for it must be his own guide."*
>
> Excerpts from the Resolution passed by the Working Committee on 8 August 1942

  - It would be also wrong to assume that the spontaneity can only be measured by the volume of immediate organisational activity as the preparedness for struggle can also be gauged by the level of organisational activity **done prior** to the main event and in this case, the Congress had been ideologically, politically and organisationally preparing for the struggle for a long time. For instance, in Bihar and Eastern UP, the areas of the most intense activity during the Quit India Movement, considerable mobilisation and organisational work had been carried out from 1937 onwards by the various associated and affiliated bodies of the Congress, like the CSP, provincial Congress Kisan Sabhas and the AITUC. Similarly, in Gujarat, Sardar Patel had been touring Bardoli and other areas since June 1942 warning the people of an impending struggle. Even Gandhiji himself, through the individual Civil Disobedience campaign in 1940–41, and more directly since early 1942 had started exhorting people to be prepared for the coming battle.
  - There are also certain documents that point out that the Congress leaders before 9 August had drafted a **12-point programme** which not only included the usual Gandhian methods of Satyagraha, but a plan to promote industrial strikes, holding up of railways and telegraphs, non-payment of taxes and setting up of parallel government, and several versions of this programme were in circulation among Congress volunteers, including the one prepared by the Andhra Provincial Congress Committee, which contained clear instructions for such subversive action. In addition, as the movement progressed, the AICC continued to issue **Instructions to peasants**, which outlined the course of action anticipating what was to eventuate in the later months of the movement.

So, on the basis of these above-mentioned points, to term the movement a spontaneous outburst or an organised rebellion is neither justified nor accurate. We can, thus, safely assume that though the movement was **largely spontaneous** in character but it was successful on account of the organisational work done in the earlier years.

- **Extent of Participation:** The Quit India Movement marked a new high in terms of popular participation in the national movement and despite variance in vision, the different classes and communities were strongly united in initiating common action against the British.
  - As in earlier mass struggles, the **youth**, especially, the students from colleges and even schools were again in the forefront of the movement. Many historians assume that the average age of participants in the 1942 struggle was even lower than that in earlier movements.
  - Another visible section was of **women volunteers**, especially college and school girls, who played a very important role in the movement. For instance, Aruna Asaf Ali and Sucheta Kripalani were two major women organisers of the movement during the underground phase, while Usha Mehta was an important member of the small group that ran the Congress Radio and Sumati Morarjee provided a lot of material support[13] to the underground volunteers.
  - On the similar lines, **workers** and **peasants** belonging to all strata played a prominent role and made considerable sacrifice by enduring long strikes and braving police repression.
  - Even the **government officials**, especially those at the lower levels of the police and the administration, extended generous assistance to the movement and provided shelter, information and monetary support to the volunteers. The Jail officials tended to be much kinder to prisoners than the earlier years, and often openly expressed their sympathy. In fact, this aspect of the **erosion of loyalty** to the British Government of its own officers was one of the **most striking aspects** of Quit India Movement.

However, there were **certain important social groups** who consciously stayed away from the movement:

- The most important of them were the **Muslims,** who under the influence of the Muslim League stood aloof from the Quit India Movement almost in all regions. However, it is pertinent to note here that though the abstention of Muslims was nearly universal, they did not oppose Quit India actively, except perhaps in some parts of Gujarat and there was no major incident of communal conflict throughout the whole period.
- **The Communist Party of India**, following the involvement of Soviet Russia in the war in December 1941, became another important political group, which did not support Quit India Movement because of their 'Peoples War' strategy. Still, many individual communists along with the affiliated trade unions and Kisan Sabhas were swayed by the patriotic emotions of the day and actively participated in the Quit India Movement but as a whole, the communist movement lost in terms of their popularity and support, since the leaders found it very difficult to convince their followers the logic of supporting a distant war by subverting a campaign for their own freedom.
- The **Princes** and most of the **landlords** were supportive of the War effort and did not sympathise with the movement.
- There were also **certain Congress leaders** like C. Rajagopalachari, who did not participate in the movement and instead supported the War effort.
- On the other hand, **Dr B. R. Ambedkar**, the leader of the dalits, who had joined the Viceroy's executive council as a labour member just before the onset of the Movement, also did not support it and so did many of his supporters. However, interestingly, there have been many evidences of dalit participation in the Quit India Movement in various regions, and cross-caste unity was never a rare occurrence in this Movement (as we have discussed earlier).

[13] It is believed that Sumati Morarjee helped Achyut Patwardhan to evade detection by providing him with a different car every day borrowed from her unsuspecting wealthy friends.

- The Movement also could not evoke much response from the **merchant**, **capitalist** and **industrialist community** who were more interested in their heavy profits arising due to the War time supplies, and in certain cases when they did appeal to the Government (through FICCI) to release Gandhiji[14] and other leaders, their main purpose was not struggle for independence but to address their concerns of escalation of the violent situation, which may in due course result in attacks on private property as well resulting in heavy losses for them.
- The **Hindu Mahasabha** not only remained aloof but also at times offered the strongest criticism to the Quit India Movement and condemned[15], it as the '*movement which is sterile, unmanly and injurious to the Hindu cause*' while stalwart Hindu leaders like V. D. Savarkar, B. S. Munje and Shyama Prasad Mukherjee whole heartedly supported the British war efforts. The other prominent Hindu organisation, RSS, remained aloof as well.

> *"The Sangh has scrupulously kept itself within the law, and in particular, has refrained from taking part in the disturbances that broke out in August 1942."*
>
> Excerpts from a memo of the Bombay Government.

- **Use of Violence**: One of the most notable characteristics of the Quit India Movement was that in contrast to all other mass movements, in this movement on the question of non-violence, **Gandhiji** was remarkably ambivalent in his approach giving impression to the masses that in 1942, the issue of non-violence was somehow less important than the call for '*Do or Die*' or the invitation to make a final sacrifice for the liberation of the nation.

> *"I do not ask from you my own non-violence. You can decide what you can do in this struggle."*
>
> Gandhiji's statement on 5 August 1942.
>
> *"I trust the whole of India today to launch upon a non violent struggle. But even if people deviated from this path of non violence, I shall not swerve. I shall not flinch."*
>
> Gandhiji speaking on the AICC resolution passed on 8 August 1942.
>
> *"I am one of those who feel that the violence of the brave is better than the non-violence of the cowardly."*
>
> Gandhiji praising Nana Patil of Satara Prati Sarkar who had evidently deviated from his path of non-violence.

- The people *accepted* the challenge and interpreted it in their own ways and devised their own methods of struggle, and gradually, the Gandhian message of non-violent struggle was pushed into the background as the local, often unknown, Congress leaders and students took over the leadership once the national and provincial leaders were all arrested between 9 and 11 August.

---

[14] Since they believed only Gandhiji had the influence to check violence and stop attacks on government properties.

[15] It is important to note here that despite this official line, a strong group of Mahasabha members led by N. C. Chatterjee seemed eager to participate in it and under their pressure, the Mahasabha Working Committee had to adopt a face saving but vague resolution stating that defence of India could not be supported unless freedom of India was recognised with immediate effect.

- There was, thus, **use of violence** at an **unprecedented scale** by the masses involving attacks on government buildings, police stations and post offices, railway stations, and sabotaging of rail lines, cutting off the telegraph wires, telephones and electric power lines, disrupting road traffic by destroying bridges, workers going on strike and so forth. For instance, according to official estimates, in Uttar Pradesh around 104 railway stations and 119 post offices were attacked and damaged, while about 100 railway tracks were 'sabotaged' and around 425 telephone and telegraph wires were destroyed. Similarly, in Bihar, 72 police stations were attacked and 332 railway stations along with 945 post offices were damaged while throughout the country there had been 664 bomb explosions.

It is, however, pertinent to note here that most of the violent attacks were to **check the movement of the military** and the police, which were being used by the Government to crush the Movement. Even Gandhiji **refused to condemn the violence** of the people as he justified it as a reaction to the much bigger violence of the state, but at the same time, he and Congress organisation disowned any responsibility for the violent acts of the people. His 21-day fast[16] commencing on 10 February 1943 restored symbolically his centrality in the movement once again, but not as a controlling figure.

The wholesale arrest of the Congress leaders seems to have made the people wild with rage to the point of losing self-control. I feel that the Government, not the Congress, are responsible for the destruction that has taken place. The only right course for the Government seems to me to release the Congress leaders, withdraw all repressive measures and expose ways and means of conciliation.

Gandhiji's letter to Viceroy Linlithgow on 23 September 1942.

Gandhi was the undisputed leader of a movement over which he had little command.

Gyanendra Pandey

- **Brutal Repression by the British Government:** The Government authorities also used violence at an unprecedented scale to brutally and ruthlessly suppress the Quit India Movement. Taking advantage[17] of the wartime emergency powers, not only **arbitrary arrests**, **detentions**, **police firings**, **burning of Congress offices**, **seizing of the monetary assets** of the Congress was done but even the **army was called in** and as many as 57 battalions of British troops were deployed to crush what was essentially a civilian agitation. The **press censorship** was brought and all the newspapers were gagged. The National Herald

---

[16] In fact, on 10 February, 1943, Gandhiji commenced a 21-day fast in jail as an answer to the constant exhortation by the Government for condemnation of the violence done by the people in the Quit India Movement. Gandhiji not only refused to condemn the people's resort to violence but unequivocally also held the Government responsible for it and it was against this violence of the state, which included the unwarranted detention of thousands of Congressmen that Gandhiji vowed to register his protest, in the only way open to him when in jail, by fasting. The popular response to the news of the fast was immediate and overwhelming and all over the country, there were *hartals,* demonstrations, strikes and sympathetic fasts. Groups of people reached Poona to offer Satyagraha outside the Aga Khan Palace where Gandhiji was being held in detention. The Government was bombarded with thousands of letters and telegrams from people from all walks of life even across the seas, including newspapers such as the *Manchester Guardian, New Statesmen, Nation, News Chronicle, Chicago Sun,* as well as by the British Communist Party, the citizens of London and Manchester, the Women's International League, the Australian Council of Trade Unions, the Ceylon State Council and the US Government demanding his release. Three Indian members of the Viceroy's Executive Council, M. S. Aney, N. R. Sarkar and H. P. Mody, resigned. But the Viceroy and his officials remained unmoved. The fast had done exactly what it had been intended to do. The public morale was raised, the anti-British feeling heightened, and an opportunity for political activity provided. A symbolic gesture of resistance had sparked off widespread resistance and exposed the Government's high-handedness to the whole world. Gandhiji was eventually released on 6 May 1944, on medical grounds.

[17] Churchill could defend this swift and ruthless repression and silence a critical world opinion by citing the needs of war.

and Harijan ceased publication for the entire duration of the struggle, while other publications ceased for shorter periods. In fact, by Government's own admission:

- By the end of 1942, in UP alone, around 16,000 people were arrested, 26,000 people were convicted and 18,000 were detained under the Defence of India Rules.
- There were countless instances of lathi charges, floggings, whipping of suspects along with allegations of burning of entire villages whose inhabitants had run away and could not be caught. Throughout India, nearly 92,000 people were arrested by the end of 1943.
- Unarmed crowds faced police and military firing on 538 occasions and the Government forces utilised low-flying aircrafts in **5 places** to machine-gun the civilians, Giriak near Patna, Bhagalpur district, near Ranaghat in Nadia district, Monghyr district and near Talcher town.
- **Collective fines**[18] were imposed to the tune of a total of ₹9,00,000 across country. For instance, from Uttar Pradesh alone, out of the 28,00,000 fines imposed, around 25,00,000 were collected by the end of February 1943.

- **Underground Activity**: Another important aspect pertaining to the Quit India Movement was the **consolidation of underground networks** in various parts of the country on account of the severe government repression forcing the agitation to move underground.
    - The local underground organisations were most active in places like Bombay, Poona, Satara, Baroda and other parts of Gujarat, Karnataka, Kerala, Andhra, UP, Bihar and Delhi and was working under the guidance of an all India underground leadership[19] whose prominent members included **Achyut Patwardhan**, **Aruna Asaf Ali**, **Ram Manohar Lohia**, **Sucheta Kripalani**, **Chootubhai Puranik**, **Biju Patnaik**, **R. P. Goenka** and later, after his escape from jail, **Jayaprakash Narayan**.
    - The Underground phase was characterised by underground activities, which primarily involved sabotaging of war efforts by dislocating communication systems and propaganda activities by using various means, including a clandestine radio station run by hitherto unknown **Usha Mehta**, one run by **Ram Manohar Lohia** operated clandestinely from different locations in Bombay city till November 1942 and Berlin Radio operated by **Subhash Bose**. Not only the educated youth were active participants in such activities but also bands of ordinary peasants, who organised such subversive actions by night, which came to be popularly known as the ***Karnataka method***.
    - As time passed, the underground activities came to be channelled into three streams:
        - With a radical group under the leadership of **Jayaprakash Narayan** organising guerrilla warfare in India Nepal border
        - A centrist group led by Congress Socialists like **Aruna Asaf Ali** mobilising volunteers throughout India for sabotage activities
        - A Gandhian group led by **Sucheta Kripalani** and others emphasising non-violent action and constructive programme.
    - It is pertinent to note here that these underground activists enjoyed so much enormous popular support and patronage that the definition of 'underground' in British official parlance virtually got expanded to cover the entire nation, as no Indian could anymore be trusted by the authorities.
- **Parallel Administration:** A significant feature of the Quit India Movement was the emergence of parallel governments in some parts of the country.

---

[18] Fines imposed by the Government on the residents of an area where 'riots' and so forth have taken place and which were often realised on the spot by looting the people's belongings.

[19] This leadership saw the role of the underground movement as being that of keeping up popular morale by continuing to a line of command and a source of guidance and leadership to activists all over the country. They also collected and distributed money as well as material like bombs, arms and dynamite to underground groups all over the country.

Region	Remarks
Ballia, eastern UP	• Leader: Chittu Pande
Tamluk, Midnapore District, Bengal	• Organisation: Jatiya Sarkar having trained volunteer corps or Bidyut Bhagini Sena or Vidyut Vahini • Mouthpiece: Biplabi
Contai, Midnapore District, Bengal	• Organisation: Swaraj Panchayat
Satara, Maharashtra	• Organisation: Prati Sarkar • Leaders: Nana Patil and Y. B. Chavan
Talcher, Orissa	• Organisation: Chasi-Mulia Raj

Significance of the Quit India Movement:

The historic movement holds a special significance in the freedom struggle of India as:

- It placed the demand for Independence on the **immediate agenda** of the national movement as after Quit India there could be no retreat and any future negotiation with the British Government could only be on the manner of the transfer of power since Independence was no longer a matter of bargain.
- Through Quit India, the commonly shared dominant tone of **anti-imperialism** was **further strengthened** among the masses overshadowing even the anti-feudal tendencies that appeared from time to time in different parts of the country.
- The Quit India Movement by promising immediate freedom from an oppressive imperial order **captured the imagination** of a significant section of the Indian population, notwithstanding their differing perceptions of freedom and mobilised them towards working tirelessly for achieving the goal of India's Independence and infused new energy and motivation in them for either achieving '***Victory or Death***'.
- The Quit India Movement made it amply clear to the British that after the War, keeping India by force would be an expensive proposition in every sense and, hence, there was a greater readiness among the British authorities to accept a negotiated settlement for a respectable and ordered withdrawal.

Apart from the Quit India Movement, an equally important movement was being fought against the British from the foreign soil: the **Indian National Army** (INA).

The INA Experiment and the Subsequent Trials (1942–45)

- During World War II, a number of Indian soldiers were fighting on behalf of the British and the Japanese after defeating the British in Southeast Asia, took a number of Indian soldiers as **prisoners of War**. Following the new changed policy[20] of Japanese, **Major Fujiwara**, a Japanese army officer, persuaded **Captain Mohan Singh**, a young officer of the Punjab Regiment of the British Indian Army who had surrendered to the Japanese in the jungles of Malaya, to work in collaboration with the Japanese for India's freedom in December 1941. Captain Mohan Singh agreed to cooperate with Fujiwara to raise an Indian army with POW's to march alongside the Japanese to liberate India.
- In June 1942, a united **Indian Independence League**, representing all Indians in Southeast Asia, was formed as a civilian political body having controlling authority over the army and **Rash Behari Bose**, a veteran Bengali revolutionary then living in Japan, was elected as its president, while **Captain Mohan Singh** was appointed as commander of the INA which now had around 40,000 Indian soldiers. Thus, by September, the INA was formally in existence.

[20] Though India originally did not figure in the Japanese policy of Greater East Asia Co-prosperity Sphere, under which the Japanese proposed to help Asians gain independence from Western Imperialism, but by 1940, Japan had developed an India policy to contact expatriate Indians who were organising themselves and to cooperate with them.

- In the meantime, **General Tojo**, the Japanese Prime Minister, made a declaration in the Diet[21] supporting Indian independence. However, **differences soon emerged** between the INA officers led by Mohan Singh and the Japanese over the role of the INA and the sub-standard treatment accorded to the INA officers by their Japanese counterparts. In fact, it was soon becoming apparent to the INA officers that the Japanese were only prepared to treat INA as a subsidiary force, rather than an allied army and thus eventually as **Mohan Singh** insisted on autonomy and allied status, he was removed from command and put under arrest along with another senior most Indian officer **Niranjan Singh Gill.** Subsequently, Rash Behari Bose did try to fill in the leadership vacuum, but he was then too aged for the task and thus, by the beginning of 1943, the **first INA experiment** virtually collapsed.
- The **second phase of the INA experiment** began when Subhash Chandra Bose[22] arrived in Southeast Asia in May 1943, and immediately took control of the situation, with **Japanese** assurance of help and equal treatment. Prime Minister Tojo even declared that Japan had no territorial designs on India. On 21 October 1943, in Singapore, **Bose** then established a Provisional Government of Free India, which was immediately recognised by **Japan** and later by eight other governments, including Germany and Fascist Italy and he became the **supreme commander** of its army, the ***Azad Hind Fauj*** (Free India Army) or the Indian National Army.
- Two INA headquarters were set up by Bose, one in **Rangoon** and another in **Singapore**, and he began to reorganise the INA by gathering funds and seeking recruitment from civilians and as a result of these tireless efforts, by 1945, around 4,000 men were recruited. Three fighting brigades of INA were named after **Gandhiji**, **Azad** and **Nehru** and later, even a women's regiment was raised called the **Rani Jhansi regiment**, named after the legendary Rani of Jhansi of 1857 fame. The slogans of the INA were '*Jai Hind*' and '*Delhi Chalo*'. One of the most famous was Subhash's declaration that '*Tum Mujhe Khoon Do Mein Tumhe Azadi Dunga*' (you give me blood I will give you freedom).

"India's last war of independence has begun. . . Father of our Nation! In this holy war of India's liberation, we ask for your blessing and good wishes."

Subhash Chandra Bose's broadcast dated 6 July 1944 on Azad Hind Radio.

- The Provisional Government declared war on Great Britain and its chief ambition was to march – as an allied army with the Japanese – through Burma to Imphal (in Manipur) and then to Assam, where it expected the Indian people to join them in an open rebellion for liberating their motherland. In fact, two INA regiments, one commanded by **Shah Nawaz** accompanied the Japan's Southern Army to the Indo-Burma border and participated in the ill-fated **Imphal campaign** on 8 March 1944, which eventually ended in a disaster.

"The reasons behind the failure of the Imphal Campaign were many: the lack of air power, breakdown in the chain of command, disruption of the supply line, the strength of Allied offensive, and finally for the INA, lack of cooperation from the Japanese."

As enumerated by Joyce Lebra.

[21] Name of Legislature of Japan.

[22] Although Subhash Chandra Bose did not like Germany's totalitarianism or racism, but believing that Germany has better chances of winning the War, he began to nurture the idea that the cause of Indian independence could be furthered with the help of the Axis powers and, thus, he started exploring various possibilities.

- The retreat which began in mid-1944 continued till mid-1945 and was even more devastating and ended only with the eventual surrender to the **British** in South-East Asia, finally ending the dream of liberating India through military campaign. However, Bose still remained optimistic, and thought of regrouping, and after Japanese surrender, contemplated seeking help from Soviet Russia. The Japanese agreed to provide him transport up to Manchuria from where he could travel to Russia. But on his way, on 18 August 1945 in Taihoku airport in Taiwan, he died in an air crash[23].
- Though the INA experiment could not achieve much in terms of its specified objectives, yet it left a significant imprint on the Indian National Movement as evident by its **political impact** unfolded during the INA Trials.

The INA Trials (1945–46)

- The **INA Trials** refer to the proceedings of prosecution and court martial initiated by the British authorities against the imprisoned members of the Indian National Army. After the ill-fated Imphal Campaign, the 20,000 INA soldiers, who had eventually surrendered to the British in South-East Asia, were interrogated and transported back to India while being classified under three heads:
  - **Whites**: Those who appeared to have been persuaded or misled by Japanese or INA propaganda were classified as 'Whites'
  - **Greys**: Those who were either released or rehabilitated in the army were put under 'Grey' head
  - **Blacks**: A few of them who were found to be the most committed were categorised as 'Blacks' and were decided to be court martial-led since the British authorities believed that if they do not try them, then it would be an indication of weakness and toleration of treason which would further put the loyalty of the Indian army at risk. It was also decided to hold the trial in public as the government hoped that during the trials, the former INA soldiers would reveal about the varied horrors perpetrated by them and in the process, the public opinion would be swerved against them. But as the events subsequently unfolded, **just the opposite happened** and instead of appearing traitors by any means, these officers were regarded as patriots of the highest order to the general public and with each passing day, it seemed certain that the government had completely miscalculated the political fallout of the INA trials.
- Altogether 10 trials took place, and in the first and most celebrated one in **Red Fort** in Delhi, three officers[24] – **Shah Nawaz Khan**, **G. S. Dhillon** and **P. K. Sehgal** – were charged of treason, murder and abetment of murder. Since the press censorship was lifted after the war, the details of the INA campaign were revealed every day before the Indian public and the demand for discontinuing the trials grew stronger by the day. There were meetings, processions, agitated speeches and angry outbursts almost everywhere, calling for immediate release of the INA Prisoners.
- The Congress leaders[25] too soon took up the issue and subsequently, at the AICC meeting in September 1945 in Bombay not only a strong resolution was passed declaring its support for the cause but it was also decided to defend the '*misguided patriots*', that is, the INA prisoners and, thus, a **Defence**

[23] Till date, the death of Subhash Bose in the air crash is a subject of intense controversy and mystery as many Indians don't believe till this day that Bose actually died in that plane crash and his death is a subject matter of even many conspiracy theories.

[24] Coincidentally belonging to three different religious communities Hindu, Muslim and Sikhs and, thus, brought all the communities together for this cause catching the public imagination.

[25] The Congress leaders, many of them just released after long incarceration since the Quit India days, could hardly ignore this issue that so profoundly touched popular emotions. In addition, with the passing away of the Subhash Chandra Bose, the emotions of the leaders regarding him also underwent changes as earlier he might have been a renegade leader who had challenged the authority of the Congress leadership and their principles. But, in death he was a martyred patriot whose memory needed to be cherished and could be an ideal tool for political mobilisation.

Committee, consisting of **Tej Bahadur Sapru**, **Bhulabhai Desai**, **Asaf Ali** and **Jawaharlal Nehru** appeared in court at the historic Red Fort Trials. The defence tried to argue that people fighting for freedom of their country could not be tried for treason. The Congress also organised an INA Relief and Enquiry Committee, which provided small sums of money and food to the men on their release, and attempted, though with marginal success, to secure employment for these men.

- In the subsequent days, as the election campaign set in, Nehru and other Congress leaders addressed numerous public meetings with large gatherings primarily focussing on two key issues:
  - one was the government excesses and the martyrs of Quit India Movement
  - the other was INA Trials[26].
- The government, however, still remained firm. The first trial opened on 5 November and continued for two months, with its progress reported everyday in Press leading to more awareness about the sacrifices made by the INA soldiers. Pamphlets, the most popular one being '*Patriots Not Traitors,*' were widely circulated, '*Jai Hind*' and 'Quit India' were scrawled on walls of buildings across the nation. Gradually, **all political parties**, like the Congress Socialists, Akali Dal, Unionist Party, Justice Party, Rashtriya Swayam Sevak Sangh, Hindu Mahasabha and even the Muslim League came out openly in support for **discontinuation of the trials**. Though the Communist party vacillated in its response, individual Communists enthusiastically participated in the demonstrations, and an **INA week** was celebrated between 5 and 11 November, while the **INA Day** was observed on 12 November in cities across the country.

"All parties have taken the same line though Congress are more vociferous than the others."

Observation by the then Viceroy

- The demonstrations also exhibited signs of remarkable communal harmony, and people from all walks of life participated in the campaign, attended protest meetings, donated money to the INA relief fund, closed shops and other commercial institutions, and in some places also refrained from celebrating Diwali. The holding of the trial in Red Fort further increased the **mass emotional upsurge** among people as it refreshed among the masses the idea of hegemonic British imperial domination since they related the INA trials with the 1858 trial of Bahadur Shah II, the last Mughal emperor and the acclaimed leader of the 1857 revolt. Slowly, the INA agitation spread to even the remotest places like **Coorg**, **Baluchistan** and **Assam**.

"In course of that time, India erupted into a mass upheaval and never before in Indian history had such unified sentiments and feelings been manifested by various divergent sections of the population as it had been done with regard to the question of the Azad Hind Fauj."

Nehru describing the emotions during the INA Trials

---

[26] Interestingly, the question of the right or wrong of the INA men's action was never debated. What was in question was the right of Britain to decide a matter concerning Indians. As Nehru often stressed, if the British were sincere in their declaration that Indo-British relations were to be transformed; they should demonstrate their good faith by leaving it to Indians to decide the INA issue. Even the appeals by liberal Indians were made in the interest of good future relations between India and Britain.

- **Violence** first erupted on 7 November, 1945 when the police opened fire on the crowd at a protest demonstration in Madura and then between 21 and 24 November, rioting broke out in various parts of the country, starting from **Calcutta** which was soon turned into a storm centre. Here, first of all, the American and British military establishments were attacked and then the rioting took a general anti-British tone. However, it is pertinent to note here that unprecedented communal harmony was exhibited, with the demonstrators flying simultaneously the **Congress**, **League** and **Communist** flags. Order could only be restored after 3 days, with 33 people dead and 200 injured. The Calcutta riots were soon followed by similar demonstrations in Karachi, Bombay, Allahabad, Patna, Banaras, Rawalpindi and almost all over the country.
- The nationwide agitation, which cut across the communal lines, did force the wavering down of the government's determination, and despite being found guilty as charged, the Commander-in-Chief **General Auchinleck** remitted their sentence and set them free on 3 January 1946. The three officers came out of the Red Fort to a hero's welcome at public meetings in Delhi and Lahore, which celebrated a moral victory against the British.

> *"Any attempt to force the sentence would have led to chaos in the country at large and probably to mutiny and dissention in the army culminating in its dissolution."*
>
> General Auchinleck's explanation to the senior British officers about the remission of the sentence of the three INA officers.

- But, as luck would have it, the INA agitation struck again in **February 1946**, and at the same epicentre – the volatile Calcutta. On 4 February, in another trial, **Captain Abdur Rashid Ali**[27] was sentenced to 7 years rigorous imprisonment, which sparked off another agitation in Calcutta between 11 and 13 February under the initial command of the student wing of the Muslim League, which was later joined by the members of the communist-led **Student Federation** and industrial workers. The protestations were soon transformed into fierce fights, and once again the demonstrations followed and large meetings were organised, where League, Communist and Congress leaders addressed the crowd with simultaneously flying of the Congress, League and red flags.
- A general anti-British sentiment again pervaded the city, which was further paralysed by transport strikes, industrial action and pitched street battles with British troops. Order was restored only after three days of **brutal repression** that had 84 people killed and 300 injured. The agitation soon spread to east Bengal, and the other parts of the country were also affected by the spirit of revolt, as sympathetic protest demonstrations and strikes took place in practically all major cities of India.
- Significance of the INA Trials: The INA agitation was landmark on many counts:
  - **First**, the high pitch or intensity at which the campaign for the release of INA prisoners was conducted was unprecedented, which was clearly evident from the **priority press coverage**[28], the **threats of revenge** that were publicly made and also from the **large number of meetings** held. For instance, around 160 political meetings were held in the Central Provinces and Berar alone in the first fortnight of October 1945 demanding for clemency for INA prisoners while around 5 to 7 lakhs people turned out for attending meetings organised under senior Congress leaders. **Initially**, the appeals in the press and the demands raised by Congress were for clemency to '*misguided*' men,

[27] Who preferred to be defended by a Muslim League Defence Committee, rather than by the Congress.

[28] Often priority coverage was given to the INA trials and to the INA campaign, eclipsing international news.

but by **November 1945**, when the first Red Fort trials began, the INA men were hailed as *patriots*, rather than '*traitors*' while the Government stand faced bitter criticism from all corners.

- The **second** significant feature of the INA campaign was its wide geographical reach and the participation of diverse social groups and political parties lending not only an **extensive nature** to the agitation but also leading to the spread of pro-INA sentiment to social groups hitherto outside the nationalist fold. For instance, in Punjab province[29], the return of the released men to their villages stimulated interest among groups, which had hitherto remained politically unaffected, and this trend was observed by none other than the Director of the Intelligence Bureau himself.

> *"There has seldom been a matter which has attracted so much Indian public interest, and, it is safe to say, sympathy. Anxious enquiries and profuse sympathies were forthcoming from the remotest villages from all men, irrespective of caste, colour and creed."*
>
> Statement of the Director of the Intelligence Bureau

- However, the most notable feature of the INA agitation was the **effect it had on the traditional bulwarks** of the Raj. Significant sections of the government employees, loyalist sections and even men of the armed forces were submerged in the tide of **pro-INA sentiment**. What really perturbed the British was the impact of the INA trials on the loyalty of the army, which in post Quit India days was their only reliable apparatus of rule. The growing political consciousness among the army personnel during and after the war emerged as a key cause of concern for the authorities. The members of the Royal Indian Air Force (RIAF) as well as some other army personnel in various centres openly donated money to the INA relief fund and on some occasions attended protest rallies in full uniform.

> *"Every day that passes now brings over more and more well-disposed Indians to the anti-British camp and with each passing day the issue is becoming more and more purely Indian versus British."*
>
> An advice of caution to the senior officers by the Governor of Northwest Frontier Province
>
> *"The sympathy for the INA is not the monopoly of those who are ordinarily against Government, and that it was usually the case that INA men and now its sympathisers belonged to families which had otherwise traditions of loyalty."*
>
> Director of the Intelligence Bureau

But what really posed a real grave challenge to the Raj was the open mutiny in the Royal Indian Navy (RIN) in February 1946.

The RIN Mutiny (18 February 1946)

- The Mutiny started in Bombay on 18 February, when the 1,100 naval ratings of **HMIS *Talwar*** went on hunger strike against the unpalatable food and racial discrimination. The next day, the ratings from Castle and Fort Barracks joined the strike and soon the rebellion spread to other naval bases all over India and to some ships on the sea where **sympathetic strikes** took place. In fact, at its peak, 78 ships, 20 shore establishments and 20,000 ratings were involved.

[29] To which 48.07 per cent of the INA men released till February 1946 belonged.

- However, what was really remarkable was the **fraternisation** between the naval ratings and common people that was clearly visible during these few days in various cities of India, a phenomenon that had immense revolutionary potential. For instance, Bombay went on strike on 22 February in sympathy with the ratings, and here along with general paralysing of the public transport system, the shops and banks were closed, roadblocks were raised, and trains were burnt. Here too, the navy rebels along with the strikers raised three flags of the **Congress**, the **Muslim League** and the **red Communist flag** simultaneously as they went round rampaging the city. Army had to be called in and though by 25 February, the city was quiet again, but by then 228 civilians were dead and 1,046 were injured.
- Similar hartals took place in **Karachi** on 23 February and in **Madras** on the 25th and in these both cities, several ratings and civilians died in police firing. Sympathetic, but less violent, one day strikes were also reported from Trichinopoly and Madurai, while workers strikes also took place in Ahmedabad and Kanpur. The RIAF men and some army personnel also went on strike at different centres, greatly perturbing the government.
- Although the RIN mutiny was short lived and it did not immediately lead to an open revolt in the Indian army, it had **dramatic psychological repercussions** as such a possibility could now never be ruled out, a fact accepted even by an official inquiry commission which later revealed that majority of ratings were not only politically conscious but were also profoundly influenced by the INA propaganda and ideals.
- With the sympathetic strikes in the air force and army, the British were gradually unravelling the harsh reality that the **Indian army** was no longer the same '*sharp sword of repression*' and in event of any other popular outburst like the 1942 movement, they could not rely on army as before, though it still is debatable as to what extent this revelation forced upon the British a change of its policy in favour of transfer of power.
- However, it is pertinent to note here that the Congress in principle was not much in support of the radical and violent happenings of 1945–46 as by now it was clear to everyone that the British would like to hand over power to Indians sooner rather than later and Congress was now looking forward to its new career as the ruling party and to its leadership, the INA officers were '*misguided patriots*' who could be taken back into the Congress, as Sardar Patel announced at a meeting in Calcutta, only if they '*put their swords back into the scabbard*'.

"Discipline in the Army cannot be tampered with .... We will want army even in free India."

The preferences of the Congress party clearly outlined by Sardar Patel

Attempts at Negotiated Settlements

By the end of 1944, the **British** realised that it would be impossible to hold India by force for long and that the Indian situation cannot be allowed to remain stagnant. Therefore, attempts were initiated for arriving at negotiated settlements for a peaceful transfer of power. Subsequently, in June 1945, Churchill permitted Viceroy **Lord Wavell**[30] to start negotiations with the Indian leaders. He, therefore, ordered on 14 June 1945, the release of all the Congress Working Committee members, and invited them along with others, notably the League leaders, to join in a conference in Simla convened to discuss about the way forward as an entirely Indian Executive Council was on cards.

[30] The previous commander-in-chief who had in 1943 replaced Linlithgow as the new viceroy. During his visit to London in March 1945 he finally convinced Churchill of the desirability of a Congress–League coalition government in India as a preemptive measure to forestall the political crisis he predicted after the war.

> *"India after the war will become a running sore which will sap the strength of the British empire. So some imaginative and constructive move needed to be taken immediately, in order to retain India as a willing member of the British Commonwealth."*
>
> Observations of Viceroy Wavell.

The Simla Conference (24 June–14 July 1945)

- The conference was convened for working out an interim political agreement and proposed that:
  - A new Executive Council at the Centre was to be set up practically Indian in composition with the **exception** of the Viceroy and the Commander in Chief.
  - The Council would have a 'balanced representation' of all Indians including 'caste-Hindus', Muslims, Depressed Classes, Sikhs and so forth. The Muslims were given 6 out of 14 members, which accounted for more than their share of the population (25 per cent).
  - The Council would function within the framework of the existing constitutional arrangement, that is, the 1935 Act, and thus, would not be responsible to the legislature.
  - The Viceroy was to exercise his veto on the advice of ministers.
  - Representatives of different parties were to submit a joint list to the Viceroy for nominations to the Executive council. If a joint list was not possible, then separate lists were to be submitted.
  - Doors would be open for negotiations on a new constitution once the war was finally won.
- However, the Simla conference **crashed** on the insistence of Jinnah's demand for parity. He claimed[31] that Muslim League **alone** had an exclusive right to nominate all the Muslim members to the Executive Council. **Congress** naturally refused to accept it, for that would reduce the Congress party to the status of only a caste Hindu party and, asserting its secular nationalist character claimed right to select the representatives of any community, including Muslims[32].
- The League also further demanded a communal veto by asking for a two-third majority in the proposed Council, instead of a simple one, on any decision opposed by the Muslim members and Muslim interests.
- Instead of bypassing the League, or making an effort to explore other possibilities, Wavell uphold-ing the virtual veto provided to Jinnah announced the breakdown of the Conference thereby further strengthening the League's position.

The Labour in Power (July 1945)

- Following a massive victory in the general elections, the British Labour Party[33], which was known for their sympathies with the nationalist cause, came into power in Britain in July, 1945. The new Prime Minister **Clement Attlee**, the new Secretary of State, Lord **Pethick Lawrence** and **Stafford Cripps**, now the President of the Board of Trade, were long committed to the cause of Indian independence and now with decisive majority in the House of Commons, it was anticipated that the time has arrived for them to redeem their pledge.

---

[31] The claim even embraced the Viceroy who felt that the loyal Unionist Muslim, or those in power in Punjab deserved some representation.

[32] Ironically, at time not only Maulana Abul Kalam Azad was the Congress President but he and Abdul Ghaffar Khan were duly present in Simla in the capacities as distinguished members of the Congress delegation.

[33] In fact, as early as 1938, the Labour party leaders (including Clement Attlee, Stafford Cripps and Harold Laski) had met Jawaharlal Nehru and V. K. Menon in Filkin's near London and agreed on the idea of an Indian Constituent Assembly elected on the basis of universal adult franchise, drafting its own constitution.

- But, the first moves that the Attlee Government made in India were hardly path-breaking and were rather somehow disappointing for the nationalist enthusiasm. Under directions from the Labour Coalition Government, the Viceroy announced on 21 August 1945, the **holding of elections**[34] for the Indian Legislatures in the approaching winter of 1945–46.
- On 19 September 1945, the Viceroy further renewed the promises of 'early full self-government,[35] for India based on the discussions with the elected legislators and the representatives of the Indian princes on the formation of a Constituent Assembly for undertaking fresh constitutional arrangements conveniently bypassing the previous Labourite assurance of electing a Constituent Assembly based on universal suffrage. He also declared that fresh efforts would be undertaken once again for setting up the Viceroy's Executive Council with nominees from the main Indian parties.
- In fact, attitude of Labour Party has been a subject of debate among the historians as while some historians and contemporary observers like **Howards Brasted**, **Carl Bridge** and **V. P. Menon** felt that a labour victory was indeed the main factor responsible for the early transfer of power, there are certain others like **R. J. Moore** and **John Darwin** who are more sceptical about the contribution of Labour Party. For instance, R. J. Moore has talked about '*Labour's imperialist inheritance which proved to be an impediment in fulfilling its promise of Indian self-government*', while John Darwin has argued that '*after the War, the new Labour government turned out to be remarkably unradical in its approach to foreign, defence and imperial policy as no-one was averse to having an empire or would dislike the glory of being a great power*'.

"In all British policy, whether it is the policy of the Coalition Government (under Attlee), there is still a marked and notable absence of a real will to help in making India free in the full sense of the term. There is too much exploitation of a partly real and partly unreal communal difference in India, partly made and partly exploited by ourselves ... there is the immensely overrated hero-worship of princes, for whom we are supposed to have sacred responsibility."

Rueful Observations on the Attlee Ministry's reactionary Indian policy by none other than its own ideologue, Harold Laski.

The Elections (1945–46)

- The elections were duly held in the winter of 1945–46 and brought a popular mandate for **Congress**, which won overwhelmingly in the General (non-Muslim) constituencies, securing 91.3 per cent votes, winning 57 out of 102 seats in the Central Legislative Assembly and obtaining majorities in all the provinces **except** Sind, Punjab and Bengal.
- On the other hand, the **Muslim League** also did reasonably well in the elections and in the whole of India, it secured 74.7 per cent of votes in the Muslim constituencies winning all the 30 Muslim seats in the Central Legislative Assembly and winning 442 out of 509 Muslim seats in the provinces, but it failed to form government in NWFP and Assam and also to dislodge the Unionists from Punjab. Although the electorate was heavily restricted (about 10 per cent of the population), this was interpreted as a popular mandate for Pakistan.
- The election results also marginalised all other non-Muslim political parties, like the **Communist Party**, which won only 8 seats, the **Hindu Mahasabha** having only 3 seats and Dr Ambedkar's **All India Scheduled Castes Federation**, which could bag just 2 of the 151 seats reserved for such castes.

---

[34] The elections were not only overdue for the centre (last elected in 1934), as well as for the provinces (last elected in 1937) but also essential for reopening the constitutional game the wrangles and squabbles in the name of negotiations.

[35] Refusing carefully to use the term 'independence'.

The Cabinet Mission Plan (March 1946–June 1946)

- Once the main parties emerged from the elections, the Attlee Government to initiate negotiations with them announced[36] a high powered mission of three British cabinet members (**Pethick Lawrence**, Secretary of State for India, **Stafford Cripps**, the President of the Board of Trade and **A. V. Alexander**, the First Lord of Admirality).
- Aided by the Viceroy, the Mission held discussions with the Indian leaders till June 1946 for deciding upon two issues:
  - The principles and procedures for the framing of a new constitution for granting independence, and
  - The formation of an interim government based on widest possible agreement among Indian political parties.
- However, **reversing** the earlier British strategy of divided India and due to the strong concern for imperial defence, along with having the implicit belief that Pakistan with six provinces would not be viable as a separate entity, a plan was drawn up by the Cabinet Mission to safeguard the interests of the Muslim minority within the overall framework of unity of the country. Thus, after wide consultation across the political spectrum, the Cabinet Mission rejected the proposal of a sovereign Pakistan and offered instead, on 16 May:
  - A three-tier structure of a loose federal government for the Union of India, including both the provinces and the princely states.
  - There would be a Union government at the top, in charge only of defence, foreign affairs and communications while all residual powers would be vested in the provincial governments, which would be free to form groups.
  - Each group could also would have their own executives and legislatures and could decide what provincial subjects to take on.
  - A Constituent Assembly was to be elected by the recently constituted provincial assemblies to draft a constitution for the whole of India, it would first meet at the Union level and then split into three sections:
    - **Section A**: containing **Hindu majority provinces** like Madras, Bombay, UP, Bihar, Central Provinces and Orissa
    - **Section B**: containing **Muslim majority provinces** in the north-west like Punjab, NWFP and Sind
    - **Section C**: would include **Bengal** and **Assam**.
  - After a constitution was finally settled for all the three levels (Province, Group and Union), the provinces would have the right to opt out of any particular group, but not from the Union, that is, after the first general elections. However, they could also reconsider the constitution after an interval of 10 years and could then demand the modification of both the group and union constitutions.
  - In the meanwhile, an Interim Government would look after the day-to-day administrative matters.
- The Mission's plan was thus intended to be a compromise as it tried to placate the Congress through the **rejection of the Pakistan scheme** and tried to mollify the League through the **creation of autonomous Muslim-majority areas** in some proximity. At the outset, therefore, both the Congress and League were inclined to accept the plan. However, soon a difficulty surfaced over the provisions for forming sections or groups of provinces.
- Since the Cabinet Mission Plan was not clear about whether grouping was compulsory or optional, disagreement arose between the Congress and the League regarding their interpretation of the Plan over the issue of grouping. While **Congress**[37] demanded that provinces should have the option of not

[36] Coincidentally on 19 February 1946, the day after the RIN mutiny broke out in Bombay. The Mission visited India between March and June 1946.

[37] Keeping in mind, the interests of NWFP and Assam, where it had won majorities in recent elections and which had been placed in sections B and C along with the Sikh majority areas of Punjab.

to join a group at a very beginning, rather than wait till general elections, the **League**, on the other hand, demanded that the right of provinces to modify the Union Constitution should be granted immediately without waiting for 10 years. The Cabinet Mission, however, deliberately refused to clarify its stand, probably in the hope that their ambivalence might reconcile the irreconcilable position of the Congress and the League, but in effect, it only complicated matters.

- The Congress, however, had also its other reservations because:
  - Its first priority had been independence of India, which the Mission had argued would follow only after the drafting of a constitution.
  - It wanted additional powers for the central government to intervene in crisis situations or extreme breakdown of law and order.
  - It was also critical of the absence of any provision for the elected members from the princely states in the proposed Constituent Assembly.
- Therefore, although the Congress Working Committee on 25 June and the AICC on 6 July announced conditional approval of the long-term plan offered by the Cabinet Mission, within a few days **Nehru**, the newly elected president, declared in a press conference on 10 July that Congress had '*agreed to nothing else*' other than **participation in the Constituent Assembly** and most probably the **group system will collapse** as the NWFP and Assam would not agree to it. The short-term plan to constitute an interim government also fell through on the sticky issue of parity, as Congress wanted to include a Muslim candidate among its nominees. For **Jinnah**, it was the ultimate betrayal by the Congress, and thus on 29 July, the League Working committee withdrew its earlier approval of the Mission long-term plan and gave a call for **direct action**.

> *"For Qaid-i-Azam, who believed throughout his life in constitutional politics, the day finally arrived to bid goodbye to constitutional methods and prepare his Muslim nation for agitational politics."*
>
> Sekhar Bandopadyay

The Interim Government and the Communal Carnage (1946)

- In the meanwhile, Viceroy Wavell in sharp departure from earlier British practice invited the Congress to form an Interim Government. Infuriated at being left out, Jinnah initiated the popular agitation for Pakistan which commenced on 16 August 1946, chosen as the **Direct Action Day**, and it was on this day that all hell was let loose on Calcutta and then in a chain of reactions spread over other areas of the country, notably in Bombay, eastern Bengal and Bihar, a certain part of the Uttar Pradesh, NWFP and Punjab. (We have already studied in detail about the communal carnage in the previous chapter.)
- In midst of this civil war, a **Congress dominated government** was sworn in on 2 September 1946 with **Jawaharlal Nehru** as the prime minister. However, it soon came to a complete impasse when in late October, the **League** was also persuaded to join. On 9 December, the Constituent Assembly started meeting, but the League decided to boycott it, as Congress refused to accommodate its demand for sectional meetings drafting group constitutions.
- The breaking point came when the **League** demanded that the Constituent Assembly be dissolved since it was unrepresentative, while the **Congress** members frustrated at the non-cooperation of League members at every juncture sent a letter to the Viceroy Wavell seeking resignation of the League ministers.

Interim Government	
Members	**Portfolios Held**
Lord Wavell (till February 1947) & Lord Mountbatten (from February 1947)	• President of the Executive Council • Viceroy and Governor-General of India
Sir Claude Auchinleck	• Commander-in-Chief
Jawaharlal Nehru (INC)	• Vice President of the Executive Council • External Affairs & Commonwealth Relations
Sardar Vallabhbhai Patel (INC)	• Home Affairs • Information and Broadcasting
Rajendra Prasad (INC)	• Agriculture and Food
Baldev Singh (INC)	• Defence
Liaquat Ali Khan (ML)	• Finance
Ibrahim Ismail Chundrigar (ML)	• Commerce
Abdur Rab Nishtar (ML)	• Railways and Communications, Post and Air
Ghazanfar Ali Khan (ML)	• Health
Jagjivan Ram (INC)	• Labour
C H Bhabha (INC)	• Works, Mines and Power
C Rajagopalachari (INC)	• Education and Arts
Jogendra Nath Mandal (ML)	• Law

Attlee's Statement (20 February 1947)

- On 20 February 1946, **Attlee** declared in British Parliament that the British would withdraw from India by 30th June 1948 to such authority or in such a way as would seem most reasonable and be in the best interests of the Indian people. He also sent **Lord Mountbatten** to Delhi on 22 March with plenipotentiary powers and a clear mandate to expedite the process of withdrawal.

The Mountbatten Plan (3 June 1947)

- Lord Mountbatten, on his arrival, quickly realised that the forced march to the demission of power further heightened communal tension and it was virtually impossible to hand over power to a united India and thus, **partition was inevitable**.
- In the middle of April, he first produced what is known as **Plan Balkan**, since it was based on the principle of demission of power to the provinces and proposed the partition of Punjab and Bengal and handing over power to the provinces and sub-provinces, which would be free to join one or more of group Constituent Assemblies on the basis of self-determination, while the Interim Government would remain until June 1948.
- It is therefore not surprising that in the absence of a strong centre, which would certainly lead to Balkanisation of India, **Nehru** rejected these proposals outrightly and Jinnah also casted them aside, as he was not yet prepared to accept the partition of Punjab and Bengal which would give him only a '*truncated or mutilated, moth-eaten Pakistan*'.
- Alternatively, on 3 June, Lord Mountbatten announced his new plan and proposed to transfer the power to two successor **Dominion governments** of India and Pakistan, along with the advance of the date of transfer of power from June 1948 to 15 August 1947.

- The plan provided for:
    - The partition of Bengal and Punjab
    - The Hindu majority provinces, which had already accepted the existing Constituent Assembly would be given no choice
    - The Muslim majority provinces, that is, Bengal, Punjab, Sind, North-West Frontier Province and Baluchistan, would decide[38] whether to join the existing or a new and separate Constituent Assembly for Pakistan.
- The following day **Nehru**, **Jinnah** and **Sardar Baldev Singh** on behalf of the Sikhs endorsed the plan and thus began the fast march to transfer of power.
- Consequently, the Bengal Assembly on 20 June and the Punjab Assembly on 23 June decided in favour of partition: West Punjab and East Bengal would go to Pakistan and the rest would remain in India. Shortly following this, Sind, Baluchistan and NWFP opted to join Pakistan. Two Boundary Commissions – one for Bengal and one for Punjab – both under **Sir Cyril Radcliffe** were appointed with a mandate of delineating the international frontiers within a strict time frame of not more than six weeks.
- It is pertinent to note here that **Nehru**, who was opposed to the idea of dominion status, was won over, although according to his biographer, he accepted it only as an '*interim arrangement*'.

> *"We were tired men and we were getting on in year too . ... We saw the fires burning in the Punjab and heard everyday of the killings. The plan for partition offered a way out and we took it."*
>
> Nehru's confession on the issue of acceptance of Partition.

India's Independence Act (18 July 1947)

- On 18 July, the India Independence Act was ratified by the Crown, which was eventually implemented on 14/15 August 1947, revealing the dual reality of independence and Partition.

Independence and Partition (15 August 1947)

- Pakistan became independent on 14 August, when in a brief ceremony in **Karachi**, the newly designated capital, Mountbatten handed over power by reading a King's message, and Jinnah took over as the **first Governor General** of the Dominion of Pakistan, while the Indian Constituent Assembly met in a special session, where at the stroke of midnight **Nehru** delivered his now famous 'Tryst with Destiny' speech.

> *"Long years ago, we made a tryst with destiny, and now the time comes when we shall redeem our pledge, not wholly or in full measure, but very substantially. At the stroke of the midnight hour, when the world sleeps, India will awake to life and freedom. A moment comes, which comes but rarely in history, when we step out from the old to new, when an age ends, and when the soul of a nation, long suppressed, finds utterance .... "*
>
> Excerpts from Nehru's 'Tryst with Destiny' speech."

---

[38] This was to be decided by the provincial assemblies, and there would be a referendum in the North West Frontier Provinces, and in case of Baluchistan, the Querta municipality and the tribal representatives would be consulted.

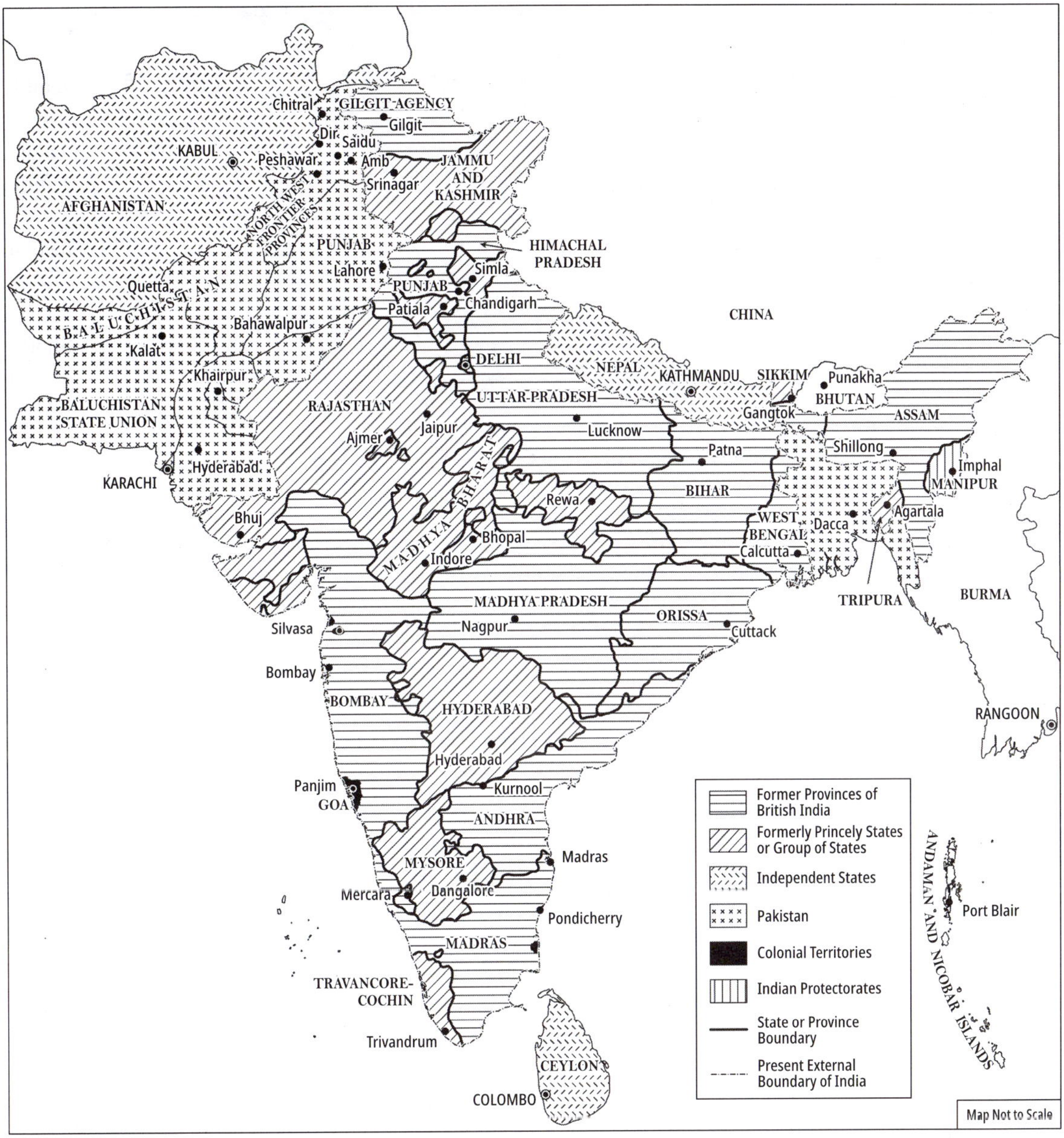

India in 1947

- The next day he was sworn in as free India's first prime minister and the country plunged into celebrations. However, there were many who were not in a mood to celebrate to register their opposition to partition and violence. For instance, Gandhiji decided not to participate in any celebration and spent the day in fasting and prayer, while the nationalist Muslims like **Maulana Azad** felt betrayed too and were not in a celebratory mood either, as revealed from the excerpts of his book *India Wins Freedom*[39] (1957). Equally unhappy were the **Hindu nationalists** like Veer Savarkar, who had once campaigned

[39] Interestingly, the thirty pages of Maulana Azad's book remained sealed for thirty years and were published only in 1988.

for *Akhand Hindustan* (undivided India), and so the **Hindu Mahasabha** and the RSS launched a campaign against the celebrations.

- But the feeling of uncertainty was most dominant in the minds of the minorities, particularly in **Punjab** and **Bengal**, where they suddenly found themselves entrapped in an alien land or indeed in an enemy territory. The next few days witnessed the worst form of communal violence and human displacement that the history of the subcontinent has ever known (we have already discussed in detail about the same in the previous chapter).

"About 1 million people were killed and seventy-five thousand or more women were raped. Trains full of dead bodies travelled across the border in both directions; more than 10 million people were displaced and began to taste bitter freedom amidst the squalor of the refugee camps. The most well known victim of this frenzy was Gandhi himself, assassinated on 30 January 1948 by a militant Hindu nationalist."

Excerpts from Sekhar Bandopadhyay.

For many Indians, freedom thus came with a sense of loss caused by the partition, while too many Muslims in Pakistan, particularly to their state ideologues, partition itself meant freedom. It is no wonder, therefore, that **Partition** happens to be one of the most contested discursive issues of India's historiography.

Historiography of Decolonisation

Critical Analysis of the Historiography of Partition

While some historians, particularly from Pakistan like Aitzaz Ahsan and Akbar Ahmed, treat the Partition as not only a libratory experience but also as a logical culmination of a long historical process that had started in the 19th century by Syed Ahmed Khan and others, when the South Asian Muslims began to discover their national identity that was articulated later in the complex subcontinental politics of the 1940s.

"Partition was a primordial divide – a divide that is 50 years young and 5,000 years old."

Aitzaz Ahsan

"The concept of Pakistan was irresistible and wide spread among the Muslims. In 1947 they forced a separation and thus claimed for themselves a separate history of their own and the chief architects of this history were Jinnah and the leaders of the Muslim League."

Akbar Ahmed

However, there are many others who have opposed this position and questioned the inevitability and legitimacy of partition. For instance, the works of **Uma Kaura** (1977), **Stanley Wolpert** (1984), **Anita Inder Singh** (1987), **R. J. Moore** (1988), **Ian Talbot** (1988), **Mushirul Hasan** (1993, 1997) and, more recently, **Sucheta Mahajan** (2000) have argued consistently over the period that while Congress and its leaders had stood all along until the very end for a secular united India, it was primarily **Jinnah** and his Muslim

League-which from 1940 began to advocate the ***two nation theory*** and were thus ultimately responsible for the sad but **avoidable vivisection** of the subcontinent. We have already discussed in the last chapter about how Jinnah's alienation from the Congress began after 1937 and after that he was not at all flexible in his approach.

However, certain historians like **Asim Roy** and **Ayesha Jalal** have come out with a 'revisionist' critique, forcefully challenging the simplistic interpretation of partition historiography, which basically rests on two fundamental assumptions or in words of Asim Roy '*the two partition myths' – **The Congress for Unity** and **the League for Partition***. Both Roy and Jalal, therefore, came up with a rather different perspective arguing that '*it was not the League but the Congress who chose, at the end of the day, to run a knife across Mother India's body*'. In fact, Ayesha Jalal[40] (1985) raised an all-important question here that '*when Pakistan was ultimately created, it contained 60 million Muslims, leaving behind another 35 million in non-Muslim India. So, how did a Pakistan come about which fitted the interests of most Muslims so poorly?*'

However, this interpretative model, as pointed out by many historians, attaches more importance to '*High Politics*' than the one it seeks to displace and relies too much on Jinnah's agency and allows too much space to the inner depths of his speculative mind. Even though we may agree that Jinnah might have first floated the idea of 'Pakistan' as a 'bargaining chip' but as asserted by even Sumit Sarkar that it is highly doubtful if he had the same bargaining autonomy once the mass mobilisation campaign began in 1944 around the emotive symbol of Muslim nationhood. The Pakistan movement, as we have already noted, had started embracing a wider public form from a much earlier period and once the riots started, the campaign only reached the point of no return. However, it will be equally fallacious to argue that Jinnah did not lead, but was led by Muslim consensus, for, as **Mushirul Hasan** has demonstrated, consensus there was none.

> *"The two-nation idea was itself grounded in the mistaken belief about such Muslim unanimity. At the political level, the League was equally faction-ridden and ideologically fragmented as the Congress was, and at the popular level, even at the height of communal distrust and conflict, there were sizeable sections of Muslim who accepted partition as an unavoidable necessity in the given circumstances."*
>
> Mushirul Hasan

Even **Sumit Sarkar** supports Hasan's view and feels that the communalism as a feeling had not yet been normalised[41] in Indian public life and indeed, there was more communal harmony at the barricade lines – as evidenced in the popular agitations, peasant struggles and industrial actions of the 1940s – than at the negotiating table. He further feels that it was a blunder on part of the Congress leadership as instead of harnessing these popular emotions and risking another round of mass movement, it accepted the tempting alternative of an early transfer of power, with partition as a necessary price for it.

---

[40] In her view, the Lahore Resolution, which neither mentioned 'Partition' nor 'Pakistan', was Jinnah's 'tactical move' – his 'bargaining counter' to have the claim of separate Muslim nationhood accepted by the Congress and the British. The ideal constitutional arrangement he preferred for India at this stage was a weak federal structure, with strong autonomy for the provinces, with Hindu–Muslim parity at the centre. His optimism was that Congress, keen on a strong unitary centre, would ultimately concede his demand to avoid his more aggressive scheme of separation, which in fact he did not really want. But that Congress or the British would never accept partition under any circumstances was a mistaken assumption. Congress in the end did accept partition and thus Jinnah was beaten in his own game of wits.

[41] Interestingly, for Sarkar, the communal riots that broke out from August 1946 do not form a part of this popular politics.

The **subaltern historians**, on the other hand, Gyanendra Pandey, for example, have argued that the conventional elitist partition historiography has been seriously constrained by its self-imposed aim of establishing 'the **causes of Partition**'. He, therefore, appeals to redirect the historical gaze away from the 'causes', to 'the meaning of Partition for those who lived through it, the trauma it produced and the transformation that it brought.'

> *"The truth of the partition lay in the violence it produced, and therefore, endeavours must be undertaken to unravel how this violence is conceptualised and remembered by those who lived through partition - as victims, aggressors or on lookers."*
>
> Gyanendra Pandey

It needs to be mentioned here that the Pandey is certainly not alone in this new discursive terrain, and in recent years, the agenda of partition historiography has significantly shifted grounds from its previous preoccupation with **causes** to a greater interest in the **experiences**. This is clearly proved by the recent spate of publications focussing on the memories of partition, on the creative literature that recaptures this traumatic experience and on the visual representations of that 'epic tragedy'.

> *"The historians are now evidently less concerned about causes, and more introspective about the aftermath of partition. In other words, they look at how partition impacted on post-colonial history and politics, how partition memory defines community identities and affect inter-community relations, thus emphasising a historical continuity. They self-consciously deny the year 1947 and the foundation of the two nation-states the privilege of being treated as the end of all history."*
>
> Shekar Bandopadhyay

Critical Analysis of the Historiography of Transfer of Power

Apart from partition, another debatable issue that figures prominently in the historiography of decolonisation in India is that **whether freedom was seized** by the Indians or **power was transferred voluntarily** by the British as an act of positive statesmanship. Well, it is certainly beyond doubt that the British decision to quit was partly based on the ungovernability of India in the 1940s **but** it is difficult to argue that there was a consistent policy of devolution of power, which came to its logical culmination in August 1947 through the granting of self-government in India.

We have already seen that the constitutional arrangements of **1919** and **1935** were meant to secure British hegemony over the Indian empire through consolidation of control over the central government, rather than to make Indians masters of their own affairs. But, at the same time, it is equally important to note here that in view of the rising tide of political resistance, it was almost impossible for the British authorities to reverse the constitutional process that inevitably gravitated towards the granting of freedom to the Indian masses. In fact, other than that there were many factors at play which made the transfer of power inevitable:

- Britain was under pressure from his own allies, particularly **America** who did not like the idea of an empire and were in favour of granting the self-government to India. The interest of **Franklin Roosevelt** in India's national movement remained as a constant pressure on an otherwise intransigent Churchill[42]. In fact, it was under pressure from Franklin Roosevelt that Churchill though unwillingly signed the Atlantic Charter in August 1941, which acknowledged the right to self-determination for all people of the world.

- Further, the rapid progress of the Japanese army in Southeast Asia during the World War II urgently demanded Indian collaboration, and the allies like Roosevelt and Chiang Kai Shek wanted the Indian problem to be sorted out on a priority basis.
- There was also pressure on the British authorities from the Labour members of the Parliament like Sir **Stafford Cripps**[43] who were committed towards Indian independence for a long time and were insisting since long time that something needs to be done about India in the line of their 1938 agreement. The massive Labour victory in July 1945 did help in creating a congenial atmosphere for such a political change.
- We have already discussed in detail about the various attempts at negotiated settlements that laid down the path for the evolution of the decolonisation like the Cripps Mission, which signified an important shift in British policy and announced that Indian independence after the war, within or outside the empire, would be the ultimate goal of British policy.
- The last years of World War II, the global political situation immediately after it with the tilting of the balance of power decisively in favour of the United States and the worldwide anti-imperialist sentiments, generated by the very struggle against Nazi Germany and enshrined in the United Nations Charter and its strict trusteeship rules, made empire **morally indefensible**.
- The drastic changes in the objective conditions in India also almost gravitated inevitably towards India's independence.

> *"Whatever pre-war tendencies may have existed, the pattern of post-war decolonisation was profoundly influenced by the course and impact of the war. In India, the Quit India movement and its brutal repression ruptured the relationship between the Raj and the Congress and destroyed whatever goodwill the former might have had among the majority of Indian population. The Bengal famine and the wartime food scarcity in other regions further damaged the moral foundations of the Raj. The subsequent agitation surrounding the INA trials showed that no resolution of the Indian question was possible without the participation of the Congress, which could neither be side lined nor coerced into silence."*
>
> John Darwin

- Another crucial aspect was that during the course of the War, the Britain's imperial relations with India had also undergone profound changes[44]. Since long, India had performed three imperial functions:
  - it provided a market for British exports
  - was a remitter of sterling

---

[42] Churchill represented the perspective of the Conservative reformer who though acknowledged the need for granting self-government to India at some stage in future preferred to postpone it as long as possible. Even after signing the Atlantic Charter, he according to his conservative interpretation, asserted that it was meant only to be applicable to the European people subjugated by Nazi Germany, and not to their colonial subjects, and just a few months later announced arrogantly that he had '*not become His Majesty's Chief Minister in order to preside over the Liquidation of the British Empire*'.

[43] Also member of the War Cabinet Britain's Labour Party.

[44] It is pertinent to note that this financial situation arose because of the increasing nationalist pressure for more resources and budgetary allocation for the development of their own country, rather than for servicing the empire.

- was a source of military strength to protect the British Empire as India was traditionally considered to be a strategic asset for maintaining control over Britain's world empire, particularly in the Middle East and Southeast Asia.

But since the 1930s, **London** had little control over Indian monetary and fiscal policies and with the imposition of protective tariffs and wartime procurement policies, India's sterling debt was gradually **replaced** by Britain's rupee debt to India. India's relevance to imperial defence was also coming under close scrutiny as a stiff opposition was emerging against the use of British Indian Army for post-war restoration of the Dutch and French empires in Indonesia and Indochina.

The military expenditure was another key issue of concern as with time, the bulk of this expenditure of fighting on foreign soil outside India was being borne by the British government when it was realised that the government of India was unable to bear the expenditure needed for modernisation of the Indian army. For instance, when the World War II broke out and Indian army had to be deployed in the Southeast Asian front, the Britain's debt to India started piling up, so much so that, by 1946 Britain owed India more than £1,300 million, almost **1/5th of Britain's GNP** eventually making the British government realise that India could only be kept under control at a heavy cost, both financial and military and to keep it henceforth as a colony would not be a profitable proposition by any means.

> *"India was no longer considered to be one of her imperial assets and was regarded as a potential or actual source of weakness."*
>
> Tomlinson
>
> *"What was dominant now in British imperial thinking vis-a-vis India was the need for a reorientation of the relationship in an orderly way within the structures of dominion status and the Commonwealth of Nations – which in a way had become a new expression for empire – so that it could serve as a model for other colonies in Asia and Africa and could safeguard long term British interests and influences, if not power."*
>
> Shekar Bandopadyay

Thus, once it was recognised that British rule could not survive on the old basis for long, a graceful withdrawal from India, to be effected after a settlement had been reached on the modalities of transfer of power and the nature of the post-imperial relationship between Britain and India, became the overarching aim of British policymakers. The British Government was clear that a settlement was a must both for good future relations and to bury the ghost of a mass movement.

Why Did Congress Accept the Partition?

It is also a point of intense speculation[45] and debate as to why the **Congress,** having strong belief in one Indian nation, accepted the division of the country. Often Nehru and Patel have been accused of accepting the Partition due to their lust for quick and easy power, which made them betray the people. However, the situation was far more complicated to be accorded a simplistic explanation.

- It is should be kept in mind that Nehru, Patel and Gandhiji in 1947 were only accepting **what had become inevitable** because of the long-term failure of the Congress to draw in the Muslim masses into the national movement and stem the surging waves of Muslim communalism, which, especially since 1937, had been

[45] That the League should assertively demand it and get it while the British authorities should concede it, being unable to get out of the web of their own making seems explicable.

beating with increasing fury. This failure was revealed with stark clarity by the 1946 elections results in which the League won 90 per cent of the Muslim seats and more so by the communal carnage carried out mercilessly on the streets of Calcutta, Rawalpindi and the village lanes of Noakhali and Bihar. The virtual collapse of the Interim Government in 1946 made 'Pakistan' as an unavoidable reality.

"In the face of the Interim Government's powerlessness to check Governors from abetting the League and the Bengal provincial Ministry's inaction and even complicity in riots, I wonder whether there was any point in continuing in the Interim Government while people were being butchered. Immediate transfer of power would at least mean the setting up of a government which could exercise the control it was now expected to wield, but was powerless to exercise."

Jawaharlal Nehru

"Congress accepted Partition because the people wanted it: The demand has been granted because you asked for it. The Congress never asked for it . . . But the Congress can feel the pulse of the people."

Gandhiji's explanation for acceptance of Partition at a prayer meeting on 4 June 1947

- There was an additional consideration in accepting immediate transfer of power to two dominions to avoid the prospect of balkanisation as the princely states given option to be independent would have meant a graver blow to Indian unity than accepting Pakistan was.
- The acceptance of Partition in 1947 can also be seen as the final act of a process of step-by-step concessions to the League's intransigent championing of a sovereign Muslim state. For instance, **Cripps Mission** accepted the autonomy of Muslim majority provinces in 1942, while **Gandhiji** went a step further and accepted the right of self-determination of Muslim majority provinces in his talks with Jinnah in 1944. Later, in June 1946, Congress conceded the possibility of Muslim majority provinces (which formed Group B and C of the Cabinet Mission Plan) setting up a separate Constituent Assembly and after clarification from the British Cabinet in December, 1946, without much demur also accepted grouping to be compulsory. The final act of surrender to the League's demands was in June 1947 when Congress ended up accepting Partition under the 3rd June Plan.

"The result was that each concession of the Congress, rather than cutting the ground from under the communalists feet, consolidated their position further as success drew more Muslims towards them."

Bipan Chandra Pal

- Another interesting aspect regarding acceptance of Partition by the Congress was the over-optimism and unreal hope[46] that once the British left, differences would be patched up and a free India could be later built by both Hindus and Muslims. Some Congress leaders also had the illusion that the **Partition would be temporary** and was reversible once the communal passions would subside and sanity returned.

---

[46] In fact, one of the most unreal beliefs, given what actually happened, was the one that Partition would be peaceful. No riots were anticipated. No transfers of population planned, as it was assumed that once Pakistan was conceded, what was there to fight over?

"But of one thing I am convinced that ultimately there will be a united and strong India. We have often to go through the valley of the shadow before we reach the sun-lit mountain tops."

Jawaharlal Nehru

"Pakistan could not exist for long if people refused to accept Partition in their hearts."

Gandhiji

The glorious struggle of India's freedom, which was both hard-fought and hard-won, thus, came to an end with India finally achieving the long-cherished dream of Independence, and despite the sorrow in their hearts for the division of their land, the people still rejoiced in the new-found freedom.

Previous Year's Questions (Prelims)

1. With reference to Indian freedom struggle, consider the following events: (2017)
   1. Mutiny in Royal Indian Navy
   2. Quit India Movement launched
   3. Second Round Table Conference

   What is the correct chronological sequence of the above events? Choose the correct answer from the following options.
   (a) 1-2-3
   (b) 2-1-3
   (c) 3-2-1
   (d) 3-1-2

2. What did the plan of Sir Stafford Cripps envisaged for after the Second World War? (2016)
   (a) India should be granted complete Independence.
   (b) India should be partitioned into two before granting Independence.
   (c) India should be made a Republic with the condition that she will join the Commonwealth.
   (d) India should be given Dominion status.

3. With reference to the Cabinet Mission, which of the following statements is/are correct? (2015)
   1. It recommended a Federal Government.
   2. It enlarged the power of the Indian courts.
   3. It provided for more Indians in the ICS.

   Choose the correct answer from the following options:
   (a) 1 only
   (b) 2 and 3
   (c) 1 and 3
   (d) None of the above

4. Quit India Movement was Launched in response to which of the following? (2013)
   (a) Cabinet Mission Plan
   (b) Cripps Proposals
   (c) Simon Commission Report
   (d) Wavell Plan

5. The Congress ministries resigned in the seven provinces in 1939 because of which of the following reasons? (2012)
   (a) The Congress could not form ministries in the other four provinces.
   (b) Emergence of a 'left wing' in the Congress made the working of the ministries impossible.
   (c) There were widespread communal disturbances in their provinces.
   (d) None of the statements (a), (b) and (c) given above is correct.

6. With reference to Indian freedom struggle, Usha Mehta is well known for (2011)

(a) running the secret Congress radio in the wake of Quit India Movement
(b) participating in the Second Round table conference
(c) leading a contingent of Indian national army
(d) assisting in the formation of Interim Government under pandit Jawaharlal Nehru

7. Which one of the following observations is not true about the quit India movement of 1942? (2011)
(a) It was a non-violent movement.
(b) It was led by Mahatma Gandhi.
(c) It was a spontaneous movement.
(d) It did not attract the labour class in general.

8. After Quit India Movement, C. Rajagopalachari issued a pamphlet entitled 'The Way Out. Which one of the following was a proposal in this pamphlet? (2010)
(a) The establishment of a 'War Advisory Council' composed of representatives of British India and the Indian states.
(b) Reconstitution of the Central Executive Council in such a way that all its members, except the Governor-General and the Commander-in-Chief should be Indian leaders.
(c) Fresh elections to the Central and Provincial Legislatures to be held at the end of 1945 and the Constitution making body to be convened as soon as possible.
(d) A solution for the constitutional deadlock.

9. Who among the following were official Congress negotiators with Cripps Mission? (2010)
(a) Mahatma Gandhi and Sardar Patel
(b) Acharya J. B. Kripalani and C. Rajagopalachari
(c) Pandit Nehru and Maulana Azad
(d) Dr Rajendra Prasad and Rafi Ahmed Kidwai

10. In the 'Individual Satyagraha', Vinoba Bhave was chosen as the first Satyagrahi Who was the second? (2009)
(a) Dr Rajendra Prasad
(b) Pandit Jawaharlal Nehru
(c) C. Rajagopalachari
(d) Sardar Vallabhbhai Patel

11. Consider the following statements: (2009)
The Cripps Proposals included the provisions for
1. Full independence for India
2. Creation of Constitution making body

Which of the statements given above is/are correct? Choose the correct answer from the following options.
(a) 1 only
(b) 2 only
(c) Both 1 and 2
(d) Neither 1 nor 2

12. During the freedom struggle, Aruna Asaf Ali was a major woman organiser of underground activity in which of the following? (2009)
(a) Civil Disobedience Movement
(b) Non-Cooperation Movement
(c) Quit India Movement
(d) Swadeshi Movement

13. Who among the following Prime Ministers sent Cripps Mission to India? (2009)
(a) James Ramsay MacDonald
(b) Stanley Baldwin
(c) Nevilli Chamberlain
(d) Winston Churchill

14. With which one of the following movements is the slogan 'Do or Die' associated? (2009)
(a) Swadeshi Movement
(b) Non-Cooperation Movement
(c) Civil Disobedience Movement
(d) Quit India Movement

15. During the Indian freedom struggle, who of the following raised an army called 'Free Indian Legion'? (2008)
(a) Lala Hardayal
(b) Rash Behari Bose
(c) Subhash Chandra Bose
(d) V. D. Savarkar

16. Which one of the following suggested the reconstitution of the Viceroy's Executive Council in which all the portfolios including that of War members were to be held by the Indian leaders? (2008)
   (a) Simon Commission
   (b) Simla Conference
   (c) Cripps Proposal
   (d) Cabinet Mission

17. Assertion (A): The Congress Ministries in all the provinces resigned in the year 1939.

   Reason (R): Congress did not accept the decision of the Viceroy to declare war against Germany in the context of the Second World War. (2008)
   (a) Both A and R are true and R is the correct explanation of A.
   (b) Both A and R are true but R is not the correct explanation of A.
   (c) A is true but R is false.
   (d) A is false but R is true.

18. Consider the following statements:

   On the eve of launch of Quit India Movement, Mahatma Gandhi (2005)
   1. asked the government servants to resign.
   2. asked the soldiers to leave their posts.
   3. asked the princes of the princely states to accept the sovereignty of their own people.

   Which of the statements given above is/are correct? Choose the correct answer from the following options.
   (a) 1 and 2
   (b) 2 and 3
   (c) 3 only
   (d) 1, 2 and 3

19. Who among the following was the Chairman of the Union Constitution Committee of the Constituent Assembly? (2005)
   (a) B. R. Ambedkar
   (b) J. B. Kripalani
   (c) Jawaharlal Nehru
   (d) Alladi Krishnaswamy Iyer

20. Consider the following statements: (2005)
   1. Lord Mountbatten was the Viceroy when Simla conference took place.
   2. Indian Navy revolt, 1946 took place when the Indian sailors in the Royal Indian Navy at Bombay and Karachi rose against the government.

   Which of the statements given above is/are correct? Choose the correct answer from the following options:
   (a) 1 only
   (b) 2 only
   (c) Both 1 and 2
   (d) Neither 1 nor 2

21. Which one of the following statements is correct? (2004)
   (a) The Constituent Assembly of India was elected by the Provincial Assemblies in the year 1946.
   (b) Jawaharlal Nehru, M. A. Jinnah and Sardar Vallabhbhai Patel were members of the Constituent Assembly of India.
   (c) The first session of the Constituent Assembly of India was held in January 1947.
   (d) The Constitution of India was adopted on 26 January 1950.

22. Which of the following was and important aspect of the Cripps mission of 1942? (2003)
   (a) All Indian state should join the Indian union as a condition to consider any degree of autonomy for India.
   (b) The creation of an Indian union with Dominion status very soon after the second world war.
   (c) The participation and co-operation of the Indian people communities and political parties in the British war effort as a condition for granting independence with full sovereign status to India after second world war.
   (d) The farming of a constitution for the entire Indian union with no separate constitution for any province and a union constitution to be accepted by all province.

23. The members of the constituent of assembly which drafted the Constitution of India were (2002)
    (a) nominated by the British Parliament.
    (b) nominated by the Governor General.
    (c) elected by the legislative assemblies of various province.
    (d) elected by the Indian National Congress. Muslim League.

24. Where did the Indian national army came into existence in 1943? (2000)
    (a) Japan
    (b) Burma
    (c) Singapore
    (d) Malaya

25. Assertion (A): Lord Linlithgow described the August movement 1942 as the most serious revolt after the sepoy mutiny.

    Reason (R): Peasants joint the movement in large number in some place. (2000)
    (a) Both A and R are true and R is the correct explanation of A.
    (b) Both A and R are true but R is not the correct explanation of A.
    (c) A is true but R is false.
    (d) A is false but R is true.

26. Which Indian nationalist leader looked upon a war between Germany and Britain as a god sent opportunity which would enable Indians to exploit the situation to their advantage? (1999)
    (a) C. Rajagopalachari
    (b) M. A. Jinnah
    (c) Subhash Chandra Bose
    (d) Jawahar W. Nehru

27. What is the correct sequence of the following events? (1998)
    1. The August offer
    2. The INA trial
    3. The Quit India Movement
    4. The Royal Indian Naval ratings revolt

    Choose the correct answer from the following options:

    Codes:
    (a) 1, 3, 2, 4
    (b) 3, 1, 2, 4
    (c) 1, 3, 4, 2
    (d) 3, 1, 4, 2

28. Assertion (A): The Congress rejected the Cripps proposal. (1998)

    Reason (R): The Cripps mission consisted solutions of whites.
    (a) Both A and R are true and R is the correct explanation of A.
    (b) Both A and R are true but R is not the correct explanation of A.
    (c) A is true but R is false.
    (d) A is false but R is true.

29. Consider the following statements about Jawaharlal Nehru: (1996)
    1. He was the president of the Congress part in 1947.
    2. He presided over the Constituent Assembly.
    3. He formed the first Congress ministry in United Province before India's Independence.

    Choose the correct answer from the following options:
    (a) 1, 2 and 3 are correct
    (b) 1 and 3 are correct
    (c) 1 and 2 are correct
    (d) None of these are correct

Previous Year's Answers (Prelims)

1. (c)	2. (d)	3. (a)	4. (b)	5. (d)	6. (a)	7. (a)	8. (d)
9. (c)	10. (b)	11. (b)	12. (c)	13. (d)	14. (d)	15. (c)	16. (d)
17. (a)	18. (c)	19. (c)	20. (b)	21. (a)	22. (b)	23. (c)	24. (c)
25. (b)	26. (c)	27. (a)	28. (b)	29. (d)			

APPENDIX 1

Congress Sessions

INC Sessions

Year	Place	President	Remarks
December, 1885	Bombay	W. C. Bannerji	• First Session attended by 72 delegates. • Under the guidance of A. O. Hume.
December, 1886	Calcutta	Dadabhai Naoroji	• First Parsi President. • Merger of Indian National Congress (INC) and Indian National Conference of Surendranath Banerjee. • Decision to set up Provincial Congress Committees across India.
December, 1887	Madras	Syed Badruddin Tyabji	First Muslim President.
December, 1888	Allahabad	George Yule	First European President.
December, 1889	Bombay	William Wedderburn	• Only foreigner to become the President of INC twice (1889 and 1910). • First INC session attended by women.
December, 1890	Calcutta	Pherozeshah Mehta	Kadambini Ganguly became the first woman to address an INC session.
December, 1891	Nagpur	Anand Charlu	• The term '*National*' added to the Congress name. • First south Indian President of INC.
December, 1892	Allahabad	W. C. Bannerji	
December, 1893	Lahore	Dadabhai Naoroji	
December, 1894	Madras	Alfred Webb	
December, 1895	Poona	Surendranath Banerjee	
December, 1896	Calcutta	Rahimatullah M. Sayani	• '*Bande Mataram*' sung for the first time by Rabindranath Tagore. • Congress officially accepted the 'drain of wealth' theory.

Year	Place	President	Remarks
December, 1897	Amravati	C. Sankaran Nair	Only Malayalee president of INC.
December, 1898	Madras	Anand Mohan Bose	Social reform was also set as a goal of INC.
December, 1899	Lucknow	Romesh Chandra Dutt	Demand for permanent fixation of Land Revenue.
December, 1900	Lahore	N. G. Chandavarkar	
December, 1901	Calcutta	Dinshaw E. Wacha	Gandhiji appeared on the Congress platform for the first time who moved a resolution on South Africa at this session.
December, 1902	Ahmedabad	Surendranath Banerjee	
December, 1903	Madras	Lal Mohan Ghosh	
December, 1904	Bombay	Henry Cotton	Protest by Congress over the violation of rules by Lord Curzon as he used revenues from India for his forward policy in Tibet.
December, 1905	Banaras	G. K. Gokhale	• Formal Proclamation of Swadeshi Movement. • Expressed resentment against Partition of Bengal.
December, 1906	Calcutta	Dadabhai Naoroji	• 'Swaraj' mentioned for the first time. • Adopted four resolutions on *swaraj*, *boycott*, *swadeshi* and *national education*.
December, 1907	Surat	Rash Behari Ghosh	• Split in Congress. • Adjournment of session due to violence among Moderates and Extremists.
December, 1908	Madras	Rash Behari Ghosh	Congress Constitution drawn.
December, 1909	Lahore	Madan Mohan Malviya	M. A. Jinnah expressed disapproval over provision of 'Separate electorates' to Muslims under the Indian Council Act 1909.
December, 1910	Allahabad	William Wedderburn	
December, 1911	Calcutta	B. N. Dhar	• First time recital of '*Jana Gana Mana*' at a Congress session. • Congress welcomed the visiting British Monarch George V.
December, 1912	Bankipur	R. N. Mudhalkar	First Congress session attended by Jawaharlal Nehru.
December, 1913	Karachi	Nawab Syed Muhammad	
April, 1914	Madras	Bhupendra Nath Bose	
December, 1915	Bombay	Satyendra Prasad Sinha	Constitution of Congress altered to admit the delegates from Extremist section.

Year	Place	President	Remarks
December, 1916	Lucknow	A. C. Majumdar	• Lucknow Pact between INC and Muslim League to build political consensus. • Readmission of Extremists to INC.
December, 1917	Calcutta	Annie Besant	First Woman President of Congress.
December, 1918	Delhi	Madan Mohan Malviya	First Congress Session held in Delhi.
December, 1919	Amritsar	Motilal Nehru	• Strong Condemnation of the Jallianwala Bagh Massacre. • Extension of support to Khilafat Movement.
December, 1920	Nagpur	C. Vijayaraghavachariar	• Radical restructuring in Congress to transform it in to a true mass organisation. • M. A. Jinnah left the INC.
December, 1921	Ahmedabad	• C. R. Das (in prison). • Hakim Ajmal Khan (Acting President).	Hakim Ajmal Khan is the only person to have been appointed president of the INC, the Muslim League and the All India Khilafat Committee.
December, 1922	Gaya	C. R. Das	Resignation of C. R. Das and M. L. Nehru to form Swaraj Party.
December, 1923	Kakinada	Maulana Muhammad Ali	
December, 1924	Belgaum	Mahatma Gandhi	Only session presided over by Gandhiji.
April, 1925	Kanpur	Sarojini Naidu	First Indian Woman President.
December, 1926	Guwahati	S. Srinivasa Iyengar	*Khadi* was made compulsory for Congress workers.
December, 1927	Madras	Dr M. A. Ansari	Adoption of: • independence resolution. • boycott of Simon Commission.
December, 1928	Calcutta	Motilal Nehru	• Ultimatum of 1 year for providing Dominion Status else Complete Independence to be demanded. • Formation of All India Youth Congress.
April, 1929	Lahore	Jawaharlal Nehru	• Passing of resolution on Complete Independence or *Purna Swaraj*. • Civil Disobedience Movement launched. • 26 January to be observed as 'Independence Day'.
1930	No Session and Jawaharlal Nehru continued as the President.		

March, 1931	Karachi	Vallabhbhai Patel	• Gandhi–Irwin Pact endorsed.
			• Resolution on:
			  • Fundamental Rights.
			  • National Economic Programme.

Year	Place	President	Remarks
December, 1932	Delhi	Amrit Ranchhordas Seth	
September, 1933	Calcutta	Nellie Sengupta (Original name: Edith Ellen Gray)	First British Woman to be the president of INC.
October, 1934	Bombay	Rajendra Prasad	Amendment in the Constitution of Congress.
1935	No Session and Rajendra Prasad continued as President.		
June, 1936	Lucknow	Jawaharlal Nehru	Push towards socialist ideas by Jawaharlal Nehru.
July, 1937	Faizpur, Maharashtra	Jawaharlal Nehru	First session to be held in a village.
February, 1938	Haripura	Subhash Chandra Bose	National Planning Committee set up under the chairmanship of Jawaharlal Nehru.
March, 1939	Tripuri	Subhash Chandra Bose defeated Gandhiji's candidate Pattabhi Sitaramayya	• Battle between Left and Right Wing of INC. • Rajendra Prasad took over as President after Bose resigned.
March, 1940	Ramgarh	Maulana Abul Kalam Azad	Proposal for Individual Satyagraha passed.
1941–45	No Session and Maulana Abul Kalam Azad continued as President making him the President holding office for the longest continuous term.		
November, 1946	Meerut	Acharya J. B. Kriplani	Was president of INC at the time of Independence.
1948	Jaipur	Dr. Pattabhi Sitaramayya	• First Congress Session in Independent India. • Appointment of JVP committee to look into the issue of linguistic reorganisation of Indian states. JVP: Jawaharlal Nehru, Vallabhbhai Patel and Pattabhi Sitaramayya.

Special Sessions of Congress

Year	Place	President	Remarks
August, 1918	Bombay	Syed Hasan Imam	Session convened to deliberate the contentious Montford Report.
1920	Calcutta	Lala Lajpat Rai	Gandhiji proposed for Non-Cooperation Movement.
September, 1923	Delhi	Maulana Abul Kalam Azad	• Formation of All India Khadi Board. • Azad was the Youngest President of INC, at the age of 35.

APPENDIX

2

Constitutional Developments

The Regulating Act (1773)

- Beginning of the parliamentary control over the Court of Directors of the East India Company.
- The status of Governor of Bengal raised to that of Governor General[1] and subordination of Bombay and Madras Presidencies to Bengal.
- Provided for the establishment of a Supreme Court of Justice at Calcutta (1774).

The Amending Act (1781)

- Attempted to define the jurisdiction of the Supreme Court more precisely.

The Pitt[2] India Act (1784)

- Reiterated the supremacy of British Parliament over the administration of Company and the Company's territories in India were termed 'British possessions'.
- Established a Board of Control and thus introduced a system of double government as:
    - Commercial Functions: to be supervised by Court of Directors
    - Political Functions: to be supervised by Board of Control
- The Presidencies of Madras and Bombay were clearly subordinated to the authority of Governor General in all matters of war, diplomatic relations and revenue.

The Amending Act (1786)

- It gave Governor General power to override his council in extraordinary circumstances.
- Governor General[3] also made Commander-in-Chief.

The Charter Act (1793)

- The Charter Act renewed the charter of the Company for 20 years.
- Civil Law, the system of government by written laws and regulations, introduced in India.

---

1 The first Governor General of Bengal was Lord Warren Hastings.
2 Named after William Pitt, the then Prime Minister of Britain.
3 The Act of 1786 was specifically enacted to satisfy Lord Cornwalli's demands.

- The Salaries for the staff and paid members of the Board of Control were now charged to the Company.

The Charter Act (1813)

- Though Company's Charter was renewed for next 20 years, it was deprived of its monopoly of trade with India, although its monopoly of tea trade and trade with China was left untouched for another 20 years.
- Provided for the spread of western education.
- Christian missionaries were allowed to preach in India.

The Charter Act (1833)

- The Governor General of Bengal became the Governor General of India[4] and all civil, and military powers were vested in him. Bombay, Madras and other regions were subjected to complete control of the Governor General in Council.
- The Company's monopoly of tea trade with China was also abolished.
- The Company's services in India were thrown open to the natives.

The Charter Act (1853)

- Last of the Charter Acts.
- Provided for the separation of the executive and the legislative functions of the Governor General's council.
- Introduction of open competition system for the recruitment of the Indian Civil Service.

The Royal Proclamation (1858)

- India to be governed directly by and in the name of the Crown through a Secretary of State for India, who was a member of the British Cabinet and would be further aided by a Council known as the India Council consisting of 15 members.
- Governor General was given the new title of Viceroy[5] and an Executive council was formed to help the Viceroy.
- Ended the system of double Government[6] by abolishing the Board of Control and Court of Directors.

The Indian Councils Act (1861)

- Beginning of representative institutions by associating Indians[7] with the law making process.
- Expansion of Viceroy's Executive Council as fifth member was added.
- Introduction of Portfolio System.
- Budget was introduced but members could not ask questions.

---

[4] Lord William Bentick was the first Governor General of India.
[5] Lord Canning became the first Viceroy of India.
[6] Introduced by Pitt's India Act of 1784.
[7] Three Indians were nominated to the Viceroy's legislative Council: Raja of Banaras, Maharaja of Patiala and Sir Dinkar Rao.

- Started the process of legislative devolution as it restored8 the legislative powers of the Governor-in-Councils of the Presidencies of Madras and Bombay.

The Indian Councils Act (1892)

- Increased the number of non-official members but retained the official majority.
- Legislative councils given power to discuss Budget and right to ask questions.
- Made indirect provision for elections as nominations were allowed on the recommendations of certain bodies like district boards and universities, etc.

The Indian Councils Act (1909)

- Also known as Morley - Minto Reforms.
- Introduced the system of communal representation and separate electorates for the Muslims.
- Considerably increased the number of elected or non-official members in both Central and Provincial legislative councils.
- Non-official majority introduced in provincial councils though official majority retained in the Governor General Council.
- For the first time, Indians[9] were provided membership to the executive Councils of the Viceroy and Governors.

The Government of India Act (1919)

- Also known as Montagu-Chelmsford Reforms.
- Introduced Dyarchy in the Provinces by dividing the provincial subjects into two:
  - Transferred Subjects: Administered by Governor on the advice of Ministers;
  - Reserved Subjects: Administered by Governor on the advice of his Executive Council.
- Introduced for the first time, direct elections and bicameralism:
  - Lower House (Legislative Assembly)
  - Upper House (Council of States)
- Separated for the first time, provincial budgets from the Central Budgets and authorised provincial legislatures to enact their budgets.
- Extended the principle of communal representation by providing separate electorates to Sikhs, Indian Christians, Anglo-Christians and Europeans.
- Provided for the establishment of the:
  - Public Service Commission
  - Office of High Commissioner for India in London

The Government of India Act (1935)

- Creation of an All India Federation and Bicameral Legislature:
  - Upper House (Council of States) based on direct election

---

[8] Earlier taken away by Charter Act (1833).

[9] Satyendra Prasad Sinha became the first Indian to become member of the Viceroy's Executive Council as Law Member.

    - Lower House (Federal Assembly) based on indirect election
- Provincial Autonomy and introduction of responsible Government[10] in the provinces.
- Abolished the system of dyarchy in the provinces but introduced at the Centre as the federal subjects were divided into two categories:
    - Reserved subjects: Administered by the Governor-General on the advice of officials.
    - Transferred subjects: Administered by the Governor-General on the advice of ministers elected by the legislature.
- Division of Powers between the Centre and the Provinces:
    - Federal List (for Centre, with 59 items);
    - Provincial List (for provinces, with 54 items);
    - Concurrent List (for both, with 36 items).
- Residuary powers were given to the Viceroy.
- Abolition of Council of India
- Establishment of New Institutions:
    - Federal Court,
    - Reserve Bank of India,
    - Federal Public Service Commission
- Separation of Burma from India and Creation of two new provinces of Sindh and Orissa.

The Indian Independence Act (1947)

- Sovereignty and responsibility of British Parliament abolished.
- Crown ceased to be source of authority.

Dominion legislatures of India and Pakistan became sovereign.

[10] The Governor was required to act with the advice of ministers responsible to the provincial legislatures.

APPENDIX 3

Governors-Generals and Significant Events during their Rule

Warren Hastings (1773–85)

- Ist Governor General of Bengal by Regulating Act of 1773 who laid down a solid foundation of the mighty British empire in India.
- Abolished Dual System of Governance (earlier introduced by Robert Clive).
- Important acts passed during his tenure:
    - The Amending Act of 1781
    - The Pitt's India Act, 1784
    - Important War, and Battles:
        - The Rohilla War (1774).
        - The First Anglo-Maratha War (1775–82) and Treaty of Salbai (1782).
        - The Second Anglo-Mysore War (1780–84) and Treaty of Mangalore (1784).
- Instrumental in the foundation of the Asiatic Society of Bengal (1784) by Sir William Jones.
- Impeachment proceedings in British Parliament in 1787 but later acquitted of all charges.

Lord Cornwallis (1786–93)

- Father of the Indian Civil Services and is credited with many administrative, revenue and judicial reforms like system of Permanent Settlement (1793), Cornwallis Code of 1793, Separation of Revenue Administration from Judicial Administration and Police Reforms.
- During his reign, the Third Anglo-Mysore War (1790–92) was fought and Treaty of Seringapatnam signed.

Sir John Shore (1793–98)

- Known for his policy of non-interference.
- The two major events during his reign were:
    - The Charter Act of 1793.
    - The Battle of Kharda (1795) between the Nizam and the Marathas, leading to the defeat of Nizam.

Lord Wellesley (1798–1805)

- Introduced Subsidiary Alliance starting from Hyderabad followed by Tanjore (1799), Surat (1800), Awadh (1801), and the Carnatic (1801).
- Maker of the Madras Presidency.
- Fought and won crucial wars:
  - The Fourth Anglo-Mysore War (1799) – death of Tipu Sultan.
  - The Second Anglo-Maratha War (1803–1805) and Treaty of Bassein (1802).

Sir George Barlow (1805–07)

- Vellore Mutiny of 1806 took place.

Lord Minto I (1807–13)

- Concluded the Treaty of Amritsar with Maharaja Ranjit Singh of Punjab in 1809.
- The Charter Act of 1813, which ended the monopoly of East India Company, was passed.

Lord Hastings (1813–23)

- Adopted vigorous forward policy and waged wars extensively:
  - Anglo Nepal War (1814–16) and Treaty of Sagauli (1816);
  - Suppression of the Pindaris (1817–18);
  - Third Maratha War (1817–19) and dissolution of Maratha confederacy.
- Maker of the Bombay Presidency (1818).
- Introduced Ryotwari system of land revenue in the Madras Presidency by Governor Sir Thomas Munroe (1820).

Lord Amherst (1823–28)

- First Anglo-Burmese War (1824–26).

Lord William Bentinck (1828–35)

- First Governor-General of India.
- Charter Act of 1833, which ended the monopoly of East India Company in tea trade and trade with China.
- Initiated an era of progress and reforms like:
  - Abolition of Sati and other cruel rites like Female Infanticide, Child Sacrifice (1829)
  - Suppression of Thugs (1830)
  - Introduction of English Education and resolution of 1835
- Annexed states of Mysore (1831), Coorg (1834) and Central Cacher and Jaintia (1834).
- Treaty of perpetual friendship with Ranjit Singh.

Lord Metcalfe (1835-36)

- Known as Liberator of Indian Press as removed restrictions on the press in India.

Lord Auckland (1836–42)

- The First Anglo–Afghan War (1836–42), in which British were defeated and led to recall of Auckland.
- Death of Maharaja Ranjit Singh (1839).

Lord Ellenborough (1842–44)

- Brought an end to First Anglo–Afghan War.
- Annexation of Sindh (1843).
- War with Gwalior (1843).
- Abolition of Slavery.

Lord Hardinge I (1844–48)

- First Anglo–Sikh War (1845–46) and concluded the Treaty of Lahore (1846).
- Credited for suppressing the barbarous practice of making human sacrifices that prevailed among the primitive tribe of Gonds.
- Introduced the policy of giving preference to English educated Indians in public employment.

Lord Dalhousie (1848–56)

- Youngest Governor-General of India.
- Annexed States through diplomatic masterstroke of 'the Doctrine of Lapse':
  - IInd Anglo–Sikh War (1848–49) and annexation of Punjab (1849);
  - IInd Anglo–Burmese War and the annexation of Lower Burma (1852);
  - Introduction of the Doctrine of Lapse and annexation of Satara (1848), Jaitpur and Sambhalpur (1849), Udaipur (1852), Jhansi (1853), Nagpur (1854) and Awadh (1856).
- Hailed as "the maker of modern India"
  - Introduced Railways, Telegraph and postage stamps;
  - Introduced Despatch of Sir Charles Wood (1854), regarded as Magna Carta of modern education in India;
  - Creating a separate Public Works Department in every province, completing the Upper Ganges Canal (1854);
  - Instrumental in passing of the Widow Remarriage Act (1856).
- Santhal Uprising (1855–56) took place during his tenure.

Lord Canning (1856–57)

- Revolt of 1857.
- Establishment of the Universities of Calcutta, Bombay and Madras in 1857.
- Last Governor General of East India Company.

- First Viceroy of India.
- Govt. of India Act,1858 passed which ended the rule of East India Company and transferred the control to British Crown.
- Indian Penal Code (IPC) and Criminal Code (CrPc) passed.
- Indian Councils Act of 1861.

Lord Elgin I (1862–63)

- Suppressed Wahabi Movement.
- Due to his premature death, Sir Charles Napier and Denison acted as Viceroys.

Lord John Lawrence (1864–69)

- Anglo–Bhutan War (1865).
- Adopted 'Policy of Masterly Inactivity' or policy of non-intervention in Afghanistan.
- Setting up of High Courts at Calcutta, Bombay, Madras (1865). Later in 1866, fourth High court set up at Agra which was later shifted to Allahabad.
- Opening of Telegraph communication with Europe.

Lord Mayo (1869–72)

- Introduced Financial Decentralisation (1870), State Railways and Prison Reforms.
- First Census of India (1871) and Indian Evidence Act (1872).
- Established:
  - Rajkot College at Kathiawar and Mayo College at Ajmer for training of Indian Princes;
  - Statistical Survey of India;
  - Department of Agriculture and Commerce.
- Only Viceroy to be murdered while in office. He was assassinated by Sher Ali Afridi, an Afghan convict during his inspection of Andaman Prisons.

Lord Thomas Baring Northbrook (1872–76)

- Kuka Rebellion in Punjab (1872).
- Famine in Bihar (1874).
- Visit of Prince of Wales, the eldest son of Queen Victoria in 1875.
- Trial of Gaekwads of Baroda over an attempt to poison estranged British Resident Colonel Robert Phayre.
- Resigned from his office due to differences with the British Cabinet over Afghanistan issue.

Lord Lytton (1876–80)

- Severe famine across India (1876–78).
- Appointment of famine Commission under Richard Strachey (1878).
- Royal Titles Act of 1876 passed and Queen Victoria assumed the title of 'Kaiser-i-Hind' or Queen Empress of India.

- Royal Durbar organised in 1877 at Red Fort to welcome Queen.
- Two repressive Acts passed:
  - The Vernacular Press Act (1878) which censored only local language newspapers.
  - The Arms Act (1878) which disallowed Indians to carry arms.
- Second Anglo–Afghan War (1878–80).

Lord Ripon (1880–84)

- Known as the father of Local Self-Government as introduced Local Self-Government in India (1882).
- Also known as the 'Good Viceroy of India' as introduced certain key reforms:
  - First Factory Act of 1881 to improve labour conditions.
  - First Regular Census conducted in 1881.
  - Rendition of Mysore (1881) as it was restored to Wodiyar dynasty.
  - Repealed the Vernacular Press Act and the Arms Act (1882).
  - Appointment of Hunter Commission (1882) under Sir William Hunter for educational reforms, especially in arena of primary education.
  - Foundation of Punjab University (1882).
  - Adopted Famine code (1883).
  - Continuation of financial decentralisation.
  - Introduction of Ilbert Bill (1883) which enabled Indian magistrates to try Europeans in court but due to strong opposition from the British could not be implemented as originally stipulated.

Lord Dufferin (1884–88)

- Formation of Indian National Congress (INC).
- Third Anglo–Burma War (1885–86) and annexation of Burma.

Bengal Tenancy Act (1885).

Lord Landsowne (1888–94)

- The Factory Act of 1891.
- Categorisation of Civil Services into Imperial, Provincial and Subordinate Services.
- Indian Councils Act of 1892.
- Setting up of Durand Commission (1893) which defined Durand line (the boundary between Afghanistan and British India. (Now, it is between Pakistan and Afghanistan.)

Lord Elgin II (1894–99)

- Great Famine of 1896–97 and appointment of Lyall Famine Commission.
- Assassination of two British officials named Rand and Lt. Ayerst by Chapekar brothers (1897).
- Mundas Uprisings (1899).

Lord Curzon (1899–1905)

- One of the most controversial and racist Viceroy who was convinced of Britain's 'civilising mission' in India and described 'Indians as inferior in character, honesty and capacity'. He brought in many controversial legislations:
    - Reduction of elected members through Calcutta Corporation Act (1899);
    - Indian Coinage and Paper Currency Act (1899) which declared British currency as legal tender in India and established a rupee ratio and the gold exchange standard;
    - Appointment of Police Commission (1902) under Andrew Fraser;
    - Appointment of Universities Commission (1902) under Raleigh and passing of India Universities Act (1904) to gain more control over the Universities;
    - Partition of Bengal (1905).
- Established:
    - Archaeological Survey of India under Ancient monuments Protection Act, 1904;
    - Department of Commerce and Industry;
    - Irrigation Commission under Moncrieff (1901);
    - Famine Commission under MacDonnell to probe causes of famine;
    - Railway Commission (1901) under Robertson which recommended handing over of Railways from PWD Department to a Railway Board.
- Curzon-Kitchener Controversy regarding the status of the military member of the council in India in which Kitchener, the Commander-in-Chief of Army, could gather support from the British Government.
- British Invasion of Tibet or Younghusband's Mission to Tibet (1904).

Lord Minto II (1905–10)

- Swadeshi and Boycott Movement.
- Formation of Muslim League (1906).
- Split in Congress (1907) at Surat session.
- Indian Councils Act of 1909, also known as Morley Minto Reforms.
- Provision of Separate electorates to Muslims.
- Alipore Conspiracy Case (1908).

Lord Hardinge II (1910–16)

- Annulment of Partition of Bengal and transfer of capital from Calcutta to Delhi (1911).
- Coronation Durbar of King George V in Delhi (1911).
- Formation of Ghadar Party (1913) and Hindu Mahasabha (1915).
- Beginning of First World War (1914–18).
- Arrival of Mahatma Gandhi from South Africa (1915).

Lord Chelmsford (1916–21)

- Formation of Home Rule Leagues (1916).
- Lucknow Session of Congress (1916) and Lucknow Pact (1916).

- Important Events and Struggles:
  - Foundation of Sabarmati Ashram (1916);
  - Champaran Satyagraha (1917;
  - Ahmedabad Mill strike (1918);
  - Kheda Satyagraha (1918);
  - Rowlatt Act and Satyagraha (1919);
  - Jallianwala Bagh Massacre and appointment of Hunter Commission (1919);
  - The Government of India Act, 1919 or Montague Chelmsford Reforms;
  - Launch of Khilafat and Non-Cooperation Movement, NCM (1919–20).
- Formation of Communist Party of India (CPI) at Tashkent by M N Roy.
- Appointment of Saddler Commission (1917) for educational reforms.
- Death of Tilak (1920).
- First Indian to be appointed as Governor (S P Sinha as Governor of Bihar).

Lord Reading (1921–26)

- Chauri-Chaura Incident and subsequent withdrawal of NCM.
- Repeal of Rowlatt Act and Press Act of 1910.
- Moplah Rebellion of Kerala (1921).
- Formation of Swaraj Party (1923).
- Lee Commission for Civil Services (1924) and holding of simultaneous examination for the ICS in England and India (from 1923).
- Formation of revolutionary Hindustan Republican Association (HRA) in 1923 and its subsequent reorganisation to Hindustan Socialist Republican Association (HSRA) in 1925 at Delhi.
- Kakori Train Robbery (1925).
- Formation of RSS (1925).

Lord Irwin (1926–31)

- Visit of Simon Commission (1927) and its eventual boycott.
- Appointment of Harcourt Butler Indian States Commission (1927).
- Formation of:
  - All India States Peoples Conference (1927);
  - All India Youth Congress (1928).
- Nehru Report (1928), Delhi Proposals and Jinnah Fourteen Points.
- Assembly Bomb Case (1929) and Lahore Conspiracy Case (1929).
- Sharda Act (1929) under which marriageable age was raised:
  - Girls (14 years);
  - Boys (18 years).
- Irwin's famous *Deepawali declaration* (31 October, 1929).
- Lahore Session of Congress declaring *Purna Swaraj* as its goal.
- Boycott of First Round Table Conference by Congress (1930).

- Dandi March (1930) and launch of Civil Disobedience Movement (CDM) (1930–34).
- Gandhi–Irwin Pact or the Delhi Pact and suspension of CDM.

Lord Willingdon (1931–36)

- Second Round Table Conference (1931) and after its failure resumption of CDM.
- Communal Award (1932), fast unto death of Gandhiji and Poona Pact (1932).
- Third Round Table Conference (1932) without Congress.
- Government of India Act, 1935 and separation of Burma from India (1935).
- Establishment of:
  - Congress Socialist Party, CSP (1934);
  - All India Kisan Sabha (1936).

Lord Linlithgow (1936–44)

- First General Elections (1936–37):
  - Spectacular performance by Congress as formed ministries in 6 provinces.
  - Dismal performance by Muslim League, Hindu Mahasabha and CPI.
- Outbreak of Second World War (1939–45).
- Resignation of Congress Ministries and observation of 'Deliverance Day' by League.
- Fight between Left and Right factions in Congress resulting in Tripuri Crisis (1939) and eventual resignation of Bose (1939) and formation of Forward Bloc.
- Pakistan or Lahore Resolution (March, 1940) by Muslim League.
- August Offer (1940).
- Individual Satyagraha (1940–41).
- Cripps Mission (1942).
- Quit India Movement (1942).
- Indian National Army (INA) Experiment.
- Observation of Pakistan Day (March 23, 1943).

Lord Wavell (1944–47)

- Rajagoplachari Formula (1944).
- Desai–Liaqat Pact (1944).
- Shimla Conference and Wavell Plan.
- INA Trials and Agitation.
- Elections to the Constituent Assembly (1945–46).
- Cabinet Mission Plan (1946).
- Nehru's July Statement and subsequent withdrawal of support by League.
- Direct Action Day (August 16,1946) and Communal Carnage at Calcutta, Noakhali, Bombay, Garhmukteshwar and NWFP.
- Formation of Interim Government.
- British PM Attlee's Statement (February 20, 1947).

Lord Mountbatten (1947–48)

- Mountbatten Plan (June 3, 1947) proposing transfer of power to:
  - Dominion Government of Pakistan;
  - Dominion Government of India
- India Independence Act (July 18, 1947).
- Independence and Partition
  - Boundary Commission under Sir Radcliffe.
  - Worse form of Communal Riots especially in Bengal and Punjab.
- Last Viceroy of India and First Governor-General of free India.

APPENDIX 4

Important Milestones in the Evolution of Relations between British and Indian States

The relations of the British with native Indian states were governed purely by expediency and British interests which varied at different times, resulting in a dynamic relationship between the two. Besides these two coefficients, the relationship was further determined by the personalities of different Governors-General and the attitudes of the British officials and residents. William Lee Warner, in his book *The Native States of India*, has categorised the policy of the British with native states up to 1919 into the following periods.

Struggle for Equality from a Position of Subordination (1740–65)

- Starting from a position of subordination, the British tried to first register their presence and later struggled with both the European powers and the dominant regional powers to assert their influence over the Indian Subcontinent.
- The struggle for equality, which primarily started with the famous *Carnatic Wars,* ended with the Treaty of Allahabad (1765), with the acquisition of the *diwani* of Bengal, Bihar and Orissa, and the emergence of the East India Company as a significant political power.

Policy of Ring Fence (1765–1813)

- The Policy of Ring Fence can be broadly understood as '*the policy of defence of one's neighbour's frontiers for safeguarding one's own territories*'. The British, thus, tried to keep the states of their allied rulers as buffer states between their territory and the territory of an enemy ruler and, later on, they attempted to manage their foreign policies to check their combination against them. For instance, under Lord Warren Hastings, the Company defended Awadh from Mysore, Hyderabad Nizams and the Marathas to safeguard its own Bengal's frontiers.
- During the period of the 'Policy of Ring Fence':
    - British claimed no sovereignty over native rulers
    - Treated them as independent
    - Allowed them freedom to manage their internal affairs (except in the case of the Hindu ruler of Mysore)
    - Signed treaties with them on an equal and reciprocal basis
- In fact, Lord Wellesley's Subsidiary Alliance was an extension of the policy of Ring Fence of Warren Hastings which now sought to reduce states to a position of dependence on British Government in India and eventually, British supremacy was established.

Policy of Subordinate Isolation (1813–57)

- Now, with the emergence of British supremacy, the theory of paramountcy began to develop, resulting in the adoption of the policy of Subordinate Isolation, wherein the native Indian states were supposed to act in subordinate cooperation with the British government and acknowledge its supremacy. They now surrendered all forms of external sovereignty and could only retain little sovereignty in matters of internal administration.
- The British residents were now transformed from diplomatic agents of a foreign power to executive and controlling officers of a superior government. Gradually, the British adopted the practice of insisting on sanction for all matters of succession.
- In fact, in 1834, the Board of Directors issued guidelines to annex states wherever and whenever possible and thus, following the guidelines, Lord Dalhousie pursued an aggressive policy of annexation, resulting in usurpation of eight states including some big states of Satara and Nagpur.

Policy of Subordinate Union (1857–1935)

- The policy of annexation was abandoned after the Revolt of 1857 due to:
    - Reward the loyalty exhibited by the states during the 1857 revolt
    - Their potential use as breakwaters in political storms of the future
- Eventually, the British Crown through the Queen's Proclamation (1858) assumed direct responsibility of governance and the new British policy outlined was now to punish or depose the States but not to annex.
- With the Royal Proclamation and the Royal Titles Act of 1876, through which the Queen proclaimed herself as the *Kaiser-i-Hind* (Queen Empress of India), the fiction of Indian princes having a status of equality with the British Crown as sovereign independent states also came to an end. The British now exercised complete and undisputed control over the external and internal affairs of Indian states.
- In 1927, Butler Committee was constituted to examine the nature of relationship between the princely states and government, which recommended:
    - Paramountcy must remain supreme and must fulfil its obligations, adopting and defining itself according to the shifting necessities of time and progressive development of states.
    - States should not be handed over to an Indian Government in British India, responsible to an Indian legislature, without the consent of states.
- The Princely States were invited and represented at all three Round Table Conferences.

Policy of Equal Federation (1935–47)

- The Government of India Act, 1935 proposed an all-India federation having 125 out of 375 seats for the princes in the Federal Assembly and the Council of States having 104 out of 160 seats for the princes. However, this scheme never came into existence and after the outbreak of World War II (September 1939), it was dropped altogether.
- With the Cripps Mission (1942) statement that the British government did not contemplate transferring paramountcy of Crown to any other party in India, the states tried various schemes to forge a union of their own, envisaging themselves as sovereign in status or as a third force in the Indian political scene. The India Independence Act of 1947 made it further clear that the states had only two options:
    - join either of the two dominions – India and Pakistan
    - continue as an independent sovereign state

Integration and Merger (1947–48)

- In 1947, there were roughly more than 500 princely states that covered 48% of the area of pre-Independent India and constituted 28% of its population. Sardar Vallabhbhai Patel (India's first deputy prime minister and the home minister), with the assistance of V.P Menon (the secretary of the Ministry of the States), was given the formidable task of integrating the princely states who utilised varied strategies:
    - invoking the patriotism of the princes
    - reminding them of the possibility of anarchy in the event of their refusal to join
    - convincing them by offering inducements like privy purses (a payment to be made to royal families for their agreement to merge with India)
- Bikaner, Baroda and a few other states from Rajasthan were the first ones to join the Union of India. By August 15, 1947, around 136 states had joined the Indian Union but others remained precariously outside such as:
    - **Travancore:** One of the first princely states to refuse accession to the Indian union. By 1946, the Dewan of Travancore, Sir C.P. Ramaswamy Aiyar declared his intention of forming an independent state of Travancore that would be open to the idea of signing a treaty with the Indian union. However, he stuck to his position till as late as July 1947 but changed his mind soon after he survived an assassination attempt by a member of the Kerala Socialist Party. On July 30, 1947, Travancore joined India.
    - **Jodhpur:** The Rajput princely state, despite having a Hindu king and a large Hindu population, strangely had a tilt towards Pakistan and was being enticed by Jinnah himself. Seeing the risks in the border state acceding to Pakistan, Patel immediately contacted the prince and offered him sufficient benefits and thus on 11th August 1947, Maharaja Hanvant Singh, the King of Jodhpur signed the Instrument of Accession and the State of Jodhpur was integrated into the Indian Dominion.
    - **Bhopal:** Was another state that wished to declare independence. Here, a Muslim Nawab, Hamidullah Khan, a close friend of the Muslim League, was ruling over a majority Hindu population. However, Lord Mountabtten snubbed his intentions stating that '*no ruler could run away from the dominion closest to him*' and thus by July 1947, the Nawab decided to join India.
- Plebiscite and Army Action:
    - **Junagarh:** The Muslim Nawab wanted to join Pakistan but a Hindu majority population wanted to join the Indian Union. In the face of repressive attitude of the Nawab, there was a plebiscite which decided in favour of India.
    - **Hyderabad:** Hyderabad, with a largely Hindu population, was under the command of Nizam Mir Usman Ali who wanted a sovereign status and signed a Standstill Agreement with India in November 1947. Things took a turn for the worse when under tacit support of Nizam, his stormtroopers, called *Razakkars*, unleashed violence targeted at Hyderabad's Hindu residents. The Indian troops were then sent to Hyderabad on September 13, 1948 under 'Operation Polo' and in the armed encounter that lasted for about four days, the Indian army gained full control of the state making Hyderabad an integral part of India. Later, in an attempt to reward the Nizam for his submission, he was made the governor of the state of Hyderabad.
    - **Kashmir:** The princely state of Jammu and Kashmir had a Hindu Maharaja Hari Singh ruling over a Muslim majority population who had remained reluctant to join either of the two dominions. As he procrastinated, Pakistan sent its forces on 24th October, 1947 behind a front of tribal militia and moved menacingly towards Srinagar. The Maharaja now sent his representative

Sheikh Abdullah to Delhi to ask for India's help. On 26th October 1947, Maharaja signed an 'Instrument of Accession' with the Indian Union and Indian troops were despatched to defend the state against the raiders from Pakistan. India's complaints to the UN Security Council regarding raids from Pakistan and the Indian offer to settle the status of the state through a plebiscite led to a ceasefire but left 84,000 square km of area under Pakistani occupation. The special status of Jammu and Kashmir was recognised under Article 370 of the Indian Constitution which implied a limited jurisdiction of the Indian Union over the state as compared to other states.

APPENDIX 5

Important Milestones in the Development of Education

Before the Advent of British

- Hindus and Muslims educated through traditional systems of *pathsala* and *madrassa*, respectively.

Initial Efforts under British East India Company (1757 onwards)

- Not much interest in the promotion of education as the focus was entirely on trading and profit-making.
- Involvement of Christian Missionaries to spread education.
- Establishment of New Institutions:
    - 1781: Calcutta Madrassa by Warren Hastings for the study of Muslim law.
    - 1784: Foundation of the Asiatic Society of Bengal by Sir William Jones.
    - 1791: Sanskrit College established by Jonathan Duncan at Benaras for the study of Hindu law and philosophy.
    - 1800: Fort William College established by Wellesley for training of civil servants of the Company in languages and customs of Indians.
    - 1817: Due to persistent efforts of Raja Rammohan Roy, grant sanctioned for Calcutta College which started imparting English education in Western humanities and sciences.

Humble Beginning by Charter Act (1813)

- Company to sanction one lakh rupees annually for encouraging education.
- The government also set up three Sanskrit colleges in Calcutta, Delhi and Agra.

Orientalist – Anglicists Controversy

- Within the General Committee on Public Instruction (1823):
    - Orientalists demanded that emphasis should be placed on the expansion of traditional Indian learning;
    - Anglicists argued that the government spending on education should be exclusively for modern studies. They were further divided over the question of medium of instruction:
        - One faction was for English language as the medium;
        - Other faction was for vernaculars languages as the medium.

Lord Macaulay's Famous Minutes (1835)

- Settled the row in favour of Anglicists.
- Govt. resources to be devoted to teaching of Western sciences and literature through the medium of English language alone.
- English education was allotted more funds as compared to oriental learning. Printings of English books were made free and available at a very low price while Persian was abolished as the court language and English was made the court language.
- Adopted *"downward filtration theory"*:
  - Plan to educate a small section of upper and middle classes to create a class "Indian in blood and colour but English in taste" who would act as interpreters between the Government and the masses.
  - Attempt to create a system of education that educates only the upper strata of society through a few English schools and colleges instead of large elementary schools, thus neglecting mass education.

Company's Efforts from 1849–1853

- Agriculture Institute was established in Pusa (Bihar) and Engineering Institute was established in Roorkee (1847).
- William Adam's reports (1835, 1836, 1838) on vernacular education in Bengal and Bihar pointed out the defects in the system of vernacular education.
- James Thomsan, Lt. Governor of NW Provinces (1843–53), developed a comprehensive system of village education through vernacular languages which included:
  - Opening of one government school as a model school in each tehsil;
  - Teacher's training school.
- In 1849, JED Bethune founded Bethune School, which did pioneering work in female education.

Woods's Despatch (1854)

- Regarded as 'Magna Carta of English Education' in India as it was the first comprehensive plan for the spread of education in India.
- Discarding the downward filtration theory and recommended:
  - The Government to assume responsibility for the education of the masses;
  - English as the medium of instruction for higher studies and Vernaculars at school level;
  - Systematised the hierarchy;
    - Vernacular primary schools in villages at bottom;
    - Anglo-Vernacular High Schools and an affiliated college at the district level;
    - Affiliating universities in the presidency towns of Calcutta, Bombay and Madras;
  - Emphasis on female and vocational education, and on teachers' training;
  - Secular education to be imparted in government institutions;
  - System of grants-in-aid to encourage private enterprise.

Transfer of Power from Company to Crown (1857)

- Universities at Calcutta, Bombay and Madras were set up in 1857 and later, departments of education were set up in all provinces.

Hunter Commission (1882–83)

- Commission set up under the chairmanship of W.W. Hunter to review the progress of education in the country since the Despatch of 1854.
- Mostly confined its recommendations to primary and secondary education.
- Recommended that:
  - State's special care is required for the extension and improvement of primary education, and it should be imparted through vernaculars;
  - The control of primary education should be transferred to newly set up district and municipal boards;
  - Secondary (High School) education should have two divisions:
    - Literary: leading up to university.
    - Vocational: for commercial careers.
- The Commission also drew attention towards inadequate facilities for female education, especially outside presidency towns and made recommendations for its spread.
- Gradually, the next two decades saw:
  - Rapid growth and expansion of secondary and collegiate education with the participation of Indians;
  - More teaching-cum-examining universities were set up like the Punjab University (1882) and the Allahabad University (1887).

Indian Universities Act (1904)

- Based on the recommendations of the Raleigh Commission (1902).
- Recommended:
  - Universities were to give more attention to study and research;
  - The number of fellows of a university and their period in office were reduced and most fellows were to be nominated by the Government;
  - Government was to have powers to veto universities, senate regulations and could amend these regulations or pass regulations on its own;
  - Conditions were to be made stricter for affiliation of private colleges; and
  - Five lakh rupees was to be sanctioned per annum for five years for the improvement of higher education and universities.
- Created a nationwide stir as the Nationalists saw it as an attempt to have greater control over universities to sabotage nationalist feelings. Gokhale called it a '*retrograde measure*'.

Introduction of Compulsory Primary Education by State of Baroda (1906)

- The state of Baroda introduced compulsory primary education throughout its territories, urging the national leaders to demand the same for British India from Government.

Government Resolution on Education Policy (1913)

- Though the government refused to take up the responsibility of compulsory education, it, however, accepted:
    - The policy of removal of illiteracy and urged provincial governments to take early steps to provide free elementary education to the poorer and more backward sections. Private efforts were also to be encouraged for the same.
    - Quality of secondary schools was to be improved.
    - Decided to establish a university in each province.

Saddler University Commission (1917–19)

- Though the Commission was set up to study and report on problems of Calcutta University, its recommendations were applicable to almost all the other universities too.
- It reviewed the entire scheme from school education to university education and advised that, for the improvement of university education, improvement of secondary education was a necessary precondition.
- Recommended:
    - School course should cover 12 years and students should enter university after an intermediate stage (rather than Matric) for a three-year degree course in university.
    - A separate board of secondary and intermediate education should be set up for administration and control of secondary and intermediate education.
    - There should be less rigidity in framing university regulations.
    - A university should function as centralised, unitary residential-teaching autonomous body, rather than as scattered, affiliated colleges.
    - Female education, applied scientific and technological education, teacher's training including those for professional and vocational colleges should be extended.

Education under Dyarchy (1920s onwards)

- Under Montagu-Chelmsford reforms, education was transferred to provincial ministries.
- Resulted in Financial difficulties as the liberal Central government grants were now stopped.
- Still education grew, especially under philanthropic efforts.

Hartog Committee (1929)

- Was set up to oversee the reports of deterioration of education standards due to large increase in the number of schools and colleges.
- Recommended:
    - Emphasis should be given to primary education but there need not be hasty expansion or compulsion in education.
    - Only deserving students should go in for high school and intermediate stage, while average students should be diverted to vocational courses after VIII standard.
    - For improvements in standards of university education, admissions should be restricted.

Wardha Scheme of Basic Education (1937)

- Formulated by Zakir Hussain Committee constituted by Congress during the National Conference on Education (October 1937) at Wardha.
- Based on:
  - The principle of 'learning through activity'
  - Gandhi's ideas published in a series of articles in the weekly Harijan
- The scheme proposed:
  - Inclusion of a basic handicraft in the syllabus.
  - First seven years of schooling to be an integral part of a free and compulsory nationwide education system (through mother tongue).
  - Teaching to be in Hindi from class II to VII and in English only after class VIII.
  - Ways to be devised to establish contact with the community around schools through service.

Sergeant Plan of Education (1944)

- Bold and comprehensive scheme based on the objective of creating, within 40 years, the same level of educational attainment as prevailed in England.
- Recommended:
  - Age wise segregation;
  - Pre-primary education (3–6 years age group);
  - Free, universal and compulsory Elementary education (6–11 years age group);
  - High school education (11–17 years age group) for selected children; and
  - University course of 3 years after higher secondary.
  - High schools to be of two types:
    - Academic
    - Technical and vocational
  - Adequate technical, commercial and arts education.
  - Abolition of intermediate course.
  - Liquidation of adult illiteracy in 20 years.
  - Stress on teacher's training, physical education, education for the divyanga.
- Demerits of the Plan:
  - Proposed no methodology for implementation;
  - The ideal of England's achievements may not have suited Indian conditions.

APPENDIX 6

Newspapers and Journals

Name of the Journal	Year from which published	Place of Publication	Founder/Editor/Remarks
Bengal Gazette (or Calcutta General Advertiser)	1780	Calcutta	James Augustus Hickey.
Madras Courier	1784	Madras	
India Gazette	1787	Madras	In later years, association of Henry Vivian Derozio when his poems were published in the India Gazette in 1827.
Bombay Herald	1789	Bombay	
Indian Herald	1795	Madras	• Started by R. Williams. • Published by Humphreys.
Digdarshana	1818	Calcutta	First Bengali Monthly.
Bengal Gazetti	1818	Calcutta	• First Bengali Newspaper. • Harish Chandra Ray.
Sambad Kaumudi	1821	Calcutta	Raja Rammohan Roy.
Mirat-ul-Akbar	1822	Calcutta	• First Persian Journal. • Raja Rammohan Roy.
Jam-i-Jahan-Numah	1822	Calcutta	First Urdu Newspaper.
Banga-doota	1822	Calcutta	• Raja Rammohan Roy, Dwarkanath Tagore and others. • Weekly in four languages: English, Hindi, Persian and Bengali.
Bombay Times	1838	Bombay	• Robert Knight and Thomas Bennett. • Post 1861, known as *The Times of India*.
Rast Goftar	1851	Calcutta	• Dadabhai Naoroji. • Gujarati fortnightly.

Name of the Journal	Year from which published	Place of Publication	Founder/Editor/Remarks
Hindu Patriot	1853	Calcutta	• Owned by Madhusudan Ray and Girish Chandra Ghosh. • Harishchandra Mukherjee became Owner-cum-Editor. • Also, supported by Ishwar Chandra Vidyasagar.
Somaprakash	1858	Calcutta	• Dwarkanath Vidyabhushan. • First Bengali political paper.
Indian Mirror	1862	Calcutta	• Debendranath Tagore. • First Indian daily paper in English.
Bengalee	1862	Calcutta	• Initially, Girish Chandra Ghosh. • Later, Surendranath Banerjee became Owner-cum-Editor.
National Paper	1865	Calcutta	Debendranath Tagore.
Amrit Bazar Patrika	1868	Jessore district, East Bengal	• Started by two brothers: • Sisir Kumar Ghosh. • Motilal Ghosh. • Changed overnight from Bengali to English to bypass the Vernacular Press Act.
Madras Mail	1868	Calcutta	First Indian Evening Newspaper.
Tahzib-ul-Akhlaq	1871	Aligarh	Sir Syed Ahmed Khan.
Bangadarshana	1873	Calcutta	Bankim Chandra Chatterjee.
Indian Statesman	1875	Calcutta	• Robert Knight. • Later, known as The Statesman.
The Hindu	1878	Madras	• G. S. Aiyar, Viraraghavachari and Subbarao Pandit. • Started as weekly.
The Tribune	1881	Lahore	Dayal Singh Majithia.
Mahratta (English weekly) *Kesari* (Marathi daily)	1881	Bombay	• Tilak, Chiplunkar, Agarkar. • Prior to Tilak, Kelkar and Agarkar were the editors of *Mahratta* and *Kesari* respectively.
Swadesh Mitram	1882	Madras	Tamil paper by G. S. Aiyar.
Paridasak	1886	-	Weekly by Bipin Chandra Pal.
Sudharak	1888	-	Newspaper by Gopal Ganesh Agarkar.
Udbodhana	1899	-	Magazine by Swami Vivekanand.

Name of the Journal	Year from which published	Place of Publication	Founder/Editor/Remarks
Indian Opinion	1903	South Africa	Newspaper by M. K. Gandhi.
Bande Mataram	1905	Calcutta	Founded by Bipin Chandra Pal. Edited by Aurobindo Ghosh.
Yugantar	1906	Bengal	• Revolutionary Newspaper. • Founded by Barindra Kumar Ghosh, Abhnash Battacharya and Bhupendranath Dutt.
Sandhya	1906	Bengal	Brahmabandhab Upadhyay.
Indian Sociologist	1905	London	Shyamji Krishan Varma.
Bande Mataram	1909	Paris	Madame Bhikaji Cama.
Talwar	1909	Berlin	Virendranath Chattopadhyay.
Kudi Arasu	1910	Tamil Nadu	Periyar E. V. Ramaswamy Naicker.
Comrade	1911	First Calcutta then Delhi	Maulana Mohammad Ali Jauhar.
Al-Hilal and Al- Balagh	1912	Calcutta	Maulana Abul Kalam Azad.
Ghadar	1913	San Fransciso	Ghadar Party (Lala Hardayal).
Pratap	1913	Kanpur	Revolutionary weekly by Ganesh Shankar Vidyarthi.
Bombay Chronicle	1913	Bombay	Daily started by Pherozeshah Mehta.
New India	1914	Madras	Annie Besant.
Young India	1916	USA	• Started by Lala Lajpat Rai. • Published by M. K. Gandhi from 1919.
Independent	1919	Allahabad	Motilal Nehru.
Mook Nayak	1920	Bombay	Marathi weekly by Dr B. R. Ambedkar.
The Hindustan Times	1920	Delhi	K. M. Pannikar.
Vanguard	1922	-	Journal started by CPI under M. N. Roy.
Bahishkrit Bharat	1927	Bombay	• Marathi fortnightly. • Dr B. R. Ambedkar.
Kranti	1927	Maharashtra	S. S. Mirajkar, K. N. Joglekar, S. V. Ghate.
Bandi Jiwan	1922	Cellular Jail, Andamans	Book written by Sachindranath Sanyal.
Nav Jeevan	1929	Gujarat	Weekly Newspaper by M. K. Gandhi.
Harijan	1932	Gujarat	Weekly Journal by M. K. Gandhi.

Name of the Journal	Year from which published	Place of Publication	Founder/Editor/Remarks
Hindustan Dainik	1936	-	Hindi Newspaper by M. M. Malviya.
National Herald	1938	Delhi and Lucknow	Jawaharlal Nehru.

APPENDIX 7

Famous Trials

Trial	Charges	Verdict
(a) Trial of Bahadur Shah Zafar (Red Fort, Delhi 1858)	Treason, conspiracy, rebellion and murder during the 1857 Revolt.	Convicted and exiled to Rangoon where he eventually died.
(b) Bal Gangadhar Tilak (1897, 1908, 1916)	Provocative articles in his journal '*Kesari*'.	• 18 months imprisonment(1897). • Six years exile to Mandalay and fine (1908). • No jail sentence was imposed as spent a year in jail as prisoner (1916).
(c) Alipore Conspiracy Case (Trial of Aurobindo Ghosh and 37 other members of Anushilan Samiti, 1908)	• Attempt to murder District Magistrate of Muzzaffarpur D. H. Kingsford. • Conspiracy and treason.	• Aurobindo acquitted of all the charges. • Death Penalty to Barindra Ghosh and Ullaskar Dutt. • Varying terms of imprisonment to 17 others while the rest were acquitted.
(d) V. D. Savarkar (1910 and 1911) (Member of Abhinav Bharat Group)	• For role in assassination of District Magistrate, Nasik A.M.T. Jackson.	• Two consecutive life transportations (50 years), though released in 1924 after several mercy petitions.
(e) Meerut Conspiracy Case (March 1929, (Arrest of 31 leading Communists and left wing leaders)	For conspiracy against the State.	Awarded sentences varying from 3 years to life sentence.
(f) Assembly Bomb Case (1929) (Bhagat Singh and B. K. Dutt)	Throwing of bombs in Central Legislative Assembly.	Sentenced to life imprisonment.
(g) Lahore Conspiracy Case (1929, Bhagat Singh and Sukhdev)	Assassination of Police official Saunders for brutally lathicharging Lala Lajpat Rai.	• Sentenced to death. • Both executed on 23 March 1931.

Trial	Charges	Verdict
(h) Red Fort Trial of INA Prisoners (1942) (Trial of Shah Nawaz Khan, Prem Kumar Sehgal, G. S. Dhillon)	Waging war against the State.	Sentenced to life but later remitted on account of INA agitation.